1996-97

EVANGELICAL SUNDAY SCHOOL LESSON COMMENTARY

FORTY-FIFTH ANNUAL VOLUME

Based on the

Evangelical Bible Lesson Series

Editorial Staff

James E. Humbertson—*EDITORIAL DIRECTOR*

Homer G. Rhea—*EDITOR IN CHIEF*

Kenneth T. Harvell—*GENERAL DIRECTOR OF PUBLICATIONS*

Lesson Exposition Writers

Eugene C. Christenbury
Jerald Daffe
Rodney Hodge
James E. Humbertson
Oliver McMahan
Homer G. Rhea

Published by
PATHWAY PRESS
Cleveland, Tennessee

Lesson treatments in the *Evangelical Sunday School Lesson Commentary* for 1996-97 are based upon the outlines of the Evangelical Bible Lesson Series prepared by the Evangelical Curriculum Commission (formerly the Curriculum Commission of the National Sunday School Association).

PATHWAY PRESS, Cleveland, Tennessee
ISBN: 0-87148-972-4

Printed in the United States of America

TABLE OF CONTENTS

SPRING QUARTER LESSONS

SUMMER QUARTER LESSONS

INTRODUCING THE 1996-97 COMMENTARY

The *Evangelical Sunday School Lesson Commentary* contains in a single volume a full study of the Sunday school lessons for the months beginning with September 1996 and running through August 1997. The 12 months of lessons draw from both the Old Testament and the New Testament in an effort to provide balance and establish relationship between these distinct but inspired writings. The lessons in this 1996–97 volume are drawn from the fifth year of a seven–year cycle, which will be completed in August 1999. (The cycle is printed in full on page 16 of this volume.)

The lessons for the *Evangelical Commentary* are based on the Evangelical Bible Lesson Series Outlines, prepared by the Evangelical Curriculum Commission. (The Evangelical Curriculum Commission is a member of the National Association of Evangelicals.) The lessons in this volume are drawn from the Old and New Testaments; and taken together with the other annual volumes of lessons in the cycle, they provide a valuable commentary on a wide range of biblical subjects. Each quarter is divided into two or more units of study.

The 1996–97 commentary is the work of a team of Christian scholars and writers who have developed the volume under the supervision of Pathway Press. All the major writers, introduced on the following pages, represent a team of ministers committed to a strictly Evangelical interpretation of the Scriptures. The guiding theological principles of this commentary are expressed in the following statement of faith:

1. WE BELIEVE the Bible to be the inspired, the only infallible, authoritative Word of God.
2. WE BELIEVE that there is one God, eternally existing in three persons: Father, Son, and Holy Spirit.
3. WE BELIEVE in the deity of our Lord Jesus Christ, in His virgin birth, in His sinless life, in His miracles, in His vicarious and atoning death through His shed blood, in His bodily resurrection, in His ascension to the right hand of the Father, and in His personal return in power and glory.
4. WE BELIEVE that for the salvation of lost and sinful men, personal reception of the Lord Jesus Christ and regeneration by the Holy Spirit are absolutely essential.
5. WE BELIEVE in the present ministry of the Holy Spirit by whose cleansing and indwelling the Christian is enabled to live a godly life.
6. WE BELIEVE in the personal return of the Lord Jesus Christ.
7. WE BELIEVE in the resurrection of both the saved and the lost—they that are saved, unto the resurrection of life; and they that are lost, unto the resurrection of damnation.
8. WE BELIEVE in the spiritual unity of believers in our Lord Jesus Christ.

USING THE 1996-97 COMMENTARY

The *Evangelical Sunday School Lesson Commentary* for 1996–97 is presented to the reader with the hope that it will become his weekly companion through the months ahead.

The fall quarter 1996 continues a seven–year cycle of lessons which will be completed with the summer quarter 1999. The 28 quarters of studies, divided into two or more units each, draw from both the Old and New Testaments. Also a number of studies will be topical in nature as attention is focused on contemporary issues. A complete listing of the themes that will be included in the seven–year cycle is printed on page 16 of this volume.

Quarterly unit themes for the 1996–97 volume are as follows:

Fall Quarter—Unit One: "Insights From 1 and 2 Timothy, Titus" Unit two: "Ministering to One Another"

Winter Quarter—Unit One: "Christ in Prophecy"; Unit Two: "Teachings From Ezekiel and Daniel"

Spring Quarter—Unit One: "Teachings of Jesus"; Unit Two: "Basic Christian Truths"

Summer Quarter—Unit One: "God's Word for Difficult Times: Jeremiah"; Unit Two: "Servanthood."

The lesson sequence used in this volume is prepared by the Evangelical Curriculum Commission. (The Evangelical Curriculum Commission is a member of the National Association of Evangelicals.)

The specific material used in developing each lesson is written and edited under the guidance of the editorial staff of Pathway Press.

STUDY TEXT: At the opening of each week's lesson, you will see printed the study text. These references point out passages of Scripture that are directly related to the lesson, and it is advisable for you to read each one carefully before beginning the lesson study.

TIME and PLACE: A time and place is given for each lesson. Where there is a wide range of opinions regarding the exact time or place, the printed New Testament works of Merrill C. Tenney and Old Testament works of Samuel J. Schultz are used to provide the information.

PRINTED TEXT and CENTRAL TRUTH: The printed text is the body of Scripture designated each week for verse–by–verse study in the classroom. Drawing on the study text the teacher delves into this printed text, expounding its content to the students. Although the printed text contains different insights for each teacher, the central truth states the single unifying principle that the expositors attempted to clarify in each lesson.

DICTIONARY: A dictionary, which attempts to bring pronunciation and clarification to difficult words or phrases, is included with most lessons. Pronunciations are based on the phonetic system used by Field Enterprises Educational Corporation of Chicago and New York in *The World Book Encyclopedia.* Definitions are generally based on *The Pictorial Bible Dictionary*, published by Zondervan Publishing Company, Grand Rapids, Michigan.

EXPOSITION and LESSON OUTLINE: The heart of this commentary—and probably the heart of the teacher's instruction each week—is the exposition of the printed text. This exposition material is preceded by a lesson outline, which indicates how the material is to be divided for study. These lesson outlines are not exhaustive but, rather, provide a skeleton for the teacher to amplify upon and to build around.

REVIEW and DISCUSSION QUESTIONS: Immediately following the expository material in each lesson are five review questions. These questions are designed as discussion starters, along with the discussion questions appearing throughout the expository material. The review questions also serve to restate the major bits of information in the text and may be supplemented by questions of your own drawn from the expository material.

GOLDEN TEXT HOMILY: The golden text homily for each week is a brief reflection on that single verse. As the word *homily* implies, it is a discourse or sermon on a particular point. The homily may often be used effectively to give the lesson a life–related slant.

SENTENCE SERMONS: Two or more sentence sermons—popular and pithy single–line thoughts on the central truth of the lesson—are included each week.

EVANGELISM APPLICATION: The evangelism application relates the general theme of the week's lesson to the ongoing task of evangelism. The theme of the lesson (but not necessarily of the lesson text) is used to make this application. At times the emphasis of the section bears on direct evangelism of class members who may not be Christians; at other times the emphasis bears upon exhorting the class members to become more involved in evangelizing others.

ILLUMINATING THE LESSON: In this section, illustrative material is provided for the teacher to use to support the lesson at whatever point seems most apropriate.

DAILY BIBLE READINGS: The daily Bible readings are included for the teacher to use in his own devotions throughout the week, as well as to share with members of his class.

EXPOSITION WRITERS

Writers for the expository materials for the 1996–97 volume are as follows:

The lesson expositions for the fall quarter (September, October, November) were prepared by the Reverend Dr. Jerald Daffe (B.A., M.A., D.Min.), who is assocate professor of pastoral studies and serves as chairman of the Department of Bible and Chrisitan Ministries, Lee College, Cleveland, Tennessee.

Dr. Daffe earned his bachelor of arts degree at Northwest Bible College, a master of arts degree at Wheaton College Graduate School, and his doctorate of ministry degree at Western Conservative Baptist Seminary. An ordained minister in the Church of God, Dr. Daffe has served in the pastoral ministry for 10 years and has been faculty member on two college campuses—Northwest Bible College and Lee College—for over 20 years.

Dr. Daffe has been recognized and listed in Outstanding Educators of America 1974-75; Outstanding Young Men of America 1984. He also received the Excellence in Teaching Award at Lee College in 1990. Recognized for his professional knowledge and communicative skills, Dr. Daffe is a popular speaker at camp meetings, retreats, seminars, and churches in many denominations. In addition to many magazine articles and Sunday school lessons, he has written two books: *Handbook for Special Services* and *Instructor's Guide for Sunday School in the 90's*

Lesson expositions for the winter quarter (December, January, February) were written by a team of Bible scholars

The Reverend Dr. Eugene C. Christenbury (see spring quarter for information on this writer); the Reverend Dr. James E. Humbertson (M.R.E., D.Min.); the Reverend Dr. Oliver McMahan (B.A., M.Div., D.Min.); the Reverend Dr. Homer G. Rhea.

The Reverend James E. Humbertson is editorial director of the *Evangelical Sunday School Lesson Commentary* at the Church of God Publishing House, Cleveland, Tennessee.

The Reverend Dr. Humbertson holds an undergraduate degree in biblical educatrion and two graduate degrees, including a master of religious education and a doctor of ministry in the field of Christian education.

Dr. Humbertson's experience includes years of service as a seminary and college professor, college administrator, a chariman of boards of Christian education, and a lecturer at writers' and educational seminars.

The Reverend Dr. Humbertson has written many articles and book chapters published in Pathway Press magazines and workers training courses. He has also written three courses including "The History and Philosophy of Christian Education" for Lee College, where he taught resident courses in Christian education from 1972-1978.

The Reverend Dr. McMahan is former dean of students and associate professor at Northwest Bible college, Minot, North Dakota. Presently, he is associate professor of pastoral studies and director of external studies at the School of Theology, Cleveland, Tennessee. He is a graduate of West Coast Bible College and of Brite Divinity School at Texas Christia University.

An ordained minister in the Church of God, Dr. McMahan has served his denomination as pastor, educator, and pastoral counselor. From 1976-1981 he served as minister of youth and outreach at the Oak Cliff Church of God, in Dallas, Texas.

Dr. McMahan has written a number of articles for the *Church of God Evangel* and is a contributor of definitions and articles for the *Complete Biblical Library*.

Dr. McMahan is a member of the Evangelical Theological Society and the Association for Clinical Pastoral Education.

The Reverend Dr. Rhea is editor in chief of the Church of God Publications. He formerly served as editor administrative assistant at the Church of God Publishing House, Cleveland, Tennessee, and in conjunction with the editor in chief, prepared the *Church of God Evangel*, the official journal of the denominatin. Reverend Rhea was reared and educated in Mississippi, where he served in the pastoral ministry for 18 years. He is an ordained minister in the Church of God and has held positions as district overseer and member of the Mississippi State Council and the State Youth and Christian Education Board.

The Reverend Dr. Rhea is author of the Instructor's Manual to the Church Training Course *Highlights of Hebrew History*, by Charles W. Conn, *A New Creation: A Study of Salvation*, and *Come, Worship With Us.*

Lesson expositions for the spring quarter (March, April, May) were written by the Reverend Dr. Eugene C. Christenbury (B.A., M.A., M.S., Ed.D.).

Dr. Christenbury earned his bachelor of arts and master of arts degrees at George Peabody College for Teachers and his doctorate of education from the University of Tennessee. He aslo earned the M.S. degree in religion from the Church of God School of Theology, Cleveland, Tennessee. An ordained minister in the Church of God, Dr. Christenbury has served as state youth and Christian education director, pastor, and assistant superintendent at the Home for Children in Sevierville, Tennessee. He is retired after serving as senior adjunct professor of education at Lee College, Cleveland, Tennessee.

Dr. Christenbury is a member of Phi Delta Kappa and the Counciil on Public Education of Religious Studies. Recognized for his academic and religious knowledge, he is a popular speaker on the Lee College campus and in the broader church community.

Lesson expositions for the summer quarter (June, July, August) were written by the Reverend Rodney Hodge, an ordained minister who has served as minister of music of music for 24 years at Northwood Temple Pentecostal Holiness Church in Fayetteville, North Carolina. He holds degrees from Emmanuel College and the University of Georgia and did graduate studies in history at the University of Georgia.

Reverend Hodge has written numerous Bible study programs, as well as dramas and music productions, and has produced an entire series of theater productions for church use.

The Reverend Hodge presently writed adult Sunday school literature for the Pentecostal Holiness Church.

GOLDEN TEXT HOMILY WRITERS 1996-967

French L. Arrington, Ph.D.
Professor of New Testament Greek and Exegesis
Church of God School of Theology
Cleveland, Tennessee

Richard Y. Bershon, Ph.D.
Chaplain, State Veterans Home
Hot Springs, South Dakota

Noel Brooks, D.D. (Retired)
Writer, Adult Sunday School Teacher Quarterly
International Pentecostal Holiness Church
Oklahoma City, Oklahoma

Eugene C. Christenbury, Ed.D. (Retired)
Former Faculty Member at Lee College
Cleveland, Tennessee

Jerald Daffe, D.Min.
Associate Professor/Pastorial Studies and Chairman/Department of Bible and Christian Ministries
Lee College
Cleveland, Tennessee

Harvey L. Davis
Sunday School Teacher
Madison, Mississippi

Brady Dennis
Former Church of God State Overseer
Greenville, South Carolina

Ralph S. Douglas (LT)
Chaplain
Virginia Beach, Virginia

James L. Durel, Captain
The Salvation Army
Roseville, California

Joel Harris
Pastor, Church of God
Mobile, Alabama

William M. Henry Jr., Former Instructor
Missions and New Testament Greek
West Coast Christian College
Fresno, California

James E. Humbertson, D.Min.
Editorial Director, *Evangelical Commentary*
Pathway Press
Cleveland, Tennessee

Willie F. Lawrence, D.D.
Pastor, Church of God
Moline, Illinois

James Leggett, Vice Chairman and Assistant General Superintendent
International Pentecostal Holiness Church
Oklahoma City, Oklahoma

William R. McCall
Missionary, Church of God
Cleveland, Tennessee

David L. Metzger
Navy Chaplain
Marion Aircraft, Japan

Aaron D. Mize, Clinical Chaplain
Alcohol and Drug Treatment Center
Parchman, Mississippi

Levy E. Moore, Mayor
City of Franklin Springs
Franklin Springs, Georgia

Richard L. Pace, Chaplain (MAJ)
Command and Staff College
Fort Leavenworth, Kansas

Ronald M. Padgett
Director of Chaplaincy Services
Mississippi Department of Corrections
Parchman, Mississippi

Luther E. Painter, D.Min.
Assistant Professor of Religion
Lee College
Cleveland, Tennessee

O.W. Polen, D.D.
Coordinator of Special Projects
Pathway Press
Cleveland, Tennessee

Wayne S. Proctor
Former Pastor
Harrisburg, Illinois

Jerry Puckett
Customer Service Representative
Pathway Press
Cleveland, Tennessee

M.E. Roberson
Former Pastor
Soddy-Daisy, Tennessee

Henry J. Smith, D.Min.
Vice President for Student Life
Lee College
Cleveland, Tennessee

Marion H. Starr
Pastor, Church of God
Marion, South Carolina

Michael S. Stewart
Senior Pastor
First Assembly of God
Winston-Salem, North Carolina

Dennis W. Watkins, Attorney at Law
Legal Services
Church of God International Offices
Cleveland, Tennessee

Fred H. Whisman (Lt. Col.)
Group II Chaplain
Civil Air Patrol
Chattanooga, Tennessee

Charles G. Wiley
Pastor, Church of God
Graham, Texas

Eugene Wigelsworth
Clinical Chaplain, Pasquotank Corr. Inst.
Elizabeth City, North Carolina

Florie Brown Wigelsworth, M.Div.
Elizabeth City, North Carolina

Sabord Woods, Ph.D.
Professor of English
Lee College
Cleveland, Tennessee

SCRIPTURE TEXTS USED IN LESSON EXPOSITION

Genesis
1: 1-3 — April 20
24: 2-4, 9, 56 — August 3

Exodus
12: 21-24 — December 8
17: 11, 12 — November 24

Numbers
21: 6-9 — December 8

Deuteronomy
15: 7, 8 — November 17
18: 15-19 — December 15

1 Samuel
3: 4-10 — August 3
16: 16, 17 — August 10

2 Samuel
7: 12-16 — December 29

Psalm
19: 1-4 — April 20
22: 1, 2, 6, 7, 11-20, 23-27 — December 1
24: 7-10 — December 15
45: 6, 7 — December 29

Proverbs
3: 11, 12 — April 27
14: 35 — August 10

Isaiah
43: 12, 13 — April 20
53: 4, 5 — May 4
59: 20, 21 — December 15
63: 7, 16 — April 27

Jeremiah
1: 4-14, 16-19 — June 1
18: 1-12 — June 15
19: 15 — June 15
20: 7-9, 11, 12 — June 22
26: 2-13 — June 8
27: 2-4, 6-9, 12-17 — July 6
31: 10-12, 31-34 — July 13
33: 14-16 — July 13
36: 1-3, 10, 16, 20, 23, 24, 27, 28, 32 — June 29
38: 17, 18 — July 20
39: 11-18 — July 27

40: 2-4	July 27
52: 8-11	July 20

Lamentations

3: 17-26, 37-40	June 22

Ezekiel

11: 17-20	January 12
14: 6-11	January 12
28: 17-19	February 2
33: 8-18	January 5
34: 2-5, 9-16	February 9
36: 25-28	February 23
37: 1, 3-6, 11-14, 21-23	February 16
47: 1-8	February 23

Daniel

1: 8-20	January 19
2: 48, 49	August 31
5: 1, 3-6, 24-30	February 2
7: 13, 14	December 29
9: 3-6, 16-22	January 26

Matthew

2: 1-12	December 22
5: 1-16	March 2
6: 1, 3-18	March 9
10: 24-41	March 16
16: 15-18	May 11
16: 27	May 25
18: 2-4	August 17
18: 15-17	November 10
20: 1-8, 11-15	August 10
20: 26-28	August 17
25: 34-40	November 3

Mark

6: 34-38, 41, 42	August 17

Luke

10: 25-37	March 23
10: 38-42	August 31
13: 11-13	May 4
15: 4-6, 8-16, 20-24	April 6
16: 13	August 3
16: 19-31	April 13

John

1: 1, 2, 14, 18	April 20
13: 1-17	August 24
14: 2, 3	May 25
14: 6-11	April 27
20: 1-12, 15-17	March 30

Acts

1: 11	May 25
2: 1-8, 12, 13, 29-33, 46, 47	May 18
6: 2-4, 7	November 3
11: 5-9	October 27
15: 1, 6-12	October 27
20: 35	November 17

Romans

1: 19, 20	April 20
12: 5-8	August 31
13: 1-4	November 24
16: 23	August 31

1 Corinthians

4: 1, 2	August 3
9: 19	August 10
12: 12-14, 26, 27	May 11

2 Corinthians

4: 5	August 10
8: 12-15	November 17
9: 6-10	November 17

Galatians

4: 6	April 27
6: 1-10	November 10

Ephesians

1: 2-4	April 27
1: 7	May 4
2: 4, 5	May 4
2: 19-22	May 11

Philippians

2: 5-8	August 17
3: 20, 21	May 25
4: 22	August 31

Colossians

3: 2-4	May 25
3: 22	August 3

1 Thessalonians

4: 16, 17	May 25

1 Timothy

1: 3-17	September 1
2: 1-4	November 24
3: 1-16	September 8
4: 1-16	September 15
5: 4	August 31
6: 3-14	September 22

2 Timothy

1: 6-14	September 29
1: 9, 10	May 4
2: 1-7, 11-21	October 6
3: 1-17	October 13
4: 5-8, 16-18	October 20

Titus

2: 1, 7, 8	September 22
2: 11-14	September 29
2: 13	May 25
3: 1-8	October 20
3: 4-7	May 4

Hebrews

1: 1, 2	April 20
2: 1-4	July 20
9: 13-15	December 8
13: 7, 17	November 24

James

1: 17	April 27
1: 27	November 3
2: 1, 8, 9	October 27
2: 14-17	November 3
5: 19, 20	November 10

1 Peter

2: 5, 9, 10	May 11
4: 9	August 31

2 Peter

1: 19-21	April 20

1 John

3: 1, 2	May 25
3: 16-18	November 17

Revelation

19: 11-16	December 29

SCRIPTURE TEXTS USED IN GOLDEN TEXT HOMILIES

Deuteronomy

18: 15	December 15

Psalm

22: 19	December 1
85: 6	February 16
119: 89	June 29

Proverbs

3: 5	January 19
16: 18	February 2

Isaiah

53: 5	December 8

Jeremiah

1: 17	June 1
18: 6	June 15
26: 15	June 8
33: 15	July 13
39: 18	July 27

Lamentations

3: 24	June 22

Ezekiel

14: 6	January 12
33: 19	January 5
34: 16	February 9
36: 27	February 23

Matthew

2: 11	December 22
5: 6	March 2
6: 1	March 9
10: 39	March 16
16: 24	October 6
25: 40	November 3

Luke

10: 27	March 23
11: 2	April 27
15: 7	April 6

John

3: 17	April 13
13: 15	August 24

Acts

2: 4	May 18

Romans

13: 1	November 24

1 Corinthians

12: 27	May 11
15: 3, 4	March 30

2 Corinthians

4: 5	August 10

Galatians

6: 1	November 10

Ephesians

6: 18	January 26

Philippians

2 : 5, 7	August 17

Colossians

3: 17	August 31
3: 23, 24	August 3

1 Timothy

6: 6	September 15

2 Timothy

1: 13	September 29
2: 15	September 1
3: 1	October 13
3: 16	September 22
4: 7	October 20

Titus

2: 13	May 25

Hebrews

1: 1, 2	April 20
1: 8	December 29
2: 1	July 20
12: 5, 6	July 6

James

2: 8	October 27

1 Peter

5: 2	September 8

2 Peter

3: 18	May 4

1 John

3: 18	November 17

ACKNOWLEDGMENTS

Many books, magazines, and newspapers have been used in the research that has gone into this 1996-97 *Evangelical Commentary*. A few of the major books that have been used are listed below.

Bibles

King James Version, Oxford University Press, Oxford, England
New American Standard Bible (NASB), A.J. Holman Co., Publishers, New York, New York
New English Bible (NEB), Oxford University Press, Oxford, England
New International Version (NIV), Zondervan Publishing House, Grand Rapids, Michigan
New King James Version, Thomas Nelson Publisher, Nashville, Tennessee
The Berkeley Version, Zondervan Publishing House, Grand Rapids, Michigan

Commentaries

Clarke's Commentary, Abingdon-Cokesbury, Nashville, Tennessee
Commentaries on the Old Testament (Keil & Delitzsch), Eerdmans Publishing Co., Grand Rapids, Michigan
Ellicott's Bible Commentary, Zondervan Publishing House, Grand Rapids, Michigan
Expositions of Holy Scriptures (Alexander MacLaren), Eerdmans Publishing Co., Grand Rapids, Michigan
The Broadman Bible Commentary, Volumes 10 and 11, Broadman Press, Nashville, Tennessee
The Interpreter's Bible, Abingdon Press, New York, New York
The Letters to the Corinthians, William Barclay, Westminster Press, Philadelphia, Pennsylvania
The Pulpit Commentary, Eerdmans Publishing Co., Grand Rapids, Michigan
The Wesleyan Commentary, Eerdmans Publishing Co., Grand Rapids, Michigan
The Expositor's Greek Testament, Eerdmans Publishing Co., Grand Rapids, Michigan

Illustrations

Dictionary of Illustrations for Pulpit and Platform, Moody Press, Chicago, Illinois
I Quote, George W. Stewart Publishers, Inc., New York, New York
3,000 Illustrations for Christian Service, Eerdmans Publishing Co., Grand Rapids, Michigan
Knight's Master Book of New Illustrations, Eerdmans Publishing Co., Grand Rapids, Michigan
Notes and Quotes, The Warner Press, Anderson, Indiana
Quotable Quotations, Scripture Press Publications, Wheaton, Illinois
The Pointed Pen, Pathway Press, Cleveland, Tennessee
The Speaker's Sourcebook, Zondervan Publishing House, Grand Rapids, Michigan
1,000 New Illustrations, Al Bryant, Zondervan Publishing Co., Grand Rapids, Michigan
The Encyclopedia of Religious Quotations, Fleming H. Revell Co., Old Tappan, New Jersey

General Reference Books

Harper's Bible Dictionary, Harper and Brothers Publishers, New York, New York
The International Standard Bible Encyclopedia, Eerdmans Publishing Co., Grand Rapids, Michigan
The Interpreter's Dictionary of the Bible, Abingdon Press, Nashville, Tennessee
The World Book Encyclopedia, Field Enterprises Education Corp., Chicago, Illinois
Pictorial Dictionary of the Bible, Zondervan Publishing House, Grand Rapids, Michigan
Word Pictures in the New Testament (Robertson), Broadman Press, Nashville, Tennessee

Evangelical Bible Lesson Series (1992-1999)

Fall Quarter September, October, November	Winter Quarter December, January, February	Spring Quarter March, April, May	Summer Quarter June, July, August
1992 Unit One—Personalities in Genesis Unit Two—Psalms, Proverbs and Ecclesiastes	**1992-93** Unit One—Following Jesus Unit Two—Evangelism	**1993** Unit One—Building Positive Relationships Unit Two—Life and Teachings of Moses	**1993** Unit One—The Church Is Launched Unit Two—Ministry in the Church
1993 Unit One—Learning From Israel's Experiences Unit Two—Living in Today's World	**1993-94** Unit One—The Gospel According to John Unit Two—Christian Growth	**1994** Unit One—Covenants in the Bible Unit Two—Joshua and Ruth	**1994** Unit One—Understanding Cultism Unit Two—Spiritual Revival and Renewal Unit Three—Ezra, Nehemiah, Ruth
1994 Unit One—Truths From Romans Unit Two—Spiritual Warfare	**1994-95** Unit One—Mosaic Law and New Testament Counterparts Unit Two—Worship in the OT and NT	**1995** Unit One—1 & 2 Corinthians Unit Two—Strengthening Marriage and Family Ties	**1995** Unit One—Principles of Godly Leadership Unit Two—Christian Values
1995 Unit One—Galatians and Ephesians Unit Two—Christian Fellowship	**1995-96** Unit One—Wisdom Literature Unit Two—Building a Consistent Devotional Life	**1996** Unit One—Triumphing Over Life's Crises Unit Two—Philippians and Colossians	**1996** Unit One—Isaiah Unit Two—God's Providential Care
1996 Unit One—Insights from 1 & 2 Timothy, Titus Unit Two—Ministering to One Another	**1996-97** Unit One—Christ in Prophecy Unit Two—Teachings from Ezekiel and Daniel	**1997** Unit One—Teachings of Jesus Unit Two—Basic Christian Truths	**1997** Unit One—God's Word for Difficult Times Unit Two—Servanthood
1997 Unit One—James, 1 & 2 Peter Unit Two—Work of the Spirit	**1997-98** Unit One—Celebrating Advent Unit Two—God's Word in Psalm 119	**1998** Unit One—The Book of Hebrews Unit Two—Lessons From the Patriarchs	**1998** Unit One—Messages of Minor Prophets Unit Two—Bible Answers to Current Issues
1998 Unit One—Life and Teachings of Paul Unit Two—Help for Life's Journey	**1998-99** Unit One—God's Plan of Redemption Unit Two—Truths From the Tabernacle	**1999** Unit One—People Who Met Jesus Unit Two—Personal Evangelism	**1999** Unit One—Understanding Revelation Unit Two—The Mission of the Church

INTRODUCTION TO FALL QUARTER

The month of September begins the fall quarter series of lessons, which is divided into two distinct units of study. Unit One (lessons 1-8) is presented under the theme "Insights From 1 and 2 Timothy, Titus." Not only is the content of these books rich in doctrinal and practical discussion, but the historical, geographical, and personal notices make the letters colorful and intensely human. Also, these epistles are the only part of the New Testament which deals with church problems from an administrative rather than a theological viewpoint.

In Unit Two (lessons 9-13) the theme "Ministering to One Another" draws from both Old and New Testament scriptures. As the name implies, the lessons are designed to help in the all-important Christian service of being ready to help others whether the individuals are of the same persuasion, laymen, or ministerial leaders.

INSIGHTS FROM
1 & 2 TIMOTHY, TITUS
(Map for General Use)

Faithful to the Truth

Study Text: 1 Timothy 1:1–20

Objective: To understand the importance of biblical truth and determine to be faithful to it.

Time: The Book of 1 Timothy was written between A.D. 62 and 64.

Place: The Book of 1 Timothy was probably written in the Macedonian city of Philippi.

Golden Text: Study to shew thyself approved unto God, a workman that needeth not to be ashamed, rightly dividing the word of truth" (2 Timothy 2:15).

Central Truth: Biblical truth is the anchor of our faith.

Evangelism Emphasis: Biblical truth leads the sinner to eternal life.

PRINTED TEXT

1 Timothy 1:3. As I besought thee to abide still at Ephesus, when I went into Macedonia, that thou mightest charge some that they teach no other doctrine,

4. Neither give heed to fables and endless genealogies, which minister questions, rather than godly edifying which is in faith: so do.

5. Now the end of the commandment is charity out of a pure heart, and of a good conscience, and of faith unfeigned:

6. From which some having swerved have turned aside unto vain jangling;

7. Desiring to be teachers of the law; understanding neither what they say, nor whereof they affirm.

8. But we know that the law is good, if a man uses it lawfully;

9. Knowing this, that the law is not made for a righteous man, but for the lawless and disobedient, for the ungodly and for the sinners, for unholy and profane, for murderers of fathers and murderers of mothers, for manslayers,

10. For whoremongers, for them that defile themselves with mankind, for menstealers, for liars, for perjured persons, and if there be any other thing that is contrary to sound doctrine;

11. According to the glorious gospel of the blessed God, which was committed to my trust.

12. And I thank Christ Jesus our Lord, who hath enabled me, for that he counted me faithful, putting me into the ministry;

13. Who was before a blasphemer, and a persecutor, and injurious: but I obtained mercy, because I did it ignorantly in unbelief.

14. And the grace of our Lord was exceeding abundant

with faith and love which is in Christ Jesus.

15. This is a faithful saying, and worthy of all acceptation, that Christ Jesus came into the world to save sinners; of whom I am chief.

16. Howbeit for this cause I obtained mercy, that in me first Jesus Christ might shew forth all longsuffering, for a pattern to them which should hereafter believe on him to life everlasting.

17. Now unto the King eternal, immortal, invisible, the only wise God, be honour and glory for ever and ever. Amen.

DICTIONARY

Ephesus (Efeh–sus)—1 Timothy 1:3—The chief city of Asia Minor.

Macedonia (Mas–eh–DOH–nee–uh)—1 Timothy 1:3—The northern part of Greece.

LESSON OUTLINE

I. TEACH THE TRUTH
   A. The Person
   B. The Place
   C. The Problem

II. FOLLOW CORRECT DOCTRINE
   A. The Goal of Love
   B. The Purpose of the Law
   C. The Glorious Gospel

III. SERVE FAITHFULLY
   A. Appointed to Serve
   B. Receiver of Grace
   C. Glorification of the King

LESSON EXPOSITION

INTRODUCTION

A close study of Timothy's actions indicates his tremendous commitment to Christ and the cause of the Cross. He remained steadfast in all the situations which occurred as a result of his being in the front lines of ministry. This is even more amazing and to his credit when one considers his youthfulness in comparison to the task.

Paul wrote this epistle to Timothy for the express purpose of providing encouragement and direction. Timothy faced a difficult task at the church in Ephesus. False teachers and their doctrines had invaded the congregation. If it had been an immature or new congregation, it would have been easier to understand these events taking place. However, the fact that it was not a new congregation underscores how false doctrine can invade any church body if the believers aren't vigilant to Satan's attacks.

This epistle to Timothy is the first of three of Paul's letters (including Titus) that have become known as the "Pastoral Epistles." In fact, this one is so relevant to pastoring that even at the end of the 20th century it has been suggested by some as necessary reading for every pastor at least once a year. It should be read each year for its methods and principles for pastoring in whatever century.

Paul wrote this letter in the period between his two Roman imprisonments. Assuming the first imprisonment was about A.D. 61–62 and the second A.D. 66–67, it may have been penned as early as A.D. 63 or 64.

Instead of writing a letter, Paul's initial intentions were to come personally and visit his "son in the faith" (v. 2) and member of his missionary team. However, some pressing matters delayed his trip. So rather than refrain from any contact at all, he sent this letter.

Right from the beginning of the epistle, Paul stressed the need for clinging to the truth. Truth is vital both in doctrine and in lifestyle. Any deviation from it places a person outside the will and Word of God. When that happens, it is only a matter of time until one's relationship with God deteriorates and disappears. You can't continue to be a Christian and adhere to beliefs that are in opposition to the Word.

In this lesson we are reminded how deeply false doctrine can become entrenched in a congregation. This situation then demands a solid leader who can deal with the situation, using both the truth of the Word and the wisdom of leadership. Sometimes, such as in this case, a younger individual is given the task of confronting those who may be both chronologically and spiritually older. When that occurs, a supportive supervisor who offers wisdom and direction makes all the difference.

I. TEACH THE TRUTH (1 Timothy 1:1–4)

A. The Person (vv. 1, 2)

(1 Timothy 1:1, 2 is not included in the printed text.)

In his usual manner Paul identified himself as the author at the beginning of the epistle. He knew and indicated that his being an apostle was not in the same manner as the original apostles. When the believers were attempting to replace Judas, Peter gave a necessary qualification for an apostle as one who had witnessed Christ's earthly ministry and His resurrection (Acts 1:22).

Paul stated that his right to apostleship came through the direct "commandment of God our Savior" (v. 1). No doubt he was referring to his Damascus–road conversion while he was on his way to persecute Christians. Jesus, the Son of God, had spoken to him. Paul's position in ministry was due to the direct call of God in a most unusual setting. Writing to the Corinthians, Paul indicated he had seen Christ (1 Corinthians 9:1; 15:8, 9).

Paul emphasized the unity of the Godhead by referring to "God our Savior." This is somewhat different from saying "Christ our Savior." It gets our attention and draws us closer to a more complete understanding of the complexities of the God we serve.

In verse 1 Paul emphasized Christ as our hope. Believers are not dabbling in the realm of wishful thinking or hopeful possibilities; we possess absolute certainty. The deity of Christ enables us to look expectantly toward the future. Then all that is currently incomplete will be complete.

In verse 2 we are introduced to Timothy, the person being given the responsibility for teaching the truth and ensuring that others were doing likewise. The description of Timothy as "my own son in the faith" attests to the intimate Christian relationship between these two men. This relationship began during Paul's first missionary journey. It appears that Timothy came to Christ under Paul's ministry (Acts 14:6; 16:1). Their relationship continued when Paul returned to Lystra on his second missionary journey and placed him on the mission team. Paul's use of this terminology also needs to be understood in terms of the contemporary society. It is especially useful in expressing the master–disciple relationship.

A thorough study of the Epistles reveals Timothy had many of the same characteristics as his spiritual father. He loved people, endured suffering, and took on difficult situations (see Philippians 2:19–23).

B. The Place (v. 3)

3. As I besought thee to abide still at Ephesus, when I went into Macedonia, that thou mightest charge some that they teach no other doctrine.

In the process of a trip Paul decided it would be best for Timothy to remain in Ephesus rather than continue with him up to Macedonia. Some believe Paul had come personally to Ephesus and, after viewing the church's situation there, realized it needed the continued pastoral care of a man like Timothy. Others believe Paul was journeying toward Macedonia and on the way asked Timothy to divert his travel plans to Ephesus. Regardless of which case it might have been, Timothy faced a tremendous challenge to teach the truth and instruct the church there.

The city of Ephesus itself existed only as a shell of its former self. At one time its harbor had enabled this port city to rival Alexandria in Egypt and Antioch of Syria in glory. But this proud heritage was only a memory of the past. Silting of the harbor had closed down its trade, and now 20 miles of reedy marshlands separated the city from the sea.

Whatever life there was at Ephesus rested on its popularity as the center of cult worship at the temple of Diana—known as Artemis to the Greeks but Diana to the Romans. A number of priestess prostitutes worked at the temple for those who came to worship the goddess of fertility. Mostly tourists and pilgrims provided a revenue lifeline for this decaying city.

Paul's familiarity with the city and the church is well documented. He spent much of his third missionary journey here (Acts 19:10). He worked to support himself and experienced a mighty move of God with many conversions taking place. If Timothy was with him at this time, it further ensured that he knew the city, the church, and the conditions he could expect there.

False doctrines in this environment can be assumed. It is only logical to expect the Greek philosophies to have some impact since Ephesus was a Hellenistic city. Ideas from former disciplines and lifestyles would remain dormant for a while and then resurface unless there was a conscious effort to eradicate them.

C. The Problem (v. 4)

4. Neither give heed to fables and endless genealogies, which minister questions, rather than godly edifying which is in faith: so do.

Paul proceeded to the major issue very quickly. It was a serious situation that he wanted to deal with immediately. In view of Timothy's experience as a ministry partner with Paul, we can assume he wasn't a stranger to the problems and types of heresy that were assailing the church. However, in times of crisis good leaders will always review the facts as part of the procedure. They also will remind their partners of the basic approach that needs to be followed.

From the information Paul provided, we assume Timothy faced two separate strains of false doctrine. The reference to "fables" seems to point to Greek ideas that were being incorporated into the church. The Greek philosophies' emphasis on knowledge became a challenge during this century and the one to follow. It was often viewed as being more important than faith and a personal experience of life in Christ.

The second reference is to "genealogies," which were important in Greek thought about the god system in the heavenlies. His mention of it also gives support to the presence of a Jewish influence. In the Jewish religion, genealogies were a vital aspect of identifying one's position as one of God's chosen people. It is logical, then, to assume there were some individuals attempting to incorporate aspects of Judaism into the new faith. The descriptive word *endless* before the word *genealogies* seems to indicate a sense of speculation, or continual wrangling.

Regardless of the type of speculation or source of the controversy, a common result existed. God's Word wasn't being glorified or edified. Speculation and controversy never enables the work of Christ to thrive. It divides! It detours! It delays!

Why do false doctrines receive such a ready hearing among many believers?

II. FOLLOW CORRECT DOCTRINE (1 Timothy 1:5–11)

A. The Goal of Love (vv. 5, 6)

5. Now the end of the commandment is charity out of a pure heart, and of a good conscience, and of faith unfeigned:

6. From which some having swerved have turned aside unto vain jangling.

Even while dealing with the specifics of the problem, Paul wanted the totality of Christianity to stand forth. To stop the false doctrine isn't sufficient. Love, the essence of life in Christ, needs to dominate and shine forth. Paul reminds all of us that love can't be evident within the controversies of false doctrine. Love originates from a threefold source:

First, love flows from a pure heart. In the Old Testament, the heart represented man's moral affections, the motives behind one's actions. Purity of heart seeks for God to be glorified. Deeds reflect the desire for a closer relationship with God rather than selfish motives. God's will stands as the dominant desire. In other words, a pure heart causes a person to witness not for the sake of convert numbers but that they may be rescued from sin and reconciled to God.

Second, love flows from a good conscience. A good conscience is one which hides nothing from God. All sin is confessed and God's forgiveness is experienced. This type of conscience commends good and condemns evil. It allows biblical judgments to occur even when facing the twisting arguments of heresy.

Third, love flows from a sincere, unfeigned faith which does not rest on the shifting sand of men's thoughts and changing current events. A truly sincere faith produces an outward appearance and public profession based on a relationship of commitment to the Lord Jesus Christ.

False doctrines cannot produce a true and genuine love. They spawn a great deal of discussion and meaningless talk but nothing positive. Lasting love can never develop from the uncertainties and inconsistencies of human thought. Thus when false doctrine infiltrates a congregation, it automatically begins to erode the love atmosphere. This is in direct contrast to what Jesus taught. Love is to be a sign of our discipleship. When we love one another, it is a witness to the world that we are Jesus' disciples.

When there is an abundance of meaningless talk, no solid foundation exists where substantial dialogue can take place. When all the eloquent verbiage ceases, nothing of substance remains. Books can be written and programs produced, but in the end there are only actions and words that fade without lasting results.

The bottom line is simply this: Without correct doctrine, true love can never flourish within the church—the body of Christ.

What are some of the results of false doctrine?

B. The Purpose of the Law (vv. 7–10)

7. Desiring to be teachers of the law; understanding neither what they say, nor whereof they affirm.

8. But we know that the law is good, if a man uses it lawfully;

9. Knowing this, that the law is not made for a righteous man, but for the lawless and disobedient, for the ungodly and for the sinners, for unholy and profane, for murderers of fathers and murderers of mothers, for manslayers,

10. For whoremongers, for them that defile themselves with mankind, for menstealers, for liars, for perjured persons, and if there be any other thing that is contrary to sound doctrine.

Following correct doctrine includes having a proper understanding of the Old Testament law. Verse 7 points out that a lack of such understanding contributes to the problem of false doctrine. Instead of understanding and propagating the gospel of Jesus Christ, individuals were attempting to follow the role of the Jewish rabbis. Not only were they unfit from the training aspect, but they also did not comprehend sacred content and purpose. They spoke confidently as though they knew; however, in reality there was a void of knowledge and an abundance of ignorance.

Paul wanted all to know that there is a positiveness in the law, provided it is used properly. The law isn't intended to be a burden for the righteous people who are striving to serve God. Instead it stands as a rule, or standard, to distinguish the actions of evildoers. Those who have been made righteous through the grace of Jesus Christ are free from guilt as determined by the law. But the evildoers are in a different situation.

Verses 9 and 10 include a partial list of evildoers whose actions are condemned under the law. Paul began with the general wrongdoers and then moved to the more specific sins. The *lawless* are those who ignore the law (also known as lawbreakers). The *disobedient* are those who refuse to be held accountable to the law. The *ungodly* are those who consciously choose to be irreverent. The *sinners* are those who oppose God and His law. The *unholy* and *profane* are those who deny and disregard sacred principles and sacred actions. The *murderers* include those who fail to honor their parents as well as those who actually take another's life.

Verse 10 begins with sexual sins including adultery and acts of sexual perversion (sodomy). It is of interest that "menstealers" (slave traders) are included, since slavery wasn't specifically denounced, while those who profited in selling others were. The final description of evildoers deals with the sins of lying in general and specifically while under oath.

The partialness of this list is emphasized by Paul's saying, "and if there be any other thing that is contrary to sound doctrine"—and there are. However, a more detailed list isn't necessary. The idea of what denotes being contrary to sound doctrine appears to be very evident.

C. The Glorious Gospel (v. 11)

11. According to the glorious gospel of the blessed God, which was committed to my trust.

Why stay burdened with the law when one has the opportunity to enjoy the glorious gospel of Jesus Christ?

Why emphasize a law built on the blood of bulls and goats when the all–cleansing blood of Jesus Christ has been shed once and for all?

To enjoy the blessings of a pure and sound doctrine, that doctrine has to be built on the salvatory work of Jesus Christ. On the cross of Calvary, Jesus suffered and died for our sins. Then He rose victoriously from the dead. He overcame death, sin, hell, and the grave. His resurrection provides joy for the present and hope for the future.

III. SERVE FAITHFULLY
(1 Timothy 1:12–17)

A. Appointed to Serve (v. 12)

12. And I thank Christ Jesus our Lord, who hath enabled me, for that he counted me faithful, putting me into the ministry.

Here Paul took time to testify of his personal experience with the glorious gospel of Jesus Christ. Personal testimonies that exalt the work of Christ always uplift and encourage those who hear or read them. They also convey that there is hope for even the worst evildoer or for the most defiant false teacher. When one considers the case of Paul (then known as Saul), one realizes there is still hope for any individual. What a transformation took place through that divine confrontation on the road to Damascus (Acts 9)!

In verse 1 Paul spoke of his divine appointment to ministry. Verse 12 is a return to his call, but this time he included a special expression of thanksgiving. Even after years of ministry which had exacted a heavy toll of personal suffering and unbelievable sacrifice, Paul could still burst out with thanksgiving.

Paul was thankful for Christ's enabling, or strengthening him. No one doubts Paul's education, intelligence, and desire. But that wasn't sufficient. There had to be that physical and emotional strength which enables an individual to continue to climb over the obstacles and opposition to the gospel. It was Christ's strengthening that initially enabled Paul to change from a persecutor of Christians to a promoter of Christians. What a dramatic turnaround!

Paul was thankful that Christ had recognized a potential for faithfulness in the transgressor Saul. Even while Saul was zealously pursuing Christians, the Lord recognized in Him the potential for trustworthiness in the propagation of the gospel. Isn't it wonderful that He can look beyond our sins and see our potential. He knows what we can be once we have received the life–changing experience of salvation. And as we continue to draw near to Him, we are strengthened and further enabled in our pursuit of faithfulness.

Paul was thankful that Christ placed him in the ministry. It wasn't a matter of personal vocational choice. It wasn't just the result of knocking on doors until one finally opened. But rather, the divine hand of God, working through the active ministry of the Holy Spirit, guided Paul's every endeavor.

The bottom line is that anyone who is appointed by God to ministry has the responsibility to serve faithfully. However, we must not overlook the context of this whole chapter––that no one can serve faithfully without adhering to and promoting doctrinal truth!

B. Receiver of Grace (vv. 13–16)

13. Who was before a blasphemer, and a persecutor, and injurious: but I obtained mercy, because I did it ignorantly in unbelief.

14. And the grace of our Lord was exceeding abundant with faith and love which is in Christ Jesus.

15. This is a faithful saying, and worthy of all acceptation, that Christ Jesus came into the world to save sinners; of whom I am chief.

16. Howbeit for this cause I obtained mercy, that in me first Jesus Christ might shew forth all longsuffering, for a pattern to them which should hereafter believe on him to life everlasting.

Paul never forgot his past life before Christ. But at the same time he never allowed it to detract from the present. No cloud of guilt hung over his head. No details of his exploits of sin were ever included. He always presented his past in such a way that there was an understanding of who he was without honoring it.

Whenever Paul began to dwell on the grace of God he had to reflect on the past. Remembering who he was and where he came from caused God's grace to shine forth even brighter.

Paul used three descriptive terms to label his past actions and life of sin in his pre–Christian condition: he was a *blasphemer*, a *persecutor*, and an *injurious* (insolent) person.

Ignorant of the truth, he spoke with the intent of defaming Jesus Christ and the Holy Spirit. His work as a persecutor evidenced a violent nature against those whom he considered enemies of Judaism. Some he put to flight. He actively pursued both men and women, with the intention of bringing them harm. Gender made no difference to him (Acts 8:3; 9:1, 2). Paul (Saul) felt that his persecuting of the believers was a favor to God.

Even in the sins of Paul's ignorance, God's mercy emerged. His being stopped on the road to Damascus really consisted of an act of love and an extension of His mercy. Instead of attempting to find some good in all his sinfulness, Paul simply stated it was only the abundance of God's grace that provided for his salvation.

It is at this point that the apostle stated a cardinal truth of Christianity (v. 15). The whole purpose for Christ's mission on earth as the God–man rests in His death, resurrection, and provision for the sins of mankind. Christ's preaching, teaching, and miracles are the overflow benefits of His compassionate heart and to give us a glimpse of the Father. We often emphasize Jesus' activities, but it is His passive mission on the cross which makes the greatest difference.

Paul couldn't seem to speak of Christ's provision without remembering his own sinfulness. Describing himself as the chief of sinners, or the worst sinner, isn't in any sense egotistical bragging. It also isn't one of those statements where rating sins becomes a kind of competition. Instead, Paul remembered his sinfulness with all its shame and guilt. Knowing how he persecuted the body of Christ caused him to believe this was some of the worst behavior anyone could have done. Yet, at the same time, if Christ could do that for this type of sinner, surely there is hope and opportunity for anyone.

Verse 16 briefly states the means of salvation. Regardless of a person's sinfulness, salvation comes by believing on Christ. Life everlasting rests initially on our believing on Him and accepting Him as our Savior and Lord. God wants to extend His mercy and love. All He requires is for us to accept and to follow Jesus.

Why is it impossible to serve God without receiving His grace and mercy?

C. Glorification of the King (v. 17)

17. Now unto the King eternal, immortal, invisible, the only wise God, be honour and glory for ever and ever. Amen.

Faithfulness to the truth necessitates knowing the truth about God. After reviewing his sinfulness and God's grace, Paul finished this section with a doxology of praise. Spontaneous praise comes naturally to believers when we contrast our sin with God's holiness and our deeds with His mercy.

In this verse Paul made four statements which are in reality a minicourse in theology, the study of God. First he recognized the *eternalness* of God. He is timeless. Never was there a time when He was not, and never will there be a time when He isn't!

Second, God is *immortal*. This is one of His great differences from mankind. Unlike us He isn't corrupted by sin. Therefore, He is free from death and provides a quality of life which stems from eternal holiness.

Third, God is *invisible*. He not only can't be seen because He is Spirit, but He also isn't confined or conformed to a particular form. We do know, however, that the image of God is seen in Christ (John 14:9; Colossians 1:15). We interpret God's image to mean likeness or representation. The characteristics of God are seen progressively clearer as we know Christ personally and study His life and example in the Scriptures.

Fourth, God is the only God. No other exists. He alone rules and dominates the universe. There can be no other genuine belief but monotheism. The belief in other gods is pure delusion, since they are the fabrication of fallen man's imagination.

Knowing these four characteristics about God leaves the believer with only one choice—to honor and to glorify our matchless King. Our response is to be forever and ever. So be it!

REVIEW QUESTIONS

1. What were the two strains of heresy facing Timothy?
2. What is the threefold source of love?
3. How should the law be viewed?
4. What is the responsibility of those who have been placed in ministry?
5. List the four descriptive statements which are a minicourse in theology.

GOLDEN TEXT HOMILY

"STUDY TO SHEW THYSELF APPROVED UNTO GOD, A WORKMAN THAT NEEDETH NOT TO BE ASHAMED, RIGHTLY DIVIDING THE WORD OF TRUTH" (2 Timothy 2:15).

In this verse Paul exhorted Timothy to strive for accreditation as a worker since the life of a Christian is set under the searching eyes of God. Christians are summoned to a twofold testing: (1) They are to test or prove what is the will of God, and if they are to be approved, they must do the will of God. (2) At the same time, Christians are summoned to a test of their own accreditation. Paul challenged the Corinthians who had celebrated the Lord's Supper in an undisciplined and unworthy manner in a similar way. They were to prove themselves in order to partake properly (1 Corinthians 11:28). Christ's work is not to be done in a careless and disorderly way.

The word translated "study" literally means to do one's best or spare no effort in presenting oneself approved unto God. There is also the sense of urgency. Timothy was to make haste to accomplish this. Zeal, earnest desire, effort, and haste are all implied in this word.

Timothy was to present himself in a genuine and acceptable way unto God. In the same way that coins and metals are tested by fire the Christian is to be tested for proper approval unto God. The worker is to be tested by trial and found to have stood the test.

The desired product is that of a workman having no cause to be ashamed. The workmen are those preachers and teachers who labor to propagate and promote Christianity among men. In their work they are to rightly divide the word of truth. The word translated "rightly dividing" means cutting straight, holding a straight course, handling aright—teaching the truth correctly and directly. It can be compared to a farmer who drives (cuts) a straight furrow, or a tailor who cuts a fabric according to a pattern. It means to preach the Word straightforwardly and not "beat around the bush." The minister must be careful not to let his energies be drained by vain and subversive wranglings. Rather, he must exert himself to the utmost to demonstrate before God that he is a competent workman.—**William M. Henry, Jr. (Retired), Former Instructor, Missions and New Testament Greek, West Coast Christian College, Fresno California**

SENTENCE SERMONS

BIBLICAL TRUTH is the anchor of the Christian's faith.

—Selected

A HALF–TRUTH is a dangerous thing, especially if you have got hold of the wrong half.

—Myron F. Boyd

MAN FINDS GOD through truth.

—Jewish Proverb

HE WHO LABORS as he prays lifts his heart to God with his hands.

—Bernard of Clairvaux

EVANGELISM APPLICATION

BIBLICAL TRUTH LEADS THE SINNER TO ETERNAL LIFE.

It was in a meeting where they were giving personal testimony. One man arose, holding a New Testament in his hand. "My story," said he, "is unlike other men. I was a pickpocket, and one day I saw a man with a definite bulge in his hip pocket. 'A fat purse,' thought I, and soon it was in my pocket. But when I arrived home, behold, it was a Book. In disgust I threw it aside; but afterward, out of curiosity, I opened it and began to read. Before many days had passed, I discovered Christ as my Savior and Lord."

Listening to this testimony, one of the volunteer colporteurs of the Bible Society became interested. After the service he asked to see the New Testament. It was the one he had carried with him for years, the one he had considered lost. Is not this evidence of the power of the Word to change and to transform man's life? What has the Word done for you?

—Gospel Herald

DAILY BIBLE READINGS

M. Essential Truth.
Exodus 20:1–17

T. Truth for the Family.
Deuteronomy 6:1–9

W. God of Truth.
Deuteronomy 32:1–4

T. Led by Truth.
Psalm 25:1–10

F. The Truth Sets Free.
John 8:28–32

S. Jesus Is the Truth.
John 14:4–7

Godly Leadership

Study Text: 1 Timothy 3:1–16

Objective: To review God's standard for leadership and adjust our lives accordingly.

Time: The Book of 1 Timothy was written between A.D. 62 and 64.

Place: The Book of 1 Timothy was probably written from the Macedonian city of Philippi.

Golden Text: "Feed the flock of God which is among you, taking the oversight thereof, not by constraint, but willingly" (1 Peter 5:2).

Central Truth: The Bible reveals specific standards for church leaders.

Evangelism Emphasis: Church leaders must reflect Christ to the lost.

PRINTED TEXT

1 Timothy 3:1. This is a true saying, If a man desire the office of a bishop, he desireth a good work.

2. A bishop then must be blameless, the husband of one wife, vigilant, sober, of good behaviour, given to hospitality, apt to teach;

3. Not given to wine, no striker, not greedy of filthy lucre; but patient, not a brawler, not covetous;

4. One that ruleth well his own house, having his children in subjection with all gravity;

5. (For if a man know not how to rule his own house, how shall he take care of the church of God?)

6. Not a novice, lest being lifted up with pride he fall into the condemnation of the devil.

7. Moreover he must have a good report of them which are without; lest he fall into reproach and the snare of the devil.

8. Likewise must the deacons be grave, not doubletongued, not given to much wine, not greedy of filthy lucre;

9. Holding the mystery of the faith in a pure conscience.

10. And let these also first be proved; then let them use the office of a deacon, being found blameless.

11. Even so must their wives be grave, not slanderers, sober, faithful in all things.

12. Let the deacons be the husbands of one wife, ruling their children and their own houses well.

13. For they that have used the office of a deacon well purchase to themselves a good degree, and great boldness in the

faith which is in Christ Jesus.

14. These things write I unto thee, hoping to come unto thee shortly:

15. But if I tarry long, that thou mayest know how thou oughtest to behave thyself in the house of God, which is the church of the living God, the pillar and ground of the truth.

16. And without controversy great is the mystery of godliness: God was manifest in the flesh, justified in the Spirit, seen of angels, preached unto the Gentiles, believed on in the world, received up into glory.

LESSON OUTLINE

I. PASTORAL LEADERSHIP
   A. The Position
   B. The Qualifications
II. LAY LEADERSHIP
   A. Deacon's Qualifications
   B. Deaconess' Qualifications
III. CONDUCT FOR LEADERSHIP
   A. Understand the Church
   B. Understand Christ

LESSON EXPOSITION

INTRODUCTION

During the 1970s leadership was a hot topic. A great deal of discussion centered on the style of leadership and the dominant principles. New books were written with the Book of Nehemiah becoming a seedbed for study. Two decades have passed and the need to look at Christian leadership again becomes necessary. The tragic spiritual failures of nationally known ministers, with their sins exposed through the worldwide media, remind us again of the need to live and minister in accord with God's Word. On a much smaller public scale are the many local pastors whose leadership qualifications fall far short of what God expects from His shepherds and messengers.

On a more positive side is the emphasis in many Pentecostal churches on having specific offices of *deacons* and *elders*. How does this fit into the church's current polity? Do all the qualifications of that time period and culture still apply today? These are just a few questions being considered.

Another area of interest arises when considering godly leadership and the qualifications listed in 1 Timothy 3. What is the role of the laity in the local congregation? Which tasks or responsibilities are to be fulfilled by the laity? And which of the offices listed in this chapter are offices for laity and which are for the clergy?

Consideration of these questions needs to be prefaced with a reminder of the status of the church when this was written. At this point in the first century there wasn't any church structure similar to our current denominational organizations. The local church depended on resident pastors from within their own congregations. The laity, in most congregations, filled the roles which we now place upon the clergy. And as will be seen in the first section, the terms change in that there is a switch from laity to clergy for at least one office.

The most important aspect of this lesson lies in the need for church leaders to meet biblical qualifications in both character and actions.

I. PASTORAL LEADERSHIP (1 Timothy 3:1–7)

A. The Position (v. 1)

1. This is a true saying, If a man desire the office of a bishop, he desireth a good work.

Paul opened this discussion on leadership with what appears to be a familiar saying among the believers. Desiring to be a bishop is seen as a worthy goal—a position worth striving for. The main issue is, was the position of a bishop that of laity or clergy?

The office of bishop is often clouded by ecclesiastical tradition and diverse denominational history and organization. At the time of Paul's writing, the New Testament (early) church did not understand the office of bishop to be such as that found in the Roman Catholic and Anglican churches today. Some Pentecostal churches also have used or are currently using the term *bishop* to describe a clerical supervisory office. However, there is every reason to believe, instead, that a bishop in the early era of the church was an office of the laity—filled by laymen.

Here is an excellent time for a reminder about the principles of biblical interpretation. The Scriptures are not to be interpreted on the patterns practiced by the church during the centuries which followed. We know how easy it is for the traditions of men to creep in. We must assure that the Scriptures are interpreted on the basis of the word meanings and context of the times in which they were written.

We are also reminded of another principle in leadership. Ambition to be in a position of responsibility within the church is commendable and a worthy effort. However, there is one necessary stipulation: The motivation for those seeking this position must be the desire to be of service rather than a desire for recognition. This ensures that the position maintains its dignity.

One other observation needs to be made. Within the New Testament are two other terms which apparently indicate the same office as *bishop*—*elders* and *overseers*. The basic meaning of *episkopos* (bishop) is "overseer" or "leader." The term *elder* reflects a spiritual maturity which when attained enables a believer to exercise oversight in a church. (See Acts 14:23; 20:17; Philippians 1:1; Titus 1:5; James 5:14.)

B. The Qualifications (vv. 2–7)

2. A bishop then must be blameless, the husband of one wife, vigilant, sober, of good behaviour, given to hospitality, apt to teach;

3. Not given to wine, no striker, not greedy of filthy lucre; but patient, not a brawler, not covetous;

4. One that ruleth well his own house, having his children in subjection with all gravity;

5. (For if a man know not how to rule his own house, how shall he take care of the church of God?)

6. Not a novice, lest being lifted up with pride he fall into the condemnation of the devil.

7. Moreover he must have a good report of them which are without; lest he fall into reproach and the snare of the devil.

In a review of the qualifications for the office of bishop, one definite concept stands forth: These are not ideas to reach toward but the minimum standards for every person desiring the office. Failure to meet even one of these disqualifies an individual until it is corrected. One is graded either *A* or *F*. You either pass or fail. Mediocrity and inferiority have no place in the leadership of Christ's body as seen through the local church. And if these are the minimum standards for lay leadership, we can accept no less of those aspiring to fulfill the divine call to clerical leadership.

Blameless means to be above reproach. It isn't synonymous with faultlessness or total perfection, however. Rather, it speaks of a person whose reputation isn't tarnished by actions that are the result of character faults. This does not mean that a person who has made major errors in the past is ineligible. Not at all! In those cases it speaks of a reputation repaired and restored over a sufficient period of time. This may include in some cases restitution along with repentance.

Also, the person's marital status plays a role in the qualification—he must be "the husband of one wife." There is some debate on this one. Is it directed toward plural marriages or toward the issue of divorce and remarriage? It almost certainly has no relation to the issue of second marriages after one's mate has died. Since plural marriages were accepted in the pagan society, it definitely speaks to this situation. If those won to Christ continued their polygamy, they could not be a leader in the local church. But this could also apply to the divorced and remarried, since it is questionable to interpret this as one wife at a time without death breaking the bonds.

The next three qualifications—*vigilance, sobriety,* and *good behavior*—are referred to in a modern translation as being *temperate, self–controlled,* and *respectable.* A vigilant person is watchful or in control of himself. This individual takes great care not to lose control of his actions. Soberness here has no reference to freedom from alcoholic beverage. It means, rather, to be of a sound mind—to be self–controlled in the processes of one's thinking. The leader must be able to think through doctrinal and practical issues facing the church. The third qualification in this trio ties into the second. A person's behavior will be respectable as a result of self–control.

The qualification of *hospitality* involves a great deal more than occasional entertaining. To understand what the writer means demands an understanding of the culture. Christian apostles and evangelists in the early church traveled from congregation to congregation, providing a special ministry to those churches lacking regular clerical leadership. These workers were almost totally dependent on the hospitality (food and shelter) offered by the lay leaders of these churches.

The *ability* to *teach* is the last qualification of verse 2. Not all bishops had the same skill level, but none were to be void of this ability. They were to have the mental ability to study and evaluate the doctrines and practices of the church and then transmit it to the congregation. Notice the practical application: The pastor and other clerical leaders aren't to be the only ones teaching the main doctrines and principles of the church.

The bishop must avoid excesses. Drunkenness, or even the regular use of wine, was not to be the pattern of a bishop. Instead of resorting to violent actions or physical blows, the one striving for this office must reflect love and restraint. The bishop also should not be quarrelsome. This is no position for the person who constantly takes the opposite view simply to argue or be different.

"Not greedy of filthy lucre [money]" speaks of the bishop candidate's view of money. Since the bishops cared for the church funds, this could become a major temptation for a person who struggled with greed or the desire for material prosperity. Anyone who constantly dreams of it and desperately wants more is deceived by riches. In chapter 6, Paul stated how this situation may cause people to wander away from the true faith.

Patience is vital to a bishop (v. 3), and it includes much more than keeping a controlled temper under continued irritation. The term here addresses the ability to reflect a spirit of gentleness and forgiveness while under pressure.

Having a good relationship with his family is also a qualification as can be seen in verses 4 and 5. Unless a bishop has cultivated discipline and respect among his own family members, how can he expect to lead the family of God? Any man who will not invest time and effort into his own family and who does not exhibit that Christ is living in him in the home environment isn't ready or fit to lead the church. Parents can't control the actions of their children once they reach the age of maturity and independence; but when they are minors, the father must invest himself in molding his own flesh and blood.

Paul says the bishop candidate is not to be a novice. Many have assumed that assigning them a position was a good way to keep new converts; thus churches have often voted them into positions of leadership before they were mature enough for the responsibility. Paul noted that the elevation to such a position of responsibility may foster pride and conceit. This opens the door to the devil (see Luke 10: 17–20).

The final requirement listed is that a bishop must have a good reputation both inside and outside the church. A person's reputation within the community directly affects his acceptability. No one is interested in becoming a part of a church in which the leadership hasn't won the respect of those around them.

Why do so many congregations neglect these qualifications when selecting their lay leadership?

II. LAY LEADERSHIP (1 Timothy 3:8–13)

A. Deacon's Qualifications (vv. 8–10, 12, 13)

(Verse 11 is discussed in section B.)

8. Likewise must the deacons be grave, not doubletongued, not

given to much wine, not greedy of filthy lucre;

9. Holding the mystery of the faith in a pure conscience.

10. And let these also first be proved; then let them use the office of a deacon, being found blameless.

12. Let the deacons be the husbands of one wife, ruling their children and their own houses well.

13. For they that have used the office of a deacon well purchase to themselves a good degree, and great boldness in the faith which is in Christ Jesus.

The qualification list for a deacon contains some of the same standards as those on the bishop's list. This reminds us that the basic characteristics of leadership need to be evident in all leaders regardless of their role.

Any study of leadership which includes deacons should begin with Acts 6. When a problem relating to the distribution of the temporal stores arose, seven men were selected for the task. Though the word *deacon* isn't used in this setting, their work is consistent with that of a deacon. An important observation about this account is that the early church apparently made a definite division of responsibility between spiritual and material matters. That doesn't mean those in each section were not concerned about or involved in the activities of the other; however, there are strong indications of a concentration in one or the other area, as indicated by a specific office.

According to verse 8, a deacon is to be *grave*, or sincere—worthy of respect. This reveals a contrast to a flippant or halfhearted approach to the temporal ministry. He is to be serious in his approach to his vital role in support of the church's members.

The deacon is to be honest and confidential in speech. That he is double–tongued should never be an accusation placed against him. In the original language, to be double–tongued this can mean to be a gossiper or to speak one thing to one individual and something different to another. Another aspect of this term can be to think one thing while speaking something else. None of these are to be true of a deacon. Because the deacon spends a lot of time in individual homes, there could easily be opportunities for all three to occur.

The deacon is also to demonstrate temperance in his use of wine. "Not given to much wine" very likely means being a total abstainer except for medicinal use.

Another qualification for a deacon is that he must have the right attitude toward materialism. Handling the church's money for charitable distributions could become a temptation toward greed. The deacon can choose to resist this temptation or succumb to greed's drawing power. Succumbing may be in the form of constantly wanting more and begrudging what others receive. In its worst form, greed leads to embezzlement of church funds and other such abuses.

Verse 9 points out that the deacon's qualifications also include a doctrinal knowledge of the Christian faith. Paul frequently referred to the mystery of the faith in his writings (see Romans 16:25, 26; Colossians 1:26, 27). The basis of this mystery is salvation through Jesus Christ and His relation to the church. As Pentecostals we cannot overlook the fact that the Holy Spirit has come to dwell in all mankind (laity and clergy), in contrast to His previously indwelling only a select few.

Blameless (v. 10) indicates being qualified—having proven to be a person worthy of the office. There is no reference here to being given a probationary period to prove acceptability. Neither is there allowance for persons of questionable character to be placed in a church position to prove their changed character. The worth of the candidate is to be evaluated prior to doing even the smallest task as a deacon. The local congregation is obligated to know candidates well prior to their being selected for the office. From the list of qualifications in this chapter it would seem logical that a person's spiritual maturity, doctrinal knowledge and purity, potential for success, and in some cases education might also enter the thoughts of those considering the eligibility of deacons.

The deacon's marital status and family discipline are also determining factors in his suitability for the office. The role of husband and father can never be separated from worthiness. The discussion of these aspects under the bishop (vv. 2, 4) also apply to the deacon.

After listing the qualifications, Paul concluded the section with special words of encouragement. In verse 13 the phrase "purchase to themselves a good degree" is translated "gain an excellent standing" in the *New International Version*. More than likely this refers to his attaining a higher standing within the Christian community. Good character evidenced in Christian actions always results in esteem. Believers and even unbelievers respect those individuals who live in actions the message they proclaim verbally.

Paul also noted that "boldness in the faith" continues to develop within the person who serves in this office. One–on–one confrontations within the privacy of homes determines the directness of one's witness and willingness to help and confront as the need arises.

How can a local church encourage doctrinal knowledge within its lay leaders?

B. Deaconess' Qualifications (v. 11)

11. Even so must their wives be grave, not slanderers, sober, faithful in all things.

How do we interpret this passage of Scripture? It could be a general description of the qualifications of the wife of a man desiring to be a deacon. Or it could be a list of the qualities of a deaconess. The author of these lessons leans toward their being the required characteristics for a deaconess.

Paul specifically singled out the wife of the deacon for a discussion of her characteristics and qualifications. Notice that nothing of the same nature occurred in his discussion of the bishop. One suggestion for this personal scrutiny, apart from her being a deaconess, is the very personal nature of her husband's work. Access to the individual homes of the congregation provides information of the most personal nature. It would be devastating if this should be leaked to other members of the congregation.

From Romans 16:1 we know there were deaconesses in the early church. If a woman became a deaconess by virtue of her husband's being a deacon, this type of intense review of her qualifications becomes absolutely necessary.

Four separate characteristics are listed. First, she is to be *grave*—a woman who is worthy of respect. Respect depends on a reputation that is built on character, Christian conduct, and seriousness of purpose. Second, she is not to be a *slanderer*—that is, prone to malicious talking. She is not to be a gossip or to speculate on private matters. She is required to watch her mouth in both public and private speech. What she knows is to be kept in the secret of her heart and prayer closet.

Third, she is to be *sober*—temperate. Self–controlled in temperament and conduct are all–inclusive in this characteristic. Finally, she is to be *faithful* in all things—trustworthy. This speaks of being honest and dependable.

III. CONDUCT FOR LEADERSHIP (1 Timothy 3:14–16)

A. Understand the Church (vv. 14, 15)

14. These things write I unto thee, hoping to come unto thee shortly:

15. But if I tarry long, that thou mayest know how thou oughtest to behave thyself in the house of God, which is the church of the living God, the pillar and ground of the truth.

These two verses along with verse 16 are considered the dividing point of this first epistle. This first section emphasizes worship and leadership qualifications, while the next provides practical instruction and specific exhortations.

It's possible that Paul's coming to Ephesus may not have followed his planned time line, and desiring that these instructions be given to Timothy at an earlier date, he choses to write this letter. This urgency reflected the importance of the concepts and his desire to be of assistance to his "son in the faith." Timothy surely knew these facts, but in this difficult situation he would have appreciated Paul's authority to lend him additional support.

Verse 15 states the need for proper conduct within the church. It isn't likely that the conduct here is in terms of behaving such as posture, gesture, and speech. More than likely Paul was speaking of knowing how to conduct the business of the church, and this business goes far beyond the financial to include its worship, selection of leaders, care for individual believers, and eradicating heresy—to name just a few items.

The importance of all these actions rests in a proper understanding of the church. First, the church is the family of God. We are not strangers but rather brothers and sisters in Christ. Second, the church is the property of the living God. God himself provides the presence which motivates and quickens individuals and the corporate group. Here we need to be reminded that a church building filled with people is just another meeting except for the spiritual empowerment of God through Jesus Christ and the Holy Spirit.

Last, the church is the custodian

of truth. Not only is it to be built on truth, but it is to operate within that truth. Thus, anytime heresy invades the church and is allowed to remain, the very nature of the church is jeopardized. Its continuance within the body guarantees the eventual separation and spiritual death of the church.

What are some ways through which we can be better informed of the nature of the church?

B. Understand Christ (v. 16)

16. And without controversy great is the mystery of godliness: God was manifest in the flesh, justified in the Spirit, seen of angels, preached unto the Gentiles, believed on in the world, received up into glory.

Godly leadership must not only understand the true nature of the church but must also understand who Christ is. Since the body (the church) is the bride of Christ, it is vital to know about the Bridegroom. In one very concise verse Paul summarized the mystery of godliness, which is Christ.

This is the second reference to "the mystery." Thus, a more extensive exploration seems appropriate. The New Testament word doesn't mean that which is mysterious and can't be known. Rather, it refers to what is out of the range of our understanding except by divine revelation. The cultural context also enters here. In the religious rites and ceremonies practiced by ancient Greek secret societies, "the mystery" referred to knowledge which had not yet been revealed to the uninitiated. Prior to Christ's coming to earth in the form of a man, the gospel message was hidden. All that could be known were the types and shadows (hints and clues) revealed in the Old Testament. But now, the fullness of the gospel has been unfolded.

Here, Paul provided an outline of Christology, beginning with the Incarnation and ending with the Ascension. His first statement reminds us of Christ's nature—"God . . . manifest in the flesh." Though difficult to understand, He is the God–man, both divine and human, without being a hybrid. Though coming in human flesh, He remained fully God. Without His becoming man there could be no provision of salvation for sin.

Being "justified [vindicated] in the Spirit" probably means it was through the agency of the Holy Spirit that He rose from the dead. However, a second interpretation is that vindication refers to the Holy Spirit's declaring Christ as the Son of God. An excellent example of this is Peter's confession of Christ (Matthew 16:16). Jesus pointed out that this knowledge didn't come by human means.

The wording "seen of angels" provides some difficulty. It could be indicating that angels opened the tomb at His resurrection. Or it may refer to the angels receiving Him back into heaven.

"Preached among the nations" indicates the impact of Christ on the whole world. This is especially interesting considering that Jesus' humanity is of the Judaistic tradition and culture. Jews were very separated, on the whole, from the other two people groups—Romans and Greeks. One would not expect the world to flock to hear of the actions and teachings of a Jew.

Then, coupled with this was the limitation of Christ's ministry. Not only was it very short—only three and a half years—but it was also restricted—to Palestine.

Next, notice how Christ was received: He was "believed on in the world." The Book of Acts records how both Jew and Gentile received Christ and the new dimension of the Holy Spirit. Roman soldiers, Jewish priests, and common people alike found Jesus as their personal Savior. All nationalities within the Roman Empire (considered the world to most) began to know Jesus.

Finally, though "received up into glory" to sit at the right hand of the Father, He clearly announced His intention to return for His own (John 14; Acts 1).

REVIEW QUESTIONS

1. How can we ensure that the office of bishop is one of dignity?
2. How many separate qualifications for a bishop are listed?
3. Why would it be so important for a deacon not to be a gossiper?
4. What are the four qualifications for the wife of a deacon?
5. What is the business of the Church?

GOLDEN TEXT HOMILY

"FEED THE FLOCK OF GOD WHICH IS AMONG YOU, TAKING THE OVERSIGHT THEREOF, NOT BY CONSTRAINT, BUT WILLINGLY" (1 Peter 5:2).

I believe the most significant word in this verse is *willingly*. The scripture bears out the fact that our attitude toward Christian service plays an important role in our relationship with Jesus Christ. Service and giving is an attitude that is common among Christian people. Moreover, these virtues are not solely relegated to pastors and church leaders. The Bible clearly addresses all of us when it states, "It is more blessed to give than to receive" (Acts 20:35).

Giving and service breathes the very air of our spiritual kingdom. It puts into language the very spirit of Jesus Christ. He points out to us that those who are only interested in receiving are living on a lower plane of human accomplishment.

When we accept Jesus Christ as our Savior we take on a Christian character and personality that is uncommon to the world. Our life should exemplify compassion and service. We should think of others, care for others, and strive to proclaim the message of Christ to the world. Such an attitude is a Christian virtue that comes from the heart of God.

Again Jesus is our example, as He lived to enlighten, to bestow, and to redeem. It was very little that He received. He simply gave everything to mankind.

Such an attitude is contrary to a worldly mentality. Obsession with personal gain will only lead to selfishness and the manipulation of others. But to be serving and concerned about others opens the door to everything that is noble and pure. To receive is to be superficial and momentarily happy, whereas a giving person is inwardly happy and blessed.

It can be said that the person who is always concerned with receiving will be a debtor to many people; but the one who gives will owe nothing to any man.—**Jerry Puckett, Customer Service**

Representative, Pathway Press, Cleveland, Tennessee

SENTENCE SERMONS

THE BIBLE REVEALS specific standards for church leaders.

—Selected

A TRUE AND SAFE LEADER is likely to be one who has no desire to lead but is forced into a position of leadership by the inward pressure of the Holy Spirit and the press of the external situation.

—A.W. Tozer

IF YOU CAN'T FACE THE MUSIC, you'll never get to lead the band.

—Draper's Book of Quotations for the Christian World

LEADERS ARE ordinary people with extraordinary determination.

—Selected

EVANGELISM APPLICATION

CHURCH LEADERS MUST REFLECT CHRIST TO THE LOST.

How important are the leaders of the church?

This question is so elementary that at first it almost appears as an insulting consideration. But when we start overlooking the elementary principles, it is only a matter of time until any structure begins to crumble.

In the Old Testament, Israel stands as a stark contrast from one era to another. Under the solid spiritual leadership of Joshua the people conquered the Promised Land. Even after his death, Israel served the Lord under the godly leadership of elders disciplined under this man. But a generation later when there was a lack of spiritual leadership, every person did what they thought was right in their own eyes.

Make this contemporary. It has often been said that the only Jesus many people will ever see or hear about is through the life we live. The preacher, the elders, and the Sunday school teachers may all speak about Christ and His claims. But the proof comes by demonstrating His love through daily living. Sometimes we can't hear what others are saying because their actions drown out their words.

Our churches won't grow when the leadership speaks of a higher life through Christ but personally lives on a much lower level. Our churches can't be "soul–saving stations" and "havens of comfort and care" unless the dynamics of the Holy Spirit are working through the congregation.

Remember, the membership is a direct reflection of the leadership.

DAILY BIBLE READINGS

M. Call to Leadership.
Exodus 3:1–14

T. Structure for Leadership.
Exodus 18:13–26

W. Leadership in the Church.
Romans 12:3–8

T. Gifted Leadership.
Ephesians 4:11–16

F. Response Toward Leadership.
1 Timothy 5:17–22

S. Motives for Leadership.
1 Peter 5:1–4

Godly Living

Study Text: 1 Timothy 4:1–16

Objective: To identify and reject ungodly influences and determine to live godly.

Time: The Book of 1 Timothy was written between A.D. 62 and 64.

Place: The Book of 1 Timothy was probably written from the Macedonian city of Philippi.

Golden Text: "Godliness with contentment is great gain" (1 Timothy 6:6).

Central Truth: Christians are to maintain a godly life in the midst of an ungodly world.

Evangelism Emphasis: A godly life is essential for an effective witness.

PRINTED TEXT

1 Timothy 4:1. Now the Spirit speaketh expressly, that in the latter times some shall depart from the faith, giving heed to seducing spirits, and doctrines of devils;

2. Speaking lies in hypocrisy; having their conscience seared with a hot iron;

3. Forbidding to marry, and commanding to abstain from meats, which God hath created to be received with thanksgiving of them which believe and know the truth.

4. For every creature of God is good, and nothing to be refused, if it be received with thanksgiving:

5. For it is sanctified by the word of God and prayer.

6. If thou put the brethren in remembrance of these things, thou shalt be a good minister of Jesus Christ, nourished up in the words of faith and of good doctrine, whereunto thou hast attained.

7. But refuse profane and old wives' fables, and exercise thyself rather unto godliness.

8. For bodily exercise profiteth little: but godliness is profitable unto all things, having promise of the life that now is, and of that which is to come.

9. This is a faithful saying and worthy of all acceptation.

10. For therefore we both labour and suffer reproach, because we trust in the living God, who is the Saviour of all men, specially of those that believe.

11. These things command and teach.

12. Let no man despise thy youth; but be thou an example of the believers, in word, in conversation, in charity, in spirit,

in faith, in purity.

13. Till I come, give attendance to reading, to exhortation, to doctrine.

14. Neglect not the gift that is in thee, which was given thee by prophecy, with the laying on of the hands of the presbytery.

15. Meditate upon these things; give thyself wholly to them; that thy profiting may appear to all.

16. Take heed unto thyself, and unto the doctrine; continue in them: for in doing this thou shalt both save thyself, and them that hear thee.

LESSON OUTLINE

- I. REJECT UNGODLINESS
  - A. False Teachers
  - B. False Teachings
- II. PROMOTE GODLINESS
  - A. Christian Heritage
  - B. Avoiding Error
  - C. Teach Truth
- III. EXEMPLIFY GODLINESS
  - A. Extraordinary Example
  - B. Public Projections
  - C. Personal Admonitions

LESSON EXPOSITION

INTRODUCTION

What is the relationship between heresy and godly living? Can it flourish side by side in the same person?

Usually when discussing the Christian lifestyle, the emphasis turns to what to eat or drink, which entertainments are acceptable, and the way we treat both believers and nonbelievers. Yet throughout both Testaments, God continues to remind His children that one's relationship to heresy impacts godliness. In the Old Testament the false prophets led people astray and into both physical destruction and spiritual damnation. In the New Testament it was the false teachers who corrupted the body of Christ and steered them into the clutches of Satan.

As we review some of the situations in which error, or heresy, proves disastrous, the classic example of Eve deserves first consideration (Genesis 3). Notice how she was led down the path of sin. First, Satan caused her to question or doubt what God had said. Second, after she stated what God had said, he responded with a counterstatement, which stood in complete opposition to the truth. What God had taught her was discarded. In its place she embraced the heresy of Satan and passed it on to her husband. Though he recognized its error, he still succumbed to its temptation.

Consider next the believers in Galatia (Galatians 1:6–9; 3:1, 2). Marvelously saved and rescued from their heathen background, they quickly deserted the gospel message. When Judaizers arrived and began to teach them the need to follow the rites and rituals of Judaism in order to be Christians, they agreed to it. The foolishness of this move appalled the apostle. How could they be deceived so quickly after possessing the truth? Didn't they realize the end effect? Once they possessed eternal life through the blood of Jesus Christ, but now they pressed for a future through human effort.

In 1 Timothy 3 Paul was concerned with the selection of church leaders, which included attention to organizational structure. Now, however (in chapter 4), Paul returned to the issues of false doctrines and false teachers. Even though there are some problems in its governmental structure, a congregation can not only survive but also experience growth. But it can never be an enduring spiritual lighthouse when there is a loss of integrity. Integrity isn't just an issue of morality in terms of honesty and sexual purity—it expands to include doctrinal correctness. In the totality of the package, a Christian's integrity rests on knowing and believing the truth of God's revealed Word.

Chapter 4 includes a number of instructions for Timothy, all with a view toward godly living. However, at the top of the list is Paul's concern about heresy in the church.

I. REJECT UNGODLINESS (1 Timothy 4:1–5)

A. False Teachers (vv. 1, 2)

1. Now the Spirit speaketh expressly, that in the latter times some shall depart from the faith, giving heed to seducing spirits, and doctrines of devils;

2. Speaking lies in hypocrisy; having their conscience seared with a hot iron.

Paul's opening statement reminds us of the gift of prophecy actively working in the body of believers. Not only was there edification and direction, but one aspect was the Spirit's warning of future events. God doesn't intend for His children to be blindsided by the attacks of Satan.

From verse 1 we see there was no need for this congregation to be surprised by the problem and presence of false teachers. On a previous occasion there were warnings of this difficulty arising within their congregation. Paul brought this to their remembrance. Instead of standing by when it took place, they should have moved quickly to eradicate it. To be forewarned is to be prepared. But apparently they hadn't benefited from the Spirit's speaking to them.

Paul's placing a time frame on this event does stimulate thought as to the timing of this event. What are the "latter times"? Usually we think of them as being sometime in the future and tied to end–time events. However, this is not necessarily the meaning here. "Latter times" should be interpreted as the period of time following the advent of Christ. Thus, the "latter times" were already in place for that body of believers.

The apostle immediately described the character and condition of these false teachers who were to come in "the latter times." They were wolves in sheep's clothing. Not only were they doctrinally incorrect, but they had departed from the faith and had become dominated by Satan. These false teachers were wandering spirits looking for an opportunity to lead people astray through deception. Their doctrines weren't just a slight difference of opinion or denominational emphasis. They were spreading untruths that came from Satan himself.

Knowing the source of these doctrines allowed Paul to uncover the hypocrisy which existed. While appearing to be a part of the church, they were nothing more than actors portraying lies. Though appearing on the outside to desire the best interest of the believers, they were nothing like that on the inside.

Some may ask, "How is this possible?" It's easy when one's conscience has been seared and thus provides no guidance for one's actions. When it loses its ability to prod and influence toward right and good, then anything is possible. Paul described their consciences as being "seared with a hot iron." There are two possible interpretations for this expression. One aspect is that of being cauterized. Instead of bleeding and showing the truth, their consciences have been cauterized so there is no sensitivity or feeling. Another possible interpretation is that of being branded. Sin marks their consciences to reflect the ownership of their master. Then they proceed to parrot the words and concepts which he projects.

B. False Teachings (vv. 3–5)

3. Forbidding to marry, and commanding to abstain from meats, which God hath created to be received with thanksgiving of them which believe and know the truth.

4. For every creature of God is good, and nothing to be refused, if it be received with thanksgiving:

5. For it is sanctified by the word of God and prayer.

In chapter 1 Paul sketched the broad aspects of the false teaching, referring to it as myths and genealogies. Now the apostle referred to some of the specifics that were being taught. The first was their teaching against marriage. This had to have come from one of the Greek philosophical views. Dualism held that matter is evil and spirit is good. Therefore anything of the flesh must be avoided where at all possible. When incorporated into some form of Christianity, possibly early Gnosticism, it spoke against marriage. Within Gnosticism there were two views; one completely opposed marriage because of the physical union between husband and wife, while the second view allowed marriage and sexual union, but only for the express purpose of procreation.

Paul chose not to respond against this false teaching. Its abnormality should be readily seen. Plus, in the previous chapter, marriage and children are discussed in a positive light in terms of qualifications. We also know that in his epistle to the Corinthians the apostle indicated that sexual union between husband and wife is a normal, desirable part of marriage. No mate is to deprive his/her partner except by mutual consent––and that only temporarily (1 Corinthians 7:3–5).

These teachers definitely had no basis for their views from the teachings and actions of Jesus. His first miracle took place at a wedding. Their view also totally disregarded that God divinely ordered marriage in the Garden of Eden. He created both a man and a woman and ordained their sexual union. Notice there was no negative hint or statement against this aspect of marriage.

The second negative teaching by these false teachers concerned the eating of certain meats. This almost certainly related to the food restrictions of the Jewish law. God did restrict the types of animals the children of Israel were to eat. These animals weren't bad in themselves, however, since when all of them were created, God viewed His work as "good" (Genesis 1:24, 25). God's restrictions served two purposes: First, they were for health reasons. Unless properly cleaned and cooked, certain of these meats could be carriers of disease and physical disorders. Second, some of these restrictions were symbolic of religious principles God wanted them to learn.

But this restrictive code on foods did not apply to Christians. Peter's vision in Joppa graphically speaks of God's sanctifying all the animals, and none of them were to be considered impure (Acts 10:9–16). Plus, 1 Timothy 4:4 emphasizes the inherent good of every creature God has created. Our only consideration is that whatever food we eat should be with thanksgiving to God for His provision.

Verses 4 and 5 provide a background or precedent for table grace. Praying a prayer of thanksgiving prior to eating was a Jewish practice that apparently carried over into Christianity, becoming a regular pattern for believers. The phrase "word of God" seems to indicate that using short portions of Scripture was a part of the prayer of thanksgiving for their food.

What are some ways to make table grace more meaningful?

II. PROMOTE GODLINESS (1 Timothy 4:6–11)

A. Christian Heritage (v. 6)

6. If thou put the brethren in remembrance of these things, thou shalt be a good minister of Jesus Christ, nourished up in the words of faith and of good doctrine, whereunto thou hast attained.

Proving oneself as a true servant of Jesus Christ involves projecting the truth in the face of false doctrine. This is neither easy nor popular when it has taken root within the body. Anyone who does not point these out to the congregation really isn't worthy to be given responsibility for the oversight of the church.

Timothy's promoting of godliness was built on a strong foundation of Christian heritage. What a positive setting! Instead of having endured the stress and uncertainty of spiritual anemia or doctrinal heresy, his Christian life had been one of spiritual nourishment and careful guidance. Paul's second epistle indicates Timothy's mother, Eunice, and his grandmother, Lois, were believers whose faith had been passed on to him (2 Timothy 1:5). A positive Christian family environment evidencing the Christian faith, lifestyle, and doctrine provides a valuable heritage when one reaches adulthood.

Timothy's Christian heritage also included his formative years as a member of Paul's missionary party. He joined Paul and Silas on the second missionary journey when he was about 20 years old. Traveling with this veteran Christian leader surely provided an environment in which spiritual maturity continued. There is no substitute for positive role models at key times in our lives.

Verse 6 also indicates why Paul trusted Timothy with the difficult task in Ephesus. He wasn't a novice in the faith, but, rather, reflected maturity in faith and doctrine. Attaining this spiritual level came partially from his Christian heritage.

What is the current application for those who have been fortunate enough to have a solid Christian heritage? The most evident concept is that we who have been so blessed have a greater responsibility to promote godliness in the face of false doctrines. It should also be easier for us to avoid false doctrine.

B. Avoiding Error (vv. 7–10)

7. But refuse profane and old wives' fables, and exercise thyself rather unto godliness.

8. For bodily exercise profiteth little: but godliness is profitable unto all things, having promise of the life that now is, and of that which is to come.

9. This is a faithful saying and worthy of all acceptation.

10. For therefore we both labour and suffer reproach, because we trust in the living God, who is the Saviour of all men, specially of those that believe.

Verse 7 begins a contrast from what had been Timothy's background. He came from a solid environment of biblical teaching and sound doctrine. But just the opposite was found among the believers of the Ephesian church. Godless, superstitious teachings were luring the believers away from truth. Myths and tales which had no relationship at all to God and true spirituality had become their foundation.

The latter part of this verse reminds us that what we believe is by choice. We train ourselves in the biblical truths or we actively gravitate toward the deceptions of Satan. The promotion of godliness in our lives and in the lives of others doesn't just happen spontaneously. It occurs as a conscious choice, and with varying degrees of effort.

Verse 8 appears out of place unless one is aware of the emphasis on physical fitness which dominated some in the Hellenic world. The emphasis on fitness for participating in sports and for appearance' sake does have some relationship to spiritual development. Paul wasn't against physical fitness. But he wanted these people through Timothy's ministry to recognize that if the same time and effort were placed in spiritual development, they would have eternal benefits.

We are aware today that physical activity stimulates not only physical health but also emotional well-being. But this pertains only to the short duration of this life. However, spiritual exercise benefits us both in this life and for eternity.

Just as physical development requires effort and fatigue, so does spiritual exercise necessitate strain and exertion. Verse 10 reminds us that with the labor of our spiritual fitness sometimes comes reproach from those in opposition to the faith. And how can we forget that false teachers with their heretical views may become another force against the believer.

The latter portion of verse 10 reminds us that the best way to avoid error is to stand on doctrinal truth. One of these truths is the unity of the Godhead. Though Jesus Christ came to earth and became the sacrificial Lamb for salvation, because of the unity of the Trinity, God can be referred to as the Savior. This title means "preserver." God's love for all men caused Him to provide the means for our eternal preservation. But to attain that position each person must follow the path of faith and repentance. Confession of our sins cannot be neglected. Simply changing our ways isn't sufficient. Every person has to recognize his/her sinful actions for what they really are—rebellion against God.

C. Teach Truth (v. 11)

11. These things command and teach.

Promoting godliness is an activity which demands a conscious effort. Paul reminded Timothy of this with a very strong directive. Those in spiritual authority have a divine obligation to speak forth the requirements of godliness. Notice that Paul instructed Timothy to both command and teach. It would be much easier if leaders were given the choice of doing one or the other depending on personality and preference. However, the importance of godliness in the lives of the believers demands both. In commanding godliness, there is an emphasis on the authority of church leaders as they fulfill their responsibility before God. In teaching, there is an emphasis on understanding the reason for the directive. God doesn't require blind obedience. He always provides a reason or purpose for what is required. Leaders have an obligation to know and to share it.

What are some reasons why church leaders may hesitate to command and teach godliness?

III. EXEMPLIFY GODLINESS
(1 Timothy 4:12–16)

A. Extraordinary Example (v. 12)

12. Let no man despise thy youth; but be thou an example of the believers, in word, in conversation, in charity, in spirit, in faith, in purity.

It isn't sufficient to simply speak the words of godliness; we have to live them as well. Our words and our actions are to be in harmony. That isn't always easy. There may be circumstances that hinder the ease by which it can be accomplished.

Verse 11 and the first part of verse 12 causes some to believe Timothy had a timid personality. To label Timothy as timid without examining the full extent of his personality would be a great injustice to him. The totality of this capable man can be seen by also studying Philippians 2:19–22. There Paul described him as being one who cared for the believers with an intensity above the rest of Paul's workers. Timothy also had distinguished himself by serving without fear for his own life or self–interest.

At the same time we need to recognize that even the most effective and experienced individuals may need special encouragement under adverse circumstances. Remember, Timothy was troubleshooting in a church with false teachers and heretical doctrine. To further complicate the matter was his age. Timothy must have been about 30 years old; however, in that society youth was a liability rather than an asset.

The term *youth* was usually applied to any person up to 40 years of age. Not only was Timothy facing a cultural handicap, but more than likely the elders in this congregation were considerably older than he was. What a challenge! Just from a general standpoint these people could look down on Timothy's position of authority and the directives he was bringing from Paul.

To counter the difficulties of this age situation, Paul provided five directives. Before we look at these instructions individually, the corporate whole of them reminds us that who we are is always more important than what we say or do. Inner character always possesses greater value than outer appearance.

Older, more reliable manuscripts do not include the word *spirit*, so we will look at the other five.

Paul exhorted Timothy to be an example in his speech ("in word") and in his conduct ("in conversation"). Notice that both of these areas are visible to those around us and easily detected. Paul encouraged Timothy to watch his speech carefully. His words needed to be carefully chosen and properly timed rather than carelessly spoken. It's a contrast between maturity and immaturity. In the same way, his actions (postures, gestures, and general conduct) were to portray maturity.

The other three qualities Timothy was to exhibit are of an inner nature; however, they do become evident in public. The quality of love develops within, but it dies unless it is allowed to overflow into the lives of others. Love evidences itself in kind deeds, a listening ear, a shoulder to cry on, along with a friendship that endures crisis.

Faith or faithfulness, is the second inner quality. This fruit of the Spirit is that virtue or grace which can be interpreted as loyalty or fidelity. Faithfulness can be seen in holding to sound doctrine without wavering. It can be displayed through consistent attendance and participation in the fellowship of the body of believers. Faithfulness begins within and then reveals itself through very definite, visible actions.

The final inner quality Paul included is purity. Usually when purity comes to our attention, we think in terms of morality and sexual wholeness. But in this case Paul was referring to setting the heart and mind on the will and work of God. Timothy was to avoid the detours of personal sovereignty and the desire to serve self. These were to be subjected to what God wanted to accomplish now in his life while stationed in Ephesus.

B. Public Projections (vv. 13–15)

13. Till I come, give attendance to reading, to exhortation, to doctrine.

14. Neglect not the gift that is in thee, which was given thee by prophecy, with the laying on of the hands of the presbytery.

15. Meditate upon these things; give thyself wholly to them; that thy profiting may appear to all.

Paul indicated his plan to return to Ephesus in the near future. But until that time he gave some directions for Timothy's public ministry. Verse 15 reminds us of the need for private preparation in order to be effective in a public ministry to believers and unbelievers.

Paul began with the need for publicly reading the Scriptures. The early church's services were similar to the synagogue services in that one individual read from the Scriptures while the rest listened. Since the New Testament canon had not been formed and all the books of Holy Scripture hadn't been written, we know Paul was encouraging Timothy to read the Old Testament as a specific part of the worship services.

It is alarming to see many Pentecostal churches minimizing or even eliminating the reading of the Scriptures as a part of their services. This lack of hearing God's Word could result in several real possibilities: (1) We miss hearing directly what God has revealed to us; (2) we only talk about the importance of God's Word to the church but never demonstrate it; (3) we fail to encourage private reading of Scripture by the lack of public reading; (4) we expect the congregation to place the working of the Holy Spirit within a biblical framework which hasn't been provided.

Paul continued by encouraging Timothy to exhort the Word. The assumption is that after the Scriptures had been read publicly, he should follow by preaching or proclaiming the truths it contained. The content needs to be highlighted, emphasized, and applied to the lives of the hearers. From a pastoral point of view this is a vital part of spiritually feeding a congregation. No pastor can claim to love his congregation and be seeking their best interests if he doesn't actively and effectively preach God's Word.

The final directive in verse 13 deals with instructing the people in the faith. Giving attendance to doctrine suggests teaching the theological truths of the gospel. One of the great dangers within a local church is that of assuming believers will know the truths of the faith. But how can they know and retain this information unless there is repeated instruction and reinforcement?

Paul also reminded Timothy about his personal giftedness (v. 14). The context of this verse doesn't indicate whether the giftedness he received was some ability or was one of the gifts of the Spirit. There are occasions when God gives the ability to speak a language never studied and it becomes part of one's normal ability. Others receive the ability to play a musical instrument. These are miracles and are intended to help them in ministry.

We know that every person who receives the Holy Spirit is a candidate for the gifts of the Spirit. Why would Timothy receive a gift in a setting where believers laid hands on him and a prophecy announced it? The logical answer is that God equips His children for their new ministry task. In His foreknowledge, God knows what will be needed in the future; however, it becomes His choice as to the timing of our being completely equipped.

What does it mean to not neglect the gift? The gifts God provides for His children are complete in themselves. But what does need maintaining is our personal spiritual condition. God works through vessels that are holy, righteous, and striving to draw nearer to Him.

In verse 15 the admonition to meditate is much broader than simply thinking about what has been presented. The connotation of the word *meditate* in that culture was to think about it and then do it diligently. Paul wanted Timothy to commit himself to this task of public ministry to a hurting congregation. If he would do this, the congregation wouldn't just notice it, but it would also profit spiritually.

What are the various methods by which teaching of doctrine needs to be occurring in the local church?

C. Personal Admonitions (v. 16)

16. Take heed unto thyself, and unto the doctrine; continue in them: for in doing this thou shalt both save thyself, and them that hear thee.

Chapter 4 ends with some of the most important admonitions in the New Testament. They show the necessary balance between doctrinal orthodoxy and practical lifestyle. These directives are specifically to ministers, but they also apply to every believer.

Verse 16 stands out as the key verse of this book. It summarizes in just a few words what needs to be the foremost concerns of the believer. No one can successfully minister to others until his/her own belief structure and current lifestyle is in harmony with God's Word. That's why doctrine and practice have to be continuing concerns.

The importance of this can be seen when we realize that our salvation depends on it. Doctrine determines practice—that is, what we believe determines what we do. It's also extremely sobering when we realize the impact we have on others. The success of their life in Christ may be in direct proportion to what they see in our lives. What you and I believe and how we live may make the difference in whether another person enjoys life everlasting.

It is not easy to review our actions and then spend the time necessary to fully evaluate our beliefs and determine whether or not they are in accordance with Scripture. This probably explains the weakness in many believers' lives. They lack the doctrinal foundations upon which they are to build their actions.

REVIEW QUESTIONS

1. Why should the Ephesian church not have been surprised by the problem of false teachers?
2. What were two of the false teachings being promoted?
3. What are several ways to promote godliness (righteousness)?
4. List the five areas in which Timothy was to be an example.
5. What are the two ways through which we may save ourself and others?

GOLDEN TEXT HOMILY

"GODLINESS WITH CONTENTMENT IS GREAT GAIN" (1 Timothy 6:6).

Godliness and contentment are great spiritual attainments.

Some people who are not Christians have the concept that if they become Christians they will have to make great sacrifices. However, the truth is that people who accept Christ as Savior give up nothing that they will miss or be harmed without. Rather, what they gain by becoming a Christian makes accepting Christ as Savior more than 100 percent worthwhile.

Many individuals have the mistaken idea that wealth alone brings contentment. This is certainly not the case. Paul, in writing to the Philippians, stated, "I have learned, in whatsoever state I am, therewith to be content" (Philippians 4:11).

The money–lover, by putting a false value on money, makes it a snare and an instrument of hurt to himself and to others and an eternal loss to his own soul. The people of God, on the other hand, by putting a true value on money, make it a joyful possession to themselves and others, a nourisher of unselfish virtue and an eternal gain.

The godly person, instead of reaching after worldly riches, procures *true* wealth and becomes rich in righteousness, godliness, faith, love, patience, and meekness.

The godly person *is rich*! He wants nothing in this world but what God has given him; thus, he has acquired riches which, unlike the riches of this world, he can take with him when he leaves this earth.

The godly man is content with what he possesses, submits meekly to God's will, and bears patiently difficult situations which he may experience in following God's direction.

The highest goal conceivable is to be like God.—**O.W. Polen, D.D., Coordinator of Special Projects, Pathway Press, Cleveland, Tennessee**

SENTENCE SERMONS

CHRISTIANS ARE to maintain a godly life in the midst of an ungodly world.

—Selected

EVIL UNCHECKED GROWS; evil tolerated poisons the whole system.

—Draper's Book of Quotations for the Christian World

THE HEART of a godly person is the sanctuary of God.

—Ann–Louise–Germaine–Da–Stael

UNCLEAN IN THE SIGHT OF GOD is everyone who is unrighteous. Clean, therefore, is everyone who is righteous.

—St. Augustine

EVANGELISM APPLICATION

A GODLY LIFE IS ESSENTIAL FOR AN EFFECTIVE WITNESS.

Walking the walk must accompany the talk.

This familiar saying emphasizes the importance of our complete witness. Its concept is the same as not being able to hear what someone is saying because his actions speak so much more loudly.

In the Scripture no one receives such scathing rebuke as the Pharisees. Though their beliefs were similar to those of Christ himself, and though they exhibited pious actions, godliness was not as dominant in their lives as it should have been. Godliness includes not only our outward actions but also our inward attitudes and thoughts.

Many people are won to Christ over an extended period of time in which the Holy Spirit is convicting their hearts and while the lives of believers are demonstrating to them the fullness of life in Christ.

DAILY BIBLE READINGS

M. Resist Temptation.
Genesis 39:7–21

T. Maintain Integrity.
Job 31:1–11

W. Walk Uprightly.
Psalm 15:1–5

T. A Heart for Godliness.
1 Peter 3:8–16

F. Reject Worldliness.
1 John 2:15–17

S. Example of Godliness.
3 John 1–14

Biblical Teachings Are Essential

Study Text: 1 Timothy 6:3–21; Titus 2:1–10

Objective: To recognize the value of scriptural teachings and conform to them.

Time: The Book of 1 Timothy was written between A.D. 62 and 64. Titus was written between A.D. 63 and 65.

Place: The Book of 1 Timothy was probably written in the Macedonian city of Philippi. Titus was possibly written from Greece or Macedonia.

Golden Text: "All scripture is given by inspiration of God, and is profitable for doctrine, for reproof, for correction, for instruction in righteousness" (2 Timothy 3:16).

Central Truth: Biblical teaching is essential for spiritual growth and recognizing false teachings.

Evangelism Emphasis: Sound biblical teaching prepares believers to take the gospel to the lost.

PRINTED TEXT

1 Timothy 6:3. If any man teach otherwise, and consent not to wholesome words, even the words of our Lord Jesus Christ, and to the doctrine which is according to godliness;

4. He is proud, knowing nothing, but doting about questions and strifes of words, whereof cometh envy, strife, railings, evil surmisings,

5. Perverse disputings of men of corrupt minds, and destitute of the truth, supposing that gain is godliness: from such withdraw thyself.

6. But godliness with contentment is great gain.

7. For we brought nothing into this world, and it is certain we can carry nothing out.

8. And having food and raiment let us be therewith content.

9. But they that will be rich fall into temptation and a snare, and into many foolish and hurtful lusts, which drown men in destruction and perdition.

10. For the love of money is the root of all evil: which while some coveted after, they have erred from the faith, and pierced themselves through with many sorrows.

11. But thou, O man of God, flee these things; and follow after righteousness, godliness, faith, love, patience, meekness.

12. Fight the good fight of faith, lay hold on eternal life, whereunto thou art also called, and hast professed a good profession before many witnesses.

13. I give thee charge in the sight of God, who quickeneth all

things, and before Christ Jesus, who before Pontius Pilate witnessed a good confession;

14. That thou keep this commandment without spot, unrebukeable, until the appearing of our Lord Jesus Christ.

Titus 2:1. But speak thou the things which become sound doctrine.

7. In all things shewing thyself a pattern of good works: in doctrine shewing uncorruptness, gravity, sincerity,

8. Sound speech, that cannot be condemned; that he that is of the contrary part may be ashamed, having no evil thing to say of you.

LESSON OUTLINE

I. CONSEQUENCES OF FALSE TEACHINGS
   A. Pride
   B. Greed
II. COMMENDATION FOR RIGHTEOUSNESS
   A. Follow Righteousness
   B. Fight the Good Fight
   C. Trust in God
   D. Lay a Good Foundation
III. COMMANDS FOR RIGHT LIVING
   A. Aged Men
   B. Aged Women
   C. Young Women
   D. Young Men
   E. Servants

LESSON EXPOSITION

INTRODUCTION

Our personal beliefs and our church teachings are matters of utmost importance. Every believer, every local church, and every denomination are challenged to remain biblical in their focus and foundation. Personal opinion and bias without a biblical basis can easily creep into the belief structure and become a foundational concept of church teachings. Even more frightening and destructive are those beliefs that are formed as the result of secular philosophies and the misinterpretation of Scripture. They can appear so convincing and truthful. But the end result is spiritual misdirection and even spiritual shipwreck.

Biblical teachings are essential for each of us individually and for the corporate group. No one can truly claim to be a Christian and a follower of Christ unless the biblical doctrines are his/her guide for belief and practice.

This brings us to a vital point of consideration. The biblical teachings that both form our doctrine and guide us in practical living need to be a continuing part of the church's program. Assuming that new converts will assimilate the necessary doctrinal truths is a dangerous position. Equally dangerous is assuming that more mature believers do not need to be reminded and refreshed in the basic doctrines of Scripture. All of us need to be regularly immersed in biblical doctrines. Not only does it keep our knowledge current but keeps false doctrine at bay.

Since this lesson moves into the epistle to Titus, some attention needs to be given to what is known about the man. Titus appears for the first time in the biblical narrative in Galatians 2. Paul was recounting the time he had taken him to Jerusalem to demonstrate that Gentile converts were worthy of being accepted in the church and that salvation by grace didn't need to be supplemented by circumcision to find acceptance in Christ. The believers at Jerusalem recognized this and did not insist on Titus' circumcision. Surely Paul made a careful choice in Titus, knowing how important this visit would be at that point and in the years to come.

Very little information is given to us, but what is available indicates Titus must have been a very close and trusted fellow minister. He stands within that inner circle of men who could step in at Paul's absence. Paul sent him to various places as a troubleshooter. We know he went to Corinth between the writing of the two canonical epistles to the Corinthians. They were a tough group, but apparently his mission was successful (see 2 Corinthians 7:6, 7, 13–16; 8:1, 6, 16–24).

His current assignment in Crete (Titus 1:5) provided another test of his ability to disciple and bring order out of chaos. The task was similar to that of Timothy's in Ephesus. Not only did the leadership of the church need to be appropriately ordered, but false doctrines had to be confronted and corrected.

Today's lesson shows three areas which biblical teaching strongly impacts—false teaching, righteousness, and right living.

I. CONSEQUENCES OF FALSE TEACHINGS (1 Timothy 6:3–10)

A. Pride (vv. 3–8)

3. If any man teach otherwise, and consent not to wholesome words, even the words of our Lord Jesus Christ, and to the doctrine which is according to godliness;

4. He is proud, knowing nothing, but doting about questions and strifes of words, whereof cometh envy, strife, railings, evil surmisings,

5. Perverse disputings of men of corrupt minds, and destitute of the truth, supposing that gain is godliness: from such withdraw thyself.

6. But godliness with contentment is great gain.

7. For we brought nothing into this world, and it is certain we can carry nothing out.

8. And having food and raiment let us be therewith content.

Before providing a listing of the characteristics and activities of false teachers, Paul gave a reminder of a general test for determining false teachers. It's relatively easy to administer and interpret. First, we know from verse 3 that anyone who differs from the practices outlined in the previous chapter should be considered a false teacher. Then we see that any deviation from the words of Jesus identifies that person as a false teacher; his teachings do not produce holiness, which evidences itself in godliness. Any lack of obedience or commitment to God's sovereignty automatically implies an erroneous path.

In verse 4 Paul began a listing of the characteristics and consequences of false teachers and their teachings. Notice that one characteristic may result in another item listed becoming a consequence. Perhaps pride, by virtue of its position at the head of the list, is the dominant characteristic, which may be the source, or at least a contributing factor, to the others.

In the Greek language the word used for *proud* can be translated as "wrapped in smoke." This literal description allows a number of applications. It may indicate a false sense of superiority—a sense of being above others. "Wrapped in smoke" allows the thought of drifting into a cloudland of conceit which causes one to look down on others. Another possibility for this translation is that a person may feel he is bigger than he really is. We usually refer to this person as having a "swollen head" due to pride.

Along with pride, these individuals are described as "knowing nothing." This doesn't mean they are ignorant in all things or even in all the dimensions of Christianity, but it does reveal aspects that are in harmony with the smoke screen of pride. False teachers generally are known for impressive words, complicated reasonings, and the misappropriation of facts. Strip all of this away and nothing remains.

Controversy and quarreling ("questions and strifes") go hand in hand with the pride of false teachers. It is so intense and frequent that Paul described it in terms of being sick or unhealthy. False teachers tend to be obsessed and argumentative concerning specific issues. This can be expected since one of the ways heresy develops is through an overemphasis on one particular doctrine or theme. Argumentation to defend a doctrine is at times necessary for the true and faithful teacher. But constant wrangling and disputing is an unhealthy practice. Constant disputing causes the first priority of Kingdom work to be neglected.

It readily becomes apparent how the consequences of false teaching multiplies. Before too long, envy becomes part of the thought process. Why envy? Most heresies eventually emphasize some gaps in degrees of authority, promotion, or privilege. With the intent of provoking animosity, these heresies are direct instruments in stimulating the rise of envy. Then it is only a matter of time until quarreling ("strifes") and personal slander ("railings") appear. Envy usually doesn't remain silent. Sooner or later it bursts forth with poisoned words and actions.

The last of the series in verse 4 is evil suspicions (surmisings). Here the sin is that of assuming more than the situation or facts allow. When a wild imagination runs unchecked, it may project possibilities far beyond the truth or reality. Once again, this comes as a logical result of pride with its ripple effect.

Verse 5 contains three distinct descriptions of the person and actions of a false teacher. First, they are constantly wrangling or in some contentious situation. They contribute to division and tension instead of promoting unity and harmony.

Second, they are individuals with corrupt minds. This sounds like a very hard accusation. But just think about it. The opposite of truthfulness and holiness is corruptness. Anyone who does not maintain and promote truth must of necessity be seen as involved in heresy. Heresy is opposite to those doctrines which bring salvation; therefore, they are corrupt and promote damnation.

The third description reflects the consequence of wanting to merchandise the gospel—"supposing that gain is godliness." They begin to use a form of godliness, or a godly facade, to accumulate personal financial gain. This isn't new to us. It can be seen throughout the past 20 centuries. Simon wanted to buy the ability to give the Holy Spirit (Acts 8:18–20). And who can forget the abuses of the church's indulgence system in the early 16th century? During the late '40s and '50s, ministry for financial gain "dogged" many of the healing revivalists. And during the last 10 years none of us can overlook the electronic church with the multiplied requests for money.

B. Greed (vv. 9, 10)

9. But they that will be rich fall into temptation and a snare, and into many foolish and hurtful lusts, which drown men in destruction and perdition.

10. For the love of money is the root of all evil: which while some coveted after, they have erred from the faith, and pierced themselves through with many sorrows.

In the preceding verses Paul discussed contentment and introduced the subject of material accumulations (vv. 6–8). After reminding us that possessions have value only in this life, Paul indicated that the basics of food and clothing are sufficient for contentment. In our current society, we consider those having only these two basics as among the most deprived. The point Paul wanted to emphasize, however, is that we are to cultivate the spiritual values which can be carried beyond the grave.

As Paul wrote verses 9 and 10 he still had false teachers in mind. Yet at the same time, all that was being said applies to Timothy and all other ministers of the gospel. Profiting from the gospel is a temptation for both the true minister and the false teacher.

Riches in themselves aren't evil. Also, being gifted in accumulating wealth and wanting to do so aren't necessarily evil. A quick review of the Old Testament provides many examples of rich individuals. Abraham, Isaac, Jacob, David, and Solomon come to mind. Even the New Testament includes individuals who must have possessed more than the average amount of this world's goods—Zacchaeus, Aquila and Priscilla, Matthew, and the fishing disciples' partnership.

The difficulty occurs when a greed for riches begins to grow and is cultivated. When allowed to remain, this desire quickly pulls one away from the principles of integrity and honesty. Unless countermanded, it can grow until the person refuses to resist, or can't resist, the illicit path to riches. The person succumbs to attitudes and actions he would never have thought possible. Lying, stealing, cheating, and even physical harm are common results. These in turn lead to mental, emotional, and spiritual destruction.

This love of money and material possessions is the root stimulus which drives individuals to a broad spectrum of sins. Paul linked those who have "erred from the faith" (false teachers) to this particular difficulty. It is logical, since truth is no longer of major importance to them. Adhering to their false teachings dominates their thinking in spiritual matters. Why shouldn't it also be seen in their views toward material gain?

One of the interesting characteristics of false teachers and their ministries is that of accumulated wealth. Followers are urged to sacrifice for the cause of Christ, but the receipts fill the heretics' pockets (bank accounts). For this reason, when a minister constantly asks for money, we should be alert to assess his true motive.

Discuss ways in which the desire for wealth may cause us to compromise the truth.

II. COMMENDATION FOR RIGHTEOUSNESS (1 Timothy 6:11–21)

A. Follow Righteousness (v. 11)

11. But thou, O man of God, flee these things; and follow after righteousness, godliness, faith, love, patience, meekness.

Paul's labeling Timothy as a man of God indicates that his life contrasted with the false teachers just described. He wasn't a man who strove for material possessions. Neither was he consumed with the desire to maintain all attention on himself. In marked contrast, Timothy fulfilled the dignity and solemn stature of an individual called to be God's servant.

In spite of Timothy's positive stature as a righteous minister of the gospel of Jesus Christ, Paul still issued a serious admonition. No one can afford to let down one's guard. For that reason he directed Timothy to avoid the evils which not only hinder but can also destroy. It wasn't a gentle suggestion to detour around or be careful of some possible pitfalls. Instead, it was a forceful directive to leave immediately whenever one of these temptations appeared.

Rather than plunging off in just any direction, Timothy was to pursue a definite goal. Special notice needs to be given to the virtues Paul listed. No one can be a committed Christian, much less a church leader, without these virtues being part of one's constant pursuit. *Righteousness* is doing what is right toward both God and man. *Godliness*, or piety, reflects a general Christlikeness in what we say or do regardless of the time of day or situation. *Faith* speaks of loyalty. It reflects a dedication that doesn't fluctuate from moment to moment. Dedication is demonstrated in a loyalty that supersedes the circumstances.

The virtue of *love* stands at the head of the list of the fruit of the Spirit (Galatians 5:22). We are to love the Lord our God and our neighbors. And once again we need to be reminded that love is to be an outward witness of our discipleship.

The final two virtues may be especially difficult for some when faced with crisis situations such as Timothy faced. *Meekness* isn't weakness. But rather it is gentleness. *Patience* comes much easier when we have been developing meekness. Extra time and second chances may become the means by which the weak are able to grow and develop in Christ.

What are some of the signs of actively working to be a righteous person?

B. Fight the Good Fight (vv. 12–16)

(1 Timothy 6:15, 16 is not included in the printed text.)

12. Fight the good fight of faith, lay hold on eternal life, whereunto thou art also called, and hast professed a good profession before many witnesses.

13. I give thee charge in the sight of God, who quickeneth all things, and before Christ Jesus, who before Pontius Pilate witnessed a good confession;

14. That thou keep this commandment without spot, unrebukeable, until the appearing of our Lord Jesus Christ.

Paul continued to emphasize the effort that has to be expended to follow righteousness. He used the allusion of athletics, more specifically, boxing in the Olympic Games. Fighting here isn't just expending effort and energy in an attempt to conquer your opponent—but it also means contending for a prize. There is something to be won or lost.

Life in Christ isn't a passive event that just happens to us. It's a struggle to keep going in the right direction. Our Savior, through the Holy Spirit, continues to guide and to strengthen us. However, we have the responsibility to do our part. God wants us to enjoy eternal life with Him. Yet, He doesn't allow us to simply stand by and let life pass us by.

Timothy was reminded of an event which occurred some time ago. The "profession" (confession) referred to in verse 12 could possibly be the time of his baptism in water. His witness of faith in Christ and renunciation of the world continued to ring clear even though the years had passed and the challenges increased.

In verse 14 Paul charged him to keep the commandment without compromise. The exact commandment isn't stated. It could be the directives which were given at the time of his baptism or the directives in verse 11—to flee and to follow.

C. Trust in God (vv. 17, 18)

(1 Timothy 6:17, 18 is not included in the printed text.)

Once again the influence of riches comes into the narrative. Those who trust in wealth and material possessions can never fully trust in God. They will never be able to experience His provision. Their joy is greatly limited in comparison to what God wants them to have.

There is a type of riches which God does require of all His children. We are to be rich in good works. This calls to mind the need to help our brothers and sisters in Christ. Good works need to begin within the household of faith (our own congregation). These good works extend to include our neighbors as well. So there can be no misunderstanding of who our neighbor is, we turn to the account of the Good Samaritan (Luke 10:29–37). As these verses demonstrate our neighbor is anyone near us who is in need of our help. Who he is and where he lives is not important.

D. Lay a Good Foundation (vv. 19–21)

(1 Timothy 6:19–21 is not included in the printed text.)

Bringing this letter to a close, Paul once again emphasized the necessity of avoiding the trap of false teachings. It isn't just those on the peripheral edges of

Christianity who become enticed with the teachings of heretics. Some of these individuals were once born–again believers striving to serve the Lord to the best of their abilities. But they erred in their beliefs by allowing themselves to be moved from the basic truths of the gospel. The ideas of men became more important than the teaching of Christ and His apostles.

Paul reminded Timothy, as well as all of us who read this epistle, that each believer's future depends on the foundation being developed today. That foundation must be the truth of the Word of God. Heretical doctrines and the riches of this world both fail. Neither enables a person to make heaven one's eternal home.

III. COMMANDS FOR RIGHT LIVING (Titus 2:1–10)

A. Aged Men (vv. 1, 2)

(Titus 2:2 is not included in the printed text.)

1. But speak thou the things which become sound doctrine.

Paul tells us how to silence false teachers and overcome the misconceptions and deceptions they have been promoting. Speak the truth! Christian leaders must demonstrate truth in their character and actions; however, they must not fail to speak it as well.

As we look at these 10 verses in Titus 2, we see the practical application of sound doctrine. All Christians are to work at ensuring that their behavior is in accord with their beliefs. Age and gender do not allow for exceptions.

Paul began with the older men in the congregation (v. 2). By virtue of their age and gender they have a responsibility to demonstrate leadership in key areas of the Christian life. They can be divided into two triads. The first three emphasize the need for seriousness of purpose, maturity, and moderation. It doesn't mean they aren't to have fun and enjoy the lighter side of life. But it does mean they are to reflect restraint, control, and direction.

The second triad reminds us somewhat of 1 Corinthians 13:13, where Paul spoke of faith, hope, and charity. In this verse (Titus 2:2) he substituted *patience* for *hope*. Each of these three virtues tends to develop along with maturation in years. These virtues do not automatically develop; they are expected, however, in individuals of advanced chronological age in combination with growth in the grace of God.

B. Aged Women (v. 3)

(Titus 2:3 is not included in the printed text.)

The older women of the congregation also share in the obligation to be leaders in their behavior. This reminds us again that the privileges of age also are accompanied by some definite responsibilities. Describing their "behaviour as becometh holiness" is a directive to reflect godliness in their behavior. This wording indicates that there is a sacredness in living one's life to the glory and honor of God. We are reminded of Romans 12:1 and our obligation to present our "bodies a living sacrifice." Worship isn't just a matter of actions or liturgy within the sanctuary; it also includes our daily living.

Paul touched on three areas. First, these women are not to be guilty of slanderous speech. Second, they were not to be bound to strong drink. The excessive use of wine creates many crises. It especially loosens the tongue and contributes to excessive, painful speech.

Third, Paul stated their role as teachers. This does not refer to a public teaching ministry. Instead it refers to teaching in the home as the women provide counsel and guidance to the members of their household. In the role of mother and grandmother, they are to teach both by example and by verbal guidance. Verses 4 and 5 indicate their impact on the younger women.

C. Young Women (vv. 4, 5)

(Titus 2:4, 5 is not included in the printed text.)

Verse 4 is a quick reminder of the cultural setting. The subservient role of women appears very quickly. Women had little choice but to enter into marriage and motherhood. In spite of the cultural norm, love in marriage is the intended Christian relationship. Being trained to love reminds us of the nature of true love (see 1 Corinthians 13:4–7). It is much more than soft words and warm fuzzy feelings. Love does have an inner dimension, but it is defined in terms of actions. In many cases individuals, both women and men, need to be trained in the expression of love.

The younger women were to be taught by the older women (v. 4). Following the need for training in love, Paul also listed other distinct characteristics which were to be found in the younger women—self–control, purity, workers at home, submission, and kindness. These provide an environment for a Christian marriage to flourish and the family to develop. Here may be an excellent time to insert a reminder for the times. Life in Christ never provides the opportunity to disregard the cultural norms and thus make the gospel appear divisive beyond its basic principles.

D. Young Men (vv. 6–8)

(Titus 2:6 is not included in the printed text.)

7. In all things shewing thyself a pattern of good works: in doctrine shewing uncorruptness, gravity, sincerity,

8. Sound speech, that cannot be condemned; that he that is of the contrary part may be ashamed, having no evil thing to say of you.

The young men were directed to be controlled and serious. Sobriety of thought and action isn't to be limited to those who are chronologically advanced. All Christian men, regardless of age, are to recognize and practice it.

Paul divided the responsibilities of the younger men into three areas: good works, sound doctrine, and wholesome speech. Their lifestyle, which includes family relationships, is to reflect life in Christ. Their doctrine was to be free of and untainted with the philosophies of the world and the deviations of the other religions around them. Their speech was to reflect a carefulness that would bring honor and glory to God rather than allow for disdain and antagonism from the world.

How do young men learn to treat wives and children in a Christian manner?

E. Servants (vv. 9, 10)

(Titus 2:9, 10 is not included in the printed text.)

Paul's specific inclusion of directives to slaves reminds us again of the society within the Roman Empire. The number of slaves in the empire were estimated to have been between one-third and one-half of the population. Many of them apparently were believers; otherwise there would be no need for including these special commands for them.

The issue here isn't whether or not slavery is just or if Christians were to have slaves. The whole context is about living as a believer—whatever one's situation is—and that is all Paul addressed. However, we can't overlook the fact that the apostle indirectly indicated that becoming a Christian didn't automatically release believers from their social status as slaves. They were to live within their environment as believers.

In verse 9 Paul exhorted them to excel in obedience and service to their masters. They were to perform their tasks to the best of their ability without talking back. Grumbling and disagreeing with their masters was seen as being inconsistent with a believer who understands all of life as service to God himself.

Right living as a believer brought several other responsibilities to slaves. They were to be honest and loyal. This means they were not to take their masters' goods and sell them for their personal gain. Loyal Christian servants in any society protect the masters' possessions rather than pilfering them—or allowing them to be pilfered by others.

REVIEW QUESTIONS

1. What are the characteristics of false teaching?
2. What are the three descriptions of false teachers?
3. How do we fight the good fight of faith?
4. List the responsibilities of the aged men and women.
5. What are the areas of concern for the younger men and women?

GOLDEN TEXT HOMILY

"ALL SCRIPTURE IS GIVEN BY INSPIRATION OF GOD, AND IS PROFITABLE FOR DOCTRINE, FOR REPROOF, FOR CORRECTION, FOR INSTRUCTION IN RIGHTEOUSNESS" (2 Timothy 3:16).

The apostle Paul presents the ultimate authority and priority of the Word of God in this verse. It is interesting to note that this verse is presented to us in the context of world conditions in the "last days." This period denotes the dramatic change in the worldview from a God-centered to a man-centered universe. Certainly the authenticity and inerrancy of the Word of God has come under more vicious attack in recent years than in any period since the canonization of the Bible.

This verse dictates the authority of the Word by stating the source of inspiration to be God. The mechanics of how this inspiration—or literally, "God-breathed" act—are not explained. However, we should be careful not to get hung up on understanding and explaining how it happened to the extent that we miss the emphasis of the verse which is the fact that all Scripture is God's truth communicated to us in written form.

The authority of Scripture establishes the necessity for the Word of

God to be a priority in our lives. This verse states that the Scriptures are profitable. God's Word is not just a compilation of religious writings. It is alive, powerful, and sharper than a two-edged sword.

The Scriptures are our primary source for doctrine or teachings. Any doctrine not in harmony with the Word of God should be discarded. The role of Scripture in the act of reproof or conviction cannot be overemphasized. When discipline is necessary, correction is made through the guidance of the Word. In fact, the total process of instruction in righteousness, which brings us to a mature understanding of God's standard of life, is based in the Word of God.

Let us be motivated as David to hide God's Word in our hearts in order that we may enjoy the powerful benefits of every scripture.—**Richard L. Pace, Chaplain (MAJ), Command and Staff College, Fort Leavenworth, Kansas**

SENTENCE SERMONS

BIBLICAL TEACHING is essential for spiritual growth and recognizing false teachings.

—Selected

GOD TAKES NOTICE of clean hands, not full hands.

—Latin Proverb

A PERSON may cause evil to others not only by his actions, but by his inaction.

—John Stuart Mill

EVANGELISM APPLICATION

SOUND BIBLICAL TEACHING PREPARES BELIEVERS TO TAKE THE GOSPEL TO THE LOST.

After being told the Pharisees were offended by His teachings, Jesus described their attitude and teachings with this illustration: "And if the blind lead the blind, both shall fall into the ditch" (Matthew 15:14). Even now it continues to be an excellent reminder that the believer needs to be doctrinally correct. No one can lead a person to Christ if he doesn't know the way himself. In the same way, no one can bring a person to Christian maturity without understanding the characteristics of the mature life in Christ.

Correct biblical teaching provides the foundation on which a new believer may build and thus mature in Christ. Maturity in turn produces the desire to fulfill the commandments of God. And when we fulfill the royal commandment to witness of the Savior whose shed blood brings salvation, we will witness of the power of the Holy Spirit, who empowers us for service, and we will want to see those without Christ come to salvation.

The application of this principle emphasizes the need for biblical preaching and teaching in the local church. This becomes the means for spiritual growth on the inside and the stimulus for evangelism on the outside.

DAILY BIBLE READINGS

M. Priority of God's Word.
2 Chronicles 34:14–28

T. Cleansed by God's Word.
Psalm 119:9–16

W. Apply God's Word.
Psalm 119:105–112

T. Power of the Word.
Hebrews 4:11–16

F. Reject False Teaching.
Revelation 2:18–29

S. The Unchangeable Word.
Revelation 22:16–21

Stand Firm for Christ

Study Text: 2 Timothy 1:1–18; Titus 1:5, 10–14; 2:11–15

Objective: To appreciate the importance of being faithful to Christ.

Time: The Book of 2 Timothy was written around A.D. 66 or 67. Titus was written between A.D. 63 and 65.

Place: The Book of 2 Timothy was probably written from a Roman prison. Titus was probably written from Greece or Macedonia.

Golden Text: "Hold fast the form of sound words, which thou hast heard of me, in faith and love which is in Christ Jesus" (2 Timothy 1:13).

Central Truth: Jesus Christ is the only foundation for Christian living.

Evangelism Emphasis: Faithfulness to Christ includes evangelizing the lost.

PRINTED TEXT

2 Timothy 1:6. Wherefore I put thee in remembrance that thou stir up the gift of God, which is in thee by the putting on of my hands.

7. For God hath not given us the spirit of fear; but of power, and of love, and of a sound mind.

8. Be not thou therefore ashamed of the testimony of our Lord, nor of me his prisoner: but be thou partaker of the afflictions of the gospel according to the power of God;

9. Who hath saved us, and called us with an holy calling, not according to our works, but according to his own purpose and grace, which was given us in Christ Jesus before the world began,

10. But is now made manifest by the appearing of our Saviour Jesus Christ, who hath abolished death, and hath brought life and immortality to light through the gospel:

11. Whereunto I am appointed a preacher, and an apostle, and a teacher of the Gentiles.

12. For the which cause I also suffer these things: nevertheless I am not ashamed: for I know whom I have believed, and am persuaded that he is able to keep that which I have committed unto him against that day.

13. Hold fast the form of sound words, which thou hast heard of me, in faith and love which is in Christ Jesus.

14. That good thing which was committed unto thee keep by the Holy Ghost which dwelleth in us.

Titus 2:11. For the grace of

God that bringeth salvation hath appeared to all men,

12. Teaching us that, denying ungodliness and worldly lusts, we should live soberly, righteously, and godly, in this present world;

13. Looking for that blessed hope, and the glorious appearing of the great God and our Saviour Jesus Christ;

14. Who gave himself for us, that he might redeem us from all iniquity, and purify unto himself a peculiar people, zealous of good works.

LESSON OUTLINE

I. BE COURAGEOUS
 A. Without Fear
 B. Without Shame
II. GUARD THE FAITH
 A. Hold Sound Teaching
 B. Appoint Elders
 C. Rebuke False Teachers
III. STAY ALERT
 A. The Stimulus
 B. The Denial
 C. The Hope

LESSON EXPOSITION

INTRODUCTION

Committed Christian living is a conscious choice. This choice necessitates understanding the foundational doctrines of the faith and then proceeding to make them one's priorities on a daily basis.

As our studies continue in the Pastoral Epistles, we enter Paul's last epistle (2 Timothy). It's only logical to remind ourselves of his situation as he wrote. Paul realized that his life and ministry on earth was drawing to a close. An overview of his work as the apostle to the Gentiles included tremendous sacrifice for the cause of the gospel. This is vividly seen in 2 Corinthians 11. This account of his sufferings is only a partial list since his ministry continued for another decade after this letter was written.

We cannot forget Paul's work as a church planter as he and his party pioneered through various parts of the Roman Empire. Then after the churches were established he continued to follow up on the spiritual development of each. Sometimes he commended them. On other occasions he disciplined them and worked hard to draw both belief and practice back in line with God's Word.

This is Paul's farewell letter to the church in general, even though it is specifically addressed to Timothy. Timothy's ministry continued in Ephesus. Surely he wanted to know of Paul's welfare and the possibility of his coming to visit him. However, that wouldn't occur, for Paul knew he wouldn't be released from prison and he wanted Timothy to come to Rome.

Thus Paul's final words are valued for their intensity and factualness. What he wrote wasn't theory or speculation. This was his life experience as a believer, spanning some three decades of preaching the gospel. Timothy's ministry with Paul included at least 15 of those years. It is these truths which have enabled him to stand firm in all crises, even when doubts and circumstances battered without mercy.

Paul's call to stand firm for Christ is more than just a rallying cry. Along with it he included the means by which it can be accomplished. Some of them we prefer not to experience, such as persecution. Others can be accomplished yet require a clear mind working in accord with a committed will.

I. BE COURAGEOUS (2 Timothy 1:6–12)

A. Without Fear (vv. 6, 7)

6. Wherefore I put thee in remembrance that thou stir up the gift of God, which is in thee by the putting on of my hands.

7. For God hath not given us the spirit of fear; but of power, and of love, and of a sound mind.

What does it mean to be courageous?

Most of us would say we understand what it means to be courageous but might have some difficulty in suggesting some synonyms. Here are a few: brave, bold, dauntless, fearless, gallant, game, heroic, lionhearted and soldierly. There is one missing, however, which needs to be added: confidence.

In the New Testament the word for *courage* is frequently interpreted as "confidence" and "boldness." But in a practical application we know courage cannot exist if fear is allowed to dominate.

Before reminding Timothy of the need for courageousness in the face of adversity, Paul brought a past event to mind. Timothy didn't need to depend only on his own abilities and personal strength. Divine assistance would provide the insight and ability necessary for the task. Knowing this enables believers to be courageous even in the most trying circumstances.

The gift Paul referred to here isn't clearly defined. Nevertheless, Paul had laid hands on Timothy at some previous time and the gift was endowed. But what was the occasion? We know that the laying on of hands speaks of conferring the responsibility of leadership. Maybe he was referring to some type of ordination service in which prayer for Timothy's future ministry accompanied the physical symbol.

There is also another possibility that needs consideration. Laying on of hands often accompanies an individual's receiving the baptism in the Holy Spirit. Ananias laid hands on Saul and he received his sight and was filled with the Holy Spirit (Acts 9:17). Many years later Paul encountered believers in Ephesus who hadn't even heard of the Holy Spirit baptism. After baptizing them in water he laid hands on them and they too received the Holy Spirit (Acts 19:1–6). Since upon receiving the Holy Spirit, a person may also be empowered or gifted as the Spirit chooses (1 Corinthians 12:7, 8), perhaps the gift referred to here is what Timothy received at the time of his Holy Spirit baptism.

Regardless of the source of this gift, Paul reminded Timothy that believers aren't gifted with fear, or timidity. We may have these weaknesses due to our personality or events that have made an impact on or shaped our thinking. Some believe this to be the case of Timothy. In spite of all his steadfastness in ministry and his history of Christian service, he may have been plagued with timidity. Therefore, he needed to constantly remember the power that God gives to replace our human weaknesses. God enables love to grow and mature in situations where it would be otherwise humanly impossible. God not only plants the seed but provides a fertile environment for its development. Those whom we could not love in our own ability or perception become lovable as the Holy Spirit makes it possible.

God also impacts our thinking. When we become a vessel open to Him, desiring His will to be done, He works through us. The concept is not that of a robot programmed to act without any self–will. Rather, He guides our thoughts so we can grasp the truth. This is a vital part of the Holy Spirit's ministry here on earth (John 16:13).

Fear cannot be a hindering factor in the believer's life unless it is allowed to be. Filling our lives with God's power and love, and properly directing our thinking, shuts out fear.

B. Without Shame (vv. 8–12)

8. Be not thou therefore ashamed of the testimony of our Lord, nor of me his prisoner: but be thou partaker of the afflictions of the gospel according to the power of God;

9. Who hath saved us, and called us with an holy calling, not according to our works, but according to his own purpose and grace, which was given us in Christ Jesus before the world began,

10. But is now made manifest by the appearing of our Saviour Jesus Christ, who hath abolished death, and hath brought life and immortality to light through the gospel:

11. Whereunto I am appointed a preacher, and an apostle, and a teacher of the Gentiles.

12. For the which cause I also suffer these things: nevertheless I am not ashamed: for I know whom I have believed, and am persuaded that he is able to keep that which I have committed unto him against that day.

A frequent companion of fear is shame. Together they can wreak havoc on a person's courage, provided they are allowed that freedom. Paul knew of this relationship between the two, so he addressed it immediately. There is no indication that Timothy had a problem with this; however, we know other believers were susceptible to it. The best way to handle some problems is to warn against them even before their arrival. Warnings against those things that rob us of both our victory and faith are always in order.

Standing firm for Christ includes a variety of attitudes and actions. In these verses Paul directed Timothy's attention to discerning between honor and disgrace. In verses 8 and 12 the apostle brought attention to his suffering and imprisonment for the sake of the gospel and in the process reminded not only Timothy but also us today that we should not be ashamed to testify of Christ or even be imprisoned for Christ's sake and our ministry. Writing to the Romans, Paul reaffirmed his commitment to the gospel and to not being ashamed. "I am not ashamed of the gospel, because it is the power of God for the salvation of everyone who believes: first for the Jew, then for the Gentile" (Romans 1:16, *NIV*).

Testifying of the grace of God and His plan of salvation for all is to be seen as an honor and blessing. Not only has God through Jesus Christ offered salvation, but He will continue to extend care and protection throughout the journey to heaven. Whatever we commit to Him will remain preserved as long as we walk faithful.

Paul understood that his imprisonment created a problem for some believers. They apparently were mortified that a minister of the gospel could be in prison just like a common criminal. And in Paul's case this was stretching into years. He was in prison in Caesarea for two years and now was continuing confinement in Rome. He didn't want this attitude to influence Timothy in any way.

Not only was Timothy not to be ashamed, but he was to willingly become a fellow sufferer for the sake of the gospel. Allegiance to Christ includes the difficult times as well as the triumphant occasions. Plus, some of the most intimate times of our relationship with Christ occur in the times of our deepest distress. Here is a good time to remember Paul's words to the Philippians: "That I may know him, and the power of his resurrection, and the fellowship of his sufferings, being made conformable unto his death" (Philippians 3:10).

Life in Christ isn't just a matter of His saving work in our lives (2 Timothy 1:9), but we are in turn to follow a life of holiness. The Lord calls us to live in opposition to the sinfulness of this world. In the process of doing so, the believer may reap the effects of sin's hatred toward those who do right. God knows from the very beginning that the call to service comes with a personal price. And we too need to expect opposition and even persecution.

Paul understood that his imprisonment stemmed directly from fulfilling his appointment as a preacher and apostle with specific responsibility to the Gentiles of the Roman Empire. Even in the midst of imprisonment his assurance continued. He knew that what he had committed (deposited) to Christ would remain safe. Regardless of what he might experience, he could not be robbed of either his joy or future in Christ. What a certainty believers have in Christ! He never fails! He always fulfills all His promises and provisions!

What are the present views of suffering held by most Christians?

II. GUARD THE FAITH (2 Timothy 1:13, 14; Titus 1:5, 10–14)

A. Hold Sound Teaching (2 Timothy 1:13, 14)

13. Hold fast the form of sound words, which thou hast heard of me, in faith and love which is in Christ Jesus.

14. That good thing which was committed unto thee keep by the Holy Ghost which dwelleth in us.

Any attempt to guard one's personal faith, or even the faith of the corporate body of believers, needs a beginning point—an initial foundation. All the other steps flow from that point. In this case, Paul directed Timothy to the basic aspect, that of consistent teaching of the gospel. But unlike what we would normally expect, Paul didn't ask Timothy to commit to memory every word preached and written. That would be impossible unless one had a photographic memory. Instead a totally different concept appears.

"Holding fast" includes knowing the pattern for interpreting the truths of God's Word. In the original language this term indicates having an outline sketch on which everything else depends. One commentator likens it to the sketch of a building which an architect designs before developing all the detailed plans of the structure. Paul's concern for Timothy and others who would follow was that they should know the standards by which Scripture had been received and how it was to be interpreted. Regardless of the context or circumstances of the decades and centuries to come, truth would continue to prevail.

Two virtues are always to accompany these standards. Proper interpretation is dependent on an environment of faith and love. Our actions and means of expression are an important part of sharing the truth. People may not accept the truth due to its inherent requirement for change; however, their nonacceptance is never to be the consequence of improper behavior on the part of believers.

Verse 14 points out that individual believers are incapable of personally fulfilling the task. Even the spiritually strong and intellectually quick need the divine empowerment of the Holy Spirit. He enables truth to develop properly in our interpretations even as cultures and centuries bring change. He keeps truth shining clearly when fear, doubt, and even sin attempt to cloud or distort the meaning. The Holy Spirit within us provides power and sustenance in many areas. One which should not be overlooked is His empowerment for truth!

From a very practical point of view we need to question who has the responsibility for maintaining sound teaching. Is it only key leaders such as Timothy who are on a special mission? Is it only ministers as they shepherd their flock? Or do all believers, regardless of their calling, have a responsibility to guard the faith through holding to the proper outline? We will look at some answers in the next section as we study the office of elders.

B. Appoint Elders (Titus 1:5)

(Titus 1:5 is not included in the printed text.)

Once again we are given a brief picture of the task Titus faced in Crete. Not only was there the problem of false teachers, but he also had to deal with disorganization. Either of these problems would be sufficient to disrupt the progress of any congregation. But having both evident at the same time ensures that it will be ineffective.

The situation in the Cretan church demanded mature leaders who would step in and provide direction. The disorganization in this congregation didn't mean there were no capable individuals. In fact, just the opposite appears true. Notice that Titus was to appoint elders. Nothing is said about training them or bringing them to the point of being able to serve. Apparently the system didn't provide for their taking office or control. It also may be suggested that they either did not have the aggressiveness to assert their leadership or that incapable individuals were dominating the scene.

When qualified individuals are serving in the position of elder, then the problems which plagued this church can be properly addressed. It may take some time to restore order and orthodox teaching. Even the wisest and most spiritual leaders cannot perform these miracles in just a few days or even weeks. However, nothing will be accomplished until they are appointed and given the power to serve.

Just to avoid any possible misunderstandings, some consideration needs to be given to the office of elder. In the Old Testament the elders were the heads and leaders of the various tribes and families (see Numbers 11:16; Deuteronomy 27:1). In the New Testament, the qualification for elders in the local churches wasn't dependent on age but on spiritual maturity and meeting the divine requirements listed in Paul's writings (1 Timothy 3:1–11; Titus 1:7–9). It should also be noted that the terms *bishop*, *presbyter*, and *elder* all refer to the same office.

C. Rebuke False Teachers (vv. 10–14)

(Titus 1:10–14 is not included in the printed text.)

Verse 13 challenges those who would suggest peaceful cooperation with all people in the church regardless of their doctrinal differences. Individuals who have strayed from orthodox teachings of the Scriptures and are spreading their views are a threat to individual and corporate spirituality. This becomes especially dangerous when these individuals project themselves as teachers and avidly seek followers.

Throughout the Scriptures the characteristics of false teachers are listed. These descriptions in themselves reflect the counterfeit nature of their teachings. In verse 10 Paul included three. First, they are unruly, or insubordinate, to the church leaders. The lack of discipline and accountability automatically places them outside of the scriptural system. Second, they are empty–headed, or "vain talkers." These individuals speak a great deal and profess to spread truth, but in reality they say nothing. Their words are empty, with little hope or truth. Third, these individuals are full of deception. Not only are they deceived, but they pour their words of deception into others.

In view of this, Paul directed Titus to sharply rebuke them. This wasn't the time to sit down and gently persuade them to take another viewpoint. This wasn't a time to encourage dialogue and the intervention of a third party. False teachers always present a crisis, but more importantly they are a dire threat to the believers' life in Christ. They are a blemish on the church, which cannot be tolerated for any period of time at any level. Their voices must be stopped. They should be stripped of any offices they hold and be given no opportunity to speak (teach) publicly within the body (the church).

Notice these individuals were not to be disfellowshipped. Their error wasn't reason to ignore their spiritual condition and needs. They could remain within the church, but restrictions applied until they became sound in the faith. People aren't simply to be discarded. False doctrine isn't confronted solely for the purpose of winning a battle and revealing the errors of false teachers. Rather, confrontation with them is to include the aspect of restoring them to the truth.

What are some steps in bringing false teachers back to the truth and fellowship with the body?

III. STAY ALERT (Titus 2:11–14)

A. The Stimulus (v. 11)

11. For the grace of God that bringeth salvation hath appeared to all men.

This final section on standing firm for Christ is both personal and theological. Too frequently we separate the two, thinking they are incompatible, when in reality they go hand in glove with each other. Our entire personal relationship with Jesus Christ comes through the truths and patterns of an established theology.

Verse 11 is the first of four verses which provide a theological basis for living the Christian life. And at the very beginning is the reality of God's grace. Everything rests on His offering undeserved favor to lawbreakers such as we all are. Paul understood and projected this concept so well. Without God's grace there is no salvation. We can't even begin to think of enjoying the relief of sins forgiven and guilt washed away except for His unearned provision.

God's provision of salvation applies to all mankind. Here we are reminded of the Bible's golden text. John 3:16 points out that God's love for all mankind caused Him to provide an opportunity for salvation to all. This provision becomes known through the witness of believers who already know the joy of having received God's grace. God's divine intervention through Jesus Christ indicates how personal this experience of salvation really is. God didn't send an angel or an impersonal book telling us what to do. Instead He sent His only Son to intervene on our behalf.

Knowing God's grace and keeping it in the forefront of our thinking serves as a stimulus for standing firm in Christ. How could we possibly betray or even disregard a God who loves us so much and paid such a price for our salvation. There are many aspects of our relationship through Christ that inspires us to good works and consistent living. These are all a result of God's grace. (Review other references to God's grace in the writings of the apostle Paul: Romans 3:24; 2 Corinthians 8:9; Ephesians 2:5, 8.)

B. The Denial (v. 12)

12. Teaching us that, denying ungodliness and worldly lusts, we should live soberly, righteously, and godly, in this present world.

Staying alert in our life as a Christian includes a balance of thought and effort. While verse 11 emphasizes the thinking or remembering aspect, verse 12 leads us to some definite actions through which we can resist evil. Avoiding Satan's schemes and the sins which attempt to ensnare, delay, and destroy us is our part. This reminds us that the effectiveness of the spiritual armor God provides (Ephesians 6:10–17) depends completely upon our picking up each piece and putting it on. In the same manner, denial is an active part of staying alert.

A theological principle to which we are to adhere is that of avoiding and rejecting the principles of the world, which present just the opposite of godliness, submission, and sacrifice. In contrast to the advertisements of the world, the good life isn't found in fulfilling the lusts of the flesh and following our own ideas.

As God's children basking in the light of His grace, we have an obligation to reject any idea or action which is in opposition to His holiness and divine will. This could mean denying some possessions and rejecting some experiences which bring short–term pleasure and the adulation of the world. Godliness doesn't just happen. It is a conscious act of choice. This choice often becomes difficult due to the culture in which we live. When the social norms, economic principles, and ethical patterns are not in harmony with God's desire for His children, it takes greater effort to deny ungodliness.

Denial consists of more than simply saying no or resisting specific actions and attitudes—there is a positive dimension as well. Verse 12 includes three positive aspects which are part of denying ungodliness and worldly lusts. The first is *living soberly*. This means a life of self–control rather than being controlled by the evil influences of the world. Frequently we perceive self–control a problem for younger people and specifically males. But notice, neither this verse nor its context has any age connotations; thus this admonition applies to all, regardless of gender or chronological age. Self–control is a standard for all believers who want to stand firm for Christ through alert living.

The second positive aspect of denial is *living righteously*. This assumes understanding God's requirements for His children. It includes our knowing the rights and wrongs, the do's and don'ts as revealed in God's Word. One's conscience can't be the guide for lifestyle. Though we value conscience, we must continually be aware of how it may be influenced, programmed, or even seared. For these reasons the written Word of God becomes the key to righteousness.

The final positive aspect of denial refers to godliness. While righteousness refers to the inherent character of the believer, godliness is living our righteousness on a daily basis in relation to others. It means exhibiting godly behavior toward our neighbors, our fellow believers, and our family members. This is the real test of our righteousness. Anyone can talk about being good and doing good. The true test is avoiding the very appearance of evil, turning the other cheek, and praying for those who despitefully use us.

C. The Hope (vv. 13, 14)

13. Looking for that blessed hope, and the glorious appearing of the great God and our Saviour Jesus Christ;

14. Who gave himself for us, that he might redeem us from all iniquity, and purify unto himself a peculiar people, zealous of good works.

It is hope that keeps believers consistent in their faith during persecution, and hope keeps believers strong in the face of overwhelming circumstances. Specifically, it is the hope of Christ's return for His saints. Christ's return is a foundational doctrine of the Christian faith. It provides believers with a motivation to stand firm and true regardless of the bombardments of Satan and his forces.

Members of the early church actively looked for Christ's return. Their expectations were for the return of Christ not just sometime in their lifetime but in the immediate future. Some of the Thessalonian believers misinterpreted

Paul's first epistle to them regarding this issue, necessitating his writing a second letter to bring to their attention several events which must occur prior to this wonderful event.

Paul reminds us that Christ's return will be a glorious event for the believers. It will be the fulfillment of His promise to return. Also this return will be in marked contrast to His first coming to earth. Then He came with the limitations of human flesh. His birth and life were in a very humble setting. And even when His public ministry began, the vast majority of people followed for the miracles and the food. The politically motivated saw Jesus as the long–awaited leader who would lead them in a victorious rebellion against Rome. Only a very few came to understand that He truly was the prophesied Messiah. But when Christ comes to earth again, it will be with all the power and glory of His position as the Son of God.

As part of our firm stand in Christ, staying alert includes maintaining our hope of His coming. Care needs to be taken that we don't lose sight of this reality. Our vision, and our desire for this coming event, is to remain in clear focus.

Verse 14 keeps the reason of this hope in the forefront. Christ willingly gave Himself to rescue us from the death grip of sin. In our lost condition, we could not bring about our own salvation. The bondage of sin is now destroyed, and we are purified and imputed with righteousness because we turned to Him in faith and repentance. Christ, through the ministry of the Holy Spirit, initiated our sanctification, purifying us and making us acceptable before God.

What are some ways to maintain our hope of Christ's returning?

REVIEW QUESTIONS

1. What does it mean to follow a life of holiness?
2. What is the beginning point for guarding one's faith?
3. Who could serve as elders?
4. Why should false teachers be rebuked?
5. What are the positive aspects of denying ungodliness?

GOLDEN TEXT HOMILY

"HOLD FAST THE FORM OF SOUND WORDS, WHICH THOU HAST HEARD OF ME, IN FAITH AND LOVE WHICH IS IN CHRIST JESUS" (2 Timothy 1:13).

If there is one thing this world needs, it is "sound doctrine." To be sound indicates a truth that man can trust. God's eternal Word is the only source that will elevate man to his highest potential. These words have proven true, and God's Word will never fail. There are many other teachings and religions, but they can never bring man to his highest calling—a personal relationship with God.

However, the Word of God is relevant to all generations. It is comforting to know there is no new plan of salvation. Once God established the plan of redemption, His plan has never changed. The same faith and commitment that established the apostles in Christ is available to us today. Such faith and commitment will bring redemption, peace, hope, and eternal life to us. That is sound doctrine!

Saving faith produces life–changing results. Our friends and family should see the change and hear from us the words of faith and redemption that now dwell in us. "Which thou hast heard of me" is a testimony to the fact that we should be eager to tell others of the saving love of Christ. This truth is a mighty force, capable of tearing down the strongholds of the Enemy. It is the only hope for this world.

Unbelievers will not find sound doctrine in the philosophies of this world. But when they see our changed lives and hear about the saving faith revealed in God's Word, they will be influenced. And Jesus said, "If I be lifted up from the earth, [I] will draw all men unto me" (John 12:32). **—Jerry Puckett, Customer Service Representative, Pathway Press, Cleveland, Tennessee**

SENTENCE SERMONS

JESUS CHRIST is the only foundation for Christian living.

—Selected

COURAGE IS the mastery of fear, not the absence of fear.

—Mark Twain

THE POWER AND AUTHORITY of your service will correspond to your dedication to a hidden life of prayer.

—Draper's Book of Quotations for the Christian World

EVANGELISM APPLICATION

FAITHFULNESS TO CHRIST INCLUDES EVANGELIZING THE LOST.

The pattern of witnessing followed by most believers is one of silence. Sad to say, most believers never share their faith in Christ with a non–Christian. Or if they do, it is either in a major crisis or after having felt such guilt that an attempt would make them feel better.

Witnessing isn't usually a high priority to the children of God. Most feel obligated to go to church, read the Bible, pray daily, and pay tithes. Doing "good deeds," such as caring for the homeless, orphans, and handicapped are also seen as important.

But when we stop to really think about life in Christ, how can we possibly be faithful to Him without witnessing regularly? He is our Savior and Lord—the most important person and focus in our life. How can we not speak openly and frequently of what He has done for us?

We are Christ's instruments for evangelism on earth. His commission to each of us is to persuade individuals to come to a saving knowledge of Him. That isn't necessarily a call to the mission field. But it is a call to tell the people we come in contact with about Jesus' love for them.

Now that's faithfulness!

DAILY BIBLE READINGS

M. Faithful to the Lord.
Job 23:1–12

T. Delivered by the Lord.
Daniel 3:13–25

W. Exalt the Lord.
John 3:30–36

T. Obey the Lord.
John 14:19–24

F. Boldness for the Lord.
Acts 4:5–22

S. Martyred for the Lord.
Acts 7:54–60

Focus on Discipleship

Study Text: 2 Timothy 2:1–21

Objective: To assess the responsibilities of discipleship and resolve to grow as a disciple.

Time: The Book of 2 Timothy was written between A.D. 66 and 67.

Place: The Book of 2 Timothy was probably written from a Roman prison.

Golden Text: "If any man will come after me, let him deny himself, and take up his cross, and follow me" (Matthew 16:24).

Central Truth: Jesus Christ calls His disciples to disciple others.

Evangelism Emphasis: Discipleship begins with accepting Jesus Christ as Savior.

PRINTED TEXT

2 Timothy 2:1. Thou therefore, my son, be strong in the grace that is in Christ Jesus.

2. And the things that thou hast heard of me among many witnesses, the same commit thou to faithful men, who shall be able to teach others also.

3. Thou therefore endure hardness, as a good soldier of Jesus Christ.

4. No man that warreth entangleth himself with the affairs of this life; that he may please him who hath chosen him to be a soldier.

5. And if a man also strive for masteries, yet is he not crowned, except he strive lawfully.

6. The husbandman that laboureth must be first partaker of the fruits.

7. Consider what I say; and the Lord give thee understanding in all things.

11. It is a faithful saying: For if we be dead with him, we shall also live with him:

12. If we suffer, we shall also reign with him: if we deny him, he also will deny us:

13. If we believe not, yet he abideth faithful: he cannot deny himself.

14. Of these things put them in remembrance, charging them before the Lord that they strive not about words to no profit, but to the subverting of the hearers.

15. Study to shew thyself approved unto God, a workman that needeth not to be ashamed, rightly dividing the word of truth.

16. But shun profane and vain babblings: for they will increase unto more ungodliness.

17. And their word will eat as doth a canker: of whom is Hymenaeus and Philetus;

18. Who concerning the truth have erred, saying that the resurrection is past already; and overthrow the faith of some.

19. Nevertheless the foundation of God standeth sure, having this seal, The Lord knoweth them that are his. And, Let every one that nameth the name of Christ depart from iniquity.

20. But in a great house there are not only vessels of gold and of silver, but also of wood and of earth; and some to honour, and some to dishonour.

21. If a man therefore purge himself from these, he shall be a vessel unto honour, sanctified, and meet for the master's use, and prepared unto every good work.

DICTIONARY

Hymenaeus (Hime–NEE–us)—2 Timothy 2:17—A professed Christian who had fallen into heresies.

Philetus (FI–LEE–tus)—2 Timothy 2:17—A professed Christian who along with Hymenaeus had fallen into heresies, and were advocating that the resurrection had already past.

LESSON OUTLINE

I. CHALLENGE OF DISCIPLESHIP
   A. Develop Disciples
   B. Value Perseverance
   C. Receive Rewards

II. COST OF DISCIPLESHIP
   A. Suffering for the Gospel
   B. Suffering for the Elect
   C. Suffering for the Future

III. GOAL OF DISCIPLESHIP
   A. Approved Workmen
   B. Holy Vessels

LESSON EXPOSITION

INTRODUCTION

What does it mean to be a disciple?

This question usually doesn't arise in our thinking. If you have been raised in the church or within Christian circles, you have heard the term. In the Gospel accounts, the word *disciples* constantly appears. So when we think about disciples, the Twelve and later the Seventy come to mind. They experienced Christ's teaching, guidance, rebuke, and general mentoring by example. They also witnessed the wondrous miracles demonstrating His power over all the forces of nature and even over the power of sin. They saw His encounters with those who doubted His identity and even sought His destruction. Truly theirs was an unforgettable experience. But what does it mean for *us* to be disciples of Christ?

Discipleship is much more than an occasional encounter with Christ. It goes beyond simply following as an interested spectator. Following isn't always synonymous with discipleship. A person may follow the career, writings, and teachings of someone out of mere curiosity. Sometimes the following is stimulated by an individual's charisma or character, or some outlandish actions or the future potential seen in a leader. In these cases there is no disciple–master relationship!

Discipleship involves commitment. It means adhering to the principles and ideas which the teacher or leader projects. A disciple becomes an adherent of the leader's philosophy and lifestyle to the point of imitating him in character and action. The true disciple will not allow a distance or gap between himself and the leader such as may be true of those who are only followers. The disciple strives to be the same in attitude and action as his leader.

Being a disciple of Christ causes a person to realize that this relationship is a total package. It's much more than praise and worship and a feeling that everything will turn out just fine. Discipleship includes submission, sacrifice, and even suffering. Being God's child, redeemed by the blood of Jesus Christ, comes with a price. But why should this be different than any other relationship of value?

Discipleship is one of those special–interest areas being emphasized within many local churches and denominations. There has arisen a generation that has avoided commitment—a people who fill the church pews and the church membership rolls but want the blessings of Christ without a solid adherence to the teachings and lifestyle of Christ. They desire that their needs be met but rebel at the thought of relinquishing their personal sovereignty to allow Christ to work in their lives.

Discipleship will always be a contemporary subject within the Christian church. However, there are decades or eras when it must be emphasized to a greater degree. It is evident that the decade of the 1990s is one of those crucial periods when discipleship needs careful consideration in our teaching and preaching. Without discipleship the church in general and our individual congregations become only a shell of pretension. Adherence to the call to follow closely after the Master is traded for following from afar. Beautiful buildings have become a facade to cover spiritual indifference. Voices parrot the words, but the hearers are far away from the Savior being proclaimed.

This second chapter of Paul's last epistle to Timothy provides an excellent overview of discipleship. The first 21 verses furnish distinct characteristics for those who are disciples and those who are going to disciple others.

I. CHALLENGE OF DISCIPLESHIP (2 Timothy 2:1–7)

A. Develop Disciples (vv. 1, 2)

1. Thou therefore, my son, be strong in the grace that is in Christ Jesus.

2. And the things that thou hast heard of me among many witnesses, the same commit thou to faithful men, who shall be able to teach others also.

The impact of verse 1 of chapter 2 appears when we consider the last four verses in chapter 1. Paul's directive to Timothy was in marked contrast to those who deserted him and possibly the faith as well (v. 15). Instead of remaining firm in their commitment to Christ and the leadership of Paul they fled to perceived safety. But on the positive side stood Onesiphorus. He risked personal safety to support and be of service to Paul (vv. 16, 17). This dedicated servant of the Lord didn't allow the presence of Roman soldiers or Paul's chains to discourage his service to him.

It's important to note that this type of strength comes from constantly recognizing the grace of God in our lives. His grace is the continuing means of our empowerment and successful living. God's grace persists throughout our Christian life. We aren't on our own! In the same way, we need the influence of mature believers to help us grow in Christ. The success and continuance of a local church depends on a program of discipleship. A teaching ministry enables individuals and the corporate body to avoid pitfalls and to overcome difficulties. Knowing this, Paul directed Timothy to develop a method for ensuring the continuance of doctrinal truth. Without truth right living can't be accomplished.

Verse 2 indicates that the preservation and transmission of the faith isn't to be simply left to chance. Though many people have heard about the faith, there may be some major hindrances in their furthering it. Some neglect what isn't popular in favor of what people want to hear. Others who are insufficient in their complete understanding of the truth want to become teachers prematurely. Still others pervert the truth for their personal gain.

To guarantee the proper discipling of believers, each local church needs to develop an appropriate program. Those chosen to develop disciples should consist of select individuals who have been loyal to the faith. Not only do they understand the principles of the Christian faith, but they have lived them on a daily basis. That's true fidelity.

These believers need to have one major ability along with their knowledge and loyalty—disciples should be able to teach others. Lifestyle example by itself isn't sufficient; they should be able to verbally communicate the basics of the faith and its practical application.

This verse points out the need to cultivate and to install individuals who are charged with the responsibility of discipling new believers in the local church. It won't happen unless the leaders recognize the challenge of discipleship and put together a working program. Our faith is too precious a possession to be left to a random approach. There are eternal rewards for and eternal repercussions of our actions. Our challenge is to teach the truth of the gospel to believers. We must teach others to pass the good news on.

B. Value Perseverance (vv. 3, 4)

3. Thou therefore endure hardness, as a good soldier of Jesus Christ.

4. No man that warreth entangleth himself with the affairs of this life; that he may please him who hath chosen him to be a soldier.

These verses bring us to the commitment part of discipleship. True discipleship isn't a part–time involvement or a fair–weather choice. Rather, it necessitates an ongoing relationship with Christ which demands separation to the task.

To demonstrate his point Paul used the analogy of a soldier, one who continues to be ready for combat. The cultural aspect of the times presents a soldier of the Roman army. These men went where they were commanded, did the task they were directed, and suffered the consequences of the environment. Keeping this in mind, we hear Paul say to "endure hardness." He wasn't speaking of training exercises which prepare both the body and the mind for combat. Instead this was to be understood as experiencing hardship while on the actual mission. He encouraged Timothy, and us as well, to understand the necessity of experiencing ill–treatment. Difficult circumstances are a part of the life of a soldier of Jesus Christ battling against sin and the efforts of Satan.

Paul's life continually demonstrated his ability and willingness to suffer hardship. He never hesitated to keep on serving God. He didn't ask for a vacation or an early retirement. He didn't take a leave of absence so he could recuperate. Instead this dynamic, selfless child of God stood firm in the face of persecution—and kept on serving. The partial list of his sufferings recorded in 2 Corinthians 11 demonstrates his having practiced what he taught. Though not called to participate in the same specific suffering as Paul, every believer is to willingly and with confidence face the ill–treatment which may come from being a child of God. We are to persevere regardless of the circumstances in which we find ourselves.

Commitment to Christ includes our pleasing Him in the same manner that a soldier strives to fulfill the directives of his commanding officer. This type of discipline comes through maintaining one's priorities and staying free from entanglements that hinder or render ineffective our ability to serve. The *New International Version* translates verse 4 as follows: "No one serving as a soldier gets involved in civilian affairs—he wants to please his commanding officer." However, we still face these questions: Which parts of our life are "civilian affairs," and how do we go about not involving ourselves in them?

The picture Paul paints for us is that of a soldier reaching for his weapon and finding it difficult to draw and fight. Somehow it has become twisted in his cloak and he struggles to free it. It would seem that there are some basic entanglements which Christians may face. The need to support one's family, also the desire to accumulate extra wealth, can hinder believers from serving Christ without reservation. The desire for personal prestige may project the ego above the need to follow the direction of God's Word and the leading of the Holy Spirit. Our potential entanglements vary from believer to believer; however, no one is exempt from the possibility of entanglement.

Being a disciple of Christ is a matter of priority and service. He must come first in our life. Otherwise, any claim to being His child is spurious and we are deceiving ourselves.

List some of the aspects of living which may become entanglements, or hindrances, in our serving Christ.

C. Receive Rewards (vv. 5–7)

5. And if a man also strive for masteries, yet is he not crowned, except he strive lawfully.

6. The husbandman that laboureth must be first partaker of the fruits.

7. Consider what I say; and the Lord give thee understanding in all things.

In this passage Paul used two more illustrations. He moved from the life of a soldier to the distinctive discipline of an athlete. The overall topic deals with reward, but in this first illustration the emphasis is that of following the rules. More than likely, this picture refers to the regulations which governed the Olympic Games. To ensure the quality of the competition, all participants were to train appropriately prior to entering the games. In some instances the athletes took an oath declaring they had been in training for 10 months.

Verse 5 reminds us that developing as a believer isn't an on–again, off–again process. Discipleship is a commitment to follow the guidelines of the Word in order that a Christlike life can come into existence. Receiving the crown of life comes only when our life has been lived within the framework of Christ's requirements. Life in Christ does have rules! Though we are not heaped with thou–shalt–nots, we are provided with guidelines which enable us to live according to what God knows is best for us.

Paul's illustration in verse 6 emphasizes the reward of work. Using the occupation of farming he pointed out how the hardworking farmer shares in the crop. The lazy unwilling worker has no right to the rewards of another's efforts. There are several applications from this verse. First, it means God will reward each of us according to our service. Second, it is understood that those who work are to be rewarded for their service even here on earth—which reminds us that a "labourer is worthy of his hire" (Luke 10:7).

The concepts within the challenge of discipleship can be grasped only through a combined effort of the human and the divine. We are told to reflect on what has been said (v. 7). Part of our spiritual understanding comes as we allow the concepts of the Word to become a part of our thought patterns. Once again we see how God will work through our own thinking to better understand the challenge to live a discipled life. He will supply the wisdom necessary to help in self–discipline and in developing the convictions we need.

II. COST OF DISCIPLESHIP (2 Timothy 2:8–14)

A. Suffering for the Gospel (vv. 8, 9)

(2 Timothy 2:8, 9 is not included in the printed text.)

Before looking at the distinctives of verses 8 and 9, consideration needs to be given to Christ's teachings on the cost of discipleship. Large crowds had been traveling with the Lord when suddenly He confronted them with the reality of discipleship—taking up and carrying one's own cross (Luke 14:25–27). He followed this with two examples—a person who is contemplating building a tower and a king deciding whether to make war against another king (14:28–33). Both of them pause to consider the cost before making the crucial decision. Failure to do so may result in bankruptcy for the builder and defeat for the king.

Being a Christian demands the

same deliberation. The question "Are we willing to pay the price of discipleship?" should be part of choosing to become a Christian. Having done so, the believer begins with a stronger foundation of commitment and a greater knowledge of what may occur. We may have pushed people into declaring a commitment before they have had the opportunity to evaluate the cost and make a firm decision based on sound calculations of the cost.

The price of discipleship may differ greatly from one believer to another. But in the case of the apostle Paul, he suffered personal harm, restriction, and indignity because of preaching the gospel of Jesus Christ. Because Paul preached Jesus as the promised Messiah, from the lineage of David, he was very unpopular in the community of the unbelieving Jews, whose image of the coming king differed drastically from the reality presented by Jesus. How could the son of a poor, insignificant carpenter be the long–awaited Messiah? Paul also preached the miraculous resurrection of Jesus from the dead, which was opposed by the Sadducees. This is the hope of all believers. Without it, Christianity fades into insignificance along with all the other religions. Christ's resurrection is the distinctive that separates Christianity from them all.

Because of preaching the gospel, Paul suffered as a common criminal. Since he was in prison, the world made no distinction. The apostle was in chains and under constant guard. He received no better treatment than a thief or murderer. The cost of discipleship for him included the harshest of suffering for the gospel.

B. Suffering for the Elect (v. 10)

(2 Timothy 2:10 is not included in the printed text.)

This verse deserves a special highlighting. Paul understood suffering for what he had already accomplished for Christ. But he also knew that the suffering of the present extended forward to include those who would be saved but had not heard or accepted the gospel at this point. "The elect" appears to refer to those who still needed to be won to Christ. No suffering was too great when one considered the salvation of all those who would one day come to Christ through the work of Paul. God wasn't done with Paul even though he understood the time of his death was drawing near. Paul's steadfastness even in the most trying circumstances would be an encouragement for other ministers to speak boldly and win the lost to Christ.

Notice how suffering continued throughout Paul's entire ministry. As he pushed the borders of Christianity further into the Roman Empire on each missionary trip, there were always those who rejected both him and his message. Of course, this wasn't unexpected. Part of his conversion experience included his being informed of his ministry and the suffering he would endure. What a way to start a ministry! The Lord told Ananias, "For I will shew him how great things he must suffer for my name's sake" (Acts 9:16).

If Paul and his party had not been willing to suffer for ministering the gospel, many people would never have become believers, and many churches would never have been planted. Whole geographical areas would have continued to remain in the darkness of heathen religions rather than experiencing the true light of Jesus Christ.

C. Suffering for the Future (vv. 11–14)

11. It is a faithful saying: For if we be dead with him, we shall also live with him:

12. If we suffer, we shall also reign with him: if we deny him, he also will deny us:

13. If we believe not, yet he abideth faithful: he cannot deny himself.

14. Of these things put them in remembrance, charging them before the Lord that they strive not about words to no profit, but to the subverting of the hearers.

It is generally believed that verses 11–13 are at least a part of a Christian hymn. How appropriate to include words from a commonly used worship hymn as part of his message. Notice how frequently this is still done as pastors incorporate various hymns and choruses into their sermons.

Life in Christ is one of paradoxes—giving to receive, humbling oneself to be exalted, and dying to live. From the spiritual standpoint, we understand that dying to self and to our own personal agenda is a must if we are going to enjoy life in Christ. One cannot retain personal sovereignty and still live the Christian life.

Suffering for Christ may even include death. Some believers are called on to be martyrs for the faith. They willingly continue to stand for Christ and Christian principles even though it means giving up their lives. For them, to do anything less is to be a traitor to their commitment and testimony. It isn't popular to speak of martyrdom today, when most prefer to hear about happiness, wealth, and a long life. However, people will continue to lose their lives for the sake of the gospel until Jesus comes.

Verse 12 provides the heart of Paul's teachings about suffering. Our present suffering serves not only the current time, but it also sets the stage for the future. Suffering in the here and now brings a specific reward at a later time. By participating in suffering for our Lord's sake, we will have the opportunity to reign with Him. Paul's words to the Romans on this subject come to mind: "I consider that our present sufferings are not worth comparing with the glory that will be revealed in us" (Romans 8:18, *NIV*). This perspective helps us understand that regardless of the severity of our suffering for Christ, it will be worth it.

In the final verses of this section we see God's faithfulness. Even though doubts may creep in and some may go so far as to deny their faith, Christ is faithful. His words and truths last eternally. This is what all believers need to concentrate on and hold closely within their hearts. Instead of wrangling over ideas and concepts that are spiritually unprofitable or destructive, we are to remember those things which build for the future.

What can the suffering believer do to help maintain steadfastness in times of persecution?

III. GOAL OF DISCIPLESHIP (2 Timothy 2:15–21)

A. Approved Workmen (vv. 15–19)

15. Study to shew thyself

approved unto God, a workman that needeth not to be ashamed, rightly dividing the word of truth.

16. But shun profane and vain babblings: for they will increase unto more ungodliness.

17. And their word will eat as doth a canker: of whom is Hymenaeus and Philetus;

18. Who concerning the truth have erred, saying that the resurrection is past already; and overthrow the faith of some.

19. Nevertheless the foundation of God standeth sure, having this seal, The Lord knoweth them that are his. And, Let every one that nameth the name of Christ depart from iniquity.

How can we know if our discipleship endeavors are successful?

The initial response would be whether or not those being discipled "walk and talk" like Christians. And this may be a good reply for a general overview; however, Paul began with a much more distinctive evaluation. The beginning and foundational test of discipleship is doctrinal. What one believes determines one's actions. Note 1 Timothy 4:16—our salvation depends on what we believe.

The goal of discipleship is to produce men and women, boys and girls who understand the truths of God's Word and their application to daily living. Verse 15 is one of the "classic" verses—frequently used and therefore readily recognized. Its importance may not be fully recognized unless its content is understood.

Every believer needs to strive to understand the doctrines of the faith. This includes both public instruction and personal study. The goal for both instructor and student is to be able to present their belief structure for God's approval without hesitancy or any sense of shame. As with a good craftsman, incompetent or flawed work is never presented with satisfaction. Anything less than the best is blushingly presented. Shoddiness is not acceptable.

It is with this same attitude that we are to work with biblical truth. "Rightly dividing" can be understood as "correctly handling." The term means to cut straight to the truth, without deviations or heresies. It denotes a moving directly, unswervingly, rather than following the twisted paths of false teachers.

This focus on correct doctrine can be seen plainly from verses 16–18 through the example of two men who had strayed and their specific errors. Notice that Paul compared their false teachings to a canker, or gangrene. We know that though certain illnesses begin in a localized area, in time the whole body is destroyed. This also holds true for false teachings in the local congregation. Perhaps initially only one believer, or at most a few, believe the heresy. But with time it spreads until the whole group is inundated with potential death.

In spite of the destructiveness of false teachers and their deviate doctrines, verse 19 offers a solid hope. Jesus Christ is both the head and the cornerstone of the church. Regardless of all of Satan's attempts to draw believers away, the church will not only survive but continue triumphant. Persecution purifies the church. The numbers may drop sporadically as partially committed church members are weeded out. Their desire for life and freedom from pain will outweigh their commitment to Christ.

The Lord knows those who are His children even though we don't. Our major concern is still to be workmen whose truth is acceptable in the sight of God.

B. Holy Vessels (vv. 20, 21)

20. But in a great house there are not only vessels of gold and of silver, but also of wood and of earth; and some to honour, and some to dishonour.

21. If a man therefore purge himself from these, he shall be a vessel unto honour, sanctified, and meet for the master's use, and prepared unto every good work.

Once again Paul used an illustration to demonstrate his point on discipleship. This time it is an affluent home in which there are a wide array of vessels—goblets. Some are made out of precious metals while others are of clay and wood. The issue here isn't their value but their cleanliness. Whether they can be used for the purpose intended isn't based on the type of material, size, or design. It all rests on their being spotless and untainted.

This illustration reflects the wide variety of people within a local church. Some are highly skilled and gifted. Others are limited in natural abilities. But this isn't the issue. What matters is their holiness! Have they set themselves apart for the Master's use? Are they striving to overcome sin and live victoriously by walking in the Spirit?

The emphasis in verse 21 isn't on self–cleansing but, rather, our putting ourselves in a position, by making right choices, so the Holy Spirit can cleanse us. He then sanctifies us and makes us righteous vessels for the Master's use. Everything rests on our being set aside for His purposes rather than our own. Our holiness rests on allowing His sanctifying power to transform our hearts and minds. Once this occurs, we become ready for service.

List various ways by which we present ourselves for cleansing by the Holy Spirit.

REVIEW QUESTIONS

1. What is the first step in the discipling process?
2. What does it mean to endure hardness as a soldier?
3. Why does the price of discipleship differ from one believer to another?
4. List some of the paradoxes of life in Christ.
5. Explain what it means to rightly divide the word of truth.

GOLDEN TEXT HOMILY

"IF ANY MAN WILL COME AFTER ME, LET HIM DENY HIMSELF, AND TAKE UP HIS CROSS, AND FOLLOW ME" (Matthew 16:24).

It is important for us to frequently review the requirements of discipleship. They are stated clearly in the text: deny self, take up the cross, follow Christ.

We must renounce, forgo, or postpone any pleasure, profit, or interest which may conflict with Christ's will for our lives. Self–denial is not carelessness about one's life, health, or family. It is not bodily abuse in any respect. It is simply the surrender of our will to Christ.

The counterpart of Christian

self–denial is the giving of one's life to God. Self–denial is a self–surrender, which, by dethroning self, enthrones Christ.

Self–denial, then, is the first step in Christian discipleship. The second step is taking up the cross.

As Christ bore His own cross to His own crucifixion, so His followers must bear their cross to their crucifixion. The great crucified leader is followed by an immense throng of crucified followers. They are crucified symbolically in all of their sufferings of mind and body in behalf of Christ and the truth.

The third step in Christian discipleship is to follow Christ wherever He may lead. Wilfred T. Grenfell, medical missionary to Labrador, at age 54 wrote: "Feeble and devious as my own footsteps have been since my decision to follow Jesus Christ, I believe more than ever that this is the only real adventure in life. No step in life do I even compare with that one in permanent satisfaction." The adventure of following Christ is a supreme effort to pattern our life after the life of Christ. May we follow Him all the days of our life. May we never think of turning back or failing Him for even one day.

We have accepted the challenge of Christian discipleship. We have dedicated ourselves to following in Christ's steps. To the Lord Jesus Christ we will be true regardless of what the future holds. We have forsaken all to follow Jesus.—**Excerpts from the *Evangelical Sunday School Lesson Commentary*, Vol. 29**

SENTENCE SERMONS

JESUS CHRIST calls His disciples to disciple others.

—Selected

SALVATION IS FREE, but discipleship costs everything we have.

—Billy Graham

WE TALK ABOUT the joys and comforts of salvation. Jesus Christ talks about taking up the Cross and following Him.

—Oswald Chambers

SELF–SACRIFICE is never entirely unselfish, for the giver never fails to receive.

—Dolores E. McGuire

DAILY BIBLE READINGS

M. Discipleship Is a Decision. Joshua 24:14–24
T. Hearing God's Call. 1 Samuel 3:1–10
W. Cleansed for Discipleship. Isaiah 6:1–8
T. Respond to the Call. Matthew 10:5–10
F. Counting the Cost. Luke 14:26–33
S. Changed by Christ. Luke 19:1–10

Facing the Last Days

Study Text: 2 Timothy 3:1–17

Objective: To be alert to conditions of the last days and equip ourselves with God's Word.

Time: The Book of 2 Timothy was written between A.D. 66 and 67.

Place: The Book of 2 Timothy was probably written from a Roman prison.

Golden Text: "This know also, that in the last days perilous times shall come" (2 Timothy 3:1).

Central Truth: Knowing God's Word equips us to face the last days.

Evangelism Emphasis: Understanding the times should cause us to be more fervent in witnessing.

PRINTED TEXT

2 Timothy 3:1. This know also, that in the last days perilous times shall come.

2. For men shall be lovers of their own selves, covetous, boasters, proud, blasphemers, disobedient to parents, unthankful, unholy,

3. Without natural affection, trucebreakers, false accusers, incontinent, fierce, despisers of those that are good,

4. Traitors, heady, highminded, lovers of pleasures more than lovers of God;

5. Having a form of godliness, but denying the power thereof: from such turn away.

6. For of this sort are they which creep into houses, and lead captive silly women laden with sins, led away with divers lusts,

7. Ever learning, and never able to come to the knowledge of the truth.

8. Now as Jannes and Jambres withstood Moses, so do these also resist the truth: men of corrupt minds, reprobate concerning the faith.

9. But they shall proceed no further: for their folly shall be manifest unto all men, as their's also was.

10. But thou hast fully known my doctrine, manner of life, purpose, faith, longsuffering, charity, patience,

11. Persecutions, afflictions, which came unto me at Antioch, at Iconium, at Lystra; what persecutions I endured: but out of them all the Lord delivered me.

12. Yea, and all that will live godly in Christ Jesus shall suffer persecution.

13. But evil men and seducers shall wax worse and worse, deceiving, and being deceived.

14. But continue thou in the things which thou hast learned and hast been assured of, knowing of whom thou hast learned them;

15. And that from a child thou hast known the holy scriptures, which are able to make thee wise unto salvation through faith which is in Christ Jesus.

16. All scripture is given by inspiration of God, and is profitable for doctrine, for reproof, for correction, for instruction in righteousness:

17. That the man of God may be perfect, thoroughly furnished unto all good works.

DICTIONARY

Jambres (JAM–brez)—2 Timothy 3:8—One of the magicians who opposed Moses before Pharaoh.

Antioch (An–tee–ack), Iconium (eye–KOH–nee–un) and Lystra (LIS–tra)—2 Timothy 3:11—Cities in which Paul preached and was opposed.

LESSON OUTLINE

I. LIVING IN DANGEROUS TIMES
 A. Environment of Vices
 B. Environment of Empty Religion

II. ENDURING DIFFICULTIES
 A. The Rescue
 B. The Reality

III. EQUIPPED BY GOD'S WORD
 A. For Salvation
 B. For Discipleship

LESSON EXPOSITION

INTRODUCTION

The concept of the "last days" brings to mind the many times calculations have been made and a date assigned for Christ's return. Augustine calculated that human history would end in A.D. 650. William Miller, forerunner of the Adventists, selected 1843. When Christ didn't come and the world didn't end, one of Miller's followers, Samuel S. Snow, changed the date to October 22, 1844. Other individuals offered the dates of 1911 and 1933. Even in the last few years, dates have been set for Christ's return—and multitudes were left disappointed.

The Scriptures speak of three "last days." (1) The "last day" referred to the eighth day of the Feast of Tabernacles, when the largest crowd assembled (John 7:37). (2) The "last day" may indicate the Day of Judgment (John 11:24). (3) The "last days" refers most often to the time period between Christ's first and second comings. We tend to think today of the last days as that period when the signs of Christ's soon coming are very evident. The danger of this modification surfaces when the signs aren't so visible and people begin to believe His coming isn't at hand—that He has delayed His coming. Self–deception and failure to understand the Scriptures result in wrong conclusions.

Paul's inclusion of the "last days" in this final epistle indicates the church's continued interest and expectation of the Lord's return. The first nine verses of chapter 3 provide a description of the condition of mankind in those days. Following them are eight verses showing how to live during this time period.

I. LIVING IN DANGEROUS TIMES (2 Timothy 3:1–9)

A. Environment of Vices (vv. 1–4)

1. This know also, that in the last days perilous times shall come.

2. For men shall be lovers of their own selves, covetous, boasters, proud, blasphemers, disobedient to parents, unthankful, unholy,

3. Without natural affection, trucebreakers, false accusers, incontinent, fierce, despisers of those that are good,

4. Traitors, heady, highminded, lovers of pleasures more than lovers of God.

Paul's writing on the "last days" wasn't necessarily new information for Timothy. How could he have been Paul's companion and not have heard him teach and preach on this subject? This is a major topic, and Paul addressed it in other situations as well. This appears to be one of those cases where a reminder is given of what one already knows. Not only do reminders further embed the teaching in one's memory, but they also emphasize the importance of what has been said. This is an important and effective way of keeping errors from creeping into the subject material.

Paul began by stating the severity of the "last days." The *New International Version* says, "But mark this: There will be terrible times in the last days" (v. 1). How are we to understand this when we already expect a degree of persecution as a normal aspect of life in Christ? To begin with, one must realize that the description which follows isn't limited to how just Christians will be treated. Rather, it describes a violent, troublesome period in which both believers and unbelievers will suffer due to a society raging out of control. However, those who seriously take devotion to Christ as the priority for their lives will find the times especially difficult.

Paul provided a list of the vices, or sins, that will dominate society. It is quite evident that the picture is one of a morally bankrupt generation caring only for *self.*

Lovers of themselves—Self-centeredness is the hub around which all that follows revolves. All the other sins are the natural outgrowth of the focus being on self, when one's personal pleasure, desires, and opinions are all that matter. This is a me-first generation, in which love for others is valued only if the greatest benefit comes to "me."

Lovers of money, (covetous)—These first two characteristics go hand in hand. Materialism tends to be the partner of selfishness. Tangible possessions are all-important, since they emphasize the ability, power, and importance of the owner. When a generation or a local group adopts this sin, charitable giving becomes only a pittance, even when individuals have the ability to give and the need is evident. When such selfishness creeps into the church, people tend to give less and their giving is directed only to programs that minister to their own needs.

Boastful and proud—These two characteristics are also a pair. Each feeds on the other. Pride causes one to boast. And the more one brags about himself, the greater the sense of pride. Both of these sins are linked directly to the opening description of self–centeredness. Also tied to this combination can be a growing sense of classism, prejudice, and haughtiness.

Abusive—The word *blasphemer* is better translated "abusive" since it means evil speaking toward one's fellowmen. It has no connotation of speaking evil toward God or defaming the sacred. To speak abusively is to tear down another while making oneself appear superior. This logically follows the previous four vices.

The following three vices listed in verse 2 are distinctly in opposition to basic Christian teachings and values:

Disobedient to parents—This is a direct violation of the commandment to honor father and mother. In addition to disregarding the authority and nurture of parents, it reflects a breakdown of family values as well. But what more can you expect when a narcissistic humanism prevails. However, lest it appear that all the blame is to be laid at the feet of the children, we need to include the responsibility of the parents as well. It is difficult to be obedient to parents who have not maintained a marital relationship and a home environment that encourages obedience.

Unthankful (ungrateful)—What a contrast to the New Testament teachings and practice of the apostle Paul! Repeatedly he burst forth in praise to God for His grace and saving power. Repeatedly he thanked those who had aided him in the ministry or had made it possible for others to be blessed. Ingratitude indicates a total lack of appreciation. It comes from the minds of those who believe they deserve or are owed more than they have received. It also can originate within a society where people think they are victims and deserve to be compensated for some supposed losses.

Unholy—The unholy life is one which delights in sin and revels in thoughts and actions that defile and make them spiritually unclean.

In verse 3 Paul listed six more vices. None of them are surprising in view of those already mentioned in the previous verse.

Without natural affection (without love)—This vice causes one to immediately think in terms of homosexual behavior; however, the emphasis here is on not loving those close to you. It speaks of being hard–hearted, callous, or inhumane toward your own kindred. When you love yourself to the extreme, it is difficult to love anyone else. Or if you have been abused or neglected by family members it is easy to feel you can't trust anyone.

Trucebreakers (unforgiving)—This vice speaks of an inherent hostility which keeps a person from entering into or keeping a covenant or treaty. Instead of trying to overcome difficulties and restore a relationship, unforgiving people will remain at odds and in conflict with others.

False accusers (slanderous)—Truth is unimportant to individuals whose priority is self. They will say anything to promote their own personal glory and position.

Incontinent (without self–control)—those who are morally powerless to maintain self–control. Sin eventually robs people of the ability to direct their own lives. They become a helpless pawn at the mercy of their passions.

Fierce (brutal)—This is just the opposite of tame and peaceful. In terms of animals the concept is one of being wild or savage. Individuals who possess this vice often become violent in their behavior. In our current society individuals of this nature are those who murder, rape, and physically abuse others simply because of their brutal nature.

Despisers of those that are good (not lovers of the good)—Anything that is good, positive, or wholesome finds contempt in the eyes of this generation. Thus, individuals who attempt to serve Christ and follow the admonition of Philippians 4:8 are looked down upon and treated as nothing.

In verse 4 Paul closed his list with four final vices, without explanation or application:

Traitors (treacherous)—Due to the evil which abounds, individuals cannot be trusted to be a person of their word or commitment. One moment they will be on your side, and the next moment they will turn and fight against you.

Heady (rash)—This characteristic can also be termed recklessness, or being headstrong. Rash individuals want to do things their way regardless of the risk or consequences.

Highminded (conceited)—Once again we come to the concept of "being wrapped in smoke" as was discussed earlier in our study of 1 Timothy 3:6. Conceit and pride logically coincide with a dominating spirit.

Lovers of pleasures more than lovers of God—The issue isn't the rejection of pleasure but making pleasure a priority. Serving God becomes secondary to serving personal desires and comforts. This vice brings us full circle to the first one listed in verse 2—lovers of self.

How is it possible that so many believers exhibit some of or all these vices in our churches?

B. Environment of Empty Religion (vv. 5–9)

5. Having a form of godliness, but denying the power thereof: from such turn away.

6. For of this sort are they which creep into houses, and lead captive silly women laden with sins, led away with divers lusts,

7. Ever learning, and never able to come to the knowledge of the truth.

8. Now as Jannes and Jambres withstood Moses, so do these also resist the truth: men of corrupt minds, reprobate concerning the faith.

9. But they shall proceed no further: for their folly shall be manifest unto all men, as their's also was.

This section could also have been titled "An Environment of Apostasy." In the last days, churches will continue to hold services, and ministers and congregations will go through a form of worship. But it will be nothing more than a vain ritual reflecting real worship of the past. Verse 5 states it so plainly. They will follow the exterior forms of godliness but deny the Person and truth which must empower them from within. An example of this is the minister who reads the Scriptures as part of the worship ritual and then in his sermon declares that these are myths and stories that never really took place.

Verse 5 describes so–called believers going through the process of church membership and participating in the sacraments without ever knowing the life–changing power of Jesus Christ and the empowerment of the Spirit. It is one of the saddest descriptions of the end times to be found anywhere. We must continue to remember that these individuals aren't our brothers and sisters in Christ! And even though their leaders are educated and continue to study aspects of the Bible and Christian faith, they haven't come to the truth. Verse 7 points out that in spite of all their time, effort, and even money spent in the process, there is a lack of truth.

Once again we are faced with the reality of believers' following after false teachers. Verse 6 describes a particular method and audience. Some males will take advantage of gullible women. Through the use of cunning and devious methods these women will be drawn into a bondage of thought, something like being prisoners of war. The King James Version describes them as "silly"; a modern translation uses the description "weak–willed" (*NIV*). This seems to indicate those who lack moral strength. Many individuals, both men and women, gravitate to false teachers rather than face up to their weaknesses and inadequacies.

In verse 8 Paul used an Old Testament example to demonstrate what will be taking place in the "last days." Jannes and Jambres are not mentioned by name anywhere else in Scripture. Most commentators believe they were Pharaoh's magicians who attempted to stand against Moses (Exodus 7:11, 12). In response to Aaron's staff becoming a snake, Pharaoh called his religious leaders. These magicians threw down their staffs and each of them became a snake also. However, Aaron's staff/snake swallowed theirs. The impact on most people would have been to think these magicians were religiously powerful if Aaron and Moses had not been there to counter the miracle through God's almighty power. Regardless of the greatness of the miracle, it was still merely part of an empty religion.

II. ENDURING DIFFICULTIES (2 Timothy 3:10–13)

A. The Rescue (vv. 10, 11)

10. But thou hast fully known my doctrine, manner of life, purpose, faith, longsuffering, charity, patience.

11. Persecutions, afflictions, which came unto me at Antioch, at Iconium, at Lystra; what persecutions I endured: but out of them all the Lord delivered me.

In a list of nine items the testimony of Paul is summarized. It indicates that voluminous script and a multitude of words aren't always necessary to tell what Christ has done through us. Since Timothy and Paul were so close, the details of each of these items were well known. Paul was bringing them to Timothy's attention once again as a reminder of the example which he had set for others to follow.

At the head of Paul's list is doctrine. The prominence it occupies isn't just happenstance. Here again we see the importance of scriptural doctrine. Without this foundation, the believer cannot live in a manner acceptable to God.

The remaining six items listed in verse 10 include Paul's personal behavior and purpose in life. From his other epistles we know that behavior and purpose always included being acceptable before Christ while sharing the gospel of Christ. The other four items are the common Christian virtues which all believers should strive to develop and exhibit. Instead of "faith, longsuffering, charity, and patience," the translation should more accurately read, "faith, patience, love, and endurance." Endurance is especially important when considering the difficulties mentioned in the following verse.

Some consideration needs to be given also to the thought of giving one's testimony of faith. It can be done without boasting and with humility and modesty. With extreme brevity Paul reviewed the facts of his life in Christ. Other believers need to hear our testimonies of faith. It encourages them, strengthens them, and lets them know they too can be successful in living for the Lord.

Timothy was well acquainted with the details of Paul's life. Remember that he appears to have become a Christian through Paul's ministry on his first missionary journey with all its suffering.

The apostle described the difficult times as persecutions and afflictions. *Afflictions* are those difficulties which may come due to circumstances related to the specific time or area. It doesn't necessarily mean that detractors are attempting to harm you. But when Paul included the word *persecutions*, he spoke of adversaries doing whatever they could to drive him away from their area.

The key point of these two verses isn't Paul's testimony; the major emphasis is the Lord's deliverance. God's coming to the rescue in the middle of our trial is what Paul wanted Timothy to continually grasp. However, deliverance doesn't always mean taking us out of the situation, but more often it means bringing us through it. At Iconium information came concerning a plot to stone the missionaries, so Paul and Barnabas fled (Acts 14:5, 6). At Lystra, Paul was stoned, dragged from the city, and left for dead (14:19). Apparently the prayers of faithful disciples raised Paul back to health, and he continued his ministry.

Why do we usually interpret rescue to mean deliverance?

B. The Reality (vv. 12, 13)

12. Yea, and all that will live godly in Christ Jesus shall suffer persecution.

13. But evil men and seducers shall wax worse and worse, deceiving, and being deceived.

Two stark realities of the last days can logically be expected after having studied the list of vices and noted the sad state of religion described in verses 1–9. Once again we face the reality of persecution. Those of us who live in countries with religious freedom tend to shy away from this one. We know it's the truth but most often see it as a situation which others must face. Paul stripped away that idea completely. His words are all–inclusive. All who want to live godly in the last days are going to experience opposition on the basis of their commitment of faith.

Here is another paradox. The more individuals strive to live in accord with Jesus Christ, the more they will be despised and rejected. Life on the outside will become more difficult because life on the inside has been transformed by Christ. This is truly following in the steps of our Savior—being rejected and persecuted just as He was. Apparently this will become much more evident and widespread as the end times approach.

Also, the Enemy will increase his efforts to draw people from the truth. The deceived will even try to deceive others. The term *seducers* can be translated as wizards. Like Jannes and Jambres, they will appear as genuine men of power, but in reality they are only impostors. Many people will be impressed with their apparent power to perform miracles, their eloquent vocabularies, and their magnetic personalities and will allow the exterior veneer of these impostors to dominate their thinking without ever seeking the truth. This will become more evident as people emphasize self rather than God.

III. EQUIPPED BY GOD'S WORD (2 Timothy 3:14–17)

A. For Salvation (vv. 14, 15)

14. But continue thou in the things which thou hast learned and hast been assured of, knowing of whom thou hast learned them;

15. And that from a child thou hast known the holy scriptures, which are able to make thee wise unto salvation through faith which is in Christ Jesus.

This lesson demonstrates that anyone who would live for Christ will experience difficult times. The storms are dangerous and can capsize your faith unless you are anchored and stabilized in Christ. The provision of a firm foundation during these times of unrest is one of God's tremendous blessings to us.

In this passage Paul wrote to Timothy about this assurance. He exhorted his son in the Lord to continue in what he had learned both factually and experientially. He spoke of the years Timothy was under the teaching of his mother and grandmother as well as his time of being discipled by Paul. Plus, his years as Paul's companion provided numerous experiences in which God's truth and provision became a fixed reality.

In the final analysis, all of our beliefs and hopes as Christians rest upon the Word of God. It alone provides the only sure foundation—one that will never crack, sink, or fade away! We can rely without hesitation on the directions and promises of God's Word.

Specific reference to Timothy's knowing the Scriptures from a child could indicate several things. It could remind him of how he learned to read through the use of them. (Many centuries later here in America, the Bible was also a vital part of the learning curriculum.) Again, this points out that Timothy was not a novice in the reading and studying of the Word of God. It had been a continuing part of his life for more than 30 years. Timothy understood the difference the Word of God makes in one's life.

The Scriptures serve a variety of purposes, as will be seen in the next verse. It is through the Scriptures that we are able to come to a knowledge of salvation. They instruct us in both our need for salvation and the means by which it can be attained. Regardless of how much wisdom we may obtain, without a knowledge of how to become saved we continue to be without hope.

Paul always emphasized the means of salvation. It is by faith in Jesus. No other means brings about a covering for sin and reconciliation with God the Father. Jesus is the only way by which a relationship with God can be initiated. There is no other way!

B. For Discipleship (vv. 16, 17)

16. All scripture is given by inspiration of God, and is profitable for doctrine, for reproof, for correction, for instruction in righteousness:

17. That the man of God may be perfect, throughly furnished unto all good works.

Even though there will be uncertainties in the last days, we need not live a life of uncertainty. There is a source which provides unchanging guidelines even when the world appears to be in chaos. The Scriptures are that bulwark of truth.

How did the Holy Scriptures come into being? Without an extended explanation, Paul simply stated they were *God–breathed.* This means God inspired humans to write the truths which He intended for us to study and to live by. Again we see how the divine and the human blend. These Bible writers weren't robots through whom God mechanically transcribed His Word. Rather, He allowed each person to write in his own personal style, using the words and phrases with which the writer was familiar. Isn't that phenomenal! All the different writers, over a span of some 1,500 years, experienced the same inspiration and wrote the coherent and undivided, divinely intended Word of God!

Verse 16 indicates the importance of the Scriptures as they relate to discipleship. There are four applications. First, the Scriptures are to be our only source of *doctrine* (teaching). The basics of the faith and their impact on our lives are to be derived solely from the Word. Anything else is man–made and can usually be classified as heresy. It isn't necessary for the believer to develop his own belief structure. All we need to do is accept it and live by it.

Second, the Scriptures are for *reproof* (rebuking). They confront us and convict us. Without a human word of exhortation or exposition, the Word of God drives deeply into our consciousness, showing us whether we have been living in accord with the Word or have a need to reevaluate our thinking.

Third, the Scriptures are given for correction. Reproof in itself has little value unless changes occur. The Scriptures help us to reform our way of life and to avoid evil. The Word changes both our inner character and our outer lifestyle.

Finally, the Scriptures provide *instruction in righteousness.* This is the aspect of training. By reading and following the directives of

Scripture, the believer is able to follow after holiness and justice. Training enables us to develop a pattern of thinking and acting which reflects Christlikeness. The constant intake of the positive reflects itself in our outward life.

The whole purpose of Scripture is summarized in verse 17. Through it we are able to become complete individuals, properly equipped for the service of our Lord and Master, Jesus Christ. Total perfection isn't a possibility until our final glorification, but through the Word of God there is a level of holiness which we can attain regardless of our humanity.

What is our responsibility in being properly equipped by the Word?

REVIEW QUESTIONS

1. List at least six of the vices of the last days.
2. What are some of the signs of empty religion?
3. How did the apostle Paul summarize his testimony?
4. What are the two general trends of the last days?
5. What is the Scripture's role in salvation?

GOLDEN TEXT HOMILY

"THIS KNOW ALSO, THAT IN THE LAST DAYS PERILOUS TIMES SHALL COME" (2 Timothy 3:1).

Having expressed hope for the recovery of those caught in the devil's snare (2:24–26), Paul now warned Timothy that opposition to the truth will continue to grow more intense. He stated that evil men will arise in the body of professed believers who will not accept redemption. Using the imperative "This know," Paul told Timothy to keep this realization before him. The emphasis is on the fact that "perilous times," hard and difficult seasons, lie ahead—a time when believers will be faced with perplexing problems and difficult responsibilities because of the abounding iniquity operating under the guise of Christianity. When will this occur? Paul indicated that it will be "in the last days." Dr. D. Edmond Hiebert writes: "The original does not have the article *the*, thus designating a characteristic state, rather than a positive time. It is not to be limited to the few years just before the Second Advent. The use of the article would have made the period too restricted; its absence enlarges the sphere to cover the closing seasons of the Christian era, however long God may be pleased to protract them."

Those who study the Bible are aware that the seeds of the evil being predicted were already sprouting when Paul wrote but that this evil will find its awful culmination in the closing seasons of this age. History indicates that there have been many times when it seemed that the fulfillment of prophecy was an exact description of those times. And today every informed believer is painfully aware of the fearful apostasy that is sweeping over the Christian church again. This verse was given as God's warning to His people to prepare themselves to confront apostasy in their own day.—**Eugene C. Christenbury, Professor of Education, Lee College, Cleveland, Tennessee**

SENTENCE SERMONS

KNOWING GOD'S WORD equips us to face the last days.

—Selected

THE BOOKS of men have their day and become obsolete. God's Word is like Himself, "the same yesterday, today, and forever."

—Robert P. Smith

DIFFICULTIES are meant to rouse, not discourage. The human spirit is to grow strong by conflict.

—William E. Channing

MANY MEN owe the grandeur of their lives to their tremendous difficulties.

—Charles H. Spurgeon

EVANGELISM APPLICATION

UNDERSTANDING THE TIMES SHOULD CAUSE US TO BE MORE FERVENT IN WITNESSING.

At least that is what logically should be happening! When you are thoroughly convinced of a danger, you usually do everything possible to save not only yourself but others as well.

There are at least two possibilities that come to mind as to why individuals may not witness even when they understand the times. First is the problem of selfishness. People become so busy doing "their own things" that everyone else becomes secondary. It happens not only in society as a whole but also in the church. We may become so busy doing the business of the local church that we neglect the business of the gospel.

Second, there is paucity of godly love. It's so much easier to stand back and say we love someone than to put our love into action. More often, we want to love indirectly rather than directly. We would rather pay than go. We would rather send than carry out the mission personally. These attitudes call our love into question.

There is also a third possibility which needs our consideration. Many believers aren't really sure these *are* the last days. We do not hear as much teaching and preaching on these passages as we used to. Perhaps believers really don't understand the times.

DAILY BIBLE READINGS

M. God Is in Control.
Psalm 2:1–12
T. Hope in God.
Isaiah 26:12–21
W. Trouble Foretold.
Matthew 24:1–8
T. Stay Alert. Luke 21:29–36
F. Deliverance Promised.
Hebrews 10:31–39
S. Presented Faultless.
Jude 17–24

Portrait of a Faithful Life

Study Text: 2 Timothy 4:1–18; Titus 3:1–8

Objective: To comprehend the rewards for faithfulness and determine to persevere.

Time: The Book of 2 Timothy was written between A.D. 66 and 67. Titus was written between A.D. 63 and 65.

Place: The Book of 2 Timothy was probably written from a Roman prison. Titus was probably written from Greece or Macedonia.

Golden Text: "I have fought a good fight, I have finished my course, I have kept the faith" (2 Timothy 4:7).

Central Truth: By God's grace, the believer remains faithful in every circumstance.

Evangelism Emphasis: Faithful believers witness to sinners.

PRINTED TEXT

2 Timothy 4:5. But watch thou in all things, endure afflictions, do the work of an evangelist, make full proof of thy ministry.

6. For I am now ready to be offered, and the time of my departure is at hand.

7. I have fought a good fight, I have finished my course, I have kept the faith:

8. Henceforth there is laid up for me a crown of righteousness, which the Lord, the righteous judge, shall give me at that day: and not to me only, but unto all them also that love his appearing.

16. At my first answer no man stood with me, but all men forsook me: I pray God that it may not be laid to their charge.

17. Notwithstanding the Lord stood with me, and strengthened me; that by me the preaching might be fully known, and that all the Gentiles might hear: and I was delivered out of the mouth of the lion.

18. And the Lord shall deliver me from every evil work, and will preserve me unto his heavenly kingdom: to whom be glory for ever and ever. Amen.

Titus 3:1. Put them to mind to be subject to principalities and powers, to obey magistrates, to be ready to every good work,

2. To speak evil of no man, to be no brawlers, but gentle, shewing all meekness unto all men.

3. For we ourselves also were sometimes foolish, disobedient, deceived, serving divers lusts and pleasures, living in malice and envy, hateful, and hating one another.

4. But after that the kindness and love of God our Saviour

toward man appeared,

5. Not by works of righteousness which we have done, but according to his mercy he saved us, by the washing of regeneration, and renewing of the Holy Ghost;

6. Which he shed on us abundantly through Jesus Christ our Saviour;

7. That being justified by his grace, we should be made heirs according to the hope of eternal life.

8. This is a faithful saying, and these things I will that thou affirm constantly, that they which have believed in God might be careful to maintain good works. These things are good and profitable unto men.

LESSON OUTLINE

I. KEEPING THE FAITH
   A. Discharge the Duties
   B. Finish the Race
   C. Remember the Crown

II. STRENGTHENED BY THE LORD
   A. Through Colleagues
   B. In Opposition

III. CALLED TO GOOD WORKS
   A. The Christian's Attitude
   B. Christ's Love
   C. The Christian's Works

LESSON EXPOSITION

INTRODUCTION

Today's lesson takes us to some dynamic testimonial verses of the apostle Paul. He not only demonstrated the reality of victorious living but reminded every believer that it comes with a price. We need to hear this type of testimony. It encourages us as believers to continue serving Christ. Others have successfully lived the life of faith, and we can as well. It reminds us that the reward far exceeds any price we may pay.

I. KEEPING THE FAITH
(2 Timothy 4:5–8)

A. Discharge the Duties (vv. 5, 6)

5. But watch thou in all things, endure afflictions, do the work of an evangelist, make full proof of thy ministry.

6. For I am now ready to be offered, and the time of my departure is at hand.

Paul knew his life would end shortly. What a change from his letter to the Philippians during the first Roman imprisonment. At that time there was uncertainty as he looked at the possibilities of both life and death. Yet prior to ending chapter 1, he stated his conviction that God would allow him to live a while longer and continue his ministry (v. 25). The apostle was still writing with conviction in this letter to Timothy; however, this time he knew beyond a shadow of doubt that death loomed on the horizon.

Verse 6 stands out as a statement of triumph. He wasn't feeling sorry for himself or wanting the pity of others. Instead he saw a fulfilled life now moving to a glorious eternity with Christ. What he had preached and lived continued to be evident even in the closing months of life.

Paul described himself as a drink offering being poured out. This is a continuation of a metaphor initiated in other biblical writings (see Philippians 2:17). It can be understood from both a biblical and cultural perspective. Throughout the Book of Numbers the children of Israel were instructed to bring a drink offering to accompany their grain offerings (see especially 6:17; 15:1–24).

This also parallels Paul's exhortation for believers to be "a living sacrifice" (Romans 12:1). Paul wasn't suggesting that Christians seek martyrdom; but rather he used this as an illustration to encourage believers to live a life of holiness, thus making them acceptable before God.

The latter half of verse 6 emphasizes the nearness of Paul's death. His choice of words continues the atmosphere of triumph. In the original language the word *departure* is one that would be used for the loosing of a ship from its dock, thus enabling a new journey to begin, which reminds us that death is not just an ending but also a beginning.

In verse 5 Paul's continued concern for Timothy and the other Christian workers as well was that they not lose sight of what it takes to keep the faith. There are four distinct directives. First is the call to watchfulness. Literally, this means to be sober. Even while preaching the truth there is a need to be morally alert. Success can blind one from seeing the path of truth and can sidetrack or derail the believer's journey with Christ. Too often the accolades of the people become more important than what God demands. King Saul illustrated this so well when he said to Samuel, "Now therefore, I pray thee, pardon my sin, and turn again with me, that I may worship the Lord" (1 Samuel 15:25). He thought worshiping the Lord in front of the people was more important than confessing his sin to God.

The second directive—"endure afflictions"—has been covered in previous lessons, but it still demands our attention. Steadfastly serving the Lord will bring opposition and even harm. A sad reality is that the affliction may come from other believers, or at least professing Christians who aren't willing to follow the biblical paths of truth.

Third is the directive for evangelism. Doing the work of an evangelist may not be a specific reference to the *office* of an evangelist. Though we know some individuals are called and gifted in evangelism (Acts 21:8; Ephesians 4:11), that does not exclude the rest of us from sharing Christ and persuading people to accept salvation. All believers are commissioned to evangelize regardless of their particular vocations (Matthew 28:19, 20). And specifically in Timothy's case as he wrestled with the problem of false teachers and organizing the congregation, the need for evangelism continued. As long as there are people around us who do not know Jesus Christ, evangelism is a constant part of our ministry portfolio.

Special emphasis needs to be given to the fourth directive—"make full proof of thy ministry." It is better translated, "Discharge all the duties of your ministry" (*NIV*). In some settings we would say, "Complete your entire job description." Paul reminded Timothy that fulfilling his calling as a minister would come only as he accomplished all that he was being asked to do. Accomplishing the job wasn't important merely because Paul had asked him to do it but because God requires obedient faithfulness of us in the present and will continue to ask it of us in the future. Meeting God's requirements also means fulfilling all the duties of one's ministry. No one can be faithful by doing only those tasks that are enjoyable and that bring the greatest satisfaction.

The duties of ministry vary according to the position to which one is called. There are primary responsibilities which are distinguished by the office. One's duties also vary according to the times and the needs of the people. Exhorting people to launch out in faith isn't feasible when they are in need of being comforted and encouraged. These factors have to be considered when evaluating whether or not we have successfully discharged our duties.

B. Finish the Race (v. 7)

7. I have fought a good fight, I have finished my course, I have kept the faith.

There is no greater conclusion or testimony of the completion of a life's assignment than these few words by the apostle Paul. He summarized in three short statements his life as a Christian. He also provided an example for all of us to follow as we strive to successfully complete our own life's commission in Christ.

Verse 7 is usually seen as a picture of an athlete competing in the Roman and Greek games. Some scholars, however, see the image of a soldier reflected in the first description.

The full significance of Paul's having "fought a good fight" comes when we understand the depth of the effort which he expressed here. In the Greek language the word *fight* means a struggle in which there is a mighty contest. It is the word from which we derive our English word *agony*. This portrays a situation in which one continues to struggle even though the pain is great and it seems impossible to continue. It's a picture of football linemen so tired they can't lift their feet, but they endure the agony and continue taking their positions and playing the game. It's runners whose lungs and muscles burn from the effort, but they continue running. It's boxers whose hands feel like lead weights, whose bodies are bruised, and whose faces are swollen, but they keep on fighting. It's the soldier who hasn't slept in hours, who lacks proper nourishment, and who has been hounded by the enemy yet never thinks of retreating.

Notice that when Paul spoke of finishing the course, he put no emphasis on being the winner. It's not a statement of having won over other runners in the race. It's not an emphasis on having run faster or smarter than anyone else. It's not a boasting of being better equipped or prepared. Instead it's a statement of endurance and completion. *Finishing* is the key word, which reminds us that life in Christ isn't one of bursts of production and great results followed by quitting. Life in Christ is a prescribed course we are to follow. And unless we finish what has been laid out, all of what we have previously done profits us nothing.

Lastly, Paul said he had "kept the

faith." In the athletic metaphor, this could refer to the oath which athletes took prior to participating in the games. They vowed to compete honestly and honorably. However, since he always admonished his circle of workers to guard the truth and keep the doctrine, this most assuredly refers to his having held firmly to the truth imparted to him.

What is the course Christ has laid out for all of us?

C. Remember the Crown (v. 8)

8. Henceforth there is laid up for me a crown of righteousness, which the Lord, the righteous judge, shall give me at that day: and not to me only, but unto all them also that love his appearing.

Keeping the faith brings rewards. God will honor His children when they complete the course He has laid for them. The stimulus for our service is to be love, but that doesn't mean we cannot look forward to the reward.

There are two possible backgrounds to which Paul referred here. The most commonly cited is the crown given to the winner of each of the sporting events in the games (see 1 Corinthians 9:24, 25). Laurel wreaths were presented to honor the competitors who achieved first place. Or he could have been referring to special rewards that Oriental kings gave to loyal subjects for outstanding service.

This is all secondary to the concept of who will receive the reward. In both of the situations mentioned, only the outstanding individuals received the reward. In the games, the winner alone received the wreath. In the sovereign court only the few citizens whose efforts were extraordinary received the king's favor. How unlike the kingdom of God! God doesn't reward just the Abrahams, the Pauls, and the Esthers. He will reward all those who are looking forward to Christ's appearing and are living for that day. No one serving God does so for a reward. We serve because it is a loving relationship, and we can't wait to be united with Him. Then all the glory will be revealed. And we will be face–to–face with our Savior and Lord! Amen!

II. STRENGTHENED BY THE LORD (2 Timothy 4:9–18)

A. Through Colleagues (vv. 9–13)

(2 Timothy 4:9–13 is not included in the printed text.)

Verse 9 begins the closing of this final epistle. After the glorious words of verses 7 and 8, one may tend to skip over what appears to be "housekeeping" information. However, to do so is to miss some of the most human aspects of being a believer. One writer suggests that this is a picture of Paul at one of his most human moments—in need of friends, physical comfort, and intellectual stimulus. This is a the same Paul who once persecuted the believers but had now become the prince of believers, and we rejoice at the success of one who overcame massive failures to become a profitable servant for his King.

Paul began by asking Timothy to come and be with him in Rome. In times of crisis all of us need close friends at our side. Who would be better to have there than his "son in the Lord," Timothy? Apparently, Timothy's work was sufficiently established to allow him to leave

Ephesus. Or perhaps since Tychicus was now on his way to Ephesus, it enabled Timothy to leave (v. 12). Timothy was asked to come as soon as possible, which further demonstrates Paul's uncertainty about his life.

Timothy was also to bring Mark (v. 11). How wonderful to know that though Mark as a young man had been a failure in difficult circumstances, he had matured in Christ and was now needed. This was the same John Mark who had deserted Paul and Barnabas on the first missionary journey. Just as they were about to enter some of the most treacherous territory of Asia Minor, Mark went home (Acts 13:13). Now, however, Paul didn't hesitate to bring him to Rome and to have him associated with a condemned prisoner.

At the beginning of the second missionary journey (15:36–40) Paul refused to allow Mark to go along. The contention became so severe that Paul and Barnabas had to separate. Notice that each followed a different philosophy of ministry. Barnabas was a discipler and encourager (as his name implies). Paul was an explorer for the gospel who needed qualified and strong men to step in as the need dictated. But he put all that in the past now; John Mark was mature enough to stand even in the most difficult environment.

Paul's loneliness is evident in verses 9 and 10. Demas provides a sad note. His "having loved this present world" doesn't necessarily mean he "backslid." There is no indication that he chose to leave the faith. He did, however, choose to leave Paul in Rome at a very difficult time in the apostle's life. We assume he either feared losing his own life or no longer wanted to be a part of the lifestyle of Paul.

Crescens and Titus were on assignment. More than likely Paul continued overseeing the church in general by writing letters and dispatching messengers.

Once again Luke enters the biblical account. He too was one of Paul's very close companions. He frequently appeared at just the right time to minister to Paul physically during times of illness or to be of service when a helping hand was needed.

Besides the need for companionship, Paul had several other requests. He asked for his cloak which he had left at Troas to be brought to him. The cloak would help Paul withstand the cold dampness of a Roman dungeon. He also asked for his book and some parchments. No doubt, Scripture would be a part of this request; however, some individuals suggest it might also include valuable legal papers as well.

The role of fellow believers (colleagues) is of inestimable importance to each of us. The Lord uses a variety of people to strengthen us and to continue in ministry even when circumstances have blocked one's own effectiveness. The walls and locks of a Roman prison couldn't dampen Paul's spirit or stop his administrative ministry. Others simply became his legs and voice. They did and said for him what he was unable to do and say personally.

B. In Opposition (vv. 14–18)

(2 Timothy 4:14, 15 is not included in the printed text.)

16. At my first answer no man

stood with me, but all men forsook me: I pray God that it may not be laid to their charge.

17. Notwithstanding the Lord stood with me, and strengthened me; that by me the preaching might be fully known, and that all the Gentiles might hear: and I was delivered out of the mouth of the lion.

18. And the Lord shall deliver me from every evil work, and will preserve me unto his heavenly kingdom: to whom be glory for ever and ever. Amen.

With little explanation Paul briefly brought Alexander the coppersmith into the narrative (vv. 14, 15). Apparently he strongly opposed Paul's ministry and the Christian faith. He may have even been a witness for the prosecution at Paul's hearing in Rome. The warning for Timothy to also beware of this man suggests his antagonism went beyond Paul and included anyone who was propagating the gospel and in a position of leadership.

Then we come face–to–face with the problem of believers who were not willing to support a brother in the Lord when he had to face the political authorities. Of great concern was the lack of response of these believers who should have been rallying to either defend or at least support Paul. It was normal for the friends of a person on trial to at least appear at the proceedings even if they remained silent. Their physical presence would lend support. Yet, no one from the Roman congregation came to be with Paul. How could these friends and brothers in the Lord stay away? How could they forsake him in his hour of need?

The apostle's attitude toward the Roman believers and Alexander deserves close consideration. Notice how he avoided any words of anger or rebuke. He didn't pray a particular form of judgment on them. Instead, he followed the advice given in his letter to the Romans: "Recompense to no man evil for evil" (12:17). In the case of Alexander he allowed God alone to judge and reward his evil actions. But in the case of his fellow believers Paul pleaded their case. Though they had failed him, he desired that God would pardon this gross oversight of Christian love. He followed the example set by Christ on the cross (Luke 23:34) and Stephen just before dying from stoning (Acts 7:60).

Even in the face of opposition and desertion Paul experienced the strength of the Lord (v. 17). The Lord stood by and delivered Paul, and He becomes our strength when no one else will help. He rescues us when no one else defends us. Paul's mention of being delivered from the mouth of the lion may be simply a reference to a common metaphor used to express extreme danger. However, we cannot overlook the reality of the colosseum and believers' being placed at the mercy of wild beasts there.

Verse 18 shows the breadth of God's power. He can overcome and deliver from any evil that may overtake the believer. God wants to preserve His children. He doesn't offer us the free gift of salvation only to leave us to work out our spiritual lives all by ourselves. Our heavenly Father wants us to be successful in running the race and to finally enjoy His kingdom forever.

No wonder Paul ended this section with a doxology. Consideration of God's provision of salvation, followed by His preservation in difficult circumstances, causes an eruption of adoration.

Why do we often want God to bring judgment on those who don't meet our expectations?

III. CALLED TO GOOD WORKS (Titus 3:1–8)

A. The Christian's Attitude (vv. 1–3)

1. Put them to mind to be subject to principalities and powers, to obey magistrates, to be ready to every good work,

2. To speak evil of no man, to be no brawlers, but gentle, shewing all meekness unto all men.

3. For we ourselves also were sometimes foolish, disobedient, deceived, serving divers lusts and pleasures, living in malice and envy, hateful, and hating one another.

The faithful life includes good works. But it is impossible to continue doing faithfully doing what is right without having a godly attitude. Those things we think in our minds and emotionally hold in our hearts become translated into actions and words. As has been noted in a previous lesson, these Cretan Christians were facing the challenge of not being like their surrounding culture. While they were still Cretans, they were now Christians and should have been demonstrating what it means to be Christlike.

In verse 1 Paul addressed community responsibility. Regardless of the country in which the believer lives, each person bears the responsibility of good citizens. Even in the middle of the worst dictator's rule, we are to remember that God ordains government. No matter how unorganized or ungodly it may be, the Christian is to follow the guidelines of proper citizenship. This includes paying our taxes and voting when elections are held, as well as serving in the armed forces if required. It also means obeying the laws of the land, provided they are not in opposition to God's law. And we are specifically instructed to pray for those in authority (1 Timothy 2:1–3; see also Romans 13:1–7; 1 Peter 2:13–17.)

Verse 2 addresses the virtue of humility, which isn't even close to weakness. Humility is gentleness and courtesy. Even when we disagree with those who advocate evil and harm, we must not become like them in attitude. If we attack with the purpose of destroying their character and position, that is not proper Christian behavior. Our motivation must be to promote truth and convert those in error. We are to avoid being a brawler. This describes someone who is combative and quarrelsome.

Remembering our past helps provide a perspective for the present and the future. In verse 3, Paul listed some of the past sins of himself and Titus. These are not uncommon to individuals prior to accepting Christ. The challenge we face is one of not allowing them to continue. Through Christ we are cleansed from all our previous unrighteousness, but it becomes our responsibility to keep our former sins from reappearing.

The list of sinful attitudes paints a common picture. These are vices found in most unbelievers. The first is *foolishness*. This refers to a lack of spiritual understanding. Sin darkens our hearts and minds to the truth and wisdom of God. *Disobedience* logically follows. Why follow God and His directives when we lack knowledge and understanding of them? *Deception* is a partner to the other characteristics mentioned. Satan deceives us into following lies, all the while believing we are in the right.

Prior to salvation people are in slavery to their own *lusts* and desire for *pleasure*. This seems normal since there is no sense of immediate destruction. *Hatred* and *envy* arise in our hearts and impact our actions toward those who have what we want.

These inner attitudes are evidence of a sin–dominated life. When they begin to form in the believer's life, they must be immediately eradicated from the heart and mind. Asking for God's forgiveness, we then open ourselves for Him to work through the Holy Spirit within us (Philippians 2:13).

B. Christ's Love (v. 4)

4. But after that the kindness and love of God our Saviour toward man appeared.

This verse fits with the previous three as a unit. However, it is necessary for us to also look at God's love alone. All that we as believers enjoy rests singularly on God's love. Without His love there would have been no provision for salvation. Without His love there would be no means of forgiveness of sins committed after salvation. Without His love there would be no ministry of the Holy Spirit. Without His love there would be no hope of a glorious life eternal.

The call to Christian attitudes and actions rests upon God's providing the means to make it all possible. Good works are possible only because God's love has been applied to our lives through Jesus Christ.

C. The Christian's Works (vv. 5–8)

5. Not by works of righteousness which we have done, but according to his mercy he saved us, by the washing of regeneration, and renewing of the Holy Ghost;

6. Which he shed on us abundantly through Jesus Christ our Saviour;

7. That being justified by his grace, we should be made heirs according to the hope of eternal life.

8. This is a faithful saying, and these things I will that thou affirm constantly, that they which have believed in God might be careful to maintain good works. These things are good and profitable unto men.

In the process of exhorting Titus and all believers to good works, Paul used these verses to emphasize the role of the Christian's deeds and lifestyle. He wanted it clearly understood that works are not the means of salvation. Regardless of all the righteous activities in which one may participate, activities, of themselves, produce no change in one's relationship with God. That comes only as a result of His divine mercy extended to us. Regeneration, that new state of being, rests solely on God's bringing about a change. This renovation of our spiritual being comes through the ministry of the Holy Spirit.

Verse 7 reminds us that our new state of righteousness and our position as heirs of eternal life comes through Jesus Christ. All of our kind deeds, positive attitudes, and thoughtful words do not bring salvation. We are to walk in His steps and follow His example. Besides the spiritual aspect, it needs to be observed that the last portion of verse 8 states, "These things are good and profitable unto men."

List some of the good works which are to be evident in the life of the believer.

REVIEW QUESTIONS

1. List the four directives in discharging our duties.
2. Why is winning not the emphasis of finishing the race?
3. How do friends strengthen us in crisis?
4. How should Christians respond to their government?
5. What is the role of works in the believer's life?

GOLDEN TEXT HOMILY

"I HAVE FOUGHT A GOOD FIGHT, I HAVE FINISHED MY COURSE, I HAVE KEPT THE FAITH" (2 Timothy 4:7).

One of the cruelest theories presented by some ministers is that if you are a Christian there will never be problems—all will be sunshine and roses. God never promised it would be easy—but that He would be with us in all we face.

Multitudes have suffered for Christ, even martyrdom. However, few have had such severe difficulties while fulfilling God's will as did Paul.

Opposition to Paul's witness was on every side, but nothing deterred him. In spite of prisons, he fought on. In spite of the "perils among false brethren" (2 Corinthians 11:26), he fought on. In spite of his thorn in the flesh, he fought on. In spite of desertions, distrust, and mistrust, he fought on. What a testimony to the grace of God!

Now all that would detract from his ministry or destroy him was ending. There was a persistence within him to finish his race, the course God had set for him. Quickly it would be a reality, coming at the hands of Nero's executioners. He did not flinch. From heaven and earth he was being cheered on. God's grace had seen him through.

Seeing ultimate victory, he acknowledged it was faith that had kept him, even as he had kept the faith. It wasn't just a faith of any kind or just any faith at all—but *the* faith—faith that Jehovah was his God, Jesus was his redeemer, and the Holy Spirit his advocate.

It is when one faces death that one realizes how important it is to know in whom one's faith lies (Acts 4:12). Sincerity is not enough.—**Fred H. Whisman, Chaplain (Lt. Col.), Group II Chaplain, Civil Air Patrol, Chattanooga, Tennessee**

SENTENCE SERMONS

BY GOD'S GRACE, the believer remains faithful in every circumstance.

—Selected

WITHOUT FAITH, we are as stained-glass windows in the dark.

—Anonymous

FAITH IS the daring of the soul to go farther than it can see.

—William Newton Clarke

THE CHURCH is a workshop, not a dormitory; and every Christian man and woman is bound to help in the common cause.

—Alexander MacLaren

EVANGELISM APPLICATION

FAITHFUL BELIEVERS WITNESS TO SINNERS.

Wow! Isn't that a straightforward statement! It doesn't allow any room for excuses or explanation. There it is. You either are or you aren't.

Since faithfulness is usually calculated in terms of other activities, we tend to forget the test of witnessing. Yet sharing our faith should be as normal as going to church, praying, reading the Bible, and paying our tithes. Of course, if these practices aren't regular parts of one's life in Christ, then witnessing regularly definitely won't be.

Faithfulness to any cause automatically carries with it some type of verbal witness. Those who like Chrysler Corporation cars laud their features. Individuals who prefer a particular store speak of the values and the selection to be found there. We all do this as part of our daily life. Should it be any different with our faith in Jesus? Absolutely not!

So how do we become faithful in our witness? First, we must choose to make it a regular part of our Christian faith. Second, we should let it be a normal part of our lifestyle. Third, whenever a conversation opens the door for us to share Christ, we should witness briefly and without apology.

ILLUMINATING THE LESSON

The effort and result of faithfulness is evident in one of the accounts of church planting by Paul H. Walker in Maryland. He describes the brush arbor and the revival as follows:

"We erected a brush arbor. We made it of brush which we piled upon stringers held up by posts. The lighting system consisted of old kerosene drums which had a gooseneck with the burner on the end. We hung these on the posts. The light had a reddish glow with fogs of smoke and soot rising above the flame.

"The altar in the brush arbor was filled. And here again we were blessed . . . with rotten eggs. But we were not deterred and the work moved forward in the revival.

"One evening the rowdies were so mean that we actually were afraid that someone would be killed. When these reports reached Salisbury, the Home Guard was sent out in uniform to protect us. They surrounded the brush arbor and the meeting continued unmolested.

"A new church was set in order and many young preachers received their first preaching experience."
—***Paths of a Pioneer***

DAILY BIBLE READINGS

M. Faithful in Evil Times.
Genesis 6:9–22

T. Test of Faith.
Genesis 22:1–14

W. Faithfulness Observed.
Ruth 2:1–13

T. Tried Faith.
Job 1:12–22

F. Heroes of Faith.
Hebrews 11:32–40

S. Focus of Our Faith.
Hebrews 12:1–3

A Heart for Ministry

Study Text: Acts 11:1–12; Acts 15:1–12; James 2:1–9

Objective: To recognize attitudes that hinder our ministry and determine to reject them.

Time: The Book of Acts was written between A.D. 61 and 63, and covers a period of time from Christ's Ascension through imprisonment of Paul about A.D. 62. James was written between A.D. 45 and 49.

Place: The Book of Acts was probably written at Caesarea or Rome. James was most likely written at Jerusalem.

Golden Text: "If ye fulfil the royal law according to the scripture, Thou shalt love thy neighbour as thyself, ye do well" (James 2:8).

Central Truth: Effective ministry flows out of a compassionate heart.

Evangelism Emphasis: Evangelism begins with a heart for ministry.

PRINTED TEXT

Acts 11:5. I was in the city of Joppa praying: and in a trance I saw a vision, A certain vessel descend, as it had been a great sheet, let down from heaven by four corners; and it came even to me:

6. Upon the which when I had fastened mine eyes, I considered, and saw fourfooted beasts of the earth, and wild beasts, and creeping things, and fowls of the air.

7. And I heard a voice saying unto me, Arise, Peter; slay and eat.

8. But I said, Not so, Lord: for nothing common or unclean hath at any time entered into my mouth.

9. But the voice answered me again from heaven, What God hath cleansed, that call not thou common.

Acts 15:1. And certain men which came down from Judaea taught the brethren, and said, Except ye be circumcised after the manner of Moses, ye cannot be saved.

6. And the apostles and elders came together for to consider of this matter.

7. And when there had been much disputing, Peter rose up, and said unto them, Men and brethren, ye know how that a good while ago God made choice among us, that the Gentiles by my mouth should hear the word of the gospel, and believe.

8. And God, which knoweth the hearts, bare witness, giving them

the Holy Ghost, even as he did unto us;

9. And put no difference between us and them, purifying their hearts by faith.

10. Now therefore why tempt ye God, to put a yoke upon the neck of the disciples, which neither our fathers nor we were able to bear?

11. But we believe that through the grace of the Lord Jesus Christ we shall be saved, even as they.

12. Then all the multitude kept silence, and gave audience to Barnabas and Paul, declaring what miracles and wonders God had wrought among the Gentiles by them.

James 2:1. My brethren, have not the faith of our Lord Jesus Christ, the Lord of glory, with respect of persons.

8. If ye fulfill the royal law according to the scripture, Thou shalt love thy neighbour as thyself, ye do well:

9. But if ye have respect to persons, ye commit sin, and are convinced of the law as transgressors.

LESSON OUTLINE

I. OVERCOME PRIDE
   A. The Indictment
   B. The Account
   C. The Spirit
II. REJECT PREJUDICE
   A. The Dissension
   B. The Consideration
   C. The Acceptance
III. AVOID PARTIALITY
   A. The Sin
   B. The Royal Law

LESSON EXPOSITION

INTRODUCTION

With this lesson we begin a second topic area in this fall quarter. The first eight lessons took us through portions of the Pastoral Epistles. Now in lessons 9 through 13 the theme is "Ministering to One Another." They probe our inner thoughts and attitudes in an attempt to reveal those characteristics which hinder successful ministry. They also force us to look at some of the actions which are a part of true ministry.

This lesson takes a look at three basic problems that obstruct ministry—pride, prejudice, and partiality. They are each important for our consideration, since we often deny their presence in our own hearts and minds. The challenge is to strip away our denial of their existence and try to overcome them. We see them in the lives of other believers but have nearsightedness when it comes to ourselves.

The sin of *pride* can be defined as being boastful, haughty, or conceited. It reflects the opposite of being modest and humble. Pride can be dominant within an individual without evidencing itself on the exterior. We generally think that pride reveals itself in one's demeanor or words; however, in reality, it may remain quietly in the recesses of a person's heart. While the person may appear normal on the outside, within there may be a poison that eats away true spirituality and the ministering spirit.

Prejudice is a problem we all face. No one is exempt although many think they have never had it or have overcome it. This attitude comes from limiting prejudice to the area of ethnic and racial differences. This type of prejudice constantly appears in the media, and attempts are made to right wrongs and contain the extremists on both sides. Those of us who are not part of these conflicts often stand by very piously and believe we are prejudice free. But there are other types of prejudice that can manifest itself with equal intensity—economic, the wealthy against those with less; geographic, North versus South, East as opposed to West; religious, Evangelicals against other Evangelicals.

Partiality could be considered prejudice in reverse. Prejudice speaks of a very strong bias, a one–sidedness which may injure and bring harm. Partiality goes the other way—a strong inclination toward someone or something you prefer. All of us have certain preferences that are just part of our individuality. We are partial to certain foods, specific brands, and even particular days. Basically there isn't anything wrong with that. It's normal. There's no doubt we tend to like some people better than others. Common interests and blending personalities causes us to gravitate to these individuals. The difficulty comes when our preferences cause division and prejudice again begins to rear its ugly head. It is a sin to make other human beings feel second–best or on a lower level socially.

I. OVERCOME PRIDE (Acts 11:1–12)

A. The Indictment (vv. 1–3)

(Acts 11:1–3 is not included in the printed text.)

How is it possible that Spirit–filled people would oppose others receiving the same fullness of the Spirit? Even good people lose proper perspective when pride influences their thinking and speaking. This becomes very evident in the account of Peter's ministry in Cornelius' household as recorded in Acts 10 and then retold in chapter 11. Pride blinds people to the truth. Pride produces selfishness.

From the very beginning of the early church, Christ's intention stood forth. Believers were to spread the gospel first to their own but then spread out both geographically and culturally. Even those who heard this commission had difficulty incorporating it into their ministry consciousness. This appears especially true of those mentioned in verse 1. Some of them were of the original 12 disciples. They too had heard of the outpouring of the Holy Spirit on the Gentiles through the ministry of Peter. Further compounding the matter was that in this group of Gentiles were a Roman centurion and his household. Even the conquerors of the Jews were experiencing the special blessing of salvation and the endowment of power by the Holy Spirit.

The news of this event preceded Peter's arrival in Jerusalem. Those opposing his actions were prepared to do battle with him upon their initial meeting. The description of their being "of the circumcision" immediately indicates a clinging to the distinction of being God's chosen people. They chose to hold on to the past mark of circumcision as a sign of God's covenant. They continued to allow the past to dominate their thinking rather than allow the new revelation of Christ to be their benchmark. This caused them to be contentious and ready to criticize.

Notice that their indictment against Peter did not even consider the spiritual events that had taken place. They accused him of stooping to eat with Gentiles. Their attack on Peter was for failing to maintain a separation from the uncircumcised.

B. The Account (vv. 4–10)

(Acts 11:4, 10 is not included in the printed text.)

5. I was in the city of Joppa praying: and in a trance I saw a vision, A certain vessel descend, as it had been a great sheet, let down from heaven by four corners; and it came even to me:

6. Upon the which when I had fastened mine eyes, I considered, and saw fourfooted beasts of the earth, and wild beasts, and creeping things, and fowls of the air.

7. And I heard a voice saying unto me, Arise, Peter; slay and eat.

8. But I said, Not so, Lord: for nothing common or unclean hath at any time entered into my mouth.

9. But the voice answered me again from heaven, What God hath cleansed, that call not thou common.

Before looking at what Peter said, we must consider what was left unsaid. There are so many ways he could have responded, but he chose a means for healing rather than further contention. He avoided any name–calling or labeling. He also refrained from questioning the spirituality of his questioners. Either of these approaches would have fanned the flames of division. We are to rise above the methods of those who haven't experienced the grace of God, or are having difficulty comprehending its fullness.

Peter recognized their need to hear the entire account. What happened in Caesarea was due to his experience at Joppa. All of his actions stemmed from a spiritual experience while praying on the housetop. His praying there was normal and logical since the flat roof served many purposes, one of which was that as a room for guests.

The apostle Peter recalled in their hearing how an object like a sheet descended. It was full of various birds, reptiles, and four–footed animals. All were in the "unclean" category and not to be used for food by Jews. Then, to Peter's amazement, a voice instructed him to kill and eat. With predictable protest, he responded with pride that no unclean food had ever entered his mouth (v. 8). God broke into this prideful boasting with a clear reminder of who determines right and wrong, clean and unclean. But even more importantly, God reminded Peter of His cleansing power. What He chooses to cleanse is clean regardless of human perspective. And the conclusion we face, then, is to do anything different from God's way is to be disobedient and in a state of rebellion.

So there could be no misunderstanding, God gave His message to Peter three times. Although the vision addressed the food laws of the Old Testament (Leviticus 11), the application of its message included the Gentiles. The ceremonial laws of separation that forbade Jews to enter the house of a Gentile were to be set aside and the gospel shared with them. Notice that the specific directive to go to Cornelius' house was lacking. Instead, God provided Peter with a principle that enabled him to make the right choice when the situation developed.

C. The Spirit (vv. 11, 12)

(Acts 11:11, 12 is not included in the printed text.)

Here again we see the marvelous phenomenon of God's timing. As soon as the vision ended, Cornelius' men came to Simon's house and inquired for Peter, as they had been instructed by their master (Acts 10:5–7). God worked on both ends to accomplish a new opportunity for the gospel. He brought together a fertile field with a gospel preacher who could reap the harvest. But He also sent the Holy Spirit to continue the work in Peter. The Spirit directed him to go without hesitation. He was able to set aside his personal pride as a strict law–abiding Jew to walk in the fullness of a Spirit–led life. Six other individuals accompanied Peter. Nothing is said as to whether or not Peter shared the distinctives of his vision with these companions. It is only reasonable to assume he did. Time was available since they didn't leave until the next morning. Besides, some explanation would be in order, since they would have known of Peter's position and practices in regard to Jewish law.

What are some ways the Holy Spirit enables us to overcome pride?

II. REJECT PREJUDICE
(Acts 15:1–12)

A. The Dissension (vv. 1–5)

(Acts 15:2–5 is not included in the printed text.)

1. And certain men which came down from Judaea taught the brethren, and said, Except ye be circumcised after the manner of Moses, ye cannot be saved.

Here we see prejudice against a group of people because they did not conform to a preconceived notion of how salvation must be obtained. The Judaizing element of the early church wanted to apply the requirements of the law to their new life in Christ. However, it didn't end there. They expected the same concepts to be applied to the Gentiles.

From verse 5 we see that this legalistic prejudice stemmed from those who were members of the Pharisee sect prior to becoming believers. Their commitment to man–made laws surrounding God's laws continued to evidence itself. They were so committed to their religious prejudice that various members traveled all over the region in an attempt to indoctrinate new believers. Not only did they travel to Antioch in Syria, but they also made their presence felt in the churches of Galatia. It was to these congregations that Paul wrote his sharpest rebuke as he addressed them as "foolish Galatians" (3:1).

The dissension over this issue expanded to such an extent that some resolution had to be found. Knowing of the experiences of Paul and Barnabas on the first missionary journey, the church at Antioch appointed them to go to Jerusalem and confer there with the church leaders. Since the 12 apostles represented the formal leadership of the entire church, it was only logical that they be consulted along with other elders. At this point, the church at Jerusalem represented the seat of authority.

On the way to Jerusalem, Paul and Barnabas apparently visited churches in two separate regions of Palestine. They shared how the gospel had been preached to and received by the Gentiles. Their response was one of great joy. They understood that whenever anyone received the message of salvation, it was a time to rejoice rather than question the validity of the experience. This enables us to understand that the vast majority of even the Jewish Christians were not committed to keeping the dietary and ritual laws of the Pharisees. However, it reveals how just a few individuals can provoke dissension and create misdirection within the body.

Upon arriving in Jerusalem, Paul and Barnabas spoke to both the leadership and the members of the church. With care and detail these returned missionaries told of the wondrous spreading of the gospel. They left nothing hidden or to be assumed. The whole story of God's marvelous intervention and the Gentile's acceptance of the gospel shone through. In spite of all this, there were still those who were not convinced that the Gentiles were free from following the law.

B. The Consideration (vv. 6–11)

6. And the apostles and elders came together for to consider of this matter.

7. And when there had been much disputing, Peter rose up, and said unto them, Men and brethren, ye know how that a good while ago God made choice among us, that the Gentiles by my mouth should hear the word of the gospel, and believe.

8. And God, which knoweth the hearts, bare witness, giving them the Holy Ghost, even as he did unto us;

9. And put no difference between us and them, purifying their hearts by faith.

10. Now therefore why tempt ye God, to put a yoke upon the neck of the disciples, which neither our fathers nor we were able to bear?

11. But we believe that through the grace of the Lord Jesus Christ we shall be saved, even as they.

Apparently the discussion between the apostles and the elders became tense. It was time for the Jerusalem Council to decide what position the church should endorse. And in the process of doing so, many of them must face the reality of their prejudice.

Verse 7 indicates a considerable amount of dialogue and reasoning. The time allotment for this consideration is not clear. Apparently after many had an opportunity to express their views, Peter stood and addressed them. He followed the Jewish pattern of using the past to determine a course for the present and the future. He began with his personal testimony which took them back to the experience at Joppa and Caesarea. They knew the story well. The details were secondary, however, to the major principle. Cornelius and his household had believed and experienced the baptism of the Holy Spirit. This had not happened because Peter had a personal desire to minister to

Gentiles. Instead, God had selected the messenger and the specific group of Gentiles who would be the first Gentiles to receive the baptism of the Holy Spirit.

Peter pointed out the contribution of Cornelius and his household. Their hearts were open and filled with faith. God honored it to the point of pouring out the Holy Spirit on them even before they verbally expressed faith. In view of this acceptance, how could God's people continue to doubt and harbor prejudice? Besides, Peter argued, they were demanding of the Gentiles that which they as Jews had difficulty fulfilling themselves. His use of the term "yoke" (v. 10) demonstrates the burden of the law. Jesus used this same concept when describing the burden the scribes and Pharisees laid on others (Matthew 23:4). In marked contrast, however, when Jesus spoke of His yoke, it was in terms of a lighter and much easier one. The Lord keeps His yoke from unnecessarily chafing and helps us carry the loads of life.

Verses 9 and 11 remind us how God is free from all prejudice in offering His salvation. He doesn't consider factors which humans consider important, such as race, skin color, economics, or gender. No one is more advantaged or disadvantaged in God's sight. The only prerequisite is faith. No one earns salvation, since God offers it on the basis of His grace; and by definition, *grace* is God's unmerited favor to the lawbreaker. So it doesn't matter whether one is a Jew or a Gentile. All experience salvation on the same grounds. Thus, if we want to be found acceptable in God's sight, we must emulate His lack of prejudice.

Paul's letter to the Galatians emphasizes the equality of all in God's plan of salvation—"There is neither Jew nor Greek, there is neither bond nor free, there is neither male nor female: for ye are all one in Christ Jesus" (3:28).

What are some steps we may take to overcome our personal prejudices?

C. The Acceptance (v. 12)

12. Then all the multitude kept silence, and gave audience to Barnabas and Paul, declaring what miracles and wonders God had wrought among the Gentiles by them.

How can anyone argue against what God has done? Who would be foolish enough to dispute with God? Why would anyone question God as to whom He chooses to bless with salvation and the Holy Spirit baptism? Yet these believers did. The report of Paul and Barnabas wasn't a dialogue on what *they* had done. Instead they spoke only of what *God* had done. Peter did the same when he recounted the events at Caesarea.

It's easy to retain one's prejudices and personal opinions when sparring with other individuals. We can use them to question their motives and evaluate the appropriateness of their methodology. But when facing the Sovereign God, these approaches are ineffective.

Peter's explanation brought silence to the group and opened the door for Paul and Barnabas to tell of other wonderful acts of God among the Gentiles. They spoke of the miracles that had accompanied the spiritual blessings. This was consistent with what God had been doing among the Jews from the Day of Pentecost (Acts 2:43; 3:7; 5:12–16; 6:8). The similarity provides another proof that this was God's doing.

Prejudice can be overcome. It isn't necessary for it to continue to blind individuals to the truth. However, a step toward its demise is to be silent and allow the truth to be heard.

III. AVOID PARTIALITY (James 2:1–9)

A. The Sin (vv. 1–7)

(James 2:2–7 is not included in the printed text.)

1. My brethren, have not the faith of our Lord Jesus Christ, the Lord of glory, with respect of persons.

Being a Christian is much more than a matter of profession. It is easy to mouth the words "I am a Christian." But the real test comes by our living a lifestyle that is genuinely pure and undefiled. In the last verse of chapter 1, James provided a twofold test. Our claim of Christianity needs proving by our ministry to the needy and oppressed—the orphans and widows. It also needs proving by our actively avoiding the imprint of the world's thought processes and lifestyles.

James carefully instructs us that acceptable Christian behavior includes both positive and negative aspects. There are areas in which we must demonstrate that we are "doers of the word" (1:22–25). Then there are also things we are told to avoid.

In chapter 2 we face the heart of James' message, the relationship of faith and works. This proves difficult for many since the tendancy is to emphasize one or the other. Some see believing as the prime necessity to be a Christian. Others believe they can score points with God through their many good deeds. But God demands a combination of the two.

In beginning this discussion on faith and works, James started with the sin of partiality. This demonstrates that the early concept of commonality (sharing all things) did not permeate the church as time went by and the church spread. Communalism, even among believers, didn't fare well. It is so easy to categorize people and then give certain individuals or groups priority treatment. The Corinthian church evidenced this sin of partiality at their love feasts. Apparently some ate the food they brought for the supper before others of a lesser economic status arrived or they chose not to share it with them. And then they proceeded to participate in Communion (1 Corinthians 11:20, 21).

James used two examples to illustrate how the sin of partiality may be evident within the church. Though couched in a culture of two millennia ago, they still ring true today. The first describes a rich man who is well dressed and evidences his material well–being by wearing gold rings. When he arrives at the location where the believers are gathered, they lavish attention on him and escort him to a good place to be seated. Treating him properly isn't the issue. Proper hospitality is always in order, especially among believers. And, of course, treating visitors kindly is a must if there is to be any chance of winning them to Christ and His church.

The difficulty comes when the

second example is presented, and the sin of partiality can be clearly seen. A poor man comes into the assembly of believers. In marked contrast to the rich man's finery, he is shabbily clothed and lacks gold jewelry. Instead of seating him on the same level as the rich man, he is relegated to sitting on the floor. When this happens, believers have taken it upon themselves to judge others solely on the basis of one's outward appearance and economic status. This differs from evaluating people on the basis of their faith, motives, and deeds! Verse 4 emphasizes that the inherent evil of this action comes from sinful thinking. The condition of one's heart and mind can be clearly demonstrated in such a simple action as where one is seated.

James then stimulates their thinking and ours with a reminder of the need to be rich in faith to inherit the kingdom of God (v. 5). It sometimes seems that those who are poor in this world's goods are better able to place their trust in God. Possessions often tend to make one feel self-sufficient rather than relying on God. Love of money robs us of the ability to love God wholeheartedly. The church's power is never in silver and gold but in the power of God through the active working of the Holy Spirit.

In verses 6 and 7 James took this a step further. He asked the church to look around them. Who are the ones taking advantage of the poor? Who are the people taking believers to court? Who are the people insulting the name of Christ? It is quite evident that the rich are guilty of all three. This doesn't mean all of the rich are doing these things. Nevertheless, the poor are seldom the instigators of such practices. It's the rich. So why should believers be so impressed with possessions and appearances that they allow the sin of partiality to enter both their thinking and their actions.

B. The Royal Law (vv. 8, 9)

8. If ye fulfill the royal law according to the scripture, Thou shalt love thy neighbour as thyself, ye do well:

9. But if ye have respect to persons, ye commit sin, and are convinced of the law as transgressors.

To avoid partiality we need to begin with the royal law of love. This deals with the two greatest commandments: "Thou shalt love the Lord thy God with all thine heart, and with all thy soul, and with all thy might" (Deuteronomy 6:5). And "Thou shalt love thy neighbour as thyself" (Leviticus 19:18).

There is no better illustration to use here than Jesus' encounter with the lawyer who was testing Him (Luke 10:25–37). After stating how to receive eternal life, Jesus was asked the question "Who is my neighbor?" He responded with the story of the Good Samaritan. After being robbed and beaten, a traveler lay helplessly on the road. Both a priest and a Levite came by. However, when they saw him, each continued on the other side of the road. Neither allowed compassion to influence his actions. Not until a Samaritan came by did help become available. Not only did he stop and bind up the man's wounds, but he also took him to the nearest inn and paid for lodging during the recuperation time.

This story illustrates not only

love and compassion, but also that our loving actions are to be given to *whoever* is in need, at the time we are available and have the resources to meet the need. Verse 9 is explicit in its directive concerning avoiding partiality: it is sin. Those practicing partiality are in complete opposition to God's law. They are transgressors (sinners) just like anyone who breaks any other of God's laws.

What are some steps that may be taken to overcome partiality?

REVIEW QUESTIONS

1. Why did some of the Jewish believers refuse to believe that Gentiles were receiving the whole gospel?

2. How did the Holy Spirit work on both Cornelius and Peter?

3. What was the yoke some were attempting to place on the Gentiles?

4. Why would it be difficult to argue against God?

5. What is the royal law? (James 2:8)

GOLDEN TEXT HOMILY

"IF YE FULFIL THE ROYAL LAW ACCORDING TO THE SCRIPTURE, THOU SHALT LOVE THY NEIGHBOUR AS THYSELF, YE DO WELL" (James 2:8).

I had reached a point in my life when I was having trouble feeling love for several individuals I was called on to relate to on a daily basis. Over time, problems had developed because of personality clashes or disagreements. Quite frankly, I had become bitter toward several of these people, having come to feel that they had wronged me and never even acknowledged the deed. I had become negative in spirit, my inner turmoil spilling over into relationships having nothing to do with the "problem people." A simple scriptural imperative was riveted into my spirit early one Friday morning during my personal devotions: I must love people and act in love toward people because I love God—not because I have been treated well by them, feel positive emotions toward them, or find it personally advantageous to "stroke" them. This simple truth was not new to me, but I had forgotten it in an operative sense. Burdened with a series of slights, hurts, and rejections, I was allowing my negative emotions to rule me instead of allowing the Holy Spirit to produce His fruit of practical love.

I would submit that if we as Christians try to love our neighbors as ourselves without first attending to our relationship with God, we will fail miserably. Ultimately, we will make for ourselves a legalistic code, a mental rule book for relationships which will quickly become burdensome and which we will begin to impose on others rather than using it as our own guide. Or we will become perfectionists, laying upon ourselves a burden of "good works" beyond what is natural and practical. But if our interactions with those individuals whom God places within our sphere of relationships are an outflow of our interaction with God in intimate devotion—as we worship and adore Him—we will know the great joy of service and devotion to other people which results from our love to Him. And, gradually, we will be able to shed those conditions we find so easy to lay on others, particularly family members—burdens for them to carry as they feel we love them *if* or *because*, not purely and unconditionally.—**Sabord Woods, Ph.D., Professor of English, Lee College, Cleveland, Tennessee**

SENTENCE SERMONS

EFFECTIVE MINISTRY flows out of a compassionate heart.

—Selected

GOD HATES THOSE who praise themselves.

—Saint Clement

PREJUDICE IS being down on something you're not up on.

—Draper's Book of Quotations for the Christian World

'TIS A MARK of great perfection to bear with the imperfection of others.

—Italian Proverb

EVANGELISM APPLICATION

EVANGELISM BEGINS WITH A HEART FOR MINISTRY.

What motivates a believer to go against the grain of society to be of service to his fellowman and to his fellow believers? The best general answer has to be "a heart for ministry." A heart for ministry stems from a variety of stimuli. First is the desire to be an obedient servant of the Lord. All the biblical directives and principles instructing us to meet the needs of others are considered as His will for us. Second is the motivation of the Holy Spirit as He urges and enables us to fulfill what we know is right. Third is the ability to minister. None of us are asked to do anything that is outside the scope of our natural abilities or enhanced spiritual giftedness. Sometimes we need to grow into a particular area of service through study and practice, but it's still within our range of possibility.

All of us are called to share our faith in God with the unbeliever. There are no exceptions to this aspect of life in Christ. However, some are directed to a more public presentation than others. Regardless of the means or place, a heart for ministry is the stimulus that makes a difference. Unless it motivates us, our evangelistic attempts will be occasional, mediocre, and unproductive.

All of us need to pray, "Lord, give me a heart for ministry."

DAILY BIBLE READINGS

M. Overcome by Pride.
Genesis 4:2–13

T. Showing Kindness.
2 Samuel 9:1–13

W. Impartial Ministry.
Luke 7:36–50

T. Bigotry Rejected.
John 4:3–14

F. Overcome Barriers.
Acts 10:1–15

S. Debtor to All.
Romans 1:11–16

Ministering to the Hurting

Study Text: Matthew 25:34–40; Acts 6:1–7; James 1:27; 2:14–17

Objective: To examine biblical examples of ministering to the hurting and dedicate our lives to serving others.

Golden Text: "Inasmuch as ye have done it unto one of the least of these my brethren, ye have done it unto me" (Matthew 25:40).

Central Truth: The Christian reflects Christ by reaching out to the hurting.

Evangelism Emphasis: The believer can reach the lost by entering through the door of their hurts.

PRINTED TEXT

Matthew 25:34. Then shall the King say unto them on his right hand, Come, ye blessed of my Father, inherit the kingdom prepared for you from the foundation of the world:

35. For I was an hungred, and ye gave me meat: I was thirsty, and ye gave me drink: I was a stranger, and ye took me in:

36. Naked, and ye clothed me: I was sick, and ye visited me: I was in prison, and ye came unto me.

37. Then shall the righteous answer him, saying, Lord, when saw we thee an hungred, and fed thee? or thirsty, and gave thee drink?

38. When saw we thee a stranger, and took thee in? or naked, and clothed thee?

39. Or when saw we thee sick, or in prison, and came unto thee?

40. And the King shall answer and say unto them, Verily I say unto you, Inasmuch as ye have done it unto one of the least of these my brethren, ye have done it unto me.

Acts 6:2. Then the twelve called the multitude of the disciples unto them, and said, It is not reason that we should leave the word of God, and serve tables.

3. Wherefore, brethren, look ye out among you seven men of honest report, full of the Holy Ghost and wisdom, whom we may appoint over this business.

4. But we will give ourselves continually to prayer, and to the ministry of the word.

7. And the word of God increased; and the number of the disciples multiplied in Jerusalem greatly; and a great company of the priests were obedient to the faith.

James 1:27. Pure religion and undefiled before God and the Father is this, To visit the fatherless and widows in their

affliction, and to keep himself unspotted from the world.

2:14. What doth it profit, my brethren, though a man say he hath faith, and have not works? can faith save him?

15. If a brother or sister be naked, and destitute of daily food,

16. And one of you say unto them, Depart in peace, be ye warmed and filled; notwithstanding ye give them not those things which are needful to the body; what doth it profit?

17. Even so faith, if it hath not works, is dead, being alone.

LESSON OUTLINE

I. COMPASSIONATE SERVICE
   A. The Action
   B. The Recipient
II. RESPONDING TO NEED
   A. The Need
   B. The Solution
   C. The Selection
III. PRACTICAL SERVICE
   A. Pure Religion
   B. Working Faith

LESSON EXPOSITION

INTRODUCTION

Hurting people may suffer from a variety of causes. Some are hurting physically. Pain generated by disease and accidents keeps them in discomfort, ranging from slight aches to sheer agony. Others are hurting emotionally. Some things that generate this type of pain are separation, failure, losses, and prejudice.

No one is exempt from the responsibility to try to alleviate the pain when it is within our resources to do so. Some situations, however, are beyond our ability, and we can only call for help or guide the hurting to those who can help. In each case we have a Christian obligation to be compassionate. And we can always pray.

What is the mission of the church regarding the suffering? What should believers as part of the body of Christ see as their task? Most Evangelicals would answer "evangelism." This comes from an emphasis on the Great Commission, recorded in Matthew 28:19, 20. Thus, meeting needs is seen only as a means of bringing the lost to Christ, and food pantries, medical missions, and benevolence funds are attractive only as tools for witnessing.

A much more balanced approach to ministering to the hurting comes from emphasizing John 17:18. As Jesus prayed, He used His own ministry as an example for the believers and the church as a whole. Not only did Jesus preach and teach, but He also fed the hungry, brought dignity to the underprivileged, and comforted the sorrowing. To follow His example, the mission of the church, then, includes concern for the plight of the homeless, the poor, and the disenfranchised. It is of interest to note how many Pentecostal churches have become much more active in these forms of ministry during the past 15 years.

We cannot hide behind

government programs or place the responsibility on someone else; we have to look at how we can serve individually and as a church effort. What am I doing to help those who are in need? That question strips away our smugness and piety that are based solely on reading the Bible and going to church as our primary works of righteousness.

The challenge for us in this lesson is to realize our personal responsibility to minister to the hurting.

I. COMPASSIONATE SERVICE (Matthew 25:34–40)

A. The Action (vv. 34–36)

34. Then shall the King say unto them on his right hand, Come, ye blessed of my Father, inherit the kingdom prepared for you from the foundation of the world:

35. For I was an hungred, and ye gave me meat: I was thirsty, and ye gave me drink: I was a stranger, and ye took me in:

36. Naked, and ye clothed me: I was sick, and ye visited me: I was in prison, and ye came unto me.

The context of these verses is the judgment of nations. Christ will judge and separate the people into groups designated as sheep and goats. The sheep will be placed on His right. This reflects their favored position with the Master. People understood this, since at a banquet the person receiving the greatest honor or recognition was always seated at the host's right hand.

Christ will address them as being blessed and will give them the inheritance provided from the beginning of time. It is then that their actions will be noted. The Lord will acknowledge their compassionate response to Him in terms of specific ministry to the hurting. Verses 35 and 36 list six individual needs or hurts to which they had responded. Each one of them can be categorized as a social need and physical in nature.

Hunger stands highest on the list. Everyone knows food is necessary to sustain life. And in a society where the majority of the people were of the lower economic status, hunger would have been much in evidence. Under the law the poor were to be allowed to glean in the fields, groves and vineyards. Farmers were to leave the corners of their fields uncut, and any heads of grain that fell to the ground were to be left for them. The same held true of the olive groves and vineyards. Any of the fruit missed on the first picking was to be left for the needy (Leviticus 19:9, 10; 23:22; Deuteronomy 24:19–21). Even an enemy was to be fed (Proverbs 25:21).

Notice how Jesus' ministry included feeding the hungry. On two occasions He fed thousands of people (Matthew 14:13–21; 15: 29–38) with only a few fish and some small loaves. It is of special interest that compassion was the compelling reason that He chose to feed the multitude rather than send them away. Jesus provided us with an example of righteousness by ministering to their hunger.

Then there is the problem of thirst. Thirst goes hand in hand with hunger. The possibility of thirst stands out vividly when you remember the overall lack of water in Palestine. Rivers, springs, and wells were highly valued and carefully used. The worth of water and its use in ministry is seen in Jesus' teaching: "I tell you the truth, anyone who gives you a cup of water in my name because you belong to Christ will certainly not lose his reward" (Mark 9:41, *NIV*; also see Matthew 10:42).

Hospitality was applauded. This benevolence applied to the stranger, or alien, who arrived in a community and had no place to stay. Since the Hebrews as a people knew the difficulties of being strangers in a distant land, God specifically directed them to care for strangers (Exodus 23:9). That can be seen in allowing them to glean the fields, groves, and vineyards. However, it went beyond that to the extent of providing shelter also. Two biblical accounts demonstrate not only the sheltering of strangers but also the type of protection to be given. Guests were considered to be a gift of God, and no sacrifice was too great for one's company. Notice how Lot invited the two angels into his home (Genesis 19:1–11) and how an elderly man in Gibeah invited a traveling Levite and concubine into his home (Judges 19:1–24).

Nakedness refers to being scantily or poorly clothed rather than being totally without clothing. The issue would be one of suffering from both cold and heat due to improper and insufficient clothing. And as would be expected, the poor are the ones who most often experience this need. In the New Testament, Dorcas stands out for her assistance to the poor. It is especially noted that she provided robes and other types of clothing for the widows (Acts 9:36, 39).

Christ also showed his concern for the sick. Illness, regardless of its length or severity, is never a pleasant experience. The intensity of the problem escalates when there is no one to care for the sick one or when the illness places the rest of the family in poverty. Then, as now, the family's monetary resources were often depleted in an attempt to find a cure. The woman with a bleeding problem who desired to touch Jesus' robe for healing had spent all she had (Luke 8:43).

Illness produces other difficulties as well. Since the activities of the sick are restricted, the ill person may become restless and even lapse into depression. In those dark hours the individual needs someone to be there, to encourage, to listen, and to understand.

The final need mentioned centers on those in prison. Not everyone in prison is a criminal. Some have been imprisoned for their faith. Others in the past have become inmates of a debtor's prison. Held in prison until their debts were paid, it became impossible for them to get out, since they could not work to make money to pay off their debts. Some are prisoners, however, because they have committed crimes. They too have needs. They especially need the comfort the message of the gospel brings.

Since the care of the hurting does not come easy for most people, there has to be a strong motive to make this more than a onetime event. Compassion makes the difference. It keeps the need before our eyes and may even drive us to keep on ministering to those hurting.

Which of the needs listed may be more difficult for you to meet?

B. The Recipient (vv. 37–40)

37. Then shall the righteous

answer him, saying, Lord, when saw we thee an hungred, and fed thee? or thirsty, and gave thee drink?

38. When saw we thee a stranger, and took thee in? or naked, and clothed thee?

39. Or when saw we thee sick, or in prison, and came unto thee?

40. And the King shall answer and say unto them, Verily I say unto you, Inasmuch as ye have done it unto one of the least of these my brethren, ye have done it unto me.

Those designated as the righteous will respond in wonderment. When were any of their actions directed toward the Lord? Apparently all their ministering appeared to be directed toward people. They didn't realize the eternal dimensions. The positive aspect of this limited perspective, however, is that the righteous can't be accused of working for a reward—that would be self–serving.

In response to the question of when they had done these things, the Lord will remind them that ministry to a brother or sister in Christ was ministry to the Lord himself. This should cause us to tear down the barriers between the secular and the sacred, the physical and the spiritual. Every action of the believer has eternal consequences.

II. RESPONDING TO NEED (Acts 6:1–7)

A. The Need (v. 1)

(Acts 6:1 is not included in the printed text.)

This sixth chapter of Acts introduces us to one of the problems of church growth along with the issue of partiality. The church was growing on a regular basis with an outreach to several major groups of Jews. Their major differences produced not only internal tension but also definite needs as one group's widows were being slighted.

The "Hebrews," in this context, were the Aramaic–speaking Jews who generally were natives of Palestine. Even before becoming part of the church, this group's main concern was to retain the Jewish language and customs in their religion. Once they were believers, their religious adherence changed, but they remained strongly Jewish. The "Grecians" were Greek–speaking Jews and generally were natives of countries other than Palestine. They reflected the language and customs of the lands in which they lived.

These cultural differences did not disappear simply because they had the commonality of Christ as Savior and Lord. Sadly, it continued and evidenced itself in the church's charitable care of its widows. Using the resources of a common treasury, the church aided those who were unable to care for themselves. Daily they received money or food as part of their provision. Without knowing any particulars, it is quite obvious there was an imbalance in the care giving. Widows of the Grecian group either did not receive the same amount or were skipped some days. Their cultural tension heightened, but even more important was the fact that there were widows who had a physical need which the church was not meeting. The leadership of the church faced both issues. How could the gap be closed and the widows cared for properly? They had to respond to this need immediately!

B. The Solution (vv. 2–4)

2. Then the twelve called the multitude of the disciples unto them, and said, It is not reason that we should leave the word of God, and serve tables.

3. Wherefore, brethren, look ye out among you seven men of honest report, full of the Holy Ghost and wisdom, whom we may appoint over this business.

4. But we will give ourselves continually to prayer, and to the ministry of the word.

Informal government under the leadership of the Twelve dealt with this situation. All believers came to hear how this problem could be overcome. Since it was a public matter to the church, they solved it in the same manner. Also they are to be commended because they did not allow time to go by and the murmuring to escalate. After everybody had gathered, the Twelve gave their decision.

Here was a situation in which the leadership made clear–cut decisions that enabled the need to be met, caused the murmuring to cease, and helped the church to grow. They projected a philosophy of ministry that allowed more people to share in the total work of the church. This type of wisdom came from the Holy Spirit's guidance. They weren't experienced administrators, but they understood the priority of their ministerial calling.

The disciples' choosing not to divide their public ministry with social actions doesn't mean they felt they were above the task. Nor does their choosing not to be personally involved in "serving tables" make such service a second–class task. Instead they understood that the designated leaders of an organization do not have time to have a hands–on approach to every situation. There are many gifted and talented people who have a personal passion for the mundane tasks of caring for the needs of people. They need to be given the opportunity to serve God and their fellow believers.

Another interesting principle came from the means used by the apostles to select workers. Instead of naming the individuals who were to serve, they entrusted this task to the people. Each of them would have an opportunity for input—thus demonstrating the ability of the body of believers to analyze and choose workers. Leaders aren't the only ones with wisdom and insight.

It is of interest that this meeting offered no advice about the undercurrent of disagreement between the two groups. Why didn't they face the issue head–on? Why didn't they direct both groups to get their act together by accepting each other and go on? It's rather simple. You can't legislate unity! You can't force people to put down decades of prejudice and be in harmony overnight. Unity comes through a moving of the Holy Spirit which draws each side together in the bonds of Christian love. It takes time and a conscious effort to grow in all the dimensions of God's grace. Knowing this, the apostolic leadership offered a solution which both eased the tension and met the need.

The believers were directed to select seven men to administer this social ministry. Instead of presenting possible names, they listed personal characteristics that needed to be evident in each applicant. There are only three, but each one designates a special area: First, being of "honest report" speaks of one's reputation. They were to be known for their just dealings. Prejudice, partiality, and personal greediness had no part in their lifestyle. Second, they were to be "full of the Holy Ghost." It means they not only had received the baptism of the Holy Spirit but were continuing to walk in the Spirit. Third, they were to be "full of wisdom." Wisdom enables a person to have understanding and insight and thus make right decisions.

What can local churches learn from this event about solving problems and selecting leaders?

C. The Selection (vv. 5–7)

(Acts 6:5, 6 is not included in the printed text.)

7. And the word of God increased; and the number of the disciples multiplied in Jerusalem greatly; and a great company of the priests were obedient to the faith.

Approving of their leadership's decision, the gathered disciples selected seven men who met the three–point criterion. Of the seven on the list, only two have any descriptions included. It is of interest that all seven have Greek names. Those widows who were being slighted would be served well. Six of them were Jewish by birth; however, Nicholas was a Gentile who had become a Jewish proselyte and later a believer. Their selection for this service doesn't mean they weren't involved in preaching or teaching. It simply designates a principal area of responsibility and ministry. Stephen's was "a man full of faith and of the Holy Ghost," a minister whose martyrdom stands out in the early church record (Acts 7).

Even though no title is given for the position or office of these seven men, they are frequently referred to as the seven deacons. Their responsibilities were very similar to the tasks of those later called deacons. These men daily served and ministered to the widows. The word *deacon* in the Greek implied service.

Verse 6 describes a formal setting forth of these men to their task. The seven were taken to the Twelve, who prayed for them and then followed the prayer with the ceremonial laying on of hands. In the Old Testament the laying on of hands indicated the bestowing of a blessing, a statement of identification, or the commissioning of a successor (see Genesis 48:13, 14; Leviticus 1:4; 3:2; Numbers 27:23). More than likely, the laying on of hands here represented their commissioning to fulfill a new role (office) in the church as part of ministering to the hurting.

Was the solution and selection successful? Definitely yes! Verse 7 describes a thriving ministry of the Word and a multiplying congregation. This would not be impossible if the church body itself were torn with divisions and the needs of the members disregarded. By caring for the body of believers, they were enabled to continue outreach and to experience both spiritual and numerical growth. The church never goes wrong when it responds to the needs of hurting believers regardless of the type of hurt. What better way to witness to the world of the love for God and for one another?

III. PRACTICAL SERVICE (James 1:27; 2:14–17)

A. Pure Religion (1:27)

27. Pure religion and undefiled before God and the Father is this, To visit the fatherless and widows in their affliction, and to keep himself unspotted from the world.

James helps us maintain balance and perspective in the Christian life. He reminds us that the true test of spirituality isn't designed by us humans. God determines the standards for acceptable living as a believer. And ministry to others stands forth as one of the two major dimensions.

Verse 27 places two criteria for our consideration. To possess a religious experience or spiritual relationship with God, we have to understand two key words: *ministry* and *separation*. Those of us raised in traditional Pentecostalism understand the aspect of *separation*. A repeated emphasis on holiness and sanctification was a constant part of the church's vocabulary and exhortation. We also are well acquainted with the word *ministry*. But usually we tend to see it in spiritual matters rather than physical care. This passage shakes our usual concept. It forces us to look at the total concept of ministry. We aren't given the luxury of ministering only to the soul.

James was very specific in naming hurting individuals who need our ministrations. He selected two related groups who are to be first on the believer's care list—orphans and widows. Why orphans? They are immature humans incapable of providing for themselves. Children are a blessing from God. When their parents are taken away, for whatever reason, others need to step in and provide adult protection and direction. They need to know the love of God through an adult and have someone to turn to in times of doubt or crisis.

Why widows? Older children have the responsibility of providing for their parents. That was true within Judaism as well as some of the other ethnic groups. But there are some situations in which the widow has only small children, has no children, or has outlived the rest of her family. Also, there are widows who have been rejected by their families due to their Christian commitment. In all of these situations, the widows of that day had very few options for a means of support.

James reminds all of us that being part of the family of God includes both benefits and responsibilities. Being brothers and sisters in Christ is more than titles used in greetings. There are both bonds and responsibilities to this relationship.

B. Working Faith (2:14–17)

14. What doth it profit, my brethren, though a man say he hath faith, and have not works? can faith save him?

15. If a brother or sister be naked, and destitute of daily food,

16. And one of you say unto them, Depart in peace, be ye warmed and filled; notwithstanding ye give them not those things which are needful to the body; what doth it profit?

17. Even so faith, if it hath not works, is dead, being alone.

As already pointed out in a previous lesson, this second chapter of James deals with the relationship between faith and works. They aren't opposites; they are partners. Without the other, each becomes void. Salvation comes by faith alone. But then, the continuing evidence of that faith is our lifestyle of works and attitudes. The author pointed this out very clearly in verse 14. Faith and works go hand in hand. Salvation begins with our faith. Faith alone places us in a right relationship with our heavenly Father. That faith continues throughout our life in Christ. We exhibit a constant trust, confidence, and obedience toward our Savior and Lord. At the same time this faith evidences itself in very visible, tangible actions—which are our works.

Those living in the Spirit can't simply walk past situations in which people are hurting. They must stop and put their faith in Christ into action for both fellow believers and unbelievers. Words of comfort and direction for the hurting are necessary, but words of comfort and direction are not enough when physical responses are needed. Individuals needing clothes for warmth and food for hunger appreciate kind words; but without other provisions, words alone are not beneficial, and may even be painful to the hearer. Words alone may only appear hypocritical. If the speaker truly cares, he will also attempt to provide food and clothing. Pious words alone leave a person still cold and still hungry.

It is heartless to speak words of warmth and peace without materially providing the necessities of life to the hurting. On many occasions Charles Schultz includes this scriptural concept in his cartoon strip, "Peanuts." One of my favorites has Charlie Brown bundled up and ice skating. He falls down, and because of all the wraps he can't get up. His friends, led by Lucy, come by to check on his condition. After visiting with him they begin to leave. As they do Lucy usually says something like "Be warmed, Charlie Brown." But nothing changes; he still lies helplessly on the cold ice.

The severity of the gap between professed faith and putting faith into action (works) cannot be overlooked. Faith can't continue to exist without works. Neither works nor faith are sufficient alone—each must be accompanied by the other.

One of the miracle accounts in Acts demonstrates an example of faith and works. About to go into the Temple, Peter and John encountered a lame man begging. These two disciples were men of faith and knew there was healing available. They commanded the man to rise and walk. But they didn't stop there. Peter took the man by the right hand and lifted him up, and then the healing occurred (3:1–7). The disciples exhibited an abundance of faith, and along with it a willingness to extend a helping hand.

Intercessory prayer is not enough when we have the resources to minister to the hurting ourselves. True spiritual service includes both our prayers and our helping hands. True spirituality evidences itself in practical service.

What are some ways that a local church as a body can demonstrate a working faith?

REVIEW QUESTIONS

1. What are the six social concerns Jesus addressed in Matthew 25?

2. What was the basic problem between the Hebrews and the Grecian Jews?

3. What would be a benefit of allowing the people to select the men responsible for the charitable disbursements?

GOLDEN TEXT HOMILY

"INASMUCH AS YE HAVE DONE IT UNTO ONE OF THE LEAST OF THESE MY BRETHREN, YE HAVE DONE IT UNTO ME" (Matthew 25:40).

What will it be like to stand before the Lord and be judged for our total being? It's difficult to describe for several reasons. First, our human finiteness makes it impossible to comprehend the glory and majesty of God himself. Second, it is also impossible to comprehend that our whole life will be scanned for its righteousness. It's this last one that comes to our attention in Matthew 25:40.

It is easy to talk about our heart being right with God. But do we recognize this also includes our actions toward individuals we don't even know? Are we aware that how we treat the unfortunate of this world will impact our status at the time of judgment? In the previous verses Jesus spoke of the hungry and thirsty, the homeless, the naked, the sick, and those in prison. The bottom line is this: Our social concern for those less fortunate and in need will impact our final judgment.

Here are some questions for our personal consideration:

1. Have I ever roughly dismissed the beggar who extends a cup for my donation?

2. Have I ever offered coins to the needy in a condescending manner?

3. Do I offer donations of clothing and furniture to charitable organizations for the tax deduction?

4. Do I avoid visiting those in prison or in hospitals and nursing homes?

All of this returns us to the second greatest commandment: We are to love our neighbors as ourselves. From the story of the Good Samaritan we know this includes anyone in need that we encounter. When we fail to meet the needs of others, we fail in the sight of God. It is as though He were in need and we passed Him by.—**Jerald Daffe, D.Min., Chairman, Bible and Christian Ministries, Lee College, Cleveland, Tennessee**

SENTENCE SERMONS

THE CHRISTIAN REFLECTS CHRIST by reaching out to the hurting.

—Selected

COMPASSION IS a sign of a truly great and generous heart.

—Megiddo Message

CHRISTIANITY DEMANDS a level of caring that transcends human inclination.

—Erwin W. Lutzer

DAILY BIBLE READINGS

M. Meeting the Need.
2 Kings 4:1–7

T. Cry of the Hurting.
Jeremiah 8:18–22

W. Who Is My Neighbor?
Luke 10:25–37

T. Giving What We Have.
Acts 3:1–10

F. Motive for Ministry.
1 Corinthians 13:1–8

S. Praying for One Another.
James 5:13–16

Restoring Those Who Fail

Study Text: Matthew 18:15–17; Galatians 6:1–10; James 5:19, 20

Objective: To develop a sensitivity to those who fail and seek to restore them.

Golden Text: "If a man be overtaken in a fault, ye which are spiritual, restore such an one in the spirit of meekness" (Galatians 6:1).

Central Truth: The church should act to restore those who have fallen.

Evangelism Emphasis: Restoration of the fallen is a witness to the unsaved.

PRINTED TEXT

Matthew 18:15. Moreover if thy brother shall trespass against thee, go and tell him his fault between thee and him alone: if he shall hear thee, thou hast gained thy brother.

16. But if he will not hear thee, then take with thee one or two more, that in the mouth of two or three witnesses every word may be established.

17. And if he shall neglect to hear them, tell it unto the church: but if he neglect to hear the church, let him be unto thee as an heathen man and a publican.

Galatians 6:1. Brethren, if a man be overtaken in a fault, ye which are spiritual, restore such an one in the spirit of meekness; considering thyself, lest thou also be tempted.

2. Bear ye one another's burdens, and so fulfil the law of Christ.

3. For if a man think himself to be something, when he is nothing, he deceiveth himself.

4. But let every man prove his own work, and then shall he have rejoicing in himself alone, and not in another.

5. For every man shall bear his own burden.

6. Let him that is taught in the word communicate unto him that teacheth in all good things.

7. Be not deceived; God is not mocked: for whatsoever a man soweth, that shall he also reap.

8. For he that soweth to his flesh shall of the flesh reap corruption; but he that soweth to the Spirit shall of the Spirit reap life everlasting.

9. And let us not be weary in well doing: for in due season we shall reap, if we faint not.

10. As we have therefore opportunity, let us do good unto all men, especially unto them who are of the household of faith.

James 5:19. Brethren, if any of you do err from the truth, and one convert him;

20. Let him know, that he which converteth the sinner from the error of his way shall save a soul from death, and shall hide a multitude of sins.

LESSON OUTLINE

I. PROCEDURE FOR RESTORING
   A. Personal Confrontation
   B. Several Witnesses
   C. Entire Body
II. ATTITUDE IN RESTORING
   A. Gentleness
   B. Carrying
   C. Testing
   D. Avoiding
   E. Goodness
III. REWARD FOR RESTORING
   A. The Rescue
   B. The Life

LESSON EXPOSITION

INTRODUCTION

Today's lesson brings us face-to-face with a topic that is receiving greater consideration than in many previous decades. Many denominations are wrestling with the subject of reconciliation, especially as it applies to "fallen" ministers. Does moral failure disqualify a person from future ministry in the local church? If we believe in restoration, what process and time limits need to be followed?

Too frequently the church is ready to discard the believer who has sinned while avidly promoting the winning of the "lost" to Christ. That seems inconsistent. In a private paper titled "After Moral Failure (Forgiveness vs. Ministerial Fitness)," Dr. R. Hollis Gause comments on this conflicting action: "It is a strange thing that a church that has been famous for its rescue of the debauched of the world does not have an equal fame for the rescue of its own who have failed."

Let's consider some reasons for our failure to achieve restoration. We must begin with the lack of forgiveness. We desire God's forgiveness when we sin. We expect Him to be merciful and restore us to fellowship with Him. But if we choose not to forgive others for their sin, we can't expect God's forgiveness either. "But if ye forgive not men their trespasses, neither will your Father forgive your trespasses" (Matthew 6:15).

Second, the uncertainty of how to approach a situation for the purpose of restoration may be another contributing factor. What do we say? Is there a specific process? How long should the process take? It may seem easier to just leave the task to other believers. Congregations must have genuine concern for their members and actively try to help them in times of failure.

Third, we may fear the anger and rejection of a brother or sister when confronted. But we must not allow fear to paralyze us into inactivity.

Fourth, it's vital to consider our love for one another. Can we really claim to love one another and not come to the rescue when a brother or sister falls into sin? First Corinthians 13:5, 6 reads, "[Love] is not rude, it is not self-seeking, it is not easily angered, it keeps no record of wrongs. Love does not delight in evil but rejoices with the truth" (*NIV*).

Fifth, consideration needs to be given to our church traditions. Some congregations, in their attempt to maintain holiness, neglect to acknowledge that individuals may easily stray from the righteous path when they fail to walk in the Spirit. Even good people who love God may succumb to temptation and commit sin. Do they deserve to be discarded? Let's personalize it. Do we deserve to be discarded by the body of believers when we sin?

This lesson produces many questions, but it also takes us through the basic biblical teachings on restoration. Included are comments on the attitudes and rewards of restoration along with the procedures necessary to accomplish them.

I. PROCEDURE FOR RESTORING (Matthew 18:15–17)

A. Personal Confrontation (v. 15)

15. Moreover if thy brother shall trespass against thee, go and tell him his fault between thee and him alone: if he shall hear thee, thou hast gained thy brother.

The impact of these verses on restoration are heightened by considering the context of this chapter. Jesus was asked by His disciples, "Who is the greatest in the kingdom of heaven?" (v. 1). Setting a child in the middle of them He proceeded to answer the question and then expanded it to include the concept of restoration. Verse 12 paints a pastoral picture to emphasize both the risk and the importance of rescuing one even when a large group remains. When a shepherd leaves the entire flock to find the one straying, it speaks of compassion, love, and responsibility. But he doesn't leave the others unguarded and unprovided for. They stay safely in the fold while he makes the treacherous trip to the mountains. The shepherd isn't content to simply keep the 99 sheep. He wants all 100 to remain within his nurture and safety.

Verse 14 emphasizes that the heavenly Father wants the very same for His children. He isn't willing for even one to be lost from His care. That brings the concept of restoration back to us. Each of us as individual believers should see ourselves as being part of the process. Restoration isn't just the responsibility of the pastor and the leaders in the church.

The first step in restoration is personal confrontation. When it becomes evident that a brother or sister is involved in sin, we have an obligation to discuss the situation with the one who has erred. Confrontation should be gentle, not authoritarian, demanding, or condemning. Restoration means loving someone so much that you, in Christian concern, inquire about his straying actions. Confrontation must be done in private. No one else needs to know what you are discussing. This avoids embarrassment. It's just between the faltering, failing believer who is caught in sin and a brother or sister who desperately wants to see that individual restored.

When we confront these individuals, it is imperative to be able to show them how their action contradicts life in Christ. Read to them from the Word what God says. His Word pierces where we can't. Never become argumentative. That often becomes hopeless wrangling and defeats the purpose of the confrontation. We want them to listen to us. That means presenting the Bible's views in such a manner that they will give us their attention and return to fellowship with God.

One final aspect of this verse deserves attention. Some manuscripts include the words "against you," thus reading, "If your brother sins against you." Other manuscripts do not include the words "against you." Without these two words, the verse speaks more broadly of restoration, which forces all of us to feel a responsibility toward any believer who becomes entangled in sin whether or not the sinful acts affect us directly.

How can we encourage believers to become active in restoring faltering believers?

B. Several Witnesses (v. 16)

16. But if he will not hear thee, then take with thee one or two more, that in the mouth of two or three witnesses every word may be established.

There is more than one step to be taken if the first encounter is not successful. Attempts at restoration can't be a "one strike and you're out" game. Genuine love doesn't give up so easily or so quickly. Love looks for ways to bring about the desired result.

When a brother or sister rejects our attempt at restoration, it may be that the individual wants the freedom to follow self–determined concepts of right and wrong rather than be subject to God's directions. Individuals' egocentrism places them on a pedestal with God himself. Some people find it difficult to admit to themselves or to others that they have sinned. Others have simply selected a path of sin and refuse to repent of it.

Jesus teaches us to establish the truth in the mouth of two or three witnesses. Deuteronomy 19:15 provides the background: "One witness shall not rise up against a man for any iniquity, or for any sin, in any sin that he sinneth: at the mouth of two witnesses, or at the mouth of three witnesses, shall the matter be established." This pattern not only provides moral support for those confronting the sinning believer, but it also provides greater reliability and accountability concerning the account of what took place during the confrontation. When two or three people affirm a particular action, it is much more difficult to deny its reality and ignore their concern. This also confirms that the initial confrontation was in order.

The individuals selected to go with the one who made the initial confrontation must be believers who also reflect the proper attitudes of restoration, which will be covered in section two of the lesson. Otherwise, this attempt will be no more successful than the first one.

C. Entire Body (v. 17)

17. And if he shall neglect to hear them, tell it unto the church: but if he neglect to hear the church, let him be unto thee as an heathen man and a publican.

Now we face an extremely difficult step. When the person refuses the concern and reconciling attempts of the church, this individual cannot be allowed the luxury of remaining without discipline within the body. Love for the erring individual requires correction. Equally important is the integrity of the whole body. How can the church witness to sinners and call for their repentance if it allows unrepentant sin to remain within? This apparent hypocrisy can quickly become a major hindrance to evangelism. Practicing what we preach includes the area of discipline.

One reason for the difficulty of this step of disfellowshipping, is the process of taking the situation before the church. What this means varies according to the polity (government) of the denomination or individual church. In some situations it means the person appears only before the leadership. In others the breach of conduct must be discussed before the assembled membership. Regardless of the method used, the supervising body who controls membership must take action. Keep in mind there is still opportunity, even in this last step, for repentance and reconciliation.

Very few churches actively pursue this third step of reconciliation. Some fear legalism to the point of neglecting their responsibility. Others allow a misconception of love and grace to overcome the need for accountability. Sadly, many congregations fail in this step because they are not convinced of the need to "go that far." The abundance of lawsuits against churches for almost any reason could possibly be another factor. This is such a touchy issue now that when a member is disfellowshipped, the wording needs to be in the general terms such as "breaking the church's covenant," in order to lessen the church's possibility of being charged with slander.

What are the practical ramifications of this step? First, it removes the failing individual from identification with the church. This individual may still attend services but has no rights of membership, nor can she/he hold any office. Second, if the individual later repents and requests membership, the believers need to restore the repentant one. Ascending to leadership also is possible after a period of proving commitment to Christ and the church. Third, it announces to the entire body that continued unconfessed sin, along with unchristian behavior, will not be tolerated within the membership. Fourth, we recognize that discipline needs to be evident in order to truly claim to be the body of Christ.

A biblical study of disfellowshipping a member and then bringing him back into the fellowship of the church can be found in Paul's epistles to the Corinthians. The severity of the offense demands excommunication or disfellowshipping (1 Corinthians 5). But when he changes his lifestyle and repents, the church is directed to welcome him back (2 Corinthians 2).

II. ATTITUDE IN RESTORING (Galatians 6:1–10)

A. Gentleness (v. 1)

1. Brethren, if a man be overtaken in a fault, ye which are spiritual, restore such an one in the spirit of meekness; considering thyself, lest thou also be tempted.

This section of the lesson deals with the people who are attempting to restore a fallen brother or sister. They must exhibit some very specific Christian attributes to qualify for this task. It definitely isn't a task for a novice or for the long–term believer who has chosen not to grow or exhibit the fruit of the Spirit. Writing to the Galatians, Paul stated that spiritual maturity is the greatest qualification necessary for those who are involved in reconciling the fallen. It would be easy to allow a debate over the definition of *spirituality* to erupt here. But it is more beneficial to consider instead a number of the attitudes that identify the mature believer.

He began with *gentleness* (KJV, *meekness*). When attempting to restore someone, the individual who is zealous against sin may approach the offending one in a demanding or condemning manner. Instead of exhibiting contrition, however, the one the church is trying to restore may be angry or hurt, which defeats the intended result. This demanding situation requires a spirit of gentleness such as a nurse or a mother exhibits toward her disobedient children. Gentleness helps us to come as friends rather than inquisitors. Remember, if we drive them further from Christ and the church, we too have sinned!

B. Carrying (vv. 2, 5)

2. Bear ye one another's burdens, and so fulfil the law of Christ.

5. For every man shall bear his own burden.

We often speak of a caring attitude, but these verses call for a carrying attitude—bearing a load or burden.

These verses bring us to the interdependence of the body of Christ. Certain dimensions of our individuality and their distinct responsibilities are never lost. Yet at the same time mature believers understand the sharing concept, which goes beyond blessings to include burdens. That is the beauty and strength of being part of the body of Christ. We suffer together. We rejoice together. We carry each other in times of weakness. We help to carry a brother's sins as we intercede for him. Moses said, "Yet now, if thou wilt forgive their sin—; and if not, blot me, I pray thee, out of thy book which thou hast written" (Exodus 32:32). Righteous Ezra interceded, "O my God, I am ashamed and blush to lift up my face to thee, my God: for our iniquities are increased over our head, and our trespass is grown up unto the heavens" (Ezra 9:6).

Even in this interdependence there are some responsibilities which only the individual can bear. It's similar to the soldier. Each carries his individual pack or gear. The believer who works to restore the failing brother needs to understand these two distinctives: You can identify with and intercede for that brother, but it is the sole responsibility of the sinner to ask for God's forgiveness. No one can do that for him.

Usually we are willing to carry our own burden (v. 5), but it is more difficult to carry someone else's burden (v. 2). Patiently we are to listen, to value, and to invest even when our caring and carrying seem to be bearing no fruit in the person's life. We are to continue to carry the burden even through repeated failures. This attitude breaks many personal barriers and opens the door for restoration to Christ and the body of believers.

C. Testing (vv. 3, 4, 6)

3. For if a man think himself to be something, when he is nothing, he deceiveth himself.

4. But let every man prove his own work, and then shall he have rejoicing in himself alone, and not in another.

6. Let him that is taught in the word communicate unto him that teacheth in all good things.

Even while recognizing the sins of others and attempting to restore them to fellowship, the mature believer must continue his own self–examination. This serves a twofold purpose. The first is to keep one from assuming a hypocritical concept of spiritual superiority. When we see the weaknesses and failures that led others to sin, it is often easy to assume we are above that and feel that it could never happen to us. Deception becomes the partner of feelings of superiority. Self–pride automatically demonstrates some critical flaws in ourselves and indicates that we are not walking in the Spirit. Not one of us is a super–Christian. It is only through the grace of God and the continuing empowerment of His Spirit that we successfully overcome sin.

The second purpose for self–examination is the need for self–appreciation. On the one hand, we are to practice self–denial. But on the other hand, we must appreciate our strengths and our accomplishments through Jesus Christ. There is no benefit in deriding and devaluing ourselves unnecessarily. When we learn to better appreciate our God–given natural talents and spiritual gifts, we can rejoice in what God continues to do in our lives.

The emphasis of verse 6 is the material support of those who serve the church through the ministry of teaching. A practical application can be found within the aspect of testing. Can a believer qualify as mature and be a restorer of others if he/she fails in the support of those who are their spiritual teachers? The implied answer is no. The verse reminds us of the totality of our responsibility as believers.

What are some practical suggestions for continued self–examination?

D. Avoiding (vv. 7, 8)

7. Be not deceived; God is not mocked: for whatsoever a man soweth, that shall he also reap.

8. For he that soweth to his flesh shall of the flesh reap corruption; but he that soweth to the Spirit shall of the Spirit reap life everlasting.

These verses frequently are referred to as the law of the harvest. It reminds us of the choices we have, depending on what type of spiritual harvest we choose to reap. Just as a farmer selects his harvest on the basis of the seed sown, so do we as believers know that the seeds we sow in life will decide our eternal reward.

We are reminded to "be not deceived." There is no way we can sow to the flesh (the carnal and sensual) and harvest the fruit of the Spirit. Those who believe and practice living in this manner hide themselves in the darkness of deception.

The attitude of avoiding isn't just a negative legalistic concept. But rather, to avoid wrong is to choose the right (the spiritual) while turning from the wrong (the fleshly). However, life in Christ requires spiritual restrictions in order that we may remain healthy and vibrant. Mature believers understand this principle of avoiding. They know it equips them for service now and entitles them to heavenly rewards. No one can successfully operate as a restorer of the fallen and continue in sin himself or constantly lean away from the good and toward the wrong.

E. Goodness (vv. 9, 10)

9. And let us not be weary in well doing: for in due season we shall reap, if we faint not.

10. As we have therefore opportunity, let us do good unto all men, especially unto them who are of the household of faith.

Here in verse 9 we explore one of those special verses of comfort and direction which reminds us of the need to endure and not to let the fatigue of the moment keep us from reaping the rewards of spiritual service. This applies very specifically to the task of restoration. It can be discouraging when those confronted deny their sin even though it is very visible. It also can be discouraging when an individual continues to be a repeat offender—when you help one to be restored to the fellowship of the body only to see him stray again.

Though fatigued for doing what is good, we must remember the underlying characteristic is *goodness*. Doing good is to flow forth from believers. This isn't to be seen as self–righteousness that is evident in words only, for goodness comes in the form of genuine words of encouragement and actions that edify and encourage spiritual growth. Goodness is words of comfort to the hurting, clothing for the naked, food for the hungry, shelter for the homeless, and jobs for the unemployed.

Goodness enables a believer to continue the process of restoration, even when the fallen brother or sister resists and other Christians question the motives. Goodness desires complete restoration and provides the incentive to continue.

III. REWARD FOR RESTORING (James 5:19, 20)

A. The Rescue (v. 19)

19. Brethren, if any of you do err from the truth, and one convert him.

In this fifth chapter of James a variety of healings are covered. Verses 13–16 deal with physical healing. Those who are ill need only call for the elders and have them pray. Prayer must be in faith and in conjunction with the confession of sins. The prayers of the righteous are both powerful and effective. When God wills to intervene and the people meet the qualifications, miraculous healings can be expected.

Verses 17 and 18 show a totally different type of intervention. They take us to the story of Elijah and his praying that there would be no rain. For the next three and one–half years a drought plagued the land of Israel. Then through a second prayer of the prophet, the climatic conditions were healed. The earth once again blossomed and bore fruit.

Then as James brought his

epistle to a close, he included the spiritual healing of restoration. Before that can happen, however, someone has to be willing to initiate the rescue. Some believer needs to recognize that this person is wandering away from the faith. Somebody must intercept the wandering one and plead for a change of direction. The *New International Version* renders verse 19 as follows: "My brothers, if one of you should wander from the truth and someone should bring him back. . . ."

Restoration is no easy task. Bringing backsliders back to God begins with the courage to confront them. This includes taking the time to persuade them of the error of their ways in the light of the Scripture. And as previously mentioned, sometimes the task includes incorporating the assistance of other believers. There's no doubt that restoration is not a job for the weak and inconsistent. Only the spiritually mature will stick with it to the end.

B. The Life (v. 20)

20. Let him know, that he which converteth the sinner from the error of his way shall save a soul from death, and shall hide a multitude of sins.

What's the bottom line? What is the reward for putting forth the effort to rescue a straying believer?

Here we come face–to–face with the true nature of reward. Usually we think of rewards in terms of monetary honorariums, trophies, plaques, and testimonials of various kinds. There is, however, another type of reward—the satisfaction of knowing you made a difference in someone's life and that through your intercession that person returned to the path of righteousness and truth. Restoring those who are drifting away really means rescuing them from spiritual death and eternal punishment.

In verse 20 a new importance is given to the restoration of wandering believers. Without restoration there is no hope and no joyous future. Love enables the Christian worker to look beyond visible sins to what the grace of God will do through repentance.

A reward for the restorers rests in knowing they have had a hand in renewing a brother or sister to the spiritual life.

How can we assist believers to understand the value of a restored believer?

REVIEW QUESTIONS

1. What should be the motivation for restoration?
2. What does it mean, in practical terms, to bring someone before the church?
3. List the five things necessary in restoring?
4. What is the twofold purpose of self–examination?
5. What is the future of the unrestored backslidden believer?

DAILY BIBLE READINGS

M. Sin Confronted.
2 Samuel 12:1–13
T. Prayer for Restoration.
Psalm 51:1–12
W. Christ Denied.
Luke 22:54–62
T. Renewed Ministry.
John 21:7–19
F. Repentance Refused.
Acts 5:1–11
S. Hope for Those Who Fail.
1 John 1:6 through 2:2

Giving to Help Others

Study Text: Deuteronomy 15:7, 8; Acts 20:35; 2 Corinthians 8:8–15; 9:6–13; 1 John 3:16–18

Objective: To discover the joy of giving and commit ourselves to meeting the needs of others.

Golden Text: "Let us not love in word, neither in tongue; but in deed and in truth" (1 John 3:18).

Central Truth: God's love motivates believers to give to others.

Evangelism Emphasis: The believer must be willing to give unselfishly to reach the lost.

PRINTED TEXT

Acts 20:35. I have shewed you all things, how that so labouring ye ought to support the weak, and to remember the words of the Lord Jesus, how he said, It is more blessed to give than to receive.

2 Corinthians 8:12. For if there be first a willing mind, it is accepted according to that a man hath, and not according to that he hath not.

13. For I mean not that other men be eased, and ye burdened:

14. But by an equality, that now at this time your abundance may be a supply for their want, that their abundance also may be a supply for your want: that there may be equality:

15. As it is written, He that had gathered much had nothing over; and he that had gathered little had no lack.

9:6. But this I say, He which soweth sparingly shall reap also sparingly; and he which soweth bountifully shall reap also bountifully.

7. Every man according as he purposeth in his heart, so let him give; not grudgingly, or of necessity: for God loveth a cheerful giver.

8. And God is able to make all grace abound toward you; that ye, always having all sufficiency in all things, may abound to every good work:

9. (As it is written, He hath dispersed abroad; he hath given to the poor: his righteousness remaineth for ever.

10. Now he that ministereth seed to the sower both minister bread for your food, and multiply your seed sown, and increase the fruits of your righteousness.)

Deuteronomy 15:7. If there be among you a poor man of one of thy brethren within any of thy gates in thy land which the Lord thy God giveth thee, thou shalt not harden thine heart, nor shut thine hand for thy poor brother:

8. But thou shalt open thine hand wide unto him, and shalt surely lend him sufficient for his need, in that which he wanteth.

1 John 3:16. Hereby perceive we the love of God, because he laid down his life for us: and we ought to lay down our lives for the brethren.

17. But whoso hath this world's good, and seeth his brother have need, and shutteth up his bowels of compassion from him, how dwelleth the love of God in him?

18. My little children, let us not love in word, neither in tongue; but in deed and in truth.

LESSON OUTLINE

I. ATTITUDE IN GIVING
   A. Christlikeness
   B. Willingness
   C. Equality

II. GENEROSITY ENCOURAGED
   A. Sowing Principle
   B. Thanksgiving Expressed

III. LOVE IN ACTION
   A. Freedom in Love
   B. Test of Love

LESSON EXPOSITION

INTRODUCTION

Ministering to one another includes our whole being and takes a variety of forms. The importance of the heart, our inner being, stood out in lesson 9. Lesson 10 reminded us of those who needed our help. Lesson 11 walked us through the ministry of restoring fallen brethren. And now in lesson 12 we face the material dimension. Ministering to the hurts of others includes investing our money and possessions so that needs can be met. It means we must be ready to give. Talking about doing something is necessary for motivation, but it's only when our checkbooks become involved that changes take place.

Today's lesson deals with believers' giving to meet the needs of fellow believers they haven't even met. And if that is an obligation, then how much more is the obligation increased in regard to those in need in our own congregations! How can we be compassionate to those in need in distant lands while overlooking those who are our "next–door" neighbors? When this occurs, it reflects a disorder or imbalance. Even well–intentioned believers may become caught in this inconsistency.

In studying the various biblical characters we tend to emphasize major points such as position, possessions, and penance. For example, we speak of Saul's position as the first king of Israel, Abraham's wealth in terms of animals and servants, and David's repentance as recorded in Psalm 51. But how often do we overlook those actions that are insignificant on a resume but have vital importance to those in need?

Providing financial assistance to the needy raises some questions. Should we give the money directly to the needy? Who should determine the amount of the need? Should the local church be the clearing agency for all financial help to the needy? What about working through agencies which aren't church–related? How long should you continue helping the needy if they make no attempt on their own to better their conditions even though they are capable of doing so?

These are reasonable questions for consideration, but they can sidetrack the potential donor from doing anything at all until coming to a definite conclusion on them. In some cases, by that time it may be too late to help. When that occurs, it seems only reasonable to believe we have sinned by virtue of our delay. Any form of hesitation which compounds or lengthens hurting and suffering can never be brushed off as "just one of those things." We must identify it as the sin it is.

In the past several decades, we Pentecostals have become much more involved in helping the hungry, the homeless, and the aged. An increasing number of local churches have food pantries and benevolence funds, which is commendable. The success of these programs is dependent largely upon the financial gifts of individuals and families.

Before looking at the individual passages, one other aspect of giving needs to be raised in the introduction—generosity. When generosity provides the foundation for giving, then amount and timing become moot points. Generosity motivated by love always fills the gaps of need. Then there is no need for repeated calls to help the suffering and hurting. Simply making a need known produces the appropriate response where there is generosity.

I. ATTITUDE IN GIVING (Acts 20:35; 2 Corinthians 8:8–15)

A. Christlikeness (Acts 20:35; 2 Corinthians 8:8, 9)

(2 Corinthians 8:8, 9 is not included in the printed text.)

Acts 20:35. I have shewed you all things, how that so labouring ye ought to support the weak, and to remember the words of the Lord Jesus, how he said, It is more blessed to give than to receive.

Once again we are reminded of Christ's example. He set the standard we are to follow. The joy of being Christlike increases as we recognize He not only spoke the words but also demonstrated how to live them. He asks nothing of us He hasn't already completed while living in human flesh.

Acts 20:35 is the conclusion of Paul's address to the Ephesian elders. Hurrying to arrive in Jerusalem for the Day of Pentecost, he chose not to stop in Ephesus. Still wanting to speak to the leaders of the Ephesian church, he called them to join him in Miletus. Following his normal pattern, Paul spoke first of his ministry in Asia. Then he moved to the uncertainty of the future. There's no doubt he understood the difficulty of the future since the Holy Spirit had already warned him of arrest and incarceration (v. 23). He also knew he would not be able to see them again (v. 25).

Beginning with verse 28 Paul exhorted the Ephesian elders on a variety of areas, beginning with guarding themselves from false teachers and their destructive doctrines. He closed with the topic of financial ministry to the needy. His final statement quoted the words of Jesus: "It is more blessed to give than to receive." This lays the foundation for the entire discussion of giving.

Most of us enjoy receiving. Regardless of the size of the gift, we know it says someone is thinking of us and wants to show appreciation for us. But before we become so engrossed in being loved and cared for, the words of Jesus remind us of the blessedness of giving. To provide for another's needs far exceeds the joy of receiving. To be blessed carries the connotation of being praised. It reflects the highest good. But if we are motivated by praise, then we have missed the intent. We should want to give since it fulfills the teaching of Jesus our Savior and Lord.

The second dimension of a Christlike attitude appears in Philippians 2:5–8, as well as 2 Corinthians 8:8, 9. Paul described Christ's giving of Himself for us. The test of sincere love is our actions. Without actions, words are meaningless. The greatest expression of Christ's love came through His sacrificing the riches of divinity to put on the poverty of human flesh. What does this mean to us in practical application? Does it mean we are to sell everything we have and give to the needy? Maybe! God deals differently with different individuals. But at the least it teaches us to give for the purpose of enriching others. And the cost to us needs to be secondary in our thinking.

B. Willingness (2 Corinthians 8:10–12)

(2 Corinthians 8:10, 11 is not included in the printed text.)

12. For if there be first a willing mind, it is accepted according to that a man hath, and not according to that he hath not.

Tightfistedness is an unacceptable attitude on the part of believers toward giving. Neither are we simply to begin to give but then delay its completion. The Corinthian church, much to Paul's dismay, were demonstrating the latter action.

To fully understand these verses, the entire situation needs to be reviewed. Possibly due to drought or persecution, the believers in Palestine were in dire financial circumstances. Paul shared this need with various congregations in Galatia, Macedonia, and Achaia. At the end of his first letter to the Corinthians the apostle went so far as to provide a way their donations could be collected on a regular basis (16:1–3). According to verse 10 of our lesson text, this congregation's response deserved commendation. Not only did they identify with the need of their brethren and desire to help, but they were the first church to do so.

But what they did so well the first year didn't continue. In verse 11 Paul directed them to complete what they had started. He wanted them to balance their willingness with the completion of what they had started. They were cautioned, however, to give according to their ability to give. No one was expected to give beyond one's means. Neither does God require us to give beyond our means just because a need is great. He knows our ability. But if He directs us to a sum that appears exceptionally large, He will also enable us to fulfill our pledge.

The key Paul stressed to the church at Corinth centered on giving what they were able to give. Then their giving would be on a regular basis rather than sporadic. Even more important, if they gave according to what they were able, true willingness to help would remain. Verse 12 states this so clearly in one of the modern translations: "For if the willingness is there, the gift is acceptable according to what one has, not according to what he does not have" (*NIV*).

At the beginning of the chapter, Paul gave an example which illustrates this concept. Several congregations in Macedonia were identified for their willing, liberal giving in view of their poverty. The amount of their gift might have been smaller than what others gave; but in comparison to what they had, their gift vaulted them into the category of riches.

Isn't it amazing that the "widow's mites" and the pennies of the poor have consistently been the financial foundation of the church! They willingly give from their poverty, and it becomes the abundance which cares for believers and promotes the gospel.

How does a spirit of willingness become a part of the believer's giving?

C. Equality (2 Corinthians 8:13–15)

13. For I mean not that other men be eased, and ye burdened:

14. But by an equality, that now at this time your abundance may be a supply for their want, that their abundance also may be a supply for your want: that there may be equality:

15. As it is written, He that had gathered much had nothing over; and he that had gathered little had no lack.

Just to make sure no one missed the point and leveled a charge of unfairness, Paul inserted verse 13 as a qualifier. He wasn't suggesting that one believer be allowed to give less while more is required of another. He didn't want anyone to believe he was suggesting that one group of people be burdened while another slipped through without sacrifice. This also wasn't a guilt trip. The willingness of the Macedonians to give from their poverty wasn't intended to make the Corinthians feel they should give beyond their means. But neither did Paul afford them the opportunity to be slackers.

This brings the concept of equality into consideration. Equality isn't based on equal amounts being given but, rather, the ability of each to give. Those with an abundance will provide a larger amount in giving than those who have considerably less. Besides, at a later time in these Corinthians' lives, they might be the ones in need. And because of God's blessings, those previously in poverty might be the ones who out of their abundance would then be able to give. It balances out.

Verse 15 further demonstrates equality. It describes God's provision of manna for the Israelites while in the wilderness (Exodus 16:18). In response to their grumbling over the food, God sent an abundance of quail. He also provided manna for them every morning, six mornings a week. The phenomenon of this provision is its equality for all. Those who gathered a great deal of manna didn't cause anyone else to have less. And those who gathered little had sufficient.

Paul wanted these believers to understand equality in the same manner. Those who have less still have sufficient to help, but they do not have to give the same amount as those with far more.

II. GENEROSITY ENCOURAGED (2 Corinthians 9:6–13)

A. Sowing Principle (vv. 6–10)

6. But this I say, He which soweth sparingly shall reap also sparingly; and he which soweth bountifully shall reap also bountifully.

7. Every man according as he purposeth in his heart, so let him give; not grudgingly, or of necessity: for God loveth a cheerful giver.

8. And God is able to make all grace abound toward you; that ye, always having all sufficiency in all things, may abound to every good work:

9. (As it is written, He hath dispersed abroad; he hath given to the poor: his righteousness remaineth for ever.

10. Now he that ministereth seed to the sower both minister bread for your food, and multiply your seed sown, and increase the fruits of your righteousness.)

Love for fellow believers is the identifying mark of Christ's followers, and it will by its very nature stimulate generous giving when others are in need. Anything less than generous sharing of one's assets in this setting must of necessity call one's love into question. This in turn suggests a spiritual warning.

Verse 6 provides an agricultural illustration which even the urban dwellers of that time understood. It still holds true today as farmers decide the amount of seed to be planted per acre. A number of factors enter the decision—the type of soil, moisture available, and the crop to be planted. Farmers always plant less seed in less fertile soil. And if irrigation is unavailable and little moisture in the form of rain is falling, the amount of seed to be planted automatically is reduced. Even while all these considerations are being calculated, one principle remains dominant: The amount of harvest one reaps depends directly upon the amount of seed sown. The same applies in our spiritual reaping. Spiritual blessings and rewards have a direct relationship to the generosity of one's giving to others in need.

The factor of choice follows the sowing principle. Just as no farmer tells another how much to plant, neither should one believer attempt to designate the amount another should give. This would have a definite impact on whether the gift stems from love and compassion or proceeds reluctantly under compulsion. No one should feel forced to give. No one should give while really wanting to keep what is being offered. This reluctant giving brings neither pleasure to the giver nor glory to God. It is directly opposed to God's preference: He loves a cheerful giver.

What does it mean to be a cheerful giver? The Greek word for *cheerful* (*hilaros*) is the word from which we derive the English word *hilarious*. This speaks of a joyous heart and a ready mind cooperating and evidencing themselves as the believer shares by giving. How could you not be generous when this spirit dominates?

The source of our liberality is the grace of God (v. 8). His unmerited favor continues to be one of the greatest illustrations of liberality. Even though we do not deserve even one of His blessings, God not only extends salvation to us, but He also continues to offer His love and care to weak and faltering humanity. His abundant provision, both spiritually and materially, provides an example for believers in generous charitable giving. In the previous chapter Paul indicated it was God's grace that spurred the Macedonian churches to give generously, even out of their poverty (8:1).

Paul quoted Psalm 112:9 to continue this emphasis on generous giving. It follows the previous metaphor of the sower. Scattering abroad paints the picture of a farmer who walks in the field picking handfuls of seed from his seed bag and spreading them over the ground in a sweeping pattern. In the same manner believers are to distribute generously to those in need. No one deserves to be left without provisions.

This passage also emphasizes the character of the giver. Giving is more than an outward action; it radiates from righteousness. Righteousness promotes kindness and benevolent actions. Right conduct to all brethren, including those in need, logically flows from a heart which is God–centered and concerned about others.

Two very important concepts are introduced in verse 10. First is the fact of God's magnificent provision for us. All that we have to share with others in need comes from God's gracious supply. Our abundance, our prosperity, our extra are all from God himself. Money in the bank and grain in the storage bins isn't just because of good luck and our hard work. It is the blessing of God. He provides the sunshine and the rain. He gives us health to provide the necessary effort to sow and to reap. As much as we may want to believe we are independent, the truth remains that all of us are dependent upon God.

The second concept reminds us of the need to plant before we can reap. That seed has to fall to the ground and die before its abundant potential can be released. Jesus taught this in John 12:24: "Verily, verily, I say unto you, Except a corn of wheat fall into the ground and die, it abideth alone: but if it die, it bringeth forth much fruit." The multiplication comes only after the sower is willing to release it to the ground.

It would be an injustice not to mention the seed's size. A very small seed generates a multiplied number of fruits, each containing seed of its own, thus dwarfing the original seed for sheer magnitude. God's plan of bringing an abundance from little can be seen repeatedly in both Testaments. A handful of meal in a barrel and a little oil in a cruse provided food for Elijah, the widow of Zarephath, and her son for many days (1 Kings 17:12, 15, 16). A small pot of oil filled all the empty vessels a widow could borrow and bring into her house. After selling the oil, she paid off the family's indebtedness and rescued her sons from being sold as slaves (2 Kings 4:1–7). And look at Christ's miraculous provision of food for the multitudes. With five loaves and two fish Jesus fed 5,000 men plus women and children, and on another occasion He used seven loaves and a few fish to feed 4,000 men as well as women and children (Matthew 14:15–21; 15:32–39).

How do we bring believers to the point of being generous givers?

B. Thanksgiving Expressed (vv. 11–13)

(2 Corinthians 9:11–13 is not included in the printed text.)

When believers generously give of their possessions to meet the needs of others, they are instruments enabling others to express their gratitude to God. Those benefiting from liberal giving surely express thanks to the individuals, but thanksgiving to God is much more important, since He is truly the source of all blessings.

Two benefits of liberal giving are pointed out in verses 11 and 12. First, the material needs of brothers and sisters are met. They are no longer in want of the necessities of life. Second, it enables those previously in need to express their thankfulness for God's provision. The importance of praise to God can be overlooked very easily. We tend to forget that the most beneficial result of our giving is enabling individuals to glorify God. It's a spiritual experience for both the giver and the receiver.

A specific benefit of this charitable act by the Corinthians is pointed out in verse 13. Many of the Jewish Christians were hesitant to accept that Gentiles were experiencing salvation and receiving the baptism in the Holy Spirit. Here would be tangible proof of their faith in Christ and brotherhood in the body of Christ. One of the tests of a profession of faith is one's actions toward other brothers and sisters. If they are without food or clothing, real faith evidences itself by meeting that need. Simply expressing concern and praying for them isn't sufficient. When the love of God and compassion dwells within, no one can withhold that which will meet another's needs (1 John 3:17).

Meeting the needs of hurting believers places a variety of items in proper perspective. More than likely the believers in Jerusalem had heard of some of the disorders in these new congregations of Gentiles. The nature of some of the problems could have led them to question whether conversion had ever taken place. But when they received the tangible, material evidence from these Gentile believers, it would perhaps bring a heightened sense of understanding about God's divine gospel being for all people. The proof would be the generosity of the gift which would feed and clothe their children as well as themselves.

The provision of the Gentile churches for the Jewish congregations points us to corporate responsibility. Not only do individual believers have a responsibility to other individual believers, but congregations need to comprehend their corporate responsibility to other congregations.

III. LOVE IN ACTION (Deuteronomy 15:7, 8; 1 John 3:16–18)

A. Freedom in Love (Deuteronomy 15:7, 8)

7. If there be among you a poor man of one of thy brethren within any of thy gates in thy land which the Lord thy God giveth thee, thou shalt not harden thine heart, nor shut thine hand for thy poor brother:

8. But thou shalt open thine hand wide unto him, and shalt surely lend him sufficient for his need, in that which he wanteth.

To better understand the content of these verses, consideration needs to be given to the context of the chapter. The topic being discussed is the sabbatical year. "Six years thou shalt sow thy field, and six years thou shalt prune thy vineyard, and gather in the fruit thereof; but in the seventh year shall be a sabbath of rest unto the land." Verse 5 goes further to direct that any grain which grew voluntarily or grapes which formed from undressed vineyards were not to be gathered by the owners. However, the poor could continue the practice of gleaning.

God's directive of a sabbath for the land follows the pattern of a weekly day of rest for the people of Israel, for beasts of burden, slaves, and foreigners. God knows that even the ground needs to lie fallow in order to regain its productive ability. The modern farming practices of summer fallowing and crop rotation were developed millennia after God's plan.

The sabbatical year encouraged faith, since the Israelites had to believe that God's bountiful provision in the sixth year would last until the next harvest, two years away. The Sabbath reminds us that rest and refreshing come through faith alone.

Verse 7 brings us face–to–face with responsibility to the poor. God warns His children not to become calloused or stingy toward their need. The poor among us deserve our generous help. Verse 8 demonstrates the openhanded provision we are to extend. The poor should be allowed to borrow sufficient for their total needs to be met rather than receive only a little and then have to come back again in want.

It's possible that some might have withheld their generous support when the sabbatical year drew near. Knowing they might not ever receive payment or have repayment delayed, they might have been tempted to offer less help (see Deuteronomy 15:1, 2). Or, in the worst scenario, no assistance might have been offered at all. However, no one can claim love for one's brothers and be guilty of such restrictive behavior. True love offers freely without any thought of the amount given or the time it will be returned.

The question facing us then is, how do we apply the exhortation of these verses in our lives as believers? First, we need to realize the distinctive obligation each of us has to others who are believers. Second, the evidence of God's love in our lives shines forth in loving action toward those less fortunate. Third, loving action always offers freely without thought of return. Fourth, love remains fresh and guards against calloused thinking and miserly giving.

One last observation appears appropriate: The abundance and/or continuance of the poor in our land isn't an excuse to do nothing. We can't personally help everyone; our resources are limited. But we can help those in our circle of acquaintances and those in the body of Christ in our local church.

B. Test of Love (1 John 3:16–18)

16. Hereby perceive we the love of God, because he laid down his life for us: and we ought to lay down our lives for the brethren.

17. But whoso hath this world's good, and seeth his brother have need, and shutteth up his bowels of compassion from him, how dwelleth the love of God in him?

18. My little children, let us not love in word, neither in tongue; but in deed and in truth.

This portion of our lesson brings us face–to–face with the reality of love. Its genuineness can be proven through specific testing. All the talk about love comes to a decisive evaluation based on definite actions.

In the last half of chapter 3 the apostle John spoke about loving one another. He first cited the negative example of Cain, who not only didn't love his brother but in anger against his brother's righteousness murdered him (v. 12). He pointed out that we are not to be surprised when the unbelievers of the world hate us (v. 13). That is the condition of those who are spiritually dead. The evidence of having passed from death to life is the love we have for our brothers and sisters in Christ.

Before making a personal application by testing the reader's love, John shared the most dynamic example of love. In verse 16 he brings us back to the definition of love. It isn't an emotion or feeling but, rather, an action. Christ's sacrificial death for unregenerate sinful mankind stands forth as the truest test of love. Only love caused God to leave all the splendor of heaven and exchange it for the limitation and frailty of human flesh. Only love enabled Christ to lay down His life in the agony and suffering of crucifixion. In the same manner believers are to be willing to die for fellow believers. John didn't share the circumstances, but we assume that "we ought to lay down our lives for the brethren" applies to being persecuted for the faith.

Dying for a fellow believer would be a rare circumstance, so the apostle provided a very practical application which everyone can use as a personal test. True love causes us to help a brother/sister in need. The implication of verse 17 indicates needs which are material or financial. Love shares of one's abundance to meet the need of those in want. Love doesn't allow you to turn away. Love doesn't allow you to simply pray for the need. And when there is no attempt made to meet the need, then the logical assumption must be that love isn't present.

The author used the word *bowels* (v. 17) as the seat of compassion (the heart). At John's point in cultural history, *bowels* spoke of tender mercies, compassion, and affection. Thus, in this verse it means that our love must be reflected in compassion and tender mercy toward those in need of our help.

Verse 18 summarizes the whole concept in just a few words. We believers need to avoid claiming a love that manifests itself only by a multitude of words. True love evidences itself in actions which stem from a genuine desire for the good of others. However, neither are deeds alone sufficent—truth and faith in God must also reside in the heart of the believer who is the doer.

How does hypocrisy often creep into the actions of the believer?

REVIEW QUESTIONS

1. What is a Christlike attitude of giving?
2. What is meant by equality in giving?
3. Describe the sowing principle.
4. What is the source of liberality in giving?
5. How do we test our love for fellow Christians?

GOLDEN TEXT HOMILY

"LET US NOT LOVE IN WORD, NEITHER IN TONGUE; BUT IN DEED AND IN TRUTH" (1 John 3:18).

As I study 1 John 3:18, several words stand out as though they were highlighted by the Holy Spirit. The first word is *love* (*agapao*), which is used in this New Testament context to convey God's will for His children concerning their attitude toward one another (cf. John 13:34) and toward all men (1 Thessalonians 3:12; cf. 1 Corinthians 16:14; 2 Peter 1:7). This word *love* expresses the essential nature of God (1 John 4:8). This love can only be known from the actions it prompts. It is practical love given by God that causes people to be drawn to Him.

John proclaims that this type of love cannot be shared properly with others only by our "word" (*logos*), which is the expression of our thoughts or our good intentions. Neither can it be conveyed by our "tongue" (*glossa*—the very word from which we transliterate "glossolalia" or "speaking in tongues"). John exhorts us that the love he is proclaiming can only be shared in "deed" (*ergon*) and in "truth" (*aletheia*). This is practical Christianity which encompasses every activity undertaken for Christ's sake (2 Thessalonians 1:11); it is the practical effect that faith in Christ has upon us (James 2:24). This "work" expresses the "truth" that Christ is indeed Lord of our life by revealing Him in concrete ways. Love knows no enemies, least of all any person in need!

This command to Christian love is demonstrated in the model that the Christian has been given to imitate nothing less than the selfless love of Christ himself (John 13:34). This duty of love cannot be fulfilled merely by profession or good intentions. It must be proven by our deeds. This is the love that has God for its source and model.—**Ralph S. Douglas (LT), Chaplain, Virginia Beach, Virginia**

SENTENCE SERMONS

GOD'S LOVE motivates believers to give to others.

—Selected

TRUE CHARITY is the desire to be useful to others without thought of recompense.

—Emmanuel Swedenborg

THIS ONLY IS CHARITY, to do all we can.

—John Donne

GIVING UNTIL IT HURTS is not a true measure of giving. Some are more easily hurt than others.

—Anonymous

DAILY BIBLE READINGS

M. Abundant Results. Exodus 36:3–7

T. Willingness to Give. 1 Chronicles 29:6–13

W. Sacrificial Giving. Mark 12:41–44

T. The Spirit of Giving. Luke 6:30–38

F. Sufficient Giving. Acts 20:32–35

S. Consistent Giving. Philippians 4:10–19

Supporting Our Leaders

Study Text: Exodus 17:8–13; Romans 13:1–7; 1 Timothy 2:1–4; Hebrews 13:7, 17

Objective: To realize that leadership is ordained of God and honor our leaders through prayer and cooperation.

Golden Text: "Let every soul be subject unto the higher powers. For there is no power but of God: the powers that be are ordained of God" (Romans 13:1).

Central Truth: The believer's cooperation with leadership is a reflection of his response to God's authority.

Evangelism Emphasis: God has given every believer the responsibility to lead others to Christ.

PRINTED TEXT

Exodus 17:11. And it came to pass, when Moses held up his hand, that Israel prevailed: and when he let down his hand, Amalek prevailed.

12. But Moses' hands were heavy; and they took a stone, and put it under him, and he sat thereon; and Aaron and Hur stayed up his hands, the one on the one side, and the other on the other side; and his hands were steady until the going down of the sun.

Romans 13:1. Let every soul be subject unto the higher powers. For there is no power but of God: the powers that be are ordained of God.

2. Whosoever therefore resisteth the power, resisteth the ordinance of God: and they that resist shall receive to themselves damnation.

3. For rulers are not a terror to good works, but to the evil. Wilt thou then not be afraid of the power? do that which is good, and thou shalt have praise of the same:

4. For he is the minister of God to thee for good. But if thou do that which is evil, be afraid; for he beareth not the sword in vain: for he is the minister of God, a revenger to execute wrath upon him that doeth evil.

Hebrews 13:7. Remember them which have the rule over you, who have spoken unto you the word of God: whose faith follow, considering the end of their conversation.

17. Obey them that have the rule over you, and submit yourselves: for they watch for your souls, as they that must give account, that they may do it with joy, and not with grief: for that is unprofitable for you.

1 Timothy 2:1. I exhort therefore, that, first all, supplications, prayers, intercessions, and giving of thanks, be made for all men;

2. For kings, and for all that

are in authority; that we may lead a quiet and peaceable life in all godliness and honesty.

3. For this is good and acceptable in the sight of God our Saviour;

4. Who will have all men to be saved, and to come unto the knowledge of the truth.

DICTIONARY

Amalek (AM-ah-lek)—Exodus 17:11—Son of Eliphaz (eldest son of Esau) by his concubine Timna.

Hur (HER)—Exodus 17:12—A friend who, with Aaron, held Moses' hands up as he prayed for victory over Amalek.

LESSON OUTLINE

I. HELP LEADERS
   A. Stress of Leadership
   B. Impact of Helpers
II. SUBMIT TO LEADERS
   A. Divinely Ordained
   B. Personal Examples
   C. Spiritual Responsibility
III. PRAY FOR LEADERS
   A. Civil Order
   B. Personal Salvation

LESSON EXPOSITION

INTRODUCTION

"It's lonely at the top."

Usually this quip is used in jest to a friend about his/her leadership position. There's no doubt, however, that it is often lonely in the top positions of leadership, but the reasons vary. Some leaders bring this problem on themselves by assuming an air of superiority and looking on everyone else as lowly subjects who are to bow to their wishes. Others separate themselves because they do not want their personal relationships to adversely affect their judgments in making difficult decisions.

By its very nature leadership often has some legitimate loneliness. There are occasions when the leader must make tough decisions. Always attempting to please certain people or all the people doesn't make for a strong, decisive leader. Some decisions alienate for the moment. In those times, the leader feels lonely.

When failure comes and the entire enterprise is threatened through no fault of your own, it's lonely. Positions of leadership are lonely when the people rebel against truth and follow a path of guaranteed destruction. Leadership positions may be lonely due to the suspicions of the people who have seen the greed and hypocrisy of other leaders. However, without leadership chaos reigns.

There can be no concentrated, united effort by any group without leadership. Closely tied to the successful effort of any leader is the support and cooperation of the people who are to be led. This holds true for the church, as it does in every other aspect of society. The logical implication, then, is that we believers need to understand the value of supporting our leadership. This becomes another dimension of ministering to each other within the body of Christ. We can't afford to choose a path of non-involvement. We are to actively help, submit to, and pray for the leaders of our local churches and the denomination.

I. HELP LEADERS (Exodus 17:8–13)

A. Stress of Leadership (vv. 8–11)

(Exodus 17:8–10 is not included in the printed text.)

11. And it came to pass, when Moses held up his hand, that Israel prevailed: and when he let down his hand, Amalek prevailed.

Up to this point, Moses had had his share of stress as a leader. He and the fledgling nation he was leading had faced danger at the Red Sea with the army of Pharaoh in swift pursuit. He had subsequently endured the people's complaining, criticism, and threatened rebellion. Then, arriving at another camping site, Rephidim, they found no water and the people had become so angry they were about to stone Moses. It's unfortunate that these ungrateful individuals always turned against their leader and always failed to turn to God. They delighted in crying *against* Moses rather than crying *to* God. But as He had done on the previous occasions, God graciously responded in spite of their rebellion and caused a stream of water to flow from the rock of Horeb to meet their needs (Exodus 17:1–7).

It was also at Rephidim the Israelites experienced the first attack by the warring Amalekites. Without provocation they attacked some of the Israelites who were straggling behind the main body and had not arrived in camp (Deuteronomy 25:17, 18). This couldn't be allowed without a retaliatory strike. No one could have the pleasure of attacking God's people without feeling His fury. Besides, these grumbling complainers needed to know God hadn't led them out into the desert to be prey for any group that happened to come by.

Yet there was a very interesting problem. Israel had no standing army. None of these men were experienced soldiers. None of them had been part of a militia. They were former slaves who had labored on the building projects of the Pharaohs. How could they overcome an experienced army? And there's another question: Where would their weapons have come from? Josephus, the Jewish historian of the first century, recorded that when the dead bodies of the Egyptians washed ashore at the Red Sea (Exodus 14:30), the Israelites armed themselves with the Egyptians' weapons.

Now Israel needed a leader who could take men into military combat. Moses appointed Joshua to the position with responsibility for the task. Nothing is known about his background and experience. All he was asked to do was select some men for the job and go fight. This reminds us that the issue wasn't military training and experience. What mattered was leadership and resources! If Joshua would lead the men, Moses would stand on the hilltop with the rod, the same symbol of authority and power God had told Moses to stretch over the Red Sea when God brought deliverance (Exodus 14:16, 21).

Scripture doesn't record that God specifically gave instructions for this situation. Moses knew by this point in his leadership that God desired to bring deliverance to His people and vengeance on the oppressors. He stood on the top of the hill as Joshua led the chosen men of Israel into battle. Sure enough, God was faithful. With the rod uplifted, God's army prevailed. In time, however, fatigue set in. Physically unable to keep the rod extended, Moses was forced to lower his arm. Immediately the army of Amalek began to prevail. No matter how much he desired to keep his rod continuously uplifted, it became humanly impossible for him to do so. Can you imagine the stress of knowing you make the sole difference in the victory or defeat of your army but are physically unable to continue doing what is necessary to assure victory? That's the stress of leadership Moses was facing.

B. Impact of Helpers (vv. 12, 13)

(Exodus 17:13 is not included in the printed text.)

12. But Moses' hands were heavy; and they took a stone, and put it under him, and he sat thereon; and Aaron and Hur stayed up his hands, the one on the one side, and the other on the other side; and his hands were steady until the going down of the sun.

Thank God for people who understand the ministry of helping. These helpers function out of the limelight and their names are often unknown. But without them the ministries of the church would quickly cease to be.

Into the setting of Moses' stressful fatigue stepped two men who quickly recognized the problem and found the solution. Instead of shaking their heads over the difficulty, or suggesting intercessory prayer, they immediately took action. Moses had been standing for hours and needed to sit down. They brought a stone, which became a seat. Then they situated themselves on each side of Moses and held up his hands. What he could not do as an individual, they accomplished as a trio. The description in Ecclesiastes 4:12 fits this situation well: "And if one prevail against him, two shall withstand him; and a threefold cord is not quickly broken."

Who were these two helpers? Aaron, of course, was the older brother of Moses. For the past several years he had been working as the assistant to his younger brother. His presence provided the assurance Moses needed to become the man who led the Hebrews out of Egyptian bondage. He served as Moses' mouthpiece. Aaron's rod became an instrument for miracles as well as the rod of Moses (Exodus 7:10, 19; 8:5, 6, 16, 17). It wasn't until later that God selected and installed him as the high priest.

Hur's identity is much more difficult to determine. We know from 1 Chronicles 2:19, 20 that he was the son of Caleb and the grandfather of Bezaleel, the chief workman on the tabernacle. When Moses went up on Mount Sinai, Hur along with Aaron served as magistrates in his absence (Exodus 24:14). However, the important factor here in the battle at Rephidim was that he helped a fatigued leader enable God's army to accomplish victory.

God chose to work through helping hands. He could have endowed Moses with supernatural strength, but He didn't. He worked through willing individuals who desired to see His will accomplished.

What are some reasons why individual believers may not want to serve as helpers?

II. SUBMIT TO LEADERS (Romans 13:1–7; Hebrews 13:7, 17)

A. Divinely Ordained (Romans 13:1–7)

(Romans 13:5–7 is not included in the printed text.)

1. Let every soul be subject unto the higher powers. For there is no power but of God: the powers that be are ordained of God.

2. Whosoever therefore resisteth the power, resisteth the ordinance of God: and they that resist shall receive to themselves damnation.

3. For rulers are not a terror to good works, but to the evil. Wilt thou then not be afraid of the power? do that which is good, and thou shalt have praise of the same:

4. For he is the minister of God to thee for good. But if thou do that which is evil, be afraid; for he beareth not the sword in vain: for he is the minister of God, a revenger to execute wrath upon him that doeth evil.

Romans 13:1–7 presents a challenge to our views of leadership in both political and ecclesiastical circles. It forces us to recognize how leaders came to a certain position and what their role is in God's plan for the organization of the world and the church.

Verses 1 and 2 set the stage by indicating that all powers are ordained by God. He institutes order for both society and the church. Without it, the political and moral situations would soon disintegrate into chaos and anarchy. Since these powers are God–ordained, we are to offer obedient submission. These verses remind us that all believers are to have a high view of authority and willingly become subservient to it.

This view of authority was especially directed to those Jews who questioned the right of the Romans to rule over God's people, the Jews, and the Promised Land, Canaan. They were being reminded of God's sovereign control and His designation of even unbelievers to positions of authority. Paul chose not to address at this point how the believer is to respond when an ungodly ruler demands actions inconsistent with Christian belief and practice. The issue here is to understand the requirement to submit to divinely ordained leaders, whether secular or religious.

Paul also addressed the purpose of authority (vv. 3, 4). Leaders are to use their authority to curb evil so the society of mankind can live quietly and at peace (1 Timothy 2:1, 2). Peace and order are the result of leaders restraining those who would bring harm and disruption.

Those who do good and refrain from evil and breaking the law have nothing to fear. The praise referred to in verse 3 doesn't mean receiving a reward. Instead, it means those who obey the law will be approved and thus not subject to reprisal. In contrast, evildoers not only should fear the authorities because of their unacceptable behavior, but they should also expect a punitive response. As individuals receiving their authority from God, a magistrates' responsibility is to uphold the law and pronounce judgment. In an organized society those who are harmed do not take the law into their own hands and seek revenge; they allow the orderly process of law and authority to operate.

Verse 5 brings the Christian conscience into the discussion. The believer's obedience is to be motivated by a higher principle than the presence of fear. As God's children saved by His love and grace, we are to hold a high view of authority which stems from our desire to be Christlike. Having the mind of Christ includes this aspect of Christian respect.

Verses 6 and 7 present some very practical dimensions of what it means to be in subjection to those in authority. We are to pay taxes for the support of government. Those who rule are to be paid like any other worker. A workman is "worthy of his hire" regardless of the job. Even when we disagree with their personality, lifestyle, and legislative or political actions, we have the responsibility to respect them for their positions. This is the sentiment of the loyal soldier: "You may hate your commanding officer, but you always respect his uniform!"

What possibilities are available to the believer who disagrees with a leader's political actions?

B. Personal Examples (Hebrews 13:7)

7. Remember them which have the rule over you, who have spoken unto you the word of God: whose faith follow, considering the end of their conversation.

Verse 7 is the first of three references to leaders in Hebrews 13. The second reference (v. 17) will be discussed later. The third reference (v. 24) sent greetings to those who were leading the people of that area.

The writer of Hebrews concluded with a wide variety of exhortations. They include topics of love, hospitality, social concern, sexual morality, and greed (vv. 1–6). Verse 7 is a continuation of these exhortations as he addressed the area of Christian leadership from the standpoint of benefits to those who follow. Implicit in the writer's words is that those leaders have already died and that they not only taught us the Word but also left us an example to follow. What should be the relationship between those former leaders and the current body of believers?

Believers are given two directions: They are to *remember* and to *consider.* It is so easy to simply let the memory of a deceased leader fade into the past. However, believers are to keep alive the memory of those who have ministered the gospel. This includes those who led us to salvation as well as those who were involved in our continued discipleship. One's spiritual life is tied directly to the actions and ministry of those individuals, although sometimes long gone.

Believers are to review these individuals' lives and follow their example of personal righteousness and witness to others. We should consider how these leaders treated their spouses and children. Were the fruits of righteousness evident to these leaders' families and friends? The success of a leader goes far beyond preaching ability and public image; it encompasses one's home, financial accountability, and general integrity.

This verse by no means demands that every leader be perfect. It doesn't even mean every leader's son and daughter will make a decision to live for Christ. At times even devout parents have children who choose not to serve Christ even though they had positive parental examples. We can't simply disregard these leaders on this basis alone. Yet, we are to consider the overall fruit of our leaders' lives.

The challenge for each of us comes after having viewed the many fine Christian men and women who have led the church. We don't have the privilege of saying "That's nice" and then going on our way. We are to follow their examples. They have paved a path that enables us to follow without having to suffer all the obstacles that may have been their lot to overcome.

What are some of the ways in which we can review examples from the past?

C. Spiritual Responsibility (Hebrews 13:17)

17. Obey them that have the rule over you, and submit yourselves: for they watch for your souls, as they that must give account, that they may do it with joy, and not with grief: for that is unprofitable for you.

As believers in the body of Christ, we have two specific obligations—we are to obey and submit to those in authority over us. No leader can fulfill his/her responsibility unless those being led fulfill their role in the framework of submission and obedience. This isn't difficult when we understand the love and sacrifice that goes into being a leader. Leadership stands for much more than a title, a position, or recognition. Leadership involves sacrifice. No cost becomes too great to the truly caring leader when he begins to realize the eternal impact of his actions. This can be seen by the author's referring to the grief or burden that leaders bear. Sleepless nights along with hours of prayer and advising are all part of the leader's task.

The particular problems faced by the leaders in this verse aren't indicated. But the reason for the writing of the epistle surely applies here. Under intense persecution many of the Hebrew Christians were considering returning to their Jewish faith. This placed a double burden on the leaders. Not only did they personally face persecution, but they carried the load of their brothers and sisters who were vacillating in their faith. It was much more serious than physical death; they were carrying the weight of spiritual life and death.

The leader is accountable not only to the congregation but, even more importantly, before God himself. Consider the prophet Ezekiel: As a watchman over the souls of people he held the responsibility to warn them of sin. Failure to do so would make him personally accountable for those persons' spiritual failure and eventual destruction (Ezekiel 33:6).

It is easy for believers to overlook the tremendous load that church leaders bear. Infatuated by traveling teachers and preachers who attempt to woo by charisma and attractive but false doctrines, many church members drift away and become hopelessly entangled in those false doctrines. But for the intervention of dedicated leaders at all levels of the church who intervene for us, lives would be wrecked. Others become complacent in their spiritual disciplines or are enticed by the attractively deceptive face of sin. Again, were it not for the intervention of dedicated leaders, spiritual disaster would occur.

III. PRAY FOR LEADERS (1 Timothy 2:1–4)

A. Civil Order (vv. 1, 2)

1. I exhort therefore, that, first all, supplications, prayers, intercessions, and giving of thanks, be made for all men;

2. For kings, and for all that are in authority; that we may lead a quiet and peaceable life in all godliness and honesty.

Praying for individuals whom we dislike or consider sinful can be a formidable task. This second chapter of 1 Timothy opens with an exhortation to believers to involve themselves in a variety of prayers. He emphasized those prayers which should be a part of one's prayer life. Supplications and requests we tend to be the most familiar with and utilize a great deal. Generally we have no difficulty in asking for God's help. We are also to employ those "regular prayers" of adoration, praise, and daily communication. Along with them should be prayers of thanksgiving, which include praises for blessings from general to very specific. But it's the prayer of intercession that often gets left out, since it necessitates praying with the same passion and intensity for others as though the need were our very own.

After pointing out the types of prayer, Paul indicated who are to be the subjects. Our prayers should not be limited to the needs of a few chosen friends. Instead, they are to be open and all–inclusive—"for all men." Some very practical applications need to be considered from the teachings of Jesus. In the Sermon on the Mount, He instructed that we are to "pray for them which despitefully use [us], and persecute [us]" (Matthew 5:44). We begin to move into a dimension of true spirituality as we respond to the more difficult aspects of life in Christ.

Believers are to pray specifically for their political rulers, beginning with the very top individual in the nation and moving down the administrative ladder. We assume that praying for them includes their salvation, as will be seen in the next verses. But the specific purpose here is for our quality of life. They are to pray for the rulers to not only look favorably on believers but also make decisions that will enable the nation to continue peacefully.

The magnitude of this directive comes to light when one considers that Nero was the Roman emperor at the time of this writing. For the first five years of his reign the atmosphere was one of peace and success. But when his mother, Agrippina, attempted to overthrow him, he arranged her murder. His egotistic temperament eventually brought chaos as his carelessness and extravagance emptied the government treasury. His solution for replenishment was one of violence and oppressive actions. The great fire in Rome (A.D. 64) is believed to have been planned arson by the emperor, thus enabling him to build his massive complex, the Golden House. Then to shift the blame he accused the Christians, bringing many of them to trial and torturing some to death by fire and wild animals.

Even this type of person is to be included in the prayers of believers. For those of us in the free world, there can be little comprehension of what Paul asked of the believers of the first century. But there are millions of believers still being crushed under the heels of dictators even now.

How do we go about praying for our rulers when we have strong opposition to their views and actions?

B. Personal Salvation (vv. 3, 4)

3. For this is good and acceptable in the sight of God our Saviour;

4. Who will have all men to be saved, and to come unto the knowledge of the truth.

Paul reminded Timothy and those who will read this epistle that it is God's intention that they pray for those in authority. Paul wasn't making up a directive for them; but, rather, God himself expects this of His children. No human being, regardless of his/her position or temperament, is to be exempt from the believer's prayer. It is the means by which lives are changed and entire environments improved.

The emphasis in verse 4 isn't on the means of salvation but on the recipients. Though God would have been justified in His sovereignty and holiness, He didn't select just a chosen few to receive salvation from sin. God loves the whole world of lost mankind—from His first created couple to the babies being born this very minute. He desires all to be reconciled to Himself through the blood of His Son, Jesus Christ. God doesn't look down with glee on sinful man, just waiting to punish him. But He looks on us with compassion and wants every human to come to a saving knowledge of Jesus. This is made clear in the golden text of the Bible—John 3:16.

Christ's example of ministering to everyone further demonstrates God's desire for all to experience salvation. Jesus associated with sinners, since they were the ones who needed a spiritual physician (Mark 2:17). In Samaria an immoral woman needed to hear the good news about living water (John 4). At Jericho, Jesus stopped under a tree to speak to a short, well-dressed tax collector named Zacchaeus, then went home with him (Luke 19:1–6).

The believers' prayers for their rulers must not stop with civil order but should also include their personal salvation. In many cases where rulers have been oppressive, it would be much easier to pray for their judgment and removal, but God desires their spiritual renovation. Their salvation would definitely be reflected in the rulers' opinions and political operations—to the believers' advantage. We are to desire an individual's salvation above anything else, for nothing is of greater value.

REVIEW QUESTIONS

1. What are some of the causes of stress in leadership?

2. Who were Aaron's two helpers, and what was the impact of their help?

3. What is the purpose of authority?

4. Why should we remember the leaders of the past?

5. What two areas should our prayers for political leaders include?

GOLDEN TEXT HOMILY

"LET EVERY SOUL BE SUBJECT UNTO THE HIGHER POWERS. FOR THERE IS NO POWER BUT OF GOD: THE POWERS THAT BE ARE ORDAINED OF GOD" (Romans 13:1).

The apostle Paul, a person highly skilled and trained in legal logic, here counsels his readers concerning obeying the civil law. He begins with simple advice: "Obey the government, because it's the right thing to do."

Paul explains another important principle—civil leadership is vicarious leadership. Governmental leaders actually derive their authority from God. That is one reason we should pray for our leaders (see 1 Timothy 2:1, 2).

Paul then points out the benefits of a law–abiding life. Simply put, a law–abiding life will be an anxiety–free life. There is no need to fear law enforcement if one is obeying the law.

A central message in this and other scriptures is that our lives should bring glory and honor to God in everything we do. Living a quiet and peaceable life is one way to bring honor to God.

It seems that lack of respect for authority is a major societal ill today. The problems this causes are very visible. Some writers contend that this is a direct result of the "de–Christianizing" of America and its rejection of God's ways.

The Bible is clear in its directives. When we honor, obey, pray for, and support our governmental and spiritual leaders, we please God. Those who please God then reap the benefits of obeying Him, individually and societally.—**Dennis W. Watkins, Legal Counsel, Church of God International Offices, Cleveland, Tennessee**

SENTENCE SERMONS

THE BELIEVER'S COOPERATION with leadership is a reflection of his response to God's authority.

—Selected

HE WHO PRAYS FOR OTHERS will be heard for himself.

—Hebrew Proverb

WE ARE NOT put on earth primarily to see through one another, but to see one another through.

—Peter DeVeres

FIND OUT WHERE you can render help to others; then render it. The rest is up to God.

—Quotable Quotations

DAILY BIBLE READINGS

M. Honoring With Tithe. Genesis 14:17–20

T. Obedience to Authority. Genesis 24:1–9

W. Allegiance Pledged. Joshua 1:12–18

T. Response to Parental Authority. Ephesians 6:1–4

F. Response to Employers. Ephesians 6:5–8

S. The Ultimate Authority. Philippians 2:5–11

INTRODUCTION TO WINTER QUARTER

The lessons for the winter quarter (December, January, February) are presented in two units under the themes "Christ in Prophecy" (lessons 1-5) and "Teachings From Ezekiel and Daniel" (lessons 6-13).

Unit One draws from the Old Testament prophetic messages that give credibility to the Christian's claim for the validity of Bible. It indeed spells out in detail the coming, suffering, and the return of the Lord Jesus. Lesson 4 comes from the Gospel According to Matthew as focus is given to the Christmas message.

Unit Two is a series of lessons from two of the Old Testament prophets—Ezekiel and Daniel. The studies, however, are of a practical nature highlighting the Christian's personal responsibility to God, oneself, and to others.

The lessons of this quarter of study are certain to make life-changing conditions for the serious student of God's Word.

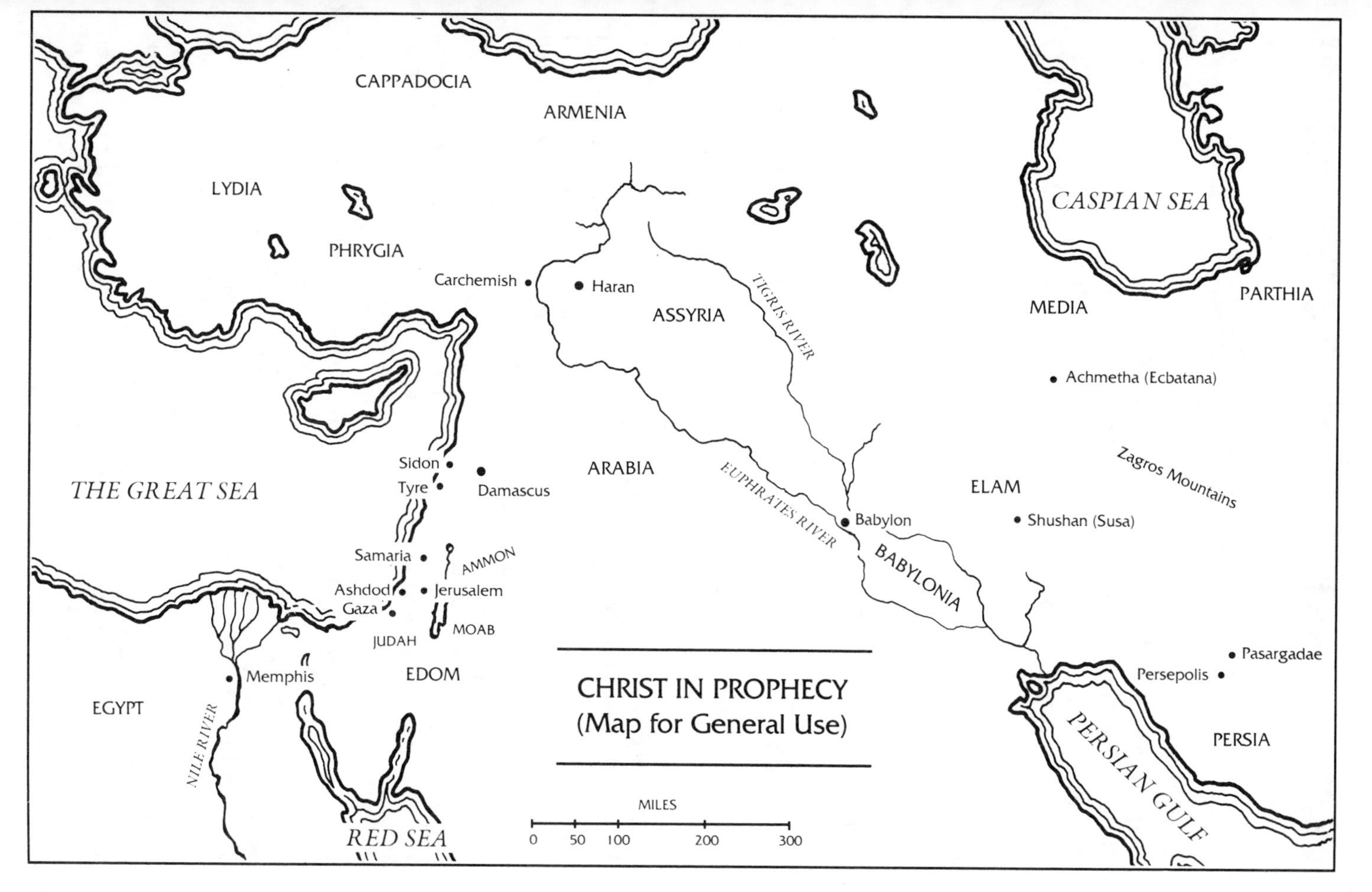
CHRIST IN PROPHECY
(Map for General Use)
CAPPADOCIA
ARMENIA
LYDIA
PHRYGIA
Carchemish
Haran
ASSYRIA
TIGRIS RIVER
CASPIAN SEA
PARTHIA
MEDIA
Achmetha (Ecbatana)
Zagros Mountains
ELAM
Shushan (Susa)
Babylon
BABYLONIA
EUPHRATES RIVER
ARABIA
Sidon
Tyre
Damascus
THE GREAT SEA
Samaria
AMMON
Ashdod
Jerusalem
Gaza
MOAB
JUDAH
EDOM
Memphis
EGYPT
NILE RIVER
RED SEA
Pasargadae
Persepolis
PERSIA
PERSIAN GULF
MILES
0
50
100
200
300

The Suffering Savior

Study Text: Psalm 22:1–31

Objective: To consider Christ's suffering on the cross and appropriate the benefits of His sacrifice.

Time: Psalm 22 is considered to be the writing of David. The date of Psalm 22 is probably between 1000 and 980 B.C.

Place: Psalm 22 was probably written at Jerusalem.

Golden Text: "Be not thou far from me, O Lord: O my strength, haste thee to help me" (Psalm 22:19).

Central Truth: Christ's atoning death is foretold in the Old Testament.

Evangelism Emphasis: Jesus suffered and died to save sinners.

PRINTED TEXT

Psalm 22:1. My God, my God, why hast thou forsaken me? why art thou so far from helping me, and from the words of my roaring?

2. O my God, I cry in the daytime, but thou hearest not; and in the night season, and am not silent.

6. But I am a worm, and no man; a reproach of men, and despised of the people.

7. All they that see me laugh me to scorn: they shoot out the lip, they shake their head, saying.

11. Be not far from me; for trouble is near; for there is none to help.

12. Many bulls have compassed me: strong bulls of Bashan have beset me round.

13. They gaped upon me with their mouths, as a ravening and a roaring lion.

14. I am poured out like water, and all my bones are out of joint: my heart is like wax; it is melted in the midst of my bowels.

15. My strength is dried up like a potsherd; and my tongue cleaveth to my jaws; and thou hast brought me into the dust of death.

16. For dogs have compassed me: the assembly of the wicked have inclosed me: they pierced my hands and my feet.

17. I may tell all my bones: they look and stare upon me.

18. They part my garments among them, and cast lots upon my vesture.

19. But be not thou far from me, O Lord: O my strength, haste thee to help me.

20. Deliver my soul from the sword; my darling from the power of the dog.

23. Ye that fear the Lord, praise him; all ye the seed of Jacob, glorify him; and fear him, all ye the seed of Israel.

24. For he hath not despised nor abhorred the affliction of

the afflicted; neither hath he hid his face from him; but when he cried unto him, he heard.

25. My praise shall be of thee in the great congregation: I will pay my vows before them that fear him.

26. The meek shall eat and be satisfied: they shall praise the Lord that seek him: your heart shall live for ever.

27. All the ends of the world shall remember and turn unto the Lord: and all the kindreds of the nations shall worship before thee.

LESSON OUTLINE

I. FORSAKEN BY GOD
   A. Deserted
   B. Reproached
   C. Derided

II. PERSECUTED BY ENEMIES
   A. Emptied
   B. Humbled
   C. Pierced
   D. Shamed

III. PROMISE OF TRIUMPH
   A. Declaration
   B. Assurance
   C. Triumph

LESSON EXPOSITION

INTRODUCTION

Psalm 22 has been called "The Psalm of the Cross." Some believe it was actually repeated word by word by our Lord while He was hanging on the cross. It is a description of Christ's saddest hour—the record of His dying words, a memorial to His finished work. David and his afflictions may be seen here in a modified sense; but just as the star is concealed by the light of the sun, the anguish of David is overshadowed by the sorrow of our Lord.

We have here both a description of the darkness and the glory of the Cross, the sufferings of Christ and the glory which should follow. The opening words of the psalm—"My God, my God, why hast thou forsaken me?"—alerts us to the extreme anguish of our Savior. The entire psalm refers to Christ; it contains much that cannot be applied to another—parting His garments, casting lots for His vesture, and so forth.

Christ is described as a kindly, meek, and beautiful hart startled by the hunter at the dawn of the day. It should be remembered that Herod began hunting Christ as soon as He was born. Poverty, the hatred of men, and the temptation of Satan joined in the pursuit. There was always some "dog" or "bull" or "unicorn" ready to attack Him. After His first sermon, the hunters gathered about Him, but He was too fast of foot; and because His time had not yet come, He escaped.

He had often been driven by the hunters to the edges of the awful precipices vowing destruction from below, while He was surrounded and held at bay by all the beasts of prey and monsters of the ominous forest.

Christ foiled all His enemies, and in His own time He bowed His head and died on a cross at Calvary, a craggy and fearful hill. When He was buried in a new grave, His assailants thought they had gained complete victory. They had not considered that He was a morning hart. At the appointed time He escaped from the hunter's net, because He lives forever.

I. FORSAKEN BY GOD (Psalm 22:1–11)

A. Deserted (vv. 1–5)

(Psalm 22:3–5 is not included in the printed text.)

1. My God, my God, why hast thou forsaken me? why art thou so far from helping me, and from the words of my roaring?

The question "My God, my God, why?" is an intensely human one. We are startled to find it upon the lips of Jesus. Yet as He hung on the cross, He took the words of the ancient psalmist and made them the vehicle for the expression of His agony. After terrible hours of suffering He flung out this age–old question: "My God, my God, why?"

Clovis Chappell writes of this question: "These words have become the very words of Jesus. We tend to forget that anyone ever uttered them except Him whose was the tenderest heart that was ever broken and whose were the purest lips that ever spoke. Surely it is our Lord who has given to these words their immortality. Let us think of them, then, not so much as those of a long dead poet, but rather as the exceedingly bitter cry of the dying Son of God" *(Sermons From the Psalms).*

According to Chappell there are two peculiarities in these words from Jesus. First, He addressed the Infinite by a name that He has never used in speaking to Him before, nor did He ever use it afterward. When He cried out His question, He addressed the Eternal as "God." "My God, my God," He called out. Now, the one word He used in speaking to or of God everywhere else is "Father." When we heard from Him for the first time in the Temple as a boy of 12, He said, "Wist ye not that I must be about my Father's business?" (Luke 2:49). When He taught us to pray, He told us to say "Our Father." When He explained to us the reasonableness of prayer, He did so by reminding us that God is our Father. The first word He uttered on the cross was "Father, forgive them; for they know not what they do." When the deathly ordeal was over, His last word was, "Father, into thy hands I commend my spirit." Almost constantly did Jesus call God "Father" in speaking of Him. Always and everywhere He did so when speaking to Him, except here, when He said, "My God."

Second, these words are peculiar because they are a question He asked God. This is the only question we have on record that Jesus ever asked God during His entire earthly ministry. We are full of questions. Jesus questioned only once. There were, of course, times when He looked at the will of God with amazement that His Father could so choose this way for Him. But always He accepted that will without question *(Sermons From the Psalms).*

2. O my God, I cry in the daytime, but thou hearest not; and in the night season, and am not silent.

These words indicate a sense of forsakenness and perplexity born of a terrible agony. There was the agony of a dimmed realization of God. There was the agony of bewilderment and the agony of physical suffering, but the cross was the most horrible torture that the fiendish ingenuity of man ever devised. The physical agony of Jesus, however, was as nothing in comparison with His spiritual suffering. It was this suffering that broke His heart. It was this suffering that brought from Him this terrible question that sounds so little like the shout of a victor and so much like the wail of one whose dreams, instead of coming true, have only led him into the quagmire of desolation and death. "My God, why?" This question was born of immeasurable heartbreak.

B. Reproached (vv. 6, 7)

6. But I am a worm, and no man; a reproach of men, and despised of the people.

Charles Spurgeon insisted this verse is a miracle in language. He observes: "How could the Lord of glory be brought to such abasement as to be not only lower than the angels but even lower than men? What a contrast between 'I AM' and 'I am a worm'! Yet such a double nature was found in the person of our Lord Jesus when bleeding upon a tree.

"He felt Himself to be comparable to a helpless, powerless, down–trodden worm, passive while crushed and unnoticed and despised by those who trod upon Him. He selected the weakest of creatures, which is all flesh, and becomes, when trodden upon, withering, quivering flesh. Utterly devoid of any might except strength to suffer.

"This was a true likeness of Himself when His body and soul had become a mass of misery—the very essence of agony—in the dying pangs of crucifixion. Man by nature is but a worm; but our Lord puts Himself even beneath man, on account of the scorn which was heaped upon Him and the weakness which He felt, and therefore He adds, 'and no man'" *(The Treasury of David)*.

7. All they that see me laugh me to scorn: they shoot out the lip, they shake their head, saying.

Men made faces at Him whom angels veil their faces and adore. The basest signs of disgrace which disdain could devise were maliciously cast at Jesus.

Who were the guilty parties? Priests and people, Jews and Gentiles, soldiers and civilians—all united in the general scoffing, and that at the time when He was prostrate in weakness and ready to die. Spurgeon asks, "Which shall we wonder at the most, the cruelty of man, or the love of the bleeding Savior?" How can we ever complain of ridicule after this?

C. Derided (vv. 8–11)

(Psalm 22:8–10 is not included in the printed text.)

The crowd derided Jesus with the words of verse 8: "He trusted on the Lord that he would deliver him: let him deliver him, seeing he delighted in him." Here the derision is cruelly aimed at the sufferer's faith in God. This is the tenderest point in a good man's soul. One of the great preachers of the last century said they must have learned the diabolical art from Satan himself, for they made rare proficiency in it.

11. Be not far from me; for trouble is near; for there is none to help.

Alexander Maclaren writes of this verse: "The request is based on the extremity of His need. The thought of the early part of the psalm undulates between complaint and trust, indicating a troubled sea of emotion–packed thought in which each mood works its opposite" *(An Exposition of the Bible)*.

What is the significance of the question "My God, why?"

II. PERSECUTED BY ENEMIES (Psalm 22:12–21)

A. Emptied (vv. 12–14)

12. Many bulls have compassed me: strong bulls of Bashan have beset me round.

13. They gaped upon me with their mouths, as a revening and a roaring lion.

14. I am poured out like water, and all my bones are out of joint: my heart is like wax; it is melted in the midst of my bowels.

The priests, elders, scribes, Pharisees, rulers, and soldiers bellowed around the cross like wild cattle, fed in the rich pastures of Bashan. Bashan was a fertile country (Deuteronomy 32:14), and the cattle that fed there were fat and strong.

Jesus was as a helpless, unarmed, naked man, cast into the midst of a herd of infuriated bulls, full of strength and fury. They stamped and foamed around Jesus on the cross and longed to gore Him to death with their cruelties.

Jesus emptied Himself and became of no reputation (see Philippians 2:7). He poured out His soul unto death. He gave all that He had. As far as His enemies were concerned, He was utterly destroyed. Second Samuel 14:14 states, "For we must needs die, and are as water spilt on the ground, which cannot be gathered up again."

St. Bernard exclaims, "What marvel that the Name of the Bridegroom should be as ointment poured forth, when He Himself, for the greatness of His love, was poured forth like water!"

Concerning the statement "All my bones are out of joint," Lancelot Andrews comments: "The rack is devised as a most exquisite pain, even for terror. And the cross is a rack, whereon He was stretched till, saith the Psalm, all His bones were out of joint. But even to stand, as He hung, three long hours together, holding up but the arms at length, would be incredible pain. But the hands and the feet being so cruelly nailed it could not but make His pain out of measure painful" *(The Treasury of David).*

B. Humbled (v. 15)

15. My strength is dried up like a potsherd; and my tongue cleaveth to my jaws; and thou hast brought me into the dust of death.

Approaching death is suggested by the dryness of the mouth, the failing of His strength, and finally giving up the ghost. He was brought to the dust, through His own voluntary humility. "He humbled himself, and became obedient unto death" (Philippians 2:8).

C. Pierced (v. 16)

16. For dogs have compassed me: the assembly of the wicked have inclosed me: they pierced my hands and my feet.

Literature and the movies portray how hunters frequently encircle their prey and gradually close in on them with an ever–narrowing ring of dogs and men. Verse 16 presents such a picture. In the center stands, not an animal, but a bleeding, fainting man, and around Him are the enraged and unpitying wretches who have hounded Him to His doom.

In commenting on the statement "They pierced my hands and my feet," John Trapp writes: "It was much for the Son of God to be bound, more to be beaten, most of all to be slain; but what shall I say to this, that He was crucified? That was the most vile and ignominious; it was also a cruel and cursed kind of death, which yet He refused not; and here we have a clear testimony for His cross."

Concerning crucifixion John Stevenson observes:

"The tearing asunder of the tender fibers of the hands and feet, the lacerating of so many nerves, and bursting so many blood vessels, must have produced intense agony. The nerves of the hand and foot are intimately connected, through the arm and leg, with the nerves of the whole body; their laceration therefore would be felt over the entire frame. Consider the result of even a single needle's puncture in one of the remotest nerves. A spasm is not infrequently produced by it in the muscles of the face, which locks the jaws inseparably.

"When, therefore, the hands of our blessed Lord were transfixed with nails, He felt the sharpest pains shoot through every part of His body. Supported only by His lacerated limbs, and suspended from His pierced hands, our Lord had nearly six hours of torment to endure."

D. Shamed (vv. 17–21)

(Psalm 22:21 is not included in the printed text.)

17. I may tell all my bones: they look and stare upon me.

G. Rawlinson observes concerning this verse: "Our Lord's active life and simple habits would give Him a spare frame, while the strain of crucifixion would accentuate and bring into relief every point of His anatomy. He might thus, if so minded, "tell all His bones" *(Pulpit Commentary).*

In dealing with the statement "They look and stare upon me," Charles Spurgeon writes: "Let us blush for human nature and mourn in sympathy with our Redeemer's shame. The first Adam made us all naked, and therefore the second Adam became naked that He might clothe our naked souls" *(The Treasury of David).*

18. They part my garments among them, and cast lots upon my vesture.

In the words of John Stevenson, "As trifling as this act of casting lots for our Lord's vesture may appear, it is most significant. It contains a double lesson. It teaches us how greatly that seamless shirt was valued [and] how little He to whom it belonged. It seemed to say, this garment is more valuable than its owner. How cheaply Christ was held."

19. But be not thou far from me, O Lord: O my strength, haste thee to help me.

The special trouble for which our Lord might conceivably have invoked God's aid having been described minutely, we hear a further plea for help, at first implored, and then strengthened by a request that the help may be given quickly.

20. Deliver my soul from the sword; my darling from the power of the dog.

The sword symbolizes authority—the authority by which Christ was actually put to death, that is the authority of Rome. G. Rawlinson suggests that this prayer was prayed with the reservations previously made in Gethsemane: "If it be possible, let this cup pass from me: nevertheless not as I will, but as thou wilt" (Matthew 26:39). The human in Christ was in favor of deliverance [from further suffering]; the Divine will, the same in Christ as in His Father, was against it" *(Pulpit Commentary).*

Satan is appropriately called a lion (v. 21), for he has all the characteristics of the lion: as bold as a lion, as strong as a lion, as furious as a lion, as terrible as the roaring of a lion. Here the devil is depicted as worse than a lion, for the lion lacks subtlety and suspicion. The lion will spare the prostrate; the devil spares none.

Thomas Adams writes: "The lion is full and forbears; the devil is full and devours. He seeks all; let not the simple say, 'He will take no notice of me'; nor the subtle, 'He cannot overreach me'; nor the noble say, 'He will not presume to meddle with me'; nor the rich, 'He dares not contest with me'; for he seeks to devour all. He is our common adversary; therefore let us cease all quarrels among ourselves, and fight with him" *(The Treasury of David).*

What was the purpose of Jesus being persecuted?

III. PROMISE OF TRIUMPH (Psalm 22:22–31)

A. Declaration (vv. 22, 23)

(Psalm 22:22 is not included in the printed text.)

23. Ye that fear the Lord, praise him; all ye the seed of Jacob, glorify him; and fear him, all ye the seed of Israel.

Verse 22 states, "I will declare thy name." The apostle Paul continued with that approach: "Wherefore [because of His sufferings and death] God also hath highly exalted him, and given him a name which is above every name" (Philippians 2:9). The preaching of His name is the preaching of His holy and wondrous saving character.

In verse 23 all the people are called upon to join in the praise which the Son will offer to the Father through eternity. The praise of God is to be joined with the fear of God, according to the universal teaching of Scripture.

B. Assurance (vv. 24–26)

24. For he hath not despised nor abhorred the affliction of the afflicted; neither hath he hid his face from him; but when he cried unto him, he heard.

Justice demanded that Christ should bear the burden which as a substitute He carried. But Jehovah, in love, laid that load upon Him with a view to His ultimate glory and to the accomplishment of the dearest wish of His heart.

25. My praise shall be of thee in the great congregation: I will pay my vows before them that fear him.

The words "of thee," in the original are "from You"—true praise is always of celestial origin. The rarest harmonies of music are nothing unless they are sincerely consecrated to God by hearts sanctified by the Spirit.

26. The meek shall eat and be satisfied: they shall praise the Lord that seek him: your heart shall live for ever.

Charles Spurgeon makes the following observations on this verse: "Mark how the dying lover of our souls solaces Himself with the result of His death! The spiritually poor find a feast in Jesus; they feed upon Him to the satisfaction of their hearts; they were famished until He gave Himself for them: but now they are filled with royal dainties."

C. Triumph (vv. 27–31)

(Psalm 22:28–31 is not included in the printed text.)

27. All the ends of the world shall remember and turn unto the Lord: and all the kindreds of the nations shall worship before thee.

The true nature of conversion is to remember and turn to the Lord and to worship Him. This is a plain and simple process.

In commenting on the words "All the ends of the world shall remember," John Stevenson writes: "This is a remarkable expression. It implies that man has forgotten God. It represents all the successive generations of the world as but one, and then it exhibits that one generation, as if it had been once in paradise suddenly remembering the Lord whom it had known there but had long forgotten. The converted nations, we learn by this verse, will not only obtain remembrance of their past loss but will be filled with the knowledge of the present duty" *(Treasury of David).*

To what extent do you think the cause of Christ has triumphed?

REVIEW QUESTIONS

1. What is the theme of Psalm 22?

2. How is Christ described in this psalm?

3. How does Christ feel in verses 1–11?

4. How is Christ persecuted by His enemies in verses 12–21?

5. What are the characteristics of triumph in verses 22–31?

GOLDEN TEXT HOMILY

"BE NOT THOU FAR FROM ME, O LORD: O MY STRENGTH, HASTE THEE TO HELP ME" (Psalm 22:19).

God's people have always been acquainted with pain, suffering, and sorrow. Some have thought that spiritual growth comes from mountaintop experiences, but others say that is not true. They have discovered that the greatest spiritual growth takes place in the valley. Many have brought their troubles to the Lord while going through valley experiences. The psalmist is an example. He felt utterly forsaken by God. Nevertheless he cried out in faith, "My God" (v. 1). It seemed as though God had ignored his unceasing cry for help in the midst of enemies and sickness. He found that suffering is very personal and painful. When it is the sharpest, he groaned, "O my God, I cry in the daytime, but thou hearest not; and in the night season, and am not silent" (v. 2).

Throughout his experience the psalmist desired to keep in touch with God. He asked, "Why art thou so far . . . ?" (v. 1). Then he pleaded, "Be not far from me" (v. 11) and even begged, "But be not thou far from me, O Lord" (v. 19). God who has promised never to forsake His own seemed to be so far away. Though he felt abandoned by God, he knew better.

Jesus also knew what it was to suffer and to feel that God had forsaken Him. Like Jesus and the psalmist, we may feel the same way when we encounter suffering or our world seems to be collapsing. We remember what God has been to us in the past. His unchanging love gives us courage to face hardships and tragedies.

I have known people who proved to be faithful to God in the most trying circumstances. Some have gone through financial reverses, a few even become bankrupt. Others have lost their homes or a child. And still others have suffered greatly from diseases that medical science had deemed incurable. But they had stayed in touch with God and remembered His goodness to them. They have kept going to church, believing in the Savior, singing the hymns, and praying the prayers. God has been faithful to them, and they are confident that He will see them through whatever may come.—**French L. Arrington, Ph.D., Professor of New Testament Greek and Exegesis, Church of God School of Theology, Cleveland, Tennessee**

SENTENCE SERMONS

CHRIST'S ATONING DEATH is foretold in the Old Testament.

—Selected

SUFFERING LOVE, the Cross, stands at the heart of the church.

—T.Z. Koo

WHEN CHRIST hung, and bled, and died, it was God saying to the world "I love you."

—Billy Graham

THE HEAD that once was crowned with thorns is crowned with glory now.

—Thomas Kelley

EVANGELISM APPLICATION

JESUS SUFFERED AND DIED TO SAVE SINNERS.

Apart from Christ there is no true life, for all men are naturally dead in sin. It is in Him that we have eternal life, for "he that hath the Son hath life; and he that hath not the Son of God hath not life (1 John 5:12). He came to give life to the world by giving His life, for He said, "I am come that they might have life, and that they might have it more abundantly" (John 10:10). "In him was life; and the life was the light of men" (John 1:4). In Christ's life, death, and resurrection alone is that life to be found—and that life is an abundant one.

ILLUMINATING THE LESSON

In Uncle Tom's Cabin one of the characters was represented as being at the bedside of a dying woman, whom he sought to comfort by the Word of God. In the course of the conversation, he quoted the words of the Savior: "Come unto me . . . and I will give you rest" (Matthew 11:28). By so doing, the attention of the dying woman was immediately arrested.

"Them is good words," she said. "Who speaks them?"

That is the point upon which their value depends: "Who speaks them?" Spoken by any other, the words in Psalm 22 would only tantalize; spoken by God, they can banish a world of sorrow and unrest, and establish a universe of bliss!

DAILY BIBLE READINGS

M. Suffering Servant. Isaiah 52:13 through 53:2

T. Man of Sorrows. Isaiah 53:3–12

W. Love Rejected. Hosea 11:1–5

T. Mocked by the World. Matthew 27:27–31

F. Death on the Cross. Matthew 27:45–50

S. Resurrection Prefigured. Matthew 27:51–54

Pictures of Christ

Study Text: Exodus 12:1–13, 21–27; Leviticus 16:3–16; Numbers 21:4–9; John 3:14, 15; 1 Corinthians 5:7; Hebrews 9:11–15

Objective: To review Old Testament types of Christ and rejoice in His fulfillment of prophecy.

Golden Text: "He was wounded for our transgressions, he was bruised for our iniquities: the chastisement of our peace was upon him; and with his stripes we are healed" (Isaiah 53:5).

Central Truth: Christ fulfills every Old Testament picture of redemption.

Evangelism Emphasis: Old Testament pictures of redemption point sinners to Christ.

PRINTED TEXT

Exodus 12:21. Then Moses called for all the elders of Israel, and said unto them, Draw out and take you a lamb according to your families, and kill the passover.

22. And ye shall take a bunch of hyssop, and dip it in the blood that is in the bason, and strike the lintel and the two side posts with the blood that is in the bason; and none of you shall go out at the door of his house until the morning.

23. For the Lord will pass through to smite the Egyptians; and when he seeth the blood upon the lintel, and on the two side posts, the Lord will pass over the door, and will not suffer the destroyer to come in unto your houses to smite you.

24. And ye shall observe this thing for an ordinance to thee and to thy sons for ever.

Numbers 21:6. And the Lord sent fiery serpents among the people, and they bit the people; and much people of Israel died.

7. Therefore the people came to Moses, and said, We have sinned, for we have spoken against the Lord, and against thee; pray unto the Lord, that he take away the serpents from us. And Moses prayed for the people.

8. And the Lord said unto Moses, Make thee a fiery serpent, and set it upon a pole: and it shall come to pass, that every one that is bitten, when he looketh upon it, shall live.

9. And Moses made a serpent of brass, and put it upon a pole, and it came to pass, that if a serpent had bitten any man, when he beheld the serpent of brass, he lived.

Hebrews 9:13. For if the blood of bulls and of goats, and the ashes of an heifer sprinkling the unclean, sanctifieth to the purifying of the flesh:

14. How much more shall the blood of Christ, who

through the eternal Spirit offered himself without spot to God, purge your conscience from dead works to serve the living God?

15. And for this cause he is the mediator of the new testament, that by means of death, for the redemption of the transgressions that were under the first testament, they which are called might receive the promise of eternal inheritance.

LESSON OUTLINE

I. PASSOVER LAMB
   A. Instructions
   B. Application
   C. Protection
   D. Remembrance
II. EXALTED HEALER
   A. Symbol
   B. Reality
III. ETERNAL HIGH PRIEST
   A. Preparation
   B. Fulfillment

LESSON EXPOSITION

INTRODUCTION

The Old Testament and the New Testament of the Bible are not two books but one—divided into two components. They have the same author (the Holy Spirit), the same God (Father, Son, and Holy Spirit—three personages eternally existing as one God). It was the Trinity of God that spoke the universe into existence and gave life to man from the dust of the earth.

The central theme of the Old Testament is a demonstration of what God can do with a people "which were not my people . . . [to make] her beloved, which was not beloved" (Romans 9:25).

From a straggling group of herdsmen who had spent 400 years in slavery, God forged a nation which, with all its regressions into sin and idolatry, would one day hold out the only candle to a dark and godless pagan world.

Among other things, Israel gave the Gentile world the Bible, an example of a moral life, a message of salvation for now, and the only eternal hope for tomorrow. They spoke to all who would listen about *one* God, who, contrary to what they had been taught, cared for them and was accessible to them.

But the most important thing the Jews would give their world was a hope in the coming of a Messiah (the Anointed One), who would bring God's salvation, healing, and peace into a sin-torn, helpless, and hopeless world.

Throughout the Old Testament there are shadows and vague shapes signifying things to come. Many of these prophecies point directly to the coming Christ, who was to be born of a virgin (Isaiah 7:14), born in Bethlehem (Micah 5:2), and would die an ignominious death (Isaiah 53).

This week's lesson is a study of those Old Testament prophecies which were fulfilled in the New Testament by the death of Jesus Christ on the cross.

I. PASSOVER LAMB (Exodus 12:1–13, 21–27; 1 Corinthians 5:7)

A. Instructions (Exodus 12:1–13)

(Exodus 12:1–13 is not included in the printed text.)

God foretold redemption in many ways. He began with the coats of skin with which He clothed the first pair in the Garden of Eden (Genesis 3:21). These were a type and a shadow. The firstborn of Abel's flock which he offered as a sacrifice to God were a type and a shadow (Genesis 4:4). This continued in the altar which Noah built on Mount Ararat after he came forth from the ark and upon which he offered clean beasts to the Lord (Genesis 8:20). Abraham joined in when he took his only son, Isaac, into the land of Moriah to offer him as a burnt offering to God and was stopped by the angel of the Lord, who provided a ram for a substitute (Genesis 22:1–13).

When God sought to deliver Israel by the hand of His servant Moses, they had been in bondage in Egypt for 400 years. He brought nine great plagues upon Egypt, but the Lord hardened Pharaoh's heart, and he refused to let the people go (Exodus 11:10).

One day God communicated to Moses and Aaron instructions for instituting the Passover. We are not told how the Lord communicated these instructions. One thing is certain, however: they did not doubt the source of the revelation. It should be noted that it is expressly stated that these rules for the Passover were given in Egypt. All the other laws regulating the Hebrew forms of worship were given outside Egypt.

In giving the instructions to Moses concerning the Passover, God, for the first time in Jewish history, called His people "the congregation of Israel" (v. 3).

There was to be one lamb for each home. If there were not enough members of a household to consume a lamb, they were to merge with another family. Later Jewish tradition stated that the number around the table for the Passover feast should be at least 10.

It should be observed that the first ordinance of the Jewish religion was a domestic service. This arrangement was divinely judicious. No nation has ever been really prosperous or permanently strong that did not cherish the importance of the family and the home.

Ancient Rome failed to resist the enemy not because her discipline had degenerated but because the home had collapsed as a viable social institution. We cannot overlook the simple and obvious fact that God has built His nation upon families.

Four days before the night when the destroying angel of death was to pass over Egypt and the Israelites were to be allowed to go out, every Hebrew household was to select a lamb. It was to be a one–year–old male lamb without blemish.

The most probable reason the lamb was to be kept four days was that the Israelites might have time to meditate upon the solemnity and significance of that divine event. The four days also gave them an opportunity to prepare for their departure from Egypt.

B. Application (Exodus 12:21, 22)

21. Then Moses called for all the elders of Israel, and said unto them, Draw out and take you a lamb according to your families, and kill the passover.

22. And ye shall take a bunch of hyssop, and dip it in the blood that is in the bason, and strike the lintel and the two side posts with the blood that is in the bason; and none of you shall go out at the door of his house until the morning.

It was important that the Israelites observe strictly the ritual in connection with the Passover. The lamb was to be killed. Then its blood was to be sprinkled on the doorposts and lintel of the house where the Israelites had stayed that night. It was not enough to shed the blood; it had to be applied. An Israelite might have selected a proper lamb, and he might have slain it; but unless he had applied the blood to the outside posts of the door, the death angel would have entered his house and slain his firstborn.

Neither is it enough for me to know that the blood of Christ was shed for the remission of sins. That a Savior was provided is not sufficient; He must be received. There must be faith in the efficacy of His blood, and faith is a personal thing. I must exercise faith. I must allow the Holy Spirit to place that blood between my sins and a holy God. I must rely on that blood as the absolute ground of my acceptance with God.

C. Protection (Exodus 12:23)

23. For the Lord will pass through to smite the Egyptians; and when he seeth the blood upon the lintel, and on the two side posts, the Lord will pass over the door, and will not suffer the destroyer to come in unto your houses to smite you.

According to this verse, God's eye was not on the house but on the blood. It might have been a big house, a strong house, a beautiful house—this made no difference. If no blood was there, the death angel entered and put to death the firstborn of each household. Its height, its strength, its magnificence did not matter—if the blood was lacking. On the other hand, the house might have been a miserable hovel, falling to pieces with age and decay; but if the blood was on the door, those within were absolutely secure and safe.

It should be noted that God's eye was not on those within the house. They might have been descendants of Abraham, they might have been circumcised on the eighth day, and they might have been walking blamelessly. But it was not on their heredity, not their ceremonial uprightness, nor their good works that guaranteed deliverance for them. It was the application of the shed blood.

D. Remembrance (Exodus 12:24–27; 1 Corinthians 5:7)

(Exodus 12:25–27 and 1 Corinthians 5:7 are not included in the printed text.)

24. And ye shall observe this thing for an ordinance to thee and to thy sons for ever.

God commanded Israel to keep the Passover throughout their generations. He gave it to them for a twofold purpose: to remind them of His delivering power and to point to the Coming One. He wanted them to look back in remembrance and to look forward in expectancy—backward with thanksgiving and forward with praise.

They were faithful in keeping the Feast of the Passover, but there came a time when they failed to look backward or forward. The Passover had degenerated into ritual.

The Jews in Egypt were delivered from death by the application of the blood of the lamb. Paul declared in 1 Corinthians 5:7 that Jesus is "our passover"—the Lamb of God—who shed His blood to deliver us from sin.

How is the Passover symbolic of Christ?

II. EXALTED HEALER (Numbers 21:4–9; John 3:14, 15)

A. Symbol (Numbers 21:4–9)

(Numbers 21:4, 5 is not included in the printed text.)

6. And the Lord sent fiery serpents among the people, and they bit the people; and much people of Israel died.

7. Therefore the people came to Moses, and said, We have sinned, for we have spoken against the Lord, and against thee; pray unto the Lord, that he take away the serpents from us. And Moses prayed for the people.

8. And the Lord said unto Moses, Make thee a fiery serpent, and set it upon a pole: and it shall come to pass, that every one that is bitten, when he looketh upon it, shall live.

9. And Moses made a serpent of brass, and put it upon a pole, and it came to pass, that if a serpent had bitten any man, when he beheld the serpent of brass, he lived.

Discouragement and murmuring reared up again among the Israelites, this time at a most untimely moment, when the people were actually on the march. They had left Mount Hor and were intending to "compass the land of Edom" (21:4), whether on the east or west is difficult to determine. They had no bread or water, and they loathed the manna. For their speaking against God and against Moses, judgment fell as a scourge of "fiery serpents" whose bite was fatal to many of the people. The general area where this scourge occurred is still known for its many venomous reptiles. Through this plague, God was restating the unchanging and universal truth that sin brings judgment, whether committed in that era or our own. The fact of God's presence on the march gave no license to commit the old sins of the wilderness. At the confession of the frightened people and the intercession of a faithful Moses, God set up a condition for the people to be delivered. A brass fiery–looking serpent was to be made and set high on a standard. When someone was bitten by a live serpent, he was spared death by looking upon the brazen serpent.

Most of the religions in these lands believed that the serpent had health–giving and healing power and was therefore worthy of worship. Hence the making of statues and objects in the form of serpents, which were appealed to for help in the heathen worship practices. However, the brazen serpent which Moses was commanded to raise on a standard had no allusion whatever to the heathen practice. The object chosen was a serpent statue because it corresponded to the deadly serpent scourge that had come to the people. It was cold and lifeless; it only represented what God was able to do for the Israelites—that is, take a fatal, hot sting and render it harmless. Also, it was set upon a pole so as to be a visible sign to the people. Finally, it was efficacious only to those who looked on it. The object itself was not to be worshiped. In fact, when the Israelites later began to regard it as an object of worship, it had to be destroyed by Hezekiah (2 Kings 18:4).

In *Numbers: Journey to God's Rest–Land*, Irving Jensen states: "In this great Old Testament type of salvation–by–faith in a Savior who died on a cross, the brazen serpent was not a medium for mass deliverance as such. Everyone was not automatically given an antibiotic for the fatal venom of the serpent. Deliverance came only to the individual who looked up at the representative symbol. The heresy of universalism is exposed here. Christ, who was in the form of sinful flesh, and yet without sin, was set up publicly on the standard of a cross, a visible sign to all the world of the guilt [of our sins] He was bearing. He died as a representative of the race of sinners, and only that individual who looks up to Him in faith is saved (John 3:14).

"So the scourge of serpents was a critical experience for the Israelites on the renewed march to Canaan. Were it not for God's grace in granting this miraculous way of deliverance from the very judgment for sin which He himself was bringing, and the people's individual faith, the march would have ended here."

B. Reality (John 3:14, 15)

(John 3:14, 15 is not included in the printed text.)

Charles Erdman said: "As it was necessary for the dying Israelites to accept God's provision, and, with submission and faith, to look upon the brazen serpent, so it is necessary for us to look, in repentance and faith, to the crucified Savior, and to commit ourselves to God as He is graciously revealed in Jesus Christ. This provision is made by the love of God, and is freely offered to everyone who will believe" *(The Gospel of John)*.

The statement "even so must the Son of man be lifted up" is a reference to the cross, on which the body of the condemned was lifted above the crowd of spectators.

The term "Son of man" comes from the prophecy of Daniel (7:13). It was Christ's favorite name for Himself. It signifies the incarnation of Deity in man—Christ was representative man and yet was God. He was lifted high on the cross of shame and agony. In referring to His crucifixion, Christ said, "And I, if I be lifted up from the earth, will draw all men unto me" (John 12:32).

Eternal life, referred to in John 3:15, is not the result of the belief, though it is given to believers alone. It flows from union with the Savior, who is life. Eternal life is God's life. It is the fullest life possible. It is a life of holiness, a life of peace and joy, a life that has no end. It is not simply life that endures forever, but life forever in God and with God.

To what extent do some believers tend to worship the cross rather than the Christ of the cross?

III. ETERNAL HIGH PRIEST (Leviticus 16:3–10, 14–16; Hebrews 9:11–15)

A. Preparation (Leviticus 16:3–10, 14–16)

(Leviticus 16:3–10, 14–16 is not included in the printed text.)

The Day of Atonement was the most solemn occasion in the Jewish year. Individual sins had been dealt with previously. Now "all the iniquities of the children of Israel, and all their transgressions in all their sins" (v. 21) were ceremonially atoned for in one solemn act. Only on this day could the high priest enter the Holy of Holies, the place where the glory of the God of Israel was visibly manifest.

Before the high priest could officiate, he must be ceremonially cleansed. No impurity could be tolerated in the holy presence of God.

The ornate priestly garments were put aside, and garments of white linen were put on for the services of the day. The Day of

Atonement was a day of humiliation. The "garments of glory" were inappropriate.

Next, Aaron offered sacrifices for himself and his family—a bullock for a sin offering, and a ram for a burnt offering. Although ceremonially cleansed, the priests of Israel were sinners and stood in need of atonement.

Then Aaron offered two male goats for a sin offering for the people, and a ram for a burnt offering. The two male goats constituted a single offering. Aaron cast two lots upon the goats: "one lot for the Lord, and the other lot for the scapegoat" (v. 8). The goat on which the lot fell "for the Lord" was offered as a sin offering. The other was released alive in the wilderness.

A young bull was presented to God for Aaron and the priests. Then a censer full of burning coals from the altar was taken with sweet incense into the Holy of Holies—"within the vail" (v. 12).

The incense was then placed on the fire so that a cloud of sweet-smelling fragrance filled the Holy of Holies. The blood of the bullock was sprinkled on the cover of the ark, the mercy seat, seven times.

The goat of the sin offering for the people was treated in a way similar to that of the bullock for the priests. Atonement was made for the Holy Place (the Holy of Holies, "within the vail") because of the uncleanness of the children of Israel. As the Tabernacle is the place where God meets sinful man, it must be ceremonially pure. No taint of the sin of man may appear in it.

B. Fulfillment (Hebrews 9:11–15)

(Hebrews 9:11, 12 is not included in the printed text.)

13. For if the blood of bulls and of goats, and the ashes of an heifer sprinkling the unclean, sanctifieth to the purifying of the flesh:

14. How much more shall the blood of Christ, who through the eternal Spirit offered himself without spot to God, purge your conscience from dead works to serve the living God?

The sin offerings presented on the Day of Atonement, or at any other time, had no effect on the consciences of those on whose behalf they were brought; they served merely in an external and symbolic manner to counteract the defilement of sin. Along with these offerings the author of Hebrews mentioned "the ashes of an heifer sprinkling the unclean." This is a reference to a purification ritual prescribed in Numbers 19, for the removal of ceremonial impurity.

But it is no mere ceremonial cleansing that is effected by the sacrifice of Christ. In verse 14 the author presented one of the most impressive instances of his "how much more" argument. The rituals of the old order effected external purification, but the blood of Christ cleanses the conscience. It does what rituals could not do.

Jesus' complete holiness and active obedience to God were essential to the effectiveness of His sacrifice. Christ's sacrifice of Himself on the cross was voluntary; it was a loving response to the holy will of God and to mankind's sinful condition. Those who believe on the Lord Jesus Christ, accepting thereby what He did for them on Calvary, are set free from inward bondage and can worship God in spirit and in truth. This is the perfection which the law could not provide.

15. And for this cause he is the mediator of the new testament,

that by means of death, for the redemption of the transgressions that were under the first testament, they which are called might receive the promise of eternal inheritance.

That Jesus was "the mediator of a better covenant" has already been stated in Hebrews 8:6. But now the basis of His mediatorship is made plain; that basis was His sacrificial death. By virtue of His death, redemption was made available to all who have broken the law of God. Christ gave His life that men might be liberated from their sins. The first covenant provided a measure of atonement and remission for sins committed under it, but it was incapable of providing eternal redemption; this blessing of God had to await the inauguration of the new covenant.

Why is sin such a great obstacle to worship?

REVIEW QUESTIONS

1. What were the instructions concerning the Passover lamb?
2. Where was the blood to be applied?
3. What was the purpose of the brazen serpent?
4. What did Jesus say about the brazen serpent?
5. Compare the work of the Old Testament priests with that of Christ.

GOLDEN TEXT HOMILY

"HE WAS WOUNDED FOR OUR TRANSGRESSIONS, HE WAS BRUISED FOR OUR INIQUITIES: THE CHASTISEMENT OF OUR PEACE WAS UPON HIM; AND WITH HIS STRIPES WE ARE HEALED" (Isaiah 53:5).

The most touching portrait of our Lord's vicarious sufferings is found in the prophetic Passion– poem of Isaiah 53 as the prophet reveals the person and passion of Jesus Christ and His provision for man's salvation.

Our Golden Text is precious to us because it depicts the passion of Jesus, the Lamb of God. The prophet used an accumulation of terms to describe the awful agony of our Savior at Calvary. He layered word upon word to enable us to grasp something of the intensity and extremity of our Lord's suffering upon the cross. With the use of the word *wounded*, the writer spoke of the piercing of Christ. The term *bruised* refers to the crushing weight of sin and woe upon the Lord, while *chastisement* tells us of the beating which left livid stripes in the flesh of Jesus. Though we read the words which describe the sufferings of our Lord, we can never fully understand all that He endured when He was beaten, bruised, and bloodied at Calvary. We simply stand in amazement at such suffering.

But the great truth here is not the revelation of those sufferings; it is the reason for such sufferings. The prophet made it clear that the Sufferer was not suffering for Himself, but for others. He was pierced, but it was for our transgressions. He was bruised or crushed, but it was for our iniquities. He was beaten, but it was for our healing and peace. It was the innocent suffering for the guilty. He took our place at Calvary and suffered the punishment we so clearly deserved—all this that we might be set free. Isaiah summed it up in verse 6: "The Lord hath laid on him the iniquity of us all." No wonder Paul declared, "The life which I now live . . . I live by the faith of the Son of God, who loved me, and gave himself for me" (Galatians 2:20).

Our Lord did not suffer and die in vain. Blessed are the results of His death. All who take His death to heart and accept Him as their sacrifice and substitute find their sins forgiven, their souls healed, and their minds resting in peace. He did it all for us that we might be made righteous in Him.

Our hearts ought to be filled with praise as we think of the unspeakable price which Christ paid at Calvary for our salvation.—**James Leggett, Vice Chairman and Assistant General Superintendent, International Pentecostal Holiness Church, Oklahoma City, Oklahoma**

SENTENCE SERMONS

CHRIST FULFILLS every Old Testament picture of redemption.

—Selected

ALL MY THEOLOGY is reduced to this narrow compass—Christ Jesus came into the world to save sinners.

—Archibald Alexander

REDEMPTION MEANS that Jesus Christ can put into any man the disposition that ruled His own life.

—Oswald Chambers

CHRIST IS THE BREAD for men's souls. In Him the church has enough to feed the whole world.

—Ian MacLaren

EVANGELISM APPLICATION

OLD TESTAMENT PICTURES OF REDEMPTION POINT SINNERS TO CHRIST.

Redemption means not only purchase by payment of the required ransom, but it also has in view particularly the deliverance, or setting free, of those who have been slaves and are in bondage. Deliverance is the prominent idea of redemption in both Testaments. All three words for *redeem* in the Old Testament enforce the truth of freedom or deliverance from bondage. One example is Psalm 136:24. The word rendered "redeem" here is "deliver" in Lamentations 5:8, and it is generally translated by the terms "break," or "rend," or "tear in pieces." At its root it signifies violent action. When applied to the work of God in redeeming Israel, it refers to His mighty power in breaking the forces of evil which held them and to His opening the Red Sea so that they might safely pass through it. There, too, His power shone forth in the destruction of their enemies, the Egyptians. In Egypt their redemption was effected by the sprinkling of the blood, which made them safe from the judgment of God; and then the passage at the Red Sea delivered them from the power of Pharaoh and his hosts. These find their fulfillment in the cross of Christ and His resurrection from the dead.

He who knew no sin was there to be made sin for us, that we might be made the righteousness of God in Him. He was there to suffer "without the gate" that He might sanctify the people with His own blood.

DAILY BIBLE READINGS

M. Provision for Sin. Genesis 22:1–14
T. Healer of Disease. Exodus 15:23–27
W. Messiah's Ministry. Isaiah 61:1–3
T. Ministry to the Hurting. Matthew 4:23–25
F. Lamb of God. John 1:29–34
S. Jesus Prays for Believers. John 17:20–26

Christ's Advent Foretold

Study Text: Deuteronomy 18:15–19; Psalm 24:7–10; Isaiah 59:20 through 60:3

Objective: To study Old Testament prophecies of Christ's first coming and praise Him for His incarnation.

Golden Text: "The Lord thy God will raise up unto thee a Prophet from the midst of thee . . . unto him ye shall hearken" (Deuteronomy 18:15).

Central Truth: Inspired by the Holy Spirit, Old Testament writers accurately announced Christ's first advent.

Evangelism Emphasis: Every Christian should tell the good news of Christ's first coming.

PRINTED TEXT

Isaiah 59:20. And the Redeemer shall come to Zion, and unto them that turn from transgression in Jacob, saith the Lord.

21. As for me, this is my covenant with them, saith the Lord; My spirit that is upon thee, and my words which I have put in thy mouth, shall not depart out of thy mouth, nor out of the mouth of thy seed, nor out of the mouth of thy seed's seed, saith the Lord, from henceforth and for ever.

60:1. Arise, shine; for thy light is come, and the glory of the Lord is risen upon thee.

2. For, behold, the darkness shall cover the earth, and gross darkness the people: but the Lord shall arise upon thee, and his glory shall be seen upon thee.

3. And the Gentiles shall come to thy light, and kings to the brightness of thy rising.

Psalm 24:7. Lift up your heads, O ye gates; and be ye lift up, ye everlasting doors; and the King of glory shall come in.

8. Who is this King of glory? The Lord strong and mighty, the Lord mighty in battle.

9. Lift up your heads, O ye gates; even lift them up, ye everlasting doors; and the King of glory shall come in.

10. Who is this King of glory? The Lord of hosts, he is the King of glory. Selah.

Deuteronomy 18:15. The Lord thy God will raise up unto thee a Prophet from the midst of thee, of thy brethren, like unto me; unto him ye shall hearken;

16. According to all that thou desiredst of the Lord thy God in Horeb in the day of the assembly, saying, Let me not hear again the voice of the Lord my God, neither let me see this great fire any more, that I die not.

17. And the Lord said unto me, They have well spoken that which they have spoken.

18. I will raise them up a Prophet from among their brethren, like unto thee, and will put my words in his mouth; and he shall speak unto them all that I shall command him.

19. And it shall come to pass, that whosoever will not hearken unto my words which he shall speak in my name, I will require it of him.

LESSON OUTLINE

I. COMING REDEEMER
   A. God's Commitment to the Redeemed
   B. Fulfilled Prophecy

II. CONQUERING KING

III. PROPHET OF THE LORD
   A. The Prophet's Coming Announced
   B. The Prophet's Message Foretold

LESSON EXPOSITION

INTRODUCTION

The lesson for next Sunday is the Christmas emphasis, which focuses on the birth of Jesus, thereby fulfilling the prophetic messages given in the Old Testament many centuries earlier. Our study today relates to prophecies concerning that momentous event.

As we study the events of Christ's first coming, it is indeed a solemn reminder that history is unfolding toward His second coming. Prophetic events that mark the end times are evident. Prophecy holds a unique place in the interests of Bible scholars, since in its pure form it is divinely inspired utterances given by a prophet who has been willing to speak a particular message for God regardless of the personal consequences. The unfolding of events as told by God's prophets builds our faith. It gives evidence that we can put total confidence in God.

Most prophecies to the Jewish people were messages of judgment, condemning sins and a lethargic mind–set. But on the benefits side are the prophecies concerning God's help and blessings as they returned and truly worshiped Jehovah.

The prophecies concerning Christ's first coming that our lesson today deals with emerged from the mix of judgments and blessings recorded in Isaiah 59 and 60, Psalm 24, and Deuteronomy 18. While limited by space, today's study provides a glimpse into what the Bible says about Christ's coming as Redeemer, Conquering King, and Prophet of the Lord.

I. COMING REDEEMER (Isaiah 59:20, 21; 60:1–3)

The prophet Isaiah's vision and concerns included the wide world reaching far beyond the borders of Judah—to Assyria, Babylon, Philistia, Moab, Egypt, Edom, Arabia, and Tyre. Many of his predictions have passed into history, but some of them remain unfulfilled yet. His book at times pictures the darkness of forthcoming storms, followed by the prediction of the rainbow shining through. And then Isaiah transports his readers on to the Golden Age that still lies ahead for the world.

Isaiah is called the messianic prophet because he was so

thoroughly imbued with the idea that his nation was to be the messianic nation through whom a great and wonderful blessing would come from God to all nations. And he was continually dreaming of that day when the great and wonderful work would be done. The New Testament says that Isaiah "saw [Christ's] glory and spoke of Him" (John 12:41, *NIV*).

Isaiah delighted himself with prophecy concerning the Messiah as Redeemer and as a Sovereign bringing both the Cross and the crown into focus. Christ is as much the Lamb of God in Isaiah's writing as He is the Lion of the tribe of Judah.

The section of Isaiah that is considered in this lesson will perhaps be more meaningful with a bit of background. The Israelites had returned from Babylon with some of the promises of Isaiah still ringing in their ears. They were expecting the Temple to be restored (see 44:28), the land to be bustling with joyful people (49:19–21), that wealth from surrounding nations would enrich them (45:14), and even that kings of surrounding lands would pay homage to them. When these promises were not immediately kept, the people lost heart and began questioning the power and goodness of God.

Isaiah challenged the people and laid the blame squarely on the people themselves. He told them that their iniquities had made a separation between them and God and that their sins had hidden God's face so that He did not hear their prayers (54:8; 59:2).

The prophet's charge against the nation is detailed in 59:1–8, followed by Israel's confession of guilt in verses 9–15a through prayer offered by Isaiah. Beginning with verse 15b a picture of God's intervention to save Israel is presented. Israel's failure as a righteous people could not defeat the purpose of God. When God finds no human helper to intervene on behalf of the downtrodden, He enters the picture and wins the victory (63:3–6)

A. God's Commitment to the Redeemed (Isaiah 59:20, 21)

20. And the Redeemer shall come to Zion, and unto them that turn from transgression in Jacob, saith the Lord.

21. As for me, this is my covenant with them, saith the Lord; My spirit that is upon thee, and my words which I have put in thy mouth, shall not depart out of thy mouth, nor out of the mouth of thy seed, nor out of the mouth of thy seed's seed, saith the Lord, from henceforth and for ever.

God is sovereign of the universe and He steps in to help the downtrodden and oppressed since they cannot help themselves. Isaiah saw that the time would come for the Incarnation, when God would raise up a true Intercessor.

The Hebrew term *ga'al*—"kinsman–redeemer"—is used in verse 20, as it is also in 41:14 and 43:1. The choice of the term is significant since the practice of redemption figured strongly into Jewish theology. The essential purpose of a redemptive act is to deliver a person or thing from captivity or loss, and it becomes an apparent image for God's saving action among men. Against the background of Hebrew law, the image had a vividness which can hardly be realized by individuals of different background and culture. "This term is one of the favorite names for God (44:24; 47:4), pointing as it does not merely to the fact that Yahweh delivers His people; but that He has an obligation to do so because of having adopted them for His own. He is their 'Next of Kin'" (*The Interpreter's Dictionary of the Bible,* Vol. 4).

The *New Century Bible* translates verse 20 as "Then a Savior will come to Jerusalem and to the people of Jacob who have turned from sin." Also, the *Peshitta* (the official and oldest Syriac versions of the Scripture) gives the same translation.

God made a new and eternal covenant with the repentant and redeemed (v. 21). God's message and the anointing will not fail. "The new covenant is to involve the gift of the Spirit that writes the law of God inwardly in the heart, as distinct from the Law, which is thought of as outside the conscience doing its work as an accuser and judge" (*Beacon Bible Commentary,* Vol. 4).

The prophet Isaiah's hope was not in man's faith, virtue, or ability, but in God's faithfulness and the power of His Word and Spirit to bring change in people, generation after generation. God is still carrying out His faithfulness with each new day.

B. Fulfilled Prophecy (vv. 60:1–3)

1. Arise, shine; for thy light is come, and the glory of the Lord is risen upon thee.

2. For, behold, the darkness shall cover the earth, and gross darkness the people: but the Lord shall arise upon thee, and his glory shall be seen upon thee.

3. And the Gentiles shall come to thy light, and kings to the brightness of thy rising.

Expressed poetically and as if the then–future event had already happened, Isaiah 60 opens with a double imperative: "Arise, shine." The command was for Zion not only to accept joyfully the proclamation of her salvation through the Redeemer but also to reflect the light of the glory of the Lord, which had risen upon her. The "glory of the Lord" stands for the revelation of His power and holiness (Exodus 24:16; Psalm 19:1; John 1:14).

In verse 2, the prophet pictured Zion (Jerusalem) as an island of light in a sea of darkness that shrouded the people in gross darkness. Darkness is here representative of sin and unrighteousness, while light is representative of righteousness and holiness. It seems that Isaiah was saying Zion was in the midst of a wicked world shaped by humanism, self–made philosophies, and unrighteousness, but God's glory would shine through the Redeemer, Jesus Christ.

Verse 3 gives assurance that the Gentile nations would come to the light, and kings would be drawn to the brightness of the dawning light. The light of Christ and the gospel are drawing powers for all nations and rulers. The prophet emphasized the nature of Zion's mission to the nations: her first task is not to go out and seek to evangelize the nations but rather to reflect the light of the glory of God with such clarity that they will be drawn to her (see 45:14, 15; Zechariah 8:20–23).

Are there modern–day examples of churches that truly reflect the light of the glory of God so intensely that people are drawn to them with little outreach effort?

II. CONQUERING KING (Psalm 24:7–10)

Psalms 22 through 24 comprise a tremendous trilogy which is basically Christological. The three psalms are ascribed to David, and the close relationship of the three has long been noted. G. Campbell Morgan, in his book *Living Messages of the Bible, Genesis to Malachi*, captions them respectively "The Savior," "The Shepherd," and "The Sovereign." Other Bible scholars refer to them in order as "The Cross," "The Crook" (shepherd's staff), and "The Crown." Certainly the emphasis of the first two gives a natural tie to the "Conquering King" focus of the verses to be considered in this section of the lesson.

From a historical perspective Psalm 24 may have been written for the occasion when the ark of the Lord was brought to the tent prepared for it on Mount Zion (2 Samuel 6:1–15). No other psalm seems to fit as well. However, the psalm was greater than that occasion if it was indeed for the movement of the ark to a new location. Leslie McCaw notes in his book *Psalms, the New Bible Commentary:* "This psalm has generally been interpreted as a prophetic expression of Christ's ascension after victory over death and sin as well as His ultimate sovereignty over all (see verse 10 and compare James 2:1; Revelation 5:11–14; and 17:14)." So in addition to the historical perspective, it is essential to consider the prophetic application of the verses of our lesson. The prophetic consideration will follow the historical commentary.

The historical setting of this psalm is apparently a call to procession, then the procession itself, and finally the entry into the Temple of Yahweh on Mount Zion. The people involved in the event are singers, priests and/or prophets, and worshipers who are counted worthy of joining the procession and entering the Temple.

In verses 1–6 the psalmist indicates the procession is called to those on their way up the slope toward the Temple, by a majestic hymn to God the Creator, to whom dominion belongs. It is likely that the hymn was sung by a part of the Temple choir, indicating the earth belongs to the Lord because He founded it and made it firm on the seas and rivers of pre–Creation chaos and was brought under His rule by the power of His command.

Then the question rings out: "Who shall ascend into the hill of the Lord? or who shall stand in his holy place?" (v. 3). The question is rhetorical and calls for priestly instruction or truth. The answer comes: "He that hath clean hands, and a pure heart; who hath not lifted up his soul unto vanity, nor sworn deceitfully" (v. 4). Such a person will receive the blessings of the Lord.

Beginning with verse 7 the procession of worshipers has made its way to the great doors of the Temple (vividly described by Ezekiel 40:5–16).

7. Lift up your heads, O ye gates; and be ye lift up, ye everlasting doors; and the King of glory shall come in.

8. Who is this King of glory? The Lord strong and mighty, the Lord mighty in battle.

9. Lift up your heads, O ye gates; even lift them up, ye everlasting doors; and the King of glory shall come in.

10. Who is this King of glory? The Lord of hosts, he is the King of glory. Selah.

The call rings out: "Lift up your heads, O ye gates." The gates are here personified and called upon to open in dignity and reverence for the entrance of the King of Glory. The expression "ye everlasting doors" is better translated "you ancient doors," referring to their duration of many years.

The call to the doors is then followed by a challenge from the gates (perhaps the gatekeeper): "Who is this King of glory?" The answer is, "The Lord strong and mighty, the Lord mighty in battle." God had proven Himself more than a match for any foe that might arise. Then the question is repeated with great rhetorical effect. The second question is answered with the words "The Lord of hosts, he is the King of glory." This is the first time in the Psalms where a familiar and beautiful title for the true God is given. He is "the Lord of hosts" (Yahweh Tsebaoth), hence the Captain both of the armies of Israel and of all the hosts of heaven—the supreme Ruler of the universe. With the assertion of Yahweh's dominion, the hymn and the procession are ended and the worshipers are moved into the sanctuary for a more intimate worship and celebration of their great God.

As mentioned earlier, it is essential also to consider the prophetic application of verses 7–10 in their Christological setting since there seems to be an unfolding revelation of future events. The concept of progressive revelation, along with evidence of revealed truths, has long been a part of sound biblical exegesis. In his book *Exposition of Holy Scriptures (Psalm)*, Alexander Maclaren states: "We must never forget that in the Old Testament we have to do with an incomplete and a progressive revelation, and that if we would understand its significance we must ever endeavor to ascertain to what point in that progress the words under consideration belong. We are not to read into Old Testament words New Testament depth and fulness of meaning; we are to take them and try to find out what they meant to the writer and to his people; and so we shall get a firm basis for any deeper significance which we may hereafter see in them."

Many Bible scholars, including Maclaren have included the prophetic application of verses 7–10, which focuses on Christ. Maclaren says, "The devout hearts in Israel felt that something more was needed than this dwelling of Jehovah within an earthly Temple, and the process of revelation familiarized them with the thought that there was to be in the future a 'coming of the Lord' in some special manner unknown to them. So that the whole anticipation and forward look of the Old Testament system is gathered into and expressed by almost its last words which prophesy that 'the Lord shall suddenly come to His Temple' and that once again this King of glory shall stand before the ancient doors and summons them to open."

For the Christian, one great memory fills the past—Christ has come. And one great hope brightens the otherwise bleak future—Christ will come again. Perhaps that hope has been cherished only by those who hold a particular opinion as to the chronology of unfulfilled prophecy. But it should be to every Christian heart the blessed hope—this appearing of Him who has come in the past. He is both with us and in us in the present, but He will come in the future 'in His glory and will then sit on the throne of His glory.

What do you think is God's purpose in giving some information by progressive steps?

III. PROPHET OF THE LORD (Deuteronomy 18:15–19)

To set this passage of Scripture in its context, it is essential to remind ourselves that the Book of Deuteronomy is basically Moses' last words to Israel. As the book opens, the people of Israel are camped on the plains just across the Jordan River from Canaan. The many people who saw God's miracles surrounding the exodus from Egypt have passed from the scene, due to their unwillingness to trust Jehovah; and a new generation has grown to maturity during the 40 years of wilderness wanderings. The new group is eager to move into Canaan and remove the opposing forces.

Moses, the leader they have come to trust, is about to die, and a new leader will be in charge of the move and occupation of the land. Much aware of his own destiny, Moses assembles the people he has loved and led to hear his final words. The words recorded on the pages of Deuteronomy sum up the central truths and basic principles Moses has come to understand through his many years of intimate relationship with the Lord. Speaking under the inspiration of God's Spirit, Moses reviews the history of God's saving work for Israel. He explains the motives behind God's choice of Israel and God's gift of the Law, but he also includes a review of the instructions for holy living.

Deuteronomy 18 is the key biblical passage dealing with the validity of Old Testament prophets. It gives the criteria to be used by Israel in recognizing a spokesman for God. The true prophet will be an Israelite, will speak in the name of the Lord and not another god, and what the true prophet predicts will come true (v. 22).

In addition to local leaders, the priests and legal experts who comprised the supreme court, and the king, Israel had other leaders. These included the ordinary priests and Levites who served brief shifts at the central sanctuary (vv. 1–8) and, most notably, the prophets. The role of prophet was not hereditary. God called and commissioned individuals as He chose, from any of Israel's tribes. The prophets provided guidance for special situations, at times to individuals, but usually to those who ruled God's people.

In the ancient world, however, it was not uncommon for people to turn to sorcery or divination in search of supernatural guidance. Some in today's world do the same thing, turning to palm readers, spiritists, or astrology. In verses 9–14 Israel was bluntly informed that such practices are detestable. God's people are not to engage in any of them.

Immediately following that admonition, God made a promise. Aware that situations will arise which had no direct answer from Scripture, God said, "I will raise them up a Prophet " (v. 18).

A. The Prophet's Coming Announced (vv. 15–17)

15. The Lord thy God will raise up unto thee a Prophet from the midst of thee, of thy brethren, like unto me; unto him ye shall hearken;

16. According to all that thou desiredst of the Lord thy God in Horeb in the day of the assembly, saying, Let me not hear again the voice of the Lord my God, neither let me see this great fire any more, that I die not.

17. And the Lord said unto

me, They have well spoken that which they have spoken.

The Prophet that Moses spoke about was to be a special prophet. While other prophets were included in the general announcement of the prophetic office, the One Moses referred to would be the Prophet who would be over all other prophets. He would be the Prophet–Messiah and would be a man "like unto" Moses himself.

Moses is a prototype prophet. He was commissioned as God's spokesman and communicated the Word of God that was to shape Israel's lifestyle in the Promised Land. The disciples of Jesus recognized that the prophecy of Moses was fulfilled in Christ (John 1:45; Acts 3:22). But Christ Jesus was more than a prophet; His role is as Prophet, Priest, and King.

Prophecy is still a viable ministry today. The dedicated minister serves as both prophet and priest. He is to speak for God (prophet) and to speak on behalf of his people to God (priest).

Verse 16 alludes to the Israelites who were present on the occasion when Moses received the Ten Commandments from God at Mount Sinai. The people were terrified to the extent that they begged God never to speak to them in that manner again. His presence had so overwhelmed them that they thought they were going to die.

God had agreed to the request of the Israelites and would send spokesmen from among them to communicate God's messages. But in the person of His Son, God again spoke face–to–face with the human family.

We are reminded through this incident, where the people were so overwhelmed by the presence of God that they asked that they be spared from such an experience again, of the compassion and mercy of the Lord. It would have been His right to retain the original approach of communicating with His people. But His love and mercy revealed what He had for the future—prophets and of course eventually Jesus—the Prophet–Messiah.

B. The Prophet's Message Foretold (vv. 18, 19)

18. I will raise them up a Prophet from among their brethren, like unto thee, and will put my words in his mouth; and he shall speak unto them all that I shall command him.

19. And it shall come to pass, that whosoever will not hearken unto my words which he shall speak in my name, I will require it of him.

In verse 18, Moses repeated the subject matter of verse 15, except this time the words are given in the words of God himself. The promise of the Prophet which Moses gave is now confirmed by the words of Jehovah. In verse 15 Moses said, "Unto him ye shall hearken," but in verse 18 the source and authority by which the Prophet will speak is given; that is, the Prophet will speak the very words of God to them—"all that I shall command him." In the New Testament we have the literal fulfillment of this promise of God when Jesus said, "I can of mine own self do nothing: as I hear, I judge: and my judgment is just; because I seek not mine own will, but the will of the Father which hath sent me" (John 5:30).

In verse 19, God was saying through His servant Moses that there would be a responsibility of obedience to the teaching and words of the future Prophet. His words are not to be rejected; but if they are, a requirement becomes necessary—hence a judgment for disobedience and rebellion.

Weldon O. Klopfenstein reminds us: "Christ's words can never be taken lightly. Not only is obedience required because of who He is, but no other one can bring salvation to sin–cursed mankind (Acts 4:12). If we disregard the message of salvation, we both lose our hope of eternal reward and place ourselves in the position where God, because of His forewarning, must punish the disobedience" (*Evangelical Sunday School Lesson Commentary,* Vol. 13).

REVIEW QUESTIONS

1. What mind–set did the Jewish people have following their return from Babylon that caused them to question the power and goodness of God?
2. What promise did God make in Isaiah 59:21 to the person who is willing to stand for righteousness?
3. In addition to the historical interpretation of Psalm 24, what prophetic interpretation does it have?
4. In what ways would the promised Prophet be like Moses?
5. What was the Israelites' reaction to the experience they had at Mount Sinai?

GOLDEN TEXT HOMILY

"THE LORD THY GOD WILL RAISE UP UNTO THEE A PROPHET FROM THE MIDST OF THEE . . . UNTO HIM YE SHALL HEARKEN" (Deuteronomy 18:15).

Many commentators, even Evangelical commentators, consider that this Mosaic prediction has in mind each true prophet of the Lord who would be raised up generation after generation in Old Testament times. The Lord was saying to His people that they must not follow the spiritistic and demonic voices by which pagan nations were ruled and guided (vv. 9–14). They must obey the true prophets of the Lord in Israel who would interpret and apply and build on the revelation which had been given through Moses.

There is a measure of truth in this explanation, but in the light of the New Testament we must go further. The ultimate prophet of the Lord, whose Spirit was the source of whatever truth came through other prophets of the Lord in Israel (see John 1:9; 1 Peter 1:10–12), was the Lord Jesus Christ (John 5:45–47; Acts 3:22, 23; 7:37; cf. John 4:25).

It seems evident that the supernatural voice which was heard on the Mount of Transfiguration— "A voice came out of the cloud, saying, 'This is My beloved Son, in whom I am well pleased. Hear Him!'" (Matthew 17:5, *NKJV*)—had Deuteronomy 18 in mind. The three apostles were told to "hear Him!" Christ is that Prophet of the Lord of whom Moses had spoken. The people of God must hear Him! Pagans (and they are not all in the Far East; there are millions of pagans in Western society today) may be tuning in to all kinds of voices. But the church must "hear Him," the Prophet of the Lord.

Moreover, all other acclaimed prophets and prophecies, even within the Pentecostal and Charismatic world, must be compared with and evaluated by the pure light of Jesus Christ, of which the New Testament is the inspired and authentic record.—**Noel Brooks, D.D. (Retired), Avon, England, Writer, *Adult Sunday School Teacher Quarterly,* International Pentecostal Holiness Church, Oklahoma City, Oklahoma**

SENTENCE SERMONS

INSPIRED BY THE HOLY SPIRIT, Old Testament writers accurately announced Christ's first advent.

—Selected

I READ IN A BOOK that a man called Christ went about doing good. It is very disconcerting to me that I am satisfied with just going about.

—Toyohiko Kagawa

CHRIST'S MESSAGE was revolutionizing; His words simple, yet profound. And His words provoked either happy acceptance or violent rejection.

—Billy Graham

EVANGELISM APPLICATION

EVERY CHRISTIAN SHOULD TELL THE GOOD NEWS OF CHRIST'S FIRST COMING.

Miss Frances Ridley Havergal, soon after she became a Christian, went to a school at Dusseldorf. Her heart was warm with love for her Savior and she was eager to speak for Him. To her dismay, however, she soon discovered that among the hundred girls she was the only Christian. Her first feeling was that she could not confess Christ in that great company of unchristian companions. Her gentle sensitive heart shrank from a duty so hard. Her second thought, however, was that she could not refrain from confessing Christ. "I am the only one He has here," she said. And this thought became a source of strength and inspiration. She felt she was Christ's witness in that school, His only witness, and she dare not fail.

—Knight's Masterbook of New Illustrations

ILLUMINATING THE LESSON

In the Rospigliosi Palace in Rome is Guido Reni's famous fresco, "The Aurora," a work unequaled in that period for nobility of line and poetry and color. It is painted on a lofty ceiling. As you stand on the pavement and look up at it, your neck stiffens, your head grows dizzy, and the figures become hazy and indistinct. And so the owner of the palace has placed a broad mirror near the floor. In it the picture is reflected and you can sit down before it and study the wonderful work in comfort.

Jesus Christ does precisely that for us when we try to get some notion of God. He is the mirror of Deity. He is the express image of God's person. He interprets God to our dull hearts. In Him God becomes visible and intelligent to us. He is God stooping down to our level and He enables our feeble thoughts to get some real hold on God himself.

—Frank M. Fairchild in *Moody Monthly*

DAILY BIBLE READINGS

M. Promise From God. Genesis 3:9–15
T. Righteous Branch. Isaiah 11:1–5
W. Honorable Ruler. Micah 5:2–5
T. Wonderful Blessing. Luke 1:39–45
F. Song of Praise. Luke 1:46–55
S. Promise of Justification. Galatians 3:19–25

Wise Men Worship Christ (Christmas)

Study Text: Matthew 2:1–23

Objective: To review the meaning of Christmas and commit to love Christ the King.

Time: Scholars differ on the time of the birth of Christ; but it is generally considered to have been 4 or 5 B.C.

Place: Bethlehem

Golden Text: "When they were come into the house, they saw the young child with Mary his mother, and fell down, and worshipped him" (Matthew 2:11).

Central Truth: Obedience to God's Word will cause people to believe in, love, and worship Jesus Christ.

Evangelism Emphasis: Obedience to God's Word will cause people to believe in, love, and worship Jesus Christ.

PRINTED TEXT

Matthew 2:1. Now when Jesus was born in Bethlehem of Judaea in the days of Herod the king, behold, there came wise men from the east to Jerusalem,

2. Saying, Where is he that is born King of the Jews? for we have seen his star in the east, and are come to worship him.

3. When Herod the king had heard these things, he was troubled, and all Jerusalem with him.

4. And when he had gathered all the chief priests and scribes of the people together, he demanded of them where Christ should be born.

5. And they said unto him, In Bethlehem of Judaea: for thus it is written by the prophet,

6. And thou Bethlehem, in the land of Juda, art not the least among the princes of Juda: for out of thee shall come a Governor, that shall rule my people Israel.

7. Then Herod, when he had privily called the wise men, enquired of them diligently what time the star appeared.

8. And he sent them to Bethlehem, and said, Go and search diligently for the young child; and when ye have found him, bring me word again, that I may come and worship him also.

9. When they had heard the king, they departed; and, lo, the star, which they saw in the east, went before them, till it came and stood over where the young child was.

10. When they saw the star, they rejoiced with exceeding great joy.

11. And when they were come into the house, they saw the young child with Mary his mother, and fell down, and worshipped him: and when they had opened their treasures, they presented

unto him gifts; gold, and frankincense, and myrrh.

12. And being warned of God in a dream that they should not return to Herod, they departed into their own country another way.

LESSON OUTLINE

I. SEEKING GOD'S SON
   - A. The Wise Men
   - B. The Birthplace
   - C. Herod's Reaction

II. WORSHIPING GOD'S SON
   - A. The Star and the Child
   - B. The Star and Their Joy
   - C. The Gifts

III. OBEYING GOD'S WILL
   - A. Warned by God
   - B. Out of Egypt
   - C. Herod Enraged
   - D. Returning to Nazareth

LESSON EXPOSITION

INTRODUCTION

Attitude is what Christmas is all about. In the passage we study today, we observe two contrasting attitudes relative to the Lord. The Magi came from the East to worship Him. Herod took what steps he could to destroy Him. This contrast between love and hate toward the Lord has been repeated many times throughout history.

Some people today are still threatened by the celebration of the birth of the Christ child. This is reflected in lawsuits to have Nativity scenes and any other reference to Christ or the Christian faith removed from government property. Schools are restricted as to how much of the Christmas story they can tell, even which songs they can sing.

The commercialization of Christmas has taken away from the true meaning of the season. For some, Christmas is no more than an opportunity to make a huge profit. Some businesses fail, while others prosper—based on how sales go during the Yuletide season. This emphasis is not bad in itself, but it is bad if profit is the only concern and Christ is left out entirely.

There are still many, however, who understand the true meaning of Christmas. To them it is more than a holiday; it is a *holy* day. Time is spent in worship and the adoration of our lovely Lord. As believers, we have a responsibility to spread the word about what Christmas is all about. Perhaps our journey back to the city of Bethlehem today will better prepare us to capture the spirit of Christmas and to display that attitude more prominently among our associates.

What is your definition of the true meaning of Christmas?

I. SEEKING GOD'S SON (Matthew 2:1–8)

A. The Wise Men (vv. 1, 2)

1. Now when Jesus was born in Bethlehem of Judaea in the days of Herod the king, behold, there came wise men from the east to Jerusalem,

2. Saying, Where is he that is born King of the Jews? for we have seen his star in the east, and are come to worship him.

Bethlehem is rich with history. It was the setting for most of the Book of Ruth. It was David's home and the scene of his anointing by Samuel. However, Bethlehem is best known as the birthplace of Jesus. It means "house of bread," and the meaning takes on added significance through Christ, who is the Bread of Life. Located five miles south of Jerusalem, a church marks the traditional site of Jesus' birth.

While Herod was king, "wise men from the east" arrived in Jerusalem bearing gifts for the newborn Messiah. Matthew made no effort to identify these men. He only said that they were from the East, which could mean Arabia, Mesopotamia, or regions beyond. These men were not Jews; they were foreigners. They were guided by a star. Jews often identified the "Star out of Jacob" with the Messiah. Balaam prophesied, "I shall see him, but not now: I shall behold him, but not nigh: there shall come a Star out of Jacob, and a Sceptre shall rise out of Israel, and shall smite the corners of Moab, and destroy all the children of Sheth" (Numbers 24:17). The psalmist also spoke of kings bearing gifts: "Because of thy temple at Jerusalem shall kings bring presents unto thee" (Psalm 68:29).

Recognizing the One to whom the star was pointing as the King of the Jews, the wise men came to worship Him.

So many things keep us from worship. Maula Powers, a storyteller, understands the Enemy well. The Germans, she says, called him "Advent Teufel" (Advent Devil). In their thinking, it is the Advent Devil who comes to try to keep people so busy in outward affairs that they lose sight of the real meaning of Christmas. He doesn't want people to have time to experience the rebirth which Christ works within.

The temptations of the Advent Devil are diabolically clever. He makes it so easy to go along with the flow of seasonal celebrations.

"There is so much rushing around during the holiday season," Powers says. "It has become the busiest time of the year. We want to read Christmas stories. We want to have time to anticipate and feel the awe and wonder of the Christmas miracle. But we're so busy we don't have time. So Christmas passes, and nothing has happened to us inside."

The Advent Devil's business is to keep us so busy with holiday obligations that we forgo daily prayer and Scripture reading. He must be resisted, and worship must be given a central place during the Yuletide season.

B. The Birthplace (vv. 3–6)

3. When Herod the king had heard these things, he was troubled, and all Jerusalem with him.

4. And when he had gathered all the chief priests and scribes of the people together, he demanded of them where Christ should be born.

5. And they said unto him, In Bethlehem of Judaea: for thus it is written by the prophet,

6. And thou Bethlehem, in the land of Juda, art not the least among the princes of Juda: for out of thee shall come a Governor, that shall rule my people Israel.

Herod received the word of the birth of the Christ child as a threat. A rival king was on the horizon. He called the chief priests and scribes together to learn more about this king and to identify His birthplace. They declared Bethlehem to be the place of His birth and further heightened the king's fears by announcing that this child would be a "Governor, that shall rule my people Israel."

From a human point of view, Herod's fear was understandable. After all, he was not the rightful king over Israel. He was not of the lineage of David; neither was He a descendant of Jacob. He had, in fact, descended from Esau and thus was an Edomite. He was hated by most of the Jews and never really accepted as their king. If it could be determined that this baby had every right to the throne of Israel, Herod would perceive his reign to be in jeopardy.

Even Herod subscribed to the idea of a Messiah. When he was told of the inquiry of the wise men about the King of the Jews, Herod associated this with the Messiah. He even asked the scholars about "the Christ." Indeed Israel had a messianic hope and believed that the Messiah would be born. Jews still embrace this hope while believers know it is fulfilled in Christ Jesus.

How do you respond to truth? When Herod heard the truth about the Christ child, he "was troubled, and all Jerusalem with him." What emotions do you feel when you hear talk about the second coming of Christ? Do you welcome such talk or does it fill you with anxiety? Rather than producing fear, the thought of our Lord's return should call us to renewed commitment. The apostle Peter challenged us with these words, "Seeing then that all these things shall be dissolved, what manner of persons ought ye to be in all holy conversation and godliness, looking for and hasting unto the coming of the day of God" (2 Peter 3:11, 12).

Why was Herod so agitated about the possible birth of a rival when he must have realized that his own time was short?

C. Herod's Reaction (vv. 7, 8)

7. Then Herod, when he had privily called the wise men, enquired of them diligently what time the star appeared.

8. And he sent them to Bethlehem, and said, Go and search diligently for the young child; and when ye have found him, bring me word again, that I may come and worship him also.

We detect a note of urgency in Herod's request as to when the star appeared. This information would allow him to know the approximate age of the child. He used this information later in his infamous slaughter of the babies.

Herod was a master of craftiness and deception. He concealed his real purpose in seeking to learn about the Christ child. When he encouraged the wise men to search diligently for the child and then report to him, he had no intentions of worshiping Jesus. His whole purpose was to get rid of Him.

In his deception, Herod was following the example of his master, Satan. He found himself in the same position as the Pharisees when Jesus said to them, "Ye are of your father the devil, and the lusts of your father ye will do. He was a murderer from the beginning, and abode not in the truth, because there is no truth in him. When he speaketh a lie, he speaketh of his own: for he is a liar, and the father of it" (John 8:44).

Don't expect Satan to reveal his real purpose when he approaches you. He disguises himself as an angel of light. He puts on his best face when he is trying to entice you away from the Lord. He wants you to believe his objectives are noble. And he is so clever and has so much experience deceiving men that he can be very persuasive. We need to put on the whole armor of God to deal with him. The Word, the Spirit, and the shield of faith are all needed to offset the devious ploys of the Evil One.

The Lord has provided us with all that we need to be victorious over the Enemy. Satan trembles in the presence of the Word of God. In His great temptation, Jesus repeatedly said, "It is written." Christ answered every half-truth or deceptive remark of the devil with a quotation from God's Word. Also, the Holy Spirit in you is greater than Satan and all his forces. The combination of the Word and the Spirit will put the Enemy to flight every time.

II. WORSHIPING GOD'S SON (Matthew 2:9–11)

A. The Star and the Child (v. 9)

9. When they had heard the king, they departed; and, lo, the star, which they saw in the east, went before them, till it came and stood over where the young child was.

How do you suppose the wise men felt when they learned that the king knew very little about the One to whom the star was leading them? He found it necessary to inquire of the priests and scribes as to the birthplace of the Christ. But because of this encounter, the wise men had more than the guidance of the star; they also had the sure word of prophecy. Centuries before, Bethlehem had been identified by the prophets as the place where the Messiah was to be born.

God's Word is a sure guide in every area of life. It shows us the way to Christ. Paul wrote to Timothy: "And that from a child thou hast known the holy scriptures, which are able to make thee wise unto salvation through faith which is in Christ Jesus" (2 Timothy 3:15). It touches all aspects of life. John Quincy Adams said: "So great is my veneration of the Bible, that the earlier my children begin to read it, the more confident will be my hope that they will prove useful citizens of their country and respectable members of society."

As soon as the wise men resumed their journey, the star appeared again to guide them. This same star that had aroused their hopes at the beginning of the journey would now take them to the end of the venture. The star led them to the very place where the new King was to be found.

B. The Star and Their Joy (v. 10)

10. When they saw the star, they rejoiced with exceeding great joy.

The *Pulpit Commentary* notes that the reappearance of the star "was the pledge of the full answer to their search, the full reward of their toilsome journey." When they saw the star again and learned that it would now direct them to the Messiah, they were exuberant.

All of us need those moments when the light shines upon our path bringing us hope and encouragement. In *Farewell to Fear*, Nelson L. Price tells about an impoverished widow awaiting eviction. She was far behind in her rent. Other bills had accumulated. Her utilities had been turned off and her eviction notice received.

There was a knock on her door. She cowered inside in absolute silence. Her doors were locked and her drapes drawn. In terror she heard again the knock on the door. Breathlessly, she trembled at the sound. Finally the knocking ceased. She gained a sense of relief. Her conditions prompted her to assume it was the officials who had come to repossess her properties and put her out on the street. The knock at the door had caused her to freeze in fright.

Had she the courage to answer, she would have found to her delight quite a different situation. The knock was by her pastor. Through the grace of friends he had accumulated enough money to pay her utilities, rent, and other bills. He had come to share the good news and offer her the relief she needed.

All of us can testify that we have had a friend to knock at the door of our life. All of us have seen a light shining in the darkness. We have found that friend and that light in the Word of God. The psalmist wrote, "Thy word is a lamp unto my feet, and a light unto my path" (Psalm 119:105).

C. The Gifts (v. 11)

11. And when they were come into the house, they saw the young child with Mary his mother, and fell down, and worshipped him: and when they had opened their treasures, they presented unto him gifts; gold, and frankincense, and myrrh.

The wise men did not find Jesus in a manger as did the shepherds, but rather in a house. Apparently, after the busy tax season, Mary and Joseph were able to find a house. The wise men had believed in Him before they saw Him when they had only His star to guide then. But when they saw the baby in His mother's arms, their faith reached its crowning point and they responded in reverent worship before Him.

The next action of the wise men was in keeping with Eastern custom. They opened their treasure chests and presented the three traditional gifts of homage to a ruler—gold, frankincense, and myrrh. Gold was a gift for a king; frankincense, a gift for deity; and myrrh, a gift with an advance warning of death. So Adam Clark could say that they gave Him "incense as their God, gold as their King, myrrh as [relating] to a human body, subject to suffering and death."

The wise men offered to Christ the very finest of gifts. In so doing, they set an example for all believers. Nothing but our best is good enough for our Lord. He deserves that we live before Him, by His grace, a life of consecration and holiness. Our life should be so permeated with Christ's presence that all we do has His stamp of approval. There should be no secret places in our life where His presence is unwelcome. Worship should be as common for us as any daily activity, yet as reverent as standing in His holy presence.

What do you suppose happened to the gifts Jesus received?

III. OBEYING GOD'S WILL (Matthew 2:12–23)

A. Warned by God (v. 12)

12. And being warned of God in a dream that they should not return to Herod, they departed into their own country another way.

By means of divine revelation, God made known to the wise men that they should not return to Herod. It is possible that their obedience saved their lives. It is certain that their obedience preserved the life of the infant Jesus and allowed Him to fulfill His mission on earth.

Dreams containing a divine message were very common in the Old Testament. They were also mentioned quite prominently in the New Testament. One of the most significant is the fulfillment of the prophecy of Joel 2:28 on the Day of Pentecost. "And it shall come to pass in the last days, saith God, I will pour out of my Spirit upon all flesh: and your sons and your daughters shall prophesy, and your young men shall see visions, and your old men shall dream dreams" (Acts 2:17).

On occasion, the Lord still communicates through dreams. Any such message must comply in every way with the Word of God. When a message comes from God, it will result in edification for the believer. This is one way we can be sure God is speaking.

The wise men returned to their country another way. Anyone who truly finds the Christ always returns "another way." The rich young ruler found Him and went away sorrowful because he did not accept Him as his personal Savior. Multiplied millions have found Him and received Him into their hearts and have gone away rejoicing at their newfound life. But none ever found Him and left Him the same.

Has the Lord ever communicated to you in a dream? If so, what was His message?

B. Out of Egypt (vv. 13–15)

(Matthew 2:13–15 is not included in the printed text.)

In a dream, an angel of the Lord warned Joseph that he should take the baby and His mother and flee to Egypt. He was to stay in Egypt until the Lord gave him further instructions. Once again, prophecy was being fulfilled in relation to the Messiah. This happening enabled the fulfillment of the words of the prophet Hosea: "When Israel was a child, then I loved him, and called my son out of Egypt" (11:1).

There were many Jews living in Egypt at this time. It is probable that Joseph sought them out and lived among them. This area provided for him a safe retreat from the outbreak of evil which Herod would carry out in an attempt to destroy the Christ child.

Every indication is that Joseph obeyed the Lord immediately. How much better our lives would be if we could learn to obey the Lord's instructions.

In the Winter 1993 issue of *Leadership*, David R. Culver tells this story. A TV news camera crew was on assignment in southern Florida filming the widespread destruction of Hurricane Andrew. In one scene, amid the devastation and debris stood one house on its foundation. The owner was cleaning up the yard when a reporter approached him.

"Sir, why is your house the only one still standing?" asked the reporter. "How did you manage to escape the severe damage of the hurricane?"

"I built this house myself," the man replied. "I also built it according to the Florida state building code. When the code called for 2 x 6 roof trusses, I used 2 x 6 roof trusses. I was told that a house built according to code could withstand a hurricane. I did, and it did."

When the sun is shining and the skies are blue, building our lives on something other than the guidelines in God's Word can be tempting. But obedience to God's Word can spare one a hurricane of trouble as it did for Joseph.

C. Herod Enraged (vv. 16–18)

(Matthew 2:16–18 is not included in the printed text.)

When Herod discovered that the wise men had not obeyed him, he was furious. He ordered the execution of all the male children in Bethlehem and all its districts under 2 years of age. His decree fulfilled yet another prophecy recorded in Jeremiah 31:15: "Thus saith the Lord; A voice was heard in Ramah, lamentation, and bitter weeping; Rahel [Rachel] weeping for her children refused to be comforted for her children, because they were not."

This action was in keeping with the nature of Herod. History records that he killed two of his 10 wives, at least three sons, his brother–in–law, his mother–in–law, and the grandfather of one of his wives.

Herod's hatred of Christ borne out of a threat to his own throne, which was in reality unfounded, has not been an uncommon attitude toward the Lord and His followers through the centuries. This attitude has caused much suffering, sorrow, and even death in the world. But Jesus reminds us, "If the world hate you, ye know that it hated me before it hated you" (John 15:18).

D. Returning to Nazareth (vv. 19–23)

(Matthew 2:19–23 is not included in the printed text.)

Herod's death was not mourned by the Jewish people both because of his cruelty and because he was not a Jew. In yet another dream, an angel of the Lord brought the news of Herod's death to Joseph and told him to return to Israel. Fearing that Herod's son who had assumed the throne would be as cruel as his father had been, Joseph did not choose to settle near Jerusalem. Rather, he returned to Nazareth in Galilee, where he and Mary had lived earlier.

Nazareth was a town of low esteem in Jesus' day. It was thought of as a place from which nothing good could come. Thus it fulfilled another prophecy related to the Messiah. (See Isaiah 11:1; Jeremiah 23:5; and Zechariah 6:12.) In this environment, Jesus lived in safety, grew to manhood, and went on to do the work for which He came into this world.

REVIEW QUESTIONS

1. Who were the wise men?
2. Why was Herod troubled at the thought of the birth of the Messiah?
3. What did the three gifts symbolize as expression of worship to Christ?
4. Why are the Old Testament references so important for Matthew's account of the life of Jesus?
5. Given what we know of the Magi, what characteristics exist today for people who wisely follow Christ?

GOLDEN TEXT HOMILY

"WHEN THEY WERE COME INTO THE HOUSE, THEY SAW THE YOUNG CHILD WITH MARY HIS MOTHER, AND FELL DOWN, AND WORSHIPPED HIM" (Matthew 2:11).

The wise men from the East had heard that the Christ child was born, and they followed a star, placed in the heavens by God to guide them to the house in Bethlehem where the Christ child was. God has also given us His Holy Word to believe in and the Holy Spirit to guide us to Him and to areas of service for Him.

The wise men then came into the house. They fell down and worshiped Him and gave gifts to Him: "gold as a token of His royalty, frankincense as a token of His divinity, and myrrh as a token of His suffering" (*Pulpit Commentary*). They loved and worshiped Him as King of the Jews, even though Christ was a young child.

God's presence is vitally important to us and is always available, for He is omnipresent. If we are to be beneficiaries of His grace, we must "come into His house"—into His presence—falling down before Him in submission, humility, and in surrender worshiping Him. And we too must give gifts to Christ. We are to give ourselves as living sacrifices and our reasonable service—our talents, our abilities, and our substance. Immanuel—"God is with us" as He was with the wise men. Our redemption is totally in God and His Son, Jesus Christ. **—Harvey L. Davis (Retired), FHA Official, Active Sunday School Teacher, Madison, Mississippi**

SENTENCE SERMONS

OBEDIENCE TO GOD'S WORD will cause people to believe in, love, and worship Jesus Christ.

—Selected

WHEN MEN SEEK a better understanding of God's revelation in Christ, it is a mark of wisdom.

—Selected

THE SON OF GOD became a man to enable men to become the sons of God.

—C.S. Lewis

HE WHO PROVIDES for this life, but takes no care for eternity, is wise for a moment, but a fool forever.

—John Tillotson

EVANGELISM APPLICATION

OBEDIENCE TO GOD'S WORD WILL CAUSE PEOPLE TO BELIEVE IN, LOVE, AND WORSHIP JESUS CHRIST.

Before the beginning of an athletic event, awaited by thousands of fans, a little dog strayed from its master onto the field. From the grandstand on one side of the field, one whistled. Presently, many were whistling to the dog from all sides of the field. In the middle of the field, the little dog, filled with confusion and fright, crouched to the ground. Then, a boy at the end of the field put two fingers into his mouth and whistled shrilly and loudly. The little dog, recognizing his master's call amidst the others, leaped to his feet. With ears erect, the dog ran swiftly to its master.

About God's children following their heavenly Master, Jesus said, "My sheep hear My voice . . . and they follow Me" (John 10:27, *NKJV*). Let us be swift to discern and obey His voice, for He is sure to bless us and others are given a living example to obey and love Christ. **—Howard H. Hamlin, M.D.**

DAILY BIBLE READINGS

M. Begin With Wisdom. Proverbs 1:1–9

T. Prince of Peace. Isaiah 9:2–7

W. Accept God's Message. Luke 1:26–38

T. Thank God for His Gift. Luke 2:8–20

F. Bear Witness to Christ. John 1:1–14

S. Learn More of Christ. Philippians 3:7–15

The Coming King

Study Text: 2 Samuel 7:12–17; Psalm 45:1–7; Daniel 7:13, 14; Revelation 19:11–16

Objective: To acknowledge that Jesus Christ is King of the universe and submit to His dominion over our lives.

Golden Text: "Thy throne, O God, is for ever and ever: a sceptre of righteousness is the sceptre of thy kingdom" (Hebrews 1:8).

Central Truth: The Bible announces that Jesus Christ will return as King of kings.

Evangelism Emphasis: Believers should warn sinners to prepare for Christ's second coming.

PRINTED TEXT

2 Samuel 7:12. And when thy days be fulfilled, and thou shalt sleep with thy fathers, I will set up thy seed after thee, which shall proceed out of thy bowels, and I will establish his kingdom.

13. He shall build an house for my name, and I will stablish the throne of his kingdom for ever.

14. I will be his father, and he shall be my son. If he commit iniquity, I will chasten him with the rod of men, and with the stripes of the children of men:

15. But my mercy shall not depart away from him, as I took it from Saul, whom I put away before thee.

16. And thine house and thy kingdom shall be established for ever before thee: thy throne shall be established for ever.

Daniel 7:13. I saw in the night visions, and, behold, one like the Son of man came with the clouds of heaven, and came to the Ancient of days, and they brought him near before him.

14. And there was given him dominion, and glory, and a kingdom, that all people, nations, and languages, should serve him: his dominion is an everlasting dominion, which shall not pass away, and his kingdom that which shall not be destroyed.

Revelation 19:11. And I saw heaven opened, and behold a white horse; and he that sat upon him was called Faithful and True, and in righteousness he doth judge and make war.

12. His eyes were as a flame of fire, and on his head were many crowns; and he had a name written, that no man knew, but he himself.

13. And he was clothed with a vesture dipped in blood: and his name is called The Word of God.

14. And the armies which were in heaven followed him upon white horses, clothed in fine linen, white and clean.

15. And out of his mouth

goeth a sharp sword, that with it he should smite the nations: and he shall rule them with a rod of iron: and he treadeth the winepress of the fierceness and wrath of Almighty God.

16. And he hath on his vesture and on his thigh a name written, KING OF KINGS, AND LORD OF LORDS.

Psalm 45:6. Thy throne, O God, is for ever and ever: the sceptre of thy kingdom is a right sceptre.

7. Thou lovest righteousness, and hatest wickedness: therefore God, thy God, hath anointed thee with the oil of gladness above thy fellows.

LESSON OUTLINE

I. THE KINGDOM PROMISED
- A. David's Successor
- B. God's Mercy
- C. An Everlasting Kingdom

II. THE KING IS COMING
- A. An Everlasting Dominion
- B. The Heavenly Horseman
- C. The King of Kings

III. THE KING IN HIS GLORY
- A. The Fair One
- B. The Awesome One
- C. The Anointed One

LESSON EXPOSITION

INTRODUCTION

The Bible is sprinkled with portraits of Christ. One such passage is Isaiah 53. There He is pictured as the Suffering Servant of Jehovah. The four Gospels show us His character and deeds. From them we may draw examples for daily living. Philippians 2 takes us inside the mind of Christ. His meekness and humility are highlighted. Revelation 1 presents a breathtaking view of the majestic Savior. John was so moved by the sight that he fell at Jesus' feet like a dead man.

The passages we study today offer a glimpse of the living Lord, Conqueror of all, King of kings and Lord of lords. As the words of Scripture form a picture in our minds, we are astonished at what we see. Our best effort cannot do justice to the marvelous image of the Master shown in these passages. Feeble though our attempt will be, we shall endeavor to describe Him who is indescribable.

The climax of His control and power are illustrated in this lesson. When men rally their most lethal weapons to do war against Him, their efforts will be in vain. Even though kings and armies the world over unite as one to stop Him, they will be totally defeated. Even the Satan–incarnates—the Antichrist and the False Prophet—are no match for the King of kings. With the greatest of ease, He will eliminate them.

And then it is Satan's turn. He has made his boasts about all that he will do to defy God. Now he thinks he can carry out his intentions. But when he comes face–to–face with God's messenger, how will he fare? He will be helpless to do anything for himself. Bound and confined to the Abyss, which is locked and sealed, he will be completely defeated.

I. THE KINGDOM PROMISED (2 Samuel 7:12–17)

A. David's Successor (vv. 12, 13)

12. And when thy days be fulfilled, and thou shalt sleep with thy fathers, I will set up thy seed after thee, which shall proceed out of thy bowels, and I will establish his kingdom.

13. He shall build an house for my name, and I will stablish the throne of his kingdom for ever.

In the context of this passage, David is shown as a man who desired to do something substantial for the Lord. Having built a house for himself, he longed to build a house for his God in Jerusalem. He told Nathan, a prophet and confidant, his thoughts. But David was a man of war, so the Lord would not allow him to build the Temple. Nathan became God's spokesman to convey this message to David.

The Lord assured David through Nathan that although he would not build a house for God's presence to dwell, his son would. Not only would his successor build a Temple, the Lord would also establish "the throne of his kingdom for ever." David's immediate successor was Solomon. He was followed on the throne by David's descendants. But the ultimate fulfillment of this promise is found in Jesus Christ.

Believers can take courage that the purposes of God will be realized. As in David's case, we may not see that in our lifetime. But God is in control, and He will work through others after we are gone, if need be, to fulfill His intentions. It does not matter how many obstacles stand in the way, our Lord is greater than them all. The Christ we serve is leading a victorious army. Charles J. Rolls has so eloquently said, "The potentialities of Christ are unpredictable, the prerogatives of Christ are unpronounceable, and the purposes of Christ are unpreventable."

B. God's Mercy (vv. 14, 15)

14. I will be his father, and he shall be my son. If he commit iniquity, I will chasten him with the rod of men, and with the stripes of the children of men:

15. But my mercy shall not depart away from him, as I took it from Saul, whom I put away before thee.

The Lord promised David that He would be as close to Solomon as a father. He would watch over him and love him as his heavenly Father. But if Solomon went astray, God would punish him for his waywardness. He also assured David that His mercy would not depart from Solomon.

Long ago, a poor woman from the slums of London was invited to go with a group of people for a holiday at the ocean. She had never seen the ocean before, and when she saw it, she burst into tears. Those around her thought it was strange that she should cry when such a lovely holiday had been given her. "Why in the world are you crying?" they asked. Pointing to the ocean she answered, "This is the only thing I have ever seen that there was enough of."

God has oceans of mercy. There is enough of it—and though none of us deserve it, God delights to show His mercy and compassion. Micah wrote: "He will turn again, he will have compassion upon us; he will subdue our iniquities; and thou wilt cast all their sins into the depths of the sea" (7:19).

The story has been told of a mother who sought from Napoleon a pardon for her son. The emperor said it was the man's second offense, and justice demanded his death. "I don't ask for justice," said the mother. "I plead for mercy."

"But," said the emperor, "he does not deserve mercy."

"Sir," cried the mother, "it would not be mercy if he deserved it, and mercy is all I ask."

"Well, then," said the emperor, "I will show mercy." And her son was saved (from *Illustrations for Biblical Preaching*, by Michael P. Green, Baker Book House).

C. An Everlasting Kingdom (vv. 16, 17)

(2 Samuel 7:17 is not included in the printed text.)

16. And thine house and thy kingdom shall be established for ever before thee: thy throne shall be established for ever.

The kingdom of God is an everlasting kingdom. When God spoke to David about his kingdom, He contrasted it with the kingdom of Saul. Saul's kingdom was earthly and, as with all earthly kingdoms, finally ceased to exist. On the other hand, the throne of David will last forever because its ultimate occupant is Jesus Christ himself.

Likewise, the church of the living God will never fail. Charles Jefferson wrote: "Jesus said, 'I will build my church.' It is His. He is the architect. He is at work. The church is no private enterprise of ours. It is His. We are co–laborers with Him. He is ever by our side. The church is not obsolescent. Humanity has not outgrown it. Its noon is not behind it. Its triumphal career has only begun.

"We are toiling amid the mists of the early morning. It is the rising sun which smites our foreheads, and we cannot even dream of the glory which is to be. We work upon an enduring institution. After the flags of republics and empires have been blown to tatters, and the earth itself has tasted death, the church of Jesus shall stand forth glorious, free from blemish and mark of decay, and the gates of Hades shall not prevail against it."

II. THE KING IS COMING (Daniel 7:13, 14; Revelation 19:11–16)

A. An Everlasting Dominion (Daniel 7:13, 14)

13. I saw in the night visions, and, behold, one like the Son of man came with the clouds of heaven, and came to the Ancient of days, and they brought him near before him.

14. And there was given him dominion, and glory, and a kingdom, that all people, nations, and languages, should serve him: his dominion is an everlasting dominion, which shall not pass away, and his kingdom that which shall not be destroyed.

In a vision Daniel saw a figure who was like a human being. He was being transported by the clouds. This method of transportation was commonly pictured involving celestial beings. The psalmist wrote: "Bless the Lord, O my soul. O Lord my God, thou art very great. . . . Who layeth the beams of his chambers in the waters: who maketh the clouds his chariot: who walketh upon the wings of the wind" (Psalm 104:1, 3).

Most Bible scholars see the term "Son of man" as representing in a collective or corporate sense the coming Kingdom and its embodiment in "the people of God." Others, however, argue that "Son of man" symbolizes both the coming messianic kingdom and the Messiah himself.

Three things are said about the Kingdom given to "one like the Son of man." First, the Kingdom will be universal. He is given authority, glory, and sovereign power. All peoples, nations, and men of every language will worship Him. Everywhere men will be touched by this Kingdom.

Second, this Kingdom will be an everlasting kingdom. It will not exist for a few years and then be replaced by another. Once it is established, it will continue. There will be no end to its dominion.

Third, this Kingdom will be indestructible. It will never be destroyed. Let its enemies use all the resources and all the power at their disposal; their attempts to overthrow this Kingdom will be in vain. They will back away wounded and defeated.

B. The Heavenly Horseman
(Revelation 19:11–14)

11. And I saw heaven opened, and behold a white horse; and he that sat upon him was called Faithful and True, and in righteousness he doth judge and make war.

12. His eyes were as a flame of fire, and on his head were many crowns; and he had a name written, that no man knew, but he himself.

13. And he was clothed with a vesture dipped in blood: and his name is called The Word of God.

14. And the armies which were in heaven followed him upon white horses, clothed in fine linen, white and clean.

Immediately following the scenes of the wedding of the Lamb and the Marriage Supper, John saw the heavens standing open and Christ was sitting upon a white horse. He was prepared to come forth as the great Conqueror.

The title ascribed to Christ in this scene is "Faithful and True." It stands in direct contrast to the forces He would encounter. His enemies are the Antichrist, the False Prophet, and the false leaders. This will be a classic conflict between good and evil.

John emphasized that the Lord would act righteously. The judgment He will mete out is based on what wicked men deserve. He is never unfair in His dealings with men. At the same time, His holiness will not allow evil to go unpunished.

John said the eyes of Jesus were like "a flame of fire." Have you ever thought of what it must be like to look into the eyes of Jesus? In those eyes could be fierce judgment or marvelous forgiveness. Think of how the adulterous woman must have felt when she saw the compassionate eyes of Jesus. One of the richest rewards of heaven will be the privilege of meeting Christ eye to eye. But the eyes of Jesus will have no mercy for those who practice sin until the end.

He who wore a crown of thorns on earth now wears many crowns. Because He humbled Himself and became obedient unto death on a cross, God has highly exalted Him and given Him a place above all others (Philippians 2).

Jesus will then be given a name that no one but He himself knows. Someone has written: "He has a glory and a character of His own, incommunicable and incomprehensible, a name written that no man knew, but He himself. Man as He is, He is also the Son of God, and thus a fullness resides in Him which no mere creature intelligence can fathom."

John saw the Lord dressed in a robe dipped in blood. The blood is symbolic of the blood of His enemies which will be shed on the battlefield. It is never a pretty sight to see men at war, and yet this is the circumstance that is brought on by sin. Evil must be conquered, and Christ is coming to produce a great victory for the right.

Christ is called the Word of God. Everything that God has said or is, is embodied in Jesus. In Him every word of God comes true. What a blessing to see the Word of God come alive in the person of the Lord.

When Jesus passes through the portals of heaven, He will not be alone. The armies of heaven will follow Him, riding white horses. Those who have been redeemed by His grace will be with Him when He carries out the victory He won at Calvary. Perhaps there will have been times when it appeared that this moment would never come. The forces of evil are described as rising to great power on the earth. Surely there were those who questioned that they could ever be stopped. The fact is that the outcome was never in doubt; the victory had already been won. It was just a matter of executing the sentence of final doom. And the saints will be there when Christ brings the evil forces down.

Not only are the saints riding white horses, but they are also wearing white garments. Have you ever heard of an army going forth dressed in white? Whatever happened to camouflaged uniforms? Why make yourself a target by dressing in a manner that will enhance your visibility? The truth is that this army will not have to fight.

C. The King of Kings
(Revelation 19:15, 16)

15. And out of his mouth goeth a sharp sword, that with it he should smite the nations: and he shall rule them with a rod of iron: and he treadeth the winepress of the fierceness and wrath of Almighty God.

16. And he hath on his vesture and on his thigh a name written, KING OF KINGS, AND LORD OF LORDS.

Christ will do the fighting in this encounter. The battle will be consummated with the spoken word of our Lord. Paul said that Christ will consume the wicked one "with the spirit of his mouth, and shall destroy with the brightness of his coming" (2 Thessalonians 2:8).

In the great crises of His life, Christ was alone. He was alone in the Temple at age 12. He was alone in the wilderness during the great temptation. And He was alone at Calvary, since no one could take His place or even offer Him assistance while He paid the debt for men's sins. Those moments, and many others, He had to face without the aid of family or friends.

In the end, in the scene that marks the climax of His dealings with evil, He will again act alone. Although the armies of heaven will be there, they will be only spectators. The victory will come through the power of the Lord.

Christ will deal sternly with the nations of earth. Their strong will must be broken, and the government of God must be established. This can be accomplished only if Christ wields an iron scepter. And so He will.

There have been other occasions when God expressed His wrath but never to the extent that He does in this Revelation scene. Here the wrath of God is poured out in its most extreme expression.

Name some of the Old Testament accounts in which God fought the battle for the Israelites.

In verse 16 we are told that Christ wore His title on His robe and on His thigh: "KING OF KINGS AND LORD OF LORDS." This title denotes universal dominion. It reminds us that He is sovereign. The rulers of the earth will call His sovereignty into question, but He will demonstrate His authority.

Jesus Christ is our one great teacher and authority on the subject of future punishment, and it is the Lamb of God himself who is represented as inflicting on men with His wrath in the great day of His wrath. Let us remember that it is the same Lamb of God who bore our shame; who took little children up into His arms and blessed them, from whose lips fell the imperishable sentences of mercy and pity, who sighed over the mute boy, who poured out His tears at the grave of Lazarus, and who wept over the doom of Jerusalem. You can pick and choose what you like or do not like in the Gospels. But no one who takes Jesus as a teacher of truth can deny that He taught future punishment (Matthew 25:31–46).

III. THE KING IN HIS GLORY (Psalm 45:1–7)

(Psalm 45:1, 2 is not included in the printed text.)

A. The Fair One (vv. 1, 2)

Psalm 45 is what is known as a messianic psalm. There are several such psalms, that is, psalms that describe some aspect of the coming of the Messiah. This psalm concentrates on the character and beauty of the Lord. Apparently, this passage was penned in connection with the wedding of King Solomon to the daughter of another king. But its meaning goes far beyond any such earthly arrangement. It is clearly a portrait of Christ in His coming.

The psalmist was eager to write about the beauty of the King. He describes himself as one whose "tongue is [like] the pen of a ready writer." He paints the Lord as an incomparable person who is fairer than the sons of men. Artists have attempted to draw likenesses of Christ. Some have shown Him as the suffering servant who hung upon the cross. Others have projected different images such as Holman's *Head of Christ.* Though we don't know what Jesus looked like, we can be sure there was an attractiveness about Him. Children clung to Him and crowds hung onto His every word. This suggests the fair One mentioned by the psalmist.

People were attracted to Him not only because of His appearance but also because of His expressions. His words captivated them. They still do. They still set men free and empower them to become all that God desires them to be.

B. The Awesome One (vv. 3–6)

(Psalm 45:3–5 is not included in the printed text.)

6. Thy throne, O God, is for ever and ever: the sceptre of thy kingdom is a right sceptre.

These verses present us with the other side of Jesus. The previous verses spoke of Him as the fair One whose words are gracious. Here He is depicted taking a sword and flexing His might. But even when called to combat His enemies, He is pictured as riding forth in meekness and righteousness defending the truth. These characteristics marked His entire journey here on earth. They are traits believers should emulate. Whether we are reaching out to win the lost or find ourselves in confrontation with the Enemy, both situations should be approached in meekness and righteousness.

We are reminded again that Christ's kingdom is an everlasting kingdom. He is superior to all other beings. He is not the highest of created beings as some would suggest. He himself is God, God made man.

C. The Anointed One (v. 7)

7. Thou lovest righteousness, and hatest wickedness: therefore God, thy God, hath anointed thee with the oil of gladness above thy fellows.

In verse 6, the Messiah is referred to as God. In verse 7, He is said to have a God, "God, thy God." In these two verses, He is shown to be both God and man. Thus, the fact of His incarnation is addressed a thousand years before His coming to earth in human form.

The apostle Paul addressed this mystery of the mighty God becoming flesh: "And without controversy great is the mystery of godliness: God was manifest in the flesh, justified in the Spirit, seen of angels, preached unto the Gentiles, believed on in the world, received up into glory" (1 Timothy 3:16).

Jesus was the Anointed One. As such He fulfilled the offices associated with the anointing—prophet, priest, and king. As prophet He spoke the truth in a manner that is unequaled. As priest He offered himself for the ultimate sacrifice. As king He demonstrated His power over death, hell, and the grave.

"The oil of gladness" represents the work of the Holy Spirit. As all who have tasted His power know, He brings joy to the human heart.

REVIEW QUESTIONS

1. What assurances did the Lord give David through Nathan concerning future events?
2. Describe the vision Daniel had concerning "one like the Son of man" in 7:13, 14.
3. How does the psalmist describe the "awesomeness" of Christ in verses 3–6?

GOLDEN TEXT HOMILY

"THY THRONE, O GOD, IS FOR EVER AND EVER: A SCEPTRE OF RIGHTEOUSNESS IS THE SCEPTRE OF THY KINGDOM" (Hebrews 1:8).

Webster's dictionary says a scepter signifies authority. We find in Luke 24:49 and Acts 1:8 that Christ has given us His power (authority), the power of His scepter. Therefore, if we will believe and take action, we will become the sons of the Scepter–Authority.

According to John 16:24, Acts 4:12, and Colossians 3:17, there is no other name as powerful as the name of Christ, and yet He has given you and me the authority to work the works of God in His name. With the scepter of His name in our hands, head, and heart at a time that speaks significantly of His coming, we find the church full of the "cult of the comfortable." This is the most hostile influence in the church and world.

There is no modern cult doing more to thwart the work of the church (the kingdom of God) than the "cult of the comfortable." However, the scepter, when used by the people of God can pull it down even though it is a well–fixed stronghold in the church. The scepter can set the captives free and bring men, women, boys and girls into the kingdom of God. His kingdom has come. His kingdom is now and eternal. There is a battle, a war to be fought, but soldiers of the scepter will win.

Our authority and right is to cast out devils and to fight off demons;

to heal the sick and raise the dead physically and spiritually.

As we leave the old year and enter the new, let us be as Orison Swett Marden said: "All men who have accomplished great things have been men of one unwavering aim, who have sacrificed all conflicting desires and ambitions to one aim." Our aim and action is to be a faithful carrier of His authority–scepter. **—Willie F. Lawrence, D.D., Pastor, Church of God, Moline, Illinois**

SENTENCE SERMONS

THE BIBLE ANNOUNCES that Jesus Christ will return as King of kings.

—Selected

THE ANGELS who bore testimony to Christ's first coming also bear testimony to His second coming.

—William Evans

THE ONE GREAT EVENT, that which supersedes all others, toward which the church is to look and for which she is to ardently long, is the second coming of Christ.

—William Evans

TO EVERY ONE MENTION of the first coming of Christ in the Bible, the second coming is mentioned eight times.

—The Great Doctrines of the Bible

ILLUMINATING THE LESSON

More than 1900 years ago there was a man born contrary to the laws of life. This man lived in poverty and was reared in obscurity. He did not travel extensively. Only once did He cross the boundary of the country in which He lived, and that was during His exile in childhood. He possessed neither wealth nor influence. His relatives were inconspicuous and had neither training nor formal education.

Yet in infancy He startled a king; in childhood He puzzled doctors; in manhood He ruled the course of nature, walked upon the billows as if pavements, and hushed the sea to sleep. He healed the multitudes without medicine and made no charge for His service.

He never wrote a book, yet all the libraries of the country could not hold the books that have been written about Him. He never wrote a song, and yet He's furnished the theme for more songs than all the songwriters combined. He never founded a college, but all the schools put together cannot boast of having so many students. He never marshaled an army nor drafted a soldier nor fired a gun, and yet no leader ever had more volunteers who have under His orders made more rebels stack their arms and surrender without a shot fired. He never practiced psychiatry, and yet He has healed more broken hearts than all the doctors far and near.

He stands forth upon the highest pinnacle of heaven's glory—proclaimed of God, acknowledged by angels, adored by saints, feared by devils—as the living, personal Lord Jesus Christ, my Lord and Savior.—Source unknown

DAILY BIBLE READINGS

M. Everlasting Kingdom.
Psalm 145:3–13

T. Peaceful Kingdom.
Isaiah 11:6–10

W. Restored Kingdom.
Jeremiah 33:14–22

T. Jesus Will Return.
Mark 13:21–31

F. Faithful Living.
1 Thessalonians 5:1–11

S. A Certain Promise.
2 Peter 3:10–18

Accept Personal Responsibility

Study Text: Ezekiel 33:1–20

Objective: To realize that God holds everyone responsible for personal sins and determine to repent and warn the lost.

Time: The Book of Ezekiel was written between 593 and 565 B.C.

Place: The Book of Ezekiel was written in Babylon.

Golden Text: "If the wicked turn from his wickedness, and do that which is lawful and right, he shall live thereby" (Ezekiel 33:19).

Central Truth: Each individual is accountable for his own sins and his response to God's plan of salvation.

Evangelism Emphasis: God's justice and compassion give every person opportunity to be saved.

PRINTED TEXT

Ezekiel 33:8. When I say unto the wicked, O wicked man, thou shalt surely die; if thou dost not speak to warn the wicked from his way, that wicked man shall die in his iniquity; but his blood will I require at thine hand.

9. Nevertheless, if thou warn the wicked of his way to turn from it; if he do not turn from his way, he shall die in his iniquity; but thou hast delivered thy soul.

10. Therefore, O thou son of man, speak unto the house of Israel; Thus ye speak, saying, If our transgressions and our sins be upon us, and we pine away in them, how should we then live?

11. Say unto them, As I live, saith the Lord God, I have no pleasure in the death of the wicked; but that the wicked turn from his way and live: turn ye, turn ye from your evil ways; for why will ye die, O house of Israel?

12. Therefore, thou son of man, say unto the children of thy people, The righteousness of the righteous shall not deliver him in the day of his transgression: as for the wickedness of the wicked, he shall not fall thereby in the day that he turneth from his wickedness; neither shall the righteous be able to live for his righteousness in the day that he sinneth.

13. When I shall say to the righteous, that he shall surely live; if he trust to his own righteousness, and commit iniquity, all his righteousness shall not be remembered; but for his iniquity that he hath committed, he shall die for it.

14. Again, when I say unto the wicked, Thou shalt surely die; if he turn from his sin, and do that which is lawful and right;

15. If the wicked restore the pledge, give again that he had robbed, walk in the statutes of life, without committing iniquity; he shall surely live, he shall not die.

16. None of his sins that he hath committed shall be mentioned unto him: he hath done that which is lawful and right; he shall surely live.

17. Yet the children of thy people say, The way of the Lord is not equal: but as for them, their way is not equal.

18. When the righteous turneth from his righteousness, and committeth iniquity, he shall even die thereby.

LESSON OUTLINE

I. WARN THE WICKED
   A. Obligation of the Watchman
   B. Responsibility of God's Watchman

II. REPENT AND LIVE
   A. How Shall We Live Before God the Judge?
   B. Failure of Human Righteousness
   C. Turning to God Yields Life

III. THE LORD IS FAIR
   A. Complaint About "Unfairness"
   B. Clarity About Human Action
   C. Correction About Judgment

LESSON EXPOSITION

INTRODUCTION

This passage is one of the most powerful calls to personal responsibility in all of Scripture. Responsibility in evangelism is not an option. Not only is the world waiting for the believer to witness, but God is also waiting for the Christian to tell others about Christ. Not only is eternal salvation for the lost at stake, but the eternal obligation to tell others about Christ is also upon every believer.

The Lord is ready and willing to redeem the sinner, but He is also looking and waiting for the believer to accept responsibility to win the lost. God uses the example of the watchman to illustrate His expectations. Just as the watchman was responsible to warn others, the child of God is also expected to cry out concerning the peril to come upon those who do not serve the Lord.

The believer is not to be an idle spectator, watching the evils of a sinful world and waiting for someone to ask him about the Lord. On the contrary, the Christian, like the watchman standing on the wall, observes the doom waiting for the lost and is solemnly charged to declare what he sees. He is to cry out the warning of impending disaster to the inhabitants of the land.

I. WARN THE WICKED (Ezekiel 33:1-9)

A. Obligation of the Watchman (vv. 1–6)

(Ezekiel 33:1–6 is not included in the printed text.)

Verses 1-6 clarify that the watchman is held accountable to sound the warning. "His blood shall be upon his own head" (v. 4), ". . . shall deliver his soul" (v. 5), and "his blood will I require at the watchman's hand" (v. 6) all indicate the serious consequences of the watchman's lack of action. The fate of the those in need of warning as well as that of the watchman is affected decisively by whether the watchman warns of the approaching danger.

What are the obligations of the watchman? To whom is the watchman most responsible in warning others?

B. Responsibility of God's Watchman (vv. 7-9)

(Ezekiel 33:7 is not included in the printed text.)

8. When I say unto the wicked, O wicked man, thou shalt surely die; if thou dost not speak to warn the wicked from his way, that wicked man shall die in his iniquity; but his blood will I require at thine hand.

9. Nevertheless, if thou warn the wicked of his way to turn from it; if he do not turn from his way, he shall die in his iniquity; but thou hast delivered thy soul.

A twofold task faced the watchman. On the one hand, he was to look for danger that was coming to the city. On the other hand he was responsible for sending a warning. The specific responsibility of the watchman was to warn others of the danger that was coming to the individual.

God holds the person who sees the danger responsible for sounding a warning to those who are unaware. After they have been warned, the wicked then bear the responsibility of listening and obeying. The spiritual watchman has been commissioned as the guardian of souls. He has been divinely appointed, and God never calls and commissions the wrong person. When God calls, God empowers, however reluctant that servant may be initially to accept the responsibility for the task. The spiritual "guardsman" must recognize that often the dangers he sees and attempts to warn others of may not seem to be a peril at all to those he is seeking to save. Nevertheless, the watchman's call is irrevocable. He must uphold God's standards whether his message meets with approval or disapproval, acceptance or rejection.

What are the consequences for the watchman who fails to properly warn others?

II. REPENT AND LIVE (Ezekiel 33:10-16)

A. How Shall We Live Before God the Judge (vv. 10, 11)

10. Therefore, O thou son of man, speak unto the house of Israel; Thus ye speak, saying, If our transgressions and our sins be upon us, and we pine away in them, how should we then live?

11. Say unto them, As I live, saith the Lord God, I have no pleasure in the death of the wicked; but that the wicked turn from his way and live: turn ye, turn ye from your evil ways; for why will ye die, O house of Israel?

The warning of the watchman was related to the judgment of God. The transgressions and sins of Israel had brought the people to the brink of danger of the judgment of God. The judgment of God is righteous, giving eternal reward to those who serve Him. The righteous judgment of God also means eternal punishment to those who have not been faithful to Him.

However, God does not hold the individual responsible for the sin and guilt of the nation. Should the individual complain that the collective guilt of the nation is so great that no one has a chance for life, God's answer is clear: "I have no pleasure in the death of the wicked." Hear Him pleading even, "Turn ye, turn ye . . . why will ye die?" God is willing to forgive the repentant sinner.

God's desire is not for eternal punishment. The prophetic message is to function primarily as a call to repentance rather than an announcement of the judgment of God. God desires that all escape the coming punishment. The way has been provided, and watchmen are crying out for all to repent that they may escape. The tragedy is that sinners ignore the pleas from God's heart and the cries of the watchmen.

B. Failure of Human Righteousness (vv. 12, 13)

12. Therefore, thou son of man, say unto the children of thy people, The righteousness of the righteous shall not deliver him in the day of his transgression: as for the wickedness of the wicked, he shall not fall thereby in the day that he turneth from his wickedness; neither shall the righteous be able to live for his righteousness in the day that he sinneth.

13. When I shall say to the righteous, that he shall surely live; if he trust to his own righteousness, and commit iniquity, all his righteousness shall not be remembered; but for his iniquity that he hath committed, he shall die for it.

Those who have lived godly in the past cannot hope to escape God's judgment if they sin. Neither will the wicked be denied God's pardon if they turn from their sinning and ask God's forgiveness. The Sovereign Lord is in no way unjust. He is merciful and will "abundantly pardon" those who truly repent.

In light of the warning of God's judgment, the only hope the sinner has for deliverance is God. Attempts at self–righteousness always spell danger. The danger is a self–deception that leads one to believe he can be good enough in his own power to merit God's approval, and thus miss the true righteousness of God.

The watchman is a herald proclaiming the perils of missing God's righteousness and issuing a plea to abandon human efforts at self-redemption and cling to divine deliverance.

What is God's role in the warning of those in danger? What is God's role in relationship to the watchman?

God's redemption cannot fail. "He shall surely live" (v. 13) is God's assurance. Redemption from God is guaranteed by God. The declaration that the danger is passed comes from God. The watchman is called to communicate this message to the person in danger of eternal punishment.

Iniquity and self-righteousness go hand in hand. God communicates this truth in this passage. An individual cannot save himself, and any attempt to do so reveals an attempt to cover sin. Self-righteousness itself is sin. Iniquity is the offspring of desiring to create one's own means of salvation, not recognizing God as the only source of righteousness.

How does self-righteous attempts at redemption affect the sinner's ability to escape God's judgment?

C. Turning to God Yields Life
(vv. 14-16)

14. Again, when I say unto the wicked, Thou shalt surely die; if he turn from his sin, and do that which is lawful and right;

15. If the wicked restore the pledge, give again that he had robbed, walk in the statutes of life, without committing iniquity; he shall surely live, he shall not die.

16. None of his sins that he hath committed shall be mentioned unto him: he hath done that which is lawful and right; he shall surely live.

The watchman is a guardian of life and godliness. It is more than the people's livelihood and prosperity he is seeking to protect; their very lives are at stake. Spiritual life, faithfulness to God, and departing from iniquity are the goals. Spiritual watchmen seek more than the physical safety and security of individuals in sounding the warning. The watchman desires to establish a right relationship with God for as many as will respond to his message.

Again, the passage communicates the depths of God's desire that individuals turn to Him. None of the sins of the person will be "mentioned unto him," or brought up against him in the judgment if he truly repents. And genuine repentance includes not only sorrow for sins committed but also a forsaking of those sins, attempting to do what is right, and making restitution for those things he has wrongfully acquired. To maintain God's permanent blessing of forgiveness and to live, he must continue to do what is lawful and right according to God's Word. Righteousness bears the fruit of freedom from condemnation.

The extent of God's desire to rescue the perishing is expressed in the term *surely*: "He shall surely live." Reminiscent of the phrase, "none of his sins," God expresses the completeness of His desire. Whosoever will may be completely delivered from anything that would bring eternal punishment.

III. THE LORD IS FAIR
(Ezekiel 33:17-20)

A. Complaint About "Unfairness"
(v. 17)

17. Yet the children of thy people say, The way of the Lord is not equal: but as for them, their way is not equal.

When people find fault with God's ways and complain that God is unfair, it is an indication of their own self–righteousness. God said it is because their own ways are not just. These complaints fly in the face of the offer of God's deliverance. It is the people's attempt to judge God rather than accepting God's judgment as just and thus coming to repentance. God's justice declared forgiveness and mercy to the repentant, although He would have been justified in destroying the wicked. His offer transcends fairness—He offers mercy! Everything that is just aligns with God's principles of justice.

"Their way is not equal" [just, fair]" affirms the futility of individuals to gain righteousness apart from God. Watchmen are to declare not only the fearsome peril but also the futile self-righteousness of the sinner.

B. Clarity About Human Action
(vv. 18, 19)

(Ezekiel 33:19 is not included in the printed text.)

18. When the righteous turneth from his righteousness, and committeth iniquity, he shall even die thereby.

Righteousness is not accumulated; it constantly depends upon one's continuing relationship with the Lord. No matter how long a person has been righteous before God, if he "turneth from his righteousness," that person will suffer eternal punishment if he does not repent to the Lord. One's past history of serving God and being in right relationship with Him does not guarantee salvation if he turns away from his righteousness and becomes evil. It is a person's spiritual status when he meets God face–to–face that will determine that person's eternal destiny. Only remaining faithful and constant in our relationship to God will be sufficient for our salvation.

C. Correction About Judgment (v. 20)

(Ezekiel 33:20 is not included in the printed text.)

Verse 20 summarizes and reaffirms the centrality of God in the judgment or deliverance of the sinner. Once again God addresses the charge of the people that He is not fair in His judgment. God says, "I will judge you"—individually, each one for his own actions. The individual will not be held accountable for the collective guilt of the nation, but each will be judged according to his own ways.

The watchman must discern the will and the commands of God. The sinner faces peril. Seeing the peril coming does nothing to rescue those in danger of destruction unless the alarm is sounded and those in danger do what is necessary to avert the disaster. The watchman must warn the sinner to turn to God in order to flee the peril to come.

REVIEW QUESTIONS

1. What is the greatest danger faced by those the watchman seeks to warn?
2. What consequences are there to those the watchman watches over if they are not properly warned?
3. What is God's desire for those whom the watchman watches over?
4. How does the self-righteousness of sinners affect the ability of the watchman to warn them?
5. What is the complaint of the self-righteous about God's judgment?

SENTENCE SERMONS

EACH INDIVIDUAL is accountable for his own sins and his response to God's plan of salvation.

—Selected

GOD'S JUSTICE AND COMPASSION give every person opportunity to be saved.

—Selected

SIN IS man's declaration of independence of God.

—Anonymous

REPENTANCE does not mean remorse alone. Repentance means giving up sin.

—W.E. Biederwolf

EVANGELISM APPLICATION

GOD'S JUSTICE AND COMPASSION GIVE EVERY PERSON OPPORTUNITY TO BE SAVED.

As severe as the punishment is for the sinner, the mercy of God is always greater. However, the mercy of God will not override the requirement of repentance. The judgment of God upon the unrepentant sinner will send that person to eternal torment in the lake of fire. The job of the watchman is great because of the severity of that punishment. Yet the task of the watchman is a blessed one because God constantly extends His mercy to whomever will heed the warning to turn from his wicked ways and repent.

The justice of God is filled not only with His wrath but also with His love. Justice is not a negative term. The justice of God makes salvation possible. The inevitability of eternal damnation is not the focus of His justice. Punishment is the consequence of rejecting the love of His justice. That love is the focus of His justice. For if a person would follow completely the desire of God in His justice, that individual would receive eternal salvation rather than punishment, for salvation is the goal of God's justice.

The opportunity to be saved is the goal of God's justice. Watchmen watch and warn, but they also encourage, because God takes "no pleasure in the death of the wicked." Rather, He pleads, "Why will ye die?" God offers to everyone the opportunity to receive divine salvation.

ILLUMINATING THE LESSON

Watchmen must be ever be alert to their task, keeping their focus on the Lord. The watchman cannot afford to be sidetracked from his divine commission. Faithfulness is vital. The following story illustrates the importance of not allowing one's attention to be diverted from a simple, clear focus:

When Edmund Gravely died at the controls of his small plane while on the way to Statesboro, Georgia, from the Rocky Mount-Wilson airport in North Carolina, his wife, Janice, kept the plane aloft for two hours until it ran out of fuel. During this time she sang hymns and prayed for help. As the plane crossed the South Carolina-North Carolina border, she radioed for help: "Help, help! Won't someone help me? My pilot is unconscious. Won't somebody help me?" Authorities who picked up her distress signal were not able to reach her by radio during the flight because she kept changing channels. Mrs. Gravely finally made a rough landing and crawled for 45 minutes to a farmhouse for help.

If she had stayed on the same channel, she could have completed her urgent mission. However, diverting her focus moved her away from her goal.

Watchmen must never be diverted from the goal of perceiving coming judgment and warning those in peril.

DAILY BIBLE READINGS

M. Covenant Promise.
Joshua 24:1–13

T. Covenant Commitment.
Joshua 24:14–18

W. Covenant Renewed.
Joshua 24:19–25

T. Heed the Warning.
Luke 3:7–18

F. Call to Repentance.
Acts 2:36–40

S. God Desires to Save.
2 Peter 3:1–9

Idolatry Forbidden

Study Text: Ezekiel 8:5–18; 11:16–20; 14:1–11

Objective: To understand that God hates idolatry and worship Him only.

Time: The Book of Ezekiel was written between 593 and 565 B.C.

Place: The Book of Ezekiel was written in Babylon.

Golden Text: "Repent, and turn yourselves from your idols; and turn away your faces from all your abominations" (Ezekiel 14:6).

Central Truth: God forbids all forms of idolatry.

Evangelism Emphasis: Believers should set an example for the lost by worshiping God only.

PRINTED TEXT

Ezekiel 14:6. Therefore say unto the house of Israel, Thus saith the Lord God; Repent, and turn yourselves from your idols; and turn away your faces from all your abominations.

7. For every one of the house of Israel, or of the stranger that sojourneth in Israel, which separateth himself from me, and setteth up his idols in his heart, and putteth the stumblingblock of his iniquity before his face, and cometh to a prophet to enquire of him concerning me; I the Lord will answer him by myself:

8. And I will set my face against that man, and will make him a sign and a proverb, and I will cut him off from the midst of my people; and ye shall know that I am the Lord.

9. And if the prophet be deceived when he hath spoken a thing, I the Lord have deceived that prophet, and I will stretch out my hand upon him, and will destroy him from the midst of my people Israel.

10. And they shall bear the punishment of their iniquity: the punishment of the prophet shall be even as the punishment of him that seeketh unto him;

11. That the house of Israel may go no more astray from me, neither be polluted any more with all their transgressions; but that they may be my people, and I may be their God, saith the Lord God.

11:17. Therefore say, Thus saith the Lord God; I will even gather you from the people, and assemble you out of the countries where ye have been scattered, and I will give you the land of Israel.

18. And they shall come thither, and they shall take away all the detestable things thereof and all the abominations thereof from thence.

19. And I will give them one

heart, and I will put a new spirit within you; and I will take the stony heart out of their flesh, and will give them an heart of flesh:

20. That they may walk in my statutes, and keep mine ordinances, and do them: and they shall be my people, and I will be their God.

LESSON OUTLINE

I. DETESTABLE PRACTICES
   A. Ezekiel's Vision
   B. God's Fury
II. IDOLATRY IN THE HEART
   A. Idolatry of Heart
   B. God's Judgment
   C. Recognition of God
III. A HEART FOR GOD
   A. Reestablishing a Sanctuary
   B. Restoration and Cleansing
   C. Newness of Spirit

LESSON EXPOSITION

INTRODUCTION

Idolatry is the great sin of our day, especially in the church. Whenever anyone or anything else is viewed as being more important than God, the stage is set for idolatry. What does the believer's life depend on more than anything else? What controls the Christian's life more than anything else? What will determine our destiny? These are the questions that face the church and the Christian?

When believers allow other attractions or superheroes to draw them away from God, their "faithfulness" becomes more a matter of what glitters than of pure gold. Then Christ is not the author and finisher of their faith, but they demand instead that He be the approver and server of their whims and wishes.

Idolatry always raises its ugly head whenever God is reduced to a secondary role. Before anything or anyone else, God should have first pirority in the minds of the Christian. One would think that this would be especially true in church; but even there, thoughts wander, hearts are distracted, and boredom is allowed to rule.

Christians are moved by so many things and personalities. The sound of the music, the flair of the teaching, or the appeal of the package sways our spirituality. Just as the heathen were in awe of the adornment of the gods they bowed to, sadly, modern–day worship has bowed to the idols of our senses. The God who created us has been put in the backseat of our spirits, while we are driven by modern–day idols.

The Scripture texts investigated in this lesson reveal that although the forms have changed, idolatry is still a matter to be dealt with and overcome. The abomination of idolatry is the bowing in worship to anyone or anything other than God—that is, depending on people or things for our necessities rather than trusting God to supply all our needs.

I. DETESTABLE PRACTICES (Ezekiel 8:5–18)

A. Ezekiel's Vision (vv. 5–16)

(Ezekiel 8:5–16 is not included in the printed text.)

The prophet was taken by the

Spirit of God to view the condition of the house of God. Verses 3 and 4 capture the scene: The glory of the God of Israel was confronted by the image that provokes jealousy. God explained to Ezekiel that the presence of the idol in the place where only God was to dwell would drive Him away: "Son of man, do you see what they are doing . . . things that will drive me far from my sanctuary?" (v. 6, *NIV*).

The great tragedy of iniquity in Israel was that the people continued a form of worship, not knowing that the glory of the Lord had departed from them. In his vision, the prophet was made to see great abominations—the false worship of Israel. They were worshiping, but not God. They were worshiping other gods, those that had been worshiped by the Canaanites and Midianites when they first came to the Promised Land. The god Tammuz (v. 14) was possibly the same god as Baal–peor referred to in Numbers 25:3. The meaning of the name *Tammuz* is "source of life." The implication is that the women were weeping for the god they had depended on for life, who perhaps by this scene had been removed from his niche. God also allowed Ezekiel to see in his vision 25 men bowing down to worship the sun as the source of their life. Some Bible scholars believe the 25 men are symbolic of the whole priesthood—that is, the high priest and the priests in general had abandoned their loyalty to God.

How would you define idolatry in ancient culture? What effects did idolatry have on people in the ancient world? How would you define idolatry in today's world?

B. God's Fury (Ezekiel 8:17, 18)

As a result of the false worship of the people of Israel, God would not hear their cries. The great abomination was that the people were crying out to God while also crying out to idols. They were mixing the worship of Jehovah with the worship of false gods, and God's wrath was kindled against them.

Worship is not pure if anything other than God is worshiped. God alone is to be glorified. The worship services must have no personal agendas. Special themes should enhance the one theme of worship to God. The house of God and our worship can easily become polluted when we bring other priorities with us to the house of worship. However, God is not only displeased with impure worship, but He also refuses our worship if our hearts are filled with hatred or our thoughts or actions toward our fellowmen are filled with violence (v. 17). Worship and morality must of necessity go hand in hand.

II. IDOLATRY IN THE HEART (Ezekiel 14:1-11)

A. Idolatry of Heart (vv. 1-5)

(Ezekiel 14:1–5 is not included in the printed text.)

The prophecies against the idolatry of Israel continue in chapter 14, the focus being on idolatry of the heart. These verses are yet another example of the truth God revealed to Samuel: "The Lord seeth not as man seeth . . . the Lord looketh on the heart" (1 Samuel 16:7). No doubt these elders of Israel came to Ezekiel with all the outward signs of deference for the man of God and reverence for the God of Israel. But God was not fooled. He saw straight through them—into their hearts.

Whatever the manifestation of idolatry—whether obvious or not so obvious, whether in its beginning stages or in full-blown blasphemy—the seedbed for idolatry is the heart. Neither doctrinal error nor the appeal of the idol itself can be effective in turning one to idolatry unless the condition of the heart allows it.

Apparently, these men of Israel wanted the freedom of walking in their own ways but yet enjoy the benefits one should only expect to receive as a result of faithfully serving the Lord. But God told Ezekiel they had no right to inquire of Him at all. Therefore, God's message exposed their insincerity and gave them a warning: His answer would not be an oracle, as they desired, but an action of judgment as weighty as the abundance of their idols.

How does idolatry begin in the heart? What is God's response to idolatry in the heart?

B. God's Judgment (vv. 6-8)

6. Therefore say unto the house of Israel, Thus saith the Lord God; Repent, and turn yourselves from your idols; and turn away your faces from all your abominations.

7. For every one of the house of Israel, or of the stranger that sojourneth in Israel, which separateth himself from me, and setteth up his idols in his heart, and putteth the stumblingblock of his iniquity before his face, and cometh to a prophet to enquire of him concerning me; I the Lord will answer him by myself:

8. And I will set my face against that man, and will make him a sign and a proverb, and I will cut him off from the midst of my people; and ye shall know that I am the Lord.

True repentance is the only solution to avoiding the promised judgment—unless idolatry is defeated, destruction will come. Our hypocrisy is revealed as we stand in the presence of God. He sees the condition of our hearts and will judge us accordingly. The heart holding idols within will soon reveal actions of abomination without. "Abominations" (v. 6) indicate behaviors that were ungodly, blasphemous, and against God.

The foreigners in the land of Israel were subject to the same calamity as predicted for the native Jew, for strangers were accepted in the land only if they forsook their idolatry and all moral abominations.

If anyone sought God with impure motives, God promised that the individual could expect to be cut off from His people. We see from this passage that idolatry in the heart did not mean that the people had completely forsaken seeking God's voice. They still sought to hear from the Lord through the prophets (v. 7). But God warned that His answer would be to speak judgment. God cannot be deceived; He knows if one is mixing idolatry with seeking the Lord. To be accepted by the Lord when we seek Him requires the forsaking of our idolatry. Otherwise we can expect to hear nothing from the Lord except the word of judgment.

C. Recognition of God (vv. 9-11)

9. And if the prophet be deceived when he hath spoken a thing, I the Lord have deceived that prophet, and I will stretch out my hand upon him, and will destroy him from the midst of my people Israel.

10. And they shall bear the punishment of their iniquity: the punishment of the prophet shall be even as the punishment of him that seeketh unto him;

11. That the house of Israel may go no more astray from me, neither be polluted any more with all their transgressions; but that they may be my people, and I may be their God, saith the Lord God.

Not only the halfhearted seekers but also any prophet who served in idolatry would receive judgment of God. The position of a prophet, or any other office, does not insulate a person from the requirement to forsake idolatry. Verse 9 describes a prophet who was "deceived" while fulfilling the functioning of the office. The person was still in the office and still functioning in that office but nevertheless deceived. The prophet who was deceived was allowed by God to reap the results of his own deception—that is, he would be destroyed along with those he had sought to placate with soothing, albeit false, predictions. God's purpose in all this was that the people of Israel learn not to desert Him and not to be polluted by sin any longer but to truly be His people and allow Him to be their God. God desires to be recognized as God.

How can an idolater mix worship of God and seeking God's blessings with idolatry? What is God's judgment upon this mixing of worship?

III. A HEART FOR GOD (Ezekiel 11:16-20)

A. Reestablishing a Sanctuary (v. 16)

(Ezekiel 11:16 is not included in the printed text.)

Still another aspect of God's character is reflected in chapter 11—His mercy. Even the dreadful sin of idolatry cannot nullify the grace of God. If the idolater will but repent, forsake his idols, and turn to God, God will receive him.

God's grace is greater than the idolatry, and He is willing to reestablish safety and protection for those who will turn to Him. Those who had turned from idolatry were still in exile in a country whose people were idolatrous. They were being threatened. Nevertheless, God in His grace and mercy not only received the repentant ones but also provided a haven for them. God said He himself would be a sanctuary to them. Today, if a person will turn from the idols that compete for his attention and worship, God will extend His grace. That grace will reestablish relationship with Him and provide shelter against the retaliatory onslaughts of Satan, who has lost his supremacy over the individual who has returned to God.

The bestowal of grace on the repentant is essential, because those who have worshiped at the shrine of pleasure, self–indulgence, position, power, or materialism have become dependent on their "idols." People become addicted to their lifestyle, lust, affluence, and greed. They fear retribution and loss if they turn from these idols. However, God will in His grace receive those who will turn from their idols and serve Him. Further, the Lord will provide a spiritual haven and sustainment in the face of any adverse effects of turning from the idols.

What are the prerequisites for turning from idolatry?

B. Restoration and Cleansing (vv. 17, 18)

17. Therefore say, thus saith the Lord God; I will even gather you from the people, and assemble you out of the countries where ye have been scattered, and I will give you the land of Israel.

18. And they shall come thither, and they shall take away all the detestable things thereof and all the abominations thereof from thence.

Reconciliation is the powerful promise God makes to those who return to Him. Idolatry isolates a person from the people of God, for God's judgment is to remove the idolater from among His people. Idolatry, however, does not remove a person from God's love or His desire for restoration.

Gather, assemble, and the giving of the *land* in verses 17 and 18 are terms describing the power of God's restoration. These terms indicate the active involvement of God in the reconciliation promise. If a person will turn away from idolatry, God will restore that individual to his former place of fellowship with God and His people.

C. Newness of Spirit (vv. 19, 20)

19. And I will give them one heart, and I will put a new spirit within you; and I will take the stony heart out of their flesh, and will give them an heart of flesh:

20. That they may walk in my statutes, and keep mine ordinances, and do them: and they shall be my people, and I will be their God.

The great climax of the restoration process is a new heart and a renewed spirit. God would give a new heart with which to worship Him. Verses 19 and 20 remind the reader today about some very important principles regarding modern-day idolatry.

Idolatry is not something that died with ancient culture; it is still rampant today. Anything or anyone that takes priority over God in our lives becomes an idol. Something or someone that we regard more highly or depend on more than God constitutes idolatry. People worship other people. People worship things. When people feel their destiny lies not in the hands of God but in themselves, in others, or in things, that is idolatry.

Idolatry is a condition of the heart. The predisposition of the heart makes a person vulnerable to idolatry. The ongoing desire of the heart sustains the idolatry. The damage of the idol is that it turns the heart of the idolater into a heart of stone (v. 19).

Stone indicates an insensitivity. The one who persists in idolatry eventually loses sensitivity to God. He refuses to hear from God and is not open to His promptings to turn from idolatry. Idolatry also turns the heart to stone in relationships with others. The idolater becomes calloused in his relationships. The commitment to his "god" is so strong that he will sacrifice relationships with other people in order to serve and maintain his relationship with the idol.

Nevertheless, the heart God gives those who turn away from idolatry is a heart sensitive to God and to others, especially to the people of God. The power of God's grace transforms the insensitivity of the "stony heart" into a heart of "flesh" (v. 19). *Flesh* indicates a tender heart, sensitive to God's promptings and willing to be in harmonious relationship with others. Though the effects of idolatry can be devastating, because it invokes the wrath and judgment of God, the transformation of the heart of the idolater is still possible if the idolater will only turn away from the idol and return to God.

REVIEW QUESTIONS

1. What are some things that might constitute modern-day idolatry?

2. How does idolatry affect the heart according to Ezekiel 14:1-5?

3. Does an office such as that of a prophet insulate a person from the temptation to become idolatrous? Discuss.

4. How is it possible to remove the effects of idolatry?

5. What is God's role in reconciliation for the person who turns from idolatry?

GOLDEN TEXT HOMILY

"REPENT, AND TURN YOURSELVES FROM YOUR IDOLS; AND TURN AWAY YOUR FACES FROM ALL YOUR ABOMINATIONS" (Ezekiel 14:6).

Our text is a command: "Repent." To repent we must first recognize that we have offended God. We must feel a godly sorrow for our offense, ask God to forgive us, and then forsake the sin. It has been described as doing an about-face. To become a Christian, we must obey this command, and to remain a Christian, we will no doubt have to repent many times.

The second part of this command is really a part of repentance: "Turn yourselves from." From what? "Your idols." What is an idol? It is anything that is more important to us than the true God. To the Israelites it was Baal, Ashtaroth, and other pagan idols, as we have seen in part one. In the 20th century we probably would not be bothered by these particular gods, but there are other things that clamor for our attention: a favorite child, the love of wealth, the desire for power, the lust for things. Ah, the lust for things! That is one of the greatest weaknesses of our consumerism society. Advertising tells us we just can't get along without it, all of our friends are buying it, we just can't afford to let the Joneses get ahead of us. But anything we let come between us and God is an idol.

The final part of the command is this: "And turn away your faces from all your abominations." Don't even look at them! Eve was tempted when she saw the fruit. The Bible lists many abominations that we should turn from. Deuteronomy speaks of several: idols; making one's children pass through the fire (classes are being given in New York on how to do this and not get burned); consulting diviners (the newspapers and the television are full of advertisements for astrologers, palm readers, and "advisers"); people with familiar spirits and necromancers (spiritualists and witches), and dishonest weights and measures (cheaters). Then Proverbs 6:16-19 lists seven more things: a proud look, a lying tongue, murder, an evil heart, a mischief hunter, a false witness, a sower of discord. Still another two are doing a holy service with a wicked mind and being a despiser of God's law. Luke nails it down in the New Testament thus: "That which is highly esteemed among men is abomination in the sight of God"(16:15). **—William R. McCall, Missionary, Church of God, Cleveland, Tennessee**

SENTENCE SERMONS

GOD FORBIDS all forms of idolatry.

—Selected

BELIEVERS should set an example for the lost by worshiping God only.

—Selected

WHENEVER WE TAKE what God has done and put it in the place of Himself, we become idolators.

—Oswald Chambers

THE GLORY of God is a living man, and the life of man consists in beholding God.

—Saint Irenaeus

EVANGELISM APPLICATION

BELIEVERS SHOULD SET AN EXAMPLE FOR THE LOST BY WORSHIPING GOD ONLY.

There are many temptations to worship idols. Discouragement sets in, and even the believer may feel as though there may be another answer besides the provision that God has given. Success occurs and a person may feel that someone or something else other than God was the reason for the success.

In the face of these temptations, the believer must resist this form of idolatry. Renouncing the allurement to accept anyone or anything else as more desirous than God is essential. Despite temptations to depend on other things, the believer can secure his faith in Christ as the source of his life and well-being.

Unbelievers are watching the level of the believer's resistance to idolatry. The unbeliever may appear unconcerned; nevertheless, the believer is always under surveillance. Will the believer be drawn by the attraction of idols? Will the believer be deceived into thinking that someone or something else can satisfy the longing soul like the Lord? Will the believer worship the creation more than the Creator? These questions are raised by unbelievers as they look to the believer for an example. The believer's example in resisting idolatry demonstrates the reward of faithful devotion to the true and living God.

ILLUMINATING THE LESSON

Arthur Pink gave seven signs of false worship. These signs are contemporary illustrations of maintaining idols of people and circumstances rather than sincerely worshiping God.

1. They bring their bodies to the house of prayer but not their souls.
2. They worship with their mouths but not in spirit and in truth.
3. They are sticklers for early-morning communion with God, but they take no thought about keeping their hearts with all diligence.
4. They boast of their orthodoxy but disregard the precepts of Christ.
5. Multitudes of professing Christians abstain from external acts of violence, yet they do not hesitate to rob their neighbors of a good name by spreading evil reports against them.
6. They contribute regularly to the church but shrink not from misrepresenting their goods and cheating their customers, persuading themselves that business is business.
7. They have more regard for the laws of man than those of God, for His fear is not before their eyes.

DAILY BIBLE READINGS

M. Beware of Idolatry.
Deuteronomy 4:23–31

T. Idolatry Brings Rejection.
1 Kings 11:26–33

W. Idols Removed.
1 Kings 15:9–14

T. Temptation to Idolatry.
Acts 14:8–18

F. Consequences of Idolatry.
Romans 1:18–25

S. Turn From Idols.
1 Thessalonians 1:5–10

Loyalty to God

Study Text: Daniel 1:1–21

Objective: To recognize the danger of worldliness and live by godly values.

Time: The Book of Daniel was written between 605 and 530 B.C., covering a time span of 60–70 years.

Place: The Book of Daniel was written at Babylon.

Golden Text: "Trust in the Lord with all thine heart; and lean not unto thine own understanding" (Proverbs 3:5).

Central Truth: Faithfulness to God results in divine blessings.

Evangelism Emphasis: A Christian's life should reflect godly values to the world.

PRINTED TEXT

Daniel 1:8. But Daniel purposed in his heart that he would not defile himself with the portion of the king's meat, nor with the wine which he drank: therefore he requested of the prince of the eunuchs that he might not defile himself.

9. Now God had brought Daniel into favour and tender love with the prince of the eunuchs.

10. And the prince of the eunuchs said unto Daniel, I fear my lord the king, who hath appointed your meat and your drink: for why should he see your faces worse liking than the children which are of your sort? then shall ye make me endanger my head to the king.

11. Then said Daniel to Melzar, whom the prince of the eunuchs had set over Daniel, Hananiah, Mishael, and Azariah,

12. Prove thy servants, I beseech thee, ten days; and let them give us pulse to eat, and water to drink.

13. Then let our countenances be looked upon before thee, and the countenance of the children that eat of the portion of the king's meat: and as thou seest, deal with thy servants.

14. So he consented to them in this matter, and proved them ten days.

15. And at the end of ten days their countenances appeared fairer and fatter in flesh than all the children which did eat the portion of the king's meat.

16. Thus Melzar took away the portion of their meat, and the wine that they should drink; and gave them pulse.

17. As for these four children, God gave them knowledge and skill in all learning and wisdom: and Daniel had understanding in all visions and dreams.

18. Now at the end of the days

that the king had said he should bring them in, then the prince of the eunuchs brought them in before Nebuchadnezzar.

19. And the king communed with them; and among them all was found none like Daniel, Hananiah, Mishael, and Azariah: therefore stood they before the king.

20. And in all matters of wisdom and understanding, that the king enquired of them, he found them ten times better than all the magicians and astrologers that were in all his realm.

DICTIONARY

eunuchs (YOU–nooks)—Daniel 1:10—The Greek word, used in both the New Testament and the Septuagint version of the Old Testament, means "bedkeeper," or "one in charge of beds and bedchambers." The Hebrew word carries the idea of physical mutilation—that is, castration. These eunuchs were often placed in charge of harems. The word came to stand for "officer," whether a eunuch or not. Some of them held a place of importance (Acts 8:27).

Melzar—Daniel 1:11—This is a transliteration of the Hebrew word, which simply means "servant" or "steward." His name is unknown.

Hananiah (han–uh–NIGH–uh)—Daniel 1:11—One of Daniel's three companions, whose Hebrew name was changed to the Babylonian name Shadrach

Mishael (MISH–ay–el)—Daniel 1:11—The Hebrew name for Meshach, the second of Daniel's companions

Azariah (az–uh–RYE–uh)—Daniel 1:11—The Hebrew name for Abednego, the third of Daniel's companions

Nebuchadnezzar (NEB–bu–kud–NEZ–zar)—Daniel 1:18—This name is often spelled with an *n* following the *d*. However, the form using the *r* more correctly represents the Hebrew name. The king of Babylon from 605 to 562 B.C., this man eventually destroyed Jerusalem (586 B.C.) and carried the inhabitants into captivity.

LESSON OUTLINE

I. CONFRONTED WITH WORLDLINESS
   A. Conquest of the Enemy
   B. In Preparation to Serve the King
   C. A Change of Names

II. CHOOSING TO HONOR GOD
   A. Purpose of Heart
   B. Potential Loss
   C. Proving the Lord

III. RESULTS OF GODLY VALUES
   A. Results of Faithfulness
   B. God's Action Toward the Faithful
   C. Demonstration of God's Faithfulness to the World

LESSON EXPOSITION

INTRODUCTION

Remaining loyal to God is the theme for both the Book of Daniel and his life. Daniel was surrounded by great power. He was held captive in the most powerful country of the world, Babylon. He was under the most powerful man in the world, Nebuchadnezzar. Daniel's country, heritage, and way of life were constantly ridiculed and challenged. Nevertheless, he remained faithful. It is possible to remain loyal to God even in the face of powerful opposition.

Daniel became very successful in the country of Israel's exile. He arose to a position of great prominence and influence—a position that caused many to become envious. Nevertheless, he gained and maintained his position of favor and power without compromising his faithfulness to God. One can be successful and still remain faithful.

The story of Daniel is even more compelling when you consider his age at the time of his captivity and his longevity in a foreign land. He came to Babylon as a young adolescent. He was probably no older than 17 and may have been as young as 14, and he outlived the Babylonian Empire. By the end of his story, the Babylonians had been defeated by the Persians, new rulers were in Babylon, and Daniel was an old man. He may have even been in his 90s when he was cast into the lions' den. Faithfulness is not limited by youth or length of years. Both young and old can be effective witnesses of their faith in God if they remain faithful to Him.

I. CONFRONTED WITH WORLDLINESS (Daniel 1:1-7)

A. Conquest of the Enemy (vv. 1, 2)

(Daniel 1:1, 2 is not included in the printed text.)

The enemy had defeated Judah. Circumstantial defeat, however, does not preclude faithfulness. Faithfulness does not depend on cloudless days and starlit nights. In fact, the faith of Daniel flourished in the midst of stormy circumstances. Many of the inhabitants of his country were taken into bondage in a far-off land. Among strangers and homesick for his native land, Daniel remained faithful to his God. And God honored the faithfulness of this individual. The treasures of the house of God in Judah were taken to the temple of the god of Babylon. But Daniel's faithfulness did not depend on access to the Temple of the Lord in Jerusalem, nor did it require that the Temple furnishings remain in their place. Daniel's faithfulness continued!

What are the requirements for loyalty and faithfulness to God in today's world?

B. In Preparation to Serve the King (vv. 3-5)

(Daniel 1:3–5 is not included in the printed text.)

Attention moves from the defeat of Judah to the one who defeated Judah, Nebuchadnezzar. The king of Babylon instructed Ashpenaz, the chief of the eunuchs of the court, to select the cream of the crop from the Israelite youth who had been captured and brought to Babylon. They were to be from the royal family and those of nobility. They were to be handsome, intelligent, knowledgeable, and free from physical defect. They were to learn the Chaldean language and be trained in court etiquette and protocol. The length of this training was to be three years, and during this period they would be fed the delicacies that the king himself subsisted on. All this was to be done to prepare these youths to serve the king in the king's palace.

C. A Change of Names (vv. 6, 7)

(Daniel 1:6, 7 is not included in the printed text.)

The focus moves now to Daniel and his three Hebrew companions. Daniel remained faithful in spite of outside circumstances (vv. 1, 2) and in the presence of the enemy (vv. 3-5). We will see that Daniel also remained loyal to God even when his captors tried to change his very identity. Changing the young men's names was an attempt by Nebuchadnezzar to transform them into Babylonians—to indoctrinate them with the Babylonian culture and lifestyle. However, even this maneuver failed to remove their love for God. All four remained loyal.

II. CHOOSING TO HONOR GOD (Daniel 1:8-14)

A. Purpose of Heart (v. 8)

8. But Daniel purposed in his heart that he would not defile himself with the portion of the king's meat, nor with the wine which he drank: therefore he requested of the prince of the eunuchs that he might not defile himself.

Much of the rest of the Book of Daniel, especially the first half of the book, explains in greater detail how Daniel was able to remain faithful throughout his life. But the foundation for his continued loyalty to God was laid when as a teenager in training in the courts of a foreign king—his people's captor—he determined "he would not defile himself with the portion of the king's meat."

Was it harder or easier for Daniel to remain faithful in the circumstances he was in than it is to remain loyal to God in the circumstances of today?

Purpose of heart was a vital factor in Daniel's ability to remain loyal. The custom of providing food from the royal table to those who would serve the king was so firmly entrenched in practice as to be akin to a law established in the land. Nevertheless, Daniel purposed in his heart that he would not defile himself.

The battleground was the heart. The defilement of the food, drink, and lifestyle offered by the pagan Nebuchadnezzar would produce its effect on the body, but that was a secondary consideration. The primary consideration was obedience to God. And this was a matter of the heart. Guarding his heart from defilement, that is, pollution and desecration, was the first task in Daniel's loyalty.

B. Potential Loss (vv. 9, 10)

9. Now God had brought Daniel into favour and tender love with the prince of the eunuchs.

10. And the prince of the eunuchs said unto Daniel, I fear my lord the king, who hath appointed your meat and your drink: for why should he see your faces worse liking than the children which are of your sort? then shall ye make me endanger my head to the king.

God's action in his life put Daniel in a favorable position with the prince of the eunuchs. In contrast to the action of Nebuchadnezzar, God's graciousness brought Daniel to be viewed with favor by the ruler of the eunuchs. "God had brought" (v. 9) indicates God's action. God made the relationship possible. The description implies that the supervisor of the eunuchs had a special respect and understanding toward Daniel.

What methods should we employ to assure our loyalty to God today? How are they like those of Daniel? What can we learn from Daniel about being loyal to God?

God acts not only in the events and circumstances of His children's lives but also in the lives of those whose decisions affect us. Faithfulness to God is still the best way to find favor among our fellowmen.

In an attempt to dissuade the prince of the eunuchs from enforcing the king's decree, Daniel made an appeal. He did not make a demand. A demand would have been rooted in self-centeredness. But a godly appeal is rooted in humble submission to God. Daniel was not passive, but neither was he aggressive. He was clear in stating his request, but he was not demanding.

The supervisor of the young men was understanding toward Daniel's request, but he was also genuinely fearful concerning the outcome. He doubted that the outcome of Daniel's request if granted would be favorable for any of them. But the task of loyalty is to demonstrate to the world's questioning mind that God's way is the best way to achieve what is best for all people. Loyalty to God enhances rather than hinders our loyalty to each other.

C. Proving the Lord (vv. 11-14)

11. Then said Daniel to Melzar, whom the prince of the eunuchs had set over Daniel, Hananiah, Mishael, and Azariah,

12. Prove thy servants, I beseech thee, ten days; and let them give us pulse to eat, and water to drink.

13. Then let our countenances be looked upon before thee, and the countenance of the children that eat of the portion of the king's meat: and as thou seest, deal with thy servants.

14. So he consented to them in this matter, and proved them ten days.

Daniel's next demonstration of his loyalty to God was to show God's loyalty to Him. He asked Melzar, the subordinate officer assigned to him and his three companions, to allow them to try the vegetable diet for 10 days, then examine them to see if they fared any the worse for forgoing the king's fancy food. Daniel was willing to carry out the discipline that God had called him to. He believed in God's loyalty to those who are faithful to Him. Daniel was faithful because God was faithful. He believed their faithfulness would result in a testimony to the king's household.

Apparently Nebuchadnezzar's food included things the Jews did not eat, especially certain meats, which were a violation of God's dietary principles found in the Old Testament Books of the Law. Melzar consented to Daniel's request, and the 10–day test period began.

III. RESULTS OF GODLY VALUES (Daniel 1:15-21)

A. Results of Faithfulness (vv. 15, 16)

15. And at the end of the ten days their countenances appeared fairer and fatter in flesh than all the children which did eat the portion of the king's meat.

16. Thus Melzar took away the

portion of their meat, and the wine that they should drink; and gave them pulse.

Daniel's spiritual victory was not the result of his own action alone. His determination to remain true to God merely set the stage for God to work in his behalf. The "fairer," or more appealing, countenance and the "fatter," or healthier, flesh came as a result of God's loyal response to Daniel's loyalty to Him. The result was not a mere biological response to a healthier diet.

The supervisor's servant was convinced of the wisdom of obeying God's directives and responded to Daniel's testimony just as the world will eventually respond to our testimony. God still responds to faithfulness. It is important to note that Melzar was not manipulated or coerced. And we must be careful today not to try to force our faith on others. That only turns individuals away from God. But if we purpose in our hearts to stand true, our life and God's favor to us will be a more convincing testimony than any attempt at forcing a confession could ever be. The testimony of God's faithfulness to Daniel as a result of his faithfulness was the basis of the servant's response.

In being loyal to God, which comes first—what we do toward God or what He does toward us? Which makes the other possible?

B. God's Action Toward the Faithful (v. 17)

17. As for these four children, God gave them knowledge and skill in all learning and wisdom: and Daniel had understanding in all visions and dreams.

The specific result of the loyalty of Daniel and the other three youths was learning, wisdom, and the understanding of visions and dreams. The emphasis of the text is still on God's own action in their lives.

A distinction is made between Daniel and the three others. This distinction is an early indication of Daniel's prophetic ministry. The other three were able to learn and discern many things; however, Daniel was given insights into and by visions and dreams. *Visions* indicate seeing something that cannot be perceived by natural sight. *Dreams* are those pictures and emotions seen or felt during sleep. God uses both methods to convey His message. Daniel's special abilities are conveyed later in the book. He interpreted dreams and saw visions.

C. Demonstration of God's Faithfulness to the World (vv. 18-21)

(Daniel 1:21 is not included in the printed text.)

18. Now at the end of the days that the king had said he should bring them in, then the prince of the eunuchs brought them in before Nebuchadnezzar.

19. And the king communed with them; and among them all was found none like Daniel, Hananiah, Mishael, and Azariah: therefore stood they before the king.

20. And in all matters of wisdom and understanding, that the king enquired of them, he found them ten times better than all the magicians and astrologers that were in all his realm.

Eventually, the witness of Daniel's loyalty reached the ultimate power of the pagan kingdom, the king himself. Daniel's loyalty was not a minor event, held in insignificance. On the contrary,

God in His faithfulness honored and rewarded Daniel's loyalty.

The definitive words *all* and *ten times better* significantly communicate the richness of God's reward for loyalty. *All* has double significance because it describes the amount of knowledge and the extent of superiority demonstrated by the Judeans. They had wisdom and understanding that superseded that of all the magicians and astrologers. God certainly takes note of His children's loyalty and often rewards their faithfulness in an obvious and immediate way.

Magicians were those who attempted to manipulate the supernatural in an effort to avoid the perils of the future they predicted. *Astrologers* gazed at the stars and sought to determine fate by their positions in the heavens. They worshiped the creation more than the Creator. No wonder the insights God provided were so far superior to theirs. Ultimate and complete wisdom and knowledge belongs only to God. God's people recognize this and are loyal to Him, confident that He will act on their behalf. He is always faithful to His people. Can we afford to do less than be faithful to Him?

REVIEW QUESTIONS

1. What is the foundation of the believer's faithfulness to God?
2. What were some of the circumstances in which Daniel found himself, yet remained loyal to God?
3. What were some of the ways Daniel demonstrated his loyalty to God?
4. In what areas are believers today being asked to compromise, and how can they remain loyal to God?

GOLDEN TEXT HOMILY

"TRUST IN THE LORD WITH ALL THINE HEART; AND LEAN NOT UNTO THINE OWN UNDERSTANDING" (Proverbs 3:5).

The great King Solomon, wisest of all men, tells us the way to happiness and success is to "trust in the Lord with all thine heart." Trusting God means that we place our confidence and dependency in Him who is able to come to our rescue at all times. Trusting Him with all our heart encompasses spiritual, physical, and material areas of life.

No man is sufficient within himself. It is God who gives life, knowledge, and understanding. Therefore, insufficient as we are, we must trust and seek God as well as do His will if we are to be successful.

Many trust in their own wisdom, ingenuity, and riches, but King Solomon tells us, "Be not wise in thine own eyes" (v. 7).

Our heavenly Father knows what we have need of and has given us direction in Matthew 6:33: "Seek ye first the kingdom of God, and his righteousness; and all these things [necessities of life] shall be added unto you."

The writer of Hebrews said it so well: "But Jesus the Son of God is our great High Priest who has gone to heaven itself to help us; therefore let us never stop trusting him. This High Priest of ours understands our weaknesses, since he had the same temptations we do, though he never once gave way to them and sinned. So let us come boldly to the very throne of God and stay there to receive his mercy and to find grace to help us in our times of need" (4:14-16, *TLB*).—**Brady Dennis (Retired), Church of God Former State Overseer, Greenville, South Carolina**

SENTENCE SERMONS

FAITHFULNESS TO GOD results in divine blessings.

—Selected

A CHRISTIAN'S LIFE should reflect godly values to the world.

—Selected

THE WORLD is a sure teacher, but it requires a fat fee.

—Finnish Proverb

TOO OFTEN the values Christ has declared to be false are brought back into evangelical favor and promoted as the very life and substance of the Christian way.

—A.W. Tozer

EVANGELISM APPLICATION

A CHRISTIAN'S LIFE SHOULD REFLECT GODLY VALUES TO THE WORLD.

The life witness of the believer is vital to reflect the principles and action of God. The Babylonians knew about the principles of the faith of Judah and even about the God of Judah. However, it was when that faith was lived through the loyalty of Daniel that they became convinced of the reality of that faith. Loyal witness is necessary if principles are to be seen as real by the unbeliever.

The witness of the believer is especially effective when loyalty persists in the face of challenges to compromise. These challenges create the opportunities in which God can demonstrate His power. The believer should not feel weak, alone, or timid when his loyalty is tested. It is at this point that God exhibits His faithfulness to those who love Him. And our loyalty is translated into witness when we stay true in the face of adversity.

Our loyalty is often challenged in the area of our values. In Daniel's case, his diet and lifestyle were assaulted. The way we live indicates the depth of our faith. For the fruit of faithfulness to remain, our faith must be strong and unwavering. The holding to our values is the visible expression of our inner faith. The Christian should reflect godly values to the world and thus reveal the presence of God within.

ILLUMINATING THE LESSON

Not everyone remains faithful to God as Daniel did. It is so easy to slip into the path of least resistance—to follow the crowd and be accepted by one's peers. But the following verse of poetry sadly points out that even those whose lifestyles did not exhibit loyalty to God often recognize how much they need Him at the crossroads of life.

Hearts that preachers could not touch
By wayside graves are raised.
And voices cry, "God be merciful"
That never cried, "God be praised."

—Anonymous

DAILY BIBLE READINGS

M. Loyalty Rewarded. Numbers 12:1–16
T. Divided Loyalty. 1 Kings 11:1–11
W. Godliness Rewarded. 2 Kings 18:1–7; 20:1–6
T. Commitment Needed. Luke 9:57–62
F. Loyal Christians. Colossians 4:7–15
S. Stand Firm in Faith. 2 Thessalonians 2:13–17

Principles of Intercession

Study Text: Ezekiel 22:30; Daniel 9:1–23

Objective: To learn God's pattern for effective prayer and commit to intercede for one another.

Time: The Book of Ezekiel was written between 593 and 565 B.C. (See time and place for Daniel, lesson 8.)

Place: The Book of Ezekiel was written in Babylon.

Golden Text: "Praying always with all prayer and supplication in the Spirit, and watching thereunto with all perseverance and supplication for all saints" (Ephesians 6:18).

Central Truth: God calls and equips intercessors.

Evangelism Emphasis: Believers are called to intercede for the salvation of the lost.

PRINTED TEXT

Daniel 9:3. And I set my face unto the Lord God, to seek by prayer and supplications, with fasting, and sackcloth, and ashes:

4. And I prayed unto the Lord my God, and made my confession, and said, O Lord, the great and dreadful God, keeping the covenant and mercy to them that love him, and to them that keep his commandments;

5. We have sinned, and have committed iniquity, and have done wickedly, and have rebelled, even by departing from thy precepts and from thy judgments:

6. Neither have we hearkened unto thy servants the prophets, which spake in thy name to our kings, our princes, and our fathers, and to all the people of the land.

16. O Lord, according to all thy righteousness, I beseech thee, let thine anger and thy fury be turned away from thy city Jerusalem, thy holy mountain: because for our sins, and for the iniquities of our fathers, Jerusalem and thy people are become a reproach to all that are about us.

17. Now therefore, O our God, hear the prayer of thy servant, and his supplications, and cause thy face to shine upon thy sanctuary that is desolate, for the Lord's sake.

18. O my God, incline thine ear, and hear; open thine eyes, and behold our desolations, and the city which is called by thy name: for we do not present our supplications before thee for our righteousnesses, but for thy great mercies.

19. O Lord, hear; O Lord, forgive; O Lord, hearken and do; defer not, for thine own sake, O my God: for thy city and thy people are called by thy name.

20. And whiles I was speaking, and praying, and confessing my sin and the sin of my people Israel, and presenting my supplication before the Lord my God for the holy mountain of my God;

21. Yea, whiles I was speaking in prayer, even the man Gabriel, whom I had seen in the vision at the beginning, being caused to fly swiftly, touched me about the time of the evening oblation.

22. And he informed me, and talked with me, and said, O Daniel, I am now come forth to give thee skill and understanding.

LESSON OUTLINE

I. IDENTIFY WITH THE NEED
- A. Seek God's Face
- B. Identify Departure From God's Precepts
- C. Identify Disgrace and Deficiency
- D. Identify Unrighteous Acts

II. INTERCEDE WITH FERVOR
- A. Necessity of a Hedge
- B. Prayer to Turn God's Anger
- C. Entreat God's Presence
- D. Cry for Forgiveness

III. EXPECT AN ANSWER
- A. God's Messenger
- B. Response of God's Love

LESSON EXPOSITION

INTRODUCTION

Prayer is a clear mark of spirituality. Daniel was used of God to see into the future, remain faithful in the present, and refuse to be discouraged about the past. That Daniel sought God in prayer is clearly the reason for much of Daniel's victory.

Daniel 9 gives some principles Daniel exercised when he interceded in prayer. These principles were the setting in which God did many mighty works of power and through which He gave insight to Daniel. It is important to study these principles of intercession in order to be effective prayer warriors today.

There is no shortcut to effective prayer. Indeed, Daniel's prayers were intense, for he was interceding in behalf of a desperate nation. To many there appeared to be no hope. Many were tempted to forsake the God of Judah. The gods of the Babylonians were awesomely displayed before them. However, through intercession, Daniel was able to see the God of Judah and behold His mighty works. In similar fashion, the believer today can commune with God despite temptations and discouragements. And in so doing he can behold what God is doing in his own life as well as in the world.

I. IDENTIFY WITH THE NEED (Daniel 9:1-15)

A. Seek God's Face (vv. 1-4)

(Daniel 9:1, 2 is not included in the printed text.)

3. And I set my face unto the Lord God, to seek by prayer and supplications, with fasting, and sackcloth, and ashes:

4. And I prayed unto the Lord

my God, and made my confession, and said, O Lord, the great and dreadful God, keeping the covenant and mercy to them that love him, and to them that keep his commandments.

Verses 1 and 2 furnish the setting for the chapter. The Medes had conquered the Babylonians, and Darius had been appointed viceroy over the Babylonians. Daniel was in his 80s, perhaps his 90s. He was aware that God had foretold the demise of the Babylonians (see Jeremiah 25:11, 12) and that the captivity would last only 70 years. However, despite the fact that the Babylonians had been overthrown, the people of Judah had not been allowed to return to their homeland.

Desiring deliverance and restoration for the people of God, Daniel bared his soul before God in intercessory prayer. Verses 3 and 4 provide valuable insight into the nature and steps of his intercession.

Daniel set (Hebrew, *nathan*) his face toward God in order to seek Him. In the word *set* is implied the giving of oneself over to someone or something. Daniel's prayerful stance was an act of commitment in which he gave himself completely to God. Prayer, for Daniel, was more than words; it was a directing of his innermost desires to God through communication with Him.

What is the mission of an intercessor? What brings a person to become an intercessor in behalf of oneself and others?

Prayer (from the Hebrew term *palal*) emphasizes intercession and mediation. Daniel was approaching God in behalf of a need for which he had a burden. *Supplication* (Hebrew, *tachanuwn*) emphasizes entreating the favor, mercy, and grace of another. Daniel was not demanding from God but was reverently approaching Him, offering his request and making confession on behalf of his countrymen.

Daniel entered this time of intercession with great awareness of the pain and suffering his fellow Jews had endured. Fasting was not an unusual discipline preparatory to prayer, especially a prayer concerning a desperate need and for which a revelation of the solution was sought. Sackcloth and ashes were the traditional signs of mourning and thus were considered appropriate as a show of contrition before God. *Ashes* (Hebrew *'epher*) signified worthlessness, depicting the worthlessness of ashes for fuel or any useful purpose. Daniel affirmed in humility that he was in himself unworthy to approach God.

Because of Daniel's lack of understanding, he turned to the One who is the source of all wisdom and knowledge. But he did not approach God casually or effortlessly. Too often our tendency today is to approach God lightly, almost nonchalantly. But prayer is itself a discipline; and the more serious the need, the more intense and agonizing our prayers must be. Our Lord himself prayed with this kind of agonizing fervor in the Garden of Gethsemane (Luke 22:44).

Daniel began his prayer by recognizing who God is. He declared four things about God: (1) He is *great*, a term emphasizing the power of God. (2) God is *dreadful* (*awesome*), a term describing fear, reverence, and awe before God. (3) He is a God of *covenant*—who had established a relationship with His people. (4) God is a God of *mercy*, a term usually translated "lovingkindness," emphasizing the unfailing, faithful love of God.

How can Daniel's prayer instruct us today as intercessors? Is it possible for people of God to intercede today as Daniel did?

In the first few lines of Daniel's prayer, we gain further insight into our responsibility to God, if we are to expect an answer to our prayers. We are to love God and keep His commandments. Communion with God and His response to our petitions require that we fulfill these two obligations. God's covenant and mercy are extended to those who are faithful to love Him and to keep His commandments. We must not forget either side of the nature of God. He is both terrible in the execution of His judgments and mercifully kind toward those who are repentant. To dwell on one of these characteristics to the exclusion of the other paints a warped image of God and is dangerously akin to heresy.

B. Identify Departure From God's Precepts (vv. 5, 6)

5. We have sinned, and have committed iniquity, and have done wickedly, and have rebelled, even by departing from thy precepts and from thy judgments:

6. Neither have we hearkened unto thy servants the prophets, which spake in thy name to our kings, our princes, and our fathers, and to all the people of the land.

After acknowledging the God to whom he was praying and affirming responsibilities to God, Daniel confessed the nation's terrible shortcomings in meeting those requirements. The summation of their failure to fulfill these responsibilities is *sin*. Specifically, Daniel named the sins—wickedness and rebellion. He admitted the people had failed to act in accordance with the precepts and judgments of God.

What a sad and terrible indictment—they didn't listen; they didn't pay heed! They had turned away from God's communication to them through the prophets, God's servants. The prophets had communicated God's message to His people, but they had turned away and would not hearken. The critical confession as Daniel approached God was that they had rebuffed God's approaches to them.

C. Identify Disgrace and Deficiency (vv. 7, 8)

(Daniel 9:7, 8 is not included in the printed text.)

Daniel confessed Israel's "confusion of faces"—that is, shame or disgrace—which had resulted from their sin and rejection of the prophets. The people were without order, strength, or dignity. They had lost face before other kings when they were taken into captivity. But their former state of respect and dignity among the nations could be reestablished only by God's intervention on their behalf.

D. Identify Unrighteous Acts (vv. 9-15)

(Daniel 9:9–15 is not included in the printed text.)

Echoing Daniel's initial approach to God is this humble confession of the shortcomings of the people in the light of God's awesome power and merciful works. Daniel's appeal was a far cry from the demands of those who specify to God the things they feel they deserve. He did not recite the reasons why God must respond to his prayer. If the people had to rely on what they deserved, they would have been pitiable indeed. Since their rebelliousness had landed them in their undesirable predicament, their only hope would have to be in God's compassion. They were thrown entirely on His mercy. Thus Daniel acknowledged that God was God, and he approached Him with repentance and humility.

What part do God's mercy and His love play in the answer to the prayer of the intercessor?

II. INTERCEDE WITH FERVOR (Ezekiel 22:30; Daniel 9:16-19)

A. Necessity of a Hedge (Ezekiel 22:30)

(Ezekiel 22:30 is not included in the printed text.)

This verse in Ezekiel provides insight concerning intercession. God sought for someone to intercede, that if the wrath of God might be averted from a land. His search was for someone who would stand between Judah and the "indignation" of God (v. 31)—someone who would "make up the hedge" and "stand in the gap." These phrases describe an intercessor.

It is important to note that the intercessor does not stand between those in danger and the danger itself. Rather, this person stands between those in danger and God, who pours out His wrath on the rebellious ones. In that position, the intercessor is not a protector but someone who approaches God in behalf of others. Correspondingly, he stands between God's response of judgment and those who would otherwise be forever cut off from God because of their rebellion. The intercessor bears much of the burden between God and a people.

God had set in place certain guidelines for the protection of His people: sound doctrine; pure worship; His own good laws; and His intention that there be godly prophets, priests, and kings. But the "hedge" God had given them was broken—there were gaps in it! Doctrine and worship had become greatly corrupted, His laws had been perverted, and the men who should have been the strong supporting posts were themselves rotten.

To become the intercessor who will make up the hedge, one must publicly oppose the corruptions that have crept in; deplore such breaches, mourn for them, and intercede to avert God's impending wrath; and make every effort to restore conditions to an acceptable state before God. This burden of intercession was what Daniel felt in Daniel 9 when he wondered if the deliverance of Judah would be completed.

B. Prayer to Turn God's Anger (Daniel 9:16)

16. O Lord, according to all thy righteousness, I beseech thee, let thine anger and thy fury be turned away from thy city Jerusalem, thy holy mountain: because for our sins, and for the iniquities of our fathers, Jerusalem and thy people are become a reproach to all that are about us.

Daniel's prayer in this verse addresses God's anger toward Judah. His specific supplication was for Jerusalem, the holy city. Again in humility, he appealed to God to turn His fury away from Jerusalem. It was to have been the crowning glory of the earth, but the people's sins had made it the object of mockery among the nations.

Daniel's intercession was an appeal to God's own righteousness. If God responded favorably to the request, it would be for the sake of His own standard of righteousness first of all, but it would also be a vindication of His name against those nations who gloated over the destruction of the city where the sanctuary of the Lord God stood.

Why does God respond to the cry of the intercessor? What is God looking for in the prayer of the intercessor?

C. Entreat God's Presence (vv. 17, 18)

17. Now therefore, O our God, hear the prayer of thy servant, and his supplications, and cause thy face to shine upon thy sanctuary that is desolate, for the Lord's sake.

18. O my God, incline thine ear, and hear; open thine eyes, and behold our desolations, and the city which is called by thy name: for we do not present our supplications before thee for our righteousness, but for thy great mercies.

Having first recognized God's righteousness, Daniel now moved to address the needs of the people. The preeminence of God's righteousness does not negate His mercy. On the contrary, God's righteousness provides His mercy. Aware that God, because of His righteousness, chooses to be merciful, Daniel pleaded for mercy. The comfort of the intercessor is to know that God, by His very nature and will, responds to a humble, repentant cry.

D. Cry for Forgiveness (v. 19)

19. O Lord, hear; O Lord, forgive; O Lord, hearken and do; defer not, for thine own sake, O my God: for thy city and thy people are called by thy name.

Daniel, in earnest intercession, cried out for forgiveness. And again, he pleaded for God's response on the basis of His own nature and "for thine own sake." He recognized that God's forgiveness does not begin with the cry of the repentant but that repentance itself is made possible by God.

God's preeminence in the process of forgiving the people of Judah and restoring Jerusalem was based on His ownership of the people. Only when Daniel confessed the sins of the people was he able to refer to the fact that they were God's own people—they bore His name. Ultimately, any glory and honor received from the forgiveness of the people and the preservation of Jerusalem and Judah would go to their owner, God himself. God does not forgive and restore because of our worthiness or because of the desperate situation we are in but because of His own nature and to bring glory to His name. Intercession not only rescues individuals, but it also brings glory to God.

III. EXPECT AN ANSWER (Daniel 9:20-23)

A. God's Messenger (vv. 20–22)

20. And whiles I was speaking, and praying, and confessing my sin and the sin of my people Israel, and presenting my supplication before the Lord my God for the holy mountain of my God;

21. Yea, whiles I was speaking in prayer, even the man Gabriel, whom I had seen in the vision at the beginning, being caused to fly swiftly, touched me about the

time of the evening oblation.

22. And he informed me, and talked with me, and said, O Daniel, I am now come forth to give thee skill and understanding.

In the midst of Daniel's intercession, God, of His own timing, sent a message to Daniel through the messenger, or angel, Gabriel. He is the same angel who had appeared to Daniel in chapter 8. He is referred to as "the man Gabriel" because when he had appeared to Daniel earlier, it was in human form. Daniel's intercession was heard. The intercessor can be assured that God, because of His righteous and merciful nature, will hear our cries and respond.

The message began with the promise that Daniel would be granted "skill and understanding." These two gifts were necessary to perceive the forthcoming explanation of God's action. Daniel's task would not be to initiate some great action. Instead, Daniel's task would be to perceive and relate the message God was conveying to him. The perception of God's merciful action toward His people would bring glory and honor to Him.

B. Response of God's Love (v. 23)

(Daniel 9:23 is not included in the printed text.)

Gabriel continued his message to Daniel. His supplication had been heard from the beginning of it, and God had sent Gabriel to deliver His message. First, he informed Daniel that he was "greatly beloved." Then, beginning in verse 24, God revealed His action throughout the end time and how Judah and Jerusalem would be delivered. However, the basis of God's action is described at the beginning of the message in verse 23. The basis was God's love.

As an intercessor, Daniel discovered that God's righteousness includes His mercy and produces a loving response. The key to Daniel's petition had been His recognition of who God is, His nature, and the need for confession from God's wayward people. If an intercessor today will approach God as God, repenting and confessing for himself and those for whom he is interceding, God will respond in love and mercy. God's will is to respond to the cry of the intercessor, grant forgiveness to the repentant, and restore His people to their intended position and right relationship to Him.

REVIEW QUESTIONS

1. What should be the priorities of an intercessor?
2. What was the method of Daniel's prayer as he interceded before God?
3. What comfort and encouragement does the righteousness of God provide to the intercessor?
4. What is the ultimate basis of God's response to intercessors?
5. How would you define an intercessor? Explain the need for a ministry of intercessory prayer today.

GOLDEN TEXT HOMILY

"PRAYING ALWAYS WITH ALL PRAYER AND SUPPLICATION IN THE SPIRIT, AND WATCHING THEREUNTO WITH ALL PERSEVERANCE AND SUPPLICATION FOR ALL SAINTS" (Ephesians 6:18).

While it is true that prayer is an attitude, it is also what we believe; and what we believe is what we become. "Praying always" means to live an active and persevering life continually. But that is not the only emphasis that this text expresses. There comes a time in our lives when it takes more than just a thought or a wish to God for a need to be answered. "Praying always with all prayer and supplication in the Spirit" means to engage all our spiritually patriotic Christian beliefs in an aggressive and persevering stand against the forces of Satan. Satan attempts to block the will of God for both believers and the lost. Sometimes we must violently attack a stronghold of the enemy of our soul with every means of spiritual strategy that God has given us. One must be determined to persevere until the victory is won and the stronghold of evil is completely torn down and destroyed.

From a Pentecostal background, I have observed that what early Pentecostals called "praying through" cannot be substituted by any other means. We must be determined to pray through if we are to become a victorious Pentecostal believer. In spiritual warfare, prayer is not so much a weapon as it is a means whereby we engage in the battle itself. Intercessory prayer is the battlefield, on which God's chief weapon, the Word of God, is employed. Many a spiritual battle has been lost because the one who is praying has not engaged himself in the battle. The apostle Paul was a Pentecostal believer who believed that praying in the Spirit was not just meaningless words but that those words are powerful, authoritative, and forceful ones coming from a heart filled with the Holy Spirit.

"Likewise the Spirit also helps in our weaknesses. For we do not know what we should pray for as we ought, but the Spirit Himself makes intercession for us with groanings which cannot be uttered" (Romans 8:26, *NKJV*). As Pentecostal believers we must revive this pattern of effective prayer if we are going to identify, intercede, and expect an answer for our needs and the needs of others. The devil and all his demonic forces cannot prevail over this powerful means of intercession. The more we intercede for others, the more we become like Christ. The Holy Spirit has gifted us with the Spirit of Christ. He has called us to intercede.**—Aaron D. Mize, Clinical Chaplain, MDOC, Parchman, Mississippi.**

SENTENCE SERMONS

GOD CALLS AND EQUIPS intercessors.

—Selected

BELIEVERS ARE CALLED to intercede for the salvation of the lost.

—Selected

AN INTERCESSOR means one who is in such vital contact with God and with his fellowmen that he is like a live wire closing the gap between the saving power of God and sinful men who have been cut off from the power.

—Hannah Hurnard

DAILY BIBLE READINGS

M. A Leader Intercedes.
Exodus 32:30–35

T. Persistent Intercession.
2 Kings 4:25–37

W. Intercession for a Nation.
Esther 4:13 through 5:3

T. God Answers Prayer.
Acts 12:1–12

F. Intercession for the Saints.
Romans 8:18–27

S. Christ, Our Intercessor.
1 John 2:1–6

Wickedness of Pride

Study Text: Ezekiel 28:6–19; Daniel 5:1–6, 22–30

Objective: To identify areas of pride in our lives and repent.

Time: The Book of Ezekiel was written between 593 and 565 B.C. (See time and place for Daniel, lesson 8.)

Place: The Book of Ezekiel was written in Babylon.

Golden Text: "Pride goeth before destruction, and an haughty spirit before a fall" (Proverbs 16:18).

Central Truth: Pride and arrogance invite divine judgment.

Evangelism Emphasis: God responds with forgiveness to a broken and contrite spirit.

PRINTED TEXT

Ezekiel 28:17. Thine heart was lifted up because of thy beauty, thou hast corrupted thy wisdom by reason of thy brightness: I will cast thee to the ground, I will lay thee before kings, that they may behold thee.

18. Thou hast defiled thy sanctuaries by the multitude of thine iniquities, by the iniquity of thy traffick; therefore will I bring forth a fire from the midst of thee, it shall devour thee, and I will bring thee to ashes upon the earth in the sight of all them that behold thee.

19. All they that know thee among the people shall be astonished at thee: thou shalt be a terror, and never shalt thou be any more.

Daniel 5:1. Belshazzar the king made a great feast to a thousand of his lords, and drank wine before the thousand.

3. Then they brought the golden vessels that were taken out of the temple of the house of God which was at Jerusalem; and the king, and his princes, his wives, and his concubines, drank in them.

4. They drank wine, and praised the gods of gold, and of silver, of brass, of iron, of wood, and of stone.

5. In the same hour came forth fingers of a man's hand, and wrote over against the candlestick upon the plaister of the wall of the king's palace: and the king saw the part of the hand that wrote.

6. Then the king's countenance was changed, and his thoughts troubled him, so that the joints of his loins were loosed, and his knees smote one against another.

24. Then was the part of the hand sent from him; and this writing was written.

25. And this is the writing that was written, MENE, MENE, TEKEL, UPHARSIN.

26. This is the interpretation of

the thing: MENE; God hath numbered thy kingdom, and finished it.

27. TEKEL; Thou art weighed in the balances, and art found wanting.

28. PERES; Thy kingdom is divided, and given to the Medes and Persians.

29. Then commanded Belshazzar, and they clothed Daniel with scarlet, and put a chain of gold about his neck, and made a proclamation concerning him, that he should be the third ruler in the kingdom.

30. In that night was Belshazzar the king of the Chaldeans slain.

DICTIONARY

Belshazzar (BEL–sha–zar)—Daniel 5:1—The name means "May Bel protect the king." Since secular history claimed that the last king of Babylon was Nabonidus, some thought that this proved the Bible wrong. Nevertheless, later archaeological findings linked the names of Nabonidus and Belshazzar as co–regents.

MENE (ME–knee), MENE, TEKEL (TEA–kel), UPHARSIN (you–FAR–sin)—Daniel 5:25—The literal translation of this is "A mina, a mina, a shekel and half–shekels," the names of three coins or weights; but the words had a double meaning. MENE meant "numbered"; TEKEL meant "weighed"; UPHARSIN meant "division."

PERES (PEA–res)—Daniel 5:28—"Divided." (*Peres* is the singular of *Upharsin.*)

Chaldeans (kal–DEE–ans)—Daniel 5:30—Citizens of Chaldea, another name for the land of Babylon

---

LESSON OUTLINE

I. ORIGIN OF PRIDE
   - A. Satan's Beauty and Resources
   - B. Lifted Up by Oneself
   - C. Horror of Pride

II. FOLLY OF PRIDE
   - A. Defiling the Things of God
   - B. Power of God's Word to Judge Pride
   - C. Reaping the Fruits of Pride

III. JUDGMENT AGAINST PRIDE
   - A. Failing to Glorify God
   - B. Pride's Accountability
   - C. Final Judgment of Pride

LESSON EXPOSITION

INTRODUCTION

Pride is not just a flaw in one's character; it is a plague that brings destruction. The whole world has been affected by pride. Going back to the fall of Satan himself, pride was the eroding factor which brought devastations of evil and wickedness.

Serious consideration should be given to the effects of pride. The believer should treat it like a time bomb and carefully avoid association with it in one's own life. The deception of pride is that it is appealing to the individual, but it is contrary to God. Left to one's own self–perception, pride gives false assurance and confidence, entrapping the soul of the person at the same time.

Pride, as discussed in this section, will not be the kind of justifiable sense of accomplishment a person may take in a job well done in the eyes of the Lord. Pride, in that meaning, is not automatically wrong. However, even this acceptable form of pride can become sinful if we become conceited in our own accomplishments and fail to give proper credit to the Lord. Our discussion of pride in this lesson will refer to a rebellious pride that is contrary to God and His Word. This kind of pride endeavors to exalt itself above God.

I. ORIGIN OF PRIDE (Ezekiel 28:11-19)

A. Satan's Beauty and Resources (vv. 11-15)

(Ezekiel 28:11–15 is not included in the printed text.)

There is much in Ezekiel's message to and description of the king of Tyre that parallels the description of Satan and what happened to him. Satan was indeed beautiful when he was first created. God's original design for him was that he should be "full of wisdom, and perfect in beauty" (v. 12). However, he ignored the truth that he was created (vv. 13, 15). He was rebellious against the One who made him, and iniquity was found in him (v. 15). That iniquity was that he tried to exalt himself above his Creator, thus rebelling against God.

Why is pride so disdained in the eyes of God? What is God's response to pride?

B. Lifted Up by Oneself (vv. 16-18)

(Ezekiel 28:16 is not included in the printed text.)

17. Thine heart was lifted up because of thy beauty, thou hast corrupted thy wisdom by reason of thy brightness: I will cast thee to the ground, I will lay thee before kings, that they may behold thee.

18. Thou hast defiled thy sanctuaries by the multitude of thine iniquities, by the iniquity of thy traffick; therefore will I bring forth a fire from the midst of thee, it shall devour thee, and I will bring thee to ashes upon the earth in the sight of all them that behold thee.

Pride is a matter of the heart, and that's where Satan's fall began. His heart took what was wholesome, God's creation of beauty, and turned it into iniquity against God. Beauty and God's creation itself were not the problem. What Satan's heart did with what God created brought the problem. The term *because* (v. 17) is to be understood as "concerning." The causal agent of Satan's fall was not his beauty, because the beauty was essentially God's creation. The cause of his fall was the pride and rebellion in Satan's heart.

Brightness (or splendor) is a description indicating the boastful nature of pride. Pride is interested in what outshines and impresses others. Those filled with pride are interested in appearances. Putting on a front becomes a major concern of the prideful, wanting to outdo others. Ultimately, pride's goal is to outshine God himself.

As we can see from our lesson text, there are many things about which individuals and nations can become proud and thus arrogantly assert—by their actions if not by their words—that they are gods. Some of these pride–causing factors are intellect, beauty, material adornment (vv. 12, 13), position and location (v. 14), superiority of trade status (vv. 16, 18), and even one's good character (v. 15).

But God's response to pride is always consuming judgment. Referring to this early event in which Satan was initially judged and then predicting the future time when Satan will be punished for eternity, God shows us that pride will not be tolerated. Like a lethal virus, pride is the enemy of God and will not be tolerated by Him.

Where does pride begin? How can one tell if he has become prideful? How does pride develop in a person's heart?

C. Horror of Pride (v. 19)

19. All they that know thee among the people shall be astonished at thee: thou shalt be a terror, and never shalt thou be any more.

Pride turns beauty into astonishment and terror. What was created by God as good and appealing is now completely reversed; it has become appalling. The sight of Satan is now one of horror. *Astonished*, from the Hebrew *shamem*, emphasizes the speechless response of being stunned at the sight of something. *Terror*, from the Hebrew root *bahal*, refers to something disturbing, producing anxiety. *Astonished* refers to external awe, and *terror* referred to internal anguish. Pride turns beauty into something grotesque and repelling.

"Never shalt thou be any more" accentuates the lost beauty. Pride's destructive force takes the beauty away and replaces it with astonishment and terror.

What does pride do to beauty? What is the source of beauty? How is it sustained?

II. FOLLY OF PRIDE (Daniel 5:1-6)

A. Defiling the Things of God (vv. 1-4)

(Daniel 5:2 is not included in the printed text.)

1. Belshazzar the king made a great feast to a thousand of his lords, and drank wine before the thousand.

3. Then they brought the golden vessels that were taken out of the temple of the house of God which was at Jerusalem; and the king, and his princes, his wives and his concubines, drank in them.

4. They drank wine, and praised the gods of gold, and of silver, of brass, of iron, of wood, and of stone.

Pride manifests itself not only in outright rebellion against God, as in the case of Satan's fall, but it can also manifest itself in the abuse of the things of God. The reign of Nebuchadnezzar had come to an end in Babylon, and Belshazzar reigned in his stead. Belshazzar gave an elaborate banquet for a thousand of his nobles, and during the festivities he ordered that the gold and silver goblets which Nebuchadnezzar had taken from the Temple in Jerusalem be brought to the feast so he and his guests could drink from them. These vessels had been consecrated to the service of Almighty God, and now they were desecrated. The defilement was not just in the fact that they had been removed from the Temple and were now used for a different purpose, but they were also profaned in the way they were used—in praising other gods.

The gods described in verse 4 represented prideful characteristics. The metals and materials were indicative of prideful luster and humanity's self-centeredness. The gods were used to reflect the king's boasting about finances and industry. The gods were also of created material, and the creature was using the creation to blaspheme the Creator, as was the case with Satan. Belshazzar's party was a blasphemous, prideful display of self-conceit and idolatry.

B. Power of God's Word to Judge Pride (v. 5)

5. In the same hour came forth fingers of a man's hand, and wrote over against the candlestick upon the plaister of the wall of the king's palace: and the king saw the part of the hand that wrote.

Even as the revelry was going on, God's judgment was declared. The event was sudden. However, although the declaration of judgment came suddenly, Belshazzar's behavior had long indicated that a fall was inevitable. His prideful blaspheming was sure to be terminated by God. The use of a person's hand to write this word from God is akin to the writing of the Ten Commandments by "the finger of God" (Exodus 31:18).

What was the reaction of God to Belshazzar's pride? How had Belshazzar demonstrated his pride?

C. Reaping the Fruits of Pride (v. 6)

6. Then the king's countenance was changed, and his thoughts troubled him, so that the joints of his loins were loosed, and his knees smote one against another.

Belshazzar was awestruck and terrified. There was no doubt in his mind that the writing was a message of doom. The fruits of pride are devastating. Pleasure initially reaped from gloating turns into the bitter fruit of trouble. *Troubled* came from the Hebrew term *behal*, indicating fright and terror. The extent of that terror was manifested in the way the king was affected physically. The ashen–faced king became weak, and his legs began to shake uncontrollably. This nervous reaction was a sign of his extreme fright. And he had just cause to be frightened. The Most High God, whom Belshazzar's ancestor Nebuchadnezzar had learned to honor and praise, had been ignored by Belshazzar. He had lifted himself up in pride instead of bowing to the God of the universe. But now the pride of the created was meeting the awesomeness of the Creator.

III. JUDGMENT AGAINST PRIDE (Daniel 5:22-30)

A. Failing to Glorify God (vv. 22, 23)

(Daniel 5:22, 23 is not included in the printed text.)

Pride rather than humility had been Belshazzar's response to the holiness of the Lord. He knew that the vessels he was defaming were from the Temple of God Jehovah. The sanctity of Jehovah had been part of the history of Babylon's kingly court. God had borne witness of Himself, especially through Daniel. Belshazzar's actions were a bold and inexcusable affront to the Lord.

"Lifted up thyself" (v. 23) describes his sin of pride. Rather than honor the God to whom the vessels of the Temple of Jerusalem belonged, Belshazzar lifted himself up. Acts of pride are actions against the Lord, and self-centeredness fails to give honor to God or give Him recognition of His rightfully exalted state.

The basis of the judgment against Belshazzar was a revelation about dependency. God's proclamation of judgment was a reminder to Belshazzar of the truth that although he had not acknowledged it, he was dependent solely upon God, even for his very breath. Pride is a self–styled assertion that one does not need God and has never needed to depend on Him. Rather than confessing his inability to be totally self–reliant, Belshazzar's pride proclaimed an independence from God. Belshazzar would be decisively proven wrong.

B. Pride's Accountability (vv. 24-28)

24. Then was the part of the hand sent from him; and this writing was written.

25. And this is the writing that was written, MENE, MENE, TEKEL, UPHARSIN.

26. This is the interpretation of the thing: MENE; God hath numbered thy kingdom, and finished it.

27. TEKEL; Thou art weighed in the balances, and art found wanting.

28. PERES; Thy kingdom is divided, and given to the Medes and Persians.

Belshazzar's bold proclamation of independence was a deceptive assumption about his worth. Pride told him that he was worth more than he really was. Humble submission to God recognizes that any worth we have is derived from God. God's judgment would clarify just how wrong Belshazzar had been in his inflated opinion of himself. Pride is a miscalculation of our own worth and a failure to acknowledge God's true worthiness and position as the One who judges the value of all things.

The interpretation of the message was that Belshazzar was "weighed in the balances" and "found wanting." The significance of this pronouncement was that it was determined by God. Every standard of measurement has a prior standard by which the measurement is made. God is His own standard of measure. In ancient times the standards of measurement were not necessarily universal but predetermined by the king, frequently according to his stature. As an example, a "foot" may have been determined by the size of the literal foot of the king. The more powerful the monarch, the more binding his standards. In the confrontation between the earthly king (Belshazzar) and the King of eternity (God Jehovah), Belshazzar was measured by God's standards.

Pride presumes a position of power and privilege exceeding the position of those around us. We think we are better than others. Though we may not intentionally be condescending of others, the peril of pride is that it introduces in our life the seeds of corruptive assumption of power. If allowed to run full course, we think we are worth more than we really are and that we can do more than we really can.

The actual words of the inscription were references to weights and measures. Although there was no specific reference to Jehovah, the sight of the hand and the dramatic inscription on the wall were a clear sign of sovereign divine action. With the interpretation of Daniel, the declaration of judgment was complete and the once-prideful Belshazzar was made to know that God was tearing down his pride.

C. Final Judgment of Pride (vv. 29, 30)

29. Then commanded Belshazzar, and they clothed Daniel with scarlet, and put a chain of gold about his neck, and made a proclamation concerning him, that he should be the third ruler in the kingdom.

30. In that night was Belshazzar the king of the Chaldeans slain.

The sad epitaph of Belshazzar is that he still failed to see the implications of God's judgment upon his sinful pride. He still thought that power and recognition were the keys to success. While it was noble of him to keep his word and recognize Daniel, proclaiming that he was the third ruler in the kingdom, the distinction he gave only indicated that he was still preoccupied with prideful shows of position and power.

The godly response would have been to repent of his blasphemy against God and try to make amends for his actions. No mention is made of his turning from pride and displaying humility. Belshazzar should have fallen down before God Jehovah, pleading for forgiveness.

The night Belshazzar was deceived by his own pride, when he thought he could presume upon the Most High God, was the night he was judged. Belshazzar was slain that very night, and the kingdom of Babylon was overthrown—"divided, and given to the Medes and Persians." When Belshazzar thought he was the strongest, God made him the weakest. The deception of pride is that we are probably, in God's reality, the very opposite of what we think we are. Pride not only deceives, but it also destroys.

REVIEW QUESTIONS

1. How would you define pride?
2. What is the condition of a prideful heart?
3. What is the relationship between pride and beauty?
4. What made Belshazzar's actions an affront to God?
5. Did Belshazzar denounce his pride?

GOLDEN TEXT HOMILY

"PRIDE GOETH BEFORE DESTRUCTION, AND AN HAUGHTY SPIRIT BEFORE A FALL" (Proverbs 16:18).

The evangelist preached on hell and the consequences of sin in a life. When the invitation was given, my friend made his way down the aisle and gave his heart to Jesus. His life had been one of running the streets, drugs, robberies and burglaries. But God changed all that; now he became busy telling other young people about Christ, giving his personal testimony. Several months later he surrendered to the call of God to preach. His denomination promoted him, and soon he was speaking at national conventions, standing before thousands of Christians and ministers. He became an outstanding evangelist.

However, like many unsuspecting Christians, he became too busy—too absorbed with life. In his rush and quest for fulfillment and prestige, he temporarily lost sight of the simple, meaningful eternal values. He became so wrapped up in his success he forgot to give credit to Jesus. Soon his life came crashing down; pride and greed had taken their toll. He faced a prison term and disgrace. The Spirit of the Lord seemed to say, "You may be fooling others, but you're not fooling Me."

But, praise be to the Lord, like the Prodigal Son, who turned his back on the father to find his own way in the world, my friend returned to the Lord—broken, yes; empty-handed, yes; but a better son than ever before! And the Lord is restoring to him what pride took away. God has strange and stringent ways of teaching His children unforgettable lessons.—**James L. Durel, Evangelist, State of California**

SENTENCE SERMONS

PRIDE AND ARROGANCE invite divine judgment.

—**Selected**

GOD RESPONDS with forgiveness to a broken and contrite spirit.

—**Selected**

BE NOT PROUD of race, face, place, or grace.

—**Charles H. Spurgeon**

CONCEIT IS a strange disease; it makes everyone sick except the person who has it.

—Draper's Book of Quotations for the Christian World

EVANGELISM APPLICATION

GOD RESPONDS WITH FORGIVENESS TO A BROKEN AND CONTRITE SPIRIT.

God's judgment for pride is more than matched in His great measure of mercy toward those who come to him with humility. As illustrated in the case of Belshazzar, God will cut off the prideful heart. However, if the same person will respond to God by being repentant and humble before God, He will respond with mercy.

Christ has paid the price for even the prideful heart, and His redemption is applied when a person repents. Repentance turns a prideful heart into one that is broken and contrite. The condition of brokenness is a reflection of the person in comparison to God. Rather than feeling greater than God or that one does not need God, the individual realizes that he must fully depend on God. The person is broken, waiting on God for restoration.

The pride of the past is gloriously forgiven when a person is broken before God. The work of Christ has satisfied the judgment of God. The heart that once tried to thrive without God now realizes that without God it cannot survive.

DAILY BIBLE READINGS

M. Pride Brings Judgment.
Leviticus 26:14–20

T. A Humble Spirit.
2 Chronicles 1:6–12

W. Pride Precedes Captivity.
Jeremiah 13:15–18

T. Pride Leads to Unbelief.
Matthew 13:53–58

F. Judgment Against Pride.
Acts 12:20–23

S. Glory in the Lord.
1 Corinthians 1:26–31

Responsibility of Spiritual Leaders

Study Text: Ezekiel 34:1–16

Objective: To learn from God's example for spiritual leaders and resolve to care for His people.

Time: The Book of Ezekiel was written between 593 and 565 B.C.

Place: The Book of Ezekiel was written in Babylon.

Golden Text: "I will seek that which was lost, and bring again that which was driven away, and will bind up that which was broken, and will strengthen that which was sick" (Ezekiel 34:16).

Central Truth: Spiritual leaders should follow the example of the Good Shepherd.

Evangelism Emphasis: The Good Shepherd seeks the lost.

PRINTED TEXT

Ezekiel 34:2. Son of man, prophesy against the shepherds of Israel, prophesy, and say unto them, Thus saith the Lord God unto the shepherds; Woe be to the shepherds of Israel that do feed themselves! should not the shepherds feed the flocks?

3. Ye eat the fat, and ye clothe you with the wool, ye kill them that are fed: but ye feed not the flock.

4. The diseased have ye not strengthened, neither have ye healed that which was sick, neither have ye bound up that which was broken, neither have ye brought again that which was driven away, neither have ye sought that which was lost; but with force and with cruelty have ye ruled them.

5. And they were scattered, because there is no shepherd: and they became meat to all the beasts of the field, when they were scattered.

9. Therefore, O ye shepherds, hear the word of the Lord;

10. Thus saith the Lord God; Behold, I am against the shepherds; and I will require my flock at their hand, and cause them to cease from feeding the flock; neither shall the shepherds feed themselves any more; for I will deliver my flock from their mouth, that they may not be meat for them.

11. For thus saith the Lord God; Behold, I, even I, will both search my sheep, and seek them out.

12. As a shepherd seeketh out his flock in the day that he is among his sheep that are scattered; so will I seek out my sheep, and will deliver them out of all places where they have been scattered in the cloudy and dark day.

13. And I will bring them out

from the people, and gather them from the countries, and will bring them to their own land, and feed them upon the mountains of Israel by the rivers, and in all the inhabited places of the country.

14. I will feed them in a good pasture, and upon the high mountains of Israel shall their fold be: there shall they lie in a good fold, and in a fat pasture shall they feed upon the mountains of Israel.

15. I will feed my flock, and I will cause them to lie down, saith the Lord God.

16. I will seek that which was lost, and bring again that which was driven away, and will bind up that which was broken, and will strengthen that which was sick: but I will destroy the fat and the strong; I will feed them with judgment.

LESSON OUTLINE

I. GOD'S PEOPLE NEGLECTED
   A. Neglectful and Self-Centered Leadership
   B. Results of Sins of Leaders

II. UNCARING LEADERS REBUKED
   A. God's Ownership of the Sheep
   B. God's Judgment on Leadership
   C. God's Deliverance

III. EXAMPLE OF GOD'S CARE
   A. Deliverance From Place of Peril
   B. Establishing a Place of Nurture
   C. The Rest of the Lord

LESSON EXPOSITION

INTRODUCTION

Change, progress, and global harmony depend to a great degree on the success of dealing with our world leaders in getting along among themselves and their effectiveness in domestic issues in their own countries. As Christians we recognize, however, that the world's view of a good leader does not necessarily parallel the principles set forth in Scripture as the criteria for responsible leadership under God.

Some of the qualities viewed as secondary by the world are of primary importance in Scripture. Submission to God is the first principle of biblical leadership. Godly character flowing out of that submission is the next important principle. Submissiveness to one another in the fear of God (Ephesians 5:21) is still another vital principle. The world, on the other hand, doesn't even consider that God has a place in the affairs of state, character and personal integrity are considered irrelevant to good government, and mutual submission is desirable and necessary only as it best serves each party. Rather than serving God, worldly leadership glorifies the individual.

Ezekiel used his people's nomadic origins to picture their leaders. This powerful and unique symbol is used only for leadership and no other function. It is that of a shepherd. Ezekiel 34, using the shepherd metaphor, can be applied to governmental leaders, church leaders, pastors, church staff, ministry group leaders, lay leaders, and others. The chapter describes both the bad shepherd and the Good Shepherd, God himself, who promised to take over the duties of the ruthless, selfish shepherds who had abused the sheep and used them for their own gain.

I. GOD'S PEOPLE NEGLECTED (Ezekiel 34:1-6)

A. Neglectful and Self-Centered Leadership (vv. 1-4)

(Ezekiel 34:1 is not included in the printed text.)

2. Son of man, prophesy against the shepherds of Israel, prophesy, and say unto them, Thus saith the Lord God unto the shepherds; Woe be to the shepherds of Israel that do feed themselves! should not the shepherds feed the flocks?

3. Ye eat the fat, and ye clothe you with the wool, ye kill them that are fed: but ye feed not the flock.

4. The diseased have ye not strengthened, neither have ye healed that which was sick, neither have ye bound up that which was broken, neither have ye brought again that which was driven away, neither have ye sought that which was lost; but with force and with cruelty have ye ruled them.

These unfaithful shepherds of Israel were guilty of feeding themselves rather than the flock. They were not concerned for the welfare of the flock; they were too interested in how they might feed themselves. The shepherds were caring for themselves instead of caring for the sheep that had been placed in their care and for which they had been given responsibility.

How does the shepherding model apply to leaders today? What was the pivotal sin of the shepherds in Ezekiel 34?

Two essential duties for the Old Testament shepherd were to nurture and protect the flock. Their foremost responsibility was to protect. Whenever sheep are depicted in Scripture without a shepherd, they are not only malnourished but also slaughtered. Ezekiel 34 bears out both of these responsibilities.

Verse 3 outlines three essential results of the shepherds' self-centered maltreatment of the sheep: (1) They had reserved the best, the "fat," for themselves. (2) They had prematurely sheared the wool off the sheep in order to clothe themselves; consequently, the sheep were without protective coats during months of harsh weather. (3) The shepherds had killed the sheep both by neglect and by intentional slaughter.

The consequences of the self-centered action of the shepherds were the neglect of several vital functions, each portraying an aspect of shepherding in the church: The first responsibility listed is to strengthen the weak. The shepherd must also care for the sick. It is his duty to bind up the wounds of the injured sheep—care for those in crisis. He is to bring back those driven away—the ministry of reconciliation. And he is to seek the lost—evangelize sinners.

Instead of carrying out their duties of care, the shepherds had crusaded in their own behalf. They had ruled the sheep with force and cruelty. This illustrates their self-justified disregard for the needs of others in order to satisfy themselves. The consequence of self-centered leadership is not only neglect of duty but, inevitably, also harm to those for whom the shepherd is responsible. Self-centeredness is a weapon against others and not just an appeasement of personal needs.

Who are the leaders in a local church? How can they guard against neglect?

B. Results of Sins of Leaders (vv. 5, 6)

(Ezekiel 34:6 is not included in the printed text.)

5. And they were scattered, because there is no shepherd: and they became meat to all the beasts of the field, when they were scattered.

The paramount responsibility of the shepherd, or of any leader in the church, is to protect those whom God has given the leader oversight. *Scattered* in this setting indicates abuse and maltreatment. "Became meat" illustrates the cruelty of the scattering. Sheep are vulnerable without leadership, open to all kinds of abuse.

Protecting functions of modern-day shepherding include sound biblical interpretation and application; discipling for integration of biblical principles into daily living; warnings against spiritual abusers and charlatans; and worshipful focus upon the one, true God revealed in Scripture, through Jesus Christ in the power and presence of the Holy Spirit.

Verse 6 indicates the greatest indictment of the shepherds, the abuse of God's own sheep. The condition of the sheep is not the greatest sin—that would only be a temporal dimension. However, there is an eternal divine dimension to the affront of the shepherds. God indicated that these were His sheep. God's interest was personal. The heart of the godly leader would be broken at the prospect of his sheep wandering helpless and unattended on the mountainside and among the hills. The good shepherd would go out and seek for even one sheep that was lost. But no one was looking for the lost sheep of Israel.

II. UNCARING LEADERS REBUKED (Ezekiel 34:7-10)

A. God's Ownership of the Sheep (vv. 7, 8)

(Ezekiel 34:7, 8 is not included in the printed text.)

Out of His own sense of ownership for the sheep, God responded to the bad shepherds' neglect. "As I live," God said, He would act in behalf of His sheep. God was all too aware of the results of neglect. His sheep had fallen prey to the wild animals. The presence of a God who broods and searches for His sheep is contrasted with self-centered leadership that left the flock with "no shepherd," forcing the sheep to fend for themselves. God's searing accusation of the shepherds' neglect was also an indication of His judgment against them.

What is God's response to the leaders' neglect? What should be the response of the flock to God's intervention when the shepherd has neglected his shepherding responsibilities?

B. God's Judgment on Leadership (vv. 9, 10a)

9. Therefore, O ye shepherds, hear the word of the Lord;

10. Thus saith the Lord God;

Behold, I am against the shepherds; and I will require my flock at their hand, and cause them to cease from feeding the flock; neither shall the shepherds feed themselves any more.

As a result of the dereliction of duty by the shepherds, God said He would remove them from their office. God was justified in His judgment against the unfaithful shepherds. His indictment against them was clearly stated, and He would hold them accountable for the trust they had held so lightly and had so grossly violated. Leadership of the people of God is a divine privilege and calling, and the maintenance of leadership is the result of God's enabling grace. To be personally gifted or talented is not the foundation of great leadership. God produces leaders for His church, and personal abilities are God–given gifts to be cultivated and used, as God directs, to care for His sheep and bring glory to Him.

C. God's Deliverance (v. 10b)

10b. For I will deliver my flock from their mouth, that they may not be meat for them.

The message of the latter portion of verse 10 is a sobering twofold word of hope and judgment. On the hope side is God's promise to personally care for the sheep. The manner and extent of His care is described in the verses that follow. However, before the fuller description of hope, one final word of judgment is given to the shepherds. This word of judgment not only reveals their end but the awful extent of their neglect and maltreatment of the sheep. Not only had the sheep become "meat" to the beasts of the field, but the shepherds themselves had also been feeding upon the sheep. Self-centered leadership consumes the very ones under one's who have been put in the leaders' charge. But God terminates such callous feasting.

III. EXAMPLE OF GOD'S CARE (Ezekiel 34:11-16)

A. Deliverance From Place of Peril (vv. 11-13)

11. For thus saith the Lord God; Behold, I, even I, will both search my sheep, and seek them out.

12. As a shepherd seeketh out his flock in the day that he is among his sheep that are scattered; so will I seek out my sheep, and will deliver them out of all places where they have been scattered in the cloudy and dark day.

13. And I will bring them out from the people, and gather them from the countries, and will bring them to their own land, and feed them upon the mountains of Israel by the rivers, and in all the inhabited places of the country.

The perfect model of godly shepherding and leadership is God himself. The tasks of the godly leader are described in three major areas: protection, which includes deliverance from peril (vv. 11-13); nurture (v. 14); and rest, epitomizing both protection and nurture (vv. 15, 16).

The text provides the shepherd leader of today with illustrations of their protective functions. First, the shepherd is to make sure the sheep remain in the protection of the flock and give them protective oversight. Second, if the sheep do stray, the shepherd should find them—seek them out and bring them back to the safety of the group or body of believers. Third, the shepherd should gather the sheep. Gathering also involves keeping the flock together.

The function of gathering highlights the protection available to the sheep when they remain together. If one remains in the body, there is protection. However, if one rebels and removes himself from the body, he is automatically in danger.

How do the various functions of shepherding illustrated in Ezekiel 34 apply to the context of shepherding today? What are some specific examples of how these functions should be carried out today?

B. Establishing a Place of Nurture (v. 14)

14. I will feed them in a good pasture, and upon the high mountains of Israel shall their fold be: there shall they lie in a good fold, and in a fat pasture shall they feed upon the mountains of Israel.

God assured Israel He would establish them in a place where they would be nurtured. The twofold nature of shepherding is conveyed in the words *good fold*, indicating protection, and *fat pasture*, indicating nurture. The word *feed* summarizes shepherding. In fact, the Hebrew term for *shepherd* is derived from this term for *feed*. Essentially, the *shepherd* was the "one who feeds." *Fold* summarizes the place where the sheep are held for safety. God is not satisfied with seeking and finding the lost; His will is not accomplished until they are safely sheltered in His everlasting fold. And the shepherd of God's flock cannot afford to settle for less than this!

C. The Rest of the Lord (vv. 15, 16)

15. I will feed my flock, and I will cause them to lie down, saith the Lord God.

16. I will seek that which was lost, and bring again that which was driven away, and will bind up that which was broken, and will strengthen that which was sick: but I will destroy the fat and the strong; I will feed them with judgment.

In feeding His flock and causing them to lie down, God was providing them with two of the great necessities of life.

Some of the responsibilities of the shepherd leader mentioned earlier are restated here: (1) Seeking the lost—the ministry of evangelism; (2) bringing back those who have been driven away—the ministry of reconciliation; (3) binding up the broken—the ministry of care; (4) strengthening the sick—the ministry of healing.

A final responsibility is added that was not mentioned previously—judgment. This judgment, as amplified in verses 17-22, is discernment within the sheepfold. God said He would judge between them. Some were crowding out others, and some were harming others in the flock. These had become fat at the expense of the others. We see, then, that the modern-day class conflict between the haves and the have-nots is no new problem. It was so serious a problem in the prophet's day that the Lord said he would judge between them. It wasn't enough for those with plenty to have eaten their fill, He accused, but they then turned and destroyed what was left, thereby preventing the less fortunate from having a chance to feed themselves. But God promised to rescue the weak ones and bring His judgment on the offending ones.

Ezekiel 34 was an indictment against the leaders in Judah who had played a part of the downfall of the nation. But the passage is also a message to all those who lead the people of God, it explicitly details and the standards by which God holds them accountable.

The leader today must take seriously the task of shepherding God's people. The shepherding model is applicable for virtually all leadership functions in the local church—clergy, laity, small group, large group, youth, the elderly, and so forth. Leaders are directly accountable to God. Spiritual leaders are responsible to God for the care of the flock.

REVIEW QUESTIONS

1. How important is leadership in the church today?
2. What are the consequences of neglect on the part of leaders in the church?
3. How does God view the shepherd leaders' neglect of the flock?
4. What are the various responsibilities of shepherding illustrated in Ezekiel 34?
5. What part do judgment and discernment play in the shepherding process?

GOLDEN TEXT HOMILY

"I WILL SEEK THAT WHICH WAS LOST, AND BRING AGAIN THAT WHICH WAS DRIVEN AWAY, AND WILL BIND UP THAT WHICH WAS BROKEN, AND WILL STRENGTHEN THAT WHICH WAS SICK" (Ezekiel 34:16).

The Lord had some very strong words for the false shepherds. This spelled trouble for those with power who had fattened themselves by oppressing the sheep.

However, He had some words of encouragement for the sheep. Though they were responsible for their own actions, they had been led astray by these brutal leaders. He declared that He would personally assume the responsibility for "shepherding" them. There are a number of people who feel that this passage from Ezekiel is the basis of our Lord's words about the Good Shepherd in John 10:11–16.

Quite often, we can hear some among us talk about how life was before they "found the Lord." However, Jesus said, "The Son of man is come to seek and to save that which was lost" (Luke 19:10). Several of His most impressive parables concerned this very matter—namely, the lost sheep, the lost coin, and the lost son (the Prodigal) (Luke 15). Notice, someone sought for the sheep and the coin, but no one sought for the boy!

He said that He would "bring again that which was driven away." Woe unto the shepherds who drive the sheep away from the fold. The Lord of Glory went all the way to Calvary in order to bring back these unfortunate ones.

Notice the next wonderful promise He makes: "I will bind up that which was broken." No one can ever care for us like Jesus. He has the ability to mend broken hearts and broken relationships, as well as restoring us to fellowship with His Father, our God. He also said He would strengthen the sick. He cares about our every need.

The remaining chapters of Ezekiel plainly refer to the siege and the Exile, but they also look forward to the future reestablishment of the nation in Palestine. However, until then, our Lord will continue His fourfold ministry as outlined in the golden text.—**Luther E. Painter, D.Min. (Retired),**

Assistant Professor of Religion, Lee College, Cleveland, Tennessee

SENTENCE SERMONS

SPIRITUAL LEADERS should follow the example of the Good Shepherd.

—Selected

EVANGELISM APPLICATION

THE GOOD SHEPHERD SEEKS THE LOST.

Christ, the Good Shepherd, seeks the lost in an effort to bring them into the safety of the fold. This, then, is also the task of His undershepherds—the leaders within the body of Christ. God seriously judged the shepherds in Ezekiel's day for their failure to seek the lost.

God seeks the lost because unless they are found, the sheep face grave consequences. They are open prey to the dangers of the world when they are separated from the flock. A person outside the household of faith is subject to manipulation, temptation, doctrinal error, and a multitude of other dangers. Ultimately, the lost sheep are open to the attack of the Enemy, whose intention is not only to brutalize the sheep but also to destroy their very life (John 10:10).

The Good Shepherd seeks the lost because the lost sheep cannot save themselves. Lost sheep are defenseless. They do not have the ability themselves to find a safe haven from danger. The plight of the lost sheep is certain—eternal destruction. A lost sheep is truly no match for the evil that awaits him.

The only hope for the lost sheep is the Good Shepherd, who offers good and safe pastures, rest, and peace. The lost sheep's comfort is that he is not abandoned.

ILLUMINATING THE LESSON

Shepherd leadership must be a caring leadership. Self-centered leaders may try to justify their lack of concern and even their cruel neglect. However, the critical question is, Have those in need been cared for? The following story illustrates the point:

A media crew composed of television and newspaper reporters in Alabama was summoned when a despondent, drunken, unemployed man indicated he was going to set himself ablaze. A photographer and sound technician responded to the call. Soon the fire began, and they had to select between two roles. They could fulfill their media role by recording the incident as impassive observers or they could fulfill a humanitarian role by smothering the flames.

For 37 seconds the team chose the former. They taped the burning man for the 6 o'clock news and did nothing to save him. By the time one of the individuals decided to change his role and began battling the flames, it was nearly too late. Fortunately, a volunteer fireman was able to extinguish the flames and save the man.

DAILY BIBLE READINGS

M. Wisdom Recognized. Genesis 41:38–46
T. Compassionate Prayer. Nehemiah 1:4–11
W. Servant Leader. Isaiah 42:1–7
T. Leadership Attitudes. Mark 9:33–37
F. Teachable Spirit. Acts 18:24–28
S. Leaders Are Examples. 1 Peter 5:1–6

Revival: From Death to Life

Study Text: Ezekiel 37:1–23

Objective: To realize that God sends revival and live by His life–changing power.

Time: The Book of Ezekiel was written between 593 and 565 B.C.

Place: The Book of Ezekiel was written in Babylon.

Golden Text: "Wilt thou not revive us again: that thy people may rejoice in thee?" (Psalm 85:6).

Central Truth: God desires to send revival to His people.

Evangelism Emphasis: Spiritual revival leads to evangelism outreach.

PRINTED TEXT

Ezekiel 37:1. The hand of the Lord was upon me, and carried me out in the spirit of the Lord, and set me down in the midst of the valley which was full of bones,

3. And he said unto me, Son of man, can these bones live? And I answered, O Lord God, thou knowest.

4. Again he said unto me, Prophesy upon these bones, and say unto them, O ye dry bones, hear the word of the Lord.

5. Thus saith the Lord God unto these bones; Behold, I will cause breath to enter into you, and ye shall live:

6. And I will lay sinews upon you, and will bring up flesh upon you, and cover you with skin, and put breath in you, and ye shall live; and ye shall know that I am the Lord.

11. Then he said unto me, Son of man, these bones are the whole house of Israel: behold, they say, Our bones are dried, and our hope is lost: we are cut off for our parts.

12. Therefore prophesy and say unto them, Thus saith the Lord God; Behold, O my people, I will open your graves, and cause you to come up out of your graves, and bring you into the land of Israel.

13. And ye shall know that I am the Lord, when I have opened your graves, O my people, and brought you up out of your graves,

14. And shall put my spirit in you, and ye shall live, and I shall place you in your own land: then shall ye know that I the Lord have spoken it, and performed it, saith the Lord.

21. And say unto them, Thus saith the Lord God; Behold, I will take the children of Israel from among the heathen, whither they be gone, and will gather them on every side, and bring them into their own land:

22. And I will make them one nation in the land upon the mountains of Israel; and one king shall be king to them all: and they shall be no more two nations, neither shall they be divided into two kingdoms any more at all:

23. Neither shall they defile themselves any more with their idols, nor with their detestable things, nor with any of their transgressions: but I will save them out of all their dwelling-places, wherein they have sinned, and will cleanse them: so shall they be my people, and I will be their God.

LESSON OUTLINE

I. IS REVIVAL POSSIBLE?
   A. Need for Revival
   B. God Makes Revival Possible
   C. The Word and Revival
   D. God's Action and Revival

II. REVIVED BY THE SPIRIT
   A. Shaking of Revival
   B. Breath of Revival
   C. Lord of Revival
   D. Spirit of Revival

III. RESULTS OF REVIVAL
   A. Unity From Revival
   B. God's Control in Revival
   C. Reconciliation and Cleansing

LESSON EXPOSITION

INTRODUCTION

Neither the skeptical world nor a cynical church believes revival is still possible. Some view revival only as a historical term, locked into a social form of the past. However, contrary to the skeptics, revival is not a reflection of ages past but is as alive as the Spirit of God. Revival is founded on the Word of God. And rather than being outdated, revival is the best hope for the church today.

The historical context of Ezekiel 37 parallels the contemporary setting of today. The text provides not only parallels of today but also principles for true spirituality. The scene that Ezekiel beheld is the same scene that God is revealing today. The message was, and is, in the midst of spiritual death, but God continually breathes newness of life.

The message of revival must be believed because it is the message of hope (v. 14). Revival brings about renewed spirituality; it is being able to see with hope, through eyes of faith, what God is doing. God is continually moving to bring life to His people. The process of renewing life, the perspective of hope in that new life—that is revival.

I. IS REVIVAL POSSIBLE? (Ezekiel 37:1-6)

A. Need for Revival (vv. 1, 2)

(Ezekiel 37:2 is not included in the printed text.)

1. The hand of the Lord was upon me, and carried me out in the spirit of the Lord, and set me down in the midst of the valley which was full of bones.

God guided Ezekiel in this experience of revival. He brought Ezekiel into a valley that was full of dry bones. Perhaps God allowed him to view the actual location of one of Judah's battlefields on which many were slain in a final attempt to resist the Babylonians. At any rate, the vision was certainly an unmistakable representation of death—in this case, the life of the nation had been snuffed out by captivity.

The valley of dry bones depicted the absolute absence of life in the nation. There was not only death but persistent death. The death had lingered to such an extent that the flesh was dried and the bones themselves had become dry and brittle.

The significant means God used to bring about this experience was His Spirit. The Spirit of God is still the means of revival today. Methods, needs, analyses, targeting populations, and any number of factors involved in revival are all secondary to the soulwinning power of the Holy Spirit. Consequently, any factor in revival is dependent upon the work of the Spirit. Revival is not dependent on favorable circumstances, for in this case there was no indication that any renewal of life was possible.

Is revival possible today? What are the hindrances to revival today?

B. God Makes Revival Possible (v. 3)

3. And he said unto me, Son of man, can these bones live? And I answered, O Lord God, thou knowest.

Ezekiel's perspective was God-centered. When God posed the question of hope, "Can these bones live?" Ezekiel focused on God. The answer of life was in God's hand. Ezekiel was affirming that revival begins with God and God alone. There was no questioning in Ezekiel's response. His was a definite affirmation of faith in the God of revival. For the believer today, revival is not in question, only one's dependence upon God.

C. The Word and Revival (v. 4)

4. Again he said unto me, Prophesy upon these bones, and say unto them, O ye dry bones, hear the word of the Lord.

God's response focused upon His word (message). Two aspects of His word are critical to remember. The word was a word of *prophecy*—"Thus saith the Lord." Ezekiel was told to prophesy although there was apparently no hope that anyone could hear. We must learn from this that we must not abandon our God-given mission even though there seems to be little or no possibility of success. The believer must establish in his heart that the word of God for revival comes from God. And if the one commissioned to prophesy will remain true to his calling, we will see that with God there is indeed the possibility of life from the dead.

How important is the Word of God in revival? What role does the Word of God play in revival?

The second aspect of the word of God was that it must be received by the bones. Hearing and receiving is assumed on the part of the bones. In this illustration the participation of the recipient is vital. God does not force revival upon anyone. Revival is begun when the message from the Lord is received. The bones were to hear and depend on God for their very renewal.

D. God's Action and Revival (vv. 5, 6)

5. Thus saith the Lord God unto these bones; Behold, I will cause breath to enter into you, and ye shall live:

6. And I will lay sinews upon you, and will bring up flesh upon you, and cover you with skin, and put breath in you, and ye shall live; and ye shall know that I am the Lord.

The declaration of the Word of God to the bones would bring God's action. God said, "I will cause breath to enter . . . and ye shall live." The initiation and sustenance of life would come from God alone.

The life–giving act of God would be in a four–step process. There would come sinews (or muscle) on the bones, flesh on the bones, skin put on the flesh, and finally breath into the body. Many times God's renewal of life is through a process. In order to achieve the fresh breath of the fullness of God, a person may go through various stages of renewal in the revival process. Just as each part of the body that was added in Ezekiel's vision was prerequisite for the next portion, the stages a person may go through are necessary in order to reach another stage on the way to the place God intends for that person.

The ultimate goal of God in revival is that individuals recognize His Lordship. In the description of the renewed bones and bodies, the climactic step is that the renewed people would acknowledge God as Lord over their lives. When we have been made alive in the Spirit, we will know that He is God. Our lives are restored and we receive blessings that we might achieve the greater goal of serving Christ as Lord. Acknowledging His lordship and continued discipleship are the tests of true revival.

How is revival given in a process in some people's lives? What is the ultimate goal of revival?

II. REVIVED BY THE SPIRIT (Ezekiel 37:7-14)

A. Shaking of Revival (vv. 7, 8)

(Ezekiel 37:7, 8 is not included in the printed text.)

Obedience is vital for revival. Ezekiel was obedient and spoke the word of prophecy from God. Obedience in revival is a foretaste of the lordship He establishes as a result of the revival. On the other hand, rebellion, dissension, and division dispel revival. The lordship of Christ does not flourish alongside disobedience. Ezekiel's obedience was a necessary part of the reception of God's life–giving action in the valley of dry bones.

As the process of revival began, a "shaking" took place. Renewal of life is not a passive, mutant process. To bring to life means activity, motion, and a breaking away from the silence of death. Revival is usually marked by strong experience, a spiritual shaking. Whether a person is silent or shouting, still or in great motion, stirring deep within is the life-giving movement of God.

B. Breath of Revival (vv. 9, 10)

(Ezekiel 37:9, 10 is not included in the printed text.)

The vitality of the Spirit of God is unmistakable and irreplaceable. Without the Spirit there is no life. There may be a miracle; the body may be shaken; but until the breath of God enters the body, there is no renewal, no life. The wind of the Spirit that fills the body transforms it, and it becomes a vibrant, living being. This was no ordinary wind that came upon the bodies, for the wind had previously been in the valley constantly. In fact, the wind had contributed to the drying process that affected the bones. Now by the command of God and the transforming breath of God, the winds became life-giving rather than life-taking.

C. Lord of Revival (vv. 11-13)

11. Then he said unto me, Son of man, these bones are the whole house of Israel: behold, they say, Our bones are dried, and our hope is lost: we are cut off for our parts.

12. Therefore prophesy and say unto them, Thus saith the Lord God; Behold, O my people, I will open your graves, and cause you to come up out of your graves, and bring you into the land of Israel.

13. And ye shall know that I am the Lord, when I have opened your graves, O my people, and brought you up out of your graves.

God spoke now to bring hope to the dry bones, that is, "the whole house of Israel." The people in exile had given up hope, as had, no doubt, those who remained in the land. Jerusalem and their Temple had both been destroyed. They may have felt they were entombed, cut off from their native land—their heritage from the Lord. But God promised He would open their graves and bring them back to the land of Israel. He was offering them hope; He would revive them. God desires to bring revival to His people.

What were the bodies without the Spirit of God? How important is obedience in true revival?

As mentioned earlier, skepticism about revival is always present. There were those among "the dry bones" who were complacent. Others, no doubt, could not see past the circumstances as they were.

Revival is dependent on a word from the Lord and the moving of the Spirit. Predictions alone cannot bring life. But we can be sure that if God speaks, God will perform. In response to those with predictions of no hope, Ezekiel declared, "Thus saith the Lord God."

The revival of Israel was brought about through the action of God. Revival is not just an individual matter in which someone receives a personal blessing. The personal dimension is part of the revival process; however, God also works in the midst of events that affect His people. That is why God's people must not only look at what God is doing to them individually, but they must also look for the hand of God in the corporate body and in events surrounding them. Revival is not just a motivation; it is a movement of God to change the course of history.

D. Spirit of Revival (v. 14)

14. And shall put my spirit in you, and ye shall live, and I shall place you in your own land: then shall ye know that I the Lord have spoken it, and performed it, saith the Lord.

In addition to the corporate dimension, God moves in a very personal way in revival. In verse 14, after describing the sweeping events of the deliverance of the nation, God said that He would place His own Spirit in each of them. He would give each one personally the breath of life. Again, the lordship of God would be affirmed, this time in their lives individually. The personal blessing of revival is vital for each person to fully know the hand of God that has given life.

III. RESULTS OF REVIVAL (Ezekiel 37:16-23)

A. Unity From Revival (vv. 16, 17)

(Ezekiel 37:16, 17 is not included in the printed text.)

Part of the corporate revival that would take place would bring the divided nations together. The prophecy given here about the two sticks representing the different parts of the nation will find its complete fulfillment during the end times. However, in part, the nation did come together in 1948 with the reestablishment of the modern nation of Israel.

Revival is an event of the body of believers. Christ declared in John 13:35 that by our love for one another others will know that we are His disciples. Without the corporate work of bringing the body of believers closer together, true revival is incomplete.

B. God's Control in Revival (vv. 18, 19)

(Ezekiel 37:18, 19 is not included in the printed text.)

"Mine hand" (v. 19) indicates that the key to unity and revival will be God's own work. No individual is the key to revival. The two sticks would be brought together in the hand of God. Merely bringing them together would not be enough. Their fusion and unity would be forged in the hand of God. The unity of the sticks required a work of transformation, not merely alignment. Revival is a radical action that produces a work that only God can do. At best, individuals can only bring the pieces together, but God does the transformation.

C. Reconciliation and Cleansing (vv. 20-23)

(Exekiel 37:20 is not included in the printed text.)

21. And say unto them, Thus saith the Lord God; Behold, I will take the children of Israel from among the heathen, whither they be gone, and will gather them on every side, and bring them into their own land:

22. And I will make them one nation in the land upon the mountains of Israel; and one king shall be king to them all: and they shall be no more two nations, neither shall they be divided into two kingdoms any more at all:

23. Neither shall they defile themselves any more with their idols, nor with their detestable things, nor with any of their transgressions: but I will save them out of all their dwellingplaces, wherein they have sinned, and will cleanse them: so shall they be my people, and I will be their God.

The nature of the transformation is delineated in verses 20-23. The nation would come together under one king. As mentioned earlier, the issues of lordship and obedience are definitely part of the work of revival. Ultimately, God is the Lord of His people, and in true revival they would confess Him as God and return to Him in obedience. The summary description is that they would be the people of God and He would be their God.

Cleansing and confession are also critical issues in the nature of the transformation of true revival. The people would renounce their sins. Their lives would be turned from transgression. Purity marks true revival. Blessings are legitimated and celebration is validated by the ongoing witness of a cleansed life.

Finally, true worship marks the transformation of true revival. Rather than worshiping idols, the people would worship God and God alone. God would be the central focus and desire of their lives. No other person or situation would attract their adoration and veneration like God himself. True revival is marked by the awe and reverent worship of God in spirit and in truth.

REVIEW QUESTIONS

1. How impossible did revival seem in Ezekiel's day?
2. What was the basis of Ezekiel's response when God asked him about the possibility of revival?
3. How important is God's action in the midst of revival?
4. What is the role of the Spirit of God in revival?
5. What are the individual and corporate dimensions of revival?

GOLDEN TEXT HOMILY

"WILT THOU NOT REVIVE US AGAIN: THAT THY PEOPLE MAY REJOICE IN THEE?" (Psalm 85:6).

The earnest prayer in Psalm 85 is for revival. This refers to something which could not be done again if it had not been done once before. Psalm 85 was written after a display of God's mercy toward Israel, but there was a desire to make the condition of the people altogether satisfactory. After considering all the former blessings (for example, six times in verses 1–3 the words "thou hast" are used), the people were still in trouble, so they appealed to God to complete what He had started.

Possibly the chief word in this verse is *revive.* Webster states that *revive* means "to restore to consciousness or life; to restore from a depressed, inactive, or unused state; to renew mentally."

Pleading for revival reveals a consciousness of need, distress because of it, a confession of that need, and confidence that God will answer.

The result sought is "that thy people may rejoice in thee." This plainly teaches that a low religious life and a joyous life are incompatible. There must be a reviving if there is to be a rejoicing. This rejoicing is to be in Him.

God alone can revive. Man may work up to a point, but he cannot impart life. This is beyond him. Only God can give life.

The prayers and promises of Scripture never grow old. So this prayer is just as apt for us to pray as it was for the psalmist. It is presumptuous not to trust God.—**Excerpts from the *Evangelical Sunday School Lesson Commentary*, Vol. 39**

SENTENCE SERMONS

GOD DESIRES to send revival to His people.

—Selected

SPIRITUAL REVIVAL should always lead to evangelism outreach.

—Selected

A RELIGIOUS AWAKENING that does not awaken the sleeper to love has roused him in vain.

—Jessamyn West

SOME PREACHERS do not believe in revivals; neither does the devil.

—Billy Sunday

EVANGELISM APPLICATION

SPIRITUAL REVIVAL LEADS TO EVANGELISM OUTREACH.

Outreach is a natural consequence of revival. God's desire is that not only will His people be blessed in revival but that they will also be a blessing. The people of God must take revival outside of the church and extend it into the community. The key is for those believers who have been working within the body of Christ to now be used by God to bless those outside of the church as well.

The key to outreach–producing revival is to continue to depend on the work of God. God's work was the key to the beginning of revival, and it will be the key to revival continuing outside the church. Outreach is desperately needed, although the task may seem impossible. However, just as the apparently impossible revival came to pass, outreach ministries can also come to pass. The principle is the same for outreach as it was for revival: depend on God and His work.

ILLUMINATING THE LESSON

The story is told of Matthew Henry leaving his countryside home and venturing into London. There he met a young lady who was of the wealthy nobility, and they fell in love. When the young woman approached her father about Matthew Henry, her father protested. He argued that young Henry was not of nobility, had no background, and she did not know where he had come from.

She replied by confirming that Henry had no regal background or stately income. "But," she further replied, "I know where he's going, and I want to go with him." Similarly, revival does not look at our background for possibilities. Revival is a message of hope, affirming that even though there may be a dead lifeless past, "these bones can live again."

DAILY BIBLE READINGS

M. Prepare for Revival.
2 Chronicles 29:15–20

T. Prayer for Revival.
Psalm 85:1–13

W. Citywide Revival.
Jonah 3:3–10

T. Obedience Leads to Revival.
Acts 4:23–31

F. Repentance and Renewal.
2 Corinthians 7:4–10

S. Revival in the Church.
Revelation 3:1–6

Life in the Spirit

Study Text: Ezekiel 36:25–29; 47:1–12

Objective: To discover the blessings of life in the Spirit and rejoice in His presence.

Time: The Book of Ezekiel was written between 593 and 565 B.C.

Place: The Book of Ezekiel was written in Babylon.

Golden Text: "I will put my spirit within you, and cause you to walk in my statutes, and ye shall keep my judgments, and do them" (Ezekiel 36:27).

Central Truth: The Holy Spirit works to conform believers to the image of Christ.

Evangelism Emphasis: The Holy Spirit empowers believers to reflect the image of Christ to the lost.

PRINTED TEXT

Ezekiel 36:25. Then will I sprinkle clean water upon you, and ye shall be clean: from all your filthiness, and from all your idols, will I cleanse you.

26. A new heart also will I give you, and a new spirit will I put within you: and I will take away the stony heart out of your flesh, and I will give you an heart of flesh.

27. And I will put my spirit within you, and cause you to walk in my statutes, and ye shall keep my judgments, and do them.

28. And ye shall dwell in the land that I gave to your fathers; and ye shall be my people, and I will be your God.

47:1. Afterward he brought me again unto the door of the house; and, behold, waters issued out from under the threshold of the house eastward: for the forefront of the house stood toward the east, and the waters came down from under from the right side of the house, at the south side of the altar.

2. Then brought he me out of the way of the gate northward, and led me about the way without unto the utter gate by the way that looketh eastward; and, behold, there ran out waters on the right side.

3. And when the man that had the line in his hand went forth eastward, he measured a thousand cubits, and he brought me through the waters; the waters were to the ankles.

4. Again he measured a thousand, and brought me through the waters; the waters were to the knees. Again he measured a thousand, and brought me through; the waters were to the loins.

5. Afterward he measured a

thousand; and it was a river that I could not pass over: for the waters were risen, waters to swim in, a river that could not be passed over.

6. And he said unto me, Son of man, hast thou seen this? Then he brought me, and caused me to return to the brink of the river.

7. Now when I had returned, behold, at the bank of the river were very many trees on the one side and on the other.

8. Then said he unto me, These waters issue out toward the east country, and go down into the desert, and go into the sea: which being brought forth into the sea, the waters shall be healed.

LESSON OUTLINE

I. BE RENEWED BY THE SPIRIT
  A. Prerequisite Cleansing
  B. Newness of Heart
  C. God's Own Work

II. GROW IN SPIRITUALITY
  A. The Source of Spirituality
  B. The Progress of Spirituality

III. LIVE BY THE SPIRIT
  A. Healing and Restoration in the Spirit
  B. Life in the Spirit
  C. Productivity by the Spirit

LESSON EXPOSITION

INTRODUCTION

The work of the Holy Spirit is the lifeline of the believer. The reality of God's presence is made known through the Holy Spirit. The believer came to Christ through the facilitation of the Holy Spirit. The Spirit's work is irreplaceable in the Christian's life. The primary means by which God reveals Himself to the believer today is through His Word and through the Holy Spirit.

Dimensions of the person and work of the Holy Spirit form the heart of the message of Ezekiel 36:25-29 and 47:1-12. The Spirit is the source of new life for the body of Christ. The theme of 36:25-29 is the restoration of life for the believer by the empowerment of the Spirit. The Spirit is the constant supply that brings renewal in Christ. The theme of 47:1-5 is that the source of spiritual growth is the Spirit. The Spirit is the life of the believer. The theme of 47:6-12 is the life of the Spirit in the believer.

Ezekiel prophesied to a nation that had been taken captive by the enemy. Judah was brought into captivity by the Babylonians. They were a dispossessed people, dominated by the strongest nation in the world.

Nevertheless, God's message to Israel was not only for physical deliverance but also further and complete deliverance by the Spirit. The message of the work of the Spirit supersedes any other cause or cry. The Lord's desire is that the Spirit should bring true deliverance. The work of the Spirit is also to maintain the spiritual life of the delivered believer. Despite the onslaught of the Enemy, the Spirit gives, sustains, and increases life in the believer.

I. BE RENEWED BY THE SPIRIT (Ezekiel 36:25-29)

A. Prerequisite Cleansing (v. 25)

25. Then will I sprinkle clean water upon you, and ye shall be clean: from all your filthiness, and from all your idols, will I cleanse you.

In Ezekiel 36 the Lord described His work of judgment and restoration. Israel was judged for wickedness. The land of Israel was purged of uncleanness, and the people were taken into exile. After the judgment, God promised to restore them. Their land was restored to them, and the people were placed back in the fruitful land.

Cleansing was a prerequisite for restoration. The land was prepared and ready, but the people themselves had to be made ready as well. The process of readiness was purification. God said He would sprinkle them with clean water and they would be clean. The people would have understood the symbolism of this message, no doubt, because of their familiarity with the ritual cleansings in the Books of the Law. The people had never really learned to be faithful to God, however. It was through their moral pollutions most of all that had profaned God's name and brought them into captivity. But instead of continuing to punish His people or cut them off from himself forever, God was willing to give them a fresh start. The purification He was willing to do would again sanctify His name and restore His people not only to their land but also to their place of favor with God. The process of God's holiness was the preparation for the work of the Spirit.

What is the nature of the work of the Spirit in the life of the believer?

B. Newness of Heart (v. 26)

26. A new heart also will I give you, and a new spirit will I put within you: and I will take away the stony heart out of your flesh, and I will give you an heart of flesh.

Cleansing leads to the Spirit's renewal. A stony condition indicates a heart in decline, ill, and near spiritual death. A stone is cold, hard, and dead. A heart of *flesh* indicates a new, vibrant heart—a warm, soft heart—ready to be used by God.

The emphasis of the work of the Spirit is on the action of God. God himself removes the prior condition of sin. The action of God brings the new heart. The old stubborn self–will gives way to the desire to know and do God's will. Whatever benefit and service the new heart may provide, the work of God will always be the source. We are not renewed because we are worthy or because we are holy. Renewal relies on the goodness of God and the work of the Spirit.

C. God's Own Work (vv. 27–29)

(Ezekiel 36:29 is not included in the printed text.)

27. And I will put my Spirit within you, and cause you to walk in my statutes, and ye shall keep my judgments, and do them.

28. And ye shall dwell in the land that I gave to your fathers; and ye shall be my people, and I will be your God.

The performance of God's work moves to the placement of His Spirit within the believer. God's Spirit within the believer is consistent with Joel 2:28 and Acts 2:17, 18 where God declared that He would pour out His Spirit upon all flesh. God's Spirit produces life, light and love. His Spirit is placed within us to influence our thoughts and our emotions—that our newly purified hearts may remain pure. And God through His Spirit will cause us to walk in His statutes—to do what He has commanded us to do.

What effect is there upon a life as a result of the work of the Spirit? How is a person's heart affected by the Spirit? What conditions does the Spirit require for indwelling a person?

The message of the Spirit is His presence—always abiding. God's work is not only to cleanse and renew a person's life; He also desires to dwell with us. Spiritual renewal leads to divine presence.

The indwelling of the Spirit of God produces power for the Christian walk and the ability to do God's will. The Spirit-filled life is not a struggle but a perception of and yielding to the enablement of God.

As an outcome of the presence of His Spirit, God would allow the people to repossess the land of their fathers. He would save them from their uncleanness and protect them from famine (v. 29). Then they would be His people and He would be their God. God will not inhabit a person that He cannot claim as His own. The work of God has moved from cleansing to renewal, then to presence, and finally to possession—all through the work of the Spirit.

II. GROW IN SPIRITUALITY (Ezekiel 47:1-5)

A. The Source of Spirituality (vv. 1, 2)

1. Afterward he brought me again unto the door of the house; and, behold, waters issued out from under the threshold of the house eastward: for the forefront of the house stood toward the east, and the waters came down from under from the right side of the house, at the south side of the altar.

2. Then brought he me out of the way of the gate northward, and led me about the way without unto the utter gate by the way that looketh eastward; and, behold, there ran out waters on the right side.

As God spoke to Ezekiel about His work among His people, He prophetically brought a word about the work of the Spirit in the process. The scene that Ezekiel saw was critical because it assaulted a primary notion of the Babylonians. Ezekiel was living under Babylonian captivity, and the Babylonians boasted that the power of their gods were connected with the mighty rivers Tigris and Euphrates. God was telling Ezekiel that there was another powerful river, from God himself, that superseded all of the claims of the Babylonians.

The river of the living God was revealed to Ezekiel as the source of change and empowerment for God's people. By contrast, the Babylonians had looked to the Tigris and Euphrates rivers for wealth, resources, transportation, and protection. The rivers were nurture, sustenance, and power to them. God's vision to Ezekiel reaffirmed that He was the source of nurture and power for Judah.

The clear message of verses 1 and 2 is that the source of the waters was the house of God. God's presence was in the Holy of Holies of the Temple. The message is that at the headwaters of the river was the very presence of God. The Babylonians believed that the headwaters of the Tigris and Euphrates rivers comprised the dwelling place of their gods. By contrast, God revealed Himself as the source of the true and living river that Ezekiel saw.

B. The Progress of Spirituality (vv. 3–5)

3. And when the man that had the line in his hand went forth eastward, he measured a thousand cubits, and he brought me through the waters; the waters were to the ankles.

4. Again he measured a thousand, and brought me through the waters; the waters were to the knees. Again he measured a thousand, and brought me through; the waters were to the loins.

5. Afterward he measured a thousand; and it was a river that I could not pass over: for the waters were risen, waters to swim in, a river that could not be passed over.

Ezekiel was led progressively into deeper and deeper levels of the water coming out of the Temple. The progression of water—ever increasing in volume, power, and effect—is the message of this section. The focus is on the comparative power of the river. Ezekiel could at first stand in the water at the level of his ankles. However, very quickly, he could not cross the mighty river. The power of God is displayed in the might of the river.

What illustration did God use to contrast His power and presence with the claim of the Babylonians to have power and might?

What others might have judged to be a relatively minor start is only the initial encounter with God's power. His presence and power only accumulate and gain momentum.

The reason the waters could continue to gain in strength was the reliability of their source. The water that flowed at the latter portion of Ezekiel's brief journey was only the collection of drops of water that began at the headwaters. The source of power is not necessarily in the place where power is exhibited. If the source is cut off, the power will be cut off. Where the power is demonstrated may vary, but the source of power must remain constant.

III. LIVE BY THE SPIRIT (Ezekiel 47:6-12)

A. Healing and Restoration in the Spirit (vv. 6-8)

6. And he said unto me, Son of man, hast thou seen this? Then he brought me, and caused me to return to the brink of the river.

7. Now when I had returned, behold, at the bank of the river were very many trees on the one side and on the other.

8. Then said he unto me, These waters issue out toward the east country, and go down into the desert, and go into the sea: which being brought forth into the sea, the waters shall be healed.

The effect of the power of the river is the message of verses 6-8. The waters had meant blessing to the regions that were touched by the flow. The waters had flowed eastward from the Temple. The significance of this direction was that barren wasteland lay eastward from Jerusalem. The power of the waters flowing from the presence of God was that even the most barren wilderness could not stop this river from yielding a harvest of blessing.

Ultimately the waters flowing east from Jerusalem would go to what is known today as the Dead Sea. Even in the days of Ezekiel, it was known as a place so barren that no life was found in its waters. The power of the river was that renewal would take place even in the Dead Sea. That stagnant, still, and lifeless body of waters would be able to produce life. The river of God would turn death into life.

B. Life in the Spirit (v. 9)

(Ezekiel 47:9 is not included in the printed text.)

Ezekiel 47:9 is a powerful declaration of the role of the Spirit of God. The river represented the life of the Spirit. Jesus would later prophesy of the Spirit in John 7:37, 38 that out of the believer would flow rivers of living water, signifying the Spirit. The river of the Spirit of God would bring life to all who would yield to it.

C. Productivity by the Spirit (vv. 10-12)

(Ezekiel 47:10–12 is not included in the printed text.)

Not only does life come from the flow of the Spirit of God but also productivity. The Spirit produces life and enables others to bring forth life as well. Verse 12 implies that the fruit of the Spirit-filled believer will remain and not fade away. Further, there would be medicine and healing produced from the leaves of the trees that were watered by the rivers of the Spirit. The depiction was that the waters came from the very presence of God—from the sanctuary, the place where the presence of God dwelt.

The apostle Peter on the Day of Pentecost (Acts 2) quoted Joel 2, which prophesied that God would pour out of His Spirit upon men and women during the last days. The flow of God's outpouring into the believer is akin to the flow of the river from God's presence in the sanctuary, depicted in Ezekiel 47. While the world, as Babylon in Ezekiel's day, may claim that they have a river, a source of power, the Spirit-filled believer in the meantime abides in the mighty flow of God's Spirit. The outpouring of the Spirit on believers today brings life and the power to be overcomers in these last days.

REVIEW QUESTIONS

1. What is the role of the Holy Spirit in cleansing the life of the believer?
2. What does the Holy Spirit produce in the believer as represented by the mighty river flowing from the Temple?
3. How does God bring His presence into a life?
4. Where did the Babylonians place dependency for divine presence and power?
5. What should the response of the believer be to the overcoming and life-giving power of the Holy Spirit today?

GOLDEN TEXT HOMILY

"I WILL PUT MY SPIRIT WITHIN YOU, AND CAUSE YOU TO WALK IN MY STATUTES, AND YE SHALL KEEP MY JUDGMENTS, AND DO THEM" (Ezekiel 36:27).

In our present generation, values such as faithfulness, reliability, and trustworthiness are looked upon as a strange remnant of bygone virtues. We are now openly encouraged through mass media to "be true to yourself" and to "be a winner" at the expense of others. If we do not feel comfortable with a commitment, an agreement, a rule, or law, the "norm" seems to be to ignore it.

In the Old Testament, God made a covenant with His people (Exodus 19:5–8), but they failed to keep their side of the agreement. As a result, they found themselves among ruin and defeat. Man, because of his evil nature, has consistently proven himself to be unworthy of God's blessings. At times it seems the only reliable aspect of humanity is its self–destructive compulsion to disobey God. Now, as then, God's power is often discredited by reason of the failure of His people.

"Behold, the days come, saith the Lord, when I will make a new covenant" (Hebrews 8:8). God promises a new covenant, a new relationship with man in which He will cause the people to obey by the power of His Holy Spirit—not because they deserve it, but for the sake of His own name (Ezekiel 36:22).

We can depend on God, for He has never yet broken His word to us. When relating His new covenant in Ezekiel 36:27, God said, "I will put my spirit within you . . . and ye shall keep my judgments." God said it and we can depend upon its happening.

"Let us hold fast the profession of our faith without wavering; (for he is faithful that promised)" (Hebrews 10:23). As a result of His forgiveness and faithfulness, may we each desire to demonstrate our gratitude and obedience. Through the power of the Holy Spirit that He has placed within us, may we be faithful in proclaiming His gospel to others.—**David L. Metzger (CDR), Navy Chaplain, Marien Aircraft, Japan**

SENTENCE SERMONS

THE HOLY SPIRIT works to conform believers to the image of Christ.

—Selected

BEFORE we can be filled with the Holy Spirit, the desire to be filled must be all–consuming.

—A.W. Tozer

THE HOLY SPIRIT empowers believers to reflect the image of Christ to lost humanity.

—Selected

THE HOLY GHOST destroys my personal private life and turns it into a thoroughfare for God.

—Oswald Chambers

EVANGELISM APPLICATION

THE HOLY SPIRIT EMPOWERS BELIEVERS TO REFLECT THE IMAGE OF CHRIST TO THE LOST.

The witness of the believer is not generated by the believer himself but by the Holy Spirit. In fact, the initial confession of a believer—that Jesus is Lord—comes only as the result of the Spirit's work upon a person (1 Corinthians 12:3). The Holy Spirit brings the experience, instruction, ability, and opportunity for the believer to tell others about Christ. Christ instructed the believers in Acts 1 that their power to witness would be subsequent to the Spirit's work.

To presume that witnessing to the lost is merely to recount facts, stories, or even doctrines is dangerous. The presumption attempts to override the work of the Holy Spirit. In fact, the work of the Holy Spirit is the heart of the believer's witness. The beginning and ending of evangelism is the Spirit's own work. The witness of the believer follows the work of the Spirit. The power to witness comes from the Spirit. And the burden to tell others about Christ is birthed by the Spirit.

ILLUMINATING THE LESSON

The Holy Spirit is the essential guide for the believer. Regardless of the changes that transpire in the landscape of life, even in the most desertlike circumstances and relationships, the Holy Spirit is our guide. Like a guide through the desert, the Holy Spirit leads the way.

It is said that a certain guide lived in the deserts of Arabia who never lost his way. He carried with him a homing pigeon with a very fine cord attached to one of its legs. When in doubt as to which path to take, he threw the bird into the air. The pigeon quickly strained at the cord to fly in the direction of home and thus led the guide accurately to his goal. Because of this unique practice he was known as "the dove man." So, too, the Holy Spirit, the heavenly Dove, is willing and able to direct us in the narrow way that leads to the more abundant life if in humble self-denial we submit to His unerring supervision.

DAILY BIBLE READINGS

M. Directed by the Spirit. 2 Chronicles 20:14–25
T. Changed by the Spirit. 1 Samuel 11:4–11
W. Outpouring of God's Spirit. Joel 2:28–32
T. Taught by the Spirit. John 14:23–31
F. Led by the Spirit. Acts 13:1–4
S. Ministry in the Spirit. 1 Corinthians 12:1–11

INTRODUCTION TO SPRING QUARTER

The spring quarter (March, April, May) lessons are presented under the unit themes "Teachings of Jesus" (lessons 1-7) and "Basic Christian Truths" (lessons 8-13). Lesson 5 is the Easter lesson, and lesson 12 is the lesson for Pentecost Sunday.

As the unit theme implies, Unit One focuses on the teachings of Jesus and draws from three of the four Gospel writers. The study of Christ's teachings is the most soul-searching and faith-building study anyone can undertake. To the Christian, it is more than just a study; it is an inexhaustible fountain of refreshment and a coffer of immeasurable treasures. To the unregenerate person, the teachings of Jesus can be a new vista of hope to set him free from sin and bondage.

The lessons for Unit two, titled "Basic Christian Truths," draw from both Old and New Testament scriptures. As earlier indicated, lessons 5 and 12 are studies on Easter and Pentecost.

Times of stress have always driven people to reexamine the basic faith by which they live. It is not strange, therefore, that in these momentous times of uncertainty and change there has been a heartening revival of interest in basic Christian truths. Perhaps these few lessons will serve as a springboard to launch you into even deeper study.

TEACHINGS OF JESUS
(Map for General Use)
Sidon
Damascus
SYRIA
Tyre
Dan
(Philip)
GAULANITIS
BASHAN
THE GREAT SEA
(Mediterranean)
Ptolemais
PHOENICIA
Capernaum
Cana
Sea of Galilee
GALILEE
Gergesa
Nazareth
Yarmuk River
Caesarea
Dothan
Beth-Shan
DECAPOLIS
Samaria
Shechem
Jabbok River
Joppa
SAMARIA
Jordan River
PEREA
(Archelais)
Pilate
Azotus
Jericho
Jerusalem
Bethlehem
(Herod Antipas)
JUDEA
Ascalon
Salt Sea
Machaerus
Hebron
Gaza
Arnon River
WILDERNESS OF JUDEA
ARABIA

Principles of the Kingdom

Study Text: Matthew 5:1-16

Objective: To understand key principles of the Kingdom and live by them.

Time: Early in A.D. 28

Place: On a hill or mountain near Capernaum in Galilee

Golden Text: "Blessed are they which do hunger and thirst after righteousness: for they shall be filled" (Matthew 5:6).

Central Truth: God's blessings rest on those who understand and apply principles of the Kingdom.

Evangelism Emphasis: Christians living by principles of the Kingdom of God will win others to Christ.

PRINTED TEXT

Matthew 5:1. And seeing the multitudes, he went up into a mountain: and when he was set, his disciples came unto him:

2. And he opened his mouth, and taught them, saying,

3. Blessed are the poor in spirit: for their's is the kingdom of heaven.

4. Blessed are they that mourn: for they shall be comforted.

5. Blessed are the meek: for they shall inherit the earth.

6. Blessed are they which do hunger and thirst after righteousness: for they shall be filled.

7. Blessed are the merciful: for they shall obtain mercy.

8. Blessed are the pure in heart: for they shall see God.

9. Blessed are the peacemakers: for they shall be called the children of God.

10. Blessed are they which are persecuted for righteousness' sake: for their's is the kingdom of heaven.

11. Blessed are ye, when men shall revile you, and persecute you, and shall say all manner of evil against you falsely, for my sake.

12. Rejoice, and be exceeding glad: for great is your reward in heaven: for so persecuted they the prophets which were before you.

13. Ye are the salt of the earth: but if the salt have lost his savour, wherewith shall it be salted? it is thenceforth good for nothing, but to be cast out, and to be trodden under foot of men.

14. Ye are the light of the world. A city that is set on an hill cannot be hid.

15. Neither do men light a candle, and put it under a bushel, but on a candlestick; and it giveth light unto all that are in the house.

16. Let your light so shine before men, that they may see your good works, and glorify your Father which is in heaven.

LESSON OUTLINE

I. PROCLAIMING KINGDOM PRINCIPLES
   A. The Essence of Kingdom Principles
   B. The Expression of Kingdom Principles
   C. The Experience of Kingdom Principles

II. APPLYING KINGDOM PRINCIPLES
   A. Being Salt
   B. Being Light

LESSON EXPOSITION

INTRODUCTION

Bible scholars generally agree that the Sermon on the Mount is the central document of the Christian faith. Most would also agree that the Beatitudes are what might be called "the center of the center."

The Sermon on the Mount has been identified as the moral law of the kingdom of Christ. Its place in the New Testament parallels that of the Ten Commandments in the Old Testament.

It is believed that Saint Augustine was the first to call this passage "The Sermon on the Mount." Others have called it "The Magna Charta of the Kingdom of God" and "The Manifesto of the King."

Some believe that the Sermon on the Mount is not a single discourse but a collection of discourses delivered on various occasions to various audiences, woven together and placed here at the beginning of the Gospel as a sort of frontispiece, illustrating the nature and character of the heavenly Teacher. Others believe that Jesus delivered the entire discourse at one time and repeated portions of it at other times. There is much to be said for this latter view. Every sermon worth preaching is worth preaching often and in many forms.

A careful study of the Sermon on the Mount reveals that it is logically constructed and forms, as it stands, a unified and powerful discourse.

Teaching, argument, and impassioned appeal provide a variety of approaches which Christ carefully used to achieve His purpose in this sermon. There can be no doubt that the basic aim and purpose is to present human character in relation to God and the life He desires for us.

This sermon was the inaugural address of the King. It was a presentation of the principles which were to govern the lives of His followers.

I. PROCLAIMING KINGDOM PRINCIPLES (Matthew 5:1-12)

A. The Essence of Kingdom Principles (vv. 1-6)

1. And seeing the multitudes, he went up into a mountain: and when he was set, his disciples came unto him:

2. And he opened his mouth, and taught them, saying.

Note the plural: *Multitudes* followed Jesus. No political campaign drew attention equal to that of the outpouring of people to hear Jesus and to be healed by Him.

Matthew identified the places from which the people came: Galilee, Decapolis, Jerusalem, Judea, and beyond Jordan (4:25). Decapolis was the region east of the Sea of Galilee. "From Jerusalem, and . . . Judaea" means that people came from as far as the deep south of Palestine. "From beyond Jordan" means the region east of the Jordan River—Perea.

From all parts of Palestine, and from beyond Palestine to the north, the sick were brought to the merciful Healer. His miracles were as bells summoning needy people to the gospel which He preached. Even so are the deeds of loving-kindness done by His followers today.

The mount on which the sermon was delivered was, according to tradition, a square-shaped hill called the Horns of Hattin, or the Mount of Beatitudes. It is located on the west side of the Sea of Galilee and is about seven miles southwest of Capernaum.

Jesus began to teach His disciples after He had sat down. William Barclay writes: "When a Jewish Rabbi was teaching officially he sat to teach. We still speak of a professor's *chair*; the Pope still speaks *ex cathedra*, from his seat. Often a Rabbi gave instruction when he was standing or strolling about; but his really official teaching was done when he had taken his seat. So, then, the very intimation that Jesus sat down to teach his disciples is the indication that this teaching is central and official" *(The Daily Study Bible)*.

3. Blessed are the poor in spirit: for their's is the kingdom of heaven.

The essence of Christian character is being "poor in spirit." These words of Jesus offer a blessing, not to the proud, whose lives revolve around themselves, but to the poor in spirit, whose motives find their fulcrum in the will of God. The kingdom of God is not promised to the self-sufficient. It is not promised to those who press toward goals of their own creation. It is promised to the humble. It is promised to those who march to the music of God. The poor in spirit are those who are self-emptied. They are those who echo the prayer from Gethsemane: "Not my will, but thine, be done."

Those who are poor in spirit have succeeded in getting out of God's way. They do not wear their feelings on their sleeve. They are not easily hurt, since they are forever thinking of others. They live by a perspective that is not self-centered. They find no comfort in the sins of others. They recognize that it is only through the extravagant benevolence of God that they are able to be counted righteous.

4. Blessed are they that mourn: for they shall be comforted.

"Blessed are they that mourn" is a hard saying. Experience is needed in order to understand this Beatitude. Everyone shrinks from sorrow at first, but everyone needs to learn its blessedness in the school of Christ. It is not only a Christian truth but also a practical, commonsense truth that sorrow is necessary for the making of character and the perfecting of life.

Pentheo is the strongest of the Greek words for *mourn*. It is the word that is used to describe grieving for the dead. It is the kind of mourning that wrings a man's heart and brings tears to his eyes. It does not mean the kind of soft, sentimental, nebulous sorrow that one can luxuriate in and half enjoy.

Three suggestions have been offered to Christ's intented meaning. It has been suggested that this blessedness is for those who mourn for this world of sin and sorrow. Others say He meant the blessedness is for those who have known sorrow, grief, and sadness. Still others indicate that this beatitude concerns those who sorrow for their own sin. Probably a combination of all three of these suggestions, with an emphasis on the last one, comes closest to the real meaning.

Comfort is a compound of two Latin words: *fortis*, meaning "strong," and *con*, meaning "together"—thus, "made strong together." Christian comfort is the strength that comes from togetherness with Christ.

5. Blessed are the meek: for they shall inherit the earth.

In classical thought, meekness was identified as helplessness; thus in the Old Testament, meekness is primarily slanted Godward. To display self-sufficiency before an omnipotent God was absolute presumption. Moses, whom Scripture describes as being meek, seems to have understood to an unusual degree the contrast between God's power and his own weakness. This understanding resulted in his humility before, and dependence upon, God. When this weak man by faith appropriated the power of God, he became the instrument for spiritual exploits for Israel.

In the New Testament, meekness acquired the moral significance of humility toward one's fellowman as well as toward God. Thus, the Son of Man, the noble example of the New Testament, in contrast to the noble Greek, washed the feet of His own disciples.

Meekness really has two sides: the passive side, which bears with provocation, controls all feelings of irritation, and refuses to regard personal injury and wrong, the active side, which strongly, bravely, and serenely discharges toward men the duties it owes to God.

Someone has described meekness as the clothing of a servant. It is the opposite of presumptuousness, arrogance, forwardness, and self-assertion. It is freedom from the loathsome disease of pride. It is the expression of those who have voluntarily surrendered their claim to independence and have humbled themselves "under the mighty hand of God" (1 Peter 5:6).

6. Blessed are they which do hunger and thirst after righteousness: for they shall be filled.

Righteousness is the highest response in man to the claim of God. The first and abiding condition for happiness is not to have what we want but to want what we have. Jesus came into the world to awaken in a man's heart a sense of his true need, which is righteousness.

Physical hunger is a condition which indicates bodily health; likewise intellectual hunger is indicative of mental health; but the quest for goodness is the only quest that is certain to be fulfilling. Goodness is the one thing that every soul may have.

Described in this beatitude is one ravenous with hunger, parched and panting with thirst. It reveals to us that when we long for goodness as much as we long for food and drink, we are among the blessed of the Lord.

What is the significance of the first four beatitudes?

B. The Expression of Kingdom Principles (vv. 7-9)

7. Blessed are the merciful: for they shall obtain mercy.

Christ did not mean that a man has to be merciful in order to receive mercy from God, but that if a man shows mercy, he will, as a result, reap mercy. Mercy is the reward for mercy. Those who are merciful receive more and more mercy in return.

J.R. Miller writes of this verse: "There must be, in some faint measure at least, a corresponding spirit in us to receive any gift or blessing from God. It is true, therefore, in relation to God, that the merciful shall obtain mercy, and the unmerciful shall find no mercy. This is taught in the petition, 'Forgive us our debts, as we forgive our debtors' (Matthew 6:12). Thus divine and human mercy are linked together" (*The Master's Blesseds*).

This is also true in our relationship with our fellowman. The merciful obtain mercy and the unmerciful do not. Those who judge others are judged (Matthew 7:1). Those who give receive (Luke 6:38).

In the world we find what we are prepared to find. A selfish person tells us everybody is selfish, while he who has a generous heart senses generosity. The unmerciful are limited by unforgiveness, while the merciful obtain mercy.

8. Blessed are the pure in heart: for they shall see God.

Purity of heart makes possible the vision of God, and the vision of God motivates us to a confession of sin and a holy life. We may tax our brain with speculations, we may study until our body is weary, we may improve ourselves for the sake of fame or gain or praise, yet we may still be no nearer to God. But if we seek first to purify our motives, to make our thoughts pure, to control the promptings of self-love and the wiles of self-deceit, we shall draw nearer to God.

A pure heart is necessary in order to live a pure life. The church can have no power apart from purity. This demands that we follow Paul's dictum: "Train yourself to be godly" (1 Timothy 4:7, *NIV*).

Statistics reveal that we live in a Corinthian, pleasure-crazed culture. And the church has not escaped, for many in today's church have wilted under the heat. In 1988 *Leadership* magazine commissioned a poll of 1,000 pastors. Twelve percent of the pastors—one out of eight—indicated that they had committed adultery while in the ministry, and 23 percent admitted they had done something they considered sexually inappropriate. *Christianity Today* surveyed 1,000 of its subscribers who were not pastors and found the figure to be nearly double, with 23 percent saying they had had extramarital intercourse and 45 percent indicating they had done something they themselves believed was sexually inappropriate. One in four Christian men are unfaithful, and nearly one-half have behaved unbecomingly. This is shocking when one knows that the readers of *Christianity Today* tend to be college-educated church leaders, elders, deacons, Sunday school superintendents, and teachers. One cannot help wondering about the average church member in light of these statistics (*Leadership* magazine, Winter 1988).

What can the church do to motivate people to be pure?

---

9. Blessed are the peacemakers: for they shall be called the children of God.

God hates war; God hates strife of any kind, on the personal or national level; and God so loves peace that He gladly receives as His true children all those who seek in every way to promote "peace on earth, good will to men" (see Luke 2:14).

It should be pointed out that

Jesus does not say, "Blessed are the peace-lovers," but "Blessed are the peacemakers." This is important, for often a peace-lover is not a peacemaker. For example, you may be in a group and know that something is very wrong and that the problem should be treated, yet someone may say; "Oh, for the sake of peace, don't do anything." That kind of person is not making peace; he is simply forestalling trouble. A peacemaker, however, is a person who knows that there may be a battle on the way to true peace. This is not the peace of evasion; it is the peace of facing a problem and getting it settled.

Before a man can be a peacemaker, he must first be at peace with himself. Another way of saying this is "Blessed is the man who is an integrated personality . . . a person who is a harmonious whole . . . a person who has gotten himself into a working harmony.

Peacemakers are the constructive agents of tranquillity. They are the efficient contributors to security and the mediators of peace. They are not merely peaceable; they are committed to the continuous and creative task of making peace.

C. The Experience of Kingdom Principles (vv.10-12)

10. Blessed are they which are persecuted for righteousness' sake: for their's is the kingdom of heaven.

11. Blessed are ye when men shall revile you, and persecute you, and shall say all manner of evil against you falsely, for my sake.

12. Rejoice, and be exceeding glad: for great is your reward in heaven: for so persecuted they the prophets which were before you.

Blessed are the persecuted! This is a rather strange statement. Yet the fact remains that Christians will always be persecuted. This is true for two reasons. First, they are different. The man who will be persecuted most of all in this world is the man who will not conform. If you want to avoid trouble, simply conform. However, if you are a Christian, you cannot conform—you have to be different, and the result will be trouble. The second reason the Christian will be persecuted is that he is the conscience of any group he happens to be in. It is not that he is critical; it is not that he is self-righteous; it is not that he says, "I'm better than you." But his very presence brings the realization that certain things are wrong and that certain actions cannot be taken. How then can a Christian be happy? He can be happy because persecution is a compliment which provides an opportunity to demonstrate loyalty to Jesus Christ.

It is not easy to be a dedicated Christian. Our society is not a friend to God or to His people. Whether we like it or not, there is conflict between us and the world. If we are for righteousness, we must expect the bitter opposition of those who are dedicated to unrighteousness.

Accusations are no blessing unless, of course, they are false. Persecution in itself brings no blessing unless it is incurred for the sake of Christ. "For my [Christ's] sake," and this only, is it a glory to endure the scoffs, revilings, and persecutions of men.

II. APPLYING KINGDOM PRINCIPLES (Matthew 5:13-16)

A. Being Salt (v. 13)

13. Ye are the salt of the earth:

but if the salt have lost his savour, wherewith shall it be salted? it is thenceforth good for nothing, but to be cast out, and to be trodden under foot of men.

The responsibility of Christ's disciples is set forth in this verse: "Ye are the salt of the earth." This metaphor needs very little explanation. It involves two things: a grave judgment as to the actual state of society and a lofty claim as to what Christ's followers are able to do for it. Society is corrupt and seems to enjoy its corruption. You do not salt a living thing; you salt a dead one, so it will not rot.

Salt does its work through close contact. Therefore, we are not to withdraw from contact with evil. The only way salt can purify is by being rubbed into the corrupted thing.

Salt does its work silently, inconspicuously, and gradually. You can never be the light of the world until you first become the salt of the earth. You have to do the humble, inconspicuous, silent work of checking corruption by your pure example before you can do the more obvious work of lighting the darkness.

Another attribute of salt is that it gives flavor to what would otherwise be tasteless or unpleasant. Christ's people are the flavoring element in the world which prevents it from being altogether loathsome to the Lord.

Little does the world know its debt to the followers of Christ. Without them the world would be a mass of corruption with nothing to heal its disorders or to stop its movement toward utter destruction. If Christians were removed, the world would soon become as Sodom and Gomorrah.

Jesus gives a warning in this verse. It is possible for salt to lose its savor and so become incapable of seasoning others. We know how a little dampness will affect the quality of salt. A little moisture in the atmosphere will deprive it of much, if not all, of its sharp, biting, seasoning power. It will leave it flat, blunt, and powerless. It will be useless, or nearly useless, for the one purpose for which it was designed. No less danger confronts the Christian. The world in which we live is not a favorable environment for us who are determined to be the salt of the earth. Many things are against us here. Many things work to cause us to dull our edge, to bring us down from our heights, to make us lose our saltiness. Christianity is an eminently practical religion. Sound doctrine is its root and foundation, and holy living should always be its fruit.

B. Being Light (vv. 14-16)

14. Ye are the light of the world. A city that is set on an hill cannot be hid.

15. Neither do men light a candle, and put it under a bushel, but on a candlestick; and it giveth light unto all that are in the house.

16. Let your light so shine before men, that they may see your good works, and glorify your Father which is in heaven.

It is the characteristic of light to be completely distinct from darkness. The least spark in a dark room can be seen at once. Of all things created, light probably is the most useful. It guides; it cheers; it warms. It was the first thing called into being. Without it the world would be a gloomy place (Genesis 1:2).

Light quickens life; light shows the way to God and leads into it.

Light develops and exhibits all the beauty of the earth. Light helps us to fellowship one with another. Light awakens the voice of adoration and praise.

This metaphor of light tells us that there is something marked, distinct, and peculiar about Christian character. There is a difference in habits, tastes, and attitudes between Christians and those in the world. We must dare to be different and unlike the world if we mean to be saved and help others to be saved.

What can the individual Christian do to be salt and light in the world?

REVIEW QUESTIONS

1. What does it mean to be poor in spirit?
2. Describe those who mourn.
3. What is meant by meekness?
4. Why is it important to show mercy?
5. Why is it important for Christians to be salt and light in today's world?

GOLDEN TEXT HOMILY

"BLESSED ARE THEY WHICH DO HUNGER AND THIRST AFTER RIGHTEOUSNESS: FOR THEY SHALL BE FILLED" (Matthew 5:6).

Scripture presents Jesus as king of a present spiritual kingdom that exists alongside and within the present rebellious universe. Wherever human beings bow to and obey Christ as Lord, there the kingdom of Jesus has come, and there Christ, the King, acts in power to guide and protect those who are citizens of His kingdom. In Matthew 5:1-12, Jesus announced the blessings for citizens of His domain, but He also declared the conditions to be met.

In verse 6, we are reminded that it is not those who are satisfied with their own righteousness that will be filled but those who hunger and thirst after a righteousness they do not feel they have achieved. Hunger and thirst are basic needs that we all experience; but unless one has experienced the need for food and water following an extended period without these basic needs, one cannot fully understand the "hunger and thirst" Christ was talking about.

We do well to note the order of progression in the Lord's admonitions. He spoke first of the consciously poor in their spirit (v. 3); next, of those who mourn over their poverty (v. 4); then, of those who are ready to receive whatever teaching or chastisement might be given them (v. 5); and, in verse 6, of those who have an earnest longing for righteousness.

The righteousness mentioned here is not that which is determined by one's own judgment, but that which is a teaching of the kingdom of Christ. If the soul's longing for righteousness is fostered, it will grow into sanctifying passion. It will become the supreme purpose of life, and it will put divinely approved character in its proper place—that is, first place. The person who seeks first the kingdom of God and His righteousness (6:33) is not made unworldly, but he does learn how to sanctify all worldly relations. **—James E. Humbertson, D.Min., Editorial Director, *Evangelical Commentary*, Pathway Press, Cleveland, Tennessee**

SENTENCE SERMONS

GOD'S BLESSINGS rest on those who understand and apply principles of the Kingdom.

—Selected

THE PRINCIPLES of the Bible are the groundwork of human freedom.

—Horace Greely

PRINCIPLES OF LIFE are like tuning forks; sound them often to bring your life up to a standard pitch.

—S.D. Gordon

THE BIBLE is a storehouse of whose contents no one can afford to be ignorant.

—Dwight Moody

EVANGELISM APPLICATION

CHRISTIANS LIVING BY PRINCIPLES OF THE KINGDOM OF GOD WILL WIN OTHERS TO CHRIST.

The church is to be a fellowship of redeeming love in the deepest sense of the word. At the same time the fellowship of Christian love is furthering and strengthening the redemption of its individual members, these same persons are called to be God's instruments to redeem the world, both in the corporate ministry of the church and in the daily secular life of its members. Redemption is not a completed fact but a continuing experience. It has a point of beginning but no ending.—**Alvin J. Lindgren, *Foundations for Purposeful Church Administration***

ILLUMINATING THE LESSON

Throughout the Sermon on the Mount, Jesus tells us that we need one another. He tells us that our strength to bear adversity, like our wisdom, is the product of many minds banded together. Approaching our problem from different directions and bringing to bear on them the varied insights of many backgrounds and differing experiences, we see together what we could never see alone. This point can be illustrated by four small boys watching an elephant pass in a circus parade. Looking at the elephant in the lead, one small boy said, "Look at his trunk"; the second, "Boy, ain't he got big feet?" "Yes," said the third, "his tusk looks wicked." The fourth boy added his bit, "He's really big all over." Each boy was impressed by one characteristic of the elephant, and each added a significant dimension to the overall picture of the elephant. Together, they saw the complete elephant. So it is with us: together we see the truth and achieve an understanding of our problems which we might otherwise miss. Our knowledge and our wisdom are neighborly achievements.

DAILY BIBLE READINGS

M. Meekness Rewarded. Psalm 37:3-11

T. Good and Evil Contrasted. Proverbs 11:1-6, 18, 19

W. Need Acknowledged. Mark 9:17-27

T. Persecution Endured. Luke 6:22-28

F. Concern for the Lost. Romans 9:1-5

S. Serving in the Kingdom. Romans 11:1-8

Establishing Right Motives

Study Text: Matthew 6:1-18

Objective: To realize that right motives are essential to Christlike living and base our actions on them.

Time: Early in A.D. 28

Place: On a high hill or mountain in Capernaum in Galilee

Golden Text: "Take heed that ye do not your alms before men, to be seen of them: otherwise ye have no reward of your Father which is in heaven" (Matthew 6:1).

Central Truth: To please God, our giving, praying, and fasting must be done with proper motives.

Evangelism Emphasis: Right motives in evangelism will result in souls for the Kingdom.

PRINTED TEXT

Matthew 6:1. Take heed that ye do not your alms before men, to be seen of them: otherwise ye have no reward of your Father which is in heaven.

3. But when thou doest alms, let not thy left hand know what thy right hand doeth:

4. That thine alms may be in secret: and thy Father which seeth in secret himself shall reward thee openly.

5. And when thou prayest, thou shalt not be as the hypocrites are: for they love to pray standing in the synagogues and in the corners of the streets, that they may be seen of men. Verily I say unto you, They have their reward.

6. But thou, when thou prayest, enter into thy closet, and when thou hast shut thy door, pray to thy Father which is in secret; and thy Father which seeth in secret shall reward thee openly.

7. But when ye pray, use not vain repetitions, as the heathen do: for they think that they shall be heard for their much speaking.

8. Be not ye therefore like unto them: for your Father knoweth what things ye have need of, before ye ask him.

9. After this manner therefore pray ye: Our Father which art in heaven, Hallowed be thy name.

10. Thy kingdom come. Thy will be done in earth, as it is in heaven.

11. Give us this day our daily bread.

12. And forgive us our debts, as we forgive our debtors.

13. And lead us not into temptation, but deliver us from evil: For thine is the kingdom, and the power, and the glory, for ever. Amen.

14. For if ye forgive men their trespasses, your heavenly Father will also forgive you:

15. But if ye forgive not men their trespasses, neither will your Father forgive your trespasses.

16. Moreover when ye fast, be not, as the hypocrites, of a sad countenance: for they disfigure their faces, that they may appear unto men to fast. Verily I say unto you, They have their reward.

17. But thou, when thou fastest, anoint thine head, and wash thy face;

18. That thou appear not unto men to fast, but unto thy Father which is in secret: and thy Father, which seeth in secret, shall reward thee openly.

LESSON OUTLINE

I. MOTIVES FOR GIVING
   A. Wrong Giving
   B. Right Giving

II. MOTIVES FOR PRAYER
   A. Contrasts in Prayer
   B. Model Prayer
   C. Sincerity in Prayer

III. MOTIVE FOR SELF-DISCIPLINE
   A. False Piety
   B. True Piety

LESSON EXPOSITION

INTRODUCTION

In this section of the Sermon on the Mount (Matthew 6), Jesus contrasted the attitude of the Pharisees with that of true citizens of His kingdom. The Pharisees were proud, ostentatious, worldly-minded; Christ's followers were to be humble, modest, heavenly-minded.

Jesus was really dealing with the motives of human behavior. Motives have been defined as that which drives us to action. They indicate a state of tension in an organism. When tension is reduced, satisfaction results, at least temporarily. Satisfaction is the result of successful tension-reducing activity that stems from motives.

Why did the Pharisees act as they did? What causes any man to behave when and as he does? The answers are many and varied because man is so complex. Because some people ascribe behavior to one thing and some ascribe it to another, conduct has been explained on the basis of instinct, tensions, needs, desires, wishes, or wants—all of which are drives to, or sources of, activity.

Human beings, by virtue of the existence of certain basic drives, are motivated to conduct themselves in such a way as to achieve certain goals. These goals, when reached, result in the reduction of the tension accompanying the drives and bring the individual varying degrees of satisfaction. This satisfaction, in turn, contributes to the mental health of that person.

The Pharisees never learned to live a balanced life. As a result, they were miserable and made those around them miserable. Some of the drives which must be considered if balance in life is to be achieved include the desire for activity, the desire for security, the desire for companionship, the desire for new experiences, the desire for accomplishment, and the desire to love and be loved. Each relates to the others, and any conflicts between them must be resolved. Each one is also relative, in the sense that too much or too little of the thing desired would probably be unpalatable. Too much activity, too much companionship, or too much work may make a person dissatisfied. Rest, solitude, play, and responsibility are essential factors in a wholesomely balanced life.

The Pharisees believed perfection to be attainable by human beings. They confused this with the realistic attempt to reach attainable goals and with the setting of standards of achievable conduct. They struggled too hard to make people good and too little to make them happy.

I. MOTIVES FOR GIVING (Matthew 6:1-4)

A. Wrong Giving (vv. 1, 2)

(Matthew 6:2 is not included in the printed text.)

1. Take heed that ye do not your alms before men, to be seen of them: otherwise ye have no reward of your Father which is in heaven.

Almsgiving played a large part in the life of the Pharisees. In fact, this was true of all Jewish people. It is said that poverty was widespread among the Jewish people. A study of the Old Testament reveals that the merciful and kindly laws of Moses provided for the support of the poor by their rich neighbors. Alms were, and still are, given in the Jewish synagogue as an appropriate act of religion. Chests for alms with mouths shaped like trumpets were placed in the Temple, in the Court for Women, and rivalry in gift-giving reached such proportions that it was necessary to limit by law the extent of giving.

B. Right Giving (vv. 3, 4)

3. But when thou doest alms, let not thy left hand know what thy right hand doeth:

4. That thine alms may be in secret: and thy Father which seeth in secret himself shall reward thee openly.

The holier-than-thou Pharisees made certain that other people saw them give alms. They proudly placed their alms in the Temple chests, and the louder the clatter they made as they fell, the more pleased they were. The Pharisees were, in all their religious deeds, *hypocrites*, a word which originally meant "playactors." They sought to make a show before men, whereas the Christian was taught to do his works before God alone.

Jesus, in opposition to all this ostentatious charity, urged secret giving. He put it very forcibly when He told them not to let their left hand know what their right hand was doing. In other words, one should not announce to others what he is doing. He indicated that the Father in heaven would know all about it and that His approval is all the reward the giver should seek.

Jesus was not condemning good deeds but rather the unworthy motive: "to be seen of men." A holy life has a persuasive eloquence, more persuasive than holy words; it must not be hidden; its influence is far too important to be lost. Men must see the good deeds that come from holiness and so be led to glorify God, from whose grace and presence all holiness comes. Good works must sometimes be done before men, but with the right motives.

How does the church promote ostentation in giving?

II. MOTIVES FOR PRAYER (Matthew 6:5-15)

A. Contrasts in Prayer (vv. 5-8)

5. And when thou prayest, thou shalt not be as the hypocrites are: for they love to pray standing in the synagogues and in the corners of the streets, that they may be seen of men. Verily I say unto you, They have their reward.

6. But thou, when thou prayest, enter into thy closet, and when thou hast shut thy door, pray to thy Father which is in secret; and thy Father which seeth in secret shall reward thee openly.

Jesus did not mean to imply that God was not in the synagogue, or even in the street corners where the hypocrites of His day were accustomed to pray, or that He is not present with us when our families meet together for prayer. There is no family altar, no prayer meeting, no church, and no street corner where God is not to be found by them that diligently call upon Him. However, our times of corporate, public prayer do not negate our need for private prayer.

Andrew Murray writes of verse 6: "The first thing the Lord teaches His disciples is that they must have a secret place for prayer; everyone must have some solitary spot where he can be alone with his God. Every teacher must have a schoolroom. . . . That inner chamber, that solitary place, is Jesus' schoolroom. That spot may be anywhere; that spot may change from day to day if we have to change our abode; but in our secret place, there must be a quiet time in which we place ourselves in the Master's presence, to be prepared for the worship of the Father. There alone—but there most surely—Jesus comes to teach us to pray.

"God is not seen with the carnal eye. As long as in our worship of God we are chiefly concerned with our own thoughts and exercises, we shall not meet Him. . . . But to the one who withdraws himself from all that is of the world, and prepares to wait upon God alone, the Father will reveal Himself" *(With Christ in the School of Prayer)*.

7. But when ye pray, use not vain repetitions, as the heathen do: for they think that they shall be heard for their much speaking.

8. Be not ye therefore like unto them: for your Father knoweth what things ye have need of, before ye ask him.

According to Jesus, all true prayer must be offered to God. The real problem of the people Jesus described was that they were praying to men and not to God. They were more concerned with impressing the people who heard them pray than with making contact with God. In essence, Jesus was saying that whether in public or private prayer, a man should have no thought in his mind and no desire in his heart but God.

Jesus stated in verse 8 that we should always remember that the God to whom we pray is a God of love who is more ready to answer than we are to pray. We do not have to beg Him to answer. His gifts and His grace do not have to be extracted from Him against His will. He does not have to be coaxed or pestered or bartered into answering our prayers. We should always remember that God desires to give us the things we need.

B. Model Prayer (vv. 9-13)

9. After this manner therefore pray ye: Our Father which art in heaven, Hallowed be thy name.

The importance of prayer cannot be overestimated. Martin Luther said, "To have prayed well is to have studied well." We may add to this: to have prayed well is to have preached well . . . to have written well . . . to have worked well . . . to have resisted well . . . to have lived well . . . and to have died well. Prayer is the key to spiritual success.

The word *Father* not only suggests our warrant for prayer but also suggests to us the spirit of filial trust, in the spirit of childlike confidence. Let us pray by prefacing every prayer with that blessed word *Father*. It is our claim upon God. No prayer can be too bold, no petition can appear presumptuous when we have begun by saying "our Father."

Our Father is in heaven. And so heaven is something more than a city, something more than a place of wondrous beauty and delight; it is our Father's house, the home prepared for His children. It may have streets of gold and it may have gates of pearl, but it is home nevertheless; and as our Father's house, it is the dearest and most sacred spot in all the universe.

The word *hallowed* means "regarded and treated as holy"—sanctified, dealt with reverentially, as a sacred thing. When we pray that God's name may be hallowed, we mean that in all whereby He makes Himself known, He may be honored, reverenced, and glorified.

10. Thy kingdom come. Thy will be done in earth, as it is in heaven.

The words "Thy kingdom come" suggest that we *ought* to pray loyally and hopefully. The kingdom of God is referred to more than 100 times in the Gospels. Matthew is preeminently the Gospel of the Kingdom. When the Jews referred to "the kingdom" they meant a political dominion, but Christ's words had no such meaning. The kingdom of God is a society of renewed men who have experienced the power of God in their lives. The natural man cannot enter that Kingdom. He must be born from above. The Kingdom is, in brief, the reign of Christ in human lives which manifests itself in love to God and to man.

Christ the King came to earth, and His own rejected Him. Now the church has its mission between the first and second coming of Christ. It is our business to be prepared and to make ready for His glorious return. It is then that He will set up a kingdom on earth.

This model prayer teaches the believer to pray submissively, "Thy will be done in earth, as it is in heaven." Christ modeled through His life and death how God's work should be done on earth and in heaven. His will is law and should never be violated. This is our standard, and we should be satisfied with nothing less.

11. Give us this day our daily bread.

The believer is dependent on God for all his needs. The Hebrew word for *daily*, which occurs only in the Lord's Prayer, has in it no thought of time. It means "needed" or "necessary." The idea is to ask for the food that is necessary, not only in quantity but also in quality.

This petition illustrates a child's faith in the Father as the great giver for both soul and body. It requests bread only, not dainties or flesh. The petition is for *our* bread, not another's—bread that is needed by us—and not another. And, as a very perceptive little girl once said, "When we eat God's bread, we are His guest.

12. And forgive us our debts, as we forgive our debtors.

The word translated *debt* means "that which is justly and legally due." The debts that God is asked to forgive are our sins, our many failures and shortcomings in our relationship to God, as well as our bold defiance of His authority and open disobedience to His commandments. We owe God all we have and all we are—our time, our strength, our money, our thoughts and feelings, our life plans and ambitions, our very best. How little of this we have paid to our heavenly Creditor. But God is ready to forgive us all this debt, on condition that we have in our hearts the spirit of forgiveness and have proved it by already forgiving those who are indebted to us in any way. If we harbor unkind feelings toward anyone—if we say, "I'll forgive but I cannot forget"—we need not ask God to do what we are unwilling to do. If we will not forgive our debtors, this prayer actually becomes a petition for God not to forgive us.

13. And lead us not into temptation, but deliver us from evil: For thine is the kingdom, and the power, and the glory, for ever. Amen.

This is a prayer for God's leading. We are told in James 1:13, 14 that God never tempts anyone but that men are tempted by their own evil desires. This petition is not in real contradiction with what James wrote, but is in effect a prayer that God will not allow us to fall into any temptation without providing for us His own great deliverance from it. As Paul wrote in 1 Corinthians 10:13, our Father will not allow His children to fall into unbearable temptations, but in every temptation will make a way of escape.

C. Sincerity in Prayer (vv. 14, 15)

14. For if ye forgive men their trespasses, your heavenly Father will also forgive you:

15. But if ye forgive not men their trespasses, neither will your Father forgive your trespasses.

The Lord's Prayer is a collection of different petitions from various parts of the Old Testament, which are concentrated so as to form a concise and comprehensive summary of all that we need to pray for. But there was added to one of the petitions a limitation which was altogether new, and which needed explanation. Jesus did not stop to explain it at the time, however. He completed the prayer first, and then added, in confirmation, the words of verses 14 and 15, showing us that the thought had not been lightly included.

It may appear strange that our own compassion toward others should be the pattern and measure of God's compassion toward us. But the Lord would have us know that it is vain to expect mercy at God's hands unless we exercise mercy toward others. This is the condition on which we can hope to be accepted by Him.

What Jesus taught about prayer is of supreme importance. If we want to pray appropriately we must evaluate our practice by His teaching and be ready to abandon anything that seems in its nature to conflict with that. Only in this way can we pray Christian prayers. The teaching of Jesus is conveyed by His words and by His example. His words teach secrecy (Matthew 6:5,

6); simplicity (6:7, 8); certainty (7:7-11); steadfastness (Luke 18:1-7; 11:5-8); a sense of unworthiness (18:13, 14); a spirit of forgiveness (Mark 11:25). The example of Christ also shows us that prayer was not with our Lord a mere glance, or sign, or attitude of mind, or passing utterance but rather a sharply defined effort, so engaging and focusing the facilities that it demanded all the time and effort required of a business engagement *(The Discipline of Prayer).*

Why is prayer so difficult for most Christians?

III. MOTIVE FOR SELF-DISCIPLINE (Matthew 6:16-18)

A. False Piety (v. 16)

16. Moreover when ye fast, be not, as the hypocrites, of a sad countenance: for they disfigure their faces, that they may appear unto men to fast. Verily I say unto you, They have their reward.

The Pharisees made much of fasting. They developed many rules to govern it. Their drawn faces were supposed to express deep sorrow for their sins. They also disfigured their faces by neglecting the usual washing and anointing, leaving their hair and beard uncared for, and even by putting ashes on their face.

It is obvious that Jesus assumed His followers would fast. This He took for granted; otherwise, why would He give direction concerning an ordinance He did not intend for them to observe or thought they would not observe? It is obvious that He expected His people to fast, as well as to give alms and pray.

But Jesus did condemn the way the Pharisees fasted. Fasting is meant to be an expression of humiliation and mourning. Under such disguise as disfigured faces, ashes, and dirt, the Pharisees made a mockery of fasting only to conceal proud and contemptuous hearts. The Pharisees sought the praise of men instead of favor with God.

B. True Piety (vv. 17, 18)

17. But thou, when thou fastest, anoint thine head, and wash thy face;

18. That thou appear not unto men to fast, but unto thy Father which is in secret: and thy Father, which seeth in secret, shall reward thee openly.

Christ recognized the positive aspects of fasting. It relieves us from worldly cares, clears our mind for deeper thought, and is a natural expression of contrition. Moreover, it is a personal thing between us and God. But it is rendered invalid by any display of self-righteousness. Therefore, Christ urged His followers, when fasting, to make no outward show of it whatever, and to be happy with the rewards of communion with God.

If we are honest with ourselves we recognize that we will never get anywhere in life without discipline—be it in the arts, business, athletics, or academics. This is doubly so in spiritual matters. In other areas we may be able to claim some innate advantage. An athlete may be born with a strong body, a musician with perfect pitch, or an artist with an eye for perspective. But none of us can claim an innate spiritual advantage. In reality, we are all equally disadvantaged. None of us naturally seeks after God, none is inherently righteous, none instinctively does good (Romans 3:9-18). Therefore, as children of grace, our spiritual discipline is everything.

Why do Christians so often shy away from self-discipline?

REVIEW QUESTIONS

1. What did Christ object to in the behavior of the Pharisees?
2. What did Christ urge in the matter of almsgiving?
3. What were Christ's rules for prayer?
4. In His model prayer, what petitions did Christ insert with regard to God?
5. What were Christ's rules concerning fasting?

GOLDEN TEXT HOMILY

"TAKE HEED THAT YE DO NOT YOUR ALMS BEFORE MEN, TO BE SEEN OF THEM: OTHERWISE YE HAVE NO REWARD OF YOUR FATHER WHICH IS IN HEAVEN" (Matthew 6:1).

Two opposite motives are seen in this text. One person is self-seeking for personal gratification—he is doing right for the wrong reasons. The other is self-giving for the glory of God—he is doing right for the right reasons.

In the case of the one who desires to be seen of men, it seems evident that there was an inner void which he hoped would find fulfillment in the applause of men.

Of this our Lord said, "Take heed." Notice four reasons why one should take heed:

1. Popular applause may becloud one's judgment and cause him to make unwise decisions.
2. The applause is temporary.
3. Applause is often treacherous. Perhaps some in the crowd that applauded Christ on His triumphal entry into Jerusalem, cried out just a few days later, "Crucify him! Crucify him!"
4. The applause of men is the only reward such a one will get. How sad!

Now consider the one who does right for the right reasons. It is evident that such a person is inwardly fortified with the basics of faith, which recognize our purpose for being: We are created for the glory and pleasure of God (Isaiah 43:7; Revelation 4:11).

With this knowledge and faith, one's primary motive is to please God and then to encourage others to join in glorifying God.

A warm glow of joy comes to a child when he or she is approved by the parents for good attitudes and conduct. The Father affirmed His pleasure in His Son when at Jesus' baptism He spoke from heaven, "This is my beloved Son, in whom I am well pleased" (Matthew 3:17). One minister paraphrased these words in a very earthly manner: "This is My boy and I am proud of Him."

Such approbation is in itself copious reward, but Jesus said, "Thy Father which seeth in secret himself shall reward thee openly" (6:4). Both here and in eternity we will be involved in unwrapping a lot of surprise reward packages which will be expressions of our Father's pleasure in us. "Godliness is profitable unto all things, having promise of the life that now is, and of that which is to come" (1 Timothy 4:8).

There is a big payoff for doing right for the right reasons.—**Excerpts from *The Evangelical Sunday School Lesson Commentary*, Vol. 36**

SENTENCE SERMONS

TO PLEASE GOD, our giving, praying, and fasting must be done with proper motives.

—Selected

THOUGH THEY MAY NOT be visible to the eye, motives are the best measure of character.

—Selected

THE MORALITY of an action depends upon the motive from which we act.

—J. Johnson

MAN SEES YOUR ACTIONS, but God knows your motives.

—Thomas `a Kempis

EVANGELISM APPLICATION

RIGHT MOTIVES IN EVANGELISM WILL RESULT IN SOULS FOR THE KINGDOM.

A businessman came to his pastor to make a confession which many other church members might also truthfully make. He said, "Ever since I united with the church, I have been what I would call an average Christian. But lately I have been thinking that I am really a drifter. I am very dissatisfied with myself."

"There is such a thing," his pastor reminded him, "as divine dissatisfaction. It is a dissatisfaction that God puts into our hearts to stir us up to achieve something better."

Soon afterward the opportunity came for this man to sponsor an effort to bring young people within the church's influence. In this work it was necessary for him to face his own personal inadequacy and to rely upon a strength and wisdom higher than his own. No longer a drifter, he was becoming a better Christian with a deeper appreciation of the great meaning of the Christian faith.

ILLUMINATING THE LESSON

It is a well-known fact that every time we do or say something wrong, we make a character groove, and thus it becomes easier to do or say that wrong thing again. The same is equally true every time we do good. When we think clean thoughts, speak kind words, do helpful things, or perform helpful acts, we are forming a character groove, making it easier for us to think, speak, or act in such a manner again.

The total result of this process is what we call character. Christian life begins when we come to the Lord in faith and ask Him to change our old character by the power of His forgiveness. This is something we cannot do for ourselves. From there on, a new character is in the making, which will be the end result of Christian speech and conduct. We may stumble and fall sometimes, and we will need daily pardon and spiritual renewal by communion with God. But our words and actions will mark us as belonging to God if we confess and keep close to the Lord.

DAILY BIBLE READINGS

M. Blindness of Hypocrisy. Isaiah 29:9-16
T. Foolish Counsel. Job 2:7-10
W. Deceptive Friendship. Psalm 55:12-18
T. Repentant Prayer. Luke 18:9-14
F. Acceptable Worship. Genesis 4:1-7
S. Self-Giving Love. Philippians 2:1-8

Challenge of Discipleship

Study Text: Matthew 10:24-42

Objective: To understand and accept the challenge of discipleship.

Time: Probably summer A.D. 28

Place: Uncertain. Jesus had just finished visiting a number of towns in Galilee.

Golden Text: "He that findeth his life shall lose it: and he that loseth his life for my sake shall find it" (Matthew 10:39).

Central Truth: The believer is called to a life of total commitment to Jesus Christ.

Evangelism Emphasis: The first step to discipleship is accepting Christ as Savior.

PRINTED TEXT

Matthew 10:24. The disciple is not above his master, nor the servant above his lord.

25. It is enough for the disciple that he be as his master, and the servant as his lord. If they have called the master of the house Beelzebub, how much more shall they call them of his household?

26. Fear them not therefore: for there is nothing covered, that shall not be revealed; and hid, that shall not be known.

27. What I tell you in darkness, that speak ye in light: and what ye hear in the ear, that preach ye upon the housetops.

28. And fear not them which kill the body, but are not able to kill the soul: but rather fear him which is able to destroy both soul and body in hell.

29. Are not two sparrows sold for a farthing? and one of them shall not fall on the ground without your Father.

30. But the very hairs of your head are all numbered.

31. Fear ye not therefore, ye are of more value than many sparrows.

32. Whosoever therefore shall confess me before men, him will I confess also before my Father which is in heaven.

33. But whosoever shall deny me before men, him will I also deny before my Father which is in heaven.

34. Think not that I am come to send peace on earth: I came not to send peace, but a sword.

35. For I am come to set a man at variance against his father, and the daughter against her mother, and the daughter in law against her mother in law.

36. And a man's foes shall be they of his own household.

37. He that loveth father or mother more than me is not worthy of me: and he that loveth son or daughter more than me is not worthy of me.

38. And he that taketh not his cross, and followeth after me, is not worthy of me.

39. He that findeth his life shall lose it: and he that loseth his life for my sake shall find it.

40. He that receiveth you receiveth me, and he that receiveth me receiveth him that sent me.

41. He that receiveth a prophet in the name of a prophet shall receive a prophet's reward; and he that receiveth a righteous man in the name of a righteous man shall receive a righteous man's reward.

LESSON OUTLINE

- I. VICTORY OVER FEAR
  - A. Opposition Will Come
  - B. God Will Reveal All
  - C. Fear God Only
  - D. God Protects His Own
- II. CONFESS CHRIST OPENLY
  - A. Christ Honors His Own
  - B. Conflict Is Inescapable
- III. REWARDS OF DISCIPLESHIP
  - A. Receiving Disciples
  - B. Supporting Disciples

LESSON EXPOSITION

INTRODUCTION

The biblical challenge of discipleship is found in Matthew 28:19, 20: "Go therefore and teach [make disciples] of all the nations . . . teaching them to observe all that I commanded you" (*NASB*). This divinely inspired challenge rests on the word *teach*, which in Matthew 28:19 comes from the Greek verb *matheteuo*, which is more properly translated "to disciple." The final mandate of the Master is to disciple men. Discipling is not giving a lecture; it is instructing.

Jesus chose 12 men with varied backgrounds and abilities to be His disciples. Many of these were unschooled, and all of them were unprepared for the great task to which they were called. But He set out to train them so that in His absence they could carry out the work that would change the world. Who would presume to improve on His methods?

Discipleship was, and is, based on invitation. Christ chose them (Luke 6:13) and He invited them to follow Him (Matthew 4:19).

These men were chosen by Jesus with much care and after intimate acquaintance. They were first called to faith in Him and in His messianic claim (see John 1:12-15). Gaines S. Dobbins records that after an interval, in which the first four believers had gone back to their usual occupation, Jesus called them again to give up their jobs and follow Him as learners (Matthew 4:17-22). And still later, after further study of these men and following a night of prayer, Jesus called His growing group of disciples about Him and from them chose 12, whom He called apostles or missionaries (Luke 6:12-16). Mark states that "He appointed twelve, that they might be with Him, and that He might send them out to preach, and have authority to cast out the demons" (Mark 3:14, 15, NASB). Later, following His death and resurrection, Jesus called these and other disciples a fourth time to "go into all the world and preach the gospel to all creation" (Mark 16:15, *NASB) (*Dobbins, *A Ministering Church)*.

Jesus used two words, *disciple* and *apostle*, to describe these called men. It is interesting that He never used *priest, rabbi*, or *scribe*. The word translated *disciple* means, literally, "a learner," but connotes more than a student. To Jesus a disciple is a convinced learner, a follower, an adherent. Literally, an *apostle* is one sent, a missionary, a person commissioned to represent another. To Jesus the apostles were those who constituted the inner circle of the disciples, chosen by Him to be fully taught and to become His special representatives in teaching and winning others *(A Ministering Church)*.

I. VICTORY OVER FEAR (Matthew 10:24-31)

A. Opposition Will Come (vv. 24, 25)

24. The disciple is not above his master, nor the servant above his lord.

25. It is enough for the disciple that he be as his master, and the servant as his lord. If they have called the master of the house Beelzebub, how much more shall they call them of his household?

Jesus Christ was persecuted by men when He was ministering on earth, so why should His followers expect anything different? The disciples of Jesus did not outrank their Master. Jesus was accused of being a cohort of Beelzebub, who was lord of the dung; so the followers of Jesus are apt to receive the same kind of treatment. And they should count it a privilege to suffer for, and with, Him.

The odds may be against the disciple of Jesus, but God will provide providential and even miraculous care and opportunity. Someone has said that "man is immortal until his work is done." A Christian disciple is even more immortal than that. When everybody says his work is done and perhaps forces his retirement, God can give him competence as intercessor to effect God's purposed spiritual results. The world, or even the church, may shut a man up; but as sure as he lives on his knees in prayer and intercession, no one can shut God out or permanently end a competence which is the channel of God at work in his life. John Bunyan was put in jail and he wrote *Pilgrim's Progress*. Samuel Rutherford was thrown in jail and he wrote those beautiful spiritual letters which are still food for the soul. The saintly Rutherford wrote, "When God puts me in the cellar of affliction, I begin to look around for His wine." He drank the heavenly wine and distilled it in words of spiritual strength.

B. God Will Reveal All (vv. 26, 27)

26. Fear them not therefore: for there is nothing covered, that shall not be revealed; and hid, that shall not be known.

27. What I tell you in darkness, that speak ye in light: and what ye hear in the ear, that preach ye upon the housetops.

Christ's enemies use secret and deceptive means to oppose the gospel. But true disciples are open and courageous in their lives and witness. Followers of Jesus have nothing to hide. They do nothing for which they feel shame. Jesus said, "In secret have I said nothing"

(John 18:20). Jesus was the victim of false witnesses at His trial, but God saw to it that the truth was revealed. True disciples have nothing to fear because the Lord will one day reveal the secrets of men's hearts and expose them and judge them (Romans 2:16). The task of disciples is to proclaim God's message, not to please men. Because we are living in the light of the future judgment of God, the present judgment of men does not frighten us.

C. Fear God Only (v. 28)

28. And fear not them which kill the body, but are not able to kill the soul: but rather fear him which is able to destroy both soul and body in hell.

The Bible has much to say about fear. The writer of Proverbs 1:7 said, "The fear of the Lord is the beginning of knowledge." The psalmist admonished that men were to "serve the Lord with fear" (Psalm 2:11) and again that "the fear of the Lord is the beginning of wisdom" (111:10). The prophet Isaiah said "the fear of the Lord is his treasure" (33:6). Peter admonished his readers, "Honour all men. Love the brotherhood. Fear God" (1 Peter 2:17). And the writer of Revelation 11:18 indicated that rewards were to be given to those who fear the name of the Lord.

These statements do not mean to suggest that the only real basis for service is a deep penetrating fear of God. Not at all. When the words of Jesus are studied, quite a different meaning becomes clear. Luke, when recording the admonition of Jesus about seeking the Kingdom and putting it first, quoted Jesus as saying, "Fear not, little flock; for it is your Father's good pleasure to give you the kingdom" (12:32). Paul declared, "Ye have not received the bondage again to fear; but ye have received the Spirit of adoption" (Romans 8:15). Even though most of us have never felt the kind of catastrophic experience that occurred to the apostle Paul, we have felt the keen sense of fear that overwhelmed him and overwhelms all men when they come into personal contact with God. The fear is the same; only the degree is different.

This deep sense of fear, however, is a part of the old order of things. Paul was saying that men are not to draw back to live in this state of impending doom. The minds of the disciples of Jesus were to be freed from the devastating effect of paralyzing fear. Christians are to be free from crippling fears. The faith of Jesus is not built on fear but on faith.

D. God Protects His Own (vv. 29-31)

29. Are not two sparrows sold for a farthing? and one of them shall not fall on the ground without your Father.

30. But the very hairs of your head are all numbered.

31. Fear ye not therefore, ye are of more value than many sparrows.

Warren Wiersbe writes, "It did not cost much to purchase sparrows in the market. If we compare these verses with Luke 12:6, we discover that sparrows were so cheap that the dealer threw in an extra one! Yet the Father knows when a sparrow falls to the ground; and the Father is there. If God cares for sparrows in such a marvelous way, will He not also care for His own who are serving Him? He certainly will! To God, we are of greater value than many sparrows."

Wiersbe continues, "God is concerned about all of the details of our lives. Even the hairs of our head are numbered—not counted in total, but numbered individually!

God sees the sparrow fall to the ground, and God sees when a hair falls from the head of one of His children. When He protects His own, He protects them down to the individual hairs (Luke 21:18). There is no need for us to fear when God is exercising such wonderful care over us" *(Meet Your King).*

What role should fear play in the life of a Christian?

II. CONFESS CHRIST OPENLY (Matthew 10:32-39)

A. Christ Honors His Own (vv. 32, 33)

32. Whosoever therefore shall confess me before men, him will I confess also before my Father which is in heaven.

33. But whosoever shall deny me before men, him will I also deny before my Father which is in heaven.

To confess is to declare a thing to be true and to commit oneself to it. A Christian confession is an open declaration of the truth of the gospel in Christ as well as a commitment to Him. Note the confession "before men." It is more than a verbal statement; it is to choose a way of life and to walk in it. If one truly confesses Christ, he is placing himself in the whole sphere of Christ.

Observe that of such a person Jesus said that He will confess him before the Father. The man in Christ and Christ in the man presents him blameless before God (see John 15:1-8). Before man, the Christian says of Christ, "He is mine." Before God, Christ says of the Christian, "He is mine." In like fashion, the man who ultimately, publicly, and finally says of Christ, "I know Him not," of him, before the Father, Christ will say, "I know him not." Note that in both confession and denial, God holds man responsible. Christ's work for man's redemption is finished. God now calls upon man to act *(Preacher's Homiletic Commentary).*

B. Conflict Is Inescapable (vv. 34-39)

34. Think not that I am come to send peace on earth: I came not to send peace, but a sword.

35. For I am come to set a man at variance against his father, and the daughter against her mother, and the daughter in law against her mother in law.

36. And a man's foes shall be they of his own household.

Warren Wiersbe declares that once we have identified with Jesus Christ and confessed Him, we are part of a war. We did not start the war; God declared war on Satan (Genesis 3:15). On the night our Lord was born, the angels declared "on earth peace" (Luke 2:14). But Jesus seemed to deny this truth: "I came not to send peace, but a sword" (Matthew 10:34). Had Israel accepted Him, He would have given them peace. But the people refused Him, and the result was "a sword." Instead of there being "peace on earth," there is "peace in heaven" (Luke 19:38). He has "made peace through the blood of his cross" (Colossians 1:20) so that men can be reconciled to God and to each other *(Meet Your King).*

Believers will often be misunderstood and persecuted even by those who are the closest to them, yet they must not permit this to affect their witness. It is important that Christians suffer for Jesus' sake, and for righteousness' sake, and not because they are difficult to live with. There is a difference between the "offence of the cross" and offensive Christians.

The Christian message unites to Christ, but it may divide from men.

Even the intimate circle may be broken. In early Christian persecution, the informants were often members of one's own household.

37. He that loveth father or mother more than me is not worthy of me: and he that loveth son or daughter more than me is not worthy of me.

38. And he that taketh not his cross, and followeth after me, is not worthy of me.

Believers must be prepared to pay a price for their faith. The word *loveth* in verse 37 has to do with choice, not with mere emotion. They must be ready even to die, if necessary, for their faith in Christ.

To take up one's cross (v. 38) meant to bear it to the place of crucifixion. In Paul's day, to confess "Jesus is Lord" rather than "Caesar is lord" could have meant death. "Faithful unto death" means faithful to the point of dying. Jesus does not ask His disciples to do more than He did, but He asks no less.

39. He that findeth his life shall lose it: and he that loseth his life for my sake shall find it.

There are no ties, draws, or stalemates in the game of life. Everyone either wins or loses. You are either victor or vanquished. However, one cannot determine the final result until the record is complete.

It often appears that a man has lost if the judgment is made on outward circumstances, financial affluence, political power, or social popularity. The size of a man's bank account, the elaborate home one lives in, the size of the car he drives, the fine texture of the clothes he wears, or the height of the office he holds are poor yardsticks by which to measure a person's success.

The psalmist declared, "A little that a righteous man hath is better than the riches of many wicked" (Psalm 37:16).

The wise man stated, "There is that maketh himself rich, yet hath nothing: there is that maketh himself poor, yet hath great riches" (Proverbs 13:7).

In writing to the Corinthians, Paul gave some strange paradoxes: "As sorrowful, yet alway rejoicing; as poor, yet making many rich; as having nothing, and yet possessing all things" (2 Corinthians 6:10).

Was Jesus referring to the same principle when He declared, "He that findeth his life shall lose it: and he that loseth his life for my sake shall find it"?

By all the standards of materialistic, political, monetary, and ecclesiastical methods of evaluation, Jesus died as a failure. He lost the good will of His own people; He lost the plaudits of the multitudes; He lost His friends; and, finally, He lost His life. He died penniless, friendless, and homeless. He was a complete failure—or was He? Conversely, He was the world's greatest success. He gave up His food for 40 days in the wilderness, but He conquered temptation. He lost His blood on the cross of Calvary, but He won salvation for every man. He lost His life on Golgotha, but He won immortality for the race.

As Jesus hung on the cross, the Jews cried out, "He saved others; himself he cannot save," and, "If thou be the Son of God, come down from the cross" (Matthew 27:40, 42). He could have saved Himself; He could have come down. By so doing He would have won temporary relief from the suffering and the admiration of onlookers. But by so doing He would have lost the battle with sin, Satan, and death. He had to lose to win.

The apostle Paul lost his seat in the Sanhedrin; he lost position, comfort, pleasure, and ease; he lost the cheers of the populace, and finally he lost his life. His life seemed a complete failure, but he won the crown of righteousness and heard the great Judge say, "Well done!"

Christians by the millions have been burned at the stake, crucified on crosses, boiled in oil, and left to rot in dirty, damp dungeons. But they won eternal life.

Martin Luther lost his place of high ecclesiastical honor; he lost the approval of the Pope; he lost the comfort and security of the church. But he won the experience of justification; he won faith in the Bible as God's Word; he won millions of people to vital religion.

John Wesley lost a place of educational honor at Oxford; he lost the approval of bishops; he lost the comfort and ease of a rich parish. But he won a heart experience, and he won thousands to God.

Nothing worthwhile can be won easily. It takes sacrifice, self-denial, and suffering. You must lose some things if you would win the most important thing—the "pearl of great price."

We must lose some things here if we would gain all things hereafter. The songwriter George Bennard put it in words we can all understand:

So I'll cherish the old rugged cross,
Till my trophies at last I lay down;
I will cling to the old rugged cross,
And exchange it someday for a crown.

The Christian life is a paradox. Jesus lives by dying; so do His disciples. Satan offered Jesus "life" (Matthew 4), but Jesus saw the fallacy. The selfish life is in reality the dying life. But he who dies to self lives unto God. Finding by losing, keeping by giving, living by dying—in so doing the Christian mounts the stairs to the throne. If a man confesses in Christ, and Christ confesses in him, there can be no other way.

Why is modeling the Christian life perhaps the best way of witnessing?

III. REWARDS OF DISCIPLESHIP (Matthew 10:40-42)

A. Receiving Disciples (vv. 40, 41)

40. He that receiveth you receiveth me, and he that receiveth me receiveth him that sent me.

41. He that receiveth a prophet in the name of a prophet shall receive a prophet's reward; and he that receiveth a righteous man in the name of a righteous man shall receive a righteous man's reward.

Not everyone will reject the witness of believers. There are those who will welcome them and receive a blessing. After all, as disciples of Christ, they are ambassadors of the King. And the King will see to it that they are rewarded for what they do. When people receive the witness, they welcome the King, for the witnesses are His representatives. Second Samuel 10 provides an example of what happens when people mistreat and reject the envoys of the King.

Alexander Maclaren writes of verse 41: "Notice the variety of the reward according to the character. The prophet has his, the righteous man has his. . . . That is to say, each level of spiritual or moral stature receives its own prize. All courses of obedient conduct have their own appropriate consequences and satisfaction. Every character is adapted to receive, and does receive, in the measure of its goodness, certain blessings and joys, here and now. 'Surely the righteous shall be recompensed in the earth' " *(A Year's Ministry).*

B. Supporting Disciples (v. 42)

(Matthew 10:42 is not included in the printed text.)

Jesus emphasized that the blessing is not automatic. It all depends on the attitude of the host. If he receives the ambassador as a prophet (a spokesman for God), then he gets one reward; if he receives him only as a righteous man, there is another reward. But even a cup of cold water, given with the right spirit, brings its own reward.

In the hot, parched land of Palestine, a cup of cold water would often be the most precious gift that could be offered, although it would cost nothing. For that reason alone, Christ says "only." And those who do this—far from losing their reward—will receive it in the most liberal measure.

How important are rewards for the believer?

REVIEW QUESTIONS

1. Why does opposition come to believers?
2. What does it mean to fear God?
3. How does God protect His own when opposition comes to them?
4. What does it mean to confess Christ?
5. Explain the rewards of discipleship.

GOLDEN TEXT HOMILY

"HE THAT FINDETH HIS LIFE SHALL LOSE IT: AND HE THAT LOSETH HIS LIFE FOR MY SAKE SHALL FIND IT" (Matthew 10:39).

Nowhere else in Scripture is the honesty of Christ more exemplified than in this passage. It is the intention of Jesus to attract people to the kingdom of heaven, but never with false impressions. The way to the Kingdom is by way of the Cross, and the Cross is by no means identified with easy achievement or access. Listen to the words of Christ in verse 38: "He that taketh not his cross, and followeth after me, is not worthy of me." Again in Matthew 16:24: "If any man will come after me, let him deny himself, and take up his cross, and follow me." Christ is explicit in stating the hardships for all who accept His invitation to follow Him.

Jesus suggests the possibility of warfare; this may include conflict in the home, with the family being divided. The Jews believed that "the day of the Lord," the day when God would directly involve Himself in the world events, would be a time of family divisions. The rabbis stated it, and Christ later confirmed it: "For I am come to set a man at variance against his father . . . and the daughter in law against her mother in law. And a man's foes shall be they of his own household" (10:35, 36).

There is always the possibility that one may eventually have to choose between his dearest earthly asset and Jesus Christ. People in every generation since Christ came have been confronted with this dilemma. John Bunyan was forced to make a choice of either remaining with his wife and children, including a blind child, or going to prison for preaching without license. He went to prison.

There are divided houses today, brought about because some members have chosen to follow Christ and others refuse to follow Him. Jesus even implied that a person's life might be in jeopardy by following Him. Again the Golden Text: "He that findeth his life shall lose it, and he that loseth his life for my sake, shall find it." The life one loses may be only the old life of sin, and the life he finds is the life of joy in Christ; but it might also mean losing one's physical life while finding eternal life. However severe the hardships, whatever price to pay, living in Christ is worth what one may be required to pay.—**Wayne S. Proctor (Retired), Former Pastor, Lexington, Kentucky**

SENTENCE SERMONS

THE BELIEVER is called to a life of total commitment to Jesus Christ.

—**Selected**

ONLY A BURDENED HEART can lead to fruitful service.

—**Alan Redpath**

WHAT WE CAN DO for Christ is the test of service. What we can suffer for Him is the test of love.

—***Speaker's Sourcebook***

THE CURE for fear is faith.

—**Norman Vincent Peale**

EVANGELISM APPLICATION

THE FIRST STEP TO DISCIPLESHIP IS ACCEPTING CHRIST AS SAVIOR.

Before people can accept Christ and become His disciples, they must first hear about Him, then they must receive the message.

One of the biggest sins on earth is for Christians to remain silent while souls are walking blindly down the road to hell. What if someone in your community were sentenced to die in the gas chamber. What if the entire community begged the governor to pardon the man. And what if, finally, the governor sent for you and said, "I'm going to pardon the man, and I am going to send the pardon by you. The man will be kept in the death cell until you deliver the pardon and he willingly accepts it."

What if you put the pardon in your pocket, went home, and became so engrossed in other things that you forgot the pardon and did nothing about it. One morning you picked up the paper to read that the man whose pardon you held had died in the gas chamber that day. You would be to blame for the death of that man.

This illustrates the neglect of lost souls all about us. God has entrusted us with the message of deliverance, and too often we keep it to ourselves.

ILLUMINATING THE LESSON

The believer is called to a life of total commitment to Jesus Christ. The nature of God demands full human commitment to Him. "God is either God of all or He is not God at all." It is His very nature to occupy all of life. "What I mean by God," says Melvin E. Wheatley, "is not the manager of a small, fourth-floor department of life called religion. What I mean by God is the owner and operator of the whole business." Halfhearted commitments deprive one of the divinely given spiritual resources. In such a case, one seeks Christian discipleship on the basis of human resources, and thus spiritual fulfillment never appears.

DAILY BIBLE READINGS

M. Courageous Faith.
Daniel 3:8-18
T. Fearless Devotion.
Daniel 6:4-10
W. Bold Witness. Acts 4:13-20
T. Steadfast in Christ.
Acts 21:8-13
F. Live Out Your Faith.
1 Peter 4:1-11
S. Rejoice in Persecution.
1 Peter 4:12-19

Overcoming Prejudice

Study Text: Luke 10:25-37

Objective: To acknowledge the sin of prejudice and eliminate it from our lives.

Time: Late in A.D. 29

Place: Perhaps Chorazin or Bethsaida

Golden Text: "Thou shalt love the Lord thy God with all thy heart, and with all thy soul, and with all thy strength, and with all thy mind; and thy neighbour as thyself" (Luke 10:27).

Central Truth: Genuine love overcomes prejudice.

Evangelism Emphasis: Christians are effective witnesses when they replace prejudice with love.

PRINTED TEXT

Luke 10:25. And, behold, a certain lawyer stood up, and tempted him, saying, Master, what shall I do to inherit eternal life?

26. He said unto him, What is written in the law? how readest thou?

27. And he answering said, Thou shalt love the Lord thy God with all thy heart, and with all thy soul, and with all thy strength, and with all thy mind; and thy neighbour as thyself.

28. And he said unto him, Thou hast answered right: this do, and thou shalt live.

29. But he, willing to justify himself, said unto Jesus, And who is my neighbour?

30. And Jesus answering said, A certain man went down from Jerusalem to Jericho, and fell among thieves, which stripped him of his raiment, and wounded him, and departed, leaving him half dead.

31. And by chance there came down a certain priest that way: and when he saw him, he passed by on the other side.

32. And likewise a Levite, when he was at the place, came and looked on him, and passed by on the other side.

33. But a certain Samaritan, as he journeyed, came where he was: and when he saw him, he had compassion on him,

34. And went to him, and bound up his wounds, pouring in oil and wine, and set him on his own beast, and brought him to an inn, and took care of him.

35. And on the morrow when he departed, he took out two pence, and gave them to the host, and said unto him, Take care of him; and whatsoever thou spendest more, when I come again, I will repay thee.

36. Which now of these three, thinkest thou, was neighbour unto him that fell among

the thieves?
37. And he said, He that shewed mercy on him. Then said Jesus unto him, Go, and do thou likewise.

LESSON OUTLINE

I. LOVE GOD AND NEIGHBOR
   A. The Question
   B. The Injunction
II. ACT WITH COMPASSION
   A. The Pious Lawyer
   B. The Robbed Traveler
   C. The Religious Cleric
   D. The Righteous Layman
   E. The Renegade Samaritan
III. SHOW MERCY TO ALL
   A. The Original Question
   B. The Personal Application

LESSON EXPOSITION

INTRODUCTION

The bias of a particular culture can be reflected in the way its people define problems and in their use of descriptive terms. Parson Thwackum, in *Tom Jones*, said, "When I mention religion, I mean the Christian religion, and not only the Christian religion but the Protestant religion, and not only the Protestant religion but the Church of England."

What is *prejudice?* The term means a value-loaded attitude toward another person because that person belongs to a different group. A prejudice is literally a prejudgment, a judgment arrived at before examining any evidence about the case or the person involved. For example, a racial prejudice is any judgment of a person based on race rather than on knowledge of his individual qualities.

Prejudice can be either positive or negative; that is, a person can be prejudiced in favor of a group as well as against it. Usually, however, when we say that someone is prejudiced, we mean that he or she looks down on or is hostile to all members of another group.

Prejudice differs from discrimination. Prejudice refers to an attitude; discrimination refers to behavior. Prejudice refers to one's judgments of others; discrimination refers to one's actions toward others.

According to sociologists there are four basic traits associated with prejudice—*ethnocentricity, stereotyping, scapegoating,* and *rationalization.*

An *ethnocentric* person tends to put his or her own group or culture on an unrealistically high pedestal and to see virtue only in that group or culture. A person is *stereotyping* when that person forms an image of a typical member of a minority group in his or her mind and then assumes that this image applies to all members of the minority group. *Scapegoating* is the tendency to blame another group for all sorts of social ills and evils. *Rationalization* is an attempt to justify some behavior. In short, prejudiced people manage to find some excuse for being prejudiced.

No one is born with prejudices. They are learned. Small children show no prejudices until they observe them in their elders. Prejudices are largely unconscious. They are acquired through contact with prejudices, not through actual contact with other groups. Prejudices are unrelated with reality.

Prejudices exist because they are satisfying. People hold prejudices because they enjoy them. Some may feel a bit guilty about them, but people enjoy many things that bring feelings of guilt. Prejudice can bring many emotional satisfactions—a feeling of superiority, an excuse for failure, an outlet for aggression and hostility—and can be a very useful weapon in power struggles between groups. But prejudice is a sin, and God is against it, as can be seen in the case of the Good Samaritan and the Jewish traveler.

I. LOVE GOD AND NEIGHBOR (Luke 10:25-28)

A. The Question (vv. 25-27)

25. And, behold, a certain lawyer stood up, and tempted him, saying, Master, what shall I do to inherit eternal life?

After leaving Galilee, Jesus started on His great mission to Perea, the region east of the lower Jordan. It was through this region that Jesus had sent not only the Twelve (Luke 9) but also the seventy (Luke 10). These messengers of the grace of God had experienced great success, and Jesus received them with joy as they returned and made their reports.

At this time, when the fame of the Great Teacher was at its height in the region of Perea, a lawyer came to Him. It is important to remember that the law of the Jews, governing all details of their lives, was not only that of Moses, as set forth in the Pentateuch, but also the commentary and interpretation of many centuries of rabbis. The Jewish lawyers were teachers. They expounded the law, and their work merged with that of the scribes, the recorders of the law. In fact, in Mark 12:28, recording a similar but later event, the questioner was a scribe.

Apparently Christ was seated on this occasion, in the posture of a teacher, with the crowd around Him—listening, asking questions, and responding to His questions. The fame of Jesus as a teacher had reached "a certain lawyer," and he wanted to see for himself if Jesus was really the teacher others claimed Him to be. The lawyer's question was not meant to badger, but to test, prove, or verify Jesus' wisdom and learning. In this situation, Jesus respected the inquiry and submitted to investigation.

The lawyer asked, "What shall I do to inherit eternal life?" The tense of the verb implies that by a single performance of some one thing, "eternal life" could be secured. In essence,"What heroic act must be performed? What great sacrifice must be made?" he inquired.

We have to remember that this man was a legalist. He conceived of eternal life as an inheritance—something to be received at some future time, as the appropriate reward for being good. He never conceived of eternal life as God's free and immediate gift to the morally bankrupt.

26. He said unto him, What is written in the law? how readest thou?

What shall I do to inherit eternal life? Ever since Adam and Eve were expelled from the Garden of Eden, this has been the most important question of fallen man. In every generation the question is asked, and sooner or later it will arise in the mind of every person who comes into contact with divine truth as revealed in the Law and the Gospels.

The very business of the man questioning Jesus was to know the Law. He should have been able to answer his own question. To the Law, which the lawyer honored, studied, and taught, Jesus turned his attention: "What is written in the Law? . . . How do you read it?" (v. 26, *NIV*).

27. And he answering said, Thou shalt love the Lord thy God with all thy heart, and with all thy soul, and with all thy strength, and with all thy mind; and thy neighbour as thyself.

The lawyer responded to Jesus by quoting from Deuteronomy 6:5 and 10:12. These words were very familiar to all Jews. They were part of the Shema, or "Hear" (6:4), so called from its opening word in the Hebrew. The Shema was repeated twice a day by every devout Jew and was also written on the parchment enclosed in the phylacteries (little boxes worn on the sleeve).

The *heart* signified the affections; the *soul*, the spiritual essence or personality; the *strength*, the physical nature; and the *mind*, the mental capacity. We are to love God with body, mind, and soul, and not merely with emotion. This is the meaning of this great statement in verse 27.

The lawyer's response also included Leviticus 19:18: "Thou shalt love thy neighbour as thyself." This was the answer to a similar question by the great Hillel (a first-centruy Jewish teacher). Love of one's neighbor summarizes morality, as love of God summarizes religion. The two together constitute the highest wisdom.

The word *love* in these verses is *agape*, the highest kind of love. Such love is selfless, sacrificial, and long-suffering (1 Corinthians 13:4-7). Its fullest expression is seen in John 15:13: "Greater love hath no man than this, that a man lay down his life for his friends."

B. The Injunction (v. 28)

28. And he said unto him, Thou hast answered right: this do, and thou shalt live.

Jesus was always ready to compliment when He could, giving even to His critics and His foes all possible commendation. It was true that perfect love to God and man would constitute godly living; it was also true that love would manifest itself in good deeds. The verb translated *do*, because of its form in the original language, should be understood as "continually do, be doing, or make a habit of doing."

Was the lawyer's question sincere? Explain your answer.

II. ACT WITH COMPASSION (Luke 10:29-35)

A. The Pious Lawyer (v. 29)

29. But he, willing to justify himself, said unto Jesus, And who is my neighbour?

The lawyer realized at once that he had convicted himself by asking a question to which he really knew the answer. In his embarrassment he asked another question to show that he really did have a point—"Who is my neighbor?" The Jews split hairs over this question and used the term conveniently. By definition a *neighbor* was a "nigh-dweller," but the Jews made racial exceptions.

The lawyer had no difficulty accepting the reality of God and the necessity of loving Him with heart, soul, strength, and mind. What troubled him was his neighbor. As a lawyer he belonged to a class of teachers who taught that no Gentile was a neighbor. For him, as a Jew, neighborliness was limited to members of the Jewish nation.

The lawyer asked the second question to justify himself, not to the crowd around him, but to his own conscience. In his own mind there lurked the suspicion that the rejection of a Gentile, simply because he was a Gentile, was not right. Dodging the issue, he tried to shift the responsibility to Jesus, who answered him with the parable of the Good Samaritan. It was far more important that the lawyer know how to be a neighbor than to identify his neighbor.

B. The Robbed Traveler (v. 30)

30. And Jesus answering said, A certain man went down from Jerusalem to Jericho, and fell among thieves, which stripped him of his raiment, and wounded him, and departed, leaving him half dead.

In His parable Jesus identified two geographical boundaries: Jerusalem and Jericho. *Jerusalem*, meaning "the vision of peace," was the seat of blessing, of history, of religion, of privilege. This was the city where God had chosen to place His name, the center of worship and communion with Himself. *Jericho* was the city of the curse (see Joshua 6:26), yet it was a scenic city where priests lived when not fulfilling their tasks in Jerusalem.

Jericho was about 20 miles from Jerusalem. The road between them led down into the Valley of Jehoshaphat, by the Garden of Gethsemane, rounded the Mount of Olives by a gradual rise, sank to the village of Bethany, and from there descended into the Jordan Valley and toward the Dead Sea—an afternoon's journey. Jericho was the hub of the Jordan Valley and was the only important city in the area. The city itself had always been notorious for its vices and for the weak, indolent character of its inhabitants. Furthermore, the road that led down to Jericho had always been extremely dangerous. It was infested with criminals who assailed the travelers, robbing and sometimes murdering them; and from these deeds of violence, it derived a ghastly name, the Ascent of Blood.

Jesus said that a man going from Jerusalem to Jericho was accosted by thieves who robbed him, beat him, left him half-dead, and departed. This was an exceptional act of violence and brutality.

Jesus had often traveled this road going up to Bethany, and the parable may well have been based on an actual occurrence.

C. The Religious Cleric (v. 31)

31. And by chance there came down a certain priest that way: and when he saw him, he passed by on the other side.

"By chance" a priest was going from Jerusalem to Jericho at this particular time. The word used here for *chance* means "coincidence." It has been described as the occurrence of one event with another, which often seems chance to us, but it is indeed the working of a higher power. The priest could not avoid meeting the man who needed help. However, he did not look upon the event as a happy coincidence, a God-planned opportunity to help a needy soul. He saw the beaten, bleeding traveler, but passed by on the other side.

D. The Righteous Layman (v. 32)

32. And likewise a Levite, when he was at the place, came and looked on him, and passed by on the other side.

The Levites were of the same tribe as the Pharisees, but they came from one of the inferior branches. They were appointed to assist the priests, but were not themselves, like Aaron and his sons, to approach the most holy things.

The priest may have known that the Levite was behind him and may have thought the care of the wounded man was more in keeping with his duties; the Levite, in turn, may have excused himself on the grounds that he was only following the example of the priest. Moved more by curiosity than by humanity, the Levite came and looked at the bleeding form, but that was all. He passed by on the other side.

E. The Renegade Samaritan (vv. 33-35)

33. But a certain Samaritan, as he journeyed, came where he was: and when he saw him, he had compassion on him,

34. And went to him, and bound up his wounds, pouring in oil and wine, and set him on his own beast, and brought him to an inn, and took care of him.

35. And on the morrow when he departed, he took out two pence, and gave them to the host, and said unto him, Take care of him; and whatsoever thou spendest more, when I come again, I will repay thee.

The third man to come along the Jericho road was a Samaritan. The Samaritans were a mixed race, descendants of idolatrous Israelites and Assyrian captives. They occupied the central position of Palestine, between Galilee and Judea. The Jews hated the Samaritans because of their mixed race and their imperfect adherence to Judaism. They would have nothing to do with them. Indeed, it was considered an act of pollution for a Jew to pass through the country of Samaria, and the feeling was mutual. The Samaritans had just recently (Luke 9:53) refused to receive Christ and His disciples because they were on their way to Jerusalem.

Undoubtedly the lawyer was amazed when Jesus introduced a Samaritan as the only one on the lonely road willing to befriend a helpless Jew. The very man from whom no needy Jew could expect the least relief was the one who gave it.

The Samaritan could have excused himself on the grounds that the road from Jerusalem to Jericho led through Jewish territory and that such cases of distress ought to be cared for by the Jews. But he did nothing of the sort. He saw a man stripped of his clothing, left half-dead. He asked no questions. He thought of no difficulties or inconveniences. He at once gave the appropriate assistance.

We are told that the Samaritan's compassion was not limited to sympathy. He took the time and trouble to give aid. He acted as well as pitied. He spared no expense. Stranger though he was, he went to the fallen, bound up his wounds, set him on his own animal, brought him to an inn, and took care of him. And that was not all. The next day he gave the host of the inn money, saying, "Take care of him; and whatsoever thou spendest more, when I come again, I will repay thee."

How do you explain the behavior of the priest and the Levite?

III. SHOW MERCY TO ALL (Luke 10:36, 37)

A. The Original Question (v. 36)

36. Which now of these three, thinkest thou, was neighbour unto him that fell among the thieves?

Jesus returned to the original question—the definition of neighbor. He asked the lawyer which one of the three was a neighbor to him "that fell among the thieves?"

B. The Personal Application (v. 37)

37. And he said, He that shewed mercy on him. Then said Jesus unto him, Go, and do thou likewise.

Notice that the lawyer avoided using the hated name *Samaritan*. Martin Luther called him a "haughty hypocrite" for this. The lawyer's answer was simply, "He that shewed mercy on him."

Jesus said to the lawyer, "Go, and do thou likewise." If these words of Christ mean anything, a Christian ought to be ready to show kindness and brotherly love to everyone in need. Our kindness must extend not merely to our families and friends, but to all men, whatever the occasion. We must avoid excessively screening possible recipients of our help. The only important questions should be, Are they in trouble? Do they really want help? If so, according to the teaching of this parable, we should help them. We should regard the whole world as our parish, and the whole race of mankind as our neighbors. We should seek to be the friend of everyone who is oppressed, neglected, afflicted, sick, poor, ignorant, starving, or dying.

The meaning of the parable is plain: The world needs more than policy; it needs healing and practical instruction and an appreciation of other people, which is the essence of applied Christianity.

Christian kindness is more than words. It reveals itself in deed and in truth. Christian love is practical. It is a love that involves self-sacrifice and self-denial, in time and in money and in trouble. It is a love that is seen not merely in talking, but in acting, not merely in profession, but in practice.

How would you define neighbor?

REVIEW QUESTIONS

1. What question did the lawyer ask Jesus?
2. How did Jesus respond to the lawyer's question?
3. Who were the Samaritans?
4. What was the attitude of the priest and Levite?
5. How did Jesus define *neighbor?*

GOLDEN TEXT HOMILY

"THOU SHALT LOVE THE LORD THY GOD WITH ALL THY HEART, AND WITH ALL THY SOUL, AND WITH ALL THY STRENGTH, AND WITH ALL THY MIND; AND THY NEIGHBOUR AS THYSELF" (Luke 10:27).

The Supreme Question Meets the Supreme Answer

The question regarding life beyond death has commanded the attention of all generations. No one has reached such lofty heights, and no one has fallen to such depraved depths, that he has not been concerned with life after death.

The Right Question

Most cultures have felt there is something that can be done in life which will affect life after death.

Some have given gifts great and small. Some have arranged to have facilities and commodities placed in their grave or in their tomb. Some have even arranged for their wives to be killed at their death so they would have companionship in the life beyond death. Many have called for a minister to whom they unburdened their soul of guilt. This list could go on and on, but the point is made that the question "What shall I do to inherit eternal life?" is of supreme importance.

To the Right Person

When one needs information concerning health problems, it is reasonable that he should consult a doctor.

When one needs information concerning legal matters, it is reasonable that he should ask a lawyer.

When one needs council regarding financial investments, it is reasonable that he should interrogate a banker.

Likewise, when the supreme question of life is to be posed, the person of top priority is the Prince of Life himself. He has the answer.

The Right Answer

The answer is a dual one which constitutes two pegs upon which all the Law and the Prophets hang.

The Master of Life cuts through the volumes and reveals the very heart: Love God right and love your fellow beings right and you will have attained eternal life. **—Excerpts from the *Evangelical Sunday School Lesson Commentary*, Vol. 32**

SENTENCE SERMONS

GENUINE LOVE overcomes prejudice.

—Selected

PREJUDICE IS the child of ignorance.

—William Hazlitt

AGAPE LOVE is profound concern for the well-being of another, without any desire to control that other, to be thanked by that other, or to enjoy the process.

—Madeline L'Engle

MERCY IMITATES GOD and disappoints Satan.

—St. John Chrysostom

ILLUMINATING THE LESSON

This parable illustrates the fact that love is the basis of correct relationship both to God and to one's fellowman. It involves the *stewardship of time*. The Good Samaritan did not hesitate to interrupt his journey and alter his plans when he saw a need. It further illustrates the *stewardship of ability*. He was not a physician, but he knew the "first aid" of the day and made good use of the skills he possessed. Also the parable exemplifies the *stewardship of possessions*. The Good Samaritan gave the use of his donkey, his food, and his money—all to minister to the needs of an absolute stranger belonging to a hostile race. And primarily it illustrates the *stewardship of the love of God*. The Samaritan had compassion on the wounded man. He carried God's tender mercy in his heart, the mercy that had been shown to him and that he was glad to share with others.

DAILY BIBLE READINGS

M. Fear Gives Rise to Prejudice. Exodus 1:7-14
T. Prejudice Displeases God. Numbers 12:1-9
W. Ministering Despite Social Barriers. John 4:5-14
T. God Loves All People. Acts 10:1-5, 9-15, 28
F. Fulfill God's Royal Law. James 2:1-9
S. Salvation for All. Revelation 5:1-10

The Empty Tomb (Easter Sunday)

Study Text: John 20:1-18

Objective: To review the events of the Resurrection and worship Christ as our risen Lord.

Time: A.D. 30

Place: Jerusalem

Golden Text: "Christ died for our sins according to the scriptures; . . . he rose again the third day according to the scriptures" (1 Corinthians 15:3, 4).

Central Truth: The resurrection of Christ is fundamental to the Christian faith.

Evangelism Emphasis: Christians must tell the unsaved the good news of Christ's resurrection.

PRINTED TEXT

John 20:1. The first day of the week cometh Mary Magdalene early, when it was yet dark, unto the sepulchre, and seeth the stone taken away from the sepulchre.

2. Then she runneth, and cometh to Simon Peter, and to the other disciple, whom Jesus loved, and saith unto them, They have taken away the Lord out of the sepulchre, and we know not where they have laid him.

3. Peter therefore went forth, and that other disciple, and came to the sepulchre.

4. So they ran both together: and the other disciple did outrun Peter, and came first to the sepulchre.

5. And he stopping down, and looking in, saw the linen clothes lying; yet went he not in.

6. Then cometh Simon Peter following him, and went into the sepulchre, and seeth the linen clothes lie,

7. And the napkin, that was about his head, not lying with the linen clothes, but wrapped together in a place by itself.

8. Then went in also that other disciple, which came first to the sepulchre, and he saw, and believed.

9. For as yet they knew not the scripture, that he must rise again from the dead.

10. Then the disciples went away again unto their own home.

11. But Mary stood without at the sepulchre weeping: and as she wept, she stooped down, and looked into the sepulchre,

12. And seeth two angels in white sitting, the one at the head, and the other at the feet, where the body of Jesus had lain.

15. Jesus saith unto her,

Woman, why weepest thou? whom seekest thou? She, supposing him to be the gardener, saith unto him, Sir, if thou have borne him hence, tell me where thou hast laid him, and I will take him away.

16. Jesus saith unto her, Mary. She turned herself, and saith unto him, Rabboni; which is to say, Master.

17. Jesus saith unto her, Touch me not; for I am not yet ascended to my Father: but go to my brethren, and say unto them, I ascend unto my Father, and your Father; and to my God, and your God.

DICTIONARY

Mary Magdalene (MAG-duh-lean)—John 20:1—A woman out of whom Jesus had cast seven devils (Mark 16:9). She was from the town of Magdala, located on the shore of the Sea of Galilee.

Sepulchre (SEP-ul-ker)—John 20:1—A tomb hewn out of solid rock. It belonged to Joseph of Arimathea.

Rabboni (rab-BOW-nigh)—John 20:16—The Hebrew word for Master. A title of respect for knowledge of the Law.

LESSON OUTLINE

I. CONFUSED DISCIPLES
   A. Discovery
   B. Perplexity
   C. Trust

II. THE RISEN LORD
   A. Persistence
   B. Seeing

III. THE MESSAGE SHARED
   A. Recognition
   B. Delivering

LESSON EXPOSITION

INTRODUCTION

The resurrection of Jesus Christ is one of the best-attested facts in history. But prejudice against believing anything that is connected with the Bible has always been great. In fact, within hours of His death men began to develop theories to deny His resurrection, and they have continued until the present. Let us review a few of these before we look at the empty tomb.

There is the theory that Jesus Christ and His friends conspired to promote the falsehood of His resurrection: "His disciples . . . stole him away" (Matthew 28:13). It is notable that the theory was so preposterous that Matthew did not even take the trouble to refute it. If that were true, those who forsook Him and fled at the time of His crucifixion must have suddenly taken on great courage to face the Roman Guard and steal His dead body! And, what about the guards themselves? Were they overpowered? Were they asleep?

Some believe that Christ never actually died—that after a short lapse of consciousness, He revived and lived long enough to see Paul and others. In answer, it is sufficient to state here that the Gospel records that He really died, and the Epistles confirm the statement.

The vision theory states that the appearances of Christ were purely subjective, caused by the excited state of mind of the disciples who longed so much to see Him that they thought they did see Him, but it was only a vision. In response to this, we may ask the question: Would it be possible that such a delusion would have done so much for the early church? It is simply impossible.

Some people accept the dream theory—that some person heard Christ was risen and told it to Peter and John, who in turn passed it on. In answer, we would suggest that for Christianity, with all its glorious accomplishments, to have come from a mere dream is absolutely incredible.

The temperature theory states that the temperature in the tomb revived the body because Christ was not dead when placed there. This theory does not take into account other significant facts concerning His death, such as the total loss of blood from His body when the soldier pierced His side.

Some argue that there were no appearances at all to be accounted for, only the very dramatic affirmation by the disciples that Christ was alive. This, it is suggested, gave rise to a misunderstanding in the early church. To refute this, we have the Scripture record that about 514 individuals saw Christ after His resurrection. Could they all have been deluded?

Finally, there is the theory that the appearances of Christ were not purely subjective but objective—that these appearances were visions He gave for the comfort of His own. It was equivalent to sending a telegram from heaven to earth to let them know that all was well. In answer to this, and all the other theories, we have the empty tomb.

I. CONFUSED DISCIPLES (John 20:1-10)

A. Discovery (vv. 1, 2)

1. The first day of the week cometh Mary Magdalene early, when it was yet dark, unto the sepulchre, and seeth the stone taken away from the sepulchre.

The first day of the week was Sunday, which has become the Christian Sabbath, in remembrance of this great event when Christ arose from the grave, replacing the Jewish Sabbath—the seventh day of the week.

One of the most remarkable proofs of the authenticity of the Gospels' account of the Resurrection is its record of our Lord's first appearance. Any false historian would have had Jesus appearing first to Peter or James or John, or perhaps to Caiaphas or to Pilate—but certainly not to a woman, and certainly not to one out of whom He had cast seven demons. It should be remembered that until the teachings of our Lord had had time to do their work, women were looked down upon. Therefore, this magnificent honor to Mary Magdalene would have seemed strange to the early Christians. No false historian would have dreamed of inventing it.

Mark and Luke recorded that there were other women at the tomb in addition to Mary. Some believe that John mentioned only Mary because he felt she was the most important. She was the woman out of whom Jesus had cast seven demons and who afterward followed Him and ministered to Him from her possessions.

The women were at the tomb early in the morning with spices to complete the embalming of the body of Jesus, hastily begun on Friday by Nicodemus and Joseph of

Arimathea, but left unfinished because the Sabbath had begun. Such work was unlawful to do on the Sabbath.

Jesus had been buried in the new tomb of Joseph of Arimathea, a member of the Sanhedrin and a secret disciple. The tomb, cut out of rock, was in a garden near Calvary. Thus, Christ made His grave "with the rich," according to the prophecy of Isaiah 53:9.

As they drew near to the tomb, the women wondered aloud how they would manage to roll back the great stone which closed the entrance. They were evidently unaware of the sealing of the stone and the posting of the guards, which would have made their task impossible. But, like most of our worries, theirs proved unnecessary, for as they reached the tomb, they saw to their surprise that the stone had been removed. They jumped to the conclusion that the Lord's body had been stolen.

2. Then she runneth, and cometh to Simon Peter, and to the other disciple, whom Jesus loved, and saith unto them, They have taken away the Lord out of the sepulchre, and we know not where they have laid him.

When she reached the tomb, Mary was surprised to find that the stone blocking the entrance had been rolled away. Fear seized her mind. After looking at the scene for a while, she ran and found Simon Peter and "the other disciple, whom Jesus loved." On meeting them, she excitedly exclaimed, "They have taken away the Lord out of the sepulchre, and we know not where they have laid him." The thought of resurrection did not enter her bewildered mind. Obviously she thought Jesus was still dead.

B. Perplexity (vv. 3-8)

3. Peter therefore went forth, and that other disciple, and came to the sepulchre.

4. So they ran both together: and the other disciple did outrun Peter, and came first to the sepulchre.

It was natural that Mary Magdalene should run with her disturbing news to Peter, for he was the leader of the apostles. It was natural that he should start instantly for the tomb, being always impulsive. It was natural that John should go with him, for all through the Gospel narratives we find these two together. It was also natural that John, being the youngest of the apostles, should outrun Peter, who was probably the oldest.

5. And he stooping down, and looking in, saw the linen clothes lying; yet went he not in.

6. Then cometh Simon Peter following him, and went into the sepulchre, and seeth the linen clothes lie,

7. And the napkin, that was about his head, not lying with the linen clothes, but wrapped together in a place by itself.

8. Then went in also that other disciple, which came first to the sepulchre, and he saw, and believed.

When John reached the open tomb, perhaps his loving reverence caused him to hesitate to enter. On the other hand, Peter the impulsive plunged right through the entrance, and John followed. What they saw was proof of some strange happening.

Peter and John discovered upon close inspection that the linen clothes were lying in a manner that informed them at once that these had not been unwound from the body of Jesus, but that Christ's body, in resurrection, had come through the linen clothes, leaving them flat on the slab of stone. The clothes no doubt still contained the undisturbed spices which Joseph of Arimathea and Nicodemus had placed there (John 19:39, 40). The napkin, a separate piece of cloth from that which was wound about the body, was resting in a place by itself; it was where Jesus' head had been.

John's decision to enter the tomb may have been because of Peter's startled exclamation. And "he saw, and believed" (v. 8). The arrangement of the clothes and the napkin assured him that Christ's body had not been removed, either by friend or foe, but that Christ himself had slipped out of His cerements and was risen from the dead. John was the first believer in the Resurrection, with Peter soon joining in that belief.

C. Trust (vv. 9, 10)

9. For as yet they knew not the scripture, that he must rise again from the dead.

10. Then the disciples went away again unto their own home.

Since the disciples did not yet understand the meaning of the Scriptures indicating that Christ would rise from the dead, it is easy to see why they would be perplexed at what they saw. Nevertheless, from our perspective it is only logical to assume that if the binding clothes had not been in the tomb, one could have concluded that the body of Jesus had been carried out. If they had been folded up in the tomb, one might conclude that someone unwound them from His body. But since they were lying undisturbed, just as they had been around the body of Christ and the body was not within, there could only be one conclusion: Christ had risen from the dead. It is significant that all the Gospels are silent as to the precise time when Christ came forth from the tomb. No one saw Him rise from the dead. But the tomb was empty early on the first day of the week after His death and burial.

The fundamental doctrine of Christianity is the resurrection of Christ. According to the Scriptures, faith in the resurrection of Christ is essential to salvation. Many who admit the necessity of the death of Christ deny the importance of His bodily resurrection.

The apostle Paul declared, "If there be no resurrection of the dead, then is Christ not risen: and if Christ be not risen, then is our preaching vain, and your faith is also vain. Yea, and we are found false witnesses of God; because we have testified of God that he raised up Christ: whom he raised not up, if so be that the dead rise not" (1 Corinthians 15:13-15).

Discuss the necessity of the bodily resurrection of Jesus.

II. THE RISEN LORD (John 20:11-16)

A. Persistence (vv. 11-13)

(John 20:13 is not included in the printed text.)

11. But Mary stood without at the sepulchre weeping: and as she wept, she stooped down, and looked into the sepulchre,

12. And seeth two angels in white sitting, the one at the head, and the other at the feet, where the body of Jesus had lain.

Some believe that Mary went on to notify other disciples after she had given her news to Peter and John; others think she may have lingered to talk with Mary the mother of Jesus, who was staying in John's house. The two disciples running to the tomb may have reached it much sooner than she could. At any rate, Mary Magdalene felt unable to remain away from the spot where the beloved form of her Savior had lain, and she came back to visit it, even though the body had been removed.

As Mary wept, she stooped to look inside the tomb. Peering into the tomb, she entertained a faint hope that the body of Jesus might be there. Instead she saw two angels sitting where Jesus had lain. They sat in mute adoration, guarding the holy spot.

It is important to remember what had happened between the burial of Jesus and His resurrection. When the Jewish rulers discovered that Joseph and Nicodemus had possession of the body of Jesus and had buried it honorably (so it would not be thrown with the bodies of criminals into the horrible valley of Gehenna), they began to worry about what the disciples of Jesus might do. Going to Pilate, they told him that Jesus had promised to rise from the grave on the third day, and they feared His disciples would steal the body and hide it, pretending a resurrection. Therefore they asked for an official sealing of the tomb and for guards to make sure the tomb would not be opened. The governor agreed to these provisions. (See Matthew 27:57-66 and John 19:38-42.).

To seal a tomb in those days, a strong cord was passed around the stone in the door of the tomb, and the two ends were drawn out to the sides of the door. Then the wax, or clay seal, was placed on the cord where it crossed in front of the stone door. This method attached the cord to the stone door and to the two sides of the door, so that the stone could not be moved without breaking the seals. The penalty for tampering with one of these seals was death. The Roman guard would also be put to death if he permitted the seal to be tampered with or fell asleep while on duty.

Pilate and the Jews thought they had taken all precautions. But there was one thing they had not counted on occurring—a supernatural event. Matthew 28 records there was a great earthquake. A shining angel descended from heaven, rolled back the stone from the entrance to the tomb and sat upon it (vv. 2-4). The Roman guards swooned in terror—so fearful was the event; and on awaking they rushed off to tell the Jewish rulers what had happened. These crafty schemers saw themselves exposed to a great peril—a Jesus risen from the dead, heading a group of exultant followers. They extricated themselves from this predicament as best they could. They bribed the soldiers to say that Christ's disciples stole the body while they were asleep, and agreed to save them from punishment by the Roman authorities. This falsehood, along with others, has persisted down to the present time (vv. 11-15).

In John 20:13, the angels asked Mary why she was weeping. Mary's response to the angels implies a complete lack of understanding of what had been happening: "Because they have taken away my Lord, and I know not where they have laid him" (v. 13). Before the angels had a chance to offer comfort and assurance, Mary interrupted them. She explained why she was heartbroken. How could she be otherwise when Christ was not there and she did not know where He was! It is interesting that she replied promptly and naturally to the angels as though she did not immediately recognize them as angels.

Note the change in Mary's language on this occasion. When she first reported to Peter and John, she said, "They have taken away the Lord" (v. 2). Now she said "*my* Lord." This indicates the depth of her devotion, but not hers to the exclusion of others. Every child of God may feel this right of fellowship in the Savior. Christ is *the* Lord, *our* Lord, and *my* Lord.

B. Seeing (vv. 14-16)

(John 20:14 is not included in the printed text.)

We are not told why Mary turned. Perhaps she heard a footstep behind her. Perhaps there was something in the gaze of the angels, looking past her, that suggested someone to be in back of Mary, out in the garden. She saw Jesus but did not recognize Him (v. 14). This is not difficult to understand. It was still early dawn, and objects were indistinct. Besides, her eyes may well have been dazzled by the sight of the angels, and she had also been weeping.

15. Jesus saith unto her, Woman, why weepest thou? whom seekest thou? She, supposing him to be the gardener, saith unto him, Sir, if thou have borne him hence, tell me where thou hast laid him, and I will take him away.

Jesus asked the same question the angels had asked (tears being so incongruous with that joyous morning), but He added a more intimate question: "Whom are you looking for?" Mary thought He was the gardener, not from His clothes or appearance but because He was there in the garden.

It is important to note that Mary did not name her Master to the supposed gardener. She simply said *Him*—"If thou have borne him hence . . . I will take him away." It is the language of one so absorbed in the thought of her Lord that she thought it unnecessary to name Him, and assumed, as a matter of course, that the gardener understood whom she meant.

16. Jesus saith unto her, Mary. She turned herself, and saith unto him, Rabboni; which is to say, Master.

The verbal exchange between Jesus and Mary is one of the most touching scenes in the Bible. Jesus responded to Mary's desire to care for the body of her Lord with one word—*Mary*. When Mary heard Jesus call her name, she recognized Him and responded immediately with *Rabboni*, which means "Master."

III. THE MESSAGE SHARED (John 20:17, 18)

A. Recognition (v. 17)

17. Jesus saith unto her, Touch me not; for I am not yet ascended to my Father: but go to my brethren, and say unto them, I ascend unto my Father, and your Father; and to my God, and your God.

Bowed down with grief, eyes filled with tears, Mary had not really looked at the supposed gardener. But suddenly her heart felt, her ears heard "Mary," her eyes saw. It was Jesus! Falling down at His feet, she probably threw her arms around His ankles and clung to Him. She would never let Him go. But Jesus gently pushed her away and said, "Touch me not." What He really said was, "Don't cling to Me." She must let Him go in the flesh, that she might receive Him in the Spirit—forever.

Jesus commissioned Mary to take a message to His disciples, who only three days before had forsaken Him and shamefully fled. Yet the risen Lord indicated by this message that all was forgiven.

B. Delivering (v. 18)

(John 20:18 is not included in

the printed text.)

Jesus' first goal was to bring back the wanderers, to bind up the wounds of their failure, to motivate them with new courage, and to restore them to their former place. This was love that passes knowledge. To trust deserters and to show confidence in failures is a love that is difficult for us to understand.

The comforting fact about all of this is that "Jesus Christ is the same yesterday, today, and forever" (Hebrews 13:8, *NKJV*). As He understood His disciples on the day of His resurrection, He understands us today. As He showed faith and trust in them, so will He deal with us until He returns. He will never break His word: "Him that cometh to me I will in no wise cast out" (John 6:37).

Why do you think Jesus selected a woman to deliver the Resurrection message?

REVIEW QUESTIONS

1. On what day of the week did Christ rise from the dead?
2. How was the stone rolled away from the tomb?
3. What did the two disciples discover in the tomb?
4. How did Mary respond to the angels?
5. How did Mary respond to Jesus?

GOLDEN TEXT HOMILY

"CHRIST DIED FOR OUR SINS ACCORDING TO THE SCRIPTURES . . . HE ROSE AGAIN THE THIRD DAY ACCORDING TO THE SCRIPTURES" (1 Corinthians 15:3, 4).

Christianity is not based on human reasoning or religious creeds, but it is based on the Word of God. It is in the Scripture where we find the real meaning and purpose for the death of Christ. We know that Christ died for the sins of the whole world, but the Scripture goes much further in explaining why it was necessary that Jesus gave His life for us. He rose again the third day as the Scriptures said He would. This lends credence to Scripture, which is sometimes viewed with skepticism.

Scripture reveals a law that deals with the absolute necessity for atonement. This law states, "Without [the] shedding of blood [there] is no remission [of sins]" (Hebrews 9:22). As we study the Scripture we realize the truth of this law. In the Old Testament, animals were brought to the altar of sacrifice and their blood was shed, before man could be forgiven of his sin. However, this was only a foreshadowing of the greatest sacrificial death in history.

The amazing thing about Jesus' sacrifice was that it was not for Himself but for you and me. Christ paid the price for the sins of the whole world. There was nothing else that would suffice, for only death could satisfy the law of God. In reality, God poured His wrath for sin upon His own Son, so that you and I, by our faith in Him, may go free. Isaiah gave us the heart of this truth when he declared that God "shalt make his [Christ's] soul an offering for sin" (Isaiah 53:10). To understand this is to understand the Atonement.

As a result of the Atonement, the only way a person may be redeemed is by his faith in Christ, who became our substitute. By our faith in Him, our penalty has been paid and we are counted righteous in the sight of God.

When Christ prayed in the Garden of Gethsemane and succumbed completely to the will of

God, He knew there was no other way that man could be redeemed. What a tragedy to reject Christ, who purchased redemption for us by dying in our place. What a Savior, what love; for what the law of God demanded, His love provided according to the Scriptures!—**Jerry Puckett, Superintendent, Customer Service and Product Assembly, Pathway Press, Cleveland, Tennessee**

SENTENCE SERMONS

THE RESURRECTION is fundamental to the Christian faith.

—**Selected**

THE RESURRECTION IS a true sunrising, the inbursting of a cloudless sky on all the righteous dead.

—**Horace Bushnell**

THE STONE was rolled away from the door, not to permit Christ to come out, but to enable the disciples to go in.

—***Draper's Book of Quotations for the Christian World***

THERE IS MORE EVIDENCE that Jesus rose from the dead than there is that Julius Caesar ever lived or that Alexander the Great died at the age of thirty-three.

—**Billy Graham**

EVANGELISM APPLICATION

CHRISTIANS MUST TELL THE UNSAVED THE GOOD NEWS OF CHRIST'S RESURRECTION.

At the battle of Inkerman a soldier was just able to crawl to his tent after he was struck down. When found, he was lying on his face, his open Bible before him, his hand glued fast to the page by his lifeblood which covered it. When his hand was lifted, the letters of the printed page were clearly traced upon it, and with the ever-living promise in and on his hand, they laid him in a soldier's grave. The words were these: "I am the resurrection, and the life: he that believeth in me, though he were dead, yet shall he live" (John 11:25).

ILLUMINATING THE LESSON

So clear is the evidence of Christ's resurrection that when Gilbert West, a celebrated infidel, selected this subject as the point of attack—sitting down to weigh the evidence and to digest the whole matter, although filled with prejudice—he was so startled with the abundant witness to the truth of this fact that he confessed himself to be a convert. He left as a heritage to the church a very valuable book titled *Observations on the Resurrection of Christ*. He studied the subject as a lawyer would examine the pros and cons in any matter of dispute. When he had finished, he declared the truth of the Resurrection, which is the fundamental doctrine of our faith, to be so exceedingly clear that he renounced his unbelief and became a convert to the Christian faith.

DAILY BIBLE READINGS

M. Living Redeemer. Job 19:21-27
T. Hope of Resurrection. Psalm 16:1-11
W. Jesus Christ Lives. Luke 24:36-44
T. Promise of Resurrection. John 5:19-29
F. Resurrection of Believers. 1 Corinthians 15:49-58
S. Newness of Life. Colossians 3:1-10

Seeking the Lost

Study Text: Luke 15:1-24

Objective: To recognize the lost condition of sinners and strive to win them to Christ.

Time: January - March A.D. 30

Place: Jerusalem

Golden Text: "Joy shall be in heaven over one sinner that repenteth, more than over ninety and nine just persons, which need no repentance" (Luke 15:7).

Central Truth: God seeks to reconcile sinners to Himself.

Evangelism Emphasis: God seeks to reconcile sinners to Himself.

PRINTED TEXT

Luke 15:4. What man of you, having an hundred sheep, if he lose one of them, doth not leave the ninety and nine in the wilderness, and go after that which is lost, until he find it?

5. And when he hath found it, he layeth it on his shoulders, rejoicing.

6. And when he cometh home, he calleth together his friends and neighbours, saying unto them, Rejoice with me; for I have found my sheep which was lost.

8. Either what woman having ten pieces of silver, if she lose one piece, doth not light a candle, and sweep the house, and seek diligently till she find it?

9. And when she hath found it, she calleth her friends and her neighbours together, saying, Rejoice with me; for I have found the piece which I had lost.

10. Likewise, I say unto you, there is joy in the presence of the angels of God over one sinner that repenteth.

11. And he said, A certain man had two sons:

12. And the younger of them said to his father, Father, give me the portion of goods that falleth to me. And he divided unto them his living.

13. And not many days after the younger son gathered all together, and took his journey into a far country, and there wasted his substance with riotous living.

14. And when he had spent all, there arose a mighty famine in that land; and he began to be in want.

15. And he went and joined himself to a citizen of that country; and he sent him into the fields to feed swine.

16. And he would fain have filled his belly with the husks that the swine did eat: and no man gave unto him.

20. And he arose, and came to his father. But when he was yet a great way off, his father saw him, and had compassion, and ran, and fell on his neck, and kissed him.

21. And the son said unto him, Father, I have sinned against heaven, and in thy sight, and am no more worthy to be called thy son.

22. But the father said to his servants, Bring forth the best robe, and put it on him; and put a ring on his hand, and shoes on his feet:

23. And bring hither the fatted calf, and kill it; and let us eat, and be merry:

24. For this my son was dead, and is alive again; he was lost, and is found. And they began to be merry.

LESSON OUTLINE

I. THE VALUE OF A SOUL
   - A. The Allegation
   - B. The Lost Sheep
   - C. The Lost Coin

II. CONSEQUENCES OF FOOLISH LIVING
   - A. The Discontent
   - B. The Waste of Sin
   - C. The Depths of Destitution

III. RESTORED TO FELLOWSHIP
   - A. The Awakening
   - B. The Return
   - C. The Welcome
   - D. The Confession
   - E. The Joy

LESSON EXPOSITION

INTRODUCTION

The unanimous testimony of Scripture is that man outside of Jesus Christ is lost. This tragic fact cannot be denied by those who accept the Word of God as authoritative and valid.

Actually, according to the Word of God there are only two classes of people—the saved and the lost. There is no middle ground. There is no halfway position. Each individual is in one or the other of these classes.

This fact is difficult for man to accept. He knows that he is not perfect, but it is difficult for him to see that his situation amounts to lostness. He believes there must be something in him, or something he can do, that will recommend him to God. There must be some other way to gain favor with God. He often concludes that God is too merciful to cast him away altogether.

The only reliable source of knowledge we have on man's lost condition is the Word of God. We cannot depend on philosophy, science, ethics, and nonbiblical religions because they are not revelational. They tend to commend man rather than convict him.

Man as a sinful creature has a depraved heart and a darkened mind; therefore, human consciousness and opinion are untrustworthy. It is impossible, apart from divine revelation, for man to form correct judgments about himself.

Man's lost condition points out his great need for salvation. Biblical salvation is the greatest concept ever to be entertained by the mind of man. The word *salva-*

tion, in its totality, includes all that God does for man, from eternity to eternity, to deliver man from sin and its consequences. Salvation is what God does for and in man.

The heavenly Father is the ultimate source of salvation. Salvation comes from God. It was God who loved the world from all eternity and sent His Son to die on Calvary for the sins of mankind. Jesus Christ as God's Son is the immediate source of salvation. Through His death on the cross, His resurrection, and His heavenly ministry, He secures our salvation. The personal source of salvation is the Holy Spirit. It is the Holy Spirit who convicts, illuminates, regenerates, and empowers us. The revealed source of salvation is the Word of God. It contains the message which is the power of God unto salvation to everyone who will believe. There are many words, phrases, and statements used in the Word of God to indicate the various aspects of salvation. For example, in the New Testament we have such words as *redemption, reconciliation, propitiation, forgiveness, regeneration, imputation, justification, sanctification, perfection, glorification.* All of these indicate some aspect of the work of God in behalf of man's salvation.

There are three aspects of salvation in relation to man's need: (1) The Bible indicates that the child of God was saved from the guilt and penalty of sin when he believed. (2) He is being saved from the power and domination of sin on the same principle of faith. (3) He is yet to be saved from the presence of sin into the presence of God.

I. THE VALUE OF A SOUL (Luke 15:1-10)

A. The Allegation (vv. 1, 2)

(Luke 15:1, 2 is not included in the printed text.)

Luke identified two classes of men as following the steps of Jesus and constantly attending them: (1) those who were attracted to Him because they liked to hear His Word, and (2) those who hated Him and His Word and yet, under the spell of an irresistible fascination, could not stay away from where He spoke. The Pharisees and scribes were as constant in attendance as the publicans and sinners who gathered together to hear Him.

Why did the publicans and sinners come to hear Christ? First of all, because He did not drive them away. He did not scorn them, as the Pharisees and scribes did. He was willing to let them come near. These publicans and sinners came near to Christ, not simply because He was willing to allow them to approach Him, but because they heard from Him words which they heard from no one else. They heard Him and marveled—"for he taught them as one having authority, and not as the scribes" (Matthew 7:29).

Note the fascination connected with envy and hatred and opposition that is indicated in verse 2. The Pharisees and scribes, observing how the publicans came around Christ, murmured. They thought themselves to be the best people in town. They were a very strict sect. They observed rigidly all ecclesiastical order. They were very careful in their observance of the prescribed feasts. They were exact in tithing all their property. And they were always certain they said their prayers and kept the feasts in the prescribed manner. However, they thought it unspeakable that this man should permit unlettered, ignorant people to come so close to Him. They said, "This man receiveth sinners, and eateth with them" (v. 2). You see, it was bad enough to receive them, but it was

10 times worse to sit down and eat with them. That miserable tax collector, that apostate Jew, that man who is epitome of submission to Rome—that he should come and be received and allowed to sit down at the same table. And that poor woman—surely, "This man, if he were a prophet, would have known who and what manner of woman this is that toucheth him: for she is a sinner" (Luke 7:39). That is the spirit of the Pharisees and the scribes. This is what motivated Jesus to tell the parables that followed.

B. The Lost Sheep (vv. 3-7)

(Luke 15:3, 7 is not included in the printed text.)

4. What man of you, having an hundred sheep, if he lose one of them, doth not leave the ninety and nine in the wilderness, and go after that which is lost, until he find it?

The sheep of this parable was lost, not because it intended to be lost, or wanted to be lost, but because it simply wandered away and could not get back. Alexander Maclaren described it this way: "It nibbled its way out of the path, out of the flock's companionship. The sheep knows only where the herbage is abundant and fresh and it goes there. Its inclinations are restrained by no sense of obligation. Many men live just so, without checking of inclination, without foresight" *(Expositions of Holy Scripture).*

Isaiah, in his portrait of the atoning work of Christ, spoke of humanity as sheep that have gone astray—everyone turning to his own way (53:6); and Jesus spoke of men as distressed and scattered because they are as sheep without a shepherd (Matthew 9:36). Unless the Shepherd seeks and finds the lost sheep, he will remain forever lost. The incarnation of the Son of God was the girding of Himself for such a task. In fact, all of His life in the flesh He followed the strays.

5. And when he hath found it, he layeth it on his shoulders, rejoicing.

6. And when he cometh home, he calleth together his friends and neighbours, saying unto them, Rejoice with me; for I have found my sheep which was lost.

The placing of the lost sheep upon the shoulders of the one finding it suggests the utter exhaustion in which the lost sheep was found. Sin always exhausts. Now that the sheep is found, the shepherd experiences joy.

The shepherd wants to communicate his joy with others, asking them to rejoice with him in the finding of the lost sheep.

God sustains a loss with every sinner that wanders away from Him. And God's great joy comes from the recovery of even one lost soul. And as George Hepworth put it, "Heaven and earth cannot be far apart if there is rejoicing in the one place over incidents which occur in the other."

C. The Lost Coin (vv. 8-10)

8. Either what woman having ten pieces of silver, if she lose one piece, doth not light a candle, and sweep the house, and seek diligently till she find it?

G. Campbell Morgan has an interesting explanation of this parable: "As the piece of silver in question represents less than a shilling in English money, or an American quarter, it does not seem feasible that the woman should search so diligently for such a small amount. But women of that time often wore upon their brow a frontlet that was called *semedi.* It was made up of coins, in themselves largely valueless . . . But it was a coin that had stamped upon it the image of authority. The frontlet signified betrothal or the marriage relationship. Whether it was of little monetary value or not, it was of priceless value to the woman who wore it. This is evidenced by the fact that she sought it diligently, sweeping the house until she found it" *(The Parables of the Kingdom).* Herbert Lockyer continues by saying, "Because the coin had sentimental value, and was an article of charm, and adornment, the woman's search for it was earnest and thorough. She was anxious to recover that which perfected the symbolism of her frontlet" *(All the Parables of the Bible).*

9. And when she hath found it, she calleth her friends and her neighbours together, saying, Rejoice with me; for I have found the piece which I had lost.

10. Likewise, I say unto you, there is joy in the presence of the angels of God over one sinner that repenteth.

In the parable of the sheep it was "Rejoice with me; for I have found my sheep which was lost"; here, it is "Rejoice with me; for I have found the piece which I had lost." In the first, it was the anguish of the sheep that was the central point of the story; in the second, it was the distress of the woman who had lost something.

In commenting on verse 10, Godet writes: "What grandeur belongs to the picture of this humble rejoicing which this poor woman celebrates with her neighbors when it becomes the transparency through which we get a picture of God himself, rejoicing with His elect and His angels over the salvation of a single sinner" *(Pulpit Commentary).*

What agencies does God use in seeking out the lost?

II. CONSEQUENCES OF FOOLISH LIVING (Luke 15:11-16)

A. The Discontent (vv. 11, 12)

11. And he said, A certain man had two sons:

12. And the younger of them said to his father, Father, give me the portion of goods that falleth to me. And he divided unto them his living.

Still seeking to make the hard-hearted Pharisees and scribes ashamed of their attitude toward the repentant publicans and sinners, Jesus told another parable. A certain man—representing the heavenly Father, whose searching love has been shown in the first two parables—had two sons. The younger son represents the publicans and sinners; the older son, the respectable and self-righteous Pharisees and scribes. The proportion of bad to good has steadily risen—one shepherd to a hundred sheep, one coin out of 10, and one of two sons to one father.

According to Jewish law (Deuteronomy 21:17) each son would receive the same proportion and inheritance from the father, except that the oldest son would receive an inheritance double that of any one of his brothers. The younger son here, then, asked for one-third of his father's estate. The request probably was not unusual, and yet it shows two things: The younger son chafed under the restraints that the home placed upon him, and he wanted to live a life which the environment of the home did not conveniently permit;

in addition to this, he needed money with which to accomplish his selfish purposes.

Concerning the attitude of the father, Godet writes: "In the father's consenting to the wish of his son, a very solemn thought is expressed, that of the sinner's abandonment to the desires of his own heart (Romans 1:24, 26, 28), the ceasing, on the part of the divine Spirit, to strive against the inclinations of a spoiled heart, which can only be cured by the bitter experiences of sin. God gives such a man over to his folly" *(Commentary on the Gospel of Luke).*

B. The Waste of Sin (vv. 13, 14)

13. And not many days after the younger son gathered all together, and took his journey into a far country, and there wasted his substance with riotous living.

14. And when he had spent all, there arose a mighty famine in that land; and he began to be in want.

The word *riotous* here means "abundant, dissolute, profligate." It is fast living without regard for the consequences. It is living wildly and carelessly, extravagantly and arrogantly, without restraint or control, a life enslaved to every debasing desire. How easy it is for a person to sink so low. It is from the word *riotous* that the parable gets its title, "The Prodigal Son"—the word *prodigal* coming from the Latin word *prodigere*, meaning "to squander." How often men must come to the end of their resources before they will throw themselves on the resources of God.

Sin is hunger. God had given this young man his heart's desire and sent leanness to his soul. The worst famine of all is not a famine of bread or thirst, but "of hearing the words of the Lord" (Amos 8:11); and in such a famine even "the fair virgins and young men faint for thirst" (8:13). The prophet Jeremiah recorded, "They have forsaken me the fountain of living waters, and hewed them out cisterns; broken cisterns, that can hold no water" (2:13).

Finding himself in want, this young man began to realize the emptiness of sin, how unsatisfactory it is, how false are its promises of pleasure and profit. Actually, he had been in want through all his months of discontent at home, but he did not know it.

C. The Depths of Destitution (vv. 15, 16)

15. And he went and joined himself to a citizen of that country; and he sent him into the fields to feed swine.

16. And he would fain have filled his belly with the husks that the swine did eat: and no man gave unto him.

Verse 15 implies that the citizen of the country, to whom he applied, was unwilling at first to give him a job and only relented after the young man's persistence.

This young man, a Jew, had now lost his independence and freedom, which, at first, he started out to fully enjoy. He had been driven to tasks which normally would have been revolting to him. Now, he who would not be treated liberally by his father, was compelled to be the servant of a foreign master. He who would not be ruled by God was compelled to serve the devil; he who would not abide in his father's palace was sent to the fields among swine.

The *husks* (v. 16) refer to the pods of the carob tree or locust tree, frequently called "St. John's bread," from the erroneous idea that its pods were the locusts which John the Baptist ate.

The swine were more important in the citizen's eyes than the one who fed them. His former companions, men and women on whom he had squandered his money, had no more use for him now that he was penniless. For true friendship one must go to God's children and not to the servants of sin.

What kind of prodigal sons do we have today?

III. RESTORED TO FELLOWSHIP (Luke 15:17-24)

A. The Awakening (v. 17)

(Luke 15:17 is not included in the printed text.)

The young man in the parable went out to *find himself,* or so he thought. But indulgence and sin so deceived him that he lost himself. Now the suffering of hunger, a consciousness of failure and shame, and hopelessness brought him back to himself. His experience illustrates the fact that life without God is madness. But he had not sunk so low that he could not still say "my father."

B. The Return (vv. 18, 19)

(Luke 15:18, 19 is not included in the printed text.)

The Prodigal was now determined to get out of the foreign country, out of his shame, out of his wasted daily life; furthermore, he was determined to go back home—back where things were right, back to the place from which he began to wander, back where love was. He was now ready to confess his sin, and that meant that he recognized the sin in his life. Going home would mean very little for him unless he went home repentant, a changed man—even willing to assume the role of a servant in his father's household instead of that of a son.

C. The Welcome (v. 20)

20. And he arose, and came to his father. But when he was yet a great way off, his father saw him, and had compassion, and ran, and fell on his neck, and kissed him.

The actual return to the father was the proper carrying out of his resolve. Note the prompt recognition, swift approach, and enthusiastic embrace by the father. The silence of the father on the question of the son's wayward and wicked behavior is most eloquent with love and compassion.

D. The Confession (v. 21)

21. And the son said unto him, Father, I have sinned against heaven, and in thy sight, and am no more worthy to be called thy son.

Genuine repentance does not spring from fear. Locked in his father's embrace, the fears of the son must have vanished entirely; and yet, he was deeply penitent. Genuine penitence is generated by exhibitions of love.

E. The Joy (vv. 22-24)

22. But the father said to his servants, Bring forth the best robe, and put it on him; and put a ring on his hand, and shoes on his feet:

23. And bring hither the fatted calf, and kill it; and let us eat, and be merry:

24. For this my son was dead, and is alive again; he was lost, and is found. And they began to be merry.

"And they began to be merry" (v. 24). Mirth is joy in high excitement, joy filling the soul to an overflow, and running into hilarity and glee. "They" would include the father, for he, indeed, originated the joy of the hour. Included in the "they" was also the son, for his was a gladness of unbounded gratitude for conscious and complete forgiveness. Gratitude is joy, and praise for mercy swells the anthems of heaven.

Luke 15 is devoted to illustrating how God, through Christ, seeks and finds the lost. Nothing brings such joy as returning to God, to obedience to God's law, to accepting as Savior God's only begotten Son.

Why was the father so quick to forgive his wayward son?

REVIEW QUESTIONS

1. What criticism prompted the parables in Luke 15?
2. Which parable condemns carelessness?
3. What do all three parables show about God?
4. Do you think the Prodigal Son always knew, deep down in his heart, that his father loved him?
5. What do you think the Prodigal learned from his waywardness?

GOLDEN TEXT HOMILY

"JOY SHALL BE IN HEAVEN OVER ONE SINNER THAT REPENTETH, MORE THAN OVER NINETY AND NINE JUST PERSONS, WHICH NEED NO REPENTANCE" (Luke 15:7).

In each of the three parables of grace in Luke 15 there is an emphasis upon joy: the joy of the shepherd and his friends and neighbors when, after long seeking, he brought his lost sheep back; the joy of the woman with her friends and neighbors when, after diligent searching with lamp and broom, she found her precious coin; the joy of the father and his household when, possibly after years of agonized waiting, praying, and yearning, the Prodigal Son came home. In all three parables, the earthly joy with which all of Christ's hearers could identify was a mirror in which was reflected the greater joy that is experienced "in heaven over one sinner that repenteth." Dr. I.H. Marshall says, "The thought is of the angels rejoicing along with God." Dean Alford thinks that possibly "the spirit of just men made perfect" is included. He also says, "The ministering spirits rejoice over every soul that is brought out of the dust of death into God's treasure-house by the searching of the blessed Spirit."

Thus Christ gives us a glimpse into heaven, both now and on the day of resurrection. We witness the rejoicing of God himself and of His angelic hosts as they gaze upon the multitude of lost souls found and redeemed and restored. In Job 38:7 the Lord said to Job, "[Where wast thou] when the morning stars sang together, and all the sons of God [the angelic beings] shouted for joy?" Thus it was when God laid the foundations of the earth. Jesus, however, paints a picture of the angelic choirs shouting with even greater joy as they behold the wondrous products of redeeming grace.

Jesus himself (the Good Shepherd) will share that joy, for "he shall see . . . the travail of his soul, and shall be satisfied" (Isaiah 53:11). He was strengthened in His earthly life and ministry during the years of searching and suffering and dying for the lost, by "the joy that was set before him" (Hebrews 12:2)—the hope of rescued sheep, found coins, and reconciled prodigals.

Paul cherished the same blessed hope. To the Thessalonian Christians he said: "For what is our hope, or joy, or crown of rejoicing? Are not even ye in the presence of our Lord Jesus Christ at his coming?" (1 Thessalonians 2:19).

And shall not all who seek with determination and sacrifice for lost sheep—who search diligently with the lamp of the Word and the broom of the Spirit for lost human coins stamped with the image of God, who pray and mourn and wait with hearts of love for lost prodigals—have their part in those joyful celebrations in the eternal presence of God?—**Noel Brooks, D.D., Avon, England, (Retired) Writer, *Adult Sunday School Teacher Quarterly*, International Pentecostal Holiness Church, Oklahoma City, Oklahoma**

SENTENCE SERMONS

GOD SEEKS to reconcile sinners to Himself.

—Selected

SEEKING FOR LOST SOULS applies a supernatural remedy for the need of the world.

—Faris Whitesesell

THE FOOL has his answer on the edge of his tongue.

—Arabian Proverb

EVERY STORY of conversion is the story of a blessed defeat.

—C.S. Lewis

EVANGELISM APPLICATION

GOD SEEKS TO RECONCILE SINNERS TO HIMSELF.

How the father received his lost son: As soon as the wanderer was recognized, on flying feet the old man ran to meet him. Before the son had time to speak a word, the father had him in his arms, pressed him to his bosom, covered his cheek with passionate kisses, and lifted up his voice and wept for joy. And this is God—God as He is drawn by the hand and seen in the face of Him whom He sent to seek and to save us, to bring us back, to open a way of reconciliation—the God who, unwilling that any should perish, invites and waits our coming.

ILLUMINATING THE LESSON

How the father rejoiced over the Prodigal! While grief retires from observation; joy must be expressed. In this parable, so true (in all its parts) to nature, this feature of joy stands out beautifully. To these servants the father had never told his grief; but now the Prodigal has come back, and the father's heart is bursting with joy and he tells them of it. So God rejoices in His ransomed, and lets them rejoice in Him. The sun that shines on you shall set, summer streams shall freeze, and the deepest wells shall go dry—but not His love. His love is a stream that never freezes, a fountain that never fails, a sun that never sets at night, a shield that never breaks in fight—whom He loves, He loves to the end.

DAILY BIBLE READINGS

M. Divine Invitation.
Deuteronomy 4:25-31

T. Eternal Choices.
Deuteronomy 30:15-20

W. Tragedy of the Lost.
Jeremiah 50:4-9

T. Compassionate Savior.
Matthew 9:35-38

F. Confronting Lost Individuals.
Luke 19:1-10

S. One Flock, One Shepherd.
John 10:14-18

Heaven or Hell?

Study Text: Luke 16:19-31

Objective: To realize that an eternal destiny awaits every person and prepare for eternity.

Time: The story of the rich man and Lazarus was told by Jesus sometime between January and March A.D. 30.

Place: Probably Jerusalem

Golden Text: "God sent not his Son into the world to condemn the world; but that the world through him might be saved" (John 3:17).

Central Truth: Our eternal destiny depends on our response to God's offer of salvation.

Evangelism Emphasis: Sinners need to know the eternal consequences of rejecting God's offer of salvation.

PRINTED TEXT

Luke 16:19. There was a certain rich man, which was clothed in purple and fine linen, and fared sumptuously every day:

20. And there was a certain beggar named Lazarus, which was laid at his gate, full of sores,

21. And desiring to be fed with the crumbs which fell from the rich man's table: moreover the dogs came and licked his sores.

22. And it came to pass, that the beggar died, and was carried by the angels into Abraham's bosom: the rich man also died, and was buried;

23. And in hell he lift up his eyes, being in torments, and seeth Abraham afar off, and Lazarus in his bosom.

24. And he cried and said, Father Abraham, have mercy on me, and send Lazarus, that he may dip the tip of his finger in water, and cool my tongue; for I am tormented in this flame.

25. But Abraham said, Son, remember that thou in thy lifetime receivedst thy good things, and likewise Lazarus evil things: but now he is comforted, and thou art tormented.

26. And beside all this, between us and you there is a great gulf fixed: so that they which would pass from hence to you cannot; neither can they pass to us, that would come from thence.

27. Then he said, I pray thee therefore, father, that thou wouldest send him to my father's house:

28. For I have five brethren; that he may testify unto them, lest they also come into this place of torment.

29. Abraham saith unto him, They have Moses and the

prophets; let them hear them.

30. And he said, Nay, father Abraham: but if one went unto them from the dead, they will repent.

31. And he said unto him, If they hear not Moses and the prophets, neither will they be persuaded, though one rose from the dead.

LESSON OUTLINE

- I. CONTRASTING CONDITIONS IN LIFE
  - A. The Rich Man
  - B. The Poor Man
- II. CONTRASTING DESTINIES
  - A. Blessedness
  - B. Anguish
  - C. Conversation
- III. GOD'S WORD BRINGS LIFE
  - A. The Five Brothers
  - B. The Verdict

LESSON EXPOSITION

INTRODUCTION

It is important to note that in this parable we do not have a complete life history of either the rich man or Lazarus. Scripture seems to assume that the luxurious self-indulgent lifestyle is characteristic of an unrenewed, worldly mind. When associated with indifference to the suffering that exists everywhere around us, self-indulgence is itself proof that the Spirit of Christ does not dwell in such a person. The rich man was not cast into torment because he was rich, but because he had given himself to pride and worldly-mindedness and selfishness, forgetting God.

It is also important to note that we do not have the complete life history of Lazarus. He was poor, he was afflicted, he was neglected and cast off by men; but so have many others, who when they died, did not find an abundant entrance into the kingdom of heaven. Worldliness of spirit may be as hidden—and disaffection toward God and holiness as inveterate and deep—as poverty and sores cloaked under a covering of fine linen and purple. It was not because he was poor that Lazarus was carried into Abraham's bosom. The real condition of the heart toward God was revealed by the test applied. If Lazarus had not been patient as well as poor, accepting as well as afflicted, he would have been refused a drop of water in the next world just as he had been refused a few falling crumbs of bread in this one; for in Christ Jesus neither riches avail anything, nor lack of riches, but a new creature.

The basic purpose of the parable is to show the inveterate stubbornness of unbelief, and the utter inadequacy of all conceivable means of removing it, when the plan of God is neglected and rejected. "If they hear not Moses and the prophets, neither will they be persuaded, though one rose from the dead" (v. 31). Unbelief is a disease of the heart. Evidence and miracles cannot reach it; but it can be reached and cured only by the enlightening and transforming power of the Spirit of God.

I. CONTRASTING CONDITIONS IN LIFE (Luke 16:19-21)

A. The Rich Man (v. 19)

19. There was a certain rich man, which was clothed in purple and fine linen, and fared sumptuously every day.

The "certain rich man" is known as Dives, which is the Latin term for *riches.* Through tradition he has been given the name Ninevis, and his contrast to Lazarus is the chief feature of the story. This unnamed man, as far as the Bible is concerned, was wealthy and of a wealthy family. It is believed that he and his five brothers, as rich as he, together formed one of the great magnates of the community. Because of his riches, this man was able to dress in the best clothes and to eat and drink sumptuously every day.

Herbert Lockyer has an interesting description of this man: "Although the rich man, along with his family, was godless, nothing is said about him being positively vicious. He is not described as being guilty of any glaring sin, or a monstrous member of society. He is not before us as a tyrant or an oppressor of the poor. Had he been notoriously selfish or uncharitable, he would not have allowed Lazarus to lie at his gate, day after day, beseeching alms. Without doubt, he lived a luxurious self-indulgent life, but he was not arbitrarily condemned because of his wealth. He went to hell because he failed to realize that he was God's trustee, with wealth and influence that could have been used for God's glory, and for the spiritual and material benefit of his fellowmen. Thus it was his wickedness and not his wealth that brought him eternal misery. His selfishness (not any conspicuous evil deeds, but his failure to have God at the center of his whole life) brought him under the condemnation of Him to whom he owed all that he possessed. No vices or crimes are laid to his charge. His sin was that he lived only for the present" *(All the Parables of the Bible).*

B. The Poor Man (vv. 20, 21)

20. And there was a certain beggar named Lazarus, which was laid at his gate, full of sores,

21. And desiring to be fed with the crumbs which fell from the rich man's table: moreover the dogs came and licked his sores.

The second man in the parable is identified by Jesus as Lazarus. He is not to be confused with the brother of Mary and Martha of Bethany; this man was a beggar. He is the only named character of the parables, and his name may have been given him because of its significance. It is a contraction meaning "helped of God" or "God help him." It is supposed he was a leper.

The word *beggar* suggests the idea of poverty. In contrast to the rich man, he was poor and destitute. The rich man was clothed in purple and fine linen; the beggar, in rags. The rich man lived in a stately mansion; the beggar was laid by sympathetic friends at the gate of the mansion. The rich man had a healthy, well-nourished body; the beggar was full of sores. The rich man fared sumptuously every day; the beggar lived on crumbs from his table. The rich man had physicians to care for him; dogs licked the sores of Lazarus.

In commenting on Lazarus, Herbert Lockyer states: "The merit of Lazarus was not in the sad fact that he was poor, helpless, and diseased. A beggar may be as vile and filthy in heart as he may be in body. No, the precious thought is that while lying at the rich man's gate, hungrily eyeing the pieces brought him, he learned contentment. As a son of Abraham, he found his help in God. As a pensioner upon divine bounty, he knew his bread and water would be sure. Ultimately he went to Paradise not because he was poor and diseased but because, in spite of his pitiful condition, he had served God, finding his constant help in Him" *(All the Parables of the Bible)*.

Is there any relationship between poverty and sainthood? Explain.

II. CONTRASTING DESTINIES (Luke 16:22-26)

A. Blessedness (v. 22a)

22a. And it came to pass, that the beggar died, and was carried by the angels into Abraham's bosom. . . .

The earthly end came for Lazarus. All Jesus said of him was, "The beggar died." Nothing was said about his burial. He was so destitute he was unable to leave anything for a decent burial. Did he have a burial, or was his diseased and emaciated body hurried away roughly and without feeling by the city officials to the potter's field?

G. Campbell Morgan says that beggars like Lazarus were not buried. "Almost inevitably the cleaners passed the dead body, unknown, unclean, and hurried it away in the early dawn until they came to Tophet, Gehenna, the rubbish and refuse heap of fire, where they flung the body in. That is a known fact of the time, and the very fact we are not told Lazarus was buried, leads us to suppose such an end for him" *(The Parables of the Kingdom)*.

Although Lazarus' body had an ignominious end, the angels came and carried his soul to the paradise of God. These angelic guardians of the righteous escorted the spirit of Lazarus to the realms of bliss.

The term "Abraham's bosom" was one of the three names common among the Jews to refer to the future state of blessedness. The other two were "paradise" and "the throne of glory." George Hodges says, "The phrase is to be understood by comparison with the account of the last supper, where the apostle whom Jesus loved leaned on his breast. That is, in the fashion of that day and place, they reclined on couches at their meals, each resting on his left arm: first the host, then next to him, leaning on his breast, the person of most honor" *(The Path of Life)*.

Lazarus had perhaps often longed for death; now his hour of redemption had come. No one missed him here below, except perhaps the dogs. But "Precious in the sight of the Lord is the death of his saints" (Psalm 116:15). Someone has aptly said that the beggar did not die, but only his misery, his diseased body. His soul entered at once into the blessed communion of the patriarchs and of all the pious Israelites in paradise. On earth nobody had taken care of him; now angels were his servants. The hope of a future rest in God's kingdom sustained his confidence amid his earthly sufferings; and now he realized that rest.

B. Anguish (vv. 22b, 23)

22b. The rich man also died, and was buried;

23. And in hell he lift up his eyes, being in torments, and seeth Abraham afar off, and Lazarus in his bosom.

The rich man's earthly life ended quite differently than Lazarus' life. He died as all men must, whether rich or poor. However, he "was buried." In all probability he had a very ornate funeral with hired mourners and all the pageantry that his riches could afford.

Herbert Lockyer writes of the rich man's burial: "Yet though his body was conveyed to an ornate tomb with all the honors, his soul on departure from earth was solitary. No angelic convoy appeared to escort him to the regions of the blest. He went straight to hell, there to endure torment. For him as a Jew, there was no height of seraphic bliss, a resting place in Abraham's bosom. All the ostentatious splendor of the rich man could not buy off the rider of the pale horse, or secure for him eternal happiness beyond the grave. In his death, the rich man was more of a pauper than Lazarus had ever been. He went into eternity stripped bare of all he had possessed and with the terrible realization that an eternal inheritance would never be his. How different it would have been if God, not gold, had been first in his life" *(All the Parables of the Bible).*

C. Conversation (vv. 24-26)

24. And he cried and said, Father Abraham, have mercy on me, and send Lazarus, that he may dip the tip of his finger in water, and cool my tongue; for I am tormented in this flame.

Lonsdale Ragg said the rich man was a typical Pharisee in hades; he claimed Abraham as his father, though he found himself on the wrong side of the chasm; and he looked for signs *(Westminster Commentary).*

It is strange that the rich man did not pray to God. Why did he not pray to God? Charles G. Finney says the rich man "knew and he most deeply felt that he had cast off God and [that] God in turn had cast him off. He could not think of speaking to God" *(Sermons on the Way of Salvation).*

The proud man was so humbled that he begged for Lazarus to come and dip the tip of his finger in water to cool his tongue. The expression suggests water falling, drop by drop, from the finger which has been immersed in it. In his own words, "I am in anguish in this flame."

Charles G. Finney says of this picture: "If any one regards this picture of Hades as too harsh, remember who painted it: the gentle, tender, compassionate, forgiving Christ, who died on the Cross to save men from an agony and misery that he fully knew. Why did he not ask for an ocean of water, or a pailful at least, or a pitcherful? Why restrict himself to the least drop? Plainly he knew himself to be placed beyond all good. He knew this was the utmost he could ask for, and even this is denied him!" *(Sermons on the Way of Salvation).*

It should be pointed out that the rich man did not confess sin, did not ask to be forgiven, did not repent, and did not ask to be in Abraham's bosom.

25. But Abraham said, Son, remember that thou in thy lifetime receivedst thy good things, and likewise Lazarus evil things: but now he is comforted, and thou art tormented.

26. And beside all this, between us and you there is a great gulf fixed: so that they which would pass from hence to you cannot; neither can they pass to us, that would come from thence.

The whole tone of Abraham's reply is certainly gentle, though firm—"[Lazarus] is comforted, and thou art tormented." Herbert

Lockyer writes: "The word for *comfort* is *parakaleo*, the word from which we get *Paraclete*, the designation of the Holy Spirit, the Divine Comforter. The word means to call near, and Lazarus had been called near to Abraham's side and to the God he had trusted. The rich man was tormented and begged Abraham to send Lazarus with relief for his anguish. This means that over the gulf dividing the two spheres, voices could be distinctly heard. With perfect spiritual intelligence Abraham knew all about the prosperity of the rich man, as well as the penury of Lazarus, and told the rich man to remember the past. He was remembering—and such memory constituted his hell and was the flame tormenting him" *(All the Parables of the Bible)*.

The great teaching of verse 26 is that there is absolutely no hope for the lost ever being brought out of hell into heaven in the next life. What men are when they leave this earth—as far as the principles of their characters are concerned, and their attitudes toward God and their fellowmen—will characterize them for all eternity.

Why was the rich man suffering torment in hades, while Lazarus was comforted in Abraham's bosom? A.B. Bruce answers with the following: "It was not because the one was rich and the other was poor, for a rich man can be a saint, and Abraham himself, the very one mentioned here as in Paradise, was exceedingly wealthy; on the other hand a poor man can live in blackest iniquity. No specific vices are assigned to the rich man, and no specific virtues are ascribed to Lazarus. All we can say about Lazarus is that, as his name indicates, his help was in God, against whom he did not murmur, even in his terrible sufferings. He was poor in this world's goods, but rich in faith. Of the rich man, much more can be said. Christ does not portray him as a monster of humanity, but simply as an average man of the world, living a self-centered life, coming short of the true ideal, while not without such small virtues as men of the world ordinarily practice" *(The Training of the Twelve)*.

In commenting on the fact of the rich man being tormented, H.A. Ironside writes: "The Scriptures tell us about hell in order that we may never go there. The Word of God makes plain the way of life and salvation through Jesus Christ, who bore, in our stead, on Calvary's cross, the bitter anguish that lost men must endure eternally after they refuse His grace. How foolish for men to reason and argue about the possibility of an end to hell when they may find One here on earth who will save them from entering upon its woe" *(The Sunday School Times)*.

Why do you think Jesus told about the rich man's suffering?

III. GOD'S WORD BRINGS LIFE (Luke 16:27-31)

A. The Five Brothers (vv. 27-30)

27. Then he said, I pray thee therefore, father, that thou wouldest send him to my father's house:

28. For I have five brethren; that he may testify unto them, lest they also come into this place of torment.

29. Abraham saith unto him, They have Moses and the prophets; let them hear them.

30. And he said, Nay, father Abraham: but if one went unto them from the dead, they will repent.

Abraham's argument was unanswerable by the rich man, and he now made an altogether different request. He asked that Lazarus be sent to his five brothers, still living on earth, to tell them of their brother's anguish so that they might not also come to the same terrible end.

W.J. Dawson has some interesting observations on these verses: "Nothing in all that Christ has to say about Dives is so striking as this, though it is usually overlooked. It is clear that whatever faults Dives had, he loved his brethren, and there is now nothing selfish in that love. If he cannot be saved himself, he thinks it at least possible that they may be saved" *(The Reproach of Christ).*

Aware of his doom, the rich man prayed that Lazarus might be liberated long enough to serve as an evangelist to his five brothers who were on their way to the same place of torment. He could not bear the thought of a reunion in hell.

Abraham said to the rich man, "They have Moses and the prophets; let them hear them" (v. 29). Nothing spectacular or miraculous can have any effect upon the life of men, if the Word of God is not believed and acted upon. We have no light beyond the revelation of God. The rich man argued that the sight of one who came from another world must surely make them believe, though the old familiar words of Moses and the prophets had been heard in vain. He thought that something sensational would appeal to the consciences of his five lost brothers. But nothing could prevent them from sharing their brother's doom apart from the revelation in Old Testament Scriptures.

B. The Verdict (v. 31)

31. And he said unto him, If they hear not Moses and the prophets, neither will they be persuaded, though one rose from the dead.

David Smith, in his book *The Days of His Flesh,* writes: "No miracle would convince one who closes his heart against the voice of conscience, which is the pleading of the Holy Spirit. The Jews did not believe when the Lord raised the widow's son at Nain, the daughter of Jairus, or Lazarus at Bethany, nor even when he himself was raised from the dead according to the Scriptures."

In fact, the Jews actually sought to kill Lazarus because of the power of his testimony to the Lord Jesus Christ after he had been raised from the dead (John 12:10, 11). As George Morrison states, "It will never be easier to believe than now. The man who is not persuaded by the gospel will never be persuaded by a ghost. Let no one wait then, before accepting Jesus, for something extraordinary to happen. That something is never going to happen, and, if it did, it would leave us as we were" *(The Wings of the Morning).*

The Scriptures contain all that we need to know in order to be saved, and a messenger from the world beyond the grave could add nothing to them. It is not more evidence that is needed in order to get men to repent, but more heart and will to make use of what they already know. The dead could tell us nothing more than what the Bible contains, if they rose from their graves to instruct us. After the novelty of their testimony wore off, we would care no more for their words than the words of any other. This constant waiting for something we have not, and neglect of what we have, is the ruin of many souls. Faith—simple scriptural faith which we already possess—is the first thing necessary to salvation. The man who has the Bible, and can read it, and yet waits for more evidence before he becomes a Christian is deceiving himself. Unless he awakens from his delusion, he will die in his sins.

Why do people persistently procrastinate regarding religious matters?

REVIEW QUESTIONS

1. What is the main teaching of the parable of the rich man and Lazarus?
2. What does it teach about the next life?
3. Why the refusal to send a messenger to the rich man's brothers?
4. According to this parable, is it wrong to possess wealth?
5. According to this parable, is it a virtue to be poor?

GOLDEN TEXT HOMILY

"GOD SENT NOT HIS SON INTO THE WORLD TO CONDEMN THE WORLD; BUT THAT THE WORLD THROUGH HIM MIGHT BE SAVED" (John 3:17).

The Bible says, "The Lord is not slack concerning his promise, as some men count slackness; but is longsuffering to us-ward, not willing that any should perish, but that all should come to repentance" (2 Peter 3:9).

I work with men every day who, if they had the opportunity, would make better decisions concerning their lives. However, some continue making wrong decisions. A good example of making a wrong decision is a young man who has been sentenced to death on two counts of murder. He is now awaiting execution in the gas chamber. He admits he has made a total wreck of his life, but still delays accepting Christ, waiting for a more convenient season. His comment to me when I witness to him of Christ is, "I'm not ready; I have some more living to do. You'll probably get me before I sit in the chamber, but I'm not ready now."

Governor Felix sent for Paul and asked about his faith concerning Christ. "And as he reasoned of righteousness, temperance, and judgment to come, Felix trembled, and answered, Go thy way for this time; when I have a convenient season, I will call thee" (Acts 24:25). It is not recorded in Scripture whether Felix ever found that convenient season. We make decisions that determine the course of our lives. Some of those decisions are made in haste, and some we would like the opportunity to go back and change. Still, many people put off correcting bad decisions until it is too late. The passage in 2 Corinthians 6:2 says, "Behold, now is the accepted time; behold, now is the day of salvation."

Our Golden Text says, "For God sent not his Son into the world to condemn the world; but that the world through him might be saved." His purpose in sending Jesus into the world was to show His love and draw men to Himself. He didn't come seeking an excuse to condemn man, but seeking a way to extend His love to man. He came to give us wisdom to know how to make right decisions, and to give us power to make them based on His Word. "Seek ye the Lord while he may be found, call ye upon him while he is near" (Isaiah 55:6). **—Ronald M. Padgett, Chaplain, Director of Religious Programs, Mississippi Department of Corrections, Parchman, Mississippi**

SENTENCE SERMONS

OUR ETERNAL DESTINY depends on our response to God's offer of salvation.

—Selected

THE ONLY ALTERNATIVE to eternal life with the Lord is eternal punishment.

—Harry W. Post

HE THAT WILL enter into paradise must come with the right key.

—Sir Thomas Fuller

HELL IS the highest reward that the devil can offer you for being his servant.

—Billy Sunday

EVANGELISM APPLICATION

SINNERS NEED TO KNOW THE ETERNAL CONSEQUENCES OF REJECTING GOD'S OFFER OF SALVATION.

The natural heart does not wish to believe in the reality of hell. This is to be expected, for men reject a belief which will condemn them. Yet the concept of hell is part and parcel of the teaching of the Bible. It is closely associated with the concept of heaven. A man who does not believe in heaven will probably refuse to believe in hell.

Opinions are important only if they agree with the facts. A man may deny the existence of God, but the denial will not alter the fact that God exists. A man may deny that there is a sun, but the denial will not change the reality of its existence. So it is with the fact of hell. Men may dislike the idea and deny it vehemently, but their denial will not alter the actuality of hell. The Bible teaches certain things about hell. To deny these truths is to call into question the rest of the scriptural teachings.

ILLUMINATING THE LESSON

Man cannot serve two masters. If he gains the world and loses his soul, his loss will be eternal.

The choice made on earth determines the life to come, and such a choice is final. The grave can work no miracle.

In the future, personality continues—feeling, knowing, seeing, reasoning, and remembering. Will these faculties aid our bliss or add to our torment?

Heaven and hell are realities; and our eternal destiny depends not upon wealth or poverty but upon our relationship to Jesus Christ, who came as prophesied by Moses and the prophets as the Savior of the world.

DAILY BIBLE READINGS

M. Forget Not God's Blessings. Deuteronomy 8:7-19

T. Judgment Upon Disobedience. 1 Samuel 13:8-14

W. Live Righteously. Isaiah 33:13-16

T. Avoid External Damnation. Matthew 23:23-33

F. Use Talents Wisely. Matthew 25:14-30

S. Point sinners to Christ. Acts 3:17-26

God's Revelation of Himself

Study Text: Genesis 1:1-3; Psalm 19:1-6; Isaiah 43:12, 13; John 1:1, 2, 14, 18; Romans 1:18- 20; Hebrews 1:1-3; 2 Peter 1:19-21

Objective: To understand that God makes Himself known to man and seek to know Him better.

Golden Text: "God . . . hath in these last days spoken unto us by his Son" (Hebrews 1:1, 2).

Central Truth: God has made known both His nature and His will.

Evangelism Emphasis: Christians must proclaim the gospel to sinners.

PRINTED TEXT

Psalm 19:1. The heavens declare the glory of God; and the firmament sheweth his handywork.

2. Day unto day uttereth speech, and night unto night sheweth knowledge.

3. There is no speech nor language, where their voice is not heard.

4. Their line is gone out through all the earth, and their words to the end of the world. In them hath he set a tabernacle for the sun.

Romans 1:19. Because that which may be known of God is manifest in them; for God hath shewed it unto them.

20. For the invisible things of him from the creation of the world are clearly seen, being understood by the things that are made, even his eternal power and Godhead; so that they are without excuse.

Genesis 1:1. In the beginning God created the heaven and the earth.

2. And the earth was without form, and void; and darkness was upon the face of the deep. And the Spirit of God moved upon the face of the waters.

3. And God said, Let there be light: and there was light.

Isaiah 43:12. I have declared, and have saved, and I have shewed, when there was no strange god among you: therefore ye are my witnesses, saith the Lord, that I am God.

13. Yea, before the day was I am he; and there is none that can deliver out of my hand: I will work, and who shall let it?

2 Peter 1:19. We have also a more sure word of prophecy; whereunto ye do well that ye take heed, as unto a light that shineth in a dark place, until the day dawn, and the day star arise in your hearts:

20. Knowing this first, that no prophecy of the scripture is of any private interpretation.

21. For the prophecy came not in old time by the will of

man: but holy men of God spake as they were moved by the Holy Ghost.

John 1:1. In the beginning was the Word, and the Word was with God, and the Word was God.

2. The same was in the beginning with God.

14. And the Word was made flesh, and dwelt among us, (and we beheld his glory, the glory as of the only begotten of the Father,) full of grace and truth.

18. No man hath seen God at any time; the only begotten Son, which is in the bosom of the Father, he hath declared him.

Hebrews 1:1. God, who at sundry times and in divers manners spake in time past unto the fathers by the prophets,

2. Hath in these last days spoken unto us by his Son, whom he hath appointed heir of all things, by whom also he made the worlds.

LESSON OUTLINE

I. REVEALED THROUGH NATURE
   - A. God's Wonderful Creation
   - B. God's Manifestation

II. REVEALED THROUGH SCRIPTURE
   - A. God Creates
   - B. God Redeems
   - C. God Inspires

III. REVEALED IN CHRIST
   - A. The Living Word
   - B. The Eternal Word

LESSON EXPOSITION

INTRODUCTION

The existence of God is a fundamental concept in religion and therefore a determinative factor in theological thought. The nature ascribed to God influences the entire system. Theology, however, can hardly be expected to furnish demonstrative proof of God's existence, for belief does not arise altogether from logical arguments. The existence of God is a first truth and that fact must logically precede and condition all observation and reasoning.

The human mind must define by limiting the object of its thought; therefore, it is evident that the human mind can never form an adequate conception of God or properly define His being. Only the infinite can comprehend the Infinite. This philosophical conclusion finds its support in the New Testament, which reveals God as "dwelling in the light which no man can approach unto; whom no man hath seen, nor can see" (1 Timothy 6:16). The nearest approach to a definition is the "I AM THAT I AM" of the Old Testament (Exodus 3:14), which asserts His existence with no attempt at proof and further implies that His essence can be known only to Himself. God, therefore, can be known to us only through a revelation of Himself; and while these manifestations are imperfect, due to our limited capacity, they are, insofar as comprehended by us, actual knowledge, which our minds attribute to God as possessing in an infinite degree. Since our conception of the attributes is to a degree indefinite, they may not in this sense be regarded as a definition; but on the other hand, insofar as they furnish a comprehensive statement of the attributes as revealed in Scripture, they may very properly be considered a definition of God (adapted from *Christian Theology*, by Orton Wiley).

Most conservative Christian believers define God as a Spirit, holy in nature and attributes, absolute in reality, infinite in efficiency, perfect in personality, and thereby the ultimate ground, adequate cause, and sufficient reason for all finite existence.

The Church of the Nazarene defines God in the following words: "We believe in one eternally existent, infinite God, Sovereign of the universe. That He only is God, creative and administrative, holy in nature, attributes, and purpose. That He, as God, is Triune in essential being, revealed as Father, Son, and Holy Spirit" (*Manual*, Article I).

The *Thirty-nine Articles* of the Church of England define God as follows: "There is but one living and true God, everlasting, without body, parts or passions; of infinite power, wisdom, and goodness; the Maker and Preserver of all things both visible and invisible. And in the unity of the Godhead there be three Persons, of one substance, power and eternity; the Father, the Son, and the Holy Ghost" (Article I).

The Christian conception of God is a conviction that the ultimate Personality of religion and the absolute of philosophy find their highest expression in Jesus Christ; and that in His person and work we have the deepest possible insight into the nature and purpose of God. "He that hath seen me hath seen the Father" (John 14:9) is Jesus' enunciation of this great truth. Stated theocentrically, Christ does not only reveal God, God reveals Himself through Jesus Christ.

I. REVEALED THROUGH NATURE (Psalm 19:1-6; Romans 1:18-20)

A. God's Wonderful Creation (Psalm 19:1-6)

(Psalm 19:5, 6 is not included in the printed text.)

1. The heavens declare the glory of God; and the firmament sheweth his handywork.

2. Day unto day uttereth speech, and night unto night sheweth knowledge.

3. There is no speech nor language, where their voice is not heard.

4. Their line is gone out through all the earth, and their words to the end of the world. In them hath he set a tabernacle for the sun.

David, the writer of this psalm, was the king of Israel, the chosen of God, and a talented warrior. Yet David felt very humble when he thought about the heavens. You do not need a telescope to be impressed with God's handiwork as it is seen in the heavens. The heavens are so vast, so beautiful, and so orderly that when we think of our own feeble abilities we wonder why God would bother to think about us. God not only thought about us, but He visited us through His Son. God is worthy to be praised.

A view of the heavens from a hilltop on a cool, clear night is a breathtaking experience. Against the darkness of empty space the stars stand out like glittering diamonds as they form infinite patterns in the sky. A casual glance at the sky may lead you to believe there is no order among the stars.

Some stars are bright; some are dim. In some areas there are many bright stars; in other areas there are few. There does not seem to be any pattern to their positions. They look as disorderly as toothpicks dropped on a table. But the more scientists study the starry heaven, the more they marvel at the order it reveals.

God has a purpose for everything He does. Why did God create all the millions of stars? Could we not live just as well without them? The Bible gives four reasons for which God created the stars:

1. The stars were created to provide measures and divisions of time. "And God said, Let there be lights in the firmament of the heaven to divide the day from the night; and let them be for signs, and for seasons, and for days, and years" (Genesis 1:14).

2. The stars were created to provide heat and light for the earth. "And let them be for lights in the firmament of the heaven to give light upon the earth: and it was so. And God made two great lights; the greater light to rule the day, and the lesser light to rule the night: he made the stars also" (Genesis 1:15, 16).

3. The stars were created to teach us God's glory and ability. "The heavens declare the glory of God; and the firmament sheweth his handywork" (Psalm 19:1).

4. The stars were created to teach us humility and our unworthiness before our great God. "When I consider thy heavens, the work of thy fingers, the moon and the stars, which thou hast ordained; what is man, that thou art mindful of him? and the son of man, that thou visitest him?" (Psalm 8:3, 4).

If every Christian on earth would grow silent and every human mouth would refuse to speak of the glory of God, the heavens above would never cease to proclaim His majesty and glory.

B. God's Manifestation (Romans 1:18-20)

(Romans 1:18 is not included in the printed text.)

19. Because that which may be known of God is manifest in them; for God hath shewed it unto them.

20. For the invisible things of him from the creation of the world are clearly seen, being understood by the things that are made, even his eternal power and Godhead; so that they are without excuse.

Men in general have always seen in nature a revelation of God. The more gifted of them have often expressed their conviction in language similar to that of psalmists, prophets, and apostles. Hume was a skeptic, but he is supposed to have said to Ferguson as they walked on a starry night: "Adam, there is a God!" Voltaire is said to have prayed in a thunderstorm. Many outstanding men in the field of the natural and biological sciences have testified to the conviction that nature reveals God. They have pointed to the universe as a manifestation of the power, glory, divinity, and goodness of God. But Christian scientists have also pointed out the limitation of the revelation of God in nature. They have insisted that this revelation alone, although leaving man without excuse, is insufficient for salvation; that it is intended, however, to incite man to search for a fuller revelation of God and His plan of salvation; and that it constitutes a general call of God to man to turn to Him (Henry C. Thiessen, *Lectures in Systematic Theology).*

The history of man began with man knowing God: the creating of man in the image of the Divine; God talking with man in the cool of the day; a face-to-face, heart-to-heart sharing. So what went wrong?

The human heart, by its own act, shut out the manifestation of the true God. It refused to worship Him and instead worshiped base creatures. In doing this, it cut itself off from its source of moral light and strength. False religion resulted, and this false religion resulted in false character. The consequence, paganism, was not simply a misfortune but a crime, with its roots in a deep hatred for God.

How do you see God revealed in nature?

II. REVEALED THROUGH SCRIPTURE (Genesis 1:1-3; Isaiah 43:12, 13; 2 Peter 1:19-21)

A. God Creates (Genesis 1:1-3)

1. In the beginning God created the heaven and the earth.

2. And the earth was without form, and void; and darkness was upon the face of the deep. And the Spirit of God moved upon the face of the waters.

3. And God said, Let there be light: and there was light.

It is interesting that the Bible does not begin with an elaborate argument to prove the existence of God. His existence is simply affirmed as a fact to be believed. In the first four words, "In the beginning God," enough truth is revealed to expose every fallacy that man has invented concerning the Deity.

Atheism is repudiated, for verse 1 postulates the existence of God. Materialism is refuted, for this verse distinguishes between God and His material creation. Pantheism is abolished, for the statement predicates that which necessitates a personal God.

The statement "In the beginning God created" tells us that God is eternal. It says that He himself was before the beginning. This statement reveals that God is a personal being, for an impersonal "first cause" could not create. It reveals that God is infinite and omnipotent, for no finite being has the power to create a universe.

The Christian's faith does not rest in the wisdom of man, and it does not stand in need of support from modern science. The impregnable rock of God's Word is the foundation of the Christian's faith, and nothing more is needed. Too many Christians have deserted their proper ground and have labored to show that the contents of Genesis 1 is in harmony with modern science. This is simply reversing things. The Word of God does not need confirming. If scientists should discover a tablet or some other object with writing upon it that agrees with what is recorded in the Bible, that confirms the historical accuracy of the finding of the scientists. If it disagrees, that is positive proof that the finding of the scientists is at fault. If the teachings of science agree with the Scriptures, that indicates science is correct; if they are in conflict, that shows science is false. Many will laugh at such reasoning, but remember the Word of God declares, "But the natural man receiveth not the things of the Spirit of God: for they are foolishness unto him: neither can he know them, because they are spiritually discerned" (1 Corinthians 2:14).

B. God Redeems (Isaiah 43:12, 13)

12. I have declared, and have saved, and I have shewed, when there was no strange god among you: therefore ye are my witnesses, saith the Lord, that I am God.

13. Yea, before the day was I am he; and there is none that can deliver out of my hand: I will work, and who shall let it?

Concerning these verses, W. Clarkson says: "God summoned His people Israel to bear witness to Him; He challenged them to come forward and testify in the absence of any possible power that could have performed it. He had foretold things which were far in the future; and He had wrought signal and splendid deliverance in their behalf—He had saved as well as declared. Thus they were in a position to maintain that He was the one living God on whom the wise would depend for guidance and redemption" *(Pulpit Commentary).*

God wants His people today to witness to His ability to redeem and to deliver from the power of sin and the Evil One.

C. God Inspires (2 Peter 1:19-21)

19. We have also a more sure word of prophecy; whereunto ye do well that ye take heed, as unto a light that shineth in a dark place, until the day dawn, and the day star arise in your hearts.

The "day star" of the knowledge of Christ had arisen in the hearts of many to whom the apostle wrote. But what about those of whom that was not true? What could they do? For them there was the "sure word of prophecy"—the Holy Scriptures—to confirm the gospel proclaimed by the apostles. Let them take heed to that, and it would bring them to the dawn. Many of the predictions in the Old Testament about the Messiah were vague and mysterious, but now that they had been fulfilled in Jesus of Nazareth, their meaning and truth were apparent. People could read and ponder with a confidence not possible before.

Christ is revealed in the Holy Scriptures. He is not revealed in nature, though He is there. He is not revealed by imagination. He is far beyond our thoughts. Nor is He revealed by our religious experiences apart from Scripture. Rev. C. New says: "For though it is through communion He makes Himself known to us, even that is through the medium of the Scripture, and in harmony with what Scripture teaches. We cannot know Christ till we come to Scripture" *(Pulpit Commentary).*

20. Knowing this first, that no prophecy of the scripture is of any private interpretation.

21. For the prophecy came not in old time by the will of man: but holy men of God spake as they were moved by the Holy Ghost.

"Holy men of God spake as they were moved by the Holy Ghost." No testimony could be more explicit to the inspiration of the Bible than this. It is the testimony of the New Testament to the Old. As such, it is the Old Testament which needs the testimony. Christians have no difficulty accepting the New Testament. We understand that the Savior spoke the words of God by direct inspiration. We understand, on the strength of Christ's own promise, that the apostles were inspired by a direct gift of the Holy Spirit. For the explanation of the inspiration of the Old Testament we look to the New. The treatment of the Old Testament by our Lord, His frequent appeals to it in controversy, His many references to it as fulfilled in Himself, and the express assertion of its inspiration by Paul and Peter are the grounds on which we believe the Old Testament is the inspired Word of God.

Why is it important to believe in the inspiration of the Bible?

III. REVEALED IN CHRIST (John 1:1, 2, 14, 18; Hebrews 1:1-3)

A. The Living Word (John 1:1, 2, 14, 18)

1. In the beginning was the Word, and the Word was with God, and the Word was God.

2. The same was in the beginning with God.

John takes us back to eternity itself and informs us not only what Christ did and suffered but also who He was. He identifies Him by a very unusual name, "the Word." In other places he refers to Him as "the Word of Life" (1 John 1:1, 2) and "the Word of God" (Revelation 19:13).

Marcus Dods states that the *Word* (Greek: *Logos*) was a term familiar to Greek philosophers which carried over into Hebrew thinking. It expressed what was meant in the Old Testament by "the angel of the Lord" and "the wisdom of God." The word *logos* already used by thoughtful men in their efforts to conceive of God's connection with the world, is utilized by John to denote the Revealer of the incomprehensible and invisible God *(The Expositor's Greek Testament)*.

In commenting on the words "and the Word was with God," J.C. Ryle states: "From all eternity there was a most intimate and ineffable union between Christ the Word and God the Father; and yet, though thus united, the Word and the Father were from all eternity two distinct persons. Augustine draws illustrations from the sun and its rays, and from fire and the light of fire, which, though two distinct things, are yet inseparably united, so that where the one is the other is. But all illustrations on such subjects halt and fail. Here, at any rate, it is better to believe than attempt to explain" *(Expository Thoughts on the Gospels)*.

In explaining the statement "and the Word was God," B.F. Wescott observes: "Christ is the thought of God toward man fully expressed. When we have seen Christ, we have seen the Father (John 14:9). He it is who reveals the Father (John 1:18). His words are the words which the Father has given him. Only the apostle John speaks of Christ as the Word of God (1 John 1:1; Revelation 19:13)" *(The Gospel According to Saint John)*.

14. And the Word was made flesh, and dwelt among us, (and we beheld his glory, the glory as of the only begotten of the Father,) full of grace and truth.

The Incarnation attests to a true conception and a real birth. The Son took on flesh and was born of a woman. It was a true acceptance of humanity with all its limitations, growth, and development.

In referring to beholding the glory of Christ, John may have been thinking of the glory that shone around Jesus on the Mount of Transfiguration. The pronoun *we* probably refers to himself and to James and Peter, who were with him.

Two essential features of the character of God in the Old Testament were grace and truth (Exodus 34:6). These also are the two features which, in John's view, distinguish the human life and the Word made flesh.

18. No man hath seen God at

any time; the only begotten Son, which is in the bosom of the Father, he hath declared him.

The meaning here is that no man has ever beheld God with his physical eye, because infinite Spirit cannot be the object of human, natural vision (Deuteronomy 4:12).

The word here translated "declared" means literally "to lead forth," and is the word from which our English word exegesis is derived. Christ as the only begotten Son of God—knowing God as no other being ever could know Him, living with God from eternity, dwelling in the very bosom of God's love—is certainly One who can unveil the glory and truth of God the Father.

B. The Eternal Word (Hebrews 1:1-3)

(Hebrews 1:3 is not included in the printed text.)

1. God, who at sundry times and in divers manners spake in time past unto the fathers by the prophets,

2. Hath in these last days spoken unto us by his Son, whom he hath appointed heir of all things, by whom also he made the worlds.

The story of divine revelation is a story of progression up to Christ, but there is no progression beyond Him. Christ possesses in Himself all the qualifications to be mediator between God and men. He is the Prophet through whom God has spoken His word; He is the Priest who has accomplished a perfect work of cleansing for His people's sins; He is the King who sits enthroned in the place of highest honor alongside the Majesty on high.

How did Christ reveal the Father?

REVIEW QUESTIONS

1. What did David think of God's work in nature?
2. What did Paul say in Romans 1:18-20 about those who refused God's revelation?
3. How does Scripture reveal God?
4. How does John present Christ as the revealer of God?
5. How does the writer of Hebrews present Christ in 1:1-3?

GOLDEN TEXT HOMILY

"GOD . . . HATH IN THESE LAST DAYS SPOKEN UNTO US BY HIS SON" (Hebrews 1:1, 2).

Someone once said that words are the most powerful force in the world. Certainly, words have been used to bring rise to nations, to silence war, to enrage hate, and to soothe fear. Words are powerful, but the Word spoken by God is unmatched. He speaks and all must listen.

God's greatest expression to mankind was not His wondrous creation, but His wonderful Son—Jesus Christ. Whereas the mountains may glorify God's greatness, Jesus Christ is the complete, clear revelation of God's glory and majesty. Jesus speaks not only of God's judgment, but also of His mercy; of His righteousness as well as of His forgiveness; of His holiness and of His grace. Jesus is God's unmistakable voice to you.

The time in which we live is full of communication. We as a society thrive on information. There are also many mixed messages about spirituality. Some have said that there are many paths to God and we must simply choose one. Others preach inner happiness and peace through self. But God has spoken in these last days. He has made a definite expression: Jesus is the Way, the Truth, and the Life; no one comes to the Father except through Him (John 14:6). Even in this time of confusing messages, God has made a relevant word of truth—a word of truth for our society, a word of truth for you in your time of need. Jesus Christ is Lord! **—Michael S. Stewart, Senior Associate Pastor, First Assembly of God, Winston-Salem, North Carolina**

SENTENCE SERMONS

GOD HAS MADE KNOWN both His nature and His will.

—Selected

GOD IS the personal Spirit who in holy love creates, sustains, and orders all.

—William Newton Clarke

WE SHOULD GIVE GOD the same place in our hearts that He holds in the universe.

—*Quotable Quotations*

THE WORD OF GOD tends to make large-minded, noble-hearted persons.

—Henry Ward Beecher

EVANGELISM APPLICATION

CHRISTIANS MUST PROCLAIM THE GOSPEL TO SINNERS.

It is God who gives us our work and calling. Isaiah heard God in the Temple, and said, "Here am I; send me" (6:8). Samuel, the little minister, heard God calling, and answered, "Speak, Lord; for thy servant heareth" (1 Samuel 3:9, 10). Paul on the way to Damascus heard the voice from heaven, and said, "Lord, what wilt thou have me to do?" (Acts 9:6). They all responded with a willingness to do whatever God asked them to do.

Our life is like that. Whatever our work may be, when God calls, we should say, "I am ready."

ILLUMINATING THE LESSON

The revelation of the true nature of God had been made gradually to the people of the Old Testament, but they had not realized that He is a God of infinite love and mercy. It was Jesus who taught His disciples to pray, "Our Father which art in heaven" (Matthew 6:9). It was Jesus who taught us that "God so loved the world, that he gave his only begotten Son" (John 3:16).

To an aged woman someone said, "Isn't it wonderful that God should give His only Son to die for us?" "It is just like Him" came her happy answer. God is not a mighty king ruling His subjects but unmindful of their needs; He is love personified, and the giving of His only Son to suffer and die for the sins of the world was "just like Him," for infinite is His love.

DAILY BIBLE READINGS

- M. God Revealed as Creator. Genesis 1:1-5
- T. God Speaks to Israel. Deuteronomy 5:23-29
- W. God Questions Job. Job 40:1-9
- T. God Is With Us. Matthew 1:18-25
- F. God's Presence Felt. Acts 4:29-33
- S. God Can Be Known. 1 John 2:12-14

The Fatherhood of God

Study Text: Proverbs 3:11, 12; Isaiah 63:7-9, 16; John 14:6-11; Galatians 4:4-7; Ephesians 1:2- 6; James 1:17, 18

Objective: To acknowledge God as our heavenly Father and accept His loving care and discipline.

Golden Text: "When ye pray, say, Our Father which art in heaven, Hallowed be thy name" (Luke 11:2).

Central Truth: We come to know God as Father by faith in Jesus Christ.

Evangelism Emphasis: The sinner can know God as Father by accepting Christ the Son.

PRINTED TEXT

Isaiah 63:7. I will mention the lovingkindnesses of the Lord, and the praises of the Lord, according to all that the Lord hath bestowed on us, and the great goodness toward the house of Israel, which he hath bestowed on them according to his mercies, and according to the multitude of his lovingkindnesses.

16. Doubtless thou art our father, though Abraham be ignorant of us, and Israel acknowledge us not: thou, O Lord, art our father, our redeemer; thy name is from everlasting.

Proverbs 3:11. My son, despise not the chastening of the Lord; neither be weary of his correction:

12. For whom the Lord loveth he correcteth; even as a father the son in whom he delighteth.

John 14:6. Jesus saith unto him, I am the way, the truth, and the life: no man cometh unto the Father, but by me.

7. If ye had known me, ye should have known my Father also: and from henceforth ye know him, and have seen him.

8. Philip saith unto him, Lord, shew us the Father, and it sufficeth us.

9. Jesus saith unto him, Have I been so long time with you, and yet hast thou not known me, Philip? he that hath seen me hath seen the Father; and how sayest thou then, Shew us the Father?

10. Believest thou not that I am in the Father, and the Father in me? the words that I speak unto you I speak not of myself: but the Father that dwelleth in me, he doeth the works.

11. Believe me that I am in the Father, and the Father in me: or else believe me for the very works' sake.

Galatians 4:6. And because ye are sons, God hath sent forth the Spirit of his Son into your hearts, crying, Abba, Father.

Ephesians 1:2. Grace be to

you, and peace, from God our Father, and from the Lord Jesus Christ.

3. Blessed be the God and Father of our Lord Jesus Christ, who hath blessed us with all spiritual blessings in heavenly places in Christ:

4. According as he hath chosen us in him before the foundation of the world, that we should be holy and without blame before him in love.

James 1:17. Every good gift and every perfect gift is from above, and cometh down from the Father of lights, with whom is no variableness, neither shadow of turning.

LESSON OUTLINE

I. FATHER OF ISRAEL
  A. God's Goodness
  B. God's Sympathy
  C. God Our Father
  D. God's Discipline
II. FATHER OF JESUS CHRIST
  A. Revelation
  B. Request
  C. Response
III. FATHER OF BELIEVERS
  A. Assurance of Sonship
  B. Source of All Good
  C. Accepted in the Family

LESSON EXPOSITION

INTRODUCTION

Fatherhood is ascribed to God with such great frequency in the New Testament, especially in the teachings of Jesus, that it has been regarded as the distinctive mark of the Christian conception of God. Its Old Testament connotation is enriched with the thought of God's fatherly readiness to forgive (Matthew 6:14; Luke 15:11-32). The question of whether the fatherhood of God, proclaimed by Jesus, is to be understood as extending to all men or only to believers has been much debated. According to George S. Hendry, "Since both views can be supported by passages in the Gospels, it is evident that the alternative is false. The Fatherhood of God is indeed universal in so far as his providential care extends to all men indiscriminately (Matthew 5:45), but it is not effectively realized as a personal relationship except where it is correlated with sonship (Matthew 11:27)."

Jesus' proclamation of the fatherhood of God is at the same time the benediction (Matthew 5:9), the challenge (5:48), and the authorization of divine sonship to men (John 1:12); for Jesus himself is the Son who alone can properly speak of God as "my Father" (Matthew 11:27) and who shares His sonship with me so that I can direct others to the Father (6:8) authorizing them to say with us "Our Father" (6:9).

The name of *Father* is applied to God with great frequency in the Gospel of John and also in the Pauline epistles, where it is expressly signified that God is primarily the Father of our Lord Jesus Christ (2 Corinthians 1:3), through whom we receive the adoption as sons (Galatians 4:5; Ephesians 1:5), and by whose indwelling Spirit we are enabled to be the sons of God (Romans 8:14-16;

Galatians 4:6).

The fatherhood of God in no way precludes His holy wrath against sin and His disciplinary treatment of sinners (Deuteronomy 8:5; Hebrews 12:5-8). However, a sentimentalized conception of the fatherhood of God has at times been used by some liberals in an attempt to do away with the Atonement.

The gospel of the fatherhood of God not only brings men into a relation of sonship to Him, but it unites them together as a family which is animated by brotherly love (Romans 12:10; 1 Thessalonians 4:9), reconciliation (Matthew 18:21-35), and mutual submission (Ephesians 5:21; Philippians 2:3). It is the ground of the universality of the church.

I. FATHER OF ISRAEL (Isaiah 63:7-9, 16; Proverbs 3:11, 12)

A. God's Goodness (Isaiah 63:7, 8)

(Isaiah 63:8 is not included in the printed text.)

7. I will mention the lovingkindnesses of the Lord, and the praises of the Lord, according to all that the Lord hath bestowed on us, and the great goodness toward the house of Israel, which he hath bestowed on them according to his mercies, and according to the multitude of his lovingkindnesses.

Reverend W. Clarkson writes of these words of Isaiah: "There is music in the sound and great comfort in the sense of these exquisite words because they tell us the greatness of God's goodness to us. 'All that the Lord hath bestowed on us.' 'The multitude of his lovingkindnesses.' His gifts night and day, in every season, through every stage of life; all material for the body, all stores of knowledge for the mind, all wealth of affection for the heart. Every house, every family, every man has special reason to speak of Divine goodness" *(Pulpit Commentary).*

What should be our response to what God does for us? We should remember for our own sakes and remind those around us of God's goodness. This is our duty. It is clearly the will of Christ that we should make known the fullness of His kindness and the riches of His grace. We exist, as His people, that we may be witnesses to the world of all that we have learned of Him. This is also our wisdom; for therein is found the one antidote to dissatisfaction, the one unfailing source of gratitude and joy.

B. God's Sympathy (v. 9)

(Isaiah 63:9 is not included in the printed text.)

All His kindnesses are "lovingkindnesses" prompted by parental affection and granted in a loving spirit. Note especially His kindness and divine sympathy in affliction: "In all their afflictions; he bare them and carried them," as a mother carries her sick child, or the shepherd a wounded lamb. Not only are His hands upon us, but underneath are His everlasting arms.

The affliction of Israel began in Egypt, probably not long after the death of Joseph. It became an intense oppression when a king arose who did not know Joseph. God's sympathy with Israel's sufferings is strongly indicated in the experience of the Exodus. He loved them so much that "the angel of his presence saved them: in his love and in his pity he redeemed them." That is, He redeemed them from bondage and brought them safely through the wilderness to Palestine.

C. God Our Father (v. 16)

16. Doubtless thou art our father, though Abraham be ignorant of us, and Israel acknowledge us not: thou, O Lord, art our father, our redeemer; thy name is from everlasting.

The name of *Father* is infrequently applied to God in the Old Testament, and mostly in a figurative sense. God is the Father of Israel because He is the Creator of Israel's existence as a people—not by physical generation (as the relationship of God to people was conceived in some heathen religions), but by sovereign divine election (Hosea 11:1). Israel was a foundling child on whom God took pity (Deuteronomy 32:10; Ezekiel 16:5, 6), and God's fatherly love toward Israel as His adopted son constituted a claim upon Israel's obedient service.

D. God's Discipline (Proverbs 3:11, 12)

11. My son, despise not the chastening of the Lord; neither be weary of his correction:

12. For whom the Lord loveth he correcteth; even as a father the son in whom he delighteth.

The motive with which God chastens His children is fatherly love. God is necessarily angry with us for our sins. His anger, however, is not the result of malignant hatred, but the expression of grieved love. For love can be angry, (in fact, sometimes must be) if it is pure and strong. The weak kindliness which is a stranger to indignation at wrongdoing is not based on deep affection.

If God chastens in love, it is for our own good. Weak love seeks the present pleasure of its objects; strong love aims at the highest welfare, although it may involve misunderstandings and even temporary estrangement.

True love is not blind to the faults of those we love; rather it is keen-sighted because it is love. Hence we may take chastening as a proof of the love and fatherhood of God. If we were not His children, God would not cause us pain. Instead of regarding trouble as proof that God has deserted us, we should see in it a sign that God lives in us and acknowledges us as His children and that He is concerned with our welfare. The worst curse a man can receive is to be deserted by God and left unchecked in his pursuit of folly.

How should the church show love in the way it disciplines its members?

II. FATHER OF JESUS CHRIST (John 14:6-11)

A. Revelation (vv. 6, 7)

6. Jesus saith unto him, I am the way, the truth, and the life: no man cometh unto the Father, but by me.

The pronoun is emphatic in this verse, "I" and no other. Jesus himself is the way between heaven and earth, the way to the Father's house, the way home, the way that leads to eternal glory (see Hebrews 10:19-22). He does not point the way—He is the way. He is also the truth. If we desire to know what God is in His essential attributes, we need but study Christ. Jesus Christ leaves us in no doubt as to whether God understands us, loves us, or wills to save us. He also leaves us no doubt as to whether man may know God, love God, or be one with God. The human soul was wearied with abstract discussions.

Jesus Christ appeared and, for all who had eyes to see, controversy ceased.

The truth that "Christ is" has never been discovered by the unaided intellect of man; yet it is the only truth that finally satisfies. He is the life in the fullest sense, the life which God intended man to have and made man capable of enjoying. Its source is God and in duration is eternal as God's own.

Thomas à Kempis was correct when he wrote: "Without the Way, there is no going; without the Truth, there is no knowing; without the Life, there is no living. [Jesus said] I am the Way which thou oughtest to follow; the Truth which thou oughtest to trust; the Life, which thou oughtest to hope for." He is the Way to the Truth and the Way to the Life. He is the Truth of the Way and the Truth of the Life; He is the Life of the Way and the Life of the Truth. He is simply the sole means to salvation.

7. If ye had known me, ye should have known my Father also: and from henceforth ye know him, and have seen him.

The emphasis in the first clause is on "known"; in the second, on "Father." The meaning is, if you had recognized Me, you would have known my Father also. The disciples knew Christ in a surface way, of course, but they did not recognize the Father in Him. If they had, they would have had no need to ask the questions that were on their lips. Earlier, Christ had given His followers hints of the great truth concerning Himself, but had never before spoken so clearly. From this time forward, they could have no excuse for not recognizing His divine nature, His union with the Father.

B. Request (v. 8)

8. Philip saith unto him, Lord, shew us the Father, and it sufficeth us.

Philip seems to have been much like Thomas, a slow-to-believe and inquiring mind. He was one of the first to be called to the band of 12 disciples (John 1:43), and he proved his zeal for Christ by immediately passing the good word along to Nathanael.

Christ had said that His disciples had seen the Father, but the mind of Philip did not understand Him. Perhaps he thought that to see God meant to have such a glorious and marvelous vision as Moses had on Mount Horeb or such a resplendent sight as Christ himself had presented on the Mount of Transfiguration—though Peter, James, and John had doubtless not yet told him of that experience. Philip had heard the voice of God speaking to Jesus at His baptism and again when he and Andrew brought the Greeks to Him (John 12:20-22, 28); now he wanted still more, to see the Infinite One with his mortal eyes. He thought that such a vision would solve all his doubts, but Christ knew that doubts are not often solved in that way.

C. Response (vv. 9-11)

9. Jesus saith unto him, Have I been so long time with you, and yet hast thou not known me, Philip? he that hath seen me hath seen the Father; and how sayest thou then, Shew us the Father?

10. Believest thou not that I am in the Father, and the Father in me? the words that I speak unto you I speak not of myself: but the Father that dwelleth in me, he doeth the works.

11. Believe me that I am in the

Father, and the Father in me: or else believe me for the very works' sake.

Christ's use of Philip's name has in it a world of loving surprise and tender disappointment. In three years Philip should have known Christ better.

In Christ dwelt all the fullness of the Father. His revelation of God was complete. When in heaven we come to see God, He will be the same as Jesus Christ. He will speak as Christ spoke and act as Christ acted.

We make Philip's unbelieving mistake if we seek any fuller revelation of God than Christ made to the world. In the New Testament we have the portrait of God. If we believe Christ and the Bible, we have no further question to ask about God. We know Him and we see Him.

In verse 10 Christ asked a question and then answered it, both in the same sentence. The fact that God was in Him, and He in God the Father, both working as one—the Son revealing the Father, and the Father accomplishing His purposes through the Son—is proved both in the fact that the very words of Christ were the words of God which He had received from His Father, and the works that He did were accomplished by the power of God working through Him. No mere man has ever spoken and ever worked such miracles as the Lord Jesus. The only way to account for His teaching and His miracles is to attribute them to His oneness with the Father.

Christ's wonderful ministry presents more than enough evidence to prove His absolute deity, and the Gospel records of His life are both sufficient argument for proving and a plea for believing Him to be the Son of God.

By "the works" (v. 11) Christ meant all that He did during the course of His ministry, including His speaking in both private and public, but especially His works of wonder, His miracles. Primarily that was why He worked them, that men might believe on Him.

Why were the disciples so slow to believe and accept what Christ said about Himself and the Father?

III. FATHER OF BELIEVERS (Galatians 4:4-7; Ephesians 1:2-6; James 1:17, 18)

A. Assurance of Sonship (Galatians 4:4-7)

(Galatians 4:4, 5, 7 is not included in the printed text.)

6. And because ye are sons, God hath sent forth the Spirit of his Son into your hearts, crying, Abba, Father.

It is one thing for God to assert that we are adopted to sonship in the family of God; it is another to give evidence of the fact. The evidence that God gives is the inner testimony of the Holy Spirit. The Holy Spirit is the witness of our sonship.

Because we are sons, God has sent into our hearts "the Spirit of his Son" (v. 6). This is another name for the Holy Spirit, who is also sometimes called "the Spirit of Christ" or "the Spirit of Jesus." The indwelling Spirit prompts the cry "Abba, Father."

A sure sign of adoption is the unerring leading of the Holy Spirit in all matters (Romans 8:14). Having the Spirit as the seal of adoption, we take on a likeness to God that marks us as His in this present evil world. We are

God-directed and Godlike as His children.

Whom God adopts, He anoints; whom He makes sons, He makes saints. When a man adopts another for a son and heir, he may give him his name, but he cannot give him his own disposition and characteristics. But when God adopts, He sanctifies. He gives not only a new name but a new nature. He turns the lion into a lamb. He works such a change as if another soul dwelt in the same body.

The termination of slavish fear (Romans 8:15) and the advent of a sense of sonship is what we call conversion. But we hardly realize at once the meaning of our inheritance. How magnificent it is to realize that God is no longer angry with us but looks at us with ineffable tenderness as our heavenly Father. We should realize that, although we have nothing of ourselves, we have become heirs of all things (8:17) and find that all things are made to work together for our good (8:20).

B. Accepted in the Family (Ephesians 1:2-6)

(Ephesians 1:5, 6 is not included in the printed text.)

2. Grace be to you, and peace, from God our Father, and from the Lord Jesus Christ.

3. Blessed be the God and Father of our Lord Jesus Christ, who hath blessed us with all spiritual blessings in heavenly places in Christ:

4. According as he hath chosen us in him before the foundation of the world, that we should be holy and without blame before him in love.

Paul said that God chose us even before He created the universe so that our salvation is wholly of His grace and not on the basis of anything we ourselves have done. He chose us in Christ, not in ourselves. And He chose us for a purpose: to be holy and without blame. In the Bible, election is always unto something. It is a privilege that carries a great responsibility.

Verse 6 says that He has accepted us. We cannot make ourselves acceptable to God, but He, by His grace, makes us accepted in Christ. This is our eternal position which will never change. One translation reads: "which He freely bestowed on us in the Beloved" (*NASB*). Or, "He has be-graced [literal translation] us in the Beloved." The idea is the same. Because of God's grace in Christ, we are accepted before Him. In writing to Philemon, Paul encouraged him to accept his runaway slave, Onesimus, using the same argument: "If he owes you anything, I will pay it. Receive him as you would receive me" (Philemon 17-19) (Warren Wiersbe, *Be Rich*).

C. Source of All Good (James 1:17, 18)

(James 1:18 is not included in the printed text.)

17. Every good gift and every perfect gift is from above, and cometh down from the Father of lights, with whom is no variableness, neither shadow of turning.

James indicated that God is not one who incites to man's destruction. He is the Great Giver of good and precious gifts. Look at the good things we enjoy—all come from God. Think of the better things we might enjoy, if God had His way. He is the Creator of the heavenly lights. He is likewise the source of all moral and spiritual light. The heavenly lights vary—sometimes there are shadows, and often they fail to give their light and warmth. But not so with our God. There is no change in Him. He is always giving good to His creatures, and the good gifts are always perfect.

In verse 18, James specified the highest good that comes from above. It is the new birth. "Of his own will"—not in response to our pleading, but putting His whole heart into it—"begat He us," or became our Father. Contrast this bringing forth with that of evil desire and sin. Death is the issue of evil desire; life and sonship are the issues of God's will. The means by which God regenerates us is "the word of truth."

What does it mean to be adopted into the family of God?

REVIEW QUESTIONS

1. What did Isaiah say about God's goodness in relation to Israel?
2. What did the wise man say about discipline?
3. Why does God discipline His children?
4. How did Jesus describe God?
5. What is the source of all goodness?

GOLDEN TEXT HOMILY

"WHEN YE PRAY, SAY, OUR FATHER WHICH ART IN HEAVEN, HALLOWED BE THY NAME" (Luke 11:2).

When we speak of the fatherhood of God, we know that God created Adam and Eve and that all mankind originated from this pair. But all men and women do not live a life that pleases God the Father.

If we live a sinful, unholy, loose, and worldly life, we give a silent, but visible, testimony that causes people to doubt our true relationship with the Father. Such a lifestyle causes others to think they can either live such a life and claim to be Christlike, or it can turn people against a true walk with God.

When we say "our Father" in prayer, we are placed in a personal relationship with Him and can claim that we are His sons and daughters. When people hear us praying, "Our Father which art in heaven," our lifestyle should be a life of holiness, honesty, and purity and should have all the other characteristics of a child of God.

We must live on a higher plane of life if we acknowledge God as our Father, so that God the Father will be accepted and glorified and placed in the highest honor to the world and sinners.

Men and women must accept God the Father as their spiritual Father and trust Him with their eternal soul.—**Charles G. Wiley, Pastor, Church of God, New Boston, Texas**

SENTENCE SERMONS

WE COME TO KNOW God as Father by faith in Jesus Christ.

—Selected

THE CONCEPT of the Fatherhood of God is filled out with rich meaning by the revealing work of Christ.

—William M. Beahm

THE SINNER can know God as Father by accepting Christ the Son.

—Selected

EVANGELISM APPLICATION

THE SINNER CAN KNOW GOD AS FATHER BY ACCEPTING CHRIST THE SON.

In response to the request "Show us the way" (see John 14:5), Christ answered Thomas by insisting that he did not need to know just where heaven is, where the Father is, or just where the Son was going. He needed only to know the way to the Father and to heaven, and that way is the Son, the only revealer of the Father and the only Guide to heaven. Note that Christ did not say "goeth" but "cometh" (v. 6). He is with the Father already, and where He is, there is the Father.

ILLUMINATING THE LESSON

By Christ we are lifted to quite a new level and rank before God. We still have God as our faithful Creator, who will supply all our necessities. The Creator is included in the Father; but in the Father we have, over and above, the assurance that our connection with Him is one of love and of lasting relationship; that we shall not be left to go adrift, but shall be brought up into His likeness, and shall live with Him; and that the ground on which this relationship is established is one of unutterable dignity, the Son of God having become our brother, our nature being now worn by the same person as wears the nature of God. The Son of God has become Son of Man, and for this very purpose—that we might receive the adoption of sons; that we might claim the same Father as Christ claims. These words, then, which the Son puts into our lips, again and again raise our hearts to the belief, that not only may we expect for His sake many blessings from God, so that it shall be a very apt simile to call Him Father, but that God enters into a relationship with us in Him, and becomes forever connected with us in a way that secures that all blessings shall be ours. It is not on account of what we receive from God that we are to think of Him with filial gratitude, and count Him a Father, but because He is in very truth our Father, we shall receive all things at His hand.—**Excerpts from Marcus Dods in *Greek New Testament***

DAILY BIBLE READINGS

M. God as Father. Deuteronomy 32:1-6
T. Rebellious Children. Isaiah 1:1-4
W. Sons of God. Hosea 1:6-10
T. Goodness of the Father. Matthew 7:7-11
F. Works of the Father. John 5:17-23
S. The Father's Provision. 1 Peter 1:1-5

Jesus Christ Our Savior

Study Text: Isaiah 53:4, 5; Luke 13:10-13; John 8:1-11; Ephesians 1:7; 2:4, 5; 2 Timothy 1:9, 10; Titus 3:4-7

Objective: To examine and appropriate the benefits of salvation through Jesus Christ.

Golden Text: "Grow in grace, and in the knowledge of our Lord and Saviour Jesus Christ" (2 Peter 3:18).

Central Truth: Jesus Christ is the Savior of sinners.

Evangelism Emphasis: Believers should testify of Christ's power to save sinners.

PRINTED TEXT

Ephesians 1:7. In whom we have redemption through his blood, the forgiveness of sins, according to the riches of his grace.

2:4. But God, who is rich in mercy, for his great love wherewith he loved us,

5. Even when we were dead in sins, hath quickened us together with Christ, (by grace ye are saved).

Luke 13:11. And, behold, there was a woman which had a spirit of infirmity eighteen years, and was bowed together, and could in no wise lift up herself.

12. And when Jesus saw her, he called her to him, and said unto her, Woman, thou art loosed from thine infirmity.

13. And he laid his hands on her: and immediately she was made straight, and glorified God.

Isaiah 53:4. Surely he hath borne our griefs, and carried our sorrows: yet we did esteem him stricken, smitten of God, and afflicted.

5. But he was wounded for our transgressions, he was bruised for our iniquities: the chastisement of our peace was upon him; and with his stripes we are healed.

2 Timothy 1:9. Who hath saved us, and called us with an holy calling, not according to our works, but according to his own purpose and grace, which was given us in Christ Jesus before the world began,

10. But is now made manifest by the appearing of our Saviour Jesus Christ, who hath abolished death, and hath brought life and immortality to light through the gospel.

Titus 3:4. But after that the kindness and love of God our Saviour toward man appeared,

5. Not by works of righteousness which we have done, but according to his mercy he saved us, by the washing of regeneration, and renewing of the Holy Ghost;

6. Which he shed on us abundantly through Jesus Christ our

Saviour;

7. That being justified by his grace, we should be made heirs according to the hope of eternal life.

LESSON OUTLINE

I. SAVIOR OF SINNERS
   A. Mercy
   B. Redemption
II. HEALER OF SICKNESS
   A. The Infirm Woman
   B. The Provision
III. RESULTS OF SALVATION
   A. Life and Immortality
   B. Heirs

LESSON EXPOSITION

INTRODUCTION

The number one news story of our day is that Jesus Christ is our Savior. However, many centuries ago His birth was announced by an angel to a band of frightened shepherds: "Fear not: for, behold, I bring you good tidings of great joy. . . . For unto you is born this day . . . a Saviour, which is Christ the Lord" (Luke 2:10, 11).

Who is this Savior? He is Jesus of Nazareth, the greatest personality ever to appear in the arena of human activity and play His part on the stage of life. No man has ever equaled Him in depth of character, breadth of soul, width of interest, or height of influence. He is the most outstanding individual who has ever trodden the dusty highways of life or trudged up the steep, jagged hillsides of earth.

The central figure of all time is this Savior of ours. He splits history into two parts—B.C. (before Christ) and A.D. (in the year of our Lord).

The imagination is staggered to realize that a child could be born in a humble home situated in an obscure little hamlet which was located in a very insignificant, small country, yet become the One the impact of whose dynamic personality should change the whole course of history, revolutionize philosophy, overthrow governments, revitalize religion, and transform men.

This Savior was born in a conquered province of the Roman Empire, held by the iron fist of military power, and subject to the yoke of a slave; yet Jesus became the great Emancipator, making freedom possible for every man and woman of Adam's race.

The mother of this Savior was a woman of lowliest station, living in the most despised city, Nazareth, from which no good had ever come. But He became the fountainhead of all goodness.

Jesus was born in a borrowed manger in the little town of Bethlehem. He worked as a carpenter with Joseph, Mary's husband. Within Jesus was the creative genius of building not just a material house but also the construction of human beings who comprise the kingdom of heaven.

This Savior lived but a brief 33 years. He was born a Jew—despised, lowly, ignoble. His emperor was Caesar, who ruled a great earthly kingdom; but little did Caesar know that One would arise and found a kingdom greater in territory, wider in scope, and richer in purpose, which would endure when the stateliest monuments and costliest palaces of Rome would be crumbled in the dust of oblivion.

This Jesus Christ is the Savior of sinners, the healer of sickness, and the provider of salvation which lasts for all eternity.

I. SAVIOR OF SINNERS (John 8:1-11; Ephesians 1:7; 2:4, 5)

A. Mercy (John 8:1-11)

(John 8:1-11 is not included in the printed text.)

The ability to penetrate the human heart and to find out its secrets and its sin and still show mercy is left to Christ alone. An example of this is seen in His dealing with the woman accused of adultery who was brought to Him by the scribes and Pharisees.

The Jews had a curious custom of consulting with a distinguished rabbi in cases of difficulty. But there was no difficulty here. The law of Moses spelled out clearly what the punishment was to be—such should be stoned.

The scribes and Pharisees thought this case presented a good opportunity to lay a trap for Christ. They could use the incident to discover how He regarded the Mosaic Law. That He was heterodox on this subject, they had reason to believe; and to satisfy themselves on this point, they asked Jesus whether or not He agreed with Moses on the subject of adultery. Jesus gave them a judgment, but it was not what they had expected. In thinking of the case, they had forgotten the woman and even the deed. What became of the criminal was unimportant to them. Toward her crime or her character they had no feeling whatsoever.

The judgment of Christ was upon them. The shame of the deed itself and the brazen hardness of the prosecutors, the legality which had no justice and did not pretend to have mercy, the religious malice that could exploit the fall and ignominious death of a fellow creature—all this was thrust upon His mind at once. The indignation He felt was demonstrated by His actions: He stooped down and began writing on the ground. His tormentors continued their clamor until He raised His head for a moment and said, "He that is without sin among you, let him first cast a stone at her" (v. 7). With astonishment, a new sense of their own condition and conduct was revealed to them, and they began to slip away. The crowd soon dissolved and left Christ and the woman to deal with the sin.

F.B. Meyer said, "There are three ways of dealing with sin: the sinner's way—to expose the sin, to scandalously and unforgivingly criticize the sinner, and to almost rejoice in the guilty one's shame; the law's way of treating the sinner—to condemn and to put to death; and the Savior's way of treating sin—to forgive, to cleanse the heart that has sinned, and to deliver from the power of that sin through the days that follow."

Christ's way was "to seek and to save that which was lost" (Luke 19:10). Mercy is justice in this case. Christ has proposed the true test: "Let him that is without sin cast the first stone" (see John 8:7). Of course, there was no one who qualified. But He interposed with His more excellent way of hope and new life. He said to the woman, "Go, and sin no more" (v. 11). Therefore, He condemned the sin and forgave the sinner.

Jesus provided for this woman a second chance. It was as though He said to her, "I know you have made a mess of things, but life is not finished yet; I am going to give you another chance, the chance to help yourself." In Jesus, through His mercy, there is the gospel of the second chance. Jesus was always intensely interested not only in what a person had been, but also in what a person could become. He did not say that what the person had done did not matter; broken laws and broken hearts always matter. But, Jesus was sure that everyone has a future as well as a past.

Jesus confronted this woman with the challenge of living a sinless life. He did not say, "It's all right; don't worry about it; just go on doing as you are doing." But, He said, "It's all wrong; go out and fight; change your life; go and sin no more." Here was no easy forgiveness. Here was a challenge which pointed a sinner to heights of goodness of which she had never dreamed. Today, as in the past, Jesus confronts the bad life with the challenge of the good life.

B. Redemption (Ephesians 1:7; 2:4, 5)

7. In whom we have redemption through his blood, the forgiveness of sins, according to the riches of his grace.

One of the most meaningful words in the Scriptures is the word *redeemed*, for it is so full of wondrous significance to the believer. Redemption is one of the great words connected with the work of Christ on the cross, expressing the blessed deliverance effected there for all under the guilt and bondage of sin. It conveys two great truths: one, the purchase or buying back by the payment of a ransom, and the other, the deliverance from bondage by the ransom paid and by the power of God.

Regarding redemption as a purchase, the prominent thought is of the price paid, but not its payment to any person. In Psalm 49, the price paid for redemption is contrasted with all the wealth possessed by rich men, showing how utterly inadequate were all the riches they possessed to pay the required ransom. "For the redemption of their soul is precious [or costly], and it ceaseth for ever" (v. 8). This last clause may be translated, "It must be let alone forever." It was far too costly for man to face, even if he possessed all the wealth that the world could give. Redemption cannot be purchased by silver or gold or any other material wealth, but by "the precious blood of Christ" (1 Peter 1:19).

The New Testament words that speak of redemption as purchase are those used to describe men buying in the market or forum. Twice, believers are reminded that they "are bought with a price" (1 Corinthians 6:20; 7:23), while false teachers are said to deny the Lord who bought them (2 Peter 2:1). In the Book of Revelation the great company seen about the throne of God is said to have been *redeemed*, or bought (Revelation 5:9; 14:4). A stronger word is used in Galatians 3:13 and 4:5, where redemption by Christ is from the law and its curse; and it means "to buy out from under," or "to buy up," which is the better translation of Ephesians 5:16 and Colossians 4:5.

The price paid for a thing often determines its value to the purchaser; and the greater the cost, the more the article is prized by its owner. No greater price could have been paid than that which God paid for our redemption, for it was the precious blood of Christ, His only begotten Son. Therefore, there can be nothing in the world so precious in His sight as those who have been bought by the payment of that great price, and it is that which makes it so very blessed to be a child of God. "Ye are not your own . . . ye are bought with a price" (1 Corinthians 6:19, 20).

Redemption means not only purchase by payment of the ransom required, but it also has in view particularly the deliverance, or setting free, of those who have been slaves and are in bondage. Deliverance is the prominent idea of redemption in both Testaments. All three words for *redeem* in the Old Testament enforce the truth of freedom or deliverance from bondage. The same Hebrew word rendered *redeem* in Psalm 136:24 is *deliver* in Lamentations 5:8 and is generally translated as "break, or rend, or tear in pieces," denoting violent action. When applied to the work of God in redeeming His people, it points to His mighty power that broke the forces of evil which held them, and then opened the Red Sea so that they might pass through it in safety. There, too, His power shone forth in the destruction of their enemies, the Egyptians. In Egypt their redemption was effected by the sprinkling of blood, which made them safe from the judgment of God, and then the passage at the Red Sea delivered them from the power of Pharaoh and his hosts. These find their fulfillment in the cross of Christ and His resurrection from the dead.

2:4. But God, who is rich in mercy, for his great love wherewith he loved us,

5. Even when we were dead in sins, hath quickened us together with Christ, (by grace ye are saved).

Grace is the fountainhead of our salvation. Because God is gracious, sinful men are forgiven, converted, purified, and saved. It is not because of anything that is or will ever be in them that they are saved, but because of the boundless love, goodness, pity, compassion, mercy, and grace of God.

Charles Spurgeon writes: "What an abyss is the grace of God! Who can measure its breadth? Who can fathom its depth? Like all the rest of the divine attributes, it is infinite. God is full of love, for 'God is love.' God is full of goodness; the very name 'God' is short for 'good.' Unbounded goodness and love enter into the very essence of the Godhead. It is because His mercy endureth forever that men are not destroyed; because His compassions fail not that sinners are brought to Him and forgiven" *(All of Grace).*

How are faith *and* grace *related in salvation?*

II. HEALER OF SICKNESS (Luke 13:10-13; Isaiah 53:4, 5)

A. The Infirm Woman (Luke 13:10-13)

(Luke 13:10 is not included in the printed text.)

11. And, behold, there was a woman which had a spirit of infirmity eighteen years, and was bowed together, and could in no wise lift up herself.

12. And when Jesus saw her, he called her to him, and said unto her, Woman, thou art loosed from thine infirmity.

13. And he laid his hands on her: and immediately she was made straight, and glorified God.

Luke is the only Gospel writer who records the healing of the infirm woman. It occurred on the Sabbath and thus stirred a lot of controversy on the part of the religious leaders.

The physical condition of the woman pit in others. She had endured her deformity for 18 long years. Luke identified her illness as a "spirit of infirmity." Herbert Lockyer explains this condition in the following way: "The phrase denotes one of those mysterious derangements of the nervous system, having their rise in the mind rather than in the body. Her physical curvature was the consequence of mental obliquity, making her melancholy. Thus her strange malady was partly physical and partly mental. She was 'bowed together, and could in no wise lift up herself.' 'Bowed together' is a phrase found nowhere else in the New Testament, and it indicates a dislocation of the vertebrae of the spine. What an expressive picture this is of every man's spiritual condition through sin—bowed down, unable to look up into the face of God, and without strength to remedy his evil plight (Psalm 40:12; Romans 5:6). Then Christ's description, 'whom Satan hath bound' [v. 16], does imply that she was a case of diabolical possession" *(All the Miracles of the Bible).*

The woman's condition appealed to the sensitive spirit of Jesus who noticed her bent form and called to her and said, "Woman, thou art loosed from thine infirmity." We do not know whether she knew Jesus or if she knew that He would be in the synagogue on the Sabbath day. She did not ask for healing; neither did He wait to be asked. Jesus saw her plight and singled her out as a special object of His mercy.

Jesus laid His hands on the woman and immediately she was made straight. Such bodily contact was a help to the woman's faith. Chrysostom said, "He laid also His hands on her, that we may learn that the holy body possessed the power and energy of the Word of God." For this unasked-for act of divine power the woman poured forth a strain of continuous praise. She glorified God.

B. The Provision (Isaiah 53:4, 5)

4. Surely he hath borne our griefs, and carried our sorrows: yet we did esteem him stricken, smitten of God, and afflicted.

5. But he was wounded for our transgressions, he was bruised for our iniquities: the chastisement of our peace was upon him; and with his stripes we are healed.

The prophet lists six assertions concerning the vicarious sufferings of Christ: (1)"He hath borne our griefs," (2)"[He has] carried our sorrows," (3)"He was wounded for our transgressions," (4)"He was bruised for our iniquities," (5)"The chastisement of our peace was upon him," (6)"With his stripes we are healed."

Christ's sufferings were the remedy for all the ills that human beings are subject to. Divine healing is a basic fundamental Christian belief and has the support of the Bible. Healing is divine—meaning that it proceeds from God. We receive healing, therefore, directly from God. The word *healing* means "the restoring of one to health." Thus, divine healing means the restoring of a sick person to health by divine means.

The vicarious death of Christ is connected with the great truths of justification, reconciliation, consecration, translation, and presentation—having in their center the great gospel message about the death, burial, and resurrection of Christ. It therefore touches every aspect of the Christian life. It is the ground of our salvation, of our justification, of our healing, and of our perfect security. It is the great incentive to holiness of walk and to earnestness in service, and it assures us of a certain hope of our translation at the coming of the Lord and of our full realization of salvation for the whole man.

Why doesn't God heal all who ask Him?

III. RESULTS OF SALVATION (2 Timothy 1:9, 10; Titus 3:4-7)

A. Life and Immortality (2 Timothy 1:9, 10)

9. Who hath saved us, and called us with an holy calling, not according to our works, but according to his own purpose and grace, which was given us in Christ Jesus before the world began,

10. But is now made manifest by the appearing of our Saviour Jesus Christ, who hath abolished death, and hath brought life and immortality to light through the gospel.

Christ is our all-sufficient Savior. We found Him to be so when we turned to Him with our burden of sins. His all-sufficiency to save is the result of His work on the cross. He bore our sins in His own body on the tree, dying as the Just One for the unjust, being made sin for us that we might be the righteousness of God in Him. "Wherefore he is able also to save them to the uttermost that come unto God by him, seeing he ever liveth to make intercession for them" (Hebrews 7:25).

This all-sufficient Savior has provided us with immortality. The fellowship of the saints on earth is with the Lord Jesus Christ, and this fellowship into which God has called us will never end. We shall see His face from eternity to eternity. We shall be with Him forever—forever being like Him, forever receiving riches of God's kindness, forever sharing all He has and possesses.

B. Heirs (Titus 3:4-7)

4. But after that the kindness and love of God our Saviour toward man appeared,

5. Not by works of righteousness which we have done, but according to his mercy he saved us, by the washing of regeneration, and renewing of the Holy Ghost;

6. Which he shed on us abundantly through Jesus Christ our Saviour;

7. That being justified by his grace, we should be made heirs according to the hope of eternal life.

All we have is in Christ; all we are is through Him; and all we shall be will be in Him, through Him, and with Him. Therefore, we can sing with the psalmist, "All my springs (my sources of life and joy) are in you" (Psalm 87:7, *Amp.*). In whom? In Him who loved me and gave Himself for me. In Him who is raised from the dead and seated at God's right hand in the highest glory, far above all principality and power and might and dominion and every name that is named. In Him who has all power in heaven and on earth. In Him, in whom all the fullness of the Godhead dwells bodily. In Him under whose feet all things are to be put and who will be crowned King of kings and Lord of lords. In such a One—wonderful, omniscient, all-loving, and all-glorious—is all our hope. To know Him means to have a never-failing and a never-ending supply of all we need in time and in eternity. Apart from Him there is nothing but death.

How would you describe the results of salvation?

REVIEW QUESTIONS

1. How did Jesus deal with the accusers of the woman in John 8?
2. Describe Jesus' attitude toward the woman?
3. How did Jesus help the woman in Luke 13?
4. What did the prophet Isaiah predict Jesus would do as the Messiah?
5. List some of the results of salvation.

GOLDEN TEXT HOMILY

"GROW IN GRACE, AND IN THE KNOWLEDGE OF OUR LORD AND SAVIOUR JESUS CHRIST" (2 Peter 3:18).

Growing in grace and in the knowledge of our Lord will help us to understand the sin problem in individual lives. As Christians we cannot solve the problem of sin or change its penalty. We can only point individuals to the Lord Jesus Christ, who alone is able to cleanse and change hearts and attitudes.

Christians are often guilty of trying to persuade sinners to stop sinning before they are born again. We look at sin through human eyes. Our attitude toward sin is that some sins are more degrading and damaging than others. We can forgive sins such as gossip, stealing, lying, and cheating as human mistakes; but sins such as adultery, murder, rape, and homosexuality we cannot forgive.

Growing in grace and in the knowledge of the Lord Jesus Christ enables us to better deal with the individual's sins and transgressions. All sin is falling short of the mark God has set for us.

When we have grown in grace and in the knowledge of Jesus Christ, we leave the forgiveness to God the Father, the Lord Jesus Christ, and the Holy Spirit to transform an individual's life from sin to righteousness.—**Charles G.Wiley, Evangelist, Weatherford, Texas**

SENTENCE SERMONS

JESUS CHRIST IS the Savior of sinners

—Selected

JESUS CHRIST is God's everything for man's total need.

—Richard Halverson

CHRIST ON OUR CROSS is the way Calvary reads: He died for us—in our place

—C. Neil Strait

CHRIST CAME to pay a debt He did not owe because we owed a debt we could not pay.

—Dayspring

EVANGELISM APPLICATION

BELIEVERS SHOULD TESTIFY OF CHRIST'S POWER TO SAVE SINNERS.

All believers can say, "He died for me." The truth of substitution is illustrated in history by the conscript's substitute. On one occasion when a man with a family was conscripted for the Army, a young unmarried man came forward and offered to go in his place. The offer was accepted and the single man went as a substitute. He was killed in action; therefore, the man in whose place he went could then say, "He died for me." Other instances of a similar nature have been recorded. Although they illustrate one side of substitution, they fail in the other; for the one taking the penalty cannot put the other fully in the place of righteousness.

Paul said, "He made Him who knew no sin to be sin on our behalf, that we might become the righteousness of God in Him" (2 Corinthians 5:21, *NASB*).

ILLUMINATING THE LESSON

Jesus Christ is the all-sufficient Savior of sinners. We believe in Him as our Savior (Acts 6:31). We confess Him as our Lord (Romans 10:9). We have redemption through His blood (Ephesians 1:7). We look to Him as our Leader (Hebrews 12:2). We follow Him as our Teacher (Ephesians 4:20, 21). We feed upon Him as our Bread (John 6:48). We go to Him in our thirst (John 6:35). We enter by Him as our door (John 10:9). We abide in Him as our Vine (John 15:5). We have in Him our example (John 13:15). We find in Him our rest (Matthew 11:28). He is our righteousness (2 Corinthians 5:21). We are succored by Him in temptation (Hebrews 2:18). We turn to Him for sympathy (Hebrews 4:15, 16). We obtain through Him our victory (1 Corinthians 15:57). We overcome the world by Him (1 John 5:5). We have in Him eternal life (1 John 5:11, 12). We gain by Him the resurrection (Philippians 3:20, 21). We appear with Him in glory (Colossians 3:4). We exult in His everlasting love (Revelation 1:5, 6).

DAILY BIBLE READINGS

M. The Savior's Coming Foretold.
Genesis 49:8-12

T. Sufferings of the Savior.
Isaiah 53:1-12

W. Justice of the Savior.
Zechariah 9:9-11

T. Compassion of the Savior.
Matthew 18:11-14

F. Reconciled by the Savior.
Romans 5:6-11

S. Triumph of the Savior.
Revelation 5:9-14

Christ's Body—The Church

Study Text: Matthew 16:15-18; 1 Corinthians 12:12-27; Ephesians 2:19-22; 1 Peter 2:5, 9, 10

Objective: To study the nature and purpose of the church and assume our place in it.

Golden Text: "Ye are the body of Christ, and members in particular" (1 Corinthians 12:27).

Central Truth: The church is composed of all believers in Christ.

Evangelism Emphasis: The church bears witness of Christ to the world.

PRINTED TEXT

Matthew 16:15. He saith unto them, But whom say ye that I am?

16. And Simon Peter answered and said, Thou art the Christ, the Son of the living God.

17. And Jesus answered and said unto him, Blessed art thou, Simon Bar-jona: for flesh and blood hath not revealed it unto thee, but my Father which is in heaven.

18. And I say also unto thee, That thou art Peter, and upon this rock I will build my church; and the gates of hell shall not prevail against it.

Ephesians 2:19. Now therefore ye are no more strangers and foreigners, but fellowcitizens with the saints, and of the household of God;

20. And are built upon the foundation of the apostles and prophets, Jesus Christ himself being the chief corner stone;

21. In whom all the building fitly framed together groweth unto an holy temple in the Lord:

22. In whom ye also are builded together for an habitation of God through the Spirit.

1 Corinthians 12:12. For as the body is one, and hath many members, and all the members of that one body, being many, are one body: so also is Christ.

13. For by one Spirit are we all baptized into one body, whether we be Jews or Gentiles, whether we be bond or free; and have been all made to drink into one Spirit.

14. For the body is not one member, but many.

26. And whether one member suffer, all the members suffer with it; or one member be honoured, all the members rejoice with it.

27. Now ye are the body of Christ, and members in particular.

1 Peter 2:5. Ye also, as lively stones, are built up a spiritual house, an holy priesthood, to offer up spiritual sacrifices, acceptable to God by Jesus Christ.

9. But ye are a chosen generation, a royal priesthood, an holy

nation, a peculiar people; that ye should shew forth the praises of him who hath called you out of darkness into his marvellous light:

10. Which in time past were not a people, but are now the people of God: which had not obtained mercy, but now have obtained mercy.

LESSON OUTLINE

I. CHRIST BUILDS THE CHURCH
   A. The Confession
   B. The Composition
II. THE CHURCH IS CHRIST'S BODY
   A. Unified Diversity
   B. Diversified Unity
III. CREATED FOR GOD'S GLORY
   A. Living Stones
   B. Royal Priesthood

LESSON EXPOSITION

INTRODUCTION

The word *church* does not mean the building in which the congregation meets; neither is it, as the Roman Catholics say, the papal system. It is not a company or a club or just an organization. The church is not an organization, but an organism.

The word *church* is used in the Scriptures in two senses: in a universal sense and in a local sense.

When it is used in the universal sense, it refers to all those who have, in this dispensation or age, been born of the Spirit of God and have by that same Spirit been baptized into the body of Christ (1 Peter 1:3, 22, 23; 1 Corinthians 12:13).

The use of the term in the universal sense can be seen in the following: Christ spoke of building His "church," not "churches" (Matthew 16:18); Paul grieved because he had persecuted "the church" (1 Corinthians 15:9; Galatians 1:13; Philippians 3:6; cf. Acts 8:3); Christ is said to have loved "the church" and to have given Himself for it (Ephesians 5:25-27); Christ is called the head of "the church" (Ephesians 1:22; 5:23; Colossians 1:18); He has set apostles, prophets, teachers, and so forth in "the church" (1 Corinthians 12:28); "the church" is making known to the principalities and powers in the heavenly places the manifold wisdom of God (Ephesians 3:10); the whole company of believers of this age is called "the church of the firstborn" who are enrolled in heaven (Hebrews 12:23).

In each of the above scriptures the Greek word *ekklesia* is used. In itself this term means simply a body of called-out people, as in an assembly of citizens in a self-governing state; but the New Testament has filled this secular term with a spiritual content, so that it means a people called out from the world and from sinful things. Although the word occurs 114 times in the Greek Testament, it is used in the secular sense only in Acts 19:32, 39, 41, and of the assembly of the Israelites only in Acts 7:38 and Hebrews 2:12. It is interesting that the English word *church* comes from the Greek word *kuriakos*, which means "belonging to the Lord." This adjective occurs only twice in the New Testament: it is used of the Lord's Supper (1 Corinthians 11:20) and of the Lord's Day (Revelation 1:10). We might, therefore, give the following as a secondary definition of the term *church*: "a group of people called out from the world and belonging to the Lord." Yet the former definition recognizes more clearly the fact that the new birth is essential to membership in the true church.

In the local sense the word *church* is used of the group of professed believers in any one locality. Thus we read of the church in Jerusalem (Acts 8:1; 11:22), the church in Antioch (Acts 13:1), the church at Ephesus (Acts 20:17), the church at Cenchrea (Romans 16:1), the church at Corinth (1 Corinthians 1:2; 2 Corinthians 1:1), the churches of Galatia (Galatians 1:2), the church of the Laodiceans (Colossians 4:16), the church of the Thessalonians (1 Thessalonians 1:1; 2 Thessalonians 1:1), the churches of Judea (1 Thessalonians 2:14), and the churches in Asia (Revelation 1:4). The local churches together ought to be a faithful replica of the true church (adapted from *Lectures in Systematic Theology*, by Henry C. Thiessen).

I. CHRIST BUILDS THE CHURCH (Matthew 16:15-18; Ephesians 2:19-22)

A. The Confession

(Matthew 16:15-18)

15. He saith unto them, But whom say ye that I am?

16. And Simon Peter answered and said, Thou art the Christ, the Son of the living God.

17. And Jesus answered and said unto him, Blessed art thou, Simon Bar-jona: for flesh and blood hath not revealed it unto thee, but my Father which is in heaven.

18. And I say also unto thee, That thou art Peter, and upon this rock I will build my church; and the gates of hell shall not prevail against it.

In the previous verses, Jesus had asked the disciples what opinion of Himself men were expressing. They had answered that some believed Him to be the murdered John the Baptist returned from the grave, while others thought Him to be the prophet Elijah come back to earth, or Jeremiah, or some other of the ancient prophets. But Christ already knew all that and was only asking that He might impress upon them the personal question—the question for which He requires an answer from each one of us, and which determines our eternal destiny: "What do you think of Christ?"

A fisherman, Peter had become a fisher of men and had been sent forth as an evangelist. He had spent two and a half years in the school of Christ and had made some progress. He had listened to many wonderful discourses delivered by the One who spoke as no other ever spoke. He had witnessed many wonderful miracles, including the cure of his own mother-in-law, stricken with a fever. He had been one of the three disciples who had witnessed the raising from the dead of the daughter of Jairus. He had gained faith enough to walk on the stormy waves of the Sea of Galilee, though his faith held out only a minute. And now he was ready to recite the lesson he had learned in Christ's school, the greatest lesson he or any other man could possibly master.

F.B. Meyer says of Peter's response: "Speaking after the manner of men, Christ's heart must have stood still for the reply. And it came instantly, emphatically, and decisively from the lips of Peter, always the spokesman for the rest. In a most significant manner the answer combined the hope of the Jew for the Anointed One, with the recognition of the unique and essential nature of our Lord, as the Only-begotten of the Eternal God. It filled the heart of Jesus with ecstasy. The bluff fisherman had been taught the secret of the mystery which in other ages had not been made known unto the sons of men, as it was now to be revealed to the holy apostles and Prophets by the Spirit" *(Peter: The Fisherman, Disciple, Apostle).*

Jesus seized upon Peter's statement at once, exalted it with His approval and praise, and held it up before the Twelve as one of the most remarkable statements of all time. Peter did not realize what a great thing he had done; nor did he understand the epochal importance of his confession. Also, the other disciples had no idea of the momentous nature of the scene they were witnessing.

Peter had not been told by any man that Jesus was the Son of God. When his brother Andrew had led him to Jesus, he had summoned Peter to follow the Messiah. If Peter had listened to those around him, he would have thought of Jesus as being John the Baptist returned from the dead, or an incarnation of one of the ancient prophets.

Christ accepted Peter's definition of Him as "the Son of the living God" and stated that none but God the Father could have revealed this to him.

Peter had given his estimate of Christ. Now Christ would give His estimate of Peter. Jesus usually called Peter by his name, Simon. But, on this occasion He used the name He had given him prophetically when Andrew brought him to Christ (John 1:42). *Peter* (both Greek and Latin in origin) means "rock," from which the English *petrified* (turned to stone) is derived. *Cephas* is Aramaic for the same thing. There was an unstable side to Peter, a fickle and uncertain side; but Christ saw the "rock" side.

Jesus told Peter He would build His church upon "this rock." Not upon Peter—the fallible, clumsy, and blundering disciple—but upon Peter's confession of Jesus as the Christ, the Son of the living God.

Jesus predicted that the church He would build could not be defeated. The word *Hades*, which is the translated term for *hell* (*KJV*), is a Greek word meaning "unseen." It means the realm of departed spirits, the invisible world, and is a synonym of *death*. From the custom of holding court at the city gates, the word gates came to mean authority or power. Therefore, Christ said in this place that against His church thus founded, the power of death would not prevail; it would stand forever.

How would you explain Peter's great confession in Matthew 16:16?

B. The Composition
(Ephesians 2:19-22)

19. Now therefore ye are no more strangers and foreigners, but fellowcitizens with the saints, and of the household of God;

20. And are built upon the foundation of the apostles and prophets, Jesus Christ himself being the chief corner stone;

21. In whom all the building

fitly framed together groweth unto an holy temple in the Lord:

22. In whom ye also are builded together for an habitation of God through the Spirit.

In the closing verses of Ephesians 2 Paul expressed that organic relationship in which Jew and Gentile find themselves united in Christ in three figures of speech: citizens of a commonwealth, members of a household, and stones of a temple. In these three metaphors there are suggested three fundamental human relationships: to the state as a subject, to the family as a child, and to God as a worshiper.

A sojourner, under Greek laws and customs, was a resident who was not a citizen in the full sense of the term and who had very restricted franchise rights. He was tolerated in the community, and that was about all. In verse 19, the term *therefore* had a meaning to the early Christians which it does not have to us. And when Paul took that word and that idea and related it to their former religious life, they did not need anyone to interpret it. They had known what it was to be on the outside—to be excluded from privilege, to be tolerated, to be snubbed. But in Christ they were such no more. In each of these metaphors Paul was using an idea he had used before. They had been "aliens from the commonwealth of Israel, and strangers from the covenants of promise" (v. 12). Now they were fellow citizens with the saints. They had full franchise rights in the kingdom of God.

Paul's choice of the word *temple* (v. 21) is significant. There were two words for *temple*. One applied to the structure in a general sense and might be used of the whole area, including the outer courts. The other word, the one he used, was restricted to the Temple proper; and that included the Most Holy Place, where the Shekinah glory had been.

Verses 21 and 22 comprise a statement which has far-reaching and mysterious implications. He compared the church to a temple in which God is taking up His abode. God dwelt in Solomon's temple in a manifest way. But the manifestation was a means to an end. The Temple was the point of contact, the way of approach between God and man. Is not the church to be, through all the ages, the vehicle of the manifestation of the grace of God to the entire universe? Is not this what the apostle implied when he said in the next chapter that he desired to see "what is the fellowship of the mystery, which from the beginning of the world hath been hid in God . . . to the intent that now unto the principalities and powers in heavenly places might be known by the church the manifold wisdom of God" (3:9, 10). And again, "That in the ages to come he might show the exceeding riches of his grace in his kindness toward us through Christ Jesus" (2:7). We are an invisible temple, a heavenly priesthood, a means of access to the universe through eternity (Adapted from *Ephesians*, by Walter Wright).

II. THE CHURCH IS CHRIST'S BODY (1 Corinthians 12:12-27)

A. Unified Diversity (vv. 12-18)

(1 Corinthians 12:15-18 is not included in the printed text.)

12. For as the body is one, and hath many members, and all the members of that one body, being many, are one body: so also is Christ.

13. For by one Spirit are we all baptized into one body, whether we be Jews or Gentiles, whether

we be bond or free; and have been all made to drink into one Spirit.

14. For the body is not one member, but many.

The apostle declared the essential unity of the church. He pointed out that the church is the body of Christ and that the basic characteristic of a healthy body is that every member in it performs its function for the good of the whole. However, he was careful to emphasize that unity does not mean uniformity. In the church there are differing gifts and differing functions, but all the gifts come from the same Spirit. Each of them is designed to bring glory to the God who gave them. Each of them is designed to help the body.

Paul was careful to indicate that there is a vast difference between various members of the body. We need each other and we should respect each other. This illustrates unity in diversity.

B. Diversified Unity (vv. 19-27)

(1 Corinthians 12:19-25 is not included in the printed text.)

26. And whether one member suffer, all the members suffer with it; or one member be honoured, all the members rejoice with it.

27. Now ye are the body of Christ, and members in particular.

Paul said that even though there are vast differences between the members of the body when one suffers, all suffer. If you have a pain in your foot as you walk along the road, what happens? Your nerves send out the signal and the whole body becomes active. Your back bends and your hands reach out to touch the part that pains. Your eyes may begin to water and your voice may begin to complain. The whole body feels the impact of the pain. This is the way the body cares one part for another. We give covering and protection to the weaker parts of our physical body in order that the life of the whole body may be preserved.

Paul could not really imagine all Christians being alike, all doing the same thing. It was his belief that the church should function as a healthy, physical body. In order for this to happen, God placed in the church those essentials that make this possible. The apostle's list in verse 28 includes apostles, prophets, teachers, miracles, gifts of healings, helps, governments, and diversities of tongues. All of these work together for the good of the whole body.

What problems arise when a church strives for uniformity rather than unity?

III. CREATED FOR GOD'S GLORY (1 Peter 2:5, 9, 10)

A. Living Stones (v. 5)

5. Ye also, as lively stones, are built up a spiritual house, an holy priesthood, to offer up spiritual sacrifices, acceptable to God by Jesus Christ.

Holiness, in addition to being a call and a growth, is a function in the temple of God. Since God chose in Old Testament times to establish fellowship with His people in a local, concrete way by means of the Tabernacle and then the Temple, it was fitting that Jesus (Matthew 16:18), Paul (1 Corinthians 3:10-17; Ephesians 2:19-22), and Peter (1 Peter 2:5) should use the figure of a building for the congregation of believers. Actually, the early Christians did not have church buildings at first. They usually met in someone's house. But they were conscious of being part of a great spiritual temple which God was erecting.

In the early days of Christianity some people thought they could achieve greater holiness by solitary effort. So they moved to deserts and caves. Later, monasteries were established as places for retreat from a sinful world. But Peter rebuked hermit asceticism. He told people to take their proper place in the life of the church. Christianity is a social faith. Fellowship with the Lord is more real when it is experienced in the group. In such a context it is also easier to give the Lord the praise which is due Him. In fact, all of the functions of worship and service have their divinely appointed center in the assembly of the saints.

B. Royal Priesthood (vv. 9, 10)

9. But ye are a chosen generation, a royal priesthood, an holy nation, a peculiar people; that ye should shew forth the praises of him who hath called you out of darkness into his marvellous light:

10. Which in time past were not a people, but are now the people of God: which had not obtained mercy, but now have obtained mercy.

Peter emphasized the priesthood of all believers. To do this he took the three basic principles underlying the priesthood in the Old Testament—divine choice, necessity for holiness, and drawing near to God—and blended them for the benefit of his readers. He told them they were a "chosen generation." They are to be spiritual and holy. They are to offer up sacrifices and to "shew forth [God's] praises."

"Ye are a chosen generation." The word *generation* here means not contemporaries, but the offspring of one common parent, the offshoots of one original stock. The Israelites were a special "generation." They had sprung from Abraham as their common progenitor. The Jews were also a "chosen generation"—called out of the darkness of Chaldean idolatry to the marvelous light of divine revelation of the one true God.

"[Ye are] a royal priesthood." The Jews were a nation of priests. In Revelation 1:6 John said that Jesus has "made us kings and priests"—kings over ourselves and priests unto God. It is a great sight to see men monarchs of themselves—ruling their own passions and keeping their lusts in subjection and, by their upright behavior and holy conversation, showing forth the character of God.

"[Ye are] a holy nation." As a people bound together for the purposes of holiness, we should show forth the excellencies of God.

In verse 10 Peter said it is the calling of God which gives unity to the church gathered out of all races and all lands and makes it the people of God. This is brought about through the mercy of God.

What is the purpose of today's church in the world?

REVIEW QUESTIONS

1. What was Peter's estimate of Christ?
2. How did Jesus praise Peter's response?
3. How did Paul describe the church in Ephesians 2:19-22?
4. What did Paul say about unity and diversity in the church in 1 Corinthians 12?
5. List the characteristics of God's people in 1 Peter 2:5, 9, 10.

GOLDEN TEXT HOMILY

"YE ARE THE BODY OF CHRIST, AND MEMBERS IN PARTICULAR" (1 Corinthians 12:27).

We have here in general terms the summation and application of the foregoing illustration of the human body as a picture of Christ's body. Paul concluded that members of the body are "members in particular."

"Now ye are the body of Christ." That which is set in the body is set in the interest of the whole body. The eye is the servant of the whole body, and so with all members. Using the human body, Paul exerted great effort to show the need of different parts to make the whole. The ear, foot, and hand are not the body; they are parts of the body. While not the body, each is necessary in making up the body. The body has many parts, but the many parts make up one body when they are all put together. Not one of the members is everything, but every member is something!

Christ is the head of the whole church. He presides over all, and individual members confirm to each other the relation of fellow members in the same body. All are subject to the same head.

Collectively, each of us in all our diversity make up the body of Christ. But our individuality and uniqueness is not lost in the union. Unlike a drop of water falling in a river and losing its identity as it becomes part of the river, we are "members in particular."

Individual members do not get lost in the union—eyes remain eyes, ears remain ears, hands remain hands. Different gifts and functions continue to operate, making the body of Christ what it is—mutually interdependent on each other. Isolated from each other, neither is complete without the other.

To belong to Christ's body means not only to belong to Him but to help each other, honor one another, and be sensitive to one another.—**Joel Harris, M.Div., Pastor, Mobile, Alabama**

SENTENCE SERMONS

THE CHURCH is composed of all believers in Christ.

—Selected

THE CHURCH bears witness of Christ to the world.

—Selected

WE WILL ONLY BE weak and stumbling believers and a crippled church unless and until we truly apply God's Word—that is, until we truly love Him and act on that love.

—Charles Colson

IN THE CHURCH two opposite dangers are to be recognized and avoided: they are a cold heart and a hot head.

—A.W.Tozer

EVANGELISM APPLICATION

THE CHURCH BEARS WITNESS OF CHRIST TO THE WORLD.

Often the best witness the Christian can provide for the world is to stand firm in his faith in Christ. The inclination of every combatant, even though victorious, is to lie down and rest after the struggle is over, but the disposition of a Christian is to stand. Every moral effort leaves a man stronger than before. There is an Indian proverb that the strength of each slain foe enters into the victor's right arm. Certainly it is true of the Christian soldier. Overcome a selfish desire in the morning, and you will travel all day with a lighter step. Fight your doubts in terrible reality, and your grip of truth will inspire fear in every skeptic. Clothe yourself with Christian principles, and dishonorable men will tempt you less. The battleground is really in your own soul. Once you have made up your mind as to your course of action, the battle is as good as won. Men entice the half-hearted, the undecided, and the hesitating, but they leave alone him whose face is steadily set toward Jerusalem.

In these 10 "ships" the Christians of the first century moved out, over stormy waters that threatened their destruction, into the broad sea of world redemption. Again the storm is on, the "ships" of the Christian faith are in peril. The contemporary church must turn to the first century to learn how to chart the course of Christianity.—**Adapted from Gaines S. Dobbins, Building Better Churches**

DAILY BIBLE READINGS

M. Benefits of Fellowship.
Psalm 84:1-10

T. Good News Foretold.
Isaiah 40:9-11

W. Message of the Church.
Isaiah 52:7-10

T. Spiritual Union With Christ.
John 15:1-8

F. Members of God's Household.
Ephesians 2:19-22

S. Destiny of the Church.
Revelation 19:6-9

Signs and Wonders at Pentecost

Study Text: Acts 2:1-47

Objective: To understand and appreciate the ministry of the Holy Spirit and live a Spirit-filled life.

Time: The Book of Acts was written between A.D. 61 and 63, recording events of A.D. 30.

Place: The Book of Acts was probably written at Rome or Caesarea about events in Jerusalem.

Golden Text: "They were all filled with the Holy Ghost, and began to speak with other tongues, as the Spirit gave them utterance" (Acts 2:4).

Central Truth: Signs and wonders accompany the ministry of the Holy Spirit in the church.

Evangelism Emphasis: The Holy Spirit empowers believers to witness for Christ.

PRINTED TEXT

Acts 2:1. And when the day of Pentecost was fully come, they were all with one accord in one place.

2. And suddenly there came a sound from heaven as of a rushing mighty wind, and it filled all the house where they were sitting.

3. And there appeared unto them cloven tongues like as of fire, and it sat upon each of them.

4. And they were all filled with the Holy Ghost, and began to speak with other tongues, as the Spirit gave them utterance.

5. And there were dwelling at Jerusalem Jews, devout men, out of every nation under heaven.

6. Now when this was noised abroad, the multitude came together, and were confounded, because that every man heard them speak in his own language.

7. And they were all amazed and marvelled, saying one to another, Behold, are not all these which speak Galilaeans?

8. And how hear we every man in our own tongue, wherein we were born?

12. And they were all amazed, and were in doubt, saying one to another, What meaneth this?

13. Others mocking said, These men are full of new wine.

29. Men and brethren, let me freely speak unto you of the patriarch David, that he is both dead and buried, and his sepulchre is with us unto this day.

30. Therefore being a prophet, and knowing that God had sworn with an oath to him, that of the fruit of his loins, according to the flesh, he would raise up Christ to sit on his

throne;

31. He seeing this before spake of the resurrection of Christ, that his soul was not left in hell, neither his flesh did see corruption.

32. This Jesus hath God raised up, whereof we all are witnesses.

33. Therefore being by the right hand of God exalted, and having received of the Father the promise of the Holy Ghost, he hath shed forth this, which ye now see and hear.

46. And they, continuing daily with one accord in the temple, and breaking bread from house to house, did eat their meat with gladness and singleness of heart.

47. Praising God, and having favour with all the people. And the Lord added to the church daily such as should be saved.

LESSON OUTLINE

I. SIGNS OF THE SPIRIT'S COMING
   A. The Sound
   B. The Sight
   C. The Speech

II. JESUS EXALTED
   A. Resurrection Predicted by God
   B. Exalted by God
   C. Honored by God

III. GOD PRAISED
   A. Through Fellowship
   B. Through Maturity
   C. Through Praise

LESSON EXPOSITION

INTRODUCTION

Pentecost was the event which completed the church and endowed it with that supernatural power which then was, and ever since has been, the source of its true life and of its greatest successes. Ever since that eventful day the term *Pentecost* has been applied to any great outpouring of the convicting and converting Spirit of God that has been enjoyed by God's people.

The word *Pentecost* is from a Greek word meaning "fiftieth," and the feast is so called because it falls 50 days after the Passover. It is also called the Feast of Weeks, 50 being a week of weeks, that is, seven weeks plus one day. It marked the end of harvest, as the Passover marked the beginning of the harvest. During the Passover the sheaves of the firstfruits of the harvest were offered to God, and during Pentecost the first two loaves made from the new grain were offered.

The city of Jerusalem was crowded at Pentecost. This was because Pentecost was one of the three annual feasts when the law required the attendance of every Jew in the Temple. Indeed, as the Passover came too early for safe navigation, more Jews from the west came to Jerusalem at Pentecost than at the Passover.

As Pentecost marked by the Jewish calendar celebrates the gathering of the firstfruits of the harvest, so, in the history of the Christian church, it speaks of the first great gathering of spiritual fruit, souls harvested for God's church.

I. SIGNS OF THE SPIRIT'S COMING (Acts 2:1-13)

A. The Sound (vv. 1, 2)

1. And when the day of Pentecost was fully come, they were all with one accord in one place.

2. And suddenly there came a sound from heaven as of a rushing mighty wind, and it filled all the house where they were sitting.

On the eve of His crucifixion, Jesus informed His disciples several times of the Spirit whom the Father would send to strengthen, instruct, and convict. Because the disciples did not realize that Jesus would be crucified so soon, they probably did not immediately understand the significance of the promise of the Spirit. Even though after the Crucifixion they may have recalled Jesus' reference to the Comforter, their joy in their Lord's resurrection probably veiled their memory of that promise.

In the opening verses of Acts we find a reiteration of that promise. This time it is in a new context. Jesus had already been crucified and resurrected, but He awaited His ascension. He again gave the promise of the coming Spirit—this time to empower His followers for witnessing at home, abroad, and to the uttermost parts of the earth (1:8).

Being assembled with the disciples, Jesus charged them not to leave Jerusalem until they had received "the promise of the Father" (Acts 1:4), which meant they would be "endued with power from on high" (Luke 24:49).

Often this commandment to wait for the promise is taken out of context and imposed upon modern believers as a condition for being baptized in the Holy Spirit. However, the stress of the command is on the words "in Jerusalem." The charge to the disciples was not as much concerned with waiting (with spiritual preparation) as with the geographical direction (in Jerusalem) and with the certainty that God would fulfill His promise of a new Spirit experience.

On the Day of Pentecost the disciples no doubt attended the Temple soon after dawn for the morning sacrifices and the offering of the firstfruits; then in a body all together, they assembled at the house which was their headquarters. The actual place of the descent of the Holy Spirit can never be determined with certainty. Many believe it was the Upper Room, where the Last Supper was held, but this cannot be dogmatically asserted.

This gathering of the 120 or more was for prayer and worship. The other Jews in Jerusalem would be engaged in similar exercises in the synagogues of the city. On Sabbath and festival days, until such services were over, they abstained from eating and drinking, not breaking their fast until the fourth hour, about 10 a.m., or even noon.

The sound heard was an extraordinary one. It came suddenly; it came from heaven. It gave forth a sound that could best be described as "a rushing mighty wind." There seems to have been no gale sweeping over the city, no wind that violently struck the sides of the building or swept furiously through the street. J.A. Alexander observes: "The word translated *rushing* is a passive participle meaning borne or carried, and is probably descriptive of involuntary motion caused by a superior power. The word *mighty* is expressive not only of a quality, but of an effect, violent, destructive. The noun itself which these words qualify is not the ordinary term for *wind*, but a stronger one answering to blast or gust. The whole phrase is therefore descriptive of a powerful, tempestuous commotion of air by some extraordinary cause" *(The Book of Acts)*.

B. The Sight (v. 3)

3. And there appeared unto them cloven tongues like as of fire, and it sat upon each of them.

Fire, like *wind*, was symbolic of the divine presence (Exodus 3:2) and of the Spirit who purifies and sanctifies (see Ezekiel 1:13; Malachi 3:2). It is not necessary to assume that these tongues were of actual material flame, but they were "as of fire."

Dr. Vernon Bartlet writes of this verse: "The fire-like appearance, originally one, broke up into tongues of flame, as it were, and distributed itself among those assembled. The phenomenon is taken in the narrative to symbolize the gift of tongues described in the next verse, viz., as one in source and essence, but various in manifested forms" *(The New Century Bible)*.

In commenting on this verse, Alexander Maclaren states: "The meaning of the Pentecostal fire is twofold: the Christian is to be purified, and he is to be fervent, zealous, enthusiastic, joyful. We are all icebergs compared with what we ought to be. Where among us are to be found lives blazing with enthusiastic devotion and earnest love? We ought to be like God himself, all aflame with love" *(Expositions of Holy Scripture)*.

Samuel Chadwick notes: "God expects us to speak, and has provided an organ of effective speech. Wherever and whenever he wants our witness, the Spirit is ready to give the right word and to clothe it with power. Fire is mightier than learning. A soul ablaze is a better guide to effective speech than much scholarship. It is fire that conquers the heart. The fire still falls from heaven. It cannot be kindled with earthly forces. There is no need to warm ourselves at other men's fires, for the Spirit fell upon all, and remained with each" *(Humanity and God)*.

The Day of Pentecost is in line with all the other days, and what God did then for the apostles and the women, He will still do for us today.

C. The Speech (vv. 4-13)

(Acts 2:9-11 is not included in the printed text.)

4. And they were all filled with the Holy Ghost, and began to speak with other tongues, as the Spirit gave them utterance.

5. And there were dwelling at Jerusalem Jews, devout men, out of every nation under heaven.

6. Now when this was noised abroad, the multitude came together, and were confounded, because that every man heard them speak in his own language.

7. And they were all amazed and marvelled, saying one to another, Behold, are not all these which speak Galilaeans?

8. And how hear we every man in our own tongue, wherein we were born?

Immediately following the audible and visible signs of the Spirit's presence, the believers were filled with the Holy Ghost. There came into evidence another manifestation or sign of the Spirit's presence in the believers: they "began to speak with other tongues, as the Spirit gave them utterance." The miraculous signs which appeared to the hearing and seeing of the believers were evidence of the Spirit's presence in their midst. The miraculous gift of being able to speak in languages they did not know was evidence of the Spirit's presence infilling each believer.

From a census taken in the time of Nero, we know that more than 2.7 million Jews were gathered at the Passover Feast, and still greater numbers came to Pentecost. Thus, at the very beginning, the disciples were witnesses for Christ to the uttermost ends of the earth, for Peter's sermon was preached to men who had their homes all over the known world.

Thomas Lindsay notes: "It is interesting that the list of countries mentioned includes all the lands to which the Israelites had been banished and where they had been settled for centuries, as well as those countries to which they had come voluntarily. Hence representatives from all the twelve tribes listened to Peter's sermon, carried back the gospel to their distant homes, and were sometime afterward confirmed in their faith by the epistle of James which is addressed to 'the twelve tribes which are scattered abroad' (James 1:1)" *(The Acts of the Apostles)*.

These verses emphasize the fact that the believers were filled with the Holy Ghost. Their speaking with other tongues occurred as a result and evidence of the fact that they were filled with the Spirit. Their speaking with other tongues was not learned or contrived or self-actuated—they spoke "as the Spirit gave them utterance." This was something more than a purely emotional experience. The Spirit-baptized believers were so completely surrendered to the Holy Spirit that even their tongues (the most unruly member of the body, James 3:8) were made by the Spirit to speak in the languages of many nations "the wonderful works of God" (Acts 2:11).

"Speaking with tongues" refers to the ability the Holy Spirit gives to speak in known or unknown languages we have not learned. Tongues-speaking may be in strange ecstatic sounds, for the Spirit can speak in any manner He chooses, but many times it is in one of the earth's known languages.

"Speaking with tongues as the Holy Spirit gives utterance" means that believers speak in another language by the power of the Holy Spirit. One scholar points out that the word *utterance* in Acts 2:4 is "a peculiar word and purposely chosen to denote clear, loud utterance [articulation] under the miraculous impulse." Another Bible scholar emphasizes that the word *utterance* includes the idea of enunciating plainly.

The ability to speak in tongues is not achieved through a heightened emotional state or through the repetition of words and phrases. It is not the result of imitating sounds made by others. We neither learn nor teach to speak in tongues by human effort. To the contrary, human effort to speak with tongues only hinders the utterance the Holy Spirit may give. He who speaks in tongues speaks only by the supernatural and motivational power of the Holy Spirit. He needs only to respond to faith and speak out as the Spirit gives the utterance. Any manipulative technique for being baptized in the Holy Spirit and speaking in tongues is without biblical pattern or propriety.

12. And they were all amazed, and were in doubt, saying one to another, What meaneth this?

13. Others mocking said,

These men are full of new wine.

The Jews could neither deny nor explain the things they saw and heard. Since it was a feast day, the Jews assumed the disciples had been drinking wine and that their strange behavior was due to drunkenness.

Dr. Doug Beacham comments: "Unless the Holy Spirit creates faith, the world can only respond with doubt to the mighty acts of God. The carnal mind does not, indeed cannot, comprehend the working of God's Spirit (1 Corinthians 2:14)" —*Evangelical Commentary*, Vol. 38.

What kind of signs have you observed accompanying the coming of the Holy Spirit?

II. JESUS EXALTED (Acts 2:29-36)

A. Resurrection Predicted by God (vv. 29-31)

29. Men and brethren, let me freely speak unto you of the patriarch David, that he is both dead and buried, and his sepulchre is with us unto this day.

30. Therefore being a prophet, and knowing that God had sworn with an oath to him, that of the fruit of his loins, according to the flesh, he would raise up Christ to sit on his throne;

31. He seeing this before spake of the resurrection of Christ, that his soul was not left in hell, neither his flesh did see corruption.

The first effect of the coming of the Holy Spirit was seen in Peter. Immediately he emerged as the wise, skillful, brave, and efficient leader of the Christian church. The news of the miracle of the tongues quickly brought together a great throng of people from at least 16 different parts of the Roman Empire. Peter was quick to seize the opportunity to preach the Christ to so many, who would carry the message so far.

This was an epoch-making sermon. It was delivered on a memorable occasion and was the first gospel message of the new church. It is an utterance of which to be proud.

In verses 14 and 15, Peter began his sermon by turning to the mockers and calling attention to the early hour, 9 o'clock, a time at which they could not be drunk, even if they were drinking men. The Jews drank wine with meat only. They ate bread in the morning and meat in the evening—basing their custom on Exodus 16:8—and so they drank no wine till late in the day. This charge being easily refuted, Peter paid no more attention to it but turned to the more serious aspect of the situation and addressed it in terms the audience could understand.

After his polite introduction (v. 14), Peter informed his audience that what they had seen had been predicted by the prophet Joel (vv. 16-21; see also Joel 2:28-32).

Rising into fierce and just indignation, Peter summarized the story of Christ's life, His miracles which proved that He was from God, the Jews wickedness in slaying Him, and the final testimony to His deity in the resurrection.

In verses 29-31 Peter, now filled with the Holy Spirit, spoke of the patriarch David and the words of Psalm 16 which he had alluded to in verses 25-28. He stressed the point that Psalm 16 did not refer to David and gave evidence of that since David did experience death and corruption and that the Jews were much aware of the sight of David's tomb.

Peter also called attention to the

fact that David was not only a king, but also a prophet who with divine anointing, was given foresight of some future events. The promise of Christ as David's descendant is found in 2 Samuel 7:11-16 and in Psalm 89:3, 4 and gives assurance that the Messiah was to sit on his throne. Peter here claimed that Jesus, who was the descendant of David, was the One to whom Jehovah referred and that He proved it by raising Jesus from the dead. David saw the resurrection prophetically. Peter declared that the resurrected Christ was bringing about the manifestations of the Spirit that they could not explain.

B. Exalted by God (vv. 32, 33)

32. This Jesus hath God raised up, whereof we all are witnesses.

33. Therefore being by the right hand of God exalted, and having received of the Father the promise of the Holy Ghost, he hath shed forth this, which ye now see and hear.

The fact that God raised Christ up is proof that God was satisfied with Him. G. Campbell Morgan states: "By the resurrection we know that whatever men may think of Jesus, God placed Him over all men from the standpoint of His life and character. He raised Him from the dead also as testimony to the perfection of His mediation. Furthermore, if by this resurrection there has been revealed God's perfect man, by that self-same resurrection God has rejected all other men" *(Expositions of Holy Scripture).*

C. Honored by God (vv. 34-36)

(Acts 2:34-36 is not included in the printed text.)

Having shown the resurrection of Christ to be the subject of ancient prophecy, Peter now proved the same of His exaltation. J.A. Alexander observes: "The argument is rendered still more parallel and uniform by drawing the proof from the Old Testament (Psalm 110:1; cf. Matthew 22:41-46). Here two signal Messianic prophecies were universally recognized and universally ascribed to David, neither of which could be applied to David as its subject, both of which must have respect to the Messiah, and both of which have been fulfilled in Jesus" *(The Acts of the Apostles Explained).*

Why did God assign Peter the task of preaching the first sermon in the Christian church?

III. GOD PRAISED (Acts 2:42-47)

A. Through Fellowship (vv. 42-45)

(Acts 2:42-45 is not included in the printed text.)

The "apostles' doctrine" (teaching) would be the recital—by those favored apostles who had known the Lord intimately, witnessed His miracles, and heard His discourses—of all that they had seen and heard. The content of the four Gospels was repeated over and over, and very likely there was much more that has not been preserved for us. "Fellowship" would be the intimate living with the apostles and other Christians, having all things common in brotherly unselfishness, as Luke goes on to describe. As Philip Schaff puts it, ". . . a few honest, plain fishermen of Galilee, raised to be the official witnesses of the Holy Ghost; transformed from illiterate men into infallible organs of the Savior of the world, teachers of all ages" *(History of the Apostolic Church).*

The phrase "in breaking of bread" is taken by some Bible scholars to refer to a common meal. These scholars believe that every such meal in the early church had a religious significance. They believe that it became a type and evidence of the kingdom of God among believers.

Some New Testament scholars say this statement is the common New Testament name for the Communion service meaning one element of the Lord's Supper being put for both. We know the Communion service is intended to promote fellowship with other Christians as well as with Christ. God receives praise through such unity of His children.

"Prayers" were a prominent feature of Christian worship in the early church. Prayers were offered at the Communion service and by groups of Christians in the Temple. Also, various groups met in the homes of the Christians just for prayer.

These early Christians were cheerful and contented; they loved one another so fervently that they sold their possessions and gave to all as they had need (v. 45). The Spirit of Christ bound these believers into one body, united in faith and love and hope. It is therefore not strange that Pentecost is regarded as the true birthday of the Christian church, nor is it surprising that such men were held in high esteem with all the people.

B. Through Maturity (v. 46)

46. And they, continuing daily with one accord in the temple, and breaking bread from house to house, did eat their meat with gladness and singleness of heart.

Christian maturity does not happen the moment one accepts Christ. In fact, those who have lived the longest for Christ are the first to admit their continued need for teaching from God's Word. A consuming desire to know more about God and His Son Jesus Christ accompanies true conversion. And they want to share this with fellow believers.

It is interesting to note the steps toward maturity in the lives of the early believers. First, they had a knowledge they were saved with the accompanying peace with God. Next followed growth in divine truth and meaningful fellowship one with another as they shared their means with those in need. Then they were able to see others saved. This growth produced gladness of heart.

C. Through Praise (v. 47)

47. Praising God, and having favour with all the people. And the Lord added to the church daily such as should be saved.

Out of this intimate communion in truth and Christian fellowship—either about the Lord's Table or in prayer on their knees or in the matter of material possessions—there came a life of extraordinary beauty and simplicity. There in the midst of religious formalism and hypocrisy were groups of men and women filled with the Holy Spirit, who, day by day, knew a glorious gladness and singleness of heart and were therefore praising God and having favor with all the people.

The last sentence of verse 47 ought to characterize the continued experience of every Christian church; for in every congregation so walking in the light of God and its members truly witnessing to the grace of His Son, newborn souls should be added daily, by the power of the Lord, who calls, convicts, and converts.

How would you compare Christians you know today with Christians of the first century?

REVIEW QUESTIONS

1. What were the signs of the Spirit's coming?
2. How did the crowd in Jerusalem react to the coming of the Holy Spirit?
3. What accusations did the crowd make toward the Christians?

GOLDEN TEXT HOMILY

"THEY WERE ALL FILLED WITH THE HOLY GHOST, AND BEGAN TO SPEAK WITH OTHER TONGUES, AS THE SPIRIT GAVE THEM UTTERANCE" (Acts 2:4).

This passage is very familiar to Pentecostals. It is one of the verses we memorized as children.

The baptism of the Holy Spirit is one of our cardinal doctrines. For many years it was the major difference between Pentecostals and other denominations. In recent years the Holy Spirit has been accepted and received by a number of what are sometimes called the "nominal" churches.

For the study in Acts 2, we will list a few points of interest concerning the Holy Spirit.

The Scripture refers to the disciples being "all with one accord in one place" (v. 1). For an outpouring of the Holy Spirit to come, these two ingredients are absolutely necessary.

Four things happened as a result of the apostles' obedience to Jesus Christ, and to their being together and in one accord:

1. "There came a sound from heaven" (v. 2).

2. "There appeared . . . cloven tongues like as of fire." They all saw the flaming tongues of fire as "it sat upon each of them" (v. 3).

3. "They were all filled with the Holy Ghost, and began to speak with other tongues, as the Spirit gave them utterance" (v. 4).

There are people who agree that all 120 heard the sound and saw the fire, but not that all spoke with tongues. The Bible specifically says they all spoke with tongues. Saint Augustine said, "The 120 all received the Holy Ghost." Lang said, "Not only the apostles, but all of the disciples were filled with the Holy Ghost." It would be wise to underscore "as the Spirit gave them utterance." God does not need the assistance of tape recorders, syllable instructors, and so forth. He needs only a sanctified vessel who desires to be filled with His Spirit.

4. The results of this outpouring were not only speaking in other tongues, but also 3,000 souls were saved (v. 41), and an evangelistic fervor that spread the good news into all parts of the world.

If only we could let the fire of the Holy Spirit burn in our hearts as Acts 2:4 describes, the Church of God would triple instead of double in a decade.—**M.E. Roberson, (Retired) Former Pastor, Soddy, Tennessee**

DAILY BIBLE READINGS

M. Led by the Spirit.
Numbers 11:25-30

T. Anointed by the Spirit.
Isaiah 61:1-11

W. Conviction by the Spirit.
John 16:7-11

T. Power Promised.
Luke 24:44-49

F. The Spirit Reveals God's Will.
Acts 16:6-12

S. The Spirit's Call.
Revelation 22:17-21

The Believer's Hope

Study Text: Matthew 16:27; John 14:1-3; Acts 1:9-11; Philippians 3:20, 21; Colossians 3:1-4; 1 Thessalonians 4:16, 17; 2 Thessalonians 1:7-10; Titus 2:11-13; 1 John 3:1, 2

Objective: To focus on the promise of Christ's coming and anticipate His return.

Golden Text: "Looking for that blessed hope, and the glorious appearing of the great God and our Saviour Jesus Christ" (Titus 2:13).

Central Truth: The Bible teaches Jesus Christ will come again.

Evangelism Emphasis: Christians should share the hope of Christ's return with sinners.

PRINTED TEXT

Matthew 16:27. For the Son of man shall come in the glory of his Father with his angels; and then he shall reward every man according to his works.

John 14:2. In my Father's house are many mansions: if it were not so, I would have told you. I go to prepare a place for you.

3. And if I go and prepare a place for you, I will come again, and receive you unto myself; that where I am, there ye may be also.

Acts 1:11. Which also said, Ye men of Galilee, why stand ye gazing up into heaven? this same Jesus, which is taken up from you into heaven, shall so come in like manner as ye have seen him go into heaven.

Philippians 3:20. For our conversation is in heaven; from whence also we look for the Saviour, the Lord Jesus Christ:

21. Who shall change our vile body, that it may be fashioned like unto his glorious body, according to the working whereby he is able even to subdue all things unto himself.

Colossians 3:2. Set your affection on things above, not on things on the earth.

3. For ye are dead, and your life is hid with Christ in God.

4. When Christ, who is our life, shall appear, then shall ye also appear with him in glory.

Titus 2:13. Looking for that blessed hope, and the glorious appearing of the great God and our Saviour Jesus Christ.

1 Thessalonians 4:16. For the Lord himself shall descend from heaven with a shout, with the voice of the archangel, and with the trump of God: and the dead in Christ shall rise first:

17. Then we which are alive and remain shall be caught up together with them in the clouds, to meet the Lord in the air: and so shall we ever be with the Lord.

1 John 3:1. Behold, what

manner of love the Father hath bestowed upon us, that we should be called the sons of God: therefore the world knoweth us not, because it knew him not.

2. Beloved, now are we the sons of God, and it doth not yet appear what we shall be: but we know that, when he shall appear, we shall be like him; for we shall see him as he is.

LESSON OUTLINE

I. CHRIST WILL COME AGAIN
   A. The Promise
   B. The Assurance
   C. Reassurance
II. LOOK FOR CHRIST'S RETURN
   A. The Anticipation
   B. The Duty
   C. The Appearing
III. EVENTS AT CHRIST'S COMING
   A. The Catching Away
   B. The Revealing
   C. Being Christlike

LESSON EXPOSITION

INTRODUCTION

The greatest fact in history is that Jesus Christ came into this world. The most important fact in contemporary times is that He is at the right hand of God now, making intercession for us. The most important fact in prophecy is that He is coming again.

The doctrine of the Second Coming of Christ has been called the polestar of the church. Paul the apostle called it "that blessed hope." No serious student of the Bible can deny its importance. In the Old Testament, it was stressed by the prophets. In the New Testament, Jesus and the apostles gave prominence to it. It was the watchword for the early Christians in the days immediately following the ascension of Christ. In fact, the early church fathers and early Christians, during the first two centuries, found it their chief source of hope and consolation. To them the belief that Jesus was coming in glory to reign with His people on the earth was almost universal.

In the third century, Origen and others developed a school of interpreters that so spiritualized those scriptures that many people ceased to believe in any literal Millennium. Although this system has been condemned by many, it has persisted down through the years and has a large following today.

When the Roman Empire became nominally Christian under Constantine, it appeared to many that the Millennium had come. Many believed that the kingdom of God was already on earth. At this point, however, hand in hand with the world, the church plunged into the Dark Ages. During this time the doctrine of the Second Coming was almost forgotten. It is to the credit of the great Reformers of the 16th century that they again began to proclaim the comforting hope and blessed promise of the coming of Christ. Since that time the doctrine has been preached and proclaimed with increasing interest. However, it is still not studied and proclaimed as much as it should be.

I. CHRIST WILL COME AGAIN (Matthew 16:27; John 14:1-3; Acts 1:9-11)

A. The Promise (Matthew 16:27)

27. For the Son of man shall come in the glory of his Father with his angels; and then he shall reward every man according to his works.

In this verse we have the personal promise that He will come again. The second coming of Christ means His personal and visible return to earth in glory. This is one of the great doctrines of the Christian faith. His return will be one of the greatest events in the future.

The Bible is the source of our knowledge of the second coming of Christ. The language used by our Lord in speaking of His return is so clear and distinct that it is difficult to see how anyone can misunderstand it to mean anything other than a literal and historical event. The Second Coming will be one of the great vindications of the truth of Scripture before an unbelieving world that considers the gospel message a failure.

There are several words used in the English Bible to describe the Lord's return, such as His *coming*, His *appearing*, His *manifestation*, and His *revelation*. This is also true in the original Greek New Testament, from which our English translation was made.

This word, *come (erchomai)*, means "to come" or "to go" and is used in this ordinary way about 700 times in the New Testament. It is used by our Lord in John 14:3, where He said, "I will come again, and receive you unto myself." It is also used by the apostle Paul in 1 Corinthians 11:26, in speaking of the Lord's Supper—"ye do shew the Lord's death till he come." In Luke 18:8 the word is used by Jesus in this statement: "When the Son of man cometh, shall he find faith on the earth?" In Acts 1:11 the word appears again: "This same Jesus . . . shall so come in like manner as ye have seen him go into heaven."

B. The Assurance (John 14:1-3)

(John 14:1 is not included in the printed text.)

2. In my Father's house are many mansions: if it were not so, I would have told you. I go to prepare a place for you.

3. And if I go and prepare a place for you, I will come again, and receive you unto myself; that where I am, there ye may be also.

In these verses we have something very definite. It is as definite as it is encouraging—"I will come again." He did not say, "I will send for you." Neither did He say, "You will come to Me when you die." To send an angel, or a legion of angels, would not be the same as coming Himself. It would be wonderful if a multitude of heavenly hosts were dispatched, with horses of fire and chariots of fire, to transport us triumphantly to heaven. But it would not be the fulfillment of His own promise, and most surely He will do what He promised to do. He will not say one thing and do another. He cannot lie or alter His word.

This assurance is full of grace. For example, if you are expecting a very valued friend by plane, you will not be satisfied with sending an empty cab to meet him. No, you will go yourself. This is precisely what Jesus means to do. He has gone to heaven, and His entrance there prepares and defines His people's place. Among the many mansions of the Father's house would be no place for us if Jesus had not gone to prepare it. Then, lest there should be any doubt on our part as to our right to be there, He said, "I will come again, and receive you unto myself; that where I am, there ye may be also." Nothing short of this can fulfill the promise Jesus made to His followers.

C. Reassurance (Acts 1:9-11)

(Acts 1:9, 10 is not included in the printed text.)

11. Which also said, Ye men of Galilee, why stand ye gazing up into heaven? this same Jesus, which is taken up from you into heaven, shall so come in like manner as ye have seen him go into heaven.

Jesus had just gone up from the earth, in the presence of His apostles, to heaven. While they looked steadfastly toward heaven, two men dressed in white stood by them with the message of verse 11.

From this message we learn that the same Jesus who left this earth and ascended into heaven, in the presence of a number of witnesses, shall come again in the same way as they had seen Him go. How did He go? He went up personally, literally, actually, the very same person who had just been talking with them—the one they had seen with their eyes, heard with their ears, handled with their hands—who had eaten in their presence and "shewed himself alive after his passion by many infallible proofs" (v. 3). This same Jesus shall come in like manner.

Who saw Jesus as He went up? Did the world? No. Not one unconverted or unbelieving person laid eyes upon Jesus, from the moment after He was laid in the tomb. The last sight the world got of Jesus was as He hung on the cross, a spectacle to the angels, men, and devils. The next sight they get of Him will be when, like lightning flashing, He shall come forth to execute judgment.

None but His own saw the ascending Savior, and only they had seen Him from the moment of His resurrection. He showed Himself to those who were dear to His heart. He assured and comforted, strengthened and encouraged their souls by the "many infallible proofs" that Luke had identified. And as someone very aptly said, "He led them to the very confines of the unseen world, just as far as men could go while still in the body; and there He allowed them to see Him ascending into heaven; and while they gazed upon this wonderful sight, He sent the testimony."

Could proof be more clear or conclusive? Either these two men in white apparel were false witnesses or Jesus shall come again in the exact same manner in which He went away. There is no middle ground between these two conclusions.

Why were unbelievers not permitted to see the ascension of Christ?

II. LOOK FOR CHRIST'S RETURN (Philippians 3:20, 21; Colossians 3:1-4; Titus 2:11-13)

A. Anticipation (Philippians 3:20, 21)

20. For our conversation is in heaven; from whence also we look for the Saviour, the Lord Jesus Christ:

21. Who shall change our vile body, that it may be fashioned like unto his glorious body, according to the working whereby he is able even to subdue all things unto himself.

There is every indication that the apostles received the promises of Christ's return as applying directly to themselves. In his letter to the Christians at Corinth, Paul wrote words applicable to the entire church throughout that age: "We shall not all sleep, but we shall all be changed, in a moment, in the twinkling of an eye" (1 Corinthians 15:51, 52). And who can prove that Paul himself did not cherish the hope of being included among those that "shall not . . . sleep"? When he wrote to the Philippians, he reminded them of citizenship ("conversation") in heaven—"from whence also we look for the Saviour" (3:20). He prayed for the Thessalonian Christians that their "whole spirit and soul and body be preserved blameless until the coming of our Lord Jesus Christ" (1 Thessalonians 5:23). He also commended them for turning "to God from idols to serve the living and true God; and to wait for his Son from heaven" (1:9, 10).

Hebrews 9:28 records, "Unto them that look for him shall he appear the second time without sin unto salvation." Paul does not ask us to look for the Tribulation or the Antichrist or for persecution or for death, but for the return of Christ.

The very fact that all generations of Christians have looked for, and are exhorted to keep looking for, the coming of the Lord gives credibility to the fact that Christ may come at any time.

B. The Duty (Colossians 3:1-4)

(Colossians 3:1 is not included in the printed text.)

2. Set your affection on things above, not on things on the earth.

3. For ye are dead, and your life is hid with Christ in God.

4. When Christ, who is our life, shall appear, then shall ye also appear with him in glory.

When Paul wrote to the Colossians, part of his theme was indicated in verse 4: "When Christ, who is our life, shall appear, then shall ye also appear with him in glory." He instructed his son in the faith, Timothy, and exhorted him to "keep this commandment [God's precepts] without spot, unrebukeable, until the appearing of our Lord Jesus Christ" (1 Timothy 6:14).

Jewish converts were reminded, "Yet a little while, and he that shall come will come, and will not tarry" (Hebrews 10:37). James exhorted those to whom he wrote: "Be ye also patient; stablish your hearts: for the coming of the Lord draweth nigh" (5:8). Peter remarked that those who scoff at the coming of the Lord are "willingly . . . ignorant" (2 Peter 3:4, 5), while John concluded the Revelation and closed the cannon of Scripture with the glad cry "He which testifieth these things saith, Surely I come quickly. Amen. Even so, come, Lord Jesus" (Revelation 22:20).

Paul told the Thessalonians it was their duty to watch for the coming of Christ: "Therefore let us not sleep, as do others; but let us watch and be sober" (1 Thessalonians 5:6). The same exhortation was given by the Lord to the church at Sardis, in Revelation 3:3: "If therefore thou shalt not watch, I will come on thee as a thief, and thou shalt not know what hour I will come upon thee." A similar command to watch is given to believers, particularly Israel, who will be under the persecution of the Beast during the Great Tribulation: "Watch therefore: for ye know not what hour your Lord doth come" (Matthew 24:42). "Blessed are those servants, whom the lord when he cometh shall find watching" (Luke 12:37). Thus, the attitude of watchfulness is appropriate for any believer in Christ, and the exhortation to watch seems to be applied to the Second Coming as a whole.

C. The Appearing (Titus 2:11-13)

(Titus 2:11, 12 is not included in

the printed text.)

13. Looking for that blessed hope, and the glorious appearing of the great God and our Saviour Jesus Christ.

For those who love the Lord, the coming of Christ is a blessed hope, a comforting hope, and a purifying hope. Those who love the Lord are constrained to look for "that blessed hope, and the glorious appearing of the great God and our Saviour Jesus Christ." According to 1 Thessalonians 4:13-18, they are not to sorrow over loved ones who are "asleep" as those who have no hope, for Christ will raise them also, "and so shall we ever be with the Lord. Wherefore comfort one another with these words." Indeed, the first comfort given to the bewildered disciples who beheld their Lord ascend into heaven and who then stood gazing into the skies was this message from the angels: "This same Jesus . . . shall so come in like manner" (Acts 1:11). Previously they had been comforted by the same hope: "Let not your heart be troubled. . . . I go to prepare a place for you. And . . . I will come again, and receive you unto myself" (John 14:1, 3). This return of the Lord is later signified by John as a purifying hope: "And every man that hath this hope in him purifieth himself, even as he is pure" (1 John 3:3).

In Titus 2:12, 13, looking for Christ is linked with living soberly, righteously, and godly. In 1 Thessalonians 5:6, the Second Coming deals with issues of sobriety; James 5:7, 8, in patience; Philippians 1:10, in sincerity; 1 John 3:3, in purity; 1 Thessalonians 3:12, 13, in brotherly love and holiness.

The value of the Second Coming in the life of the believer is well summarized by James H. Brookes: "If we heartily and practically believe that our Lord may come for His people at any moment, [then] it must separate us from the world, and kill selfishness, and blast the roots of selfish ambition, and increase brotherly love, and intensify zeal, and deepen concern for the salvation of the lost, and give comfort in affliction, and put us in a state of preparedness for the great interview, like a bride arraying herself to meet her bridegroom. Oh, there is no truth in the Bible that can bring greater blessing to the soul, when received in the power of the Holy Ghost" *(Maranatha)*.

What is the value of preachers today expounding more on the second coming of Christ? Explain.

III. EVENTS AT CHRIST'S COMING (1 Thessalonians 4:16, 17; 2 Thessalonians 1:7-10; 1 John 3:1, 2)

A. The Catching Away (1 Thessalonians 4:16, 17)

16. For the Lord himself shall descend from heaven with a shout, with the voice of the archangel, and with the trump of God: and the dead in Christ shall rise first:

17. Then we which are alive and remain shall be caught up together with them in the clouds, to meet the Lord in the air: and so shall we ever be with the Lord.

In verse 13, Paul wrote concerning "them which are asleep" (or those who fall "asleep" from time to time). *Sleep* is the softened word used in Scripture for the death of a believer, as when Jesus said, "Our friend Lazarus sleepeth; but I go, that I may awake him out of sleep" (John 11:11). The sleep of death will have its conclusion at the resurrection. The word *cemetery* comes from the Greek word *koimeterion*, or "sleeping place." It is said that the following words were found inscribed upon one of the tombs at

Thessalonica: "When our life on earth is passed, we enter into eternal sleep." Christians, however, look past the sleep of death to physical resurrection, and thus glorious reunion, and therefore are not "as others which have no hope" (1 Thessalonians 4:13). Those who sleep shall be raised, and the living ones will not precede, or go before those who sleep in Jesus. Paul's point was that the living shall in no way have an advantage over the dead.

Christ will not send an angel for us; it is to be the Lord himself, the same One who died and rose again who will come [for us]. No other will do to meet the bride than the Bridegroom himself, who has redeemed her.

Three sounds will herald Christ's coming, the first of which is a "shout." We do not know who will give the shout. Some believe it will be Christ; others, Michael the archangel. Some believe it will be like a military command. Thayer's *Lexicon* gives the meaning from classical Greek as the cry of charioteers to their horses, of hunters to their hounds, or of a captain to the rowers of his vessel. It may also mean the cry of a captain to his soldiers.

It is sufficient to understand this "shout" simply as a signal cry, heard only by the church. It will be accompanied by "the voice of the archangel" and "the trump of God." Indeed, these three may be descriptive of only one great signal from heaven, as it has been paraphrased: "a shout in the archangel's voice, even with the voice of the trump of God." It is the signal to the church, both dead and living; and if it is heard by the world at all, it will not be recognized or understood and will engender no response. This is a catching-up, not a coming-down: it is the Day of Christ, not the Day of the Lord.

B. The Revealing (2 Thessalonians 1:7-10)

(2 Thessalonians 1:7-10 is not included in the printed text.)

The second coming of Christ consists of two main phases. The first phase, called the Rapture, includes the coming of Christ in the air for His church (1 Thessalonians 4:13-17). This is the private phase as it is the Bridegroom coming for His bride. The second phase is the revelation when Christ returns to the earth with His bride (1 Thessalonians 3:13; 2 Thessalonians 1:7-10). This is the Second Coming's public aspect because every eye shall see Him (Revelation 1:7). Both of these phases are set forth in 2 Thessalonians 2:1, 8 and Titus 2:13.

Paul's concern in 2 Thessalonians 1:7-10 is not the rapture of the church but Christ's post-tribulation coming, when He brings judgment on those who do not know God. Here Christ is said to come "in flaming fire taking vengeance" (v. 8). What brought Paul to speak of this occasion was the affliction which the Thessalonian Christians were experiencing. He introduced the subject by referring to the "patience and faith" (v. 4) of the Thessalonians in the midst of this suffering as a "manifest token" (v. 5) that God would in due time bring judgment on their oppressors. The Thessalonians could take comfort in knowing that the time was coming when those who were now making them suffer would experience even worse suffering themselves and that, when this was true for them, the Thessalonians would be enjoying blessed rest and relief. Paul continued the subject by describing the time of Christ's coming, when this contrasting situation would come true—a time when all enemies of Christ would be dealt with in wrath and when Christ would "come to be glorified in his saints" (v. 10).

C. Being Christlike (1 John 3:1, 2)

1. Behold, what manner of love the Father hath bestowed upon us, that we should be called the sons of God: therefore the world knoweth us not, because it knew him not.

2. Beloved, now are we the sons of God, and it doth not yet appear what we shall be: but we know that, when he shall appear, we shall be like him; for we shall see him as he is.

We are already God's children since He has called us so, has adopted us in His great love, and has revealed to us the Father. As children of this wonderful Father we have a great future. We are to share in the riches of the Father. His glory is to be our glory. His riches and power are to be ours. We are to sit on His throne and inherit His kingdom.

"We shall be like him; for we shall see him as he is." This refers to the second coming of Christ. We will have greater powers for understanding spiritual truth when we are in our new spiritual bodies. Then we shall see Christ in all His glory. Beholding Him and understanding all that He is, we shall be like Him.

What is Christ's purpose in coming to the earth the second time?

REVIEW QUESTIONS

1. What promise did Jesus make in Matthew 16:27?
2. What assurance did Jesus give His disciples in John 14:1-3?
3. How did the angels reassure the disciples in Acts 1:9-11?
4. What does it mean to look for Christ's return?
5. How will believers be like Christ when He returns?

GOLDEN TEXT HOMILY

"LOOKING FOR THAT BLESSED HOPE, AND THE GLORIOUS APPEARING OF THE GREAT GOD AND OUR SAVIOUR JESUS CHRIST" (Titus 2:13).

Among the words of consolation spoken by Jesus before leaving His disciples was the promise that He would come again and receive them unto Himself (see John 14:3). Since these words were spoken, time has sped noiselessly along; events of vast magnitude have rapidly succeeded each other and left their lessons for the ages to ponder; nations have endured suffering, war, and revolution; generation after generation has gone down to the grave; for nearly 2,000 years the church of the living God has been intensely and anxiously expectant. But still the promise remains unfulfilled.

Though the promise is yet unfulfilled, the church has not lost confidence in the powerful words of Christ. Faith in the second advent of Christ is still firmly held by born-again believers. Long waiting has only sharpened the longing, brightened the hope, and clarified the vision. The church is still looking for the soon return of the Lord of the church.

Paul the apostle declared that the return of Christ is the "blessed hope" of the church. He used the word *hope* not to indicate merely that it is wished for but that it is assured. This sure hope is the glorious appearing of our Lord and Savior Jesus Christ.

Because we have this hope we can say no to ungodliness and worldly passions. We can live self-controlled, upright, and godly lives in this present age. We can so live while we are waiting for the appearing of the Son of God.

When He comes, those who are waiting in faith will behold Him. His appearance will be one of glory and power. He will "come in his own glory, and in his Father's, and of the holy angels" (Luke 9:26). He will not only come in divine majesty; He will come to bestow this majesty on those who have believed in Him and who have looked for His return.—**Henry J. Smith, D.Min., Vice President for Student Life, Lee College, Cleveland, Tennessee**

SENTENCE SERMONS

THE BIBLE TEACHES that Jesus Christ will come again.

—Selected

CHRISTIANS SHOULD SHARE the hope of Christ's return with sinners.

—Selected

CHRIST'S COMING for His church will be sudden and unannounced. "Blessed," said Jesus, "are those servants whom the Lord . . . shall find watching."

—Leon J. Wood

HOPE IS FAITH holding out its hand in the dark.

—George Iles

EVANGELISM APPLICATION

CHRISTIANS SHOULD SHARE THE HOPE OF CHRIST'S RETURN WITH SINNERS.

Did you know that God knows your exact measurements? He has gone to prepare a place for you. It will be a place that will satisfy every longing and desire of your heart. You do not have to worry about not being suited for the place that Christ has ready for you. He knows each of His followers personally, and He is able to equip heaven just for you.

The question is, "Are you ready for heaven?"

ILLUMINATING THE LESSON

It is generally agreed among Pentecostals that the coming of Christ is twofold—that is, the Rapture and the Revelation. *Rapture* means "to be caught up," or "to be caught away." *Revelation* means "appearing," "shining forth," or "manifestation." The Rapture occurs when the church is caught up to meet Christ in the air, before the Tribulation. The Revelation occurs when Christ comes with His saints, to end the Tribulation by the execution of righteous judgment upon the earth. At the Rapture, Christ comes in the air for His saints; at the Revelation, He comes to the earth with them. He must come *for* them before He can come *with* them.

The Rapture may happen at any moment; the Revelation cannot occur until the Antichrist is revealed and until the times and seasons which point to the Day of the Lord are fulfilled. The Rapture is full of comfort and hope for the believer; the revelation of Christ is full of solemnity and terror to those who do not obey the gospel.

DAILY BIBLE READINGS

M. Vision of Christ's Coming. Daniel 7:9-14
T. Lord Over All the Earth. Zechariah 14:3-9
W. Time of Christ's Coming Unknown. Matthew 24:36-42
T. Prepare for Christ's Coming. Luke 12:35-40
F. Rewards at Christ's Coming. 1 Peter 1:7-13
S. Expect Christ's Return. 2 Peter 3:1-10

INTRODUCTION TO SUMMER QUARTER

The month of June begins the summer quarter series of lessons, which is divided into two units of study. Unit One (lessons 1-9) is presented under the theme "God's Word for Difficult Times: Jeremiah." Unit Two of the spring quarter and Unit One of this summer quarter tie together well, inasmuch as basic truths are so essential in difficult times.

Jeremiah lived and served in times that were difficult not only for Judah but also for himself. Yet he was a champion for the cause of Jehovah and did not shrink from the boldness needed to face even personal persecution. His unwavering commitment to God and his love and desire to help God's people will surely challenge each of us to view our opportunities more seriously.

Unit Two (lessons 10-14) is presented under the theme "Servanthood." Drawing from both Old and New Testament examples, these lessons give the theological foundation as well as the reward for following the example of Christ in servanthood.

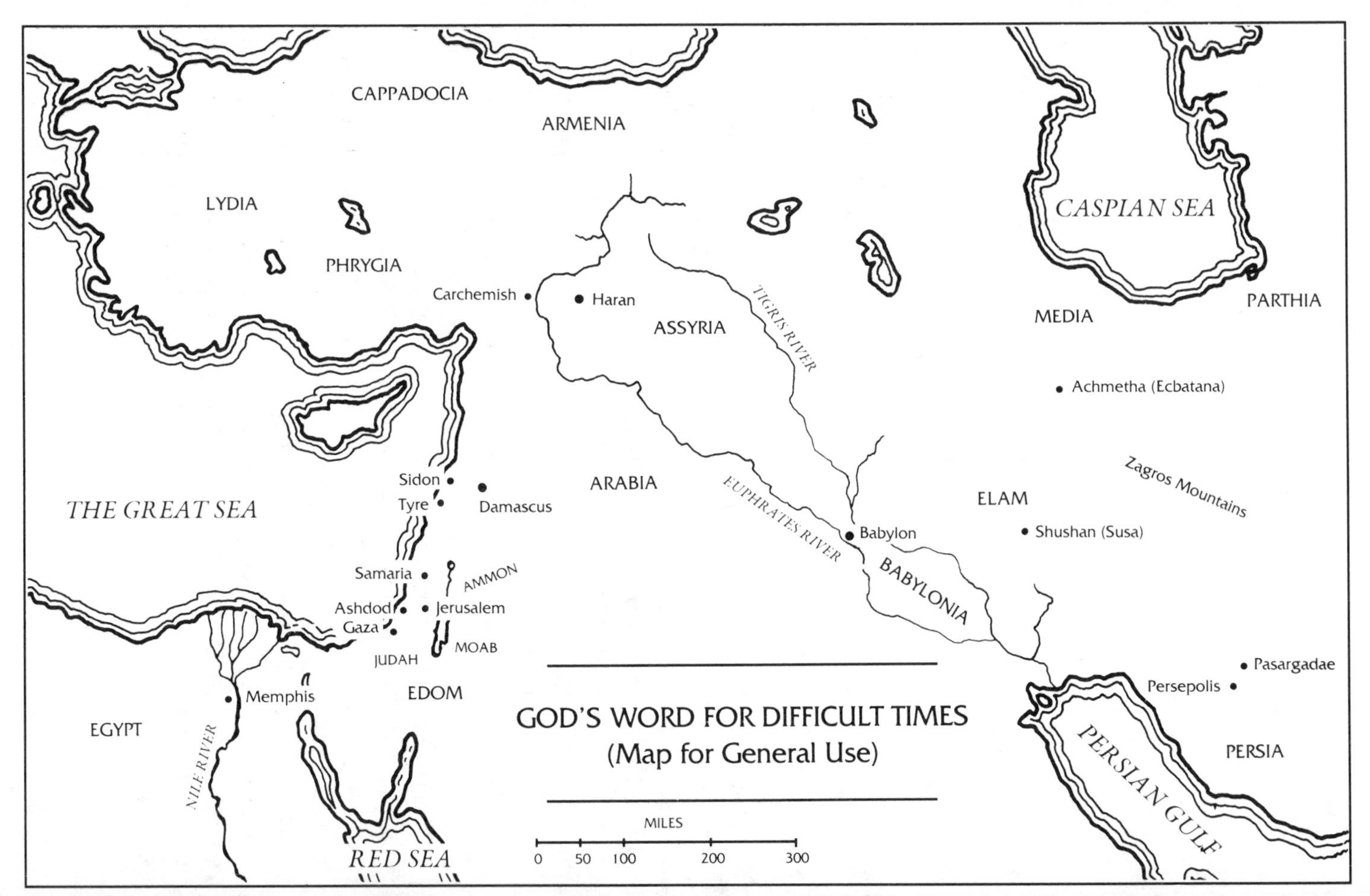

CAPPADOCIA
ARMENIA
LYDIA
PHRYGIA
Carchemish
Haran
ASSYRIA
TIGRIS RIVER
CASPIAN SEA
PARTHIA
MEDIA
Achmetha (Ecbatana)
Zagros Mountains
THE GREAT SEA
Sidon
Tyre
Damascus
ARABIA
EUPHRATES RIVER
ELAM
Babylon
Shushan (Susa)
Samaria
AMMON
Ashdod
Jerusalem
Gaza
JUDAH
MOAB
BABYLONIA
Memphis
EDOM
EGYPT
NILE RIVER
RED SEA
Pasargadae
Persepolis
PERSIA
PERSIAN GULF
GOD'S WORD FOR DIFFICULT TIMES
(Map for General Use)
MILES
0
50
100
200
300

Hearing From God

Study Text: Jeremiah 1:1-19

Objective: To hear and obey God's call for each believer to evangelize the lost.

Time: The Book of Jeremiah was written between 627 and 580 B.C.

Place: The Book of Jeremiah was probably written in Jerusalem.

Golden Text: "Speak unto them all that I command thee: be not dismayed at their faces" (Jeremiah 1:17).

Central Truth: Obedience to God's call ensures the believer's participation in God's plan.

Evangelism Emphasis: God calls believers to witness to the lost.

PRINTED TEXT

Jeremiah 1:4. Then the word of the Lord came unto me, saying,

5. Before I formed thee in the belly I knew thee; and before thou camest forth out of the womb I sanctified thee, and I ordained thee a prophet unto the nations.

6. Then said I, Ah, Lord God! behold, I cannot speak: for I am a child.

7. But the Lord said unto me, Say not, I am a child: for thou shalt go to all that I shall send thee, and whatsoever I command thee thou shalt speak.

8. Be not afraid of their faces: for I am with thee to deliver thee, saith the Lord.

9. Then the Lord put forth his hand, and touched my mouth. And the Lord said unto me, Behold, I have put my words in thy mouth.

10. See, I have this day set thee over the nations and over the kingdoms, to root out, and to pull down, and to destroy, and to throw down, to build, and to plant.

11. Moreover the word of the Lord came unto me, saying, Jeremiah, what seest thou? And I said, I see a rod of an almond tree.

12. Then said the Lord unto me, Thou hast well seen: for I will hasten my word to perform it.

13. And the word of the Lord came unto me the second time, saying, What seest thou? And I said, I see a seething pot; and the face thereof is toward the north.

14. Then the Lord said unto me, Out of the north an evil shall break forth upon all the inhabitants of the land.

16. And I will utter my judgments against them touching all their wickedness, who have forsaken me, and have burned incense unto other gods, and

worshipped the works of their own hands.

17. Thou therefore gird up thy loins, and arise, and speak unto them all that I command thee: be not dismayed at their faces, lest I confound thee before them.

18. For, behold, I have made thee this day a defenced city, and an iron pillar, and brasen walls against the whole land, against the kings of Judah, against the princes thereof, against the priests thereof, and against the people of the land.

19. And they shall fight against thee; but they shall not prevail against thee; for I am with thee, saith the Lord, to deliver thee.

LESSON OUTLINE

I. GOD'S CALL
   A. The Kings of Jeremiah's Day
   B. Jeremiah's Call and Ordination
   C. Jeremiah's Response
   D. God's Promise
   E. A Prophet to the Nations
II. IMPENDING JUDGMENT
III. PROMISE OF PROTECTION

LESSON EXPOSITION

INTRODUCTION

If the ministries of the major prophets were judged by the success they achieved, Isaiah would possibly be considered the "prince of prophets." He moved in royal circles and was greatly respected (though sometimes feared and hated) by the five kings through whose reigns he prophesied. He was a leader, opinion maker, and counselor to the southern kingdom of Judah. He has become known as the "Messiah prophet," because he saw grand revelations of the coming of Jesus Christ.

In contrast to Isaiah is Jeremiah. In terms of success, this prophet was a terrible failure. Like Isaiah, he prophesied during the reigns of five kings of Judah. However, whereas Isaiah walked among the royal courts, Jeremiah never received recognition for his calling. His name does not even appear in the historical books of 1 and 2 Kings, though he is mentioned in 2 Chronicles, Daniel, and Ezra.

Also like Isaiah, Jeremiah was called by God to be a prophet to Judah, and he faithfully confronted the people and their leaders with their sin. Isaiah had promised punishment from God if the people did not repent, but the nation continued its slide into apostasy. His ministry had lasted from 740 B.C. to about 681 B.C., a total of nearly 60 years. Jeremiah began his prophetic ministry around 627 B.C., and continued through the last five kings of Judah, a period of over 40 years. The nation fell and Jerusalem was destroyed in 586 B.C.

In this lesson we will examine the call on Jeremiah's life and search for understanding of how God speaks to men to anoint their ministries.

I. GOD'S CALL
(Jeremiah 1:1-10)

A. The Kings of Jeremiah's Day
(vv. 1-3)

(Jeremiah 1:1-3 is not included in the printed text.)

To better understand the message and life of Jeremiah, a certain knowledge of the kings of Judah who reigned during his ministry is necessary (see 2 Kings 22--24; 2 Chronicles 34--36). Josiah came to the throne at 8 years old. The nation had fallen into such a terrible state of apostasy that there was not even a known copy of the Law. In spite of this, Josiah was godly and led the nation wisely, even in his youth. When he was 26 years old, he set about to repair the Temple. Hilkiah, the high priest at the time, discovered a copy of the Law. Upon reading it, Josiah was seized with terror as conviction ripped his heart. After hearing the reading of the Law, he set about to change the course of the nation. During his 31-year reign he instituted the greatest religious reforms Judah had ever seen. No other king matched his sincere repentance and efforts to restore godliness.

Despite his godliness, Josiah made the fatal mistake of getting involved in international politics and marched into battle against the Egyptian king, Neco. Jeremiah urged against this campaign. Josiah was killed in the battle and his army defeated. The nation chose his third son, Jehoahaz, to be king, but the tiny country quickly became nothing more than a vassal to Egypt. Neco did not favor Jehoahaz and had him deported to Egypt. Jehozhaz reigned for only three months.

Jehoiakim was chosen to replace Jehoahaz. This son of Josiah was evil, dishonest, greedy, and merciless with his own people. During his reign Babylon defeated Egypt in battle, and they eventually invaded Judah. Daniel and the brightest of the Hebrew children were carried off to Babylon. Jehoiakim stubbornly tried to have Jeremiah killed but was unsuccessful. He eventually tried to revolt against Nebuchadnezzar and was captured and killed. He reigned 11 years.

Jehoiakim's son Jehoiachin succeeded Him. After only three months the Babylonian armies carried Jehoiachin away captive to Babylon, along with many others, including the prophet Ezekiel. He lived in exile in Babylon for 40 years before dying there.

Zedekiah was the last king of Judah. He reigned over the ravaged and impoverished kingdom of Judah for the final 11 years of its existence. He ignored Jeremiah's advice to remain loyal to the Babylonian overlords and joined a rebellion against that empire. Finally, Nebuchadnezzar laid siege to Jerusalem for almost two years, bringing the people to the point of starvation. Eventually the invaders breached the walls and overran the city, destroying the Temple, the king's palace, and other important buildings. Everything of value was taken back to Babylon and the city left decimated and desolate.

Judah was not a pleasant place during the years Jeremiah prophesied there. Although Josiah's reign brought hope and revival, most of Jeremiah's ministry was to a rebellious, destruction-bound people who were bent on forsaking God. There were no accolades for a man in Jeremiah's position, for the message he brought was never popular.

B. The Call and Ordination of Jeremiah (vv. 4, 5)

4. Then the word of the Lord came unto me, saying,

5. Before I formed thee in the belly I knew thee; and before thou camest forth out of the womb I sanctified thee, and I ordained thee a prophet unto the nations.

Notice that, unlike Isaiah, Jeremiah had no vision of heaven or of the Lord. Instead, he heard the Lord speak to him. How he knew for certain it was God speaking we cannot determine—but he knew. Four distinct points are made in this passage that clarify God's call to Jeremiah.

1. *God knew him.* God knows every man, long before he is born. He has known all of us even before time began. Every person ever born has been in God's plans since before the foundations of the world. (See Matthew 25:34; Revelation 17:8). No one should ever let himself feel inadequate or discouraged. Each individual is valuable in God's sight, and each has a purpose in His kingdom. This is confirmed profoundly in Psalm 139:13-16.

2. *God's claim on his life superseded all other relationships.* Since God knew Jeremiah first, even before his parents knew him, His plans had first priority. This is a strong argument against the terrible holocaust in America known as abortion. Abortion kills a life that the infinitely wise and eternal God planned in eternity past.

3. *God sanctified him.* He set him apart for a divine purpose.

4. *God appointed him.* All believers in God's kingdom are sanctified, but certain ones are anointed and appointed (ordained) to carry out very specific tasks. We are all called to ministry, and we should do the general works of the church that need to be done. However, not all of us will be pastors, evangelists, prophets, and so forth. These are appointed for special purposes. Their call includes not only the general call but also a very specific one.

The Scriptures are replete with examples of men God has called to very distinct works. Moses, Samuel, David, John the Baptist, and Paul were all men with fires burning in them. They had missions to fulfill and carried them out with zeal. Others who were not given such specific assignments as these nevertheless trusted God and served Him at whatever task they found to do. If God has never given you an explicit calling or assignment, then continue to fulfill the mission common to all believers—to serve God and obey Him.

C. Jeremiah's Response (v. 6)

6. Then said I, Ah, Lord God! behold, I cannot speak: for I am a child.

Jeremiah was struck with terror over the magnitude of the task God was putting before him. This is not an uncommon reaction for any man. Fears of inadequate ability, training, and experience bring tremendous self-doubts. Jeremiah thought himself too young and ignorant to be God's spokesman to Judah. However, God promised to be with him. One should never allow feelings of inadequacy to keep him from obeying God.

Isaiah's reaction to his call (Isaiah 6) was similar to that of Jeremiah. Both men were confronted with the holiness of God's presence. They both reacted with a fearful sense of powerlessness and moral impurity. Isaiah had already been doing the work of the Lord, but he suddenly realized how sinful his heart was. In the same way, Jeremiah was not simply using his youth and inexperience and an excuse; he felt unequipped and unworthy to be considered for the task.

D. God's Promise (vv. 7-9)

7. But the Lord said unto me, Say not, I am a child: for thou

shalt go to all that I shall send thee, and whatsoever I command thee thou shalt speak.

8. Be not afraid of their faces: for I am with thee to deliver thee, saith the Lord.

9. Then the Lord put forth his hand, and touched my mouth. And the Lord said unto me, Behold, I have put my words in thy mouth.

God did not promise Jeremiah an easy time, but He did promise that He would be with him and see him through. God does not make mistakes. He empowers those whom He calls, and He will always provide encouragement when it is needed.

God's message to Jeremiah was much like His message to Moses had been. He promised to supply the words that would be needed when it came time to speak. Notice, too, that the Lord touched Jeremiah's mouth. This resembles the experience of Isaiah (6:6, 7). Before one ever tries to speak for God, he had best submit to God his most unruly member—the tongue. The words a true prophet speaks have the power to inspire, infuriate, or frighten. As a spokesman for the Lord, he must make sure he has accurately heard from above.

Spiritual leadership is a heavy responsibility. The prophet Hosea leveled harsh indictments against the religious leaders of his day for not accurately giving out the Word of God: "My people are destroyed for lack of knowledge" (Hosea 4:6).

These men were supposed to be spiritual leaders; however, they were leading the people into sin. God deals harshly with men who supposedly serve Him but who have never confessed, submitted to God, and forsaken their own sinfulness.

E. A Prophet to the Nations (v. 10)

10. See, I have this day set thee over the nations and over the kingdoms, to root out, and to pull down, and to destroy, and to throw down, to build, and to plant.

God appointed Jeremiah to be a prophet and carry His word to the "nations." Jeremiah would warn not only the Jews of Judah but also the nations of the world about God's judgment against sin. Throughout the Old Testament, God was working through Judah and Israel to unfold a plan to bring salvation to the entire world. Everyone is included in Jeremiah's prophecies of judgment and hope.

Once God calls a man to serve Him, can that individual ever be happy or content if he refuses to heed the call?

II. IMPENDING JUDGMENT (Jeremiah 1:11-16)

(Jeremiah 1:15 is not included in the printed text.)

11. Moreover the word of the Lord came unto me, saying, Jeremiah, what seest thou? And I said, I see a rod of an almond tree.

12. Then said the Lord unto me, Thou hast well seen: for I will hasten my word to perform it.

13. And the word of the Lord came unto me the second time, saying, What seest thou? And I said, I see a seething pot; and the face thereof is toward the north.

14. Then the Lord said unto me, Out of the north an evil shall break forth upon all the inhabitants of the land.

16. And I will utter my judgments against them touching all

their wickedness, who have forsaken me, and have burned incense unto other gods, and worshipped the works of their own hands.

Jeremiah began his active ministry during the reign of Josiah. Known as one of the most godly kings during all of Judah's history, Josiah instituted a number of reforms to rid the nation of idolatry and reestablish the worship of Jehovah (2 Kings 22, 23). The Law had been completely lost to the people for many years. Josiah likely knew of Jehovah only through the oral traditions passed on by the priests and Levites. Obviously, there was little knowledge of God's commands among the people themselves. They had syncretized their Jewish traditions with heathen idol worship. Still, there was enough convicting power in what Josiah did know to help him realize that Jehovah was all-powerful and real. A malleable heart will find its way to God. A means will be provided for a true seeker to meet the Savior.

It was during the years of revitalization under Josiah that Jeremiah began to preach. The words of verses 14 and 15 stand in stark contrast to the revival effort that was taking place under Josiah. No wonder Jeremiah was hesitant to take on the call to the office of prophet. People thought the nation was in the midst of renewal. All was going well. No one wants to be a spoilsport when the team is winning. Yet God had called Jeremiah to sound a warning—however unpleasant the task may have been.

The reign of Josiah and the accompanying revival had been wonderful in some respects. Although it did not last or bring permanent change in the nation as a whole, there were those who made legitimate dedications to the Lord. Also, God's judgment was held off for a period of time. We should always remember, though, that He is looking for more than a casual commitment. He calls us for eternity, not just for the present.

Jeremiah had to learn (and we should remember) that God knows the big picture—past, present, and future. The wonderful efforts of Josiah (which Jeremiah heartily supported) did not reach deep enough into the people's souls to produce a lasting effect. Josiah did all he could, but immediately after his death the nation fell back into idolatry. God had known their hearts all along. It is possible that at the time of his call Jeremiah himself did not realize how shallow the outward revival had been.

Also, Jeremiah did not comprehend the volatile political climate that was brewing. The Assyrian Empire had been the great power for many years. However, it was now in great decline, and Babylon was rising to fill the power vacuum. Josiah's reign coincided with the point of balance between the two.

The first vision God gave Jeremiah was of an almond branch. This indicated that God's judgment was about to begin, since the almond tree is one of the first to blossom in the spring. God saw the sins of Judah and of all the other nations, and promised to carry out swift judgment. The second vision, a boiling pot tilting away from the north and pouring itself out in the direction of Judah, was a picture of Babylon pouring out steaming judgment against the Hebrew nation.

What a frightening task Jeremiah had. Yet he exhibited great courage by faithfully carrying God's message to the people. Likewise those ministering the gospel today must be courageous, for the world does not want to hear the message that it is sinful—that it is on its way to hell.

The people of Jeremiah's day were carried away with heathen idols. The idols we encounter in preaching the gospel today are just as real, though clothed in deception. Material possessions, selfish dreams for the future, approval of others, and personal pleasures are all altars that demand worship. It would appear an impossible task to proclaim that God must be worshiped above all other things in this climate. Like Jeremiah, however, we must remain faithful.

Would a preacher with such a negative message as Jeremiah fare well today on the American scene?

III. PROMISE OF PROTECTION (Jeremiah 1:17-19)

17. Thou therefore gird up thy loins, and arise, and speak unto them all that I command thee: be not dismayed at their faces, lest I confound thee before them.

18. For, behold, I have made thee this day a defenced city, and an iron pillar, and brasen walls against the whole land, against the kings of Judah, against the princes thereof, against the priests thereof, and against the people of the land.

19. And they shall fight against thee; but they shall not prevail against thee; for I am with thee, saith the Lord, to deliver thee.

The magnitude of rejection Jeremiah would encounter in his 40 years of service to God was enormous. He faced opposition, isolation, beatings, imprisonment—by his own countrymen. However, these two things gave him the strength to endure such torture: (1) He knew absolutely the message he was proclaiming was true. Otherwise, the temptation to regard his own personal safety would have outweighed any false prophetic ambitions. (2) He knew beyond a doubt that God would protect him. God had made this promise in verse 8: "Do not be afraid of them, for I am with you and will rescue you" (*NIV*). The key word in this pledge was *rescue*. Jeremiah would not be insulated from insults, pain, deprivation, sorrow, jailings, and deportations. He would not be protected from the storm but *would* be seen through it.

Jeremiah had an extraordinary encounter with the God of the universe. When God calls men to extreme ministries, He also gives them an equal assurance of His divine protection.

Isaiah's experience in the Temple likewise demonstrates an encounter with God (Isaiah 6). Elisha was another prophet who experienced the supernatural. In 2 Kings 6, the king of Syria had dispatched a large military expedition of soldiers, chariots, and horses to surround Dothan at night. Elisha's servant arose in the morning and was terrified to see they were encompassed by a Syrian horde. He quickly roused Elisha and described to him their peril. Elisha, however, could see something else—divine protection. He calmly spoke to his servant: "Fear not: for they that be with us are more than they that be with them. And Elisha prayed, and said, Lord, I pray thee, open his eyes, that he may see. And the Lord opened the eyes of the young man; and he saw: and, behold, the mountain was full of horses and chariots of fire round about Elisha" (vv. 16, 17).

God let Elisha see beyond human perception into another

dimension of reality. The same was true for Jeremiah. We are not given the details of just how he was confronted by God—but he was strengthened by what he saw.

Josephus, the Jewish historian, gives an account of a dramatic historical situation of a similar nature. Though not recorded in the Bible, it is nevertheless indicative of how God allows individuals to see beyond normal human comprehension. When Jerusalem was under siege by the Roman armies under Titus, this incident was recorded by an eyewitness:

"Then again, not many days after the feast, on the 21st of the month of Artemisium, a supernatural apparition was seen, too amazing to be believed. What I am now to relate would, I imagine, have been dismissed as imaginary, had this not been vouched for by eyewitnesses, then followed by subsequent disasters that deserved to be thus signalized. For before sunset, chariots were seen in the air over the whole country, and armed battalions speeding through the clouds and encircling the cities. Then again, at the feast called Pentecost, when the priests had entered the inner courts of the Temple by night to perform their usual ministrations, they declared that they were aware, at first, of a violent commotion and din, then of a voice as of a host crying, 'We are departing hence'" (Flavius Josephus, *The Jewish War*).

The heavenly hosts of God announced their departure from Zion just before its worst catastrophe ever. Israel had rejected the Messiah, and now the Glory was departing the city. Devastation followed quickly on the heels of this departure.

God can give assurance and vision to the men He calls to do great works. Jeremiah received his credentials as a prophet by divine appointment. Along with his call came great assurance of protection and strength.

Has God spoken to you in some way about a work He has for you to do?

REVIEW QUESTIONS

1. Should a believer feel slighted if his experience with God has not included dramatic visions and prophecies from above?
2. How should a believer serve in the Kingdom when there has not been a direct call to a specific ministry?
3. Can there ever be an excuse for refusing to obey a call by God on one's life?
4. When we commit our lives to the ministry, how much material comfort and possession can we expect? Can we evaluate the success of our ministries by these criteria?

GOLDEN TEXT HOMILY

"SPEAK UNTO THEM ALL THAT I COMMAND THEE: BE NOT DISMAYED AT THEIR FACES" (Jeremiah 1:17).

It was no easy matter for Jeremiah, young, modest, and sensitive, to come boldly forward and threaten the judgment of God against his country. But if God calls a man to any task, He will help him through with it, and Jeremiah received encouragements proportionate to his duty.

Consider what the duty of faithful service laid upon the prophet included. Jeremiah was to gird up his loins and arise. God is not satisfied with passive submission to

His will. God cannot be faithfully served by the indolent. All our powers are required for His service, and they must be employed without distraction. Jeremiah was to speak just what God commanded him. Fidelity is not simply devotion to God; it is devotion according to His will—the devotion of servants, not that of patrons.

The prophet was to speak "all" that God commanded him. It is treason for the ambassador to suppress those elements of his commission which are displeasing to himself. The servant of God must not select from the revelation of divine truth the words which suit his purpose and neglect the rest. He is not to shun to declare "the whole counsel of God"—threats as well as promises, difficult sayings and mysteries as well as plainly acceptable doctrines. The prophet was to speak without fear: "Be not dismayed." Fear is not only painful, it is also injurious, because it paralyzes effort. Cowardice is sin.

It is our duty to be faithful, even if fidelity should bring our ruin; but such a result will not follow it. Consider the encouragement Jeremiah received to a faithful discharge of his difficult task. The young prophet learned to expect opposition. It is foolish to ignore the approach of trouble. A surprise sometimes leads to a defeat from very inferior foes. Danger foreseen is danger (Luke 10:3). No ground of confidence is more inspiring than the knowledge that the danger clearly, fully apprehended will yet be certainly overcome. This was the assurance given to Jeremiah. The same assurance is offered to every faithful servant of God (Isaiah 43:1).—**Excerpts from the *Pulpit Commentary*, Vol. 11**

SENTENCE SERMONS

OBEDIENCE TO GOD'S CALL ensures the believer's participation in God's plan.

—Selected

OBEDIENCE TO GOD will mean that some time or other you must enter into desolation.

—Oswald Chambers

A YEAR OF self-surrender and obedience will bring larger blessings than fourscore years of selfishness.

—The Encyclopedia of Religious Quotations

GOD AND MAN exist for each other, and neither is satisfied without the other.

—A.W. Tozer

DAILY BIBLE READINGS

M. Call to Deliver. Exodus 3:1-12
T. Call to Go. Isaiah 6:1-8
W. Call to Witness. Matthew 28:16-20
T. Call to Evangelize. Luke 5:1-11
F. Call to Follow. John 1:43-51
S. Call to Preach. Acts 9:10-22

Personal Witness; Personal Risk

Study Text: Jeremiah 7:1 through 8:3; 26:1-24

Objective: To understand and accept the responsibility of proclaiming God's truth regardless of the risk.

Time: The Book of Jeremiah was written between 627 and 580 B.C.

Place: The Book of Jeremiah was probably written at Jerusalem.

Golden Text: "If ye put me to death, ye shall surely bring innocent blood upon yourselves, . . . for of a truth the Lord hath sent me unto you to speak all these words in your ears" (Jeremiah 26:15).

Central Truth: Believers must share the good news in spite of difficult circumstances.

Evangelism Emphasis: The reward of bringing people to Christ is greater than any risk involved.

PRINTED TEXT

Jeremiah 26:2. Thus saith the Lord; Stand in the court of the Lord's house, and speak unto all the cities of Judah, which come to worship in the Lord's house, all the words that I command thee to speak unto them; diminish not a word:

3. If so be they will hearken, and turn every man from his evil way, that I may repent me of the evil, which I purpose to do unto them because of the evil of their doings.

4. And thou shalt say unto them, Thus saith the Lord; If ye will not hearken to me, to walk in my law, which I have set before you,

5. To hearken to the words of my servants the prophets, whom I sent unto you, both rising up early, and sending them, but ye have not hearkened;

6. Then will I make this house like Shiloh, and will make this city a curse to all the nations of the earth.

7. So the priests and the prophets and all the people heard Jeremiah speaking these words in the house of the Lord.

8. Now it came to pass, when Jeremiah had made an end of speaking all that the Lord had commanded him to speak unto all the people, that the priests and the prophets and all the people took him, saying, Thou shalt surely die.

9. Why hast thou prophesied in the name of the Lord, saying, This house shall be like Shiloh, and this city shall be desolate without an inhabitant? And all the people were gathered

against Jeremiah in the house of the Lord.

10. When the princes of Judah heard these things, then they came up from the king's house unto the house of the Lord, and sat down in the entry of the new gate of the Lord's house.

11. Then spake the priests and the prophets unto the princes and to all the people, saying, This man is worthy to die; for he hath prophesied against this city, as ye have heard with your ears.

12. Then spake Jeremiah unto all the princes and to all the people, saying, The Lord sent me to prophesy against this house and against this city all the words that ye have heard.

13. Therefore now amend your ways and your doings, and obey the voice of the Lord your God; and the Lord will repent him of the evil that he hath pronounced against you.

DICTIONARY

Shiloh (SHY-lo)—Jeremiah 26:6—A town north of Jerusalem; location of the Tabernacle with the ark of the covenant (Jeremiah 7:12).

LESSON OUTLINE

I. BOLD PROCLAMATION
   A. Exposing Hypocrisy
   B. God Offers Forgiveness
   C. A Curse to All the Nations
II. UNWAVERING WITNESS
   A. Efforts to Kill Jeremiah
   B. Jeremiah's Defense
III. OBEDIENCE MAY BRING RISK
   A. Jeremiah's Life Spared
   B. The Death of a Prophet

LESSON EXPOSITION

INTRODUCTION

Lack of self-confidence holds many people back from accomplishing their goals in life. They think they have inadequate ability, experience, or training. Jeremiah felt this way when God called him. He saw himself as too young and inexperienced to be God' mouthpiece to Judah and the world. However, God promised to be with him if he would remain obedient. *God qualifies those He calls.*

Jeremiah absolutely needed the assurance of the Lord's help, because what he was sent to do brought tremendous risks to his own life. He would have a frightening burden to carry throughout his years.

This lesson takes place during the reign of Jehoiakim. Jeremiah had begun his prophetic ministry in 627 B.C., during the reign of King Josiah (a good king who had instituted many religious reforms). However, Josiah was killed in battle in 609 B.C., and Judah for a time became a puppet state of Egypt. The Egyptian king (Neco) established Jehoiakim as a vassal ruler. Jehoiakim was materialistic and self-centered. He persecuted and murdered innocent people, and even stubbornly tried to kill Jeremiah. The episode we will study occurred at the beginning of

Jehoiakim's 11-year reign.

I. BOLD PROCLAMATION (Jeremiah 26:1-7)

A. Exposing Hypocrisy (vv. 1, 2)

(Jeremiah 26:1 is not included in the printed text.)

2. Thus saith the Lord; Stand in the court of the Lord's house, and speak unto all the cities of Judah, which come to worship in the Lord's house, all the words that I command thee to speak unto them; diminish not a word.

God commanded Jeremiah to stand in front of the Temple and preach a message of doom and despair. This was the perfect spot to expose the people's hypocrisy. They believed that the Temple was "holy ground." They thought their religious ritual would be enough to save them. They might even have conceded that one day Judah would fall, but never the Temple. Surely, God would protect its borders, they thought, and they would be safe as long as they were within its perimeters.

How easy it is to flirt with disaster—to go to the very limit of what is acceptable behavior, and even bump this line with the idea that God will always preserve. The people of Judah were following a worship ritual but were continuing a sinful lifestyle. Theirs was a religion without personal commitment to God. This should be a strong warning to anyone who says, "I can do this and still be a Christian." We should never use our Christian freedom to see how lax in our commitment to Christian principles we can become. Neither should we let exemplary Christian activities—church attendance, teaching Sunday school, singing in the choir, even sharing Communion—become substitutes for true worship.

God warned Jeremiah: "Tell them everything I command you; do not omit a word" (v. 2, *NIV*). In the face of such opposition, it would have been easy for Jeremiah to soft-pedal the harsh prophecy God had given him—if for no other reason than to save his own life. However, God insisted that he preach the entire message. This had to be difficult for Jeremiah—always having to be the bearer of bad news, and always being rejected. Jeremiah was continually mocked by the people for bringing nothing but words of condemnation. The only comfort he had was the knowledge that what he was saying was the truth and that God had promised to be with him.

How do we respond to critics? People mocked Jeremiah because of the depressing criticism he always brought and the prediction of destruction unless they turned from their wicked ways. Had they accepted it as truth and turned from their evil directions, they would have been spared. However, this required change, self-discipline, and denying oneself. No one wants to do that—especially when the messenger is so unappealing.

Our reaction to most critics is something like the following: "I just consider the source" or "I don't pay attention to him because he has a critical spirit." Generally, however, behind every harsh word, no matter how unjustified, there is a nugget of truth. If we will listen carefully to what our critics are saying, we will often find help in correcting our ways. Look beyond the critic and see his words for the merit they might have. Then respond logically, not emotionally.

The people of Judah, however, refused to hear Jeremiah. They were ready to kill the man who was offering them their only hope for survival.

B. God Offers Forgiveness (v. 3)

3. If so be they will hearken, and turn every man from his evil way, that I may repent me of the evil, which I purpose to do unto them because of the evil of their doings.

God's promises are always conditional upon obedience. Likewise, His pronouncements of punishment can be averted if the conditions of repentance are met. God never enjoys disciplining His children, and He is long-suffering and patient. In Isaiah's ministry this provisionary tenderness was seen in the very first prophecy he gave: "Come now, and let us reason together, saith the Lord: though your sins be as scarlet, they shall be as white as snow; though they be red like crimson, they shall be as wool. If ye be willing and obedient, ye shall eat the good of the land" (Isaiah 1:18, 19).

As harsh as Jeremiah's words were in our present text, there was still room for a change of attitude by the people. The same mercy was echoed in Jeremiah 18:7-10: "If at any time I announce that a nation or kingdom is to be uprooted, torn down and destroyed, and if that nation I warned repents of its evil, then I will relent [KJV, repent] and not inflict on it the disaster I had planned. And if at another time I announce that a nation or kingdom is to be built up and planted, and if it does evil in my sight and does not obey me, then I will reconsider [KJV, repent] the good I had intended to do for it" (*NIV*).

When the Scriptures say that God "will repent" (vv. 8, 10), we have to understand that this is a different type of repentance from the human kind, for God never does anything wrong. God's character is consistent: "God is not a man, that he should lie, nor a son of man, that he should change his mind [KJV, repent]. Does he speak and then not act? Does he promise and not fulfill?" (Numbers 23:19, *NIV*).

God's thoughts and intentions toward man are based on men's deciding to obey Him. If men repent, God automatically recants from plans to punish them. "With God repentance is not a change of mind but his consistent response according to his changeless nature to the change in the nation's conduct" (Zondervan, *NIV Bible Commentary*).

The prophet Jonah was deeply disturbed when God recanted of the punishment He had intended for the Ninevites: "When God saw what they did and how they turned from their evil ways, he had compassion [KJV, repented] and did not bring upon them the destruction he had threatened" (Jonah 3:10, *NIV*). Jonah knew of God's hesitancy to punish, and was angry at Him when the people of Nineveh repented: "He prayed to the Lord, 'O Lord, is this not what I said when I was still at home? That is why I was so quick to flee to Tarshish. I knew that you are a gracious and compassionate God, slow to anger and abounding in love, a God who relents [repents] from sending calamity'" (4:2, *NIV*).

Again, God's dealings with man is conditioned upon his obedience or disobedience. This is why Jeremiah was commanded to continue to plea with the nation of Judah. God knew very well that the people would not change, but His consistent nature had to allow for the opportunity.

C. A Curse to All the Nations (vv. 4-7)

4. And thou shalt say unto them, Thus saith the Lord; If ye

will not hearken to me, to walk in my law, which I have set before you,

5. To hearken to the words of my servants the prophets, whom I sent unto you, both rising up early, and sending them, but ye have not hearkened;

6. Then will I make this house like Shiloh, and will make this city a curse to all the nations of the earth.

7. So the priests and the prophets and all the people heard Jeremiah speaking these words in the house of the Lord.

The threatened calamity for Judah that God was preparing was exile to Babylon. However, the people refused to heed the warning signals. They were so caught up in the pleasures of sin that they were blinded to the handwriting on the wall.

Shiloh (v. 6) was the place where the Tabernacle had been set up after the conquest of Canaan. It was destroyed by the Philistines in 1050 B.C. God's words: "Then will I make this house like Shiloh" indicates that Jerusalem and the Temple would be destroyed. The priests and false prophets were outraged at Jeremiah's words. The Temple, originally meant to be the dwelling place of God's presence, had become the symbol of their power over the people, and he was thus undermining their authority. It is interesting to note that Jesus received the same response when He prophesied another destruction of the Temple and Jerusalem (Matthew 24:2; Mark 14:57-59).

Just as sinful men can be indifferent to their wickedness, believers can also be guilty of a similar complacency. Christian complacency takes the form of resting on the laurels of small victories. An illustration from World War II points this out: After Britain had suffered so terribly at the hands of Hitler's bombing raids, there was an intense need to hear something positive. This came with the triumph in the Battle of North Africa in 1942. While the people were cheering the good news, Winston Churchill sobered them with a warning: "Now this is not the end. It is not even the beginning of the end. But it is, perhaps, the end of the beginning" (from a speech at the Lord Mayor's Day Luncheon, London). Only one battle had been won. There were still three more years of fighting left.

A present complacency can be illustrated with the culture war in the United States. There is no doubt that there has been tremendous degeneration of morality and decency. Things that once would have shocked Christians are now commonplace. There is much that does not disturb the church like it once did. Many Christians have been lulled into believing that all is well—just as the people of Judah did. There may be small victories—a revival here, a church doing a good work there—but where is the moral outrage necessary to petition God for a new Reformation or another Great Awakening?

What are some ways that the church has become indifferent to the sins that go on within its walls?

II. UNWAVERING WITNESS (Jeremiah 26:8-15)

A. Efforts to Kill Jeremiah (vv. 8-11)

8. Now it came to pass, when Jeremiah had made an end of speaking all that the Lord had commanded him to speak unto all the people, that the priests and the prophets and all the people took him, saying, Thou shalt surely die.

9. Why hast thou prophesied in the name of the Lord, saying, This house shall be like Shiloh, and this city shall be desolate without an inhabitant? And all the people were gathered against Jeremiah in the house of the Lord.

10. When the princes of Judah heard these things, then they came up from the king's house unto the house of the Lord, and sat down in the entry of the new gate of the Lord's house.

11. Then spake the priests and the prophets unto the princes and to all the people, saying, This man is worthy to die; for he hath prophesied against this city, as ye have heard with your ears.

Jeremiah's words enraged the people. He challenged their social and moral behavior. He held his ground and was not afraid to give them unpopular criticism. They could either listen or they could silence him—but he would not hold back what God had commanded him to say. They chose to silence him: "They said, 'Come, let's make plans against Jeremiah; for the teaching of the law by the priest will not be lost, nor will counsel from the wise, nor the word from the prophets. So come, let's attack him with our tongues and pay no attention to anything he says'" (Jeremiah 18:18, *NIV*).

The people reasoned that they did not need Jeremiah. Instead, they would depend on their own prophets who gave them what they wanted to hear. They were totally willing to blind themselves to the truth. We live in a similar generation. Modern-day prophets and social engineers are giving man's vilest nature what he wants to hear—justification to do exactly as he pleases with no regard to a day of reckoning.

Judah's citizens branded Jeremiah as a traitor because he prophesied destruction—both of the Temple and the city of Jerusalem. They were determined to believe what they wanted to believe. This is much the same as the prevailing philosophy of our day—that perception equals reality. In other words, if the majority of the people think something is the truth, then it must be the truth. Courage is redefined to mean standing for the most far-out ideas—even if they lead to destruction. The "courageous" people of Judah refused Jeremiah's godly advice and pushed for a foreign alliance to fight Babylon in an attempt to hold on to their independence. This led them straight down a course to captivity.

Today we have people "courageously" doing the same sort of things. The media praise those who "boldly" assert their independence to do exactly as they please—even when such behavior leads to self-destruction. Rock stars wreck their bodies with drugs and wild living—pushing themselves to premature graves. Yet, instead of learning lessons from such excess, our culture praises their boldness to "do it my way." Our day is not so different from that of Judah when Jeremiah prophesied.

B. Jeremiah's Defense (vv. 12-15)

(Jeremiah 26:14, 15 is not included in the printed text.)

12. Then spake Jeremiah unto all the princes and to all the people, saying, The Lord sent me to prophesy against this house and against this city all the words that ye have heard.

13. Therefore now amend your ways and your doings, and obey the voice of the Lord your God; and the Lord will repent him of the evil that he hath pronounced against you.

By this time Jeremiah had come to have little regard for his own life.

He was resigned to carry out God's will. He saw himself as a dead man—dead to his own will and ideas—but alive to carry out God' purposes. This is exactly the same attitude Paul expressed in Galatians 2:20: "I am crucified with Christ: nevertheless I live; yet not I, but Christ liveth in me: and the life which I now live in the flesh I live by the faith of the Son of God, who loved me, and gave himself for me." Like Paul, Jeremiah had dedicated himself to the total purposes of the One who had called him.

The three Hebrew children in the Book of Daniel had centered themselves on the same obedience: "If we are thrown into the blazing furnace, the God we serve is able to save us from it, and he will rescue us from your hand, O king. But even if he does not, we want you to know, O king, that we will not serve your gods or worship the image of gold you have set up" (3:17, 18, *NIV*).

This is what is truly necessary of every believer—to live our lives in such a way as to made Christ's will for us the absolute focus of our existence. "When God's living Word becomes 'fire in your bones,' you will feel compelled to share it with others, whatever the results'" (*Life Application Bible*, Tyndale House, Notes on Jeremiah 20:7-18).

How committed are you to speak boldly for the Lord in adverse situations?

III. OBEDIENCE MAY BRING RISK (Jeremiah 26:16-24)

A. Jeremiah' Life Spared (vv. 16-19)

(Jeremiah 26:16-19 is not included in the printed text.)

Jeremiah's life was in serious danger, and there was no way of determining just how far his inflammatory remarks would incite the people to react. Providentially, there were elders and wise men in the crowd who still exerted enough influence over the unruly mobs to keep them from murdering him. They knew the Scriptures and their history well enough to recognize that Jeremiah's words had precedence from the past. They reminded the people that the prophet Micah (742 to 687 B.C.) had prophesied virtually the same thing some years earlier during the reign of Hezekiah.

The people had forgotten their history—or likely had not ever been taught it. The old axiom that says "History repeats itself" was true in Judah, and remains so today. Every nation is destined to relive the mistakes of the past if it refuses to learn hard lessons—and then teach them to the next generation. Although both accounts of Hezekiah's reign (2 Kings 18-20; 2 Chronicles 29-32) describe Hezekiah as a great reformer, neither attributes any influence to prophets. Nor do they ever mention Micah. Here, however, in Jeremiah 26:18, Micah is presented as a prophet with hard words to say—much like Jeremiah. His warnings (see Micah 3:12) seem to have been heeded and coming disaster diverted—at least for a time. It was only by God's grace that the elders remembered what had happened and intervened for Jeremiah.

Our generation, too, has lost contact with its history—primarily because modern historians choose to rewrite it to suit their social agendas. For instance, as the 20th century comes to a close there is a tremendous effort by many to deny that the Holocaust ever occurred. If successful, such absurdity will cause the same hard lessons of history to have to be learned all over again.

B. The Death of a Prophet (vv. 20-24)

(Jeremiah 26:20-24 is not

included in the printed text.)

Another prophet, Urijah, was not so fortunate as Jeremiah. The incident recorded here probably has nothing to do with the Temple sermon Jeremiah had given. It likely took place somewhere later in the reign of Jehoiakim. Why did Jeremiah not suffer the same fate? He had friends in high places, the family of Shaphan in particular. Ahikam, son of Shaphan used his influence to protect the prophet. Likely, this was a family with some sensitivity and knowledge of past history in Judah. They had wisdom enough to know that Jeremiah was truly speaking the Lord's words.

Jeremiah survived. He was not heeded like Micah had been under Hezekiah. However, neither was he murdered like Urijah. He survived, only to be ignored until it was too late for the nation to avert disaster.

Why does God allow some prophets to be martyred, while others survive?

REVIEW QUESTIONS

1. Is the church in danger of being just like Judah in Jeremiah's day?

2. Do you have trouble handling criticism? Have you ever considered that behind even the most ridiculous faultfinding there might be a nugget of truth?

3. How can we keep reminding our children of the hard lessons that were learned in our history, yet seem to be forgotten today?

4. If Micah was such an important prophet during the reign of Hezekiah, why was he not mentioned in either Kings or Chronicles?

GOLDEN TEXT HOMILY

"IF YE PUT ME TO DEATH, YE SHALL SURELY BRING INNOCENT BLOOD UPON YOURSELVES, . . . FOR OF A TRUTH THE LORD HATH SENT ME UNTO YOU TO SPEAK ALL THESE WORDS IN YOUR EARS" (Jeremiah 26:15).

Beware of seeking popularity or fame in eyes of people around you. We most often associate "peer pressure" with teens or young people, but any social person (even church members) will be subject to experiencing the expectations of the folks around them to conform to their standards and practices. We can be pressed into thinking that the acknowledgment of people is more beneficial than attaining the acknowledgment of God.

Reputation meant so much to one young man that it got him into prison. Seeking to be a highly esteemed gang member, he robbed and beat a man with his bare hands. He thought he had to acquire a reputation of living without fear, until the Holy Ghost arrested him and humbled him like a child. His worldly reputation went out the door as Jesus came into his heart. Now he is not ashamed to share his testimony of acknowledging Christ as his personal Savior, even in prison! Some reputation! He couldn't even make it as a good loser in the world's perception. But now he has a new identity as a prisoner for Christ!

What does your reputation say about you? Do you compromise your gospel words with your worldly ways? Are you willing to be like Jeremiah and give your life for a testimony of truth? If we have any agenda to please our neighbor rather than to serve our Master, may God grant us repentance and grace! Our prayer as the chosen ones of God ought to be for help to become overcomers "by the blood of the Lamb, and by the word of [our] testimony" (Revelation 12:11). While there is yet time, let us build a testimony, a reputation as a witness for Christ's glory.

"To walk in darkness, to live in the light, To know what is wrong, and to live what is right, The hope of the Gospel is Christ living in me, Walking in the Spirit for all the world to see."—**Eugene Wigelsworth, Clinical Chaplain, Pasquotank Correctional Institution, Elizabeth City, North Carolina**

SENTENCE SERMONS

BELIEVERS MUST SHARE the good news in spite of the risk.

—Selected

IT IS NO USE walking anywhere to proclaim the gospel unless we preach as we walk.

—St. Francis of Assisi

CHILDLIKE OBEDIENCE moves toward every command of God, as the needle points where the loadstone draws.

—Thomas Watson

THE WAY OF THE WORLD is to praise dead saints and persecute living ones.

—Draper's Book of Quotations for the Christian World

EVANGELISM APPLICATION

THE REWARD OF BRINGING PEOPLE TO CHRIST IS GREATER THAN ANY RISK INVOLVED.

I remember reading once about a war correspondent who was obsessed with talking to men who had been hit by enemy fire. He always asked these kinds of questions: "Did you hear the bullet coming? What kind of noise did it make? Did you know you were about to go down?" Then one day the reporter himself was caught in the crossfire of battle and was mortally wounded. His last words to a buddy were, "I never heard a thing."

Isn't this a picture of the lives of many Christians? They seek for experiences all their lives, watching for visions, callings, grand revelations, and angel sightings. If this is all that one's spiritual journey consists of, he will most likely be disappointed with his Christian experience.

At the same time, God does very definitely reveal Himself to some with "bigger than life" confrontations. When He speaks dramatically, though, it is for a purpose—generally a great work to be accomplished. He is never frivolous in His dealings with men. Jeremiah was called to do a frightening task—that of issuing stern warnings of punishment coming to Judah for their sins.

No less today are we required to sound the warning to sinners to turn from their sins and come to Christ. In so doing, we, like Jeremiah, risk ridicule and rejection. But the reward of bringing even one soul to salvation far outweighs the difficulties we encounter: "If any of you do err from the truth, and one convert him; let him know, that he which converteth the sinner from the error of his way shall save a soul from death, and shall hide a multitude of sins" (James 5:20).

DAILY BIBLE READINGS

M. Personal Testimony. Psalm 103:1-12

T. Personal Responsibility. Ezekiel 3:17-21

W. Commission to Witness. Mark 16:15-20

T. ower to Witness. Acts 1:1-8

F. Prayer for Boldness. Acts 4:24-30

S. Ministry of Reconciliation. 2 Corinthians 5:11-21

Responding to God

Study Text: Jeremiah 18:1-12; 19:1-15

Objective: To realize that all people must choose how they will respond to God and determine to submit to Him.

Time: The Book of Jeremiah was written between 627 and 580 B.C.

Place: The Book of Jeremiah was probably written in Jerusalem.

Golden Text: "Cannot I do with you as this potter? saith the Lord. Behold, as the clay is in the potter's hand, so are ye in mine hand" (Jeremiah 18:6).

Central Truth: God requires obedience from His children.

Evangelism Emphasis: God will judge the disobedient but will be merciful to those who repent.

PRINTED TEXT

Jeremiah 18:1. The word which came to Jeremiah from the Lord, saying,

2. Arise, and go down to the potter's house, and there I will cause thee to hear my words.

3. Then I went down to the potter's house, and, behold, he wrought a work on the wheels.

4. And the vessel that he made of clay was marred in the hand of the potter: so he made it again another vessel, as seemed good to the potter to make it.

5. Then the word of the Lord came to me, saying,

6. O house of Israel, cannot I do with you as this potter? saith the Lord. Behold, as the clay is in the potter's hand, so are ye in mine hand, O house of Israel.

7. At what instant I shall speak concerning a nation, and concerning a kingdom, to pluck up, and to pull down, and to destroy it;

8. If that nation, against whom I have pronounced, turn from their evil, I will repent of the evil that I thought to do unto them.

9. And at what instant I shall speak concerning a nation, and concerning a kingdom, to build and to plant it;

10. If it do evil in my sight, that it obey not my voice, then I will repent of the good, wherewith I said I would benefit them.

11. Now therefore go to, speak to the men of Judah, and to the inhabitants of Jerusalem, saying, Thus saith the Lord; Behold, I frame evil against you, and devise a device against you: return ye now every one from his evil way, and make your ways and your

doings good.

12. And they said, There is no hope: but we will walk after our own devices, and we will every one do the imagination of his evil heart.

19:15. Thus saith the Lord of hosts, the God of Israel; Behold, I will bring upon this city and upon all her towns all the evil that I have pronounced against it, because they have hardened their necks, that they might not hear my words.

LESSON OUTLINE

I. MOLDED BY GOD'S HAND
   A. The Potter's Workshop
   B. God Molds Israel

II. GOD'S SOVEREIGN MERCY
   A. God's Judgment of Nations
   B. Repentance Averts Judgment

III. LISTEN TO GOD
   A. When There Is No Hope
   B. Shattering the Clay Jar

LESSON EXPOSITION

INTRODUCTION

Jeremiah had confronted the people by standing in front of the Temple and preaching a message of doom. This had been the perfect spot to expose their hypocrisy. They thought their religious ritual would be sufficient to save them. In their minds they were God's people, worshiping within the protection of His holy Temple.

As a result of his hard stand, Jeremiah's life had been put in real danger, but the city officials and wise men had kept cool heads to protect him. God was not finished with Jeremiah, and no one could touch him until he had completed all that Jehovah planned for him.

In this lesson we continue with Jeremiah' warnings to the nation during the reign of King Jehoiakim, all of which were to no avail. No matter how stern the threats came from God, the people were still determined to continue in their sinful ways. There is, however, a wonderful thread of God's mercy exhibited through all this, for He constantly made the effort to convince the people of their sin and to turn from it. Had they heeded the message and repented, all the terrible years of destruction, captivity, and disarray that eventually came would have been avoided. In the text of this lesson we see Jeremiah using parables and object lessons to illustrate the message God had given him to deliver.

I. MOLDED BY GOD'S HAND (Jeremiah 18:1-6)

A. The Potter's Workshop (vv. 1-4)

1. The word which came to Jeremiah from the Lord, saying,

2. Arise, and go down to the potter's house, and there I will cause thee to hear my words.

3. Then I went down to the potter's house, and, behold, he wrought a work on the wheels.

4. And the vessel that he made of clay was marred in the hand of the potter: so he made it again another vessel, as seemed good to the potter to make it.

One of the most familiar features of life in the ancient world was the potter's workshop. There was always a demand for the products a good craftsman could produce. Pottery was fragile and had to be replaced in every home regularly. Modern archeology owes much of its success to the relics of this trade that have survived the centuries. Broken pieces of pots, jars, and utensils have helped us build a picture of what ancient life was like.

The potter was a fascinating person to watch. He would sit in his workshop spinning a large circular stone with an apparatus operated by his feet. On the stone he placed the clay and then shaped it with his hands as the contraption turned. Once the clay had been molded into a vessel that satisfied the potter, it was glazed and baked in a furnace.

The Lord told Jeremiah to go "down" to a potter's shop. We can infer from this that Jeremiah left the Temple area of Jerusalem (in the upper part of the city) and walked down the slopes of the Valley of Hinnom (south of the city) to where water and clay were found. This was the location of the potters' shops. At the pottery Jeremiah saw what was already familiar to him. The potter was making a vessel on his wheel, and as would happen often, the clay had not turned out to the potter's liking. There might be a defect or piece of trash in the clay, or perhaps the design was not coming out as the potter had envisioned it. Whatever the case, he pressed the clay back into one large lump and started the process again.

B. God Molds Israel (vv. 5, 6)

5. Then the word of the Lord came to me, saying,

6. O house of Israel, cannot I do with you as this potter? saith the Lord. Behold, as the clay is in the potter's hand, so are ye in mine hand, O house of Israel.

Jeremiah had likely stopped to look in at the potter's shop many times, but on this particular day the Lord sent him there for a specific purpose. Jeremiah suddenly saw that the potter's work was a picture of God and His creation. The infinite power of Jehovah held Israel in His hands like a piece of clay.

But what does this mean? Israel, like the clay, was totally under the control of the Potter; God could do with her exactly as He pleased. God created the Jews as His people, and He could certainly shape them as He willed. This might be seen as a message of hope, but it could also serve as an omen of judgment. Israel existed on earth to serve God; God did not exist to serve Israel, as the people of Judah had come to believe. Israel had no more right to dictate to God than clay has to tell the potter how to shape it.

This same metaphor of the potter and clay is found in Isaiah 45:9: "Woe to him who quarrels with his Maker, to him who is but a potsherd among the potsherds on the ground. Does the clay say to the potter, 'What are you making?' Does your work say, 'He has no hands'?" (*NIV*). The Hebrews were guilty of presuming on the faithfulness of God. There is a fine but firm line between presumption and faith. Presumption expects God to act in one's behalf, no matter the attitude or lifestyle the individual has chosen. *Faith* trusts in God but remains humble and malleable, ever realizing that the Creator has the right to mold and break as He chooses. The people of Judah were *presuming* on God's graciousness.

Paul picked up the illustration of the clay and potter and adapted it to the individual: "But who are you, O man, to talk back to God? 'Shall what is formed say to him who formed it, "Why did you make me like this?"' Does not the potter have the right to make out of the same lump of clay some pottery for noble purposes and some for common use?" (Romans 9:20, 21, *NIV*).

Paul was not implying that some people are more valuable than others, but simply that God has control over His creation. No one has a right to demand anything of God, for our very existence depends entirely on Him. It would be wise if Christians took this to heart when claiming the promises of God in their lives. Certainly the Bible is full of wonderful assurances, pledges, and rewards to those who believe. However, we should never approach the Lord with a demanding spirit. The promises of God are most available to those who present themselves as humble servants.

Paul further developed the potter-clay, creator-created metaphor in 2 Timothy 2:20, 21: "In a large house there are articles not only of gold and silver, but also of wood and clay; some are for noble purposes and some for ignoble. If a man cleanses himself from the latter, he will be an instrument for noble purposes, made holy, useful to the Master and prepared to do any good work" (*NIV*). God creates different vessels for different roles in His kingdom. It is His choosing, not ours, that determines that purpose for our lives.

The people of Judah were guilty of attempting to use God to satisfy their own ambitions and desires. Anyone who ever claims to be God's people must carefully avoid this attitude.

Have you ever been guilty of demanding from God something that you thought you deserved?

II. GOD'S SOVEREIGN MERCY (Jeremiah 18:7-10)

A. God's Judgment of Nations (v. 7)

7. At what instant I shall speak concerning a nation, and concerning a kingdom, to pluck up, and to pull down, and to destroy it.

Jeremiah carried the potter-and-clay illustration one step further by making it clear that God exercises control over all nations of the earth, not just Judah. This was not new to Jeremiah, for God had told him he would prophesy to other nations when He called him: "See, I have this day set thee over the nations and over the kingdoms, to root out, and to pull down, and to destroy, and to throw down, to build, and to plant" (Jeremiah 1:10).

God is the absolute authority over the universe. No people can exist unless He allows it. He can mold nations until they conform to His wishes. Kings and dictators may appear as power figures, but one sweep of the "potter's hand" will cause economies to fail, armies to be defeated, and tyrants to fall.

Natural disasters of the catastrophic kind have been abundant in recent years. Floods, hurricanes, earthquakes, volcano eruptions, fires—all these "acts of God" are firm reminders that man's control of his domain is fragile indeed. The One who made us can make us or break us in a moment. Man may arrogantly declare control of his destiny, but God can step in at any time and prove otherwise.

B. Repentance Averts Judgment (vv. 8-10)

8. If that nation, against whom I have pronounced, turn from their evil, I will repent of the evil that I thought to do unto them.

9. And at what instant I shall speak concerning a nation, and concerning a kingdom, to build and to plant it;

10. If it do evil in my sight, that it obey not my voice, then I will repent of the good, wherewith I said I would benefit them.

It is God's freedom (like the potter and the clay) that also allows for God to "repent" (relent) of any punishment He has pronounced upon a nation. A nation that turns to God and repents of its evil may avert a sentence of death (v. 8), while another that has sought God's favor for a long period of time may be destroyed if it falls into sin.

Like Judah, all the nations surrounding Judah were given both a negative and a positive message. If they continued in their sin, they would see the same destruction and deportation that Judah would receive. If they repented of their evil, punishment would be nullified. The total destiny of man and nation is dependent upon a sincere repentance and turning away from sin.

There is a limit to how far the implications of *potter and clay* can be taken. Clay is a passive material in the potter's hand, but the *human will* is anything but passive. What God can do with a life is determined by the willingness of the individual to be molded. Has God's omnipotence thus been nullified? No, for it was God himself who gave man the right of choice. Therefore, man can refuse to be fashioned into a clay vessel that is useful. The quality of the clay, then, becomes an important element in carrying out the metaphor. Clay with trash, imperfections, pebbles, inconsistency of materials, and so forth, will never be useful for making anything of value.

The quality of the clay is determined by its willingness to repent: "Upon a person's repentance, God can rework him or her into a vessel of honor. The position is not one of absolute fatalism (blotting out human freedom), nor is it one where God's sovereignty is wholly dependent on a person's choice. Ultimately, no human being is free. But God in his mysterious working in human life has ordered it so that humanity may freely choose" (Zondervan *NIV Bible Commentary*, Vol. 1, Old Testament).

When repentance occurs, God then begins the reshaping of men and nations into useful vessels. For God to "repent" (and not administer a promised punishment) does not mean He has changed His mind; rather it is a consistent response of His nature to a law He established—repentance brings forgiveness.

How has God used heathen nations to administer His will?

III. LISTEN TO GOD (Jeremiah 18:11, 12; 19:1-3, 10, 11, 15)

A. When There Is No Hope (18:11, 12)

11. Now therefore go to, speak to the men of Judah, and to the inhabitants of Jerusalem, saying, Thus saith the Lord; Behold, I frame evil against you, and devise a device against you: return ye now every one from his evil way, and make your ways and your doings good.

12. And they said, There is no hope: but we will walk after our own devices, and we will every one do the imagination of his evil heart.

Jeremiah had declared God's sovereignty over both Judah and

the other nations. All of creation was the clay and God was the potter. Now he applied the parable directly to Judah. Responsibility for their future rested clearly with them. They had to make a decision. God said, "I frame evil against you." The Hebrew word for *frame* has the same root as *potter*. Literally, then, the meaning is "I am molding a terrible catastrophe for you." That calamity would be exile and servitude to Babylon.

The people reacted with a sense of resignation. They had committed themselves so completely to their selfish ways that even they recognized they had insufficient character to change their ways. They had sunk so low that they condemned themselves. Jonah 2:8 accurately describes their condition: "Those who cling to worthless idols forfeit the grace that could be theirs" (*NIV*). And 2 Kings 17:15 presents the same thought: "They rejected his decrees and the covenant he had made with their fathers and the warnings he had given them. They followed worthless idols and themselves became worthless" (*NIV*). This is the problem of sin. It is an addiction like drugs. Such a dependency is developed that Satan convinces the individual that there is no possible turning back.

Jeremiah had to have felt extreme pain and rejection. The people saw that there was truth in his words but were unwilling to respond. What a disheartening response after giving everything he had! However, his grieving could be no greater than that of God himself: "My people have committed two evils; they have forsaken me the fountain of living waters, and hewed them out cisterns, broken cisterns, that can hold no water" (Jeremiah 2:13).

B. Shattering the Clay Jar
(Jeremiah 19:1-3, 10, 11, 15)

(Jeremiah 19:1-3, 10, 11 is not included in the printed text.)

15. Thus the Lord of hosts, the God of Israel; Behold, I will bring upon this city and upon all her towns all the evil that I have pronounced against it, because they have hardened their necks, that they might not hear my words.

Like the parable of the potter and the clay, God again instructed Jeremiah to use the same imagery for another lesson. This time He told Jeremiah to buy a clay jar. The receptacle when broken could not be made usable again. He was to take with him the "ancients" (v. 1)—the elders who had lived through Josiah's reforms—and go to the Valley of Hinnom by way of the Potsherd Gate. This valley was the garbage dump for Jerusalem. It was also a place where children were sacrificed to the god Molech (Jeremiah 7:31, 32; 32:35). Jeremiah was taking the people to a place of waste and carnage to give a vivid demonstration of what God was planning.

Why were these older priests and elders to accompany Jeremiah? Likely because they did know what was right. They had been a part of Josiah's revival. They should have already had the courage to stand against the younger generation of idolaters. There is a price that goes with knowledge of the Lord: "That servant who knows his master's will and does not get ready or does not do what his master wants will be beaten with many blows. But the one who does not know and does things deserving punishment will be beaten with few blows. From everyone who has been given much, much will be demanded; and from the one who has been entrusted with much, much more will be asked" (Luke 12:47, 48, *NIV*).

The more resources, talents, teachings, and understandings of God's Word one has, the more responsible he must become. For the older priests and elders to have passively allowed (or even participated in) the terrible spiritual condition of the people was a disgrace.

Jeremiah predicted a terrible carnage to come on Jerusalem (vv. 3-9). Interestingly, this prophecy had two separate fulfillments:

1. Babylonian invasion—Nebuchadnezzar destroyed the city in 586 B.C. During the siege of the city, food was so scarce that people became cannibals, eating their own children (see Lamentations 2:20).

2. The Roman siege of Titus in A.D. 70 .

After predicting a great carnage, Jeremiah was to smash the jar he had bought (vv. 10, 11). This was not an unusual thing to do in the Near East: "It is still the practice to break a jar near a person who has wronged one and voice the hope that he will be similarly broken. Such an action is intended to bring about the downfall of one's enemies" (Zondervan *NIV Bible Commentary*, Vol. 1).

Jeremiah was illustrating that God had activated His plans for Judah's destruction. The people had passed the point of no return. The broken jar could not be mended, only thrown away. Judah had now been rejected, and just as this valley was a place of defilement, the entire nation would be the same because the people were stiffnecked and wouldn't heed God's warning to turn from their evil ways.

REVIEW QUESTIONS

1. Is it proper to label hurricanes, earthquakes, floods, and other disasters as "acts of God?"

2. For a nation to repent of its sins, must all the people repent? How much of a remnant of praying people is required for God to withhold judgment?

3. If God is Lord over this entire earth, how do we relate to other religions in our "multicultural" nation?

4. Is it possible for people or a nation to sink so low that they are beyond the reaches of God's grace?

GOLDEN TEXT HOMILY

"CANNOT I DO WITH YOU AS THIS POTTER? SAITH THE LORD. BEHOLD, AS THE CLAY IS IN THE POTTER'S HAND, SO ARE YE IN MINE HAND" (Jeremiah 18:6).

The contented Christian is one who submits to Christ first, then responds with a heart of love to the world around him. Contentment is found not in the world but through submission to Jesus, who is Lord of every circumstance for the faithful believer.

A Christian cannot halt between two opinions—there is no other path but to trust and obey. Through trust we learn to receive the provision of God; through trust and obedience we learn to apply God's principles and promises to whatever need arises. "Christ in us" is the hope exhibited by servants of God.

Sometimes as clay vessels we become concerned about the molds offered by the values of this world. Fame, fortune, success—all these attract; but the glitter is tarnished by sin unless we have allowed Christ to mold us. As frail creatures, we are prone to be molded by many temporary rewards, but as Christians we look beyond the temporary to the eternal.

Picture Christ on the cross—perhaps a failure in the eyes of humanistic philosophers. To the unbeliever it looks like foolishness; but to us who are saved, He is the author and the finisher of our faith (Hebrews 12:2). No longer should a believer be shaped by worldly pleasures or temporal rewards but by God himself, who calls us to become more Christlike. Let us take up our individual cross and allow Him to mold us according to His will. **—Florie Brown Wigelsworth, M.Div., Elizabeth City, North Carolina**

SENTENCE SERMONS

GOD REQUIRES OBEDIENCE from His children.

—Selected

OBEDIENCE TO GOD is the most infallible evidence of sincere and supreme love to Him.

—Nathanael Emmons

HE WHO NEGLECTS true worship neglects that which separates man from the lower forms of life.

—Hugh Blair

MERCY does not always express itself by withholding punishment.

—Ernest M. Ligon

EVANGELISM APPLICATION

GOD WILL JUDGE THE DISOBEDIENT BUT WILL BE MERCIFUL TO THOSE WHO REPENT.

Can we ever discern when a person has so trampled on God's grace that he passes a point of no return? We like to think that as long as there is breath there is still hope. We cannot be the judge, for only God is capable of that. However, there are times when we have probably witnessed such hardness.

Even as this lesson is being written, the author is watching what is possibly one such hopeless situation. A young man in the community is nearing the final stages of AIDS, contracted from years of hard living. However, the greater monster in his life is drug addiction. Though death is just around the corner, he will still go to any lengths—beg, steal, borrow, intimidate, or frighten anyone he sees—in order to obtain money for his next fix. He has made a mockery of every attempt others have made to help him. Having resigned himself to his fate, he appears to have no fears, but has, rather, sold his soul to narcotics.

As we sit and watch helplessly, we catch a glimpse of what Jeremiah must have felt. We want to help, but realize that the sin has taken total control. The dependence on drugs has wiped away any strength of character or resistance to the temptation. It is at these times we grasp just how merciful God has been to us all. We must always guard our hearts from becoming so captivated by sin that we no longer hear Him calling us to repentance.

DAILY BIBLE READINGS

M. Choose the Lord. Joshua 24:14-24
T. Used by God. Esther 4:6-17
W. Come as a Child. Mark 10:13-16
T. Living Sacrifices. Romans 12:1-8
F. Humble Yourselves. James 4:1-10
S. Submit and Serve. 1 Peter 5:1-7

Dealing With Discouragement

Study Text: Jeremiah 20:1-18; Lamentations 3:1-40

Objective: To acknowledge that God's people can experience discouragement and allow God to rekindle hope.

Time: The Book of Jeremiah was written between 627 and 580 B.C. Lamentations was written around 585 B.C.

Place: The Books of Jeremiah and Lamentations were probably written at Jerusalem.

Golden Text: "The Lord is my portion, saith my soul; therefore will I hope in him" (Lamentations 3:24).

Central Truth: Trust in God restores hope to the discouraged.

Evangelism Emphasis: Jesus Christ brings hope to those bound by sin.

PRINTED TEXT

Jeremiah 20:7. O Lord, thou hast deceived me, and I was deceived: thou art stronger than I, and hast prevailed: I am in derision daily, every one mocketh me.

8. For since I spake, I cried out, I cried violence and spoil; because the word of the Lord was made a reproach unto me, and a derision, daily.

9. Then I said, I will not make mention of him, nor speak any more in his name. But his word was in mine heart as a burning fire shut up in my bones, and I was weary with forbearing, and I could not stay.

11. But the Lord is with me as a mighty terrible one: therefore my persecutors shall stumble, and they shall not prevail: they shall be greatly ashamed; for they shall not prosper: their everlasting confusion shall never be forgotten.

12. But, O Lord of hosts, that triest the righteous, and seest the reins and the heart, let me see thy vengeance on them: for unto thee have I opened my cause.

Lamentations 3:17. And thou hast removed my soul far off from peace: I forgat prosperity.

18. And I said, My strength and my hope is perished from the Lord:

19. Remembering mine affliction and my misery, the wormwood and the gall.

20. My soul hath them still in remembrance, and is humbled in me.

21. This I recall to my mind, therefore have I hope.

22. It is of the Lord's mercies that we are not consumed, because his compassions fail not.

23. They are new every morning: great is thy faithfulness.

24. The Lord is my portion, saith my soul; therefore will I hope in him.

25. The Lord is good unto them that wait for him, to the soul that seeketh him.

26. It is good that a man should both hope and quietly wait for the salvation of the Lord.

37. Who is he that saith, and it cometh to pass, when the Lord commandeth it not?

38. Out of the mouth of the most High proceedeth not evil and good?

39. Wherefore doth a living man complain, a man for the punishment of his sins?

40. Let us search and try our ways, and turn again to the Lord.

LESSON OUTLINE

I. REJECTION BRINGS DISCOURAGEMENT
   A. A Cry of Despair
   B. Deserted by Friends
   C. Confident Faith

II. DESPAIR FOSTERS COMPLAINT
   A. Cursing Oneself
   B. The Bitterness of Despair

III. TRUST BRINGS HOPE
   A. Remembering God's Faithfulness
   B. Learning From Discipline
   C. God's Sovereignty in Discipline

LESSON EXPOSITION

INTRODUCTION

After delivering God's message through the object lessons of the potter and his clay and the breaking of the clay jar, Jeremiah left the Valley of Hinnom and went back up the Temple mount. In front of the Temple he stopped and reiterated what God had said. However, Jeremiah's obedience suddenly attracted the wrong ears, and the prophet was arrested. His bold words were becoming a political threat to those in power. His subsequent frustrations and feelings while under extreme duress are the subject of this lesson. Even though he was assuredly anointed to deliver God's word, the rejection he received exposed his humanity and need for acceptance.

Preaching the full message of God's Word is never easy. When we bring the truths of His love, grace, and compassion, we can usually find a receptive audience. However, when we have to expose sin and hypocrisy, it is hard to attract sympathetic ears. It is at times like these that the ministry can be a very lonely calling.

Anyone who has ever experienced God's anointing power to preach, teach, or prophesy (or to be a vessel for any of the other gifts of the Spirit) knows the wonderful sense of fulfillment that accompanies God's presence. However, there is a downside. The anointing can be extremely draining on the body and spirit. Men and women of God are often at their most vulnerable point just after experiencing a great anointing in their ministries.

Jeremiah was an example of this. Though he was being used as God's mouthpiece, he was paying an immense personal price. We will see in this lesson that sometimes our Christianity requires a determination and regimen that goes beyond feeling God's presence. The Christian life is a war—not a love feast.

Pashur, the priest assigned with responsibility for policing the Temple area, was so angered by Jeremiah's prophecies that he had the prophet locked in stocks overnight. This was both for punishment and to stop Jeremiah from further preaching. Pashur's reaction is typical of people who refuse to listen when their guilt is exposed. They have resisted the truth for so long that their very guilt expresses itself as indignation. They will go to great lengths to try to prove their lies are the truth.

This can be a lesson for all of us. How we react to criticism reflects our maturity and willingness to be molded by God. Often there is a small nuggett of truth behind the criticism directed our way—no matter how ridiculous or how obnoxious the critic. If we can look beyond the critic and acknowledge the flaw, we will be all the more wise and mature.

Also, in watching those such as Pashur go berserk in defending their lies and ungodly lifestyles, we should learn a valuable lesson in how we defend the truth. We need never get so upset that we lose control of ourselves. The gospel is best defended when there is logic and quiet assurance of its truth. Public outrage that gets out of control puts the Christian on the same level as the world he is fighting against. In recent years we have seen this demonstrated in the United States. When so-called Christians resort to murdering abortion doctors and using violence to demonstrate against other wrongs, their insane actions are as vile as the sins they are attempting to eradicate.

Christian apologetics should be simply grounded in the truth of God's Word. When we know the truth, and know that everything He has said will ultimately prevail, we can rise above the madness of those around us and see them as Christ does—wayward children who need the Savior.

As we will see in our lesson, Jeremiah went through a time of frustration and anger over the message God gave him to preach. However, he never let this show publicly. He carried his complaints privately to the only One who could answer them—the Lord himself.

I. REJECTION BRINGS DISCOURAGEMENT (Jeremiah 20:7-13)

A. A Cry of Despair (vv. 7-9)

7. O Lord, thou hast deceived me, and I was deceived: thou art stronger than I, and hast prevailed: I am in derision daily, every one mocketh me.

8. For since I spake, I cried out, I cried violence and spoil; because the word of the Lord was made a reproach unto me, and a derision, daily.

9. Then I said, I will not make mention of him, nor speak any more in his name. But his word was in mine heart as a burning fire shut up in my bones, and I was weary with forbearing, and I could not stay.

Jeremiah had just spent a very difficult night. He had been whipped and put in stocks in the cold outdoors at the Benjamin gate of the city (vv. 1, 2). Yet the Lord had apparently visited with him during those dark hours, for when Pashur came to release him the next day, the prophet had a fresh word to give to his wicked captor (vv. 3-6). This message must have been burning in his breast, for the easier route would have been to say nothing until he was released. Fear of continued restraint in the stocks did not seem to faze the prophet.

Jeremiah gave Pashur a prophecy of both national and personal disaster to come. Judah would be destroyed and her inhabitants carried off into captivity. It should be noted that this was the first time Babylon was specifically mentioned as the nation who would conquer Judah. Whenever this would come to pass, it would be obvious to all that Pashur's irresponsible policies had helped lead to the disaster. Pashur would be remembered in Jewish history as a deceiver of the people. Babylon invaded Judah in three waves. The first took place within a year of this incident (605 B.C.). Pashur himself was likely exiled during the second wave in 597 B.C., the same time that King Jehoiakim was taken captive. The final invasion came in 586 B.C. Just as Jeremiah predicted, Pashur and his family became slaves and died in Babylon.

Once released, Jeremiah cried out in lament to the Lord (vv. 7-9). As said earlier, however, he did this privately. He never let the world see his personal struggles with the Lord. There is nothing wrong with bringing everything, including frustrations and fears, before God. He is never angry with us for asking sincere questions.

Jeremiah was not the first to argue with God. David did this in Psalm 22, going all the way to the point of crying out, "My God, my God, why hast thou forsaken me?" (v. 1). Yet, mixed with this lament, Jeremiah knew he was imprisoned by the very message he hated to deliver. There was a "burning fire shut up in [his] bones" that compelled him to keep on preaching, whether he wanted to or not.

B. Deserted by Friends (v. 10)

(Jeremiah 20:10 is not included in the printed text.)

Declaring God's punishment against those who were persecuting him did not bring Jeremiah happiness or satisfaction. Instead, he cried out in despair to God for giving him such a thankless task. He was feeling the total burden of personal rejection, and he hated having to be the bearer of such terrible tidings. What made the situation worse was that even those who had been his friends also turned on him. The *New International Version* translation of this verse reads: "All my friends are waiting for me to slip, saying, 'Perhaps he will be deceived; then we will prevail over him and take our revenge on him.'" Nothing is more shattering than for your closest associates to let you down. We can thus imagine how despondent Jesus felt in His last hours before and during the Crucifixion. He had no one to turn to but the Father. Jeremiah experienced a measure of the same loneliness.

C. Confident Faith (vv. 11-13)

(Jeremiah 20:13 is not included in the printed text.)

11. But the Lord is with me as a mighty terrible one: therefore my persecutors shall stumble, and they shall not prevail: they shall be greatly ashamed; for they shall not prosper: their everlasting confusion shall never be forgotten.

12. But, O Lord of hosts, that triest the righteous, and seest the reins and the heart, let me see thy vengeance on them: for unto thee have I opened my cause.

Because of his ultimate confidence in the One who "seest the reins and the heart," Jeremiah knew he was clear of any wrong. He had committed all his own ways to the Lord and had nothing to be ashamed of. This is similar to what David expressed in Psalm 7:8-10: "Judge me, O Lord, according to my righteousness, according to my integrity, O Most High. O righteous God, who searches minds and hearts, bring to an end the violence of the wicked and make the righteous secure. My shield is God Most High, who saves the upright in heart" (*NIV*).

Like David, Jeremiah could take solace in the fact that nothing is hidden from God. Because God knows every motive, men's minds are like open books to Him. This could be terrible for anyone trying to hide from God, but Jeremiah knew that he had done everything he could to be obedient. He did not have to put on a front to impress the Lord. He could be completely honest.

How honest are we before the Lord? Do we not catch ourselves carefully wording our prayers to conceal our real motives? We had just as well be totally open with Him. He knows us all too well to be conned. Maybe you are ashamed to be honest. We all deal with attitudes, feelings, temptations, and proclivities that we don't like to admit to—but there is no need to try to conceal them from the One who made us.

Jeremiah never held back when expressing himself to God. Notice that he wanted his enemies humiliated and shamed. However, he was wise enough to know that he could not in himself accomplish this. God would have to be his defender. We should recognize this truth for ourselves. If we try to rectify all the inequities that life throws at us, all we will ever do is flail our fists into the air. The best approach is to give our problems to the Lord. Let Him diffuse the bomb that is trying to detonate inside us.

Jeremiah never tried to take the situation into his own hands by striking back at his accusers. Instead, he vented his anger and frustration to the Lord. The best way we can ever respond to slander against us is to pray.

It appears from verse 13 that Jeremiah experienced a sudden brief relief from his sense of desolation, isolation, and being abandoned by his friends. He broke forth in praise to God, with confidence in His deliverance. Often God gives us a sense desolation even as we are in the midst of a deep trial. He has a way of encouraging us even when the circumstances appear exceedingly bleak.

Do you find yourself holding on to grudges and ill feelings that you know are wrong but you hate to admit them—even to the Lord? If so, what steps are necessary to rid yourself of them?

II. DESPAIR FOSTERS COMPLAINT (Jeremiah 20:14-18; Lamentations 3:17-20)

A. Cursing Oneself (Jeremiah 20:14-18)

(Jeremiah 20:14-18 is not included in the printed text.)

Mood swings are a factor in every person's life, and Jeremiah was no different. He had just committed his problem to the Lord, but then almost immediately fell back into a state of despondency. His depression was so severe he fervently wished he had never been born. His circumstances caused him to despair of life itself. Though some might want to criticize the prophet for apparent fickleness, all of us are guilty of the same struggle. We make resolutions, declarations of faith, promises of new beginnings, and then find the same monsters facing us. Whether we like it or not, we catch ourselves overwhelmed again and again by the same problems and enemies.

There is nothing inherently wrong with such mood swings, as long as they are part of the process of pouring one's entire self out to the Lord. Jeremiah was like David in this respect. Psalm 42 is an excellent picture of how the great king was able to work his way through terrible depression. In this psalm we see him move from triumph to dejection, joy to melancholia, faith to anxiety—and back again. Every time his thoughts turned negative, he would remind himself of the goodness of God as an antidote to what he was feeling.

This is what each of us should do when we face difficult moments—focus our hearts on God's ability and faithfulness.

How should Christians deal with mood swings and moments of depression?

B. The Bitterness of Despair (Lamentations 3:17-20)

17. And thou hast removed my soul far off from peace: I forgat prosperity.

18. And I said, My strength and my hope is perished from the Lord:

19. Remembering mine affliction and my misery, the wormwood and the gall.

20. My soul hath them still in remembrance, and is humbled in me.

Jeremiah is often called the "weeping prophet." His heart was broken by the people of Judah. They refused to hear the truth he brought from the Lord, and thus they led themselves to destruction and captivity. While the book that bears the prophet's name predicts this terrible calamity, his second book, Lamentations, looks back on it. Lamentations is a funeral dirge written for the fallen city of Jerusalem.

Jeremiah felt no vindication in what had happened. The prophecies he had spoken had come to pass, but there was no "I told you so" in his voice. He truly wanted the people to repent.

Many preachers use the gospel as ammunition to condemn people, but this should never be our motive. Neither was it indicative of Jeremiah. We must always remember that behind every discipline and punishment the Lord sends is the motive of restoration.

III. TRUST BRINGS HOPE (Lamentations 3:21-40)

A. Remembering God's Faithfulness (vv. 21-26)

21. This I recall to my mind, therefore have I hope.

22. It is of the Lord's mercies that we are not consumed, because his compassions fail not.

23. They are new every morning: great is thy faithfulness.

24. The Lord is my portion, saith my soul; therefore will I hope in him.

25. The Lord is good unto them that wait for him, to the soul that seeketh him.

26. It is good that a man should both hope and quietly wait for the salvation of the Lord.

There was a glimmer of hope in all the sorrow and sin that Jeremiah had seen: *God's compassion never ends.* God always offered restitution if there was repentance, and He had preserved the prophet throughout all the problems the nation of Judah had faced. Jeremiah could look down through the years to the future and see that a plan for restoration and blessing was in the future.

Notice that the verses above provided the text for one of the greatest hymns of the church—"Great Is Thy Faithfulness." These words were spoken from a heart that had been through more than seemed possible to bear, yet Jeremiah saw God's preserving hand at work.

B. Learning From Discipline (vv. 27-33)

(Lamentations 3:27-33 is not included in the printed text.)

God's compassion never ends, even when He leads us through extreme circumstances. In the middle of any trial we ever face, we need only remind ourselves of His enduring love. He will never leave us—no matter what.

Jeremiah could look back and see the positive results of God's working. He was now able to recognize that a long-term plan was actually unfolding. Again, we should remember that *restoration* is the motive behind God's discipline. He never intends that we be left alone to die. His plan is that we come through the trials of life into ultimate victory.

Jeremiah's words here are reminiscent of those of the writer of Psalm 90: "Teach us to number our days aright, that we may gain a heart of wisdom" (v. 12, *NIV*). A young man should recognize just how short his life really is and concentrate on using his time on earth for eternal good, not just the pleasures available to him. We should all number our days and ask, "What am I doing with my life that has eternal value?"

C. God's Sovereignty in Discipline (vv. 34-40)

(Lamentations 3:34-36 is not included in the printed text.)

37. Who is he that saith, and it cometh to pass, when the Lord commandeth it not?

38. Out of the mouth of the most High proceedeth not evil and good?

39. Wherefore doth a living man complain, a man for the punishment of his sins?

40. Let us search and try our ways, and turn again to the Lord.

Over and over, the Scriptures are clear that God takes no delight in harming humans. Ezekiel 18:32 aptly states His feelings: "For I have no pleasure in the death of him that dieth, saith the Lord God: wherefore turn yourselves and live ye." The same thought is expressed in Ezekiel 33:11: "Say unto them, As I live, saith the Lord God, I have no pleasure in the death of the wicked; but that the wicked turn from his way and live: turn ye, turn ye from your evil ways; for why will ye die, O house of Israel?"

In the New Testament the writer of Hebrews gives us the true purpose for all of God's actions in our lives: "Our fathers disciplined us for a little while as they thought best; but God disciplines us for our good, that we may share in his holiness" (12:10, *NIV*).

God's will is that we all reign with Him throughout eternity. It was never in His plan that any should be lost.

Ultimately, we are in God's hands whether we like it or not. Lamentations 3:37 says, "Who can speak and have it happen if the Lord has not decreed it?" (*NIV*). We should realize that we are fighting a losing battle when we struggle against our Creator. The only hope we have—and what a glorious hope it is—is in giving ourselves totally to the Lord Jesus so that we may be molded into useful vessels for His kingdom.

In light of God's love and discipline, how should we react when difficulties arise in our lives?

REVIEW QUESTIONS

1. How should Christians vent their anger and frustrations at the sinfulness around them?
2. Is it wrong to "argue" with God? Explain.
3. What should we do when we feel we have lost sight of God's plan for our lives?
4. How can we examine ourselves to make sure that the activities of our lives have eternal value?

GOLDEN TEXT HOMILY

"THE LORD IS MY PORTION, SAITH MY SOUL; THEREFORE WILL I HOPE IN HIM" (Lamentations 3:24).

Hope is a great source of motivation and contentment. Very little is undertaken or accomplished in this world without some hope of success. To be bereft of hope is to be filled with despair.

To many people, hope is just a wish for a favorable outcome of some endeavor or that some good fortune will come their way. It is this unrealistic type of hope that causes some people to gamble their hard-earned money on lottery tickets. In the same way, people expect to go to heaven without any real basis for such a belief. Hope, in their thinking, refers only to uncertain good. All worldly hopes are tottering, built on the sand, and the worldly person's hopes of heaven are blind and groundless conjectures. Such hopes may be characterized as dead hopes, having no reasonable expectation of fulfillment.

In contrast, Jeremiah based his hope on the Lord who was his portion—the Lord he knew to be merciful, compassionate, and faithful. The Christian has an even greater basis of hope than did the prophet. As the apostle Peter wrote: "Blessed be the God and Father of our Lord Jesus Christ, which according to his abundant mercy hath begotten us again unto a lively [living] hope by the resurrection of Jesus Christ from the dead" (1 Peter 1:3). As Christians our hope is not based on wishful thinking or groundless conjectures, but on the historical fact of our Lord's resurrection.—**Richard Y. Bershon, Ph.D., Chaplain, State Veterans Home, Hot Springs, South Dakota**

SENTENCE SERMONS

TRUST IN GOD restores hope to the discouraged.

—Selected

THE MAJOR CAUSE of discouragement is a temporary loss of perspective. Restore proper perspective, and you take new heart.

—J. Francis Peak

BEWARE OF DESPAIRING about yourself: you are commanded to put your trust in God, and not in yourself.

—St. Augustine

A RELIGIOUS HOPE does not only bear up the mind under her sufferings, but makes her rejoice in them.

—Joseph Addison

EVANGELISM APPLICATION

JESUS CHRIST BRINGS HOPE TO THOSE BOUND BY SIN.

We like to think that sincerity is a

necessary part of commitment toward doing a job well. However, people can be sincere yet be sincerely wrong. Pashur probably felt that he was right in his persecution of Jeremiah, but what he did not realize was how deeply he himself had fallen into sin and misguided belief. That passion for the wrong cause brought about his own destruction.

Saul of Tarsus had a great zeal for God, but it was entirely mistaken. Until he met Jesus Christ on the road to Damascus, his life was committed to an utterly destructive set of values. He was willing to see believers murdered (remember he watched as Stephen was stoned) to promote what he thought was a purification of Judaism. But when Christ shone His light from heaven on Saul's path, the brightness—although it caused temporary physical blindness—opened Saul's spiritual eyes to his terrible sin. This encounter with Christ so changed his life that it was he who later wrote, "If in this life only we have hope in Christ, we are of all men most miserable" (1 Corinthians 15:19). By this he meant we now have the sure hope of an eternity with Christ in glory.

Misguided zeal will do nothing but get us in trouble. Sincerity is only as good as the cause for which it stands. We should always make sure that we have heard from the Lord—not from anyone else—before we involve ourselves in causes. We should study God's Word and listen for His voice to see what He wants us to say, do, think, and believe.

ILLUMINATING THE LESSON

Jeremiah could endure the trials he faced in Judah because he had a burning fire in his bones. Just such a witness as Jeremiah is described in Isaiah 55:4: "Behold, I have given him for a witness to the people, a leader and commander to the people." The great responsibility of a witness is to report honestly what he has seen or experienced, and this the prophet did faithfully. In the same light, Jesus commanded, "Ye shall be witnesses unto me" (Acts 1:8).

One great problem in Christian ministry is that many of those who are active are not true witnesses for God. "There are those who are qualified counselors, adept administrators, methodical organizers, and even powerful preachers who are not true witnesses, because they have not experienced a personal confrontation with the Almighty. They have never seen a burning bush, as Moses did; they have never heard the divine voice, as Samuel did; and they have never been on the mountain with God like Elijah. They have the written record of God's Word, but it has never burned within them like a fire as it did with Jeremiah" (Judson Cornwall, *Profiles of a Leader*).

This is not to indicate that everyone has to see a burning bush to work for the Lord. However, to be able to stand the trials and persecutions of proclaiming the truth to a rebellious people, we must seek an absolute confirmation from the Lord. Otherwise, all we will ever do is share the testimonies of others, and that is not enough. Let us seek His face so that we can be firsthand witnesses of His Word for this world.

DAILY BIBLE READINGS

M. Be Strong and Courageous. Joshua 1:1-9
T. God Is There. 1 Kings 19:9-18
W. God Brings Help. Psalm 31:19-24
T. Trust in God. Psalm 42:1-11
F. Hope Amidst Darkness. 1 Thessalonians 5:1-11
S. Anchor of the Soul. Hebrews 6:13-20

God Protects His Word

Study Text: Jeremiah 36:1-32

Objective: To affirm the importance of God's Word and honor the Word in our lives.

Time: The Book of Jeremiah was written between 627 and 580 B.C.

Place: The Book of Jeremiah was probably written at Jerusalem.

Golden Text: "For ever, O Lord, thy word is settled in heaven" (Psalm 119:89).

Central Truth: God's Word will expose, convict, and overcome evil.

Evangelism Emphasis: Christians honor God's Word by proclaiming it to the lost.

PRINTED TEXT

Jeremiah 36:1. And it came to pass in the fourth year of Jehoiakim the son of Josiah king of Judah, that this word came unto Jeremiah from the Lord, saying,

2. Take thee a roll of a book, and write therein all the words that I have spoken unto thee against Israel, and against Judah, and against all the nations, from the day I spake unto thee, from the days of Josiah, even unto this day.

3. It may be that the house of Judah will hear all the evil which I purpose to do unto them; that they may return every man from his evil way; that I may forgive their iniquity and their sin.

10. Then read Baruch in the book the words of Jeremiah in the house of the Lord, in the chamber of Gemariah the son of Shaphan the scribe, in the higher court, at the entry of the new gate of the Lord's house, in the ears of all the people.

16. Now it came to pass, when they had heard all the words, they were afraid both one and other, and said unto Baruch, We will surely tell the king of all these words.

20. And they went in to the king into the court, but they laid up the roll in the chamber of Elishama the scribe, and told all the words in the ears of the king.

23. And it came to pass, that when Jehudi had read three or four leaves, he cut it with the penknife, and cast it into the fire that was on the hearth, until all the roll was consumed in the fire that was on the hearth.

24. Yet they were not afraid, nor rent their garments, neither the king, nor any of his ser-

vants that heard all these words.

27. Then the word of the Lord came to Jeremiah, after that the king had burned the roll, and the words which Baruch wrote at the mouth of Jeremiah, saying,

28. Take thee again another roll, and write in it all the former words that were in the first roll, which Jehoiakim the king of Judah hath burned.

32. Then took Jeremiah another roll, and gave it to Baruch the scribe, the son of Neriah; who wrote therein from the mouth of Jeremiah all the words of the book which Jehoiakim king of Judah had burned in the fire: and there were added besides unto them many like words.

DICTIONARY

Jehoiakim (jeh-HO-uh-kim)—Jeremiah 36:1—King of Judah around 600 B.C.

Josiah (jo-SY-uh)—Jeremiah 36:1—King of Judah about 640 to 609 B.C.

Baruch (BAH-rook)—Jeremiah 36:10—A friend of the prophet Jeremiah who rewrote for Jeremiah the prophecies that King Jehoiakim had burned in anger.

Gemariah (GEM-ah-RYE-ah) the son of Shaphan (SHA-fan)—Jeremiah 36:10—Gemariah was the prince son of Shaphan. Shaphan served as a faithful scribe under Josiah.

Elishama (ee-LISH-ama)—Jeremiah 36:20—A scribe or secretary to Jehorakim.

Jehudi (jee-HU-dye)—Jeremiah 36:23—Jehudi sat with the princes in Jehoiakim's court and secured from Baruch the prophecies of Jeremiah and read them to the king.

LESSON OUTLINE

I. GOD GIVES HIS WORD
   - A. Writing Down the Word
   - B. Declaring the Written Word

II. PROCLAIMING GOD'S WORD
   - A. Wise Ears Listen
   - B. Wise Advice to Baruch

III. GOD'S WORD PRESERVED
   - A. The Scroll Read to the King
   - B. The Prophecy Scroll Rewritten

LESSON EXPOSITION

INTRODUCTION

Josiah, the last good king of Judah, had been killed in battle against the Egyptians in 609 B.C. One of his sons, Jehoahaz, was then chosen as king. The Egyptians were not satisfied with Jehoahaz and had him deported to Egypt. Another son of Josiah, Jehoiakim, was placed on the throne. This was all still in the year 609 B.C.

The events of this lesson took place in the summer of 605 B.C., four years later. King Nebuchadnezzar of Babylon had just defeated the Egyptian army at

Carchemish. This brought an end to Egyptian domination of Palestine by Pharaoh Neco. Jeremiah 25 describes the occurrences that set the stage for our discussions. Several points of importance are found there that will broaden the understanding of the lesson text.

1. Jeremiah said that he had been preaching the message of the Lord for 23 years. Since this was 605 B.C., he had thus been prophesying since 627 B.C. He also said that the people had not heeded his words, nor those of other godly prophets. He then went on to review the things he had been declaring during those years. Events in Judah began to sour with the death of Josiah. Jeremiah preached the coming disaster for nearly 20 years before his prophecies started to transpire (initiated with the death of Josiah).

2. Looking back over the years of his work, Jeremiah realized that he had failed. The people of Judah had continually shunned his warnings of coming judgment. They had been deaf to any calls for repentance. Anyone who has ever had romantic ideas of living in Bible times should check more carefully what the Bible actually tells us. Robert Davidson writes, "Sometimes people look back longingly and say, 'If only we had been there when Jesus was teaching in Galilee, how much easier faith would have been!' Would it? It was not easier in ancient Israel; and how many of the people who met Jesus saw in him anything unusual or anything that made them say, 'Here is God in our midst.' Israel was a living example of the truth that 'there's none so blind as those who will not see'" *(The Daily Bible Series—Jeremiah, Vol. 2, and Lamentations)*.

There is never a better time to find God than the present, whatever age one lives in. No one in any other generation has any advantage over us today. "For he says, 'In the time of my favor I heard you, and in the day of salvation I helped you.' I tell you, now is the time of God's favor, now is the day of salvation" (2 Corinthians 6:2, *NIV*).

Jeremiah had preached God's message for 23 years and was rejected throughout the period. However, because he had committed his life to God, he continued to do as he had been commanded. This was the middle of his career as a prophet, and many more difficult days lay ahead for him. The punishment he was forewarning the people of was twofold: (1) a loss of the blessing of God and (2) a loss of the Promised Land.

3. Nebuchadnezzar's invasion of Palestine in 605 B.C. was the beginning of the "times of the Gentiles" (cf. Luke 21:24). Jeremiah, for the first time in chapter 25, made it clear to the people that their punishment would come by the hands of the Babylonian king. Three times in the Book of Jeremiah (25:9; 27:6; 43:10), Nebuchadnezzar is called the Lord's servant. As God's instrument he would carry out the divine plan for Judah and the surrounding nations. He was unaware of it, but he was doing God's will by destroying entire populations.

God chose to use a heathen king to carry out His purposes. It is noteworthy that Jeremiah had been speaking of a mysterious judgment coming from God in the form of a threatening enemy from the north. As his ministry moved through the years, it became evident that this enemy would be the Babylonian empire. Jeremiah finally spoke out and identified the foe. In watching the prophesied events taking place, Jeremiah might have been tempted to feel some vindication for all the years of preaching he had done. However, there is no indication of this. He was still interested in seeing the people repent.

4. Jeremiah indicated for the first time that the captivity would be for 70 years (25:11). It started when Nebuchadnezzar swept into Palestine in September of 605 B.C. and made a vassal state out of Judah. To prove his dominance of the region, he took many of the brightest and wisest men (as well as the most beautiful women) and carried them to Babylon as captives. Daniel was among these prisoners. He had been born during the middle of Josiah's reign (2 Kings 22, 23) and grew up during the good king's reforms. He likely heard Jeremiah preaching during the years before the invasion. After he grew to be an old man in Babylon, he remembered what Jeremiah had written about a 70-year captivity. Realizing that those years were nearly over, Daniel was motivated to pray that God would return His people to their homeland: "In the first year of his [Darius] reign, I, Daniel, understood from the Scriptures, according to the word of the Lord given to Jeremiah the prophet, that the desolation of Jerusalem would last seventy years. So I turned to the Lord God and pleaded with him in prayer and petition, in fasting, and in sackcloth and ashes" (Daniel 9:2, 3, *NIV*).

Jeremiah spoke out in 605 B.C. (apparently just prior to Nebuchadnezzar's invasion) that the Babylonians would do just what they did. He insisted that God would not allow the captives to return to their land for a full 70 years (Jeremiah 25:11). Daniel now read this prophecy and knew that God had spoken the truth. The ministry of Jeremiah had finally been vindicated.

I. GOD GIVES HIS WORD (Jeremiah 36:1-7)

A. Writing Down the Word (vv. 1-4)

(Jeremiah 36:4 is not included in the printed text.)

1. And it came to pass in the fourth year of Jehoiakim the son of Josiah king of Judah, that this word came unto Jeremiah from the Lord, saying,

2. Take thee a roll of a book, and write therein all the words that I have spoken unto thee against Israel, and against Judah, and against all the nations, from the day I spake unto thee, from the days of Josiah, even unto this day.

3. It may be that the house of Judah will hear all the evil which I purpose to do unto them; that they may return every man from his evil way; that I may forgive their iniquity and their sin.

It is likely that Jeremiah had been preaching for over 20 years before he sensed any need to write down what he had been saying. Everything prior to this time had been by word of mouth. Now the Lord was telling him to write the messages down. Why now? Possibly because Jeremiah was barred from the religious and political establishment. With his unpopular Temple sermons (chapters 7 and 26), he had received threats to his life and was forbidden to preach in or near the Temple.

To make sure His word remained unchained, God instructed Jeremiah to write the messages down. Convinced of the urgency of the times, Jeremiah dictated a scroll to Baruch (v. 4). Baruch could read it to the people, even if the prophet wasn't allowed to speak.

There is power in the written word, be it God's Word or falsehood.

People are more prone to believe what they see in print more than simply what they hear. Most people in the ancient world were illiterate, so those who could read and write were generally respected. More often than not, they held positions of importance and were revered for their knowledge. As a scribe, Baruch could muster more respect reading Jeremiah's words aloud from a scroll than perhaps even the prophet himself could. It is interesting to note that after the Exile, scribes became famous teachers of the Law. By the time of Jesus, they had become a powerful political party.

The fact that none of Jeremiah's prophecies were written down until at least halfway into his ministry explains why this book is so hard to understand for the casual reader. Jeremiah recalled in no particular order, words and messages God had given him, and thus were they recorded. This is not important to the larger picture, however, for the main thrust of his three-point message—threat of impending punishment, need for repentance, and hope of restoration—are all firmly intact.

B. Declaring the Written Word (vv. 5-7)

(Jeremiah 36:5-7 is not included in the printed text.)

In sending Baruch to read the scroll in public, Jeremiah was not unwise in picking a time. The occasion would be a "fasting day" (v. 6), when people from all over the country would crowd into Jerusalem. These were generally called for in times of crisis—to appeal for God's help. In the previous year the Babylonians had defeated the Egyptians at Carchemish. News had likely now reached Jerusalem that Ashkelon (on the coastal plain) had fallen to the Babylonians. People would be flocking to Jerusalem to beg for some positive word from the Lord.

The message Jeremiah had dictated for Baruch to read was a call for repentance, the same message he had been preaching for years. By this time Baruch had become a trusted friend of the prophet, and it is likely that from his pen came the accounts of Jeremiah's activities during the first 20 years of ministry.

Why do you suppose God waited so long to tell Jeremiah to write down the messages he had been preaching? Might a written account carry more weight at this time?

II. PROCLAIMING GOD'S WORD (Jeremiah 36:8-19)

A. Wise Ears Listen (vv. 8-18)

(Jeremiah 36:8, 9, 11-15, 17, 18 is not included in the printed text.)

10. Then read Baruch in the book the words of Jeremiah in the house of the Lord, in the chamber of Gemariah the son of Shaphan the scribe, in the higher court, at the entry of the new gate of the Lord's house, in the ears of all the people.

16. Now it came to pass, when they had heard all the words, they were afraid both one and other, and said unto Baruch, We will surely tell the king of all these words.

Baruch did exactly what Jeremiah had told him to do, and his actions got the attention of the highest officials in the land. We catch a glimpse of an Old Testament "Cabinet meeting."

Interestingly, these were very wise men. Michaiah had heard Baruch read the scroll (vv. 11, 13). He was the grandson of Shaphan, a scribe who had been instrumental in helping King Josiah with his reforms. We learn about Shaphan in 2 Kings 22:3-14. One of Shaphan's sons, Ahikam, helped intervene to keep Jeremiah from being put to death by a mob (Jeremiah 26:24); he was also the father of Gedaliah, who would later become the governor of Judah after the Captivity began (2 Kings 25:22). The family of Shaphan were godly men of integrity. Another man present was Elnathan, whose father, Achbor, had also held high office under Josiah (Jeremiah 36:12). This family, too, had a history of strong principle.

These were receptive ears. They treated Baruch with respect. They asked him to read the scroll to them, and they were disturbed by what they heard (vv. 14-16). The men in the "Cabinet" meeting had watched the deterioration of Judah for a number of years. They knew this message was from the Lord. Obviously, however, they had little influence over their wicked king. They did, however, want him to hear it—possibly hoping that somehow its truth might get through to his hardened heart.

B. Wise Advice to Baruch (v. 19)

(Jeremiah 36:19 is not included in the printed text.)

The officials suspected what the king's reaction would be, thus advising Baruch to go into hiding—and to take Jeremiah with him. This was one of a number of occasions when Jeremiah providentially had "friends in high places." It would not be the only time an Old Testament prophet had to go into hiding. Elijah did so when he was being chased by Ahab and Jezebel (1 Kings 17—19). Obadiah also hid 100 prophets in remote caves from this evil pair (18:4). One of Jeremiah's contemporaries, Urijah, hid from King Jehoiakim, but was found and executed (Jeremiah 26:20-23). A verse from Proverbs adequately describes wicked men and their times: "When the righteous triumph, there is great elation; but when the wicked rise to power, men go into hiding" (28:12, *NIV*).

Is it a sign of cowardice for men and women of God to go into hiding while being pursued by evil people? Is there a time to avoid your enemies as well as a time to confront them?

III. GOD'S WORD PRESERVED (Jeremiah 36:20-32)

A. The Scroll Read to the King (vv. 20-26)

(Jeremiah 36:21, 22, 25, 26 is not included in the printed text.)

20. And they went in to the king into the court, but they laid up the roll in the chamber of Elishama the scribe, and told all the words in the ears of the king.

23. And it came to pass, that when Jehudi had read three or four leaves, he cut it with the penknife, and cast it into the fire that was on the hearth, until all the roll was consumed in the fire that was on the hearth.

24. Yet they were not afraid, nor rent their garments, neither the king, nor any of his servants that heard all these words.

As expected, King Jehoiakim was hostile to the message contained in the scroll. Unlike his father, Josiah, who had been humbly moved by the

Word of the Lord (2 Kings 22; 23), Jehoiakim had no interest in revival, but rather in a political alliance with Egypt. He looked to human resources for his deliverance.

The king was in his winter house, warming himself in a room heated by a brazier, or firepot. This was in December of 604 B.C. Jehoiakim reacted violently as the words were read aloud. He took a knife and cut off consecutive strips of the scroll as they were read, and tossed them into the fire. It is noteworthy that most of the court officials present were indifferent to this, sharing with the king his contempt for God's Word. Three, however, did oppose the blasphemous act (Jeremiah 36:25). One of these, Elnathan, had been the leader of the search party sent to Egypt to find the prophet Urijah when he went into hiding (26:22). Apparently this heretofore ally of the king had seen the light of truth and now supported Jeremiah.

In an even further act of defiance King Jehoiakim ordered the arrest of both Jeremiah and Baruch. However, the Lord used faithful friends to hide them (see 36:19, 26).

B. The Prophecy Scroll Rewritten (vv. 27-32)

(Jeremiah 36:29-31 is not included in the printed text.)

27. Then the word of the Lord came to Jeremiah, after that the king had burned the roll, and the words which Baruch wrote at the mouth of Jeremiah, saying,

28. Take thee again another roll, and write in it all the former words that were in the first roll, which Jehoiakim the king of Judah hath burned.

32. Then took Jeremiah another roll, and gave it to Baruch the scribe, the son of Neriah; who wrote therein from the mouth of Jeremiah all the words of the book which Jehoiakim king of Judah had burned in the fire: and there were added besides unto them many like words.

From his place of hiding, Jeremiah made a twofold response to the king's action. First, at the Lord's command, he dictated the words of the offensive scroll to Baruch, and added many words to them (v. 32). Second, since the king had chosen to ignore the warnings of coming judgment, Jeremiah added a further word of coming disaster: No descendant of Jehoiakim would ever sit on the throne (v. 30).

Jehoiakim's son, Jehoiachin, did reign as king for three months, but was then taken into captivity. This did not qualify him as "sitting on the throne of David" (see 2 Kings 24:6-16).

The next king in Judah, Zedekiah, was Jehoiachin's uncle (v. 17). Thus, the line of kings from David through his son Solomon came to an ignominious end. However, God's Word remains true, and an eternal lineage of David came 600 years later when Jesus was born. Jesus' earthly ancestry was through Solomon's brother, Nathan (Luke 3:31).

Jehoiakim's burning of the scroll was only one of many attempts made through the centuries to destroy God's Word. Men have constantly tried to "exterminate the idea of God, only to realize that He rises up to outlive His pallbearers" (Ravi Zacharias, *Can Man Live Without God?*).

How do you suppose Jeremiah felt upon hearing the scroll had been burned?

REVIEW QUESTIONS

1. Jeremiah's life was put in danger by his writing of the scroll, but Baruch was also taking a great personal risk by reading it in the Temple courts. Discuss the risks and Barach's willingness to read the unpopular message God had given Jeremiah.

2. Why was Jeremiah banned from the Temple? Had he done anything wrong?

3. What was achieved by writing the message in a second scroll?

4. What are some examples of ways God has preserved His Word intact throughout the centuries?

GOLDEN TEXT HOMILY

"FOR EVER, O LORD, THY WORD IS SETTLED IN HEAVEN" (Psalm 119:89).

There are very few things in this world that remain steadfast and settled. Men may build, but the destructive forces of time and of other men tear down all that men build.

All we have to do is look at the evening news—wars, AIDS, riots, hunger—to know that we are living in uncertain times here in our own nation and internationally.

Our day bears the marks and characteristics of the end times. The cry goes out from an unbelieving world, "What is there that we can rely on?" The church can answer! There is God; He is unchanging. There is His Word, which is forever settled in heaven. It was revealed through lawgivers, kings, priests, prophets, apostles, and most of all through His only begotten Son. There is the dictated Word of God—inerrant, without fault or flaw, and without variables. Upon it we can base all our hopes for the past, present, and future.

We do not have to investigate the Word or scrutinize its pages to see if there are any flaws in them. Here is the Word of God—applicable to every soul. God's Word is for the rich, the poor, the Jew, and the Gentile.

It is universal in its warnings, applications, directions, promises, and blessings. It is forever established in heaven.**—James L. Durel, Captain, The Salvation Army, Roseville, California**

SENTENCE SERMONS

GOD'S WORD will expose, convict, and overcome evil.

—Selected

MEN DO NOT reject the Bible because it contradicts itself, but because it contradicts them.

—Everett Harris

THE BIBLE is forever true whether anyone ever reads or believes it.

—Robert A. Cook

AS IN PARADISE, God walks in the Holy Scriptures seeking man.

—Saint Ambrose

DAILY BIBLE READINGS

M. Power to Create. Psalm 33:1-9
T. Power to Heal. Psalm 107:17-22
W. Power to Bear Fruit. Matthew 13:18-23
T. Power to Make Holy. John 17:6-19
F. Power to Save. 2 Timothy 3:10-17
S. Power to Overcome. Revelation 19:11-15

Heed God's Warning

Study Text: Jeremiah 27:2 through 28:17

Objective: To recognize that God's Word is true and live in anticipation of its fulfillment.

Time: The Book of Jeremiah was written between 627 and 580 B.C.

Place: The Book of Jeremiah was probably written at Jerusalem.

Golden Text: "Despise not thou the chastening of the Lord, nor faint when thou art rebuked of him: for whom the Lord loveth he chasteneth" (Hebrews 12:5, 6).

Central Truth: God disciplines His people for their good.

Evangelism Emphasis: Believers must warn sinners of God's judgment.

PRINTED TEXT

Jeremiah 27:2. Thus saith the Lord to me; Make thee bonds and yokes, and put them upon thy neck,

3. And send them to the king of Edom, and to the king of Moab, and to the king of the Ammonites, and to the king of Tyrus, and to the king of Zidon, by the hand of the messengers which come to Jerusalem unto Zedekiah king of Judah;

4. And command them to say unto their masters, Thus saith the Lord of hosts, the God of Israel; Thus shall ye say unto your masters;

6. And now have I given all these lands into the hand of Nebuchadnezzar the king of Babylon, my servant; and the beasts of the field have I given him also to serve him.

7. And all nations shall serve him, and his son, and his son's son, until the very time of his land come: and then many nations and great kings shall serve themselves of him.

8. And it shall come to pass, that the nation and kingdom which will not serve the same Nebuchadnezzar the king of Babylon, and that will not put their neck under the yoke of the king of Babylon, that nation will I punish, saith the Lord, with the sword, and with the famine, and with the pestilence, until I have consumed them by his hand.

9. Therefore hearken not ye to your prophets, nor to your diviners, nor to your dreamers, nor to your enchanters, nor to your sorcerers, which speak unto you, saying, Ye shall not serve the king of Babylon:

12. I spake also to Zedekiah king of Judah according to all

these words, saying, Bring your necks under the yoke of the king of Babylon, and serve him and his people, and live.

13. Why will ye die, thou and thy people, by the sword, by the famine, and by the pestilence, as the Lord hath spoken against the nation that will not serve the king of Babylon?

14. Therefore hearken not unto the words of the prophets that speak unto you, saying, Ye shall not serve the king of Babylon: for they prophesy a lie unto you.

15. For I have not sent them, saith the lord, yet they prophesy a lie in my name; that I might drive you out, and that ye might perish, ye, and the prophets that prophesy unto you.

16. Also I spake to the priests and to all this people, saying, Thus saith the Lord; Hearken not to the words of your prophets that prophesy unto you, saying, Behold, the vessels of the Lord's house shall now shortly be brought again from Babylon: for they prophesy a lie unto you.

17. Hearken not unto them; serve the king of Babylon, and live: wherefore should this city be laid waste?

DICTIONARY

Edom (Ee-dum) . . . Moab (Moab) . . . Ammorites (AM-or-ites) . . . Tyrus (TIE-rus) . . . Zidon (Zi-don)—Jeremiah 27:3—Territories and peoples having kings to whom Jeremiah's message was to be sent.

Zedekiah (zed-ee-KY-uh)—Jeremiah 27:3—The last king of Judah.

Nebuchadnezzar (neb-you-kud-NEZ-zur)—Jeremiah 27:6—King of Babylon.

LESSON OUTLINE

I. SUBMIT TO GOD'S CHASTENING
   - A. A Message to the Emissaries
   - B. Listening to False Prophets
   - C. Accept Babylonian Rule

II. WARNING AGAINST REBELLION
   - A. A Word for King Zedekiah
   - B. A Warning to the Priests and the People

III. GOD'S WORD PREVAILS

LESSON EXPOSITION

INTRODUCTION

The 70-year captivity period began with Nebuchadnezzar's invasion of Judah in 605 B.C., although the entire nation would not be destroyed until 586 B.C. In actuality there were three separate invasions of the land by the Babylonians:

1. 605 B.C.—At this time many of the nation's brightest and best were carried away.

2. 597 B.C.—King Jehoiakim rebelled against Babylon and caused a second invasion. He was captured and killed, and his son Jehoiachin then came to the

throne. He faced the greatest army on earth just three weeks after he was crowned. He held out for three months against the invaders, only to finally surrender and be deported to Babylon, along with many others. The Temple was also raided at this time and many important vessels taken.

3. 586 B.C.—Even the large precious objects of the Temple were taken this time. The city was ransacked and left in ruins. There was not even the semblance of a vassal kingdom remaining in the land.

As stated earlier, the 70-year captivity began with the first invasion in 605 B.C. It ended in 535 B.C. with the arrival of the exiles back in Jerusalem. Some scholars believe the Captivity should be dated from the last invasion (586 B.C.). Still others think the 70 years is a symbolic number meaning a lifetime, or the life span of one generation.

The Babylonians invaded Judah three times (2 Kings 24:1; 24:10; 25:1), just as the Assyrians had invaded the northern kingdom of Israel three times. Interestingly, the Babylonian policy for deporting captives was different from that of Assyria. The Assyrians moved the native peoples out and resettled the land with foreign captives. This is why in later centuries the Jews would hate the Samaritans. There were descendants of Assyria's invasion policy of deportation and resettlement. The Babylonians, however, took the strong and skilled back to Babylon, leaving only the weak and poor to rule the land. The effort was to win the loyalty of these more common people by giving them positions of authority. The elite and educated who were taken to Babylonian cities were, however, allowed to live together, find jobs, and become part of Babylonian society.

God used this policy to keep the Jews united throughout their captivity. They were able to maintain their identity as the chosen people of God, thus setting up the possibility of their return to Palestine later under Zerubbabel and Ezra.

In our present lesson text we see Jeremiah attacking the false optimism that was being spread in Judah. This was in the fourth year of the reign of King Zedekiah (594-593 B.C.). Foreign emissaries were coming to Jerusalem promoting a united confederacy against Babylon. Judah was being pressured by her neighbors to join the doomed enterprise, and were being encouraged by the false prophets of the time. The thought was that Babylon could be overpowered, that it would be unable to resist an allied effort. Nebuchadnezzar proved them wrong, and Zedekiah was taken bound and blind to Babylon and required to explain, no doubt, what part he had in the plot.

I. SUBMIT TO GOD'S CHASTENING (Jeremiah 27:2-11)

A. A Message to the Emissaries (vv. 2-8)

(Jeremiah 2:5 is not included in the printed text.)

2. Thus saith the Lord to me; Make thee bonds and yokes, and put them upon thy neck,

3. And send them to the king of Edom, and to the king of Moab, and to the king of the Ammonites, and to the king of Tyrus, and to the king of Zidon, by the hand of the messengers which come to Jerusalem unto Zedekiah king of Judah;

4. And command them to say unto their masters, Thus saith the Lord of hosts, the God of

Israel; Thus shall ye say unto your masters;

6. And now have I given all these lands into the hand of Nebuchadnezzar the king of Babylon, my servant; and the beasts of the field have I given him also to serve him.

7. And all nations shall serve him, and his son, and his son's son, until the very time of his land come: and then many nations and great kings shall serve themselves of him.

8. And it shall come to pass, that the nation and kingdom which will not serve the same Nebuchadnezzar the king of Babylon, and that will not put their neck under the yoke of the king of Babylon, that nation will I punish, saith the Lord, with the sword, and with the famine, and with the pestilence, until I have consumed them by his hand.

Jeremiah gave a message from God to the ambassadors who had come to Jerusalem from the surrounding small nations. Edom, Moab, Ammon, Tyre, and Sidon had all experienced Babylon's massive assault just as Judah had. They were now trying to form a coalition to rebel against the mighty terrible invaders.

It appears from Babylonian documents that just two years prior to this time Nebuchadnezzar had his attention diverted to deal with an attempted internal revolution. "No wonder the small vassal states in the western Babylonian Empire thought that now was an appropriate time to make a bid for independence. Jerusalem was at the center of a network of intrigue. Envoys came from several of the adjacent countries to consult with Zedekiah. The patriotic ticket in Jerusalem was no doubt firmly convinced that there would never be a more favorable time to throw off the yoke of Babylon" (Robert Davidson, *The Daily Bible Series—Jeremiah, Vol. 2, and Lamentations*).

In our own American history we need only look back to 1861 to see a similar situation. The Confederacy's rebellion against the Union was ultimately a complete tragedy. This is what Jeremiah saw coming in Palestine.

At the Lord's command Jeremiah took a yoke, much like those attached to the neck of an ox by leather thongs, and tied it around his own neck. With dramatic symbolism he used a visual image to show the power of Babylon. God had declared that Nebuchadnezzar was His agent and that nothing would stop him. God had decreed that all the world must come under submission to this king for the present time; rebellion would be futile.

B. Listening to False Prophets (vv. 9, 10)

(Jeremiah 27:10 is not included in the printed text.)

9. Therefore hearken not ye to your prophets, nor to your diviners, nor to your dreamers, nor to your enchanters, nor to your sorcerers, which speak unto you, saying, Ye shall not serve the king of Babylon.

The fact that Nebuchadnezzar was having his own problems at home caused the vassal nations to think they could rise up in rebellion. The false prophets were adding to this faint hope with their prophecies that tickled the ears. They were simply giving the people what they wanted to hear, even though there was no way this could be true. God had spoken, but they did not want to believe He would carry through with what He had promised. Jeremiah was going against the tide of public sentiment by insisting that the people put themselves under Babylon's yoke. Jeremiah was actually a true friend—one who brought

God's word, even though it might be painful. True friends speak the truth, even though the truth may be temporarily painful. To tell a pleasant untruth that will later bring disaster is not being a true friend. But if telling a present unpleasant truth can avert future destruction, to tell it is being a real friend.

There are five types of soothsayers mentioned in verse 9. They represent the various pagan methods for predicting the future. The people of Judah should have been well aware from their past history that God forbade any type of sorcery and divination (Deuteronomy 18:10, 11). He was to be their only source for prophetic knowledge.

C. Accept Babylonian Rule (v. 11)

(Jeremiah 27:11 ins not included in the printed text.)

God had appointed Nebuchadnezzar as His instrument. Resistance would be virtual suicide. The duration of this domination would be from Nebuchadnezzar to the third generation. It passed from him down to Evil-Merodach, and then to Belshazzar. To think that these small nations could successfully rebel when God had already declared a 70-year rule was purely wishful thinking. However, this was what the false prophets promised.

To resist Babylon would bring a threefold stroke of sword, famine, and plague. Life would be ever so much harder by trying to resist God's discipline. Moved by what he knew was the truth from the Lord, Jeremiah stood firm in opposing the great majority of false leaders who assembled in Jerusalem.

Do you think Jeremiah felt foolish wearing the yoke around his neck in public? On what do you base your opinion?

II. WARNING AGAINST REBELLION (Jeremiah 27:12-22)

A. A Word for King Zedekiah (vv. 12-15)

12. I spake also to Zedekiah king of Judah according to all these words, saying, Bring your necks under the yoke of the king of Babylon, and serve him and his people, and live.

13. Why will ye die, thou and thy people, by the sword, by the famine, and by the pestilence, as the Lord hath spoken against the nation that will not serve the king of Babylon?

14. Therefore hearken not unto the words of the prophets that speak unto you, saying, Ye shall not serve the king of Babylon: for they prophesy a lie unto you.

15. For I have not sent them, saith the Lord, yet they prophesy a lie in my name; that I might drive you out, and that ye might perish, ye, and the prophets that prophesy unto you.

Zedekiah was in an unenviable position. All the neighboring nations wanted him to join them in a rebellion. How could he save face as a king by surrendering to the Babylonians? Would it not appear disgraceful to give in and look like a coward? This was a perfect opportunity for the false prophets to take advantage of his ego and encourage him to fight. They insisted that God would never let the great city of Jerusalem and the Temple be destroyed.

Jeremiah gave Zedekiah the meaning of the yoke around his neck—that it was actually meant for the king's own neck. To submit to the king of Babylon would be the only way to survive, shameful as it might appear. Otherwise, the sword, famine, and pestilence would be the result of rebellion. Jeremiah blasted the false prophets for the lie they were inflicting on the nation. God had not sent them, and His Word against such heathen devices is strong and certain. Zedekiah should have recognized this, for God never goes against His Word.

God spoke to Zedekiah clearly through Jeremiah. Resistance was useless because Nebuchadnezzar was God's instrument: "To resist the known will of God is always spiritual suicide" (Zondervan, *NIV Bible Commentary*, Vol. 1).

B. A Warning to the Priests and the People (vv. 16-22)

(Jeremiah 27:18-22 is not included in the printed text.)

16. Also I spake to the priests and to all this people, saying, Thus saith the Lord; Hearken not to the words of your prophets that prophesy unto you, saying, Behold, the vessels of the Lord's house shall now shortly be brought again from Babylon: for they prophesy a lie unto you.

17. Hearken not unto them; serve the king of Babylon, and live: wherefore should this city be laid waste?

Jeremiah considered his message from the Lord so important that he repeated it to the priests and the people. The false prophets were taunting the populace with feelings of national pride by holding on to a hope that Babylon would return the Temple vessels that had been carried away earlier. The Temple and its furnishings were priceless treasures in Judah. They were the rallying point, the "grand old flag" of the nation, so to speak. To play on such emotion lifted the people's spirits, but the false prophets pretty-sounding words were hopelessly unfounded. Instead of the vessels being returned, those that remained would be carried away as well in 597 B.C. (2 Kings 24:13).

Jeremiah chided the false prophets by suggesting they pray that the remaining vessels not be carried away as the others had. He was making a mockery of their baseless predictions. He did prophesy, however, that all these treasures would be returned at the end of Babylon's dominance. This happened just as he said when Cyrus helped the exiles return in 536 B.C. (Ezra 1:7-11). Some 5,400 articles of gold and silver were brought back to Jerusalem at that time (Ezra 1:11). This promise concerning the treasures indicates a certain measure of hope. If the people would only take their punishment and learn from it, God would then restore them to their land.

We must be careful, however, not to let ourselves be captivated by the promises of God at the expense of His commandments. His promises are real, but so are His laws. We must balance our hopes and expectations with a disciplined life that is obedient to His Word.

Can we claim the promises of the Word when we have unconfessed sin in our lives?

III. GOD'S WORD PREVAILS (Jeremiah 28:12-17)

(Jeremiah 28:12-17 is not included in the printed text.)

Jeremiah 28 records an episode that no doubt happened after the events of the previous chapter. Jeremiah was apparently still wearing his yoke, but another prophet, Hananiah, brought a message to the people that contradicted everything Jeremiah had been saying. He spoke just as boldly as Jeremiah—and in the name of the Lord—but gave a totally opposite message. Hananiah was from the town of Gibeon, just six miles northwest of Jerusalem. He likely well represented the apostate religious establishment of the day. We could probably consider him the grand master of the prophetic lodge attached to the Jerusalem Temple. His name means "the Lord is gracious," and the graciousness of God toward his people was the theme of his message.

Hananiah insisted that within two years Judah's troubles would be over and everything and everyone taken to Babylon would be returned (vv. 1-4). This was the very false prophecy Jeremiah had warned against three times—to the emissaries, to the king, and to the priests and people.

There were two reasons Hananiah's prophecy could not be true. First, it did not line up with all the previous prophets of Israel (vv. 5-9). All other prophets in times past had warned of war, famine, and plague. The books of Amos, Hosea, and Micah are full of such elements. Whatever points of hope these prophets gave would come only after judgment or repentance. Hananiah was predicting good news that required no remorse for sin. Second, a true test of a prophet was that everything he said came true (Deuteronomy 18:22). Obviously, history would not go in Hananiah's favor. When two years had passed, Judah's problems were far from being over.

As if to steal the thunder from Jeremiah, Hananiah tried his own hand at an object lesson. He took Jeremiah's yoke off his neck and broke it (vv. 10, 11). Jeremiah had used the visual symbol of the yoke to punctuate his message. Hananiah was not above copying this to draw attention to himself.

Jeremiah chose not to refute Hananiah any further at the time, apparently feeling that enough had been said. Certainly the people had a clear decision to make. The author of Ecclesiastes had a word for such situations: "There is a time for everything . . . a time to be silent and a time to speak" (Ecclesiastes 3:1, 7, *NIV*). Jeremiah chose simply to walk away. He would wait for a word from the Lord, and it was not long in coming.

Verses 12-16 present the Lord's message for Hananiah. Here Jeremiah refuted both Hananiah's message and his object lesson. Hananiah may have broken the wooden yoke Jeremiah had carried, but this would be replaced by a yoke of iron. It would be unbreakable. Hananiah, in thinking he was helping the people with his encouraging words, instead was carrying them further into bondage. He was promoting a lie, which strengthened the people's rebellion against God. Instead of the people being freed in two years, the false prophet himself would be dead in two months.

Nothing is said about how Hananiah died, but the curse Jeremiah had pronounced on him through the words the Lord had told him to speak proved true. Sadly, however, this incident did nothing to vindicate Jeremiah in the eyes of the people. Their hearts were set on their sin, and they refused to hear the hard message he offered—which would have spared lives, much heartache, and their nation if they had heeded it.

Why do you suppose Jeremiah walked away from Hananiah without argument?

REVIEW QUESTIONS

1. Why was it so wrong for the people of Judah to trust the predictions of the pagan prophets?

2. What should the Christian's attitude be toward modern psychics, fortune-tellers, and so forth?

3. What do you think is the

proper balance between preaching from God's Word His exhortation and His warnings?

4. Why are false prophecies so dangerous?

5. How can we distinguish between true and false prophets today?

GOLDEN TEXT HOMILY

"DESPISE NOT THOU THE CHASTENING OF THE LORD, NOR FAINT WHEN THOU ART REBUKED OF HIM: FOR WHOM THE Lord LOVETH HE CHASTENETH" (Hebrews 12:5, 6)

While serving as a chaplain for the Church of God at Mississippi State Penitentiary, a young man shared with me this testimony: "Chaplain, I thank God for this prison because I'd be dead or, worse, I'd have killed someone else if I hadn't got caught." Sound strange? A young man thanking God for punishment? No, it's not strange or even abnormal; it's reality! This young man was about 21 years old, and he had been saved from drugs, from sin, from death, and given time to reflect upon his life. Now he had come to the place where he saw that God himself cared so much that He provided a way of repentance and change. This young man received a second chance; he learned to thank God for the disciplines of life.

The writer of the Epistle to the Hebrews was reminding his readers that God loved them like a father. Because of His love for them, they had to endure the suffering of a disciplined life. This was not because God desired to hurt them or be cruel to them but to perfect them in the image of Christ, the only begotten Son of the Father!

The Greek terminology used here for *discipline* means "instruction," the training and discipline given to a child. The Hebrew Christians were being reminded that their sufferings were tokens of God's fatherly love and concern. Even the best of God's children need discipline. I'd rather spank my child's hand than to see her get burned by a hot iron. That's how my love tries to discipline her in the right direction. How much more does God love us, His children, born of His Spirit! We are the children of God in whom He delights. He is preparing us for a righteous and holy life, an everlasting relationship, an eternal kingdom. How pale grows the momentary setback of this life! Let us rejoice in our circumstance, knowing we are loved.

Not every prisoner can praise God for chastening in a penitentiary. Let us be like the young man who has learned to appreciate what God is doing even though we suffer afflictions while in this life. Let us look forward to that day when we will be with Him forever. Don't let discouragement or disappointment separate you from knowing the love of God in your life!—**Eugene Wigelsworth, Clinical Chaplain, Pasquotank Correctional Institution, Elizabeth City, North Carolina**

SENTENCE SERMONS

GOD DISCIPLINES His people for their good.

—Selected

GOD DOES NOT discipline us to subdue us, but to condition us for a life of usefulness and blessedness.

—Billy Graham

GOD,WHO TRULY LOVES, will chastise well.

—Draper's Book of Quotations for the Christian World

THE DISCIPLINE of the sanctified life consists of suffering, loneliness, patience, and prayer.

—Oswald Chambers

EVANGELISM APPLICATION

BELIEVERS MUST WARN SINNERS OF GOD'S JUDGMENT.

Ours is an age when mediums, fortune-tellers, witches, magicians, and the like, have again become popular. However, God's Word is just as strong as ever against involvement with such pagan practices. We must constantly remind our families and Christian friends that under no circumstances should they consult such Satan-inspired people. Even though newspapers, television, and other media are becoming saturated with this evil, we must avoid it.

The tricks of the trade for these practitioners are no different from what they were in biblical days. Any predictions they make concerning the future comes purely from the devil—and he is not omniscient. Only God knows what the future holds. Yes, occasionally some fortune-teller may happen on a correct forecast, but remember this: Satan and his demons know enough of what is happening in the spiritual realm to accurately predict some events—but they are not all-knowing.

God is the Master of all creation. We must trust Him with our future, laying our life in His hands, and putting our faith in His Love for us. And we who know the ultimate future of judgment for the unconverted and eternal bliss for those who commit their lives to Christ are obligated to warn the sinner of impending doom unless he repents. The good news, of course, is that no one is ever turned away who comes penitently to Him.

ILLUMINATING THE LESSON

King Zedekiah and the people of Judah were looking for guidance in the wrong places. They missed God's direction. We often do the same thing today. There are several major questions to ask yourself when seeking the Lord's will for decisions and direction:

1. *Does this direction or decision agree with God's Word?* If what you are contemplating goes against principles of the Bible, forget it! For instance, if a man is considering leaving his wife for another relationship, no amount of praying will bring God's blessing. Always check decisions to make sure they measure up to the Word.

2. *Does this decision pass the test of godly advice from individuals whose spiritual maturity you trust?* Consult solid Christians for their opinion. Get honest godly advice.

3. *Do you feel right in your spirit about this decision? Do you really want to do this? Do you sense God's leading in this direction?* For instance, if God were calling you to be a missionary to Africa, He will put a love for that mission field in your heart. The Lord will not force something on you against your will.

4. *Are the circumstances right?* If you cannot seem to bring the decision to pass, God is likely telling you something. Sometimes Satan throws hurdles in the way of doing right, but God will pull the circumstances together if He wants a thing accomplished.

If all of these questions cannot be answered positively, hold back. Wait for further directions from the Lord.

DAILY BIBLE READINGS

M. Victory Prophesied. 2 Chronicles 20:14-25
T. Precious Word. Psalm 19:7-11
W. Wise Builders. Matthew 7:24-29
T. Victory Over Sorcery. Acts 19:11-20
F. Accept Discipline. Hebrews 12:3-13
S. Remain Faithful. Revelation 3:7-13

Promise of Restoration

Study Text: Jeremiah 31:10-17, 31-34; 33:14-22

Objective: To review God's plan for restoration and accept the redemption provided through Jesus Christ.

Time: The Book of Jeremiah was written between 627 and 580 B.C.

Place: The Book of Jeremiah was probably written at Jerusalem.

Golden Text: "In those days, and at that time, will I cause the Branch of righteousness to grow up unto David; and he shall execute judgment and righteousness in the land" (Jeremiah 33:15).

Central Truth: Jesus Christ came to redeem lost humanity.

Evangelism Emphasis: Jesus Christ came to save sinners.

PRINTED TEXT

Jeremiah 31:10. Hear the word of the Lord, O ye nations, and declare it in the isles afar off, and say, He that scattered Israel will gather him, and keep him, as a shepherd doth his flock.

11. For the Lord hath redeemed Jacob, and ransomed him from the hand of him that was stronger than he.

12. Therefore they shall come and sing in the height of Zion, and shall flow together to the goodness of the Lord, for wheat, and for wine, and for oil, and for the young of the flock and of the herd: and their soul shall be as a watered garden; and they shall not sorrow any more at all.

31. Behold, the days come, saith the Lord, that I will make a new covenant with the house of Israel, and with the house of Judah:

32. Not according to the covenant that I made with their fathers in the day that I took them by the hand to bring them out of the land of Egypt; which my covenant they brake, although I was an husband unto them, saith the Lord:

33. But this shall be the covenant that I will make with the house of Israel; After those days, saith the Lord, I will put my law in their inward parts, and write it in their hearts; and will be their God, and they shall be my people.

34. And they shall teach no more every man his neighbour, and every man his brother, saying, Know the Lord: for they shall all know me, from the least of them unto the greatest of them, saith the Lord: for I will forgive their iniquity, and I will remember their sin no more.

33:14. Behold, the days

come, saith the Lord, that I will perform that good thing which I have promised unto the house of Israel and to the house of Judah.

15. In those days, and at that time, will I cause the Branch of righteousness to grow up unto David; and he shall execute judgment and righteousness in the land.

16. In those days shall Judah be saved, and Jerusalem shall dwell safely: and this is the name wherewith she shall be called, The Lord our righteousness.

LESSON OUTLINE

- I. RESTORATION FORETOLD
  - A. Comparison to Isaiah
  - B. Redeemed and Ransomed
  - C. Rachel's Weeping
- II. PROMISE OF A NEW COVENANT
  - A. Parties to the New Covenant
  - B. Nature of the New Covenant
  - C. Basis of the New Covenant
- III. PROMISED MESSIAH

LESSON EXPOSITION

INTRODUCTION

For all the terrible prophecies the Lord gave Jeremiah concerning punishment for Israel, there was nevertheless a silver lining in the doomsday clouds. Jeremiah caught a glimpse of a threefold restoration for Israel. What he saw is covered in the three major outline points of this lesson: a promise of restoration, a promise of a new covenant, and a promise of a coming Messiah.

Chapters 30—33 of Jeremiah have come to be called the Book of Consolation.

To understand the context of the three promises mentioned, we need to look at chapter 32. Jerusalem was in the final 18 months of siege by the Babylonians. Most other Judean cities had already fallen. An Egyptian attempt at intervention had proved fruitless, and the people were now helpless, hungry, and disillusioned.

Up to this point Jeremiah had been prophesying doleful punishments. Now, as these thing were finally taking place, his tone changed to wonderful things to come. This is extremely dramatic, for Jeremiah was still in prison and the city was in dire straits—hardly a time when one would expect to see the positive side. Yet he saw that in the future Israel would not perish as a nation, that a new covenant was coming, the Davidic kingship would be restored, and the Gentiles would be brought to a knowledge of truth.

Chapter 31 opens with "'At that time,' declares the Lord, 'I will be the God of all the clans of Israel, and they will be my people'" (*NIV*). Although it had been many years since the northern tribes had been carried off into captivity by the Assyrians, here the Lord promised a reunited people. The God who does not change was maintaining His faithfulness to all the Israelites in describing a future reunion.

There is a strong influence of the prophet Hosea in Jeremiah's words. Hosea had preached to the northern kingdom (753-715 B.C.). He had talked about God's love for all His people: "When Israel was a child, then I loved him, and called my son out of Egypt" (Hosea 11:1). He also described the people's unfaithfulness: "What can I do with you, Ephraim? What can I do with you, Judah? Your love is like the morning mist, like the early dew that disappears" (Hosea 6:4, *NIV*). Ephraim was one of the major tribes of the northern kingdom. The term was used poetically to depict the entire area. God would still be faithful to people who had many years earlier totally rejected Him and were sent off into captivity. The day would come when a remnant would return to the Promised Land, but not in arrogance and pride. Instead, it was prophesied, "They will come with weeping; they will pray as I bring them back. I will lead them beside streams of water on a level path where they will not stumble, because I am Israel's father, and Ephraim is my firstborn son" (Jeremiah 31:9, *NIV*).

This was a hope based purely on the character of God. Hosea had described the fickleness of the people when he said, "Your love is like the morning mist, like the early dew that disappears" (6:4, *NIV*). God, however, is not fickle; He is faithful and full of compassion for His people.

I. RESTORATION FORETOLD (Jeremiah 31:10-17)

A. Comparison to Isaiah (v. 10)

10. Hear the word of the Lord, O ye nations, and declare it in the isles afar off, and say, He that scattered Israel will gather him, and keep him, as a shepherd doth his flock.

Jeremiah's words are reminiscent of those of Isaiah in describing the people of Israel returning from distant lands. "But you, O Israel, my servant, Jacob, whom I have chosen, you descendants of Abraham my friend, I took you from the ends of the earth, from its farthest corners I called you. I said, 'You are my servant'; I have chosen you and have not rejected you. So do not fear, for I am with you; do not be dismayed, for I am your God. I will strengthen you and help you; I will uphold you with my righteous right hand" (Isaiah 41:8-10, *NIV*).

These words, like Jeremiah's, describe a people with hope of restoration. This was a hope, however, that had experienced disaster. The returning souls had been greatly and well deservedly punished for their sins, but they were now returning to a new life of security in God himself. This security lay in the character of Israel's God, who is faithful in every circumstance.

The imagery of a shepherd tending his flock also is similar to Isaiah's word pictures: "He shall feed his flock like a shepherd: he shall gather the lambs with his arm, and carry them in his bosom, and shall gently lead those that are with young" (Isaiah 40:11). Everything both prophets had to say pointed to a renewed sense of community in a people who had strayed from the fold, had gotten caught on the precipices of death, and now had been found and brought home by the faithful, loving shepherd.

B. Redeemed and Ransomed (vv. 11-14)

(Jeremiah 31:13, 14 is not included in the printed text.)

11. For the Lord hath

redeemed Jacob, and ransomed him from the hand of him that was stronger than he.

12. Therefore they shall come and sing in the height of Zion, and shall flow together to the goodness of the Lord, for wheat, and for wine, and for oil, and for the young of the flock and of the herd: and their soul shall be as a watered garden; and they shall not sorrow any more at all.

Verse 11 includes two words that are often used in the Bible to describe what God does for His people—*redeem and ransom.* Both of the original Hebrew words are similar in meaning. However, there is a subtle difference between the two, indicating two separate things God did for Israel:

1. *redeem—ga'al*—this speaks of the ability of the next of kin (according to the Oriental law of kinship) to buy back a relative's property, marry his widow, and so forth.

2. *ransom—padah*—to release, preserve. This was a legal term. It had to do with what one paid in money to secure release, or what one paid to get a possession back from someone else.

The first word *(ga'al)* is associated with the life of a family. It indicates a member of the family to whom is assigned the responsibility for securing another family member's release from debt slavery, or the one who keeps a piece of family property from being sold, or the one who marries the childless widow of a deceased brother (note the example of Ruth and Boaz). The second word (*padah*) is a legal word, carrying the connotation of money paid to get a possession back that someone else has taken. God paid the ransom price (*padah*) to restore Israel and also served as the kinsman redeemer (*ga'al*) to buy Israel out of slavery. This reiterates the thought that God never punishes or disciplines purely for the sake of anger and frustration. There is always the ultimate motivation or restoration to full relationship.

There is also a deeper interpretation that can be found in the two terms just discussed. Both words "were to be given yet profounder spiritual meaning, not least in the New Testament where they are used to describe what God in Christ has done for us" *(The Daily Bible Series—Jeremiah, Vol. 2, and Lamentations).*

C. Rachel's Weeping (vv. 15-17)

(Jeremiah 31:15-17 is not included in the printed text.)

The tribes of Ephraim and Manasseh were descendants of Joseph's two sons. Their descendants became two of the northern tribes. Joseph's mother was Rachel, Jacob's favorite wife. Interestingly, Rachel became the symbolic mother of the northern tribes because of this connection. However, she was also associated with the southern kingdom because of her second son, Benjamin (the southern kingdom was made up of Judah and Benjamin). She is here pictured as crying for the exiles at Ramah. Ramah was a town five miles north of Jerusalem that was used by the Babylonians as a collection point for captives about to be exiled (see lesson 9). Rachel was buried near there. In these verses the Lord bids Rachel to stop her mourning and comfort herself because the captives would return.

Matthew quoted Jeremiah to describe the sadness of the mothers of Bethlehem when their children had been killed by Herod (2:18). The town of Bethlehem was also near Rachel's tomb.

Symbolically, Rachel was seen in Jeremiah's prophecy as weeping because she had lost her children. God interrupts her tears to promise her that they would not be gone forever. They would return home.

Why were the northern tribes included in the words of consolation in Jeremiah's prophecy?

II. PROMISE OF A NEW COVENANT (Jeremiah 31:31-34)

A. Parties to the New Covenant (v. 31)

31. Behold, the days come, saith the Lord, that I will make a new covenant with the house of Israel, and with the house of Judah.

This passage from Jeremiah (vv. 31-34) is regarded as one of the most important in the entire Old Testament. The concept of a new covenant is probably the greatest contribution Jeremiah gave to biblical truth. The fact that he spoke of a new covenant suddenly positioned the Mosaic covenant as being the old covenant. Also, the new one would be eternal: "National covenants do not die because of old age. The old covenant spoke of a great physical deliverance from Egypt through the blood of lambs and the power of God; the new covenant proclaims a great spiritual deliverance from sin and death through the efficacious blood of the Lamb of God and the power of God. The Passover Feast memorialized the first; the Lord's Supper memorializes the second" *(Zondervan New International Version Bible Commentary, Vol. 1: Old Testament)*.

Jeremiah noted three parties to this covenant: the Lord, the people of Israel, and the people of Judah. The entire nation was included (northern and southern kingdoms), thus encompassing all of the "chosen people" who had been in the old covenant. A question for many certainly arises: Are Christians included in the new covenant? Certainly they are! Christ died to institute a new covenant for all sinners. The Jews would reject this contract in Jesus' first coming, but the Gentiles would step in to take advantage of its provisions: "What then shall we say? That the Gentiles, who did not pursue righteousness, have obtained it, a righteousness that is by faith; but Israel, who pursued a law of righteousness, has not attained it. Why not? Because they pursued it not by faith but as if it were by works. They stumbled over the 'stumbling stone.' As it is written: 'See, I lay in Zion a stone that causes men to stumble and a rock that makes them fall, and the one who trusts in him will never be put to shame'" (Romans 9:30-33, *NIV*).

Jesus was the stumbling block for the Jews. They refused Him because they had different expectations for their Messiah. However, Israel will finally accept the new covenant when history climaxes. Two verses from Zechariah confirm this: "And I will pour up on the house of David, and the inhabitants of Jerusalem, the spirit of grace and of supplications: and they shall look upon me whom they have pierced, and they shall mourn for him, as one mourneth for his only son, and shall be in bitterness for him, as one that is in bitterness for his firstborn" (Zechariah 12:10); "On that day there shall be a fountain opened to the house of David and to the inhabitants of Jerusalem for sin and for uncleanness" (Zechariah 13:1).

There will come an awakening among the Jews as to who Jesus really is. They will realize that the man they killed was indeed the Messiah. He will be clearly revealed to them "that at the name of Jesus every knee should bow, of things in heaven, and things in earth, and things under the earth; and that every tongue should confess that Jesus Christ is Lord, to the glory of God the Father" (Philippians 2:10, 11).

Paul wrote in his letter to the Romans: "I do not want you to be ignorant of this mystery, brothers, so that you may not be conceited: Israel has experienced a hardening in part until the full number of the Gentiles has come in. And so all Israel will be saved, as it is written: 'The deliverer will come from Zion; he will turn godlessness away from Jacob' (Romans 11:25, 26, *NIV*). Some interpret this scripture to mean that the Jews in the final generation will all turn to Christ. Others think that Israel here means the spiritual nation, including both Jews and Gentiles who have received Christ. "God chose the nation of Israel, and he has never rejected it. He also chose the church, through Jesus Christ, and he will never reject it either. This does not mean, of course, that all Jews or all church members will be saved. It is possible to belong to a nation or to an organization without ever responding in faith to Jesus" *(Life Application Bible)*.

Romans 11:17-21 gives an excellent explanation of how both Jew and Gentile fit into the new covenant. All believers in Christ are grafted into the new covenant and as such are part of the seed of Abraham. No one—neither Jew nor Gentile—has anything to boast of except God's graciousness toward us. Paul warned Gentile Christians not to feel superior because they had replaced unbelieving Jews. Gentiles have been grafted into a tree that has Jewish roots, but both Jews and Gentiles must look to Christ for life. No one can rest on race, heritage, or theological beliefs to provide salvation.

B. Nature of the New Covenant (vv. 32, 33)

32. Not according to the covenant that I made with their fathers in the day that I took them by the hand to bring them out of the land of Egypt; which my covenant they brake, although I was an husband unto them, saith the Lord:

33. But this shall be the covenant that I will make with the house of Israel; After those days, saith the Lord, I will put my law in their inward parts, and write it in their hearts; and will be their God, and they shall be my people.

Israel failed completely in living up to the terms of the old covenant. Even before Moses had come down from Mount Sinai, they were breaking the first commandment. God had taken the Israelites by the hand as a loving Father would, but they resisted His love. The breakdown of the old covenant was purely the fault of Israel and Judah. God had been faithful; but in spite of this, the relationship was doomed.

Instead of rewriting the old covenant with the people returning from exile, God would establish an entirely new basis for relationship with His people. He would write the law on their hearts. No longer would it be engraved in stone; instead, the new covenant would bring a change of heart to the individual. "The motivation for obeying God's law is inner knowledge of His will, coupled with an enablement to perform it—all founded on the assurance that sins are forgiven" *(Zondervan New International Version Bible Commentary, Old Testament)*.

C. Basis of the New Covenant (v. 34)

34. And they shall teach no more every man his neighbour, and every man his brother, saying, Know the Lord: for they shall all know me, from the least of them unto the greatest of them, saith the Lord: for I will forgive their iniquity, and I will remember their sin no more.

The basis for this new covenant would be love, not fear. Also, knowledge of the Lord would not be rooted in religious instruction or adherence to rules and laws. Rather, it would be grounded in a heartfelt experience in which grace is imparted to the believer by the Holy Spirit. The Holy Spirit would also give assurance of acceptance into God's family through the forgiveness of sin. Everyone, from the least to the greatest, is eligible to participate in this covenant, and all have access to God through Jesus Christ, the High Priest (see Hebrews 4:16; 10:19-22).

Jeremiah predicted a new covenant coming for Israel. Why couldn't the Jews understand that its fulfillment was in Christ?

C. Promised Messiah (Jeremiah 33:14-22)

(Jeremiah 33:17-22 is not included in the printed text.)

14. Behold, the days come, saith the Lord, that I will perform that good thing which I have promised unto the house of Israel and to the house of Judah.

15. In those days, and at that time, will I cause the Branch of righteousness to grow up unto David; and he shall execute judgment and righteousness in the land.

16. In those days shall Judah be saved, and Jerusalem shall dwell safely: and this is the name wherewith she shall be called, The Lord our righteousness.

Jeremiah saw the future that God promised through the eyes of faith. Everything physically around him indicated that the final end of Israel and Judah as a people and a nation was near. Destruction was imminent, and there seemed no possible way that the line of David could continue to rule. Nevertheless, Jeremiah understood the heart of God. The punishment and discipline at hand was not for the sake of destruction but for restoring relationship. Even though the people had deserted God, God would never really desert them (see Jeremiah 31:36, 37). Jeremiah knew this and thus caught a glimpse of a time to come when the Davidic dynasty would be restored.

In 2 Samuel 7:16, God had promised David that his kingdom would last forever. Luke 1:32, 33 shows how this was fulfilled. The angel Gabriel appeared to the Virgin Mary and promised that she would bear a son: "He shall be great, and shall be called the Son of the Highest: and the Lord God shall give unto him the throne of his father David: and he shall reign over the house of Jacob for ever; and of his kingdom there shall be no end."

The priesthood was just as permanent as the Davidic dynasty. David himself had understood that the priesthood would never end. In Psalm 110 he had prophetically given the credentials for the Messiah: "The Lord has sworn and will not change his mind: 'You are a priest forever, in the order of Melchizedek'" (Psalm 110:4, *NIV*). Jeremiah reiterated this theme. God showed him that David would never lack a descendant to occupy his throne. Despite an interruption brought about by the Exile, the dynasty would ultimately continue—Christ himself will be the fulfillment of these promises as both Priest and King.

How do you explain the interruption of the throne of David? Was the permanent throne God promised to David physical or spiritual?

REVIEW QUESTIONS

1. Is it possible for Jews to be saved today outside of faith in Jesus Christ?
2. What makes the new covenant so much easier to live by than the old? Was it possible for anyone to follow the Old Testament law completely?
3. How important to Christianity was Jeremiah's prophecy of a new covenant?
4. Why have the Jews continued to be blinded to Jesus through the centuries?

GOLDEN TEXT HOMILY

"IN THOSE DAYS, AND AT THAT TIME, WILL I CAUSE THE BRANCH OF RIGHTEOUSNESS TO GROW UP UNTO DAVID; AND HE SHALL EXECUTE JUDGMENT AND RIGHTEOUSNESS IN THE LAND" (Jeremiah 33:15).

God's timing is very important in the lives of those who trust in Him and allow His Word to direct their lives. This was so true for Jeremiah, for he lived in very difficult times. His nation was experiencing the truth of God's Word that states that the "wages of sin is death." Because of the sin of His people and their rebellion, God allowed a heathen or ungodly nation to destroy their nation and place them in captivity.

God is faithful to His Word! He had warned His people so many times, but they did not obey His Word. Difficult times came to the Jews and relief came only as a result of God's message of grace to them. Jeremiah 33:15 is such a word of God's grace. During this very difficult time when no hope or help seemed to be in sight, God's word came to the prophet, "in those days, and at that time," and promised that He would "cause the Branch of righteousness to grow up unto David; and he shall execute judgment and righteousness in the land." This was God's word of grace, hope, and comfort.

Christians today go through difficult times—sometimes because of our sin and rebellion, but sometimes these difficult times come to us for no apparent reason. We can be assured, however, that God's word of grace, hope, and comfort is available to us, just as His word has always been there for His people during hard and difficult times. **—Levy E. Moore, Mayor, City of Franklin Springs, Franklin Springs, Georgia**

DAILY BIBLE READINGS

M. Judah's Scepter. Genesis 49:8-12
T. Everlasting Reign. Isaiah 9:1-7
W. God Remembers His People. Isaiah 49:8-16
T. New Heart, New Spirit. Ezekiel 36:24-30
F. Horn of Salvation. Luke 1:67-79
S. Christ, the Mediator. Hebrews 9:11-22

Rebellion Brings Judgment

Study Text: Jeremiah 37:1 through 38:28; 52:1-34; Hebrews 2:1-4

Objective: To realize rebellion brings judgment and exercise obedience in the midst of a sinful society.

Time: The Book of Jeremiah was written between 627 and 580 B.C. The Book of Hebrews was written around A.D. 64-70.

Place: The Book of Jeremiah was probably written at Jerusalem. The Book of Hebrews was possibly written at Rome.

Golden Text: "We ought to give the more earnest heed to the things which we have heard, lest at any time we should let them slip" (Hebrews 2:1).

Central Truth: Obedience to God's warnings brings deliverance from His judgment.

Evangelism Emphasis: Rebellion brings eternal judgment but faith and obedience bring life.

PRINTED TEXT

Jeremiah 38:17. Then said Jeremiah unto Zedekiah, Thus saith the Lord, the God of hosts, the God of Israel; If thou wilt assuredly go forth unto the king of Babylon's princes, then thy soul shall live, and this city shall not be burned with fire; and thou shalt live, and thine house:

18. But if thou wilt not go forth to the king of Babylon's princes, then shall this city be given into the hand of the Chaldeans, and they shall burn it with fire, and thou shalt not escape out of their hand.

52:8. But the army of the Chaldeans pursued after the king, and overtook Zedekiah in the plains of Jericho; and all his army was scattered from him.

9. Then they took the king, and carried him up unto the king of Babylon to Riblah in the land of Hamath; where he gave judgment upon him.

10. And the king of Babylon slew the sons of Zedekiah before his eyes: he slew also all the princes of Judah in Riblah.

11. Then he put out the eyes of Zedekiah; and the king of Babylon bound him in chains, and carried him to Babylon, and put him in prison till the day of his death.

Hebrews 2:1. Therefore we ought to give the more earnest heed to the things which we have heard, lest at any time we should let them slip.

2. For if the word spoken by angels was stedfast, and every transgression and disobedience received a just recompence of reward;

3. How shall we escape, if we neglect so great salvation; which at the first began to be spoken by the Lord, and was confirmed unto us by them that heard him;

4. God also bearing them witness, both with signs and wonders, and with divers miracles, and gifts of the Holy Ghost, according to his own will?

DICTIONARY

Riblah (RIB-lah)—Jeremiah 52:9—A city at the head waters of the Orontes River, a stronghold for the Egyptians and Assyrians.

Hamath (HAY-math)—Jeremiah 52:9—One of the most ancient surviving cities on the earth. It had been under both Babylonian and Assyrian rule.

LESSON OUTLINE

- I. JUDGMENT FORETOLD
  - A. A Reply to the King
  - B. The Wounded Rise Up
  - C. Surrender Brings Safety
  - D. Fear of One's Own People
- II. WARNINGS IGNORED
  - A. Jerusalem Besieged
  - B. The King's Capitulation
- III. REBEL OR OBEY
  - A. Conspirators Punished
  - B. A Toll of People
  - C. Ignoring God's Word

LESSON EXPOSITION

INTRODUCTION

Nebuchadnezzar's first invasion of Judah had taken place in 605 B.C. At this time many of the brightest and best of Judah's citizens were carried off to Babylon (including Daniel, Shadrach, Meshach, and Abednego). The second invasion came in 597 B.C., when King Jehoiakim rebelled against the conquering empire. He was captured and killed, however, and his son, Jehoiachin, then came to the throne. Just three weeks after his crowning he faced the Babylonian army. He held out for three months, only to surrender and be deported to Babylon, along with many others. Many of the important Temple vessels were taken in this sacking.

What then remained of the pitiful kingdom was ruled over by Zedekiah, another son of Josiah. Nebuchadnezzar laid siege to Jerusalem in Zedekiah's ninth year. This lasted for almost two years, with the people reaching starvation. Finally, the invaders breached the walls and overran the city, completely destroying the Temple, the king's palace, and other major buildings. Anything of value was carried off to Babylon; the city was totally looted.

The account of Zedekiah's reign in 2 Kings adds some interesting details. When Nebuchadnezzar had taken Jehoiachin as a captive to Babylon, he also took the king's mother, his wives, his officials, and all the leading men of the land, including 7,000 fighting men and 1,000 craftsmen. Judah was, in essence, drained of its most capable people. There was not much left for Zedekiah to preside over. He was not even recognized by those who remained as being their king—as long as Jehoiachin was still alive in Babylon.

Zedekiah had been placed on the throne purely as a puppet to Babylon. He had pledged his loyalty to Nebuchadnezzar. However, there was a strong Egyptian influence in his court, and Zedekiah was caught in a vise grip between those wanting him to rebel and those who saw the nation's only hope in submission to Babylon. Jeremiah, of course, insisted that he surrender to the discipline God had already ordained.

In the face of such difficult circumstances the evil Zedekiah had two choices: He could surrender to God's will and heed Jeremiah's advice or he could take a defiant attitude and follow his own desires and the advice of ungodly counselors. He chose the latter. This is typical of so many who have become entrapped in the bondage of sin. To break free just seems too difficult. To follow the path of least resistance is usually the decision chosen. The individual continues headlong toward destruction, often knowing full well what is ahead. Many a man has lost his soul by believing that there was no use in trying to change his ways. This is the high cost of lost hope; it is also one of Satan's greatest deceptions.

I. JUDGMENT FORETOLD (Jeremiah 37:6-10; 38:17-20)

A. A Reply to the King (Jeremiah 37:6-9)

(Jeremiah 37:6-9 is not included in the printed text.)

The siege of Jerusalem had been in effect for some time, but the approach of the Egyptian army had temporarily brought about the withdrawal of Babylonian forces. This had lifted the people's spirits and had given them false hopes. Zedekiah condemned Jeremiah's predictions of disaster as wrong. He had inflated hopes of rebuilding the kingdom through an alliance with Egypt.

Despite the appearance of Egyptian forces and the withdrawal of the Babylonians, Jeremiah held to his convictions based on a word from the Lord and continued to warn the people that the Babylonians would return. This was only a temporary reprieve; God's word that Jerusalem would be defeated and burned were just as sure as ever.

Judah was in great physical trouble but in even deeper spiritual trouble. The saying "There is none so blind as he who will not see" fits Zedekiah and the remaining people of Judah well. Zedekiah wanted his own way, but he also wanted God to bless him. In spite of his refusal to repent and heed what God had already said, He asked Jeremiah to pray for him (v. 3).

What Zedekiah really wanted was for the Lord to make the Babylonians withdraw permanently. He wanted God's blessings without bowing to God's laws and restrictions.

B. The Wounded Rise Up (v. 10)

(Jeremiah 37:10 is not included in the printed text.)

One of the great misconceptions of our own day is the notion that "perception equals reality." Nothing could be further from the truth. However, there is "nothing new under the sun," and the people of Judah were blinded by the same misconception when they saw the Egyptian army march into Judah.

They thought their saviors had arrived. Zedekiah had asked Pharaoh Hophra to come to Judah's aid. However, as soon as the Babylonians turned on them, the Egyptians fled. And Judah's plight was just as God had predicted. What God speaks will come to pass, despite what appears to be taking place. We must always trust God's word and not the prevailing circumstances.

C. Surrender Brings Safety (Jeremiah 38:17, 18)

17. Then said Jeremiah unto Zedekiah, Thus saith the Lord, the God of hosts, the God of Israel; If thou wilt assuredly go forth unto the king of Babylon's princes, then thy soul shall live, and this city shall not be burned with fire; and thou shalt live, and thine house:

18. But if thou wilt not go forth to the king of Babylon's princes, then shall this city be given into the hand of the Chaldeans, and they shall burn it with fire, and thou shalt not escape out of their hand.

Many people of Judah had already been taken to Babylon as captives. How much the remaining residents knew of their fellow countrymen's conditions is not known. Interestingly, the Babylonians had a lenient policy for the people they took as prisoners. They were permitted to live together, find jobs, and even take important positions in society. This kept them united in their heritage and fostered a new faithfulness to God. The actual captivity was not as bad as it might have appeared.

Had the people who remained in Judah understood that God still loved them and had they not resisted His discipline so fiercely, the outcome would not have been so difficult—the city would not have been burned. Surrender to God's will and obedience to His commands always produce the best results.

D. Fear of One's Own People (vv. 19, 20)

(Jeremiah 38:19, 20 is not included in the printed text.)

Zedekiah feared the Jews who had allied themselves with Babylon. There had always been a number of people in Judah who advised submission to the invaders. Whether these had capitulated because of Jeremiah's warnings, or whether they were simply protecting their own lives—we do not know. However, the handwriting was on the wall. Survival in any fashion depended on letting down their pride and surrendering to those who had the power. Zedekiah's enemies among his own people knew he was further contributing to the destruction on Judah by his rebellion.

Jeremiah tried to convince the king that his fears of reprisal from his countrymen were unfounded. The only thing he should fear was God's wrath for not submitting to what had already been decreed—that is, the Babylonians would rule over them.

Zedekiah was trapped by his own sins. Is there ever a way of avoiding the consequences of one's misdeeds? Explain.

II. WARNINGS IGNORED (Jeremiah 52:4-11)

A. Jerusalem Besieged (vv. 4-7)

(Jeremiah 52:4-7 is not included in the printed text.)

Chapter 52 is an epilogue to the historical events that took place throughout Jeremiah's ministry. It tells of the fall of Jerusalem and what the Babylonians did to the city and the Temple (as well as its vessels). It also describes how Nebuchadnezzar treated Zedekiah and his officials. We see a complete fulfillment of all the prophecies Jeremiah had been speaking for 40 years. Everything was just as he had predicted, according to the words the Lord had spoken to him.

The city had been under siege for nearly two years, and by the time of its capitulation it had become a death trap. Finally, Zedekiah proved his cowardice and tried to escape. This is a sad commentary on the character of a man who brought such destruction to his people. He tried to save his own life while letting those he was supposed to be serving face disaster.

B. The King's Capitulation (vv. 8-11)

8. But the army of the Chaldeans pursued after the king, and overtook Zedekiah in the plains of Jericho; and all his army was scattered from him.

9. Then they took the king, and carried him up unto the king of Babylon to Riblah in the land of Hamath; where he gave judgment upon him.

10. And the king of Babylon slew the sons of Zedekiah before his eyes: he slew also all the princes of Judah in Riblah.

11. Then he put out the eyes of Zedekiah; and the king of Babylon bound him in chains, and carried him to Babylon, and put him in prison till the day of his death.

Zedekiah was given many opportunities to repent, but he refused them all. Now he had to pay the consequences of his rebellion. His escape attempt was quickly discovered, although the Babylonians did have to chase him all the way to the plains of Jericho to catch him. In the confusion he got separated from the soldiers who were with him (2 Kings 25:5). They scattered quickly as the pursuers caught up, and Zedekiah was captured.

The rebellious king was taken to Riblah, some 200 miles north of Jerusalem. This was Nebuchadnezzar's headquarters for ruling the region. There, all of Zedekiah's sons were slaughtered before his eyes. Since he had come to the throne at age 21 and had reigned only 11 years before this capture, his sons had to be very young. The cost of his sin was proving incredibly high.

Nebuchadnezzar had Zedekiah's eyes put out and threw him into prison. Here he remained until his death. The prophet Ezekiel had also prophesied these same events but added a further detail. "I will bring him to Babylon to the land of the Chaldeans; yet shall he not see it, though he shall die there" (12:13). Zedekiah never actually saw Babylon because his eyes had been put out and he was blind when he arrived there.

Can you explain why Zedekiah had his heart so set on disobedience? Do you think he really believed he could outwit the Lord himself?

III. REBEL OR OBEY (Jeremiah 52:24-30; Hebrews 2:1-4)

A. The Conspirators Punished (Jeremiah 52:24-27)

(Jeremiah 52:24-27 is not included in the printed text.)

Nebuchadnezzar apparently was aware that it had been the priests and false prophets in Judah who had incited Zedekiah to rebel. They now paid the price for their selfish dreams. The Babylonians extracted anyone from the land who might give them further trouble. Among those was Seraiah, the high priest. Of interest is the fact that Seraiah was executed but his sons were only deported. In Ezra 7:1 we find that the great scribe was a descendant of Seraiah.

There is no doubt that these religious leaders of Judah were convinced they knew the word of the Lord for the people. They were sincere—but they were sincerely wrong. They probably reflected the prevailing sentiment and majority opinion of the day. It is often an easy thing to confuse God's will with our own.

We must be careful to remember that it is not necessarily the evangelist or pastor who has actually heard from the Lord that draws the greatest crowds. People long to hear assurances and exhortations from their religious leaders. The preacher who gives the greatest lift generally has the most listeners. However, the Bible contains a balanced message—and our preaching and teaching should likewise be balanced. The true word from the Lord comes to those "prepared to wait and to wrestle with God, rather than to those who speak with easy assurance and untroubled certainty" (Robert Davidson, *The Daily Bible Series—Jeremiah, Vol. 2 and Lamentations*).

B. A Toll of People (vv. 28-30)

(Jeremiah 52:28-30 is not included in the printed text.)

The three different deportations are listed in these last verses of the Book of Jeremiah. The numbers do not appear very large, but it is possible they reflect a counting of only the able-bodied men. It is likely that a total of between 15,000 and 20,000 Jews were actually taken to Babylon.

The center of Jewish life now shifted from Jerusalem to Babylon. After the initial turmoil and adjustment to life in a foreign land, the deported Jews had much to rethink in terms of what God wanted from a people who claimed to be His. Those who would return to Judah 70 years later would do so with a renewed determination to obey God's laws.

Interestingly, after the return, and for the next several hundred years until the birth of Christ, there was never again a rebellion against God's Word. The people came to reverence the law—to the point that it became their god. Thus, they would miss the Messiah when He came as a baby in Bethlehem.

The Book of Jeremiah closes with the relating of the release of King Jehoiachin from prison. The new king of Babylon, Evil-Merodach looked kindly on him and treated him well the rest of his life. This confirms the fact that God had not forgotten the Davidic line, even though it was now in exile.

C. Ignoring God's Word
(Hebrews 2:1-4)

1. Therefore we ought to give the more earnest heed to the things which we have heard, lest at any time we should let them slip.

2. For if the word spoken by angels was stedfast, and every transgression and disobedience received a just recompence of reward;

3. How shall we escape, if we neglect so great salvation; which at the first began to be spoken by the Lord, and was confirmed unto us by them that heard him;

4. God also bearing them witness, both with signs and wonders, and with divers miracles, and gifts of the Holy Ghost, according to his own will?

The hard lesson to be learned from Jeremiah is a challenge to be careful not to confuse what God is saying with what we want to hear. There was no shortage of religion in Judah, but it was meaningless. The people thought the rituals of their Temple in Jerusalem fully constituted their spiritual life. They were sure that the holy city could not possibly fall and that by positioning themselves in the proximity of the Temple, which was built as a place for God's presence to dwell, they were actually drawing near to Him. However, as the writer of Hebrews said, we must be careful not let the basics slip away.

We are no different from the people of Judah; it is just as easy for us today to get caught up in the activities of church life and miss the essence of a relationship with Jesus Christ. Our involvement in Christian activities will be of no value to us unless we focus our hearts on knowing Christ.

The writer of Hebrews was afraid that his readers might slip into false teaching. He pointed out that although angels had served as messengers to bring the law to Moses, they were not as important as Jesus Christ. The message He brings is the only One that can provide us an escape from God's judgment. If we become indifferent to the life that is found only in Christ, we will fare no better than the people of Judah did.

Why did the people of Judah have such a mind-set against listening to the word from God that Jeremiah spoke?

REVIEW QUESTIONS

1. Why did the people of Judah think that God would not destroy their Temple and their holy city?
2. Did the people who were captured and sent to Babylon feel that God had failed them—or rather that they had failed God? On what do you base your opinion?
3. Discuss the outcome of the captive Jews' rethinking of God's plan for Israel while they were in Babylon.
4. What is the overall lesson to be learned from Jeremiah's faithful preaching to the people?
5. Discuss the consequences of altering the message of God to suit what people want to hear.

GOLDEN TEXT HOMILY

"WE OUGHT TO GIVE THE MORE EARNEST HEED TO THE THINGS WHICH WE HAVE HEARD, LEST AT ANY TIME WE SHOULD LET THEM SLIP" (Hebrews 2:1).

We should heed the gospel truths which we have heard, lest we drift away from them. Matthew Henry said, "If we do not well attend, we shall not long retain the word of God; inattentive hearers will soon be forgetful hearers."

Inattention takes various forms. For example, we can indulge in daydreaming, criticizing, or other distractions while a minister is preaching or a teacher is teaching. We miss, therefore, at least a part of the sermon or lesson. It could be that the part we miss is just what we need to strengthen us spiritually or to equip us intellectually for the situations we will face in the coming week.

Older Christians may allow their minds to wander when a speaker is relating some Bible story or quoting some Bible passage which they have heard many times. The important thing for all of us to do when we hear a Bible truth, whether we have heard it 10 times or a hundred times, is to allow God's Spirit to minister to us while that truth is being presented. We should keep our ears open and our hearts receptive as God's Word goes forth. Afterward, we should ponder what we have heard, and we should put into practice the truths which have been presented to us.

Perhaps the truest test of how well we have heard God's truths is how well we regulate our words and actions in accordance with the Scriptures. We should be "doers of the word, and not hearers only" (James 1:22).**—Excerpts from the *Evangelical Sunday School Lesson Commentary,* Vol. 27**

SENTENCE SERMONS

OBEDIENCE to God's warnings brings deliverance from His judgment.

—Selected

IT IS ONLY by obedience that we understand the teaching of God.

—Oswald Chambers

THE UNSURRENDERED CHRISTIAN stands condemned for what he does not do more than for what he does.

—Billy Graham

IT COST GOD nothing, as far as we know, to create nice things; but to convert rebellious wills cost Him the crucifixion of His dear Son.

—C.S. Lewis

ILLUMINATING THE LESSON

I once knew two different men who each faced the prospects of bankruptcy. Both had gone into business for themselves and were successful for a time but with changing economies found themselves strapped. How they handled their individual situations is a classic illustration of our lesson from Jeremiah.

The first businessman had gotten into heavy debt carelessly. He had not disciplined himself to budget while his work was flourishing. When the demand for his services suddenly fell off, he found himself unable to pay his bills. He decided to take the bankruptcy course without hesitation. Being a young man, he figured he had plenty of time to recover from the consequences of such action. Several years later he was still struggling—both to manage his present finances and to overcome the penalties of having taken such a drastic measure.

The second individual was in even deeper financial trouble. He was already in his middle-age years when his venture went sour. He had budgeted and worked hard, but the recession had carried him down. He went to his aged father for advice. The old gentlemen told his son, "Stick with it. The Lord will help you through this. Offer to pay your creditors a little at a time. Don't ever let your good name be destroyed!" Following his father's advice, he struggled for several years to catch up. Finally, despite some lean times, he is back on his feet again.

DAILY BIBLE READINGS

M. Intercession for the Rebellious. Numbers 14:11-20

T. God Judges Rebellion. 1 Samuel 12:14-18

W. Seek God's Forgiveness. 1 Samuel 12:19-25

T. Rebellion Punished. Psalm 78:56-64

F. Submit to Authority. Romans 13:1-5

S. Suffer Only for Christ. 1 Peter 4:12-19

Be Faithful in Adversity

Study Text: Jeremiah 39:1 through 40:6

Objective: To consider God's protective power and trust Him with our lives.

Time: The Book of Jeremiah was written between 627 and 580 B.C.

Place: The Book of Jeremiah was probably written at Jerusalem.

Golden Text: "I will surely deliver thee, and thou shalt not fall by the sword, . . . because thou hast put thy trust in me, saith the Lord" (Jeremiah 39:18).

Central Truth: God rewards those who are faithful.

Evangelism Emphasis: God's faithfulness provides a reason for all people to trust in Him.

PRINTED TEXT

Jeremiah 39:11. Now Nebuchadrezzar king of Babylon gave charge concerning Jeremiah to Nebuzar-adan the captain of the guard, saying,

12. Take him, and look well to him, and do him no harm; but do unto him even as he shall say unto thee.

13. So Nebuzar-adan the captain of the guard sent, and Nebushasban, Rabsaris, and Nergal-sharezer, Rab-mag, and all the king of Babylon's princes;

14. Even they sent, and took Jeremiah out of the court of the prison, and committed him unto Gedaliah the son of Ahikam the son of Shaphan, that he should carry him home: so he dwelt among the people.

15. Now the word of the Lord came unto Jeremiah, while he was shut up in the court of the prison, saying,

16. Go and speak to Ebed-melech the Ethiopian, saying, Thus saith the Lord of hosts, the God of Israel; Behold, I will bring my words upon this city for evil, and not for good; and they shall be accomplished in that day before thee.

17. But I will deliver thee in that day, saith the Lord: and thou shalt not be given into the hand of the men of whom thou art afraid.

18. For I will surely deliver thee, and thou shalt not fall by the sword, but thy life shall be for a prey unto thee: because thou hast put thy trust in me, saith the Lord.

40:2. And the captain of the guard took Jeremiah, and said unto him, The Lord thy God hath pronounced this evil upon this place.

3. Now the Lord hath

brought it, and done according as he hath said: because ye have sinned against the Lord, and have not obeyed his voice, therefore this thing is come upon you.

4. And now, behold, I loose thee this day from the chains which were upon thine hand. If it seem good unto thee to come with me into Babylon, come; and I will look well unto thee: but if it seem ill unto thee to come with me into Babylon, forbear: behold, all the land is before thee: whither it seemeth good and convenient for thee to go, thither go.

DICTIONARY

Nebuchadrezzar (NEB-you-kad-REZ-zur) king of Babylon (BAB-uh-lun)—Jeremiah 39:11—A minor variant of the word Nebuchadnezzer, who was king of Babylon.

Nebuzar-adan (NEB-you-azr-AA-dan)—Jeremiah 39:11—Nebuchadnezer's general when the Babylonians beseiged Jerusalem.

Nebushasban (NEB-you-SHAS-ban), Rabsaris (RAB-sah-ris), Nergal-sharezer (NAR-gal-shar-REE-zer), Rab-mag (RAB-nag)—Jeremiah 39:13—This group represents officials and/or relatives of king Nebuchadnezzar.

Gedaliah (GED-ah-LIE-ah) the son of Ahikam (ah-HIGH-kam), the son of Shaphan (SHA-fan)—Jeremian 39:14—Gedaliah, an officer of high rank protected Jeremiah, whose views he shared.

Ebed-melech (Eebed-me-lek)—Jeremiah 39:16—An Ethiopian eunuch who was moved to ask the king for permission to pull Jeremiah out of the miry dungeon he had been cast into.

LESSON OUTLINE

I. REWARDED FOR FAITHFULNESS
   A. Babylon's View of the Prophet
   B. Jeremiah's New Freedom

II. PRESERVED BY GOD
   A. Jeremiah's Concern for Others
   B. As Unto the Lord

III. FREEDOM GRANTED
   A. Babylon Recognizes God's Hand
   B. Jeremiah's Choice

LESSON EXPOSITION

INTRODUCTION

It was all finally happening just as Jeremiah had predicted. He had preached the same message since 627 B.C. It was now 586 B.C.—41 years of preaching one sermon. For the last two years now Judah and Jerusalem had been under siege by Nebudchadnezzar's armies. Just days ago, when all the food in the city was gone and the invaders were breaking the city gates down, the still rebellious King Zedekiah had tried to make a break for it—only to be captured in the fields around Jericho.

We might think that Jeremiah had a right to feel vindicated. He had preached God' message faithfully and had seen it all come to pass—despite the ostracism and rejection of his fellow countrymen. God had preserved him, and now he would be a free man—to the point of being viewed as a mystical figure that even the Babylonians looked upon with reverence. He could live as he pleased and walk with an aura of pride in knowing that he had been right. But could he really? Is there any consolation in having been right when those you love are reaping the wages of their sins? Just because you warned them it was coming, it brings no comfort to see the tragedy come to pass.

No, Jeremiah still had a burden to carry. To do otherwise would have negated the integrity of the entire life he had lived. He loved these people, despite what they had done and the terrible things they had said about him. He had no personal animosity toward any of them, even the ones who had hurt him, humiliated him, thrown in a cistern, tried to kill him, and publicly attacked him.

How Jeremiah chose to live out his days, now that the invasion and captivity had finally come, would be just as important as all the years of preaching God's message had been. God is not finished with a man until the breath is gone out of his body. What Jeremiah did now would prove or disprove the integrity of all he had stood for in years past.

I. REWARDED FOR FAITHFULNESS (Jeremiah 39:11-14)

A. Babylon's View of the Prophet (vv. 11, 12)

11. Now Nebuchadrezzar king of Babylon gave charge concerning Jeremiah to Nebuzaradan the captain of the guard, saying,

12. Take him, and look well to him, and do him no harm; but do unto him even as he shall say unto thee.

After a siege of two years, the Babylonians finally breached the city walls and looted Jerusalem. The first 10 verses of this chapter tell the story of Nebuchadnezzar's invasion, although chapter 52 gives a more detailed version. King Zedekiah, realizing the end was near, still hoped to save his own life. He and his entourage tried to escape through an opening between the two city walls bordering the palace garden. This was near the Pool of Siloam. Obviously the escape plan was attempted in secret—but something went amiss. Possibly someone inside royal circles informed the invaders, hoping for better treatment for himself. No one has ever been able to figure out the exact escape route, for there is no other recording of it.

How the Babylonians discovered the fleeing king's plan no one knows, but the invaders were soon in swift pursuit. They caught up with Zedekiah on the plains of Jericho. After his arrest he was taken to Riblah, the location of Nebuchadnezzar's headquarters. This was the same strategic sight where Pharaoh Necho had kept his military headquarters when he lost his campaign against Assyria (see 2 Kings 23:33).

At Riblah, Zedekiah was forced to witness the execution of his sons and officers, and then he himself was blinded and sent in chains to Babylon, where he would later die in prison (Jeremiah 52:11; see also 2 Kings 24, 25; 2 Chronicles 36). Nebuchadnezzar's punishment of those who rebelled would seem terribly cruel by today's standards, but it was typical of pagan practices in the ancient world—especially since Judah had caused so much trouble for Babylon.

Two prophecies by two prophets were thus fulfilled. Jeremiah had made it clear that Zedekiah would be captured by the king of Babylon and would also be taken to that city (32:3-5). Ezekiel had prophesied that Zedekiah would die in Babylon without having ever seen the city (12:13). This proved true, because his eyes had been put out after he was captured but before he reached the city of Babylon.

To avoid total destruction of the country, Nebuchadnezzar left the poorest people behind, giving them high positions, thus assuring their loyalty to the conquerors. This policy was designed to keep subjugated populations from rebelling.

But what about Jeremiah? How was he faring through all this turmoil? The Babylonians were apparently quite superstitious and held magicians, fortune-tellers, seers, and prophets in high regard. They had undoubtedly heard about Jeremiah, especially how he had encouraged cooperation with Babylon. Those who had deserted Judah during the siege had likely reported and embellished this information. Because Jeremiah had been imprisoned by his own people, the invaders assumed that he would likewise desert his country.

Ironically, Jeremiah was now being treated better by the foreigners than he had been by his own countrymen, whom he loved. He was released and his care entrusted to Gedaliah, the appointed governor of Judah.

The fates of Jeremiah and Zedekiah have an ironic twist. Jeremiah was freed, Zedekiah imprisoned. Jeremiah received respect, Zedekiah condemnation. Jeremiah could finally live in comfort, while Zedekiah died a prisoner. Jeremiah had always been concerned for others; Zedekiah had thought only of himself. He had tried to ignore God, but eventually his rebellion caught up with him.

B. Jeremiah's New Freedom (vv. 13, 14)

13. So Nebuzaradan the captain of the guard sent, and Nebushasban, Rabsaris, and Nergal-sharezer, Rab-mag, and all the king of Babylon's princes;

14. Even they sent, and took Jeremiah out of the court of the prison, and committed him unto Gedaliah the son of Ahikam the son of Shaphan, that he should carry him home: so he dwelt among the people.

As already stated, the Babylonian invaders were well informed about Jeremiah's humble attitude and efforts to persuade the people of his country to submit to Babylon. Jewish deserters would have passed on much of what Jeremiah had been saying over the years.

A Babylonian military tribunal authorized the prophet's release from "the court of the prison," and he was handed over to Gedaliah, the son of Ahikam. Interestingly, this was the second time that this family had played a positive role in Jeremiah's life. Ahikam (Gedaliah's father), was the royal secretary who had stood with the prophet and persuaded the courts of Judah to protect the prophet from a mob that was trying to kill him (26:24). Also, both Ahikam and Shaphan (Gedaliah's grandfather) had been instrumental in informing Josiah of the discovery of the scroll of the Law and the institution of reforms in the country (see 2 Kings 22, 23). Three generations of this family had remained faithful to the Lord.

Since God had promised the fall of Zedekiah, is there any escape plan he could have ever come up with that would have worked? If it was mostly the poor left in the country, why did Gedaliah escape deportation?

II. PRESERVED BY GOD (Jeremiah 39:15-18)

A. Jeremiah's Concern for Others (vv. 15-17)

15. Now the word of the Lord came unto Jeremiah, while he was shut up in the court of the prison, saying,

16. Go and speak to Ebed-melech the Ethiopian, saying, Thus saith the Lord of hosts, the God of Israel; Behold, I will bring my words upon this city for evil, and not for good; and they shall be accomplished in that day before thee.

17. But I will deliver thee in that day, saith the Lord: and thou shalt not be given into the hand of the men of whom thou art afraid.

Jeremiah was still in prison awaiting release when this incident occurred. The prison was a dungeon underneath the king's palace. He had apparently been here for most of the two-year siege by Nebuchadnezzar: "The army of the king of Babylon was then besieging Jerusalem, and Jeremiah the prophet was confined in the courtyard of the guard in the royal palace of Judah" (Jeremiah 32:2, *NIV*). It was during this incarceration that God had told him to buy a field outside Jerusalem. This was land that was already occupied by the invaders, but Jeremiah was investing his faith in God's promise to restore the nation and rebuild Jerusalem.

Jeremiah had never allowed his being in prison to chain his message. From prison he had dictated a scroll to Baruch to be read in the Temple (ch. 36). Prison might be an inconvenience, but it did not stop his preaching. The Word of God will always find its intended recipient. This reminds us of Paul's words written to Timothy that carry the same flavor: "This is my gospel, for which I am suffering even to the point of being chained like a criminal. But God's word is not chained" (2 Timothy 2:8, 9, *NIV*).

Even before the Babylonians arrived to release Jeremiah from the dungeon, the Lord gave him a word for Ebed-Melech, the man who had risked his own life to save Jeremiah some time earlier. Jeremiah 38:1-13 tells the story of how the prophet was lowered into a cistern and left to die. Ebed-Melech interceded with the fickle King Zedekiah and got permission to rescue the prophet from the cruel death sentence. This noble effort had likely made many enemies for Ebed-Melech. His life had probably been in great danger for having associated himself with the hated prophet. In the present turmoil he needed a message of hope, and the Lord provided it. Because of his compassionate acts for Jeremiah, he would surely escape death.

B. As Unto the Lord (v. 18)

18. For I will surely deliver thee, and thou shalt not fall by the sword, but thy life shall be for a prey unto thee: because thou hast put thy trust in me, saith the Lord.

Although Jeremiah was about to be released from prison, his first thoughts were not for himself but for those who had risked themselves for his safety. He realized that Ebed-Melech's noble act had, in essence, been for the larger purpose of honoring God. This brings to mind the words of Jesus: "I tell you the truth, whatever you did for one of the least of these brothers of mine, you did for me" (Matthew 25:40, *NIV*).

Had he been asked why he risked his own life for Jeremiah's, Ebed-Melech would likely not have viewed his bravery as worship. However, in God's sight this man's actions took on a larger purpose. By doing for the "least of these," he had done it also for the Lord.

Why was Ebed-Melech's life in so much apparent danger? Whom did he have to fear the most—the Babylonian invaders or Jeremiah's enemies?

III. FREEDOM GRANTED (Jeremiah 40:1-6)

A. Babylon Recognizes God's Hand (vv. 1-3)

(Jeremiah 40:1 is not included in the printed text.)

2. And the captain of the guard took Jeremiah, and said unto him, The Lord thy God hath pronounced this evil upon this place.

3. Now the Lord hath brought it, and done according as he hath said: because ye have sinned against the Lord, and have not obeyed his voice, therefore this thing is come upon you.

This passage gives a different accounting of Jeremiah's release from prison than what was seen in the last chapter. Here we find Jeremiah crowded among a group of other prisoners in chains. They were in a transit camp at Ramah, a Benjamite town some five miles north of Jerusalem. It is apparent that in the process of screening the deportees, Nebuzaradan discovered Jeremiah among them. How did the prophet get here, and how do we reconcile this account with the earlier version of his release?

The likelihood is that after his initial discharge from prison, Jeremiah was accidentally arrested by Babylonian troops in Jerusalem as they rounded up potential deportees. The authorities realized their mistake when Nebuzaradan discovered the prophet's identity at Ramah. This is plausible, given the chaotic situation in Jerusalem immediately after the city's capture.

How did Nebuzaradan know about the Lord's decree against Judah? Could the Babylonians have actually known that they were being used as God's instruments to bring down Judah? Jeremiah's reputation and message were probably well known to the invaders. Every conquering nation has its spies, and it certainly would not have been difficult to hear of the dissident prophet's words. After all, he had been preaching this same message for 40 years.

Nebuzaradan did not know God, but he still acknowledged that the Lord had given victory to Babylon. It has not been uncommon throughout history for men to see the hand of the Almighty at work and yet refuse to personally accept Him. The demons in hell certainly understand who is Lord of the Universe—yet they do not worship Him.

B. Jeremiah's Choice (vv. 4-6)

(Jeremiah 40:5, 6 is not included in the printed text.)

4. And now, behold, I loose thee this day from the chains which were upon thine hand. If it seem good unto thee to come with me into Babylon, come; and

I will look well unto thee: but if it seem ill unto thee to come with me into Babylon, forbear: behold, all the land is before thee: whither it seemeth good and convenient for thee to go, thither go.

Nebuzaradan freed Jeremiah and gave him a choice of where he would live. Jeremiah could go to Babylon as a respected seer, or he could remain in Judah and live in poverty. The Babylonians were prepared to treat him well. They understood his value as a forecaster of future events. Everything now taking place had been predicted by Jeremiah many years before. Also, they likely saw him as a trustworthy collaborator.

Jeremiah, however, was neither a Babylonian sympathizer nor a traitor to his own country. His entire life had been given to proclaiming the "word of the Lord," however the chips might fall. In the end he chose to turn down what Babylon offered him. In Judah he would live out his days in poverty, but the remnant of Jews living there would know that he had not been a traitor. Also, he realized that there was still unfinished business ahead. There could still be hope for his beloved countrymen in the midst of this disaster. Perhaps some of the people remaining in Judah would see the magnitude of their sins and repent. There was still the possibility of a renewed faith in a ravaged country.

Though his reputation as the weeping prophet was well founded, Jeremiah still realized that it was only God's mercy that prevented total annihilation. Through all the adversities and afflictions, both national and personal, the prophet held to his faith and trust in God.

How do you think the exiled Jews in Babylon would have viewed Jeremiah if he had accepted the hospitality offered to him there?

REVIEW QUESTIONS

1. Did Jeremiah feel any vindication at having been right when the Babylonians invaded and carried away so many into captivity? Did he feel any sense of satisfaction at the destruction of his homeland? Discuss?
2. Could Jeremiah have allowed himself to feel vindicated even if he had been inclined to do so?
3. Could Jeremiah rejoice in any part of what the Lord had told him, or was he destined to be the weeping prophet throughout his life?
4. Should Jeremiah's difficult experiences discourage believers from taking a hard stand for the Lord? Explain your answer.

GOLDEN TEXT HOMILY

"I WILL SURELY DELIVER THEE, AND THOU SHALT NOT FALL BY THE SWORD, . . . BECAUSE THOU HAST PUT THY TRUST IN ME, SAITH THE Lord" (Jeremiah 39:18).

The faithfulness of Jeremiah to believe God and to trust Him with his very life brought safety to him and to a remnant of the people of God. We do not understand why God works the way He does in different situations, but we do know that God is at work in protecting and preserving His people—whether it was the Jewish people of Jeremiah's day or whether it is the family of God today. We simply cannot become discouraged and give up, because God is still the same today as He was yesterday. When we faithfully fulfill our promises and commitments to Him, the Lord will surely fulfill His promises to us and keep us from the hand of the spoiler. He will provide us with daily blessings from His good resources.

The situation that Jeremiah and the people of God were in was far more severe than the circumstances we in America are personally familiar with. The atrocities and brutish actions of the enemy in that day were far more severe than most of us can imagine. Yet the devil is an enemy that takes no prisoners. His goal is to destroy God's creation and to seige the authority that rightfully belongs to God. We are to resist Satan's efforts by knowing the Word of the Lord and doing what God tells us in His Word.

When we are faithful and obedient, we too shall eat the good of the land (see Isaiah 1:19). God protected and preserved Jeremiah. He will also be faithful to us and will not allow us to fall by the way of Satan's sword if we will put our trust in Him. God will protect us and not allow Satan to destroy us even though the battle will rage fiercely around us at times. Our lives are safe in God because He says to us, "I will surely deliver thee."—**Marion H. Starr, Pastor, Marion, South Carolina**

SENTENCE SERMONS

GOD REWARDS those who are faithful.

—Selected

FAITHFULNESS in little things is a big thing.

—Archibald Alexander

IF WE ARE correct and right in our Christian life at every point, but refuse to stand for the truth at a particular point where the battle rages—then we are traitors to Christ.

—Oswald Chambers

A WISE MAN, though he be a slave, is at liberty; though a fool rule, he is in slavery.

—Saint Ambrose

EVANGELISM APPLICATION

GOD'S FAITHFULNESS PROVIDES A REASON FOR ALL PEOPLE TO TRUST IN HIM.

In looking over the years of Jeremiah's ministry, many things stand out for us to learn from his courage, honesty, faithfulness, determination, and even his loneliness. However, beyond these noble traits of integrity are also a couple of principles that we should use for guidelines in our own lives as Christians:

1. *We must be careful to discern the absolute essentials of the faith.* Many people in Judah would have listened if the priesthood and monarchy had been in tune with the truth. The leaders, however, had a total misconception of what God wanted from His people. They thought religiosity was their salvation. There was no shortage of religion in Jeremiah's day—but there was a shortage of truth within the religion. The people were taught that Temple rituals would save them. They thought because they were God's chosen, they would be spared. They missed the truth that obedience is better than sacrifice (see 1 Samuel 15:22), that a show of religion without the heart can lead only to destruction.

2. *Not all prophets who claim to have heard from God have necessarily done so.* There were many people in Judah who were convinced that they had heard a word of truth from God. They were perhaps

earnest, but their conviction came purely from the consensus of public opinion. It is possible to be sincere and yet be sincerely wrong. We must search the Scriptures to find the truth.

God reveals Himself to those who wait on Him, study His Word, wrestle with Him, and obey Him—even when such obedience puts individuals at odds with the prevailing culture.

ILLUMINATING THE LESSON

There are three great principles concerning the nature of God that we can learn from Jeremiah's experience:

1. *God will do what He says:* "But do not forget this one thing, dear friends: With the Lord a day is like a thousand years, and a thousand years are like a day" (2 Peter 3:8, *NIV*). The people of Judah did not take into account that God is eternally present and that time is of little meaning to Him. Peter described those of all ages who forget this principle: "They will say, 'Where is this "coming" he promised? Ever since our fathers died, everything goes on as it has since the beginning of creation'" (2 Peter 3:4, *NIV*). The wheels of God's justice grind slowly, but they grind exceedingly fine. Jeremiah preached his message for over 40 years before his words came to pass. Many perhaps thought that time had proved him wrong—but then God intervened.

2. *God will withhold punishment if men repent.* Jeremiah continued to preach a coming judgment in the hope that some would listen. God knew that the people of Judah would not let go of their sin, but the opportunity to repent was nevertheless given to them. Again, Peter summarized this: "The Lord is not slow in keeping his promise, as some understand slowness. He is patient with you, not wanting anyone to perish, but everyone to come to repentance" (2 Peter 3:9, *NIV*).

3. *God will protect through all circumstances.* Jeremiah's life was difficult, but he nevertheless survived. As believers, our times are in God's hands. Nothing can touch us without His approval. We need not fear an untimely death, for He numbers our days and determines when our work is finished. We can trust Him entirely to give us the ability, power, and endurance to complete His call on our lives.

Jeremiah's life shows us that there are serious consequences to human sin. However, in the midst of every tragedy there is still hope, for God can turn wrong around and make it right. We also see the timeless importance of continued prayer and confession of sin. Tragedy comes to all lives at one time or another, but there is always hope in God.

DAILY BIBLE READINGS

M. Choose to Obey.
Deuteronomy 11:22-28

T. Charge to Be Faithful.
1 Kings 2:1-4

W. Promise to the Faithful.
Psalm 37:25-34

T. Declare God's Faithfulness.
Psalm 89:1-11

F. Be Faithful in Service.
2 Timothy 4:1-8

S. Be an Overcomer.
Revelation 2:5-11

Profile of a Servant

Study Text: Genesis 24:1-9, 32-38, 56; Exodus 21:2-6; 1 Samuel 3:1-10; Luke 16:13; 1 Corinthians 4:1, 2; Colossians 3:22-24

Objective: To discover the attributes of a servant and desire to emulate them.

Golden Text: "Whatsoever ye do, do it heartily, as to the Lord, and not unto men; . . . for ye serve the Lord Christ" (Colossians 3:23, 24).

Central Truth: Servanthood is required of every Christian.

Evangelism Emphasis: Service to God involves a personal commitment to reach lost humanity.

PRINTED TEXT

Luke 16:13. No servant can serve two masters: for either he will hate the one, and love the other; or else he will hold to the one, and despise the other. Ye cannot serve God and mammon.

1 Samuel 3:4. That the Lord called Samuel: and he answered, Here am I.

5. And he ran unto Eli, and said, Here am I; for thou calledst me. And he said, I called not; lie down again. And he went and lay down.

6. And the Lord called yet again, Samuel. And Samuel arose and went to Eli, and said, Here am I; for thou didst call me. And he answered, I called not, my son; lie down again.

7. Now Samuel did not yet know the Lord, neither was the word of the Lord yet revealed unto him.

8. And the Lord called Samuel again the third time. And he arose and went to Eli, and said, Here am I; for thou didst call me. And Eli perceived that the Lord had called the child.

9. Therefore Eli said unto Samuel, Go, lie down: and it shall be, if he call thee, that thou shalt say, Speak, Lord; for thy servant heareth. So Samuel went and lay down in his place.

10. And the Lord came, and stood, and called as at other times, Samuel, Samuel. Then Samuel answered, Speak; for thy servant heareth.

Colossians 3:22. Servants, obey in all things your masters according to the flesh; not with eyeservice, as menpleasers; but in singleness of heart, fearing God.

Genesis 24:2. And Abraham said unto his eldest servant of his house, that ruled over all that he had, Put, I pray thee, thy hand under my thigh:

3. And I will make thee swear by the Lord, the God of heaven, and the God of the earth, that thou shalt not take a wife unto

my son of the daughters of the Canaanites, among whom I dwell:

4. But thou shalt go unto my country, and to my kindred, and take a wife unto my son Isaac.

9. And the servant put his hand under the thigh of Abraham his master, and sware to him concerning that matter.

56. And he said unto them, Hinder me not, seeing the Lord hath prospered my way; send me away that I may go to my master.

1 Corinthians 4:1. Let a man so account of us, as of the ministers of Christ, and stewards of the mysteries of God.

2. Moreover it is required in stewards, that a man be found faithful.

LESSON OUTLINE

I. SERVES ONLY ONE MASTER
   - A. Hebrew Slaves
   - B. Slavery and Purposes of God
   - C. One Lord and Master

II. SUBMITS TO THE MASTER'S WILL
   - A. Hearing the Master's Voice
   - B. Samuel's Availability
   - C. Samuel's Response
   - D. Obedience as Worship

III. SHOWS LOYALTY AND FAITHFULNESS
   - A. A Faith to Be Imitated
   - B. Completing the Job
   - C. Faithful Ministers

LESSON EXPOSITION

INTRODUCTION

The perfect profile of a true servant can be found in the character of Eliezer, the aged servant of Abraham (Genesis 24). He was the chief, or oldest servant, and could be trusted to take charge of everything in his master's household. The story of Abraham's sending him to find a wife for Isaac is one of the most beautiful in the Bible. Single-mindedness to carry out Abraham's instructions demonstrates not only his devotion to his master but also his understanding and personal knowledge of the God of Abraham. He submitted his actions to Jehovah, prayed for guidance in carrying out his task, set up a strategy that left room for God to operate, waited patiently for God to move, was thankful when the answer came, made haste to complete the work assigned, and ultimately followed through with the entire plan.

Slavery was not a hindrance to Eliezer in living a fulfilled existence. Evidently, Eliezer did not consider his lot in life a great handicap. It was simply a fact, not a determinant. In the New Testament, Paul expressed much the same attitude. In 1 Timothy 6:1, 2 he did not speak against the institution of slavery but simply gave guidelines for Christian slaves and Christian masters. His counsel is valid for any employer-employee relationship. Employees, the same as slaves, should respect their masters, strive to exemplify a valid witness to the saving power of Jesus Christ, and work very hard. One's station in life is not in question.

Rather, one's attitude and behavior are what matter for eternity. Faithfulness and love for Christ far outweigh any handicap position, financial means, or social status. When God judges lives, His judgment is based on what has been done with what the individual has been given.

I. SERVE ONLY ONE MASTER (Exodus 21:2-6; Luke 16:13)

A. Hebrew Slaves (Exodus 21:2, 3)

(Exodus 21:2, 3 is not included in the printed text.)

Slavery has been a fact of life in many societies since time began. The Bible never gives its seal of approval to the practice but simply gives guidelines concerning it within the context of the times. For instance, most conservative Christians today realize the potential harm of alcohol, yet Jesus himself lived out His earthly ministry in a culture in which wine was an accepted drink, both socially and medicinally. However, the Scriptures are clearly against its excessive use and abuse. The same is true for slavery. God obviously hated slavery. That fact became especially evident when His chosen people, the Jews, suffered through hundreds of years of slavery at the hands of the Egyptians. Yet the institution of slavery itself is not addressed in the pages of the Bible.

Of interest in this particular text is the fact that the Hebrews also owned slaves, though they themselves had just recently been freed from its horror. Individuals could become slaves because of indebtedness, poverty, crime, or a variety of other reasons. However, God commanded that these "Hebrew" slaves be treated as humans, not chattel. They were allowed to work their way back to freedom. Leviticus 25:39, 40 specifies how this was to be carried out. Hebrews could not be enslaved by their countrymen on a permanent basis. God always made provision for them to regain their freedom, by both hard work and the Year of Jubilee. The Israelites were also allowed to have Gentile slaves from other nations, but they had rights as well. Deuteronomy 23:15 gives instructions that runaway slaves were not to be returned to their masters, a strong factor in determining how a master should treat his servants.

God is merciful and always desires to bless His children. In Leviticus 26:13, He identified Himself as "the Lord your God, which brought you forth out of the land of Egypt." He had watched the terrible ordeal the descendants of Abraham had suffered through, and He had heard their cries for help. He brought His people out of bitter slavery and gave them freedom and dignity. The Promised Land would be a total contrast to the hundreds of years of abuse they had endured, and they were never to forget where they had been brought from and that they should treat others with the same mercy God had extended to them. Moses reminded the people in Deuteronomy 15:12-18 to not only free their slaves after a six-year term of service but to also be generous in giving them enough foodstuffs, animals, and supplies to get them started in a life of freedom.

This is a perfect picture of the sacrifice Jesus made for us. Through His death and resurrection we also have been lifted from slavery—the slavery to sin. Our deliverance comes when we accept Christ's payment that redeems us.

B. Slavery and the Purposes of God (Exodus 21:4-6)

(Exodus 21:4-6 is not included in

the printed text.)

God made provision that the Hebrews themselves were to never become permanent slaves to another Hebrew. If they were forced into slavery because of sudden poverty, the law required that they be freed after six years. Leviticus 25:42 states God's position on this. Because the Israelites were His servants, they could not be slaves to another. The principle of servitude to only one master is demonstrated here.

Slaves from other nations could be purchased and even passed on to the next generation through inheritance, but the laws governing their care were strict and humane. The institution was allowed within the context of the times, but slaves owned by God's people were to be treated always with dignity, and not as animals. They even took part in religious festivals and rested on the Sabbath Day.

The only way Hebrews could be made lifetime slaves was voluntarily on their part. It was then that an ear was pierced to designate such. This protected the owner from criticism and was a symbol of lifetime commitment. As believers we might pray, "Lord, pierce my ear," as an act of commitment to serving Him all the days of our lives.

No man fully knows the ways of God. Through the centuries God has used what could be considered evil institutions to spread His Word. As terrible as slavery is, God has used it to bring millions out of pagan religions to a saving knowledge of Him. So often God turns unjust and cruel circumstances into glorious victories and blessings for those who were victimized and treated unfairly. That is so characteristic of our loving heavenly Father.

C. One Lord and Master
(Luke 16:13)

13. No servant can serve two masters: for either he will hate the one, and love the other; or else he will hold to the one, and despise the other. Ye cannot serve God and mammon.

In this verse Jesus was speaking of servitude in the context of money. Finances put an individual's integrity to its greatest test. Money, wealth, and the power that wealth brings can easily usurp God's place in our lives. Yet we have been "bought with a price" and are not to be enslaved to anyone but Jesus himself. Money is a deceptive, controlling, hard master yet never provides permanent health, happiness, or eternal life. Jesus sternly warned us that we must be careful not to let anything, especially wealth, become a master over us.

How we utilize our financial resources can generally be viewed as an accurate picture of how we accept the lordship of Christ in our lives. We should always use what we have been given, be it a little or a lot, wisely. God has promised that He would care for us, so we should be thankful for the resources He has given. We should not complain, for that insinuates that God does not provide.

A massive effort was launched in the 1990s to repay entire classes and races of people for injustices of the past. However, no amount of remorse or accusations on the part of any group can rectify the wrongs of generations past. We can grieve for the wrongs our ancestors inflicted on others or for the wrongs our ancestors suffered at the hands of others. But bitterness over past sufferings cannot solve the ills of the present. Nor is it pleasing to the Father. As children of the King we must resolve to treat all individuals of His creation with love, respect, and kind acceptance, vowing that for the future as well as the present we will never perpetuate or retaliate for the wrongs of the past. God provides for His own, and we should not resent our state in life but, rather, wisely utilize what God is presently providing for us so that we can build a greater future of harmony among all people in preparation for His coming Kingdom.

There are many forms of slavery. We all have weaknesses, handicaps, proclivities—Achilles' heels—that have to be submitted to God or they will enslave us.

Have you dealt with the potential slave driver in your life? Is that thing that would try to be your master been fully submitted to God?

II. SUBMITS TO THE MASTER'S WILL (1 Samuel 3:1-10; Colossians 3:22-24)

A. Hearing the Master's Voice (1 Samuel 3:1)

(1 Samuel 3:1 is not included in the printed text.)

God spoke audibly at times in both the Old and New Testaments. Moses and Joshua led the children of Israel through direct conversations with Jehovah. However, during the period of the judges a word from the Lord was a rare thing indeed. By Eli's day, no prophets were giving messages. This was because of the attitude of those in priestly positions. The sons of Eli mocked the very roles they played in the Tabernacle ministry. They had allowed greed and personal gain to get in the way of any relationship with the very God they were supposedly serving.

Desiring to hear from God and listening for His voice are prerequisites for real communication with Him. One might question this if he looked at Paul's experience on the road to Damascus (Acts 9). It would appear that Paul was doing anything but seeking the face of God. However, Paul sincerely believed he was doing God a service in his early treatment of Christians. He firmly believed he was doing God's will by persecuting believers. He was a sincere seeker, but he was searching in the wrong direction—when God intervened. Paul's heart was bent upon serving God, but his zeal was misplaced until Jesus appeared to him and spoke to him directly.

B. Samuel's Availability (1 Samuel 3:2-7)

(1 Samuel 3:2, 3 is not included in the printed text.)

4. That the Lord called Samuel: and he answered, Here am I.

5. And he ran unto Eli, and said, Here am I; for thou calledst me. And he said, I called not; lie down again. And he went and lay down.

6. And the Lord called yet again, Samuel. And Samuel arose and went to Eli, and said, Here am I; for thou didst call me. And he answered, I called not, my son; lie down again.

7. Now Samuel did not yet know the Lord, neither was the word of the Lord yet revealed unto him.

Eli was an old man and had been a priest of the Lord for many years. However, rote service had replaced devotion. After not hearing a direct message from the Lord for many years, one might be tempted to think that God no longer cared. However, might not the silence from God be attributable to a lack of sincere devotion? In any event, Eli was still at fault. He was not the master of his own household, never taking strong disciplinary action with his sons. This was wrong enough, but these sons were also priests under his ministry. Eli had lost the moral fortitude to be a proper spokesman for God.

Although Eli had given all his life to service, he had missed the very purpose of it. If a man is not the priest of his own home, how can he ever oversee public worship? Jesus said that he who is faithful over a few things will be granted responsibility over many. Every minister should take the lesson of Eli to heart. Paul was careful to make sure that elders and pastors were strong in their own homes as a prerequisite to public leadership.

Samuel's reverent heart made him the perfect candidate for God to use. Although he did not know at first who was calling him, he was willing and ready to listen. Interestingly, the proper instruction came from the old priest Eli. Despite his own hardness of heart, he was able to recognize that this was God moving in the child's life.

C. Samuel's Response
(1 Samuel 3:8-10)

8. And the Lord called Samuel again the third time. And he arose and went to Eli, and said, Here am I; for thou didst call me. And Eli perceived that the Lord had called the child.

9. Therefore Eli said unto Samuel, Go, lie down: and it shall be, if he call thee, that thou shalt say, Speak, Lord; for thy servant heareth. So Samuel went and lay down in his place.

10. And the Lord came, and stood, and called as at other times, Samuel, Samuel. Then Samuel answered, Speak; for thy servant heareth.

The word *heareth* means to "listen with a heart toward obeying." Samuel would not only be a hearer of the word but a doer as well (James 1:25). When God spoke the fourth time, He apparently appeared to Samuel visibly as well. Interestingly, Eli had told Samuel to respond with "Speak, Lord; for thy servant heareth." However, the boy's response left out the word *Lord*. The young child was being introduced to the Almighty, but it would take time for the relationship to grow. Samuel at this point knew the voice as authoritative, but he did not yet understand the intimacy of the relationship that would develop between himself and his Creator. His availability and willingness set in motion a friendship that would last his entire lifetime.

D. Obedience as Worship
(Colossians 3:22-24)

(Colossians 3:23, 24 is not included in the printed text.)

22. Servants, obey in all things your masters according to the flesh; not with eyeservice, as menpleasers; but in singleness of heart, fearing God.

Like other biblical writers, Paul neither condemned nor condoned slavery. The driving force of Paul's mission was spiritual rather than the tearing down or reformation of existing institutions. He was not even aware that a platform from which he could launch an assault against the evil institution of slavery was available to him. Paul was nevertheless greatly concerned about how members of the family of God treated their fellowman. Hence, he built a framework for conduct within the established institutions.

Paul instructed slaves to work hard—just as if their master were Christ himself. This attitude should pervade every employee-employer relationship. We should always do the best possible job we are capable of, leaving the discipline of an unfair or wicked employer in the hands of God. We should consider our work as an act of worship and service to our Creator. We must remember that our few years on this earth, be they in splendor or in slavery, are but temporary preparations for eternal life. The circumstances of life that we are placed in are not as important as how we deal with them.

In reviewing your work for your employer during the past week, did you give your best effort? Were your efforts to serve the Lord done with all your heart?

III. SHOWS LOYALTY AND FAITHFULNESS (Genesis 24:1- 9, 32-38, 56; 1 Corinthians 4:1, 2)

A. A Faith to Be Imitated (Genesis 24:1-9)

(Genesis 24:1, 5-8 is not included in the printed text.)

2. And Abraham said unto his eldest servant of his house, that ruled over all that he had, Put, I pray thee, thy hand under my thigh:

3. And I will make thee swear by the Lord, the God of heaven, and the God of the earth, that thou shalt not take a wife unto my son of the daughters of the Canaanites, among whom I dwell:

4. But thou shalt go unto my country, and to my kindred, and take a wife unto my son Isaac.

9. And the servant put his hand under the thigh of Abraham his master, and sware to him concerning that matter.

Though the content of these verses deal mainly with Abraham's plans for Eliezer to find a wife for Isaac, the wonderful relationship between master and slave is obvious—it is one equivalent to that of trusted friends. Eliezer questioned Abraham for details, not out of reluctance to obey but in an effort to find the exact parameters of his master's wishes. The old servant wanted to know everything he could find out in order to carry out the task more expeditiously. He also recognized the need for divine guidance in completing the mission. He apparently had learned from Abraham to trust in God, for he too asked God for direction.

It seems noble that a slave would come to believe in the God of his master—but this is as it should be. As Christians, there is no more effective witness for the Lord than a life that attracts others to imitate it. Abraham has set an example of faith; and to Eliezer's credit, he followed his master's example.

B. Completing the Job (Genesis 24:32-38, 56)

(Genesis 24:32-38 is not included in the printed text.)

56. And he said unto them, Hinder me not, seeing the Lord hath prospered my way; send me away that I may go to my master.

Even though he was speaking to a ranking superior, Eliezer begged not to be diverted from quickly completing the mission his master had assigned him. It was unthinkable for him to refuse to heed the request of the girl's family to allow her to remain at home for a few days; yet he persisted in his desire to fulfill his master's wishes. There was no offense taken by Laban at the rigid stance of the old man, especially after Rebekah agreed to go. Eliezer's dedication to Abraham was apparent to Laban. Otherwise, he would never have considered giving his daughter to go to a foreign country, likely never to see her again.

Eliezer could easily have stayed at the home of Laban and enjoyed their hospitality. Abraham would not have objected. But this was not in the character of the loyal servant. He had been sent on a mission, and he would not rest until it was completed.

C. Faithful Ministers
(1 Corinthians 4:1, 2)

1. Let a man so account of us, as of the ministers of Christ, and stewards of the mysteries of God.

2. Moreover it is required in stewards, that a man be found faithful.

Much is required of those in God's kingdom who have been given anointing and authority. Paul urged the Corinthians to think of their leaders (including himself, Peter, and Apollos) as servants whom Christ had entrusted with the secrets of the Kingdom. But because they had been given this trust, they must wisely use their leadership. Every minister of the gospel should take this admonition as a standard. He is, in essence, a slave like Eliezer and is responsible to obey the wishes of the Master, Jesus Christ. He must work daily to learn God's will from the Scriptures and follow the leading of the Holy Spirit. He should never abuse the privileges given to him, for he will be disciplined by the One he serves.

Ministers and other Christian leaders are often put on pedestals by their parishioners. This is an easy position to mistreat. It can be tempting to take advantage of the love and favors given to them. However, a servant's heart should keep the true man of God from abusing the affections of the people he serves.

As a church member, how do you treat your pastor? Do you see him as God's servant, and respect him as such?

REVIEW QUESTIONS

1. Why did God allow the Hebrew children to go through hundreds of years of slavery?
2. What stipulations did God put on the children of Israel regarding slavery in the Promised Land?
3. When God said, "No man can serve two masters," why was money spoken of as the competing master?
4. In what ways can the servant Eliezer be seen as a picture of the perfect servant, Jesus Christ?

GOLDEN TEXT HOMILY

"WHATSOEVER YE DO, DO IT HEARTILY, AS TO THE LORD, AND NOT UNTO MEN; . . . FOR YE SERVE THE LORD CHRIST" (Colossians 3:23, 24).

To understand the thought of Paul's message, one must understand the heart of the apostle's conversion. Paul was a slave to the law. Enforcing the law on others was his way of serving God. It was later revealed to him that he was not serving God but was serving sin. Sin was his master, and he was bound by the power of that he justly earned, which was death. "For the wages of sin is death" (Romans 6:23). He worked for a self-earned wage with no hope of justification.

Under an ancient law the master who owned slaves freed one of those slaves once every seven years. The slave that was given his freedom could either go his way or could choose to serve his master out of a heart of gratitude as a free slave.

The apostle Paul had been a Pharisee of Pharisees, meaning that he had tried to justify himself by judging others by the law that he himself could not fulfill. He tried to prove himself righteous by seeking recognition from men, which was his reward for service. In all of Paul's struggles to fulfill the law, he still had condemnation in his heart. Then one day he was given the opportunity to meet with the Master Savior, who had fulfilled the law that Paul could never live up to. Paul, who was then known as Saul, asked to be allowed to serve this new Master. From that day forward the man called Saul became a willing and obedient servant of the Lord Christ. He had a new Master and an eternal inheritance. Paul became a free slave by the grace of God through Jesus Christ. Paul began to serve from the heart willingly, and so it is with all who have been set free from the bondage of sin.

The free slave thus became a part of the kingdom, or the Master's: "For ye have not received the spirit of bondage again to fear; but ye have received the Spirit of adoption, whereby we cry, Abba, Father" (Romans 8:15). "Now we have received, not the spirit of the world, but the spirit which is of God; that we might know the things that are freely given to us of God" (1 Corinthians 2:12). As a Christian our service is not to receive an earned wage but is a privilege and a joy unto the Lord.—**Aaron D. Mize, Clinical Chaplain, MDOC, Parchman, Mississippi**

SENTENCE SERMONS

SERVANTHOOD is required of every Christian.

—Selected

GIVE ME the ready hand, rather than the ready tongue.

—Giuseppe Garibaldi

GOD DID NOT save you to be a sensation. He saved you to be a servant.

—John E. Hunter

NOTHING IN LIFE can take the place of faithfulness and dependability.

—Wallace Fridy

DAILY BIBLE READINGS

M. Loyalty to a Cause.
1 Samuel 17:28-40

T. Loyalty to a King.
1 Samuel 24:6-13

W. Loyalty to Another.
2 Kings 5:1-10

T. Faithful in Service.
2 Chronicles 34:9-13

F. Faithful in Small Things.
Luke 16:10-13

S. Faithful to Witness.
Acts 4:5-13

Examples of Servanthood

Study Text: 1 Samuel 16:15-17; 2 Samuel 12:18, 19; 2 Chronicles 24:12, 13; Proverbs 14:35; Matthew 20:1-15; 1 Corinthians 9:19-23; 2 Corinthians 4:5; Romans 6:22; Galatians 5:13

Objective: To study biblical examples of servanthood and commit to serving God and others.

Golden Text: "We preach not ourselves, but Christ Jesus the Lord; and ourselves your servants for Jesus' sake" (2 Corinthians 4:5).

Central Truth: Service to God is shown by our willingness to serve others.

Evangelism Emphasis: Service to others often provides opportunities for effective witness.

PRINTED TEXT

1 Samuel 16:16. Let our lord now command thy servants, which are before thee, to seek out a man, who is a cunning player on an harp: and it shall come to pass, when the evil spirit from God is upon thee, that he shall play with his hand, and thou shalt be well.

17. And Saul said unto his servants, Provide me now a man that can play well, and bring him to me.

Proverbs 14:35. The king's favour is toward a wise servant: but his wrath is against him that causeth shame.

Matthew 20:1. For the kingdom of heaven is like unto a man that is an householder, which went out early in the morning to hire labourers into his vineyard.

2. And when he had agreed with the labourers for a penny a day, he sent them into his vineyard.

3. And he went out about the third hour, and saw others standing idle in the marketplace,

4. And said unto them; Go ye also into the vineyard, and whatsoever is right I will give you. And they went their way.

5. Again he went out about the sixth and ninth hour, and did likewise.

6. And about the eleventh hour he went out, and found others standing idle, and saith unto them, Why stand ye here all the day idle?

7. They say unto him, Because no man hath hired us. He saith unto them, Go ye also into the vineyard; and whatsoever is right, that shall ye receive.

8. So when even was come, the lord of the vineyard saith unto his steward, Call the labourers, and

give them their hire, beginning from the last unto the first.

11. And when they had received it, they murmured against the goodman of the house,

12. Saying, These last have wrought but one hour, and thou hast made them equal unto us, which have borne the burden and heat of the day.

13. But he answered one of them, and said, Friend, I do thee no wrong: didst not thou agree with me for a penny?

14. Take that thine is, and go thy way: I will give unto this last, even as unto thee.

15. It is not lawful for me to do what I will with mine own? Is thine eye evil, because I am good?

1 Corinthians 9:19. For though I be free from all men, yet have I made myself servant unto all, that I might gain the more.

2 Corinthians 4:5. For we preach not ourselves, but Christ Jesus the Lord; and ourselves your servants for Jesus' sake.

LESSON OUTLINE

I. KING'S SERVANTS
   A. David Serves Saul
   B. David's Servants
   C. Wise and Foolish Servants
II. HIRED SERVANTS
   A. Integrity and Pride in Their Work
   B. Servants Who Complain
III. SERVANTS OF GOD
   A. A Servant to All
   B. A Servant of Christ Jesus

LESSON EXPOSITION

INTRODUCTION

The Bible is full of wonderful examples of servanthood. God's greatest leaders were all put through the discipline of serving others as part of the development of their potential. David served King Saul, even though the rebellious monarch was demented and tried to kill him. David had already been anointed to be the next king of Israel, yet he humbly strove to please the one he was to replace.

Paul was possibly the most educated man of his day when Jesus appeared to him on the road to Damascus. After his conversion Paul willingly gave up the honor and position his brilliance could have afforded him and went instead as a servant to take the gospel to the Gentiles. It was unthinkable to the average Jew to have anything to do with Gentiles, yet Paul saw this as no sacrifice.

Jesus himself became the ultimate servant by leaving his Father's side to serve the very people who would crucify Him. He had no regard for His own wishes while on earth but carried out His Father's plan—a plan that would restore man to renewed fellowship with the Father.

We have great examples to emulate as we strive to serve the Lord. Servanthood requires that we sacrifice our own desires, placing others ahead of ourselves so that we may win them to Christ.

I. KING'S SERVANTS (1 Samuel 16:15-17; 2 Samuel 12:18, 19; Proverbs 14:35)

A. David Serves Saul (1 Samuel 16:15-17)

(1 Samuel 16:15 is not included in the printed text.)

16. Let our lord now command thy servants, which are before thee, to seek out a man, who is a cunning player on an harp: and it shall come to pass, when the evil spirit from God is upon thee, that he shall play with his hand, and thou shalt be well.

17. And Saul said unto his servants, Provide me now a man that can play well, and bring him to me.

David had already been anointed by Samuel to be the next king of Israel, but this was done in secret. It would be many years before he would be publicly anointed and accepted as monarch (2 Samuel 2:4; 5:3). At the point in the story where the above incident took place, Saul was still legally on the throne. However, Saul was a condemned man. The mold had been set; he would not change. God knew the hardness of his heart and the futility of continuing to deal with him. This is not to say that Saul was not given opportunity to repent but simply that God in His omniscience knew the future and was preparing a king for the throne who would be faithful.

How can we explain the evil spirit that haunted Saul? Perhaps the simple fact that the Holy Spirit had left Saul created a vacuum where an evil spirit could quickly take up residence and torment him. If so, many years later David (because he also failed God) would be able to look back at the situation and beg that God would not let the same thing happen to him. When confronted by the prophet Nathan over his sin with Bathsheba, David's heart was cut to the core. He prayed desperately, "Cast me not away from thy presence; and take not thy holy spirit from me" (Psalm 51:11). There is no such thing as a spiritual vacuum. If the Holy Spirit is not present, the forces of hell move quickly to fill the gap.

The servants of Saul were concerned for their king. Obviously, they had no knowledge that David was being prepared the very throne they served. They were faithful in their service to the monarch and were discreet in protecting him from public exposure for his apparent insanity. If they recognized that the Spirit of the Lord had departed from Saul, they were wise not to make this known publicly.

Saul's invitation to David gave him an excellent opportunity as Israel's future king to study first-hand the responsibilities of the throne. He would obtain much experience in learning to lead the nation—even if it was from a negative example. Interestingly, David was a servant during these years. Even though he knew he would be king, he held the insane Saul in high reverence. This was a noble attitude on his part—and one he maintained until Saul's death.

B. David's Servants (2 Samuel 12:18, 19)

(2 Samuel 12:18, 19 is not included in the printed text.)

David had humbly and remorsefully confessed his sin to the prophet Nathan when confronted. He could have denied it or rationalized it, but he fully accepted responsibility for his actions. However, this did not release him from the penalty of his adultery with Bathsheba and the murder of

Uriah. Although his own life would be spared and his sin forgiven, the life of the child conceived by his waywardness would be taken. God forgives confessed sin and restores our relationship with Him, but He does not eliminate the consequences of our wrongdoing. There are certain laws of the universe that are constant. The laws of gravity and thermodynamics are no more changeable than the law of sin and its end result. Sin brings its own punishment. God does not refute His own laws.

David and Bathsheba deserved to die, but God spared them and took the child instead. Possibly this was an even greater punishment for David than his own death would have been.

Despite Nathan's pronouncement that the child's fate was sealed, David was unwilling to resign himself to the death of his son. He interceded and fasted for days. On the seventh day the child died. David's servants were hesitant to tell him of the boy's death, fearing that he might do something desperate. They had stood beside him faithfully and tried to encourage him. Likely, they themselves understood that he deserved this ordeal, but they still felt for the man they served. Compassion for our fellowman should not die in our hearts just because the harsh circumstances he is experiencing is the result of his own wrongdoing. And despite his sin, David was still their king and master. The very fact that it took Nathan's confronting David to elicit an acknowledgement of his sin indicates that this was not a well-known scandal outside the royal courts. The servants had evidently protected their master's privacy.

Aware of the whisperings of the servants around him, David quickly assessed the situation and confronted them. The servants confirmed his nightmare. The child was dead. He then arose and pulled himself together, realizing that nothing he had done had changed God's mind. Realizing that the child would not come back, his only option was to serve God so that he might go to where the child was.

David's servants saw true repentance by David, but they had remained loyal and served him well, even during his sin.

C. Wise and Foolish Servants (Proverbs 14:35)

35. The king's favour is toward a wise servant: but his wrath is against him that causeth shame.

The word here translated "favour" means delight or pleasure; "wise," circumspect or intelligent; "wrath," anger or rage. The king being referred to is God himself. Jesus probably best demonstrated the meaning of this verse with his parable of the wise and faithful servants, in Matthew 24:45-51, and the parable of the talents, in Matthew 25:14-28. In both of these passages, as well as the proverb above, it is apparent that the servant who is intelligent, competent, faithful, and industrious will win favor in God's sight. "The wise servant is a delight, for he is the skillful, clever one. But the incompetent one is the bungler who botches the king's business and whose indiscretions and incapacity expose his master to scandal and criticism" (Note on Proverbs 14:35, *Zondervan Bible Commentary, Vol. 1: Old Testament*).

One might argue that intelligence and competence are attributes of mental capacity, not a gauge of industriousness and faithfulness.

God determines the aptitude and acumen of each individual on a scale all the way from idiocy to genius. However, it is not ability that is being judged. The very fact that one servant was given 10 talents to utilize, another five, and the third only one, indicates that judgment was based on what was done with what was possessed.

As servants of God we should never get caught in the trap of comparing our work with that of others. There will always be someone who is smarter, more talented, more gifted, and so forth. We work with what we have, not what others have. Excellence in servanthood is doing the best with what you have.

Even when there was doubt about the king's integrity, how was the servant to treat his master?

II. HIRED SERVANTS
(2 Chronicles 24:12, 13; Matthew 20:1-15)

A. Integrity and Pride in Their Work (2 Chronicles 24:12, 13)

(2 Chronicles 24:12, 13 is not included in the printed text.)

Joash, the king of Judah from 835 to 796 B.C., came to the throne at age seven. When he was only one year old his grandmother, Athaliah, tried to slaughter all her descendants in a wicked bid for power. Joash was her only survivor because his uncle, Jehoiada, a priest in the Temple, hid him there for six years. Finally Jehoiada was able to orchestrate the overthrow of Athaliah and the crowning of Joash. For many years following, Joash did an excellent job as king, primarily because his uncle made most of the kingdom's decisions.

However, when Jehoiada died, Joash was left without direction. He listened to unwise counsel and was carried into evil. He even ordered the death of Jehoiada's son Zechariah. Eventually his army was defeated, and his own officials assassinated him. He so disgraced himself that he was not even buried among the kings of Judah, and his name is not listed in the genealogy of Jesus in the New Testament.

Joash began his career by doing right, but he eventually fell into sin. He followed the ways of his godly uncle as long as the old man lived, but he was guilty of never establishing a relationship with God himself. His knowledge of the Lord was secondhand.

The incident in our text took place during those early years when Joash and Jehoiada were making repairs to the Temple. The hired workmen were so honest that no accounting of their expenditures was needed. Their integrity was above reproach (see v. 14). Also 2 Kings 12:15 brings out further commendation for these tradesmen. They were seen in contrast to the Levites who could not be trusted with the financial matters of the Temple. These priests were not necessarily dishonest, but were not committed enough to handle the responsibilities given to them. The hired tradesmen gave a better accounting of themselves than those who supposedly had been called to a lifetime of service to the Lord.

Is this not in some instances a picture of the church? Often it is the laymen who are more devoted to the Kingdom than those in ministerial positions.

B. Servants Who Complain (Matthew 20:1-15)

(Matthew 20:9, 10 is not included in the printed text.)

1. For the kingdom of heaven is like unto a man that is an householder, which went out early in the morning to hire labourers into his vineyard.

2. And when he had agreed with the labourers for a penny a day, he sent them into his vineyard.

3. And he went out about the third hour, and saw others standing idle in the marketplace,

4. And said unto them; Go ye also into the vineyard, and whatsoever is right I will give you. And they went their way.

5. Again he went out about the sixth and ninth hour, and did likewise.

6. And about the eleventh hour he went out, and found others standing idle, and saith unto them, Why stand ye here all the day idle?

7. They say unto him, Because no man hath hired us. He saith unto them, Go ye also into the vineyard; and whatsoever is right, that shall ye receive.

8. So when even was come, the lord of the vineyard saith unto his steward, Call the labourers, and give them their hire, beginning from the last unto the first.

11. And when they had received it, they murmured against the goodman of the house,

12. Saying, These last have wrought but one hour, and thou hast made them equal unto us, which have borne the burden and heat of the day.

13. But he answered one of them, and said, Friend, I do thee no wrong: didst not thou agree with me for a penny?

14. Take that thine is, and go thy way: I will give unto this last, even as unto thee.

15. Is it not lawful for me to do what I will with mine own? Is thine eye evil, because I am good?

What a difference in the attitude of the hirelings in this story from that of the workers hired to repair the Temple! Here the servants are less concerned with the quality of the work they do than with the benefits someone else might receive.

Upon a cursory reading of the parable, it would seem unfair that those who had worked the entire day were getting the same pay as those who had labored very little. However, Jesus was talking about entrance into heaven, not rewards for exemplary service. Our membership in God's kingdom is not established by how much we do or how long we have done it but by grace alone. God is the landowner and we as believers are the workers. He is gracious and fair to all, ever wishing that everyone would come into the Kingdom. Those who feel superior because of long service to Christ have forgotten how undeserving they were themselves when saving grace was offered to them.

Jesus was talking about salvation, not rewards. None of us deserves God's generosity, so we should never begrudge it to anyone else, even though they may not turn to God until the very last moments of life. The dying thief on the cross (Luke 23:40-43) is a perfect example of the fact that there will be many in heaven who might not be expected by those who serve the Lord for many years. Praise God that He is the Righteous Judge—and not we ourselves!

Our attitude should be that of thankful servants, never comparing ourselves to anyone else but, rather, concentrating on giving everything we have in faithful service to the One who has redeemed us and given a place in His kingdom.

Have you ever resented God's grace to someone who obviously does not deserve it? Have you ever felt like the older brother of the Prodigal Son?

III. SERVANTS OF GOD (1 Corinthians 9:19-23; 2 Corinthians 4:5)

A. A Servant to All (1 Corinthians 9:19-23)

(1 Corinthians 9:20-23 is not included in the printed text.)

19. For though I be free from all men, yet have I made myself servant unto all, that I might gain the more.

The Christian life is a paradox. It includes both freedom and slavery. Jesus Christ's sacrificial death gave us freedom from sin and the law. As believers, we have been liberated from nonessential rules, rituals, and regulations. However, that freedom does not allow us to do whatever we please. If that were so, our selfish natures would lead us right back into slavery to sin. Galatians 5:1 says, "It is for freedom that Christ has set us free. Stand firm, then, and do not let yourselves be burdened again by a yoke of slavery" (*NIV*). Those who do abuse their Christian freedom by living out their selfish passions eventually fall back into sin. The true believer has been redeemed from evil slavery but has at the same time given himself over to the disciplined life of a servant to righteousness.

In this passage Paul had just finished asserting his own freedom in Christ. However, preaching the gospel was his gift and calling; and he was, in essence, enslaved to that calling. He said in 1 Corinthians 9:16, "When I preach the gospel, I cannot boast, for I am compelled to preach" (*NIV*). Though he was constrained to preach, this was a willing enslavement on his part. He said in Romans 1:16, "I am not ashamed of the gospel, because it is the power of God for the salvation of everyone who believes" (*NIV*). Paul's life was consumed with spreading the good news—that salvation is available to all. He had chosen to obligate himself to Jesus Christ.

Because of this tremendous commitment to the gospel, Paul was willing to do whatever necessary to win others to Christ. His personal needs, desires, and comforts were strictly disciplined. He avoided any entanglement that might cause him to get sidetracked from his one purpose in life. For him, freedom and discipline were combined into one unit—*commitment*.

Paul gave several principles here for anyone else willing to commit to the ministry of the gospel: (1) Make yourself amenable to others so that you can find common ground, (2) accept others and make them feel accepted, (3) be interested in the needs of others, and (4) watch for opportunity to share your faith.

Paul made himself a servant to all mankind so that he could win them to Christ. He never sacrificed his integrity or principles, but he made every effort to relate to others so that he might give witness to the gospel.

B. A Servant of Christ Jesus (2 Corinthians 4:5)

5. For we preach not ourselves, but Christ Jesus the Lord; and ourselves your servants for Jesus' sake.

Paul had no interest in glory for himself. He placed little stock in his own accomplishments but gave credit for all to the One he served.

This same attitude was demonstrated by Jesus during His earthly ministry. In John 7:18, He said, "He who speaks on his own does so to gain honor for himself, but he who works for the honor of the one who sent him is a man of truth; there is nothing false about him" (*NIV*). John the Baptist echoed similar sentiments by refusing to let the crowds believe he was the Messiah. He gave glory to the One he was preceding: "I baptize you with water for repentance. But after me will come one who is more powerful than I, whose sandals I am not fit to carry. He will baptize you with the Holy Spirit and with fire" (Matthew 3:11, *NIV*). Similar words were spoken by Peter in Acts 3:12 and again in Acts 10:25, 26.

Paul made his motive equally clear in a passage to the Romans: "Therefore I glory in Christ Jesus in my service to God. I will not venture to speak of anything except what Christ has accomplished through me in leading the Gentiles to obey God by what I have said and done" (Romans 15:17, 18, *NIV*).

Paul could boast not of himself but of the work God had done in and through him. He did not glory in himself but rather in the One he served.

Can you look at the work you have done in the Kingdom and honestly give all the glory to the Lord?

REVIEW QUESTIONS

1. Have you ever had to swallow your pride and be submissive to an employer whom you did not respect?
2. Have you ever held a grudge against someone else who advanced in his career more easily and faster than you?
3. How much do you try to make yourself amenable to others in order to win them?
4. Are you equally proud of the work God is doing in others as of that He is doing in you?

GOLDEN TEXT HOMILY

"WE PREACH NOT OURSELVES, BUT CHRIST JESUS THE LORD; AND OURSELVES YOUR SERVANTS FOR JESUS' SAKE" (2 Corinthians 4:5).

The minister who preaches "himself" soon learns the futility or foolishness of his effort. This does not mean he should not tell any of his personal experiences in giving illustrations. It does mean, however, that Christ must be the central theme of his message. The pulpit is not the place for the exhibition of one's talent and learning. It is the place to lift up Jesus Christ as the mediator between God and man and the example for men to follow.

Note the reason for the apostle Paul's comment in 2 Corinthians 4:5. Two accusations had been made against him during his absence from Corinth. First, he was accused of wanting the praises of men. To this charge Paul replied that he had not been preaching in his own interest but for the glory of the Son of God.

The apostle was also accused of domineering the churches—lording over them. To this charge Paul replied that he was their servant for Jesus' sake.

Paul, of course, was wrongly accused. The reasons for wrong accusations are many: jealousy, a front or cover-up for one's own lack of dedication, and so forth. Wrong accusations can come easily, and for this reason it is important that the servant of God be very cautious not to do anything, say anything, or act in a manner that could easily be misunderstood.

Paul realized that there is no glory in man. We in ourselves cannot offer men and women anything eternal because we are not divine. If we want to help people, we must preach Jesus—the Savior, the healer, the Holy Ghost Baptizer, and our coming King. He is the answer to the needs of mankind. Guidance in morality cannot lift men out of themselves or out of a life of sin. Sinners must draw help from somewhere, and the only source of spiritual help is faith in the Lord Jesus Christ. The urgency and the importance of preaching Jesus Christ cannot be overemphasized.

The successful minister is aware that he is servant of the people to whom he ministers. And in order for the minister to win lost souls, he must sacrifice. He must be willing to go the second, the third, and the fourth mile, and sometimes even farther if he is to win the lost to Christ. Paul made a sincere effort to impress upon the Corinthian church that whatever they thought his actions to be, he was certainly not domineering the people. He was attempting to serve them in the best possible manner.

The minister is to preach the message and to live the life.

He must believe, love, follow, preach, live, and obey Christ; and in his preaching and daily living, he must seek to always glorify Christ.—**O.W. Polen, D.D., Coordinator of Special Projects, Pathway Press, Cleveland, Tennessee**

ILLUMINATING THE LESSON

I remember learning a hard lesson in servanthood during the first years I was on a church staff. When budget time came around each year I would go through tremendous anguish and frustration. I never seemed to be paid what I felt like I was worth. I knew I was doing a good job, going far beyond what was required. Yet faithful service seemed to matter nothing. A token raise might be approved, but I was barely making enough to subsist on, and no one seemed to care.

A boiling point finally came one Christmas. I was usually brought before the church and given a week's salary as a bonus. However, this time I was given a check equivalent to what the prior year's weekly salary had been. It wasn't the few dollars' difference that upset me. It was the fact that no one cared enough to even check to see what my current salary was.

I was so upset that I finally had to release the problem to the Lord. I determined that in the future I would give myself totally to Him, let Him take care of my needs, and forget about the issue.

Things began to change. Slowly, yet surely, salaries improved and my work was recognized. I also began to see how God was blessing me in other ways.

When I took my eyes off the inequities and put them purely on the Lord, I saw that I was loved and appreciated—and I could love those in return whom I had previously blamed for my problems.

DAILY BIBLE READINGS

M. Work—Ordained by God.
Genesis 2:8-15

T. Work—A Lifelong Task.
Psalm 90:9-17

W. God Honors Honest Labor.
Proverbs 27:23-27

T. Zeal for God's Work.
Nehemiah 2:11-20

F. Support for God's Work.
Philippians 4:10-20

S. Command to Work.
2 Thessalonians 3:6-12

Our Model for Service

Study Text: Matthew 18:1-4; 20:20-28; Mark 6:30-44; Philippians 2:3, 5-8

Objective: To view Christ as the supreme example of servanthood and adopt the attitude He demonstrated.

Golden Text: "Christ Jesus . . . took upon him the form of a servant" (Philippians 2:5, 7).

Central Truth: Jesus Christ demonstrated true servanthood.

Evangelism Emphasis: Jesus Christ came to serve and save all people.

PRINTED TEXT

Mark 6:34. And Jesus, when he came out, saw much people, and was moved with compassion toward them, because they were as sheep not having a shepherd: and he began to teach them many things.

35. And when the day was now far spent, his disciples came unto him, and said, This is a desert place, and now the time is far passed:

36. Send them away, that they may go into the country round about, and into the villages, and buy themselves bread: for they have nothing to eat.

37. He answered and said unto them, Give ye them to eat. And they say unto him, Shall we go and buy two hundred pennyworth of bread, and give them to eat?

38. He saith unto them, How many loaves have ye? go and see. And when they knew, they say, Five, and two fishes.

41. And when he had taken the five loaves and the two fishes, he looked up to heaven, and blessed, and brake the loaves, and gave them to his disciples to set before them; and the two fishes divided he among them all.

42. And they did all eat, and were filled.

Philippians 2:5. Let this mind be in you, which was also in Christ Jesus:

6. Who, being in the form of God, thought it not robbery to be equal with God:

7. But made himself of no reputation, and took upon him the form of a servant, and was made in the likeness of men:

8. And being found in fashion as a man, he humbled himself, and became obedient unto death, even the death of the cross.

Matthew 18:2. And Jesus called a little child unto him, and set him in the midst of them,

3. And said, Verily I say unto you, Except ye be converted, and become as little children, ye shall not enter into the kingdom of heaven.

4. Whosoever therefore shall humble himself as this little child, the same is greatest in the kingdom of heaven.

20:26. But it shall not be so among you: but whosoever will be great among you, let him be your minister;

27. And whosoever will be chief among you, let him be your servant:

28. Even as the Son of man came not to be ministered unto, but to minister, and to give his life a ransom for many.

LESSON OUTLINE

I. COMPASSIONATE SERVICE
  A. The Need for Rest
  B. The Needs of the Multitude
  C. The Hunger of the Multitude
  D. Feeding the Hungry Multitude

II. HUMBLE SERVICE
  A. A Humble Attitude
  B. A Likeness of Christ
  C. A Childlike Attitude

III. WILLING SERVICE
  A. A Selfish Request
  B. A Selfish Response by the Others
  C. The Greatest Must First Be the Least

LESSON EXPOSITION

INTRODUCTION

There are two words that are key to understanding this particular lesson on servanthood: *serve* and *compassion*. *Serve* is a verb, meaning to furnish or supply with something needed or desired. *Compassion* is a noun, meaning the sympathetic consciousness of the distress of others, together with a desire to alleviate it. Together, these two words help form a composite picture of the ideal servant.

Implied in servanthood is the concept of *selflessness*. Jesus was the most giving person who ever lived. In spite of His own feelings of fatigue, loneliness, grief, and disappointment with humanity, He was always ready to meet the needs of others. Even as He writhed in pain on the cross, He was more concerned for His mother's welfare (John 19:26, 27), for the eternal future of the man dying next to Him (Luke 23:42, 43), and for the souls of all those who stood accusing Him (Luke 23:34) than with His own suffering.

During His three years of earthly ministry, Jesus daily demonstrated a deep concern for all human beings. Our first Scripture passage in today's lesson outline (Mark 6:30-44) illustrates His compassion as He fed the multitude with the loaves and fishes. However, to understand just how deep these feelings went, we need to review the events of that entire day. Except for the day of His crucifixion, this particular day was probably the most stressful one that He lived on this earth. Max Lucado has written an entire book on this 24-hour period. He described it as follows: "As soon as one alarm was disarmed, another began blinking. The rulers threatened. The crowds pressed. The followers doubted. The people demanded. When you see what he endured that day, you will wonder how he kept his cool. Somehow, though, he did. Although the people pressed and the problems monsooned, Jesus didn't blow up or bail out. In fact, he did just the opposite. He served people, thanked God, and made cool-headed decisions" (Max Lucado, *In the Eye of the Storm*).

The days and weeks leading up to this one had been extremely difficult for Jesus. He had just experienced rejection in His hometown of Nazareth (Mark 6:1-6). He had also received the news that John the Baptist had been beheaded. "Imagine losing the one person who knows you better than anyone else, and you will feel what Jesus is feeling. Reflect on the horror of being told that your dearest friend has just been murdered, and you will relate to Jesus' sorrow. Consider your reaction if you were told that your best friend had just been decapitated by a people-pleasing, incestuous monarch, and you'll see how the day begins for Christ. His world is beginning to turn upside down" (Lucado).

In addition, Jesus got word that Herod was after Him as well. He knew that the coming days would only accelerate with turmoil. This is how He faced the crowds that day. Yet the Messiah forgot about Himself and reached out to them. We should grasp in this lesson how true servanthood operates. It moves beyond one's personal needs and finds its fulfillment in meeting the needs of others.

I. COMPASSIONATE SERVICE (Mark 6:30-44)

A. The Need for Rest (vv. 30-32)

(Mark 6:30-32 is not included in the printed text.)

Mark used the word *apostles* here to describe the disciples. It means "one who is sent" and became the official designation for the Twelve in the early church (see also 3:14). In this passage they had been sent out for the first time and given authority by Jesus. Despite their failure in the coming months, they (except for Judas Iscariot) would ultimately live up to the title after the Lord's death and resurrection.

They were excited to share with the Master the things they had seen, but Jesus was equally happy to see them. Even though He was God in the flesh, Jesus still needed the love and sustenance of friends. It was His suggestion that they slip away for a time of rest.

Anyone in ministry knows there are times when fatigue strikes; and unless a time is set aside for relaxation, rest, and renewal, a debilitating physical and emotional exhaustion can set in, which will slow effective ministry or bring it to a complete standstill. For the average pastor, Monday is a good day to schedule this much-needed recuperation time. Christian workers should never feel guilty about "lying low" for a short period of rest.

B. The Needs of the Multitude (vv. 33, 34)

(Mark 6:33 is not included in the printed text.)

34. And Jesus, when he came out, saw much people, and was moved with compassion toward them, because they were as sheep not having a shepherd: and he began to teach them many things.

Geographically, it was four miles across the lake by boat and 10 miles around to the other side by foot. The energetic, motivated crowd reached the same destination walking that Jesus and the disciples did by water. Both Jesus and the disciples had to feel a certain sense of dismay when their planned time of privacy was interrupted.

Despite His fatigue (as well as His need to be alone to mourn the loss of His cousin), Jesus felt deep compassion for the crowds coming toward Him. This mass of humanity no longer looked like an intrusion; instead, they resembled helpless sheep in need of a shepherd. Perhaps Jesus remembered the imagery of David's Twenty-third Psalm. He might even have glimpsed Himself as the fulfillment of Isaiah's prophecy concerning the Messiah: "We all, like sheep, have gone astray, each of us has turned to his own way; and the Lord has laid on him the iniquity of us all" (Isaiah 53:6, *NIV*). Whatever the case, He quickly forgot His own feelings and delved into helping those who were reaching out longingly for what only He could do. They were lost sheep; they were wandering aimlessly—without purpose. This was indicated by the fact that as evening approached they had made no plans for food and shelter for themselves and their families.

We might be tempted to say it was easy for Jesus to put His own needs aside to minister to the people's needs, since He was God. However, He was still human as well. He too experienced fatigue; he knew frustration and all the other human emotions.

In Matthew's account of this same incident we learn that He "was moved with compassion toward them, and he healed their sick" (Matthew 14:14). That Jesus was moved with compassion suggests something of the miraculous itself. Most of us would be moved to irritation if we were in desperate need of quietness and the clamoring crowd had ruined the purpose of our trip. But not Jesus! The overwhelming emotion in that gentle heart of His was compassion. But as noble as the sentiment of compassion is, it is not enough to simply feel sympathy or pity for those with needs. If it is within our power to help them, then we are obligated to do so. There is never *nothing* we can do; we can always pray. However, if we have the means to help, we dare not "say unto them, Depart in peace, be ye warmed and filled; notwithstanding ye give them not those things which are needful to the body" (James 2:16).

Jesus healed their sick and fed them. And He is our example.

C. The Hunger of the Multitude (vv. 35-38)

35. And when the day was now far spent, his disciples came unto him, and said, This is a desert place, and now the time is far passed:

36. Send them away, that they may go into the country round about, and into the villages, and buy themselves bread: for they have nothing to eat.

37. He answered and said unto them, Give ye them to eat. And they say unto him, Shall we go and buy two hundred pennyworth of bread, and give them to eat?

38. He saith unto them, How many loaves have ye? go and see. And when they knew, they say, Five, and two fishes.

The stress that came as the day wore on did not seem to affect Jesus, but it certainly did the disciples. The excitement they had felt earlier had now dissipated, and they became "weary in doing good" (Galatians 6:9, *NIV*). They seemed flabbergasted when Jesus suggested that they feed the multitude. They now viewed the crowd as a problem, not an opportunity, and wanted to wash their hands of the responsibility to meet their physical needs.

Jesus used this predicament to show them what could be done even when circumstances indicated it was impossible. The disciples could see only the immensity of the task, not the resources that were available to them through God's hand.

The "two hundred pennyworth of bread" represented about eight months' wages. This was the human-eye view of what it would cost to feed the crowds. Interestingly, though, when Jesus told them to see what was available, they did come back with a seed of faith. The fact that they presented the meager fish and loaves to Jesus hints that they suspected something wonderful might be about to happen.

All Jesus asks us to bring is what we have. We cannot give to Him talents and resources we haven't been blessed with; but if we bring what we do possess, He can perform the miraculous. It has been said that some of the greatest achievers in every area of endeavor have not been those who were most qualified—but rather those who used what they had. When we face impossible tasks, Jesus only asks that we bring what we have available.

D. Feeding the Hungry Multitude (vv. 39-44)

(Mark 6:39, 40, 43, 44 is not included in the printed text.)

41. And when he had taken the five loaves and the two fishes, he looked up to heaven, and blessed, and brake the loaves, and gave them to his disciples to set before them; and the two fishes divided he among them all.

42. And they did all eat, and were filled.

The fact that the grass was green indicates it was springtime. The people sat down in an orderly fashion, much like rows in a vegetable garden. The crowds were not rowdy but, rather, were very cooperative. The meek and willing spirit they expressed shows that their hearts were ready to receive. We see nothing of a demanding spirit at this point, only yearning. This should be a lesson for all of us when we come to Jesus with our needs. A humble disposition will touch the Master's heart. The Greek derivative of the word *compassion* means "an intense internal yearning." Jesus was certainly moved internally by the longing attitude the crowd was expressing.

Were the disciples less than compassionate for wanting to send the multitudes away to buy food? Try to identify with them in this situation and explain your answer.

II. HUMBLE SERVICE (Philippians 2:3, 5-8; Matthew 18:1-4)

A. A Humble Attitude (Philippians 2:3)

(Philippians 2:3 is not included in the printed text.)

Paul was in the process of encouraging the Philippian believers to be unified, contending together for the faith and the spreading of the gospel. One of Satan's greatest weapons against the church is to divide the people into factions, ever fighting one another instead of solidly facing the real opponent.

The only way to avoid strife is to put others ahead of oneself. Paul emphasized that there was no place for selfish ambition in the church. This does not mean that the individual should demean himself. Putting others first is simply a part of becoming a living sacrifice. In Romans 12:3, Paul instructed every believer, "Do not think of yourself more highly than you ought, but rather think of yourself with sober judgment" (*NIV*). An honest evaluation and a healthy self-respect enables the believer to be secure enough that he can lay aside his personal ambitions and give way to the plans and ideas of others. The key to such confidence is found in having one's identity in Christ. We must remember that apart from Christ none of us are capable of accomplishing much. Our value is not in who we are, no matter what our talents or resources. Our worth comes, rather, from who lives in us. We are useful because Christ lives in us. "We have this treasure in jars of clay to show that this all-surpassing power is from God and not from us" (2 Corinthians 4:7, *NIV*).

B. A Likeness of Christ (vv. 5-8)

5. Let this mind be in you, which was also in Christ Jesus:

6. Who, being in the form of God, thought it not robbery to be equal with God:

7. But made himself of no reputation, and took upon him the form of a servant, and was made in the likeness of men:

8. And being found in fashion as a man, he humbled himself, and became obedient unto death, even the death of the cross.

Jesus was the supreme example of one who was confident enough in who He was that He could lay it all aside. He expressed the ultimate humility, giving up His rights as the Son of God in order to obey the Father and serve humanity. He was not forced to make this sacrifice; He did so willingly.

A person who demands his rights and insists on putting himself first is generally insecure and often frightened. As Christians we must decide to exhibit a different attitude—a willingness to lay aside our rights. Servanthood is a conscious decision to follow Christ in attitude. This is not an inbred disposition; it must be developed and disciplined.

C. A Childlike Attitude
(Matthew 18:1-4)

Matthew 18:1 is not included in the printed text.)

2. And Jesus called a little child unto him, and set him in the midst of them,

3. And said, Verily I say unto you, Except ye be converted, and become as little children, ye shall not enter into the kingdom of heaven.

4. Whosoever therefore shall humble himself as this little child, the same is greatest in the kingdom of heaven.

Children can be the most trusting people on earth. "If my daddy said it, it must be so" describes the attitude of a child toward his parents. Children are willing to accept as fact whatever their parents tell them about the world around them. Fairy tales are not just imaginative stories, but rather are larger-than-life adventures in their minds—because they see them as possible. They can express great faith because they willingly believe. They have not yet developed the sense of skepticism that so often characterizes adults. Jesus insisted that his followers take on this nature—having humble and sincere hearts.

Does humble service come as a natural outgrowth of Christian character, or is this something we have to work at achieving?

III. WILLING SERVICE (Matthew 20:20-28)

A. A Selfish Request (vv. 20-23)

(Matthew 20:20-23 is not included in the printed text.)

One wonders whether the mother of the two disciples was really worshiping Jesus when she knelt at His feet or whether her ulterior motive was to get what she wanted from Him. We must guard against coming to the Lord purely to have our requests granted. Religious games never work for us anyway, for the Lord sees right through our outward actions to our very thoughts and purposes. Real worship praises Christ for who He is, not for what He can do for us. Jesus knew that the mother had no idea what she was asking. Interestingly, Matthew 27:56 tells us that she was among those who were at the Lord's crucifixion; so, apparently, even though her ambition for her sons was misguided, her devotion to the Lord was sincere. She possibly remembered her request as she watched Him hanging there, and she could well have realized then how foolish her request had been.

At that time the two disciples and their mother did not grasp the idea that position in the Kingdom requires sacrifice and servanthood. The cup from which Jesus would have to drink was suffering and death on the cross. James and John ultimately proved themselves true disciples of Christ and found their place in the Kingdom. They too drank from the cup of suffering. James was executed, and John was exiled.

B. A Selfish Response by the Others (vv. 24)

(Matthew 20:24 is not included in the printed text.)

For all their indignation at the brazen request made by the two disciples' mother, the other disciples exhibited an equally poor attitude. They all wanted to be the greatest. At this point in their walk with Jesus they were all ambitious, self-serving, and jealous of one another.

C. The Greatest Must First Be the Least (vv. 25-28)

(Matthew 20:25 is not included in the printed text.)

26. But it shall not be so among you: but whosoever will be great among you, let him be your minister;

27. And whosoever will be chief among you, let him be your servant:

28. Even as the Son of man came not to be ministered unto, but to minister, and to give his life a ransom for many.

Jesus here presented an idea to the disciples that was revolutionary. Instead of using people, we are to serve people. In order to be a leader, we must seek the highest good for those we aspire to lead. Leadership in God's kingdom is for the benefit of those being led, not for the ambitions of the leader.

A *ransom* was the price required to secure a slave's freedom from bondage. Jesus had spoken before to the disciples about His own impending death, but here He gave them the reason—to redeem all mankind from the slavery of sin. Only in His death—the ultimate price of servanthood—could such a ransom be paid.

Was the attitude of the other 10 disciples any less selfish in motive than that of the two who made the presumptuous request?

REVIEW QUESTIONS

1. What do you think the disciples' first reaction was when Jesus forsook His plans for a rest period and reached out to minister to the crowds?
2. How did Jesus himself feel about and respond to this intrusion into His privacy?
3. What can the believer do to "take on the mind of Christ"?
4. Did the two disciples have any comprehension of what they were asking when they made their request to Jesus for prominence in the Kingdom?
5. Do you think the mother of these two disciples had a selfish motivation herself, or was she merely concerned for the future of her sons?

GOLDEN TEXT HOMILY

"CHRIST JESUS . . . TOOK UPON HIM THE FORM OF A SERVANT" (Philippians 2:5, 7).

The purpose of this letter to the Philippians seems to be twofold: (1) Paul wanted to express appreciation to the members of the Philippian church for their generosity in their financial support of his ministry. (2) He made an effort to correct the problems of disunity and rivalry (2:2-4).

This letter was probably written while Paul was in the Roman Mamertine Prison. As we recall, the apostle Paul was an important person in the Jewish religious hierarchy. However, following his conversion to Christ, he was expelled from all of his lofty positions, and now had descended all the way to that of a prisoner. This was quite a descent from a position of honor and respectability to one considered to be that criminal.

It is possible that as he sat in prison, he began thinking about his own decline, which reminded him of the enormous decline Christ made from heaven to earth, and even into death in His redemption of mankind.

Philippians might be called the epistle of joy and encouragement in the midst of adverse circumstances. Paul freely expressed his affection for the Philippians for their testimony and support. He then lovingly urged them to settle their differences in a Christlike spirit. He set his heart to expel this evil by expounding the humility of Jesus Christ. Motives which caused Christ to surrender and serve as he did, and which likewise actuated the apostle himself, were and are the only effective safeguard against pride and rivalry in the church today.—**Wayne S. Proctor, State Coordinator, Autumn Ministries, Church of God, Harrisburg, Illinois**

SENTENCE SERMONS

JESUS CHRIST demonstrated true servanthood.

—Selected

CHRISTIANITY DEMANDS a level of caring that transcends human inclinations.

—Erwin W. Lutzer

THE DEW of compassion is a tear.

—Lord Byron

HUMILITY is a divine veil that covers our good deeds and hides them from our eyes.

—Climacus Saint John

EVANGELISM APPLICATION

JESUS CHRIST CAME TO SERVE AND SAVE ALL PEOPLE.

We live in a materialistic society that is obsessed with moving up the ladder—socially, financially, politically. A popular term of the age is "upward mobility." Jesus, however, lived out His earthly life by becoming "downwardly mobile." He crossed the impossible class chasm between God and man. He moved from a position of ultimate power to a position of human frailty. He made Himself a servant to mankind.

When it seemed He could not possibly lower Himself any further, He made one more descent. By His death on the cross, He moved from the sinless to the sin-stained. He descended all the way into hell so that we could go to heaven.

Jesus actively embraced a life of servitude—and He calls on us to do the same thing. The only way for us to achieve real greatness in His kingdom is to make ourselves a servant just as He did. The two greatest commands He gave are to love God and love others. We must learn to view servanthood as a strength, not a weakness. Second Corinthians 12:9 puts this in total perspective: "My strength is made perfect in weakness."

ILLUMINATING THE LESSON

Dr. Evan O'Neill Kane performed thousands of appendectomies over the long span of his medical career, but none so dramatic as the one on February 15, 1921. He had long been a crusader against the abuse of general anesthesia. He felt that a local anesthetic was far more practical in many situations. However, he had great difficulty in finding a volunteer on which to try out his hypothesis.

He was finally able to prove his point with this particular surgery. As he had done many times before, he carried out the procedure with the patient experiencing only some minor discomfort. Two days later the patient was dismissed and soon back to complete health.

What made this so exciting was not just the fact that he had proved his point and medical science would be forever changed for the better. The unique aspect of the surgery was that Dr. Kane had made himself the patient. He had taken out his own appendix.

DAILY BIBLE READINGS

M. Man of Sorrows. Psalm 22:1-11
T. Righteous Servant. Isaiah 42:1-4
W. Compassionate Savior. Isaiah 63:1-9
T. Healing the Sick. Mark 1:29-39
F. Saving Sinners. John 8:1-11
S. The Good Shepherd. John 10:7-14

A Lesson in Servanthood

Study Text: John 13:1-17

Objective: To examine Christ's demonstration of servanthood and resolve to serve others in the same manner.

Time: The Gospel According to John was written between A.D. 85 and 96.

Place: The Gospel According to John was probably written at Ephesus.

Golden Text: "I have given you an example, that ye should do as I have done to you" (John 13:15).

Central Truth: Christians are to follow Christ's example in serving others.

Evangelism Emphasis: Loving service to others, however menial, can be an effective witness.

PRINTED TEXT

John 13:1. Now before the feast of the passover, when Jesus knew that his hour was come that he should depart out of this world unto the Father, having loved his own which were in the world, he loved them unto the end.

2. And supper being ended, the devil having now put into the heart of Judas Iscariot, Simon's son, to betray him;

3. Jesus knowing that the Father had given all things into his hands, and that he was come from God, and went to God;

4. He riseth from supper, and laid aside his garments; and took a towel, and girded himself.

5. After that he poureth water into a bason, and began to wash the disciples' feet, and to wipe them with the towel wherewith he was girded.

6. Then cometh he to Simon Peter: and Peter saith unto him, Lord, dost thou wash my feet?

7. Jesus answered and said unto him, What I do thou knowest not now; but thou shalt know hereafter.

8. Peter saith unto him, Thou shalt never wash my feet. Jesus answered him, If I wash thee not, thou hast no part with me.

9. Simon Peter saith unto him, Lord, not my feet only, but also my hands and my head.

10. Jesus saith to him, He that is washed needeth not save to wash his feet, but is clean every whit: and ye are clean, but not all.

11. For he knew who should betray him; therefore said he, Ye are not all clean.

12. So after he had washed their feet, and had taken his

garments, and was set down again, he said unto them, Know ye what I have done to you?

13. Ye call me Master and Lord: and ye say well; for so I am.

14. If I then, your Lord and Master, have washed your feet; ye also ought to wash one another's feet.

15. For I have given you an example, that ye should do as I have done to you.

16. Verily, verily, I say unto you, The servant is not greater than his lord; neither he that is sent greater than he that sent him.

17. If he know these things, happy are ye if ye do them.

LESSON OUTLINE

I. MOTIVATED BY LOVE
   - A. Knowledge of the Father's Will
   - B. The Betrayer's Heart
   - C. Knowledge of His Own Identity
   - D. A Slave's Task

II. MISUNDERSTOOD SERVICE
   - A. Peter's Confusion
   - B. Knowledge of the Betrayer

III. CHALLENGE TO SERVE

LESSON EXPOSITION

INTRODUCTION

The headline in the newspaper reads: "Study Raises Unexpected Questions About Beta Carotene's Cancer Risk." And we are led to believe that another long-expounded idea—that vitamin A helps protect the body from cancer—has been disproved by a scientific research group. Regularly we see this happening—some cherished theory that has long been held as truth is suddenly exposed as false, or at least is seriously questioned. In another section of the same newspaper another tradition accepted as fact is debunked. But then next week these studies may themselves be overturned and another new idea held up as truth.

As silly as this sounds, the same pattern takes place regularly within the church. Over the past few years we have gone through many religious fads, pop theologies, experimental worship forms, church marketing plans, and so forth. However, many have not passed the test of time. Before long, the latest therapeutic book for healing some spiritual malady will be just another forgotten volume on a shelf, discarded in the wake of shattered lives who tried it and realized it didn't work. Spiritual fads fail because they don't measure up to the Word of God. Ministries and preachers fall because their works were built on selfish motives and doctrines that were not biblically sound.

There are some things, however, that never fail—and one of those is servanthood. The greatest picture of a servant can be found in the actions of Jesus as He washed His disciples' feet just before His own crucifixion. This was a demonstration of how all believers should view themselves and treat each other.

Jesus was and is the epitome of all truth. The Greek word for "truth" is *aletheia*. This means "the unveiled reality lying at the base of appearance." In essence, then, truth is the reality that lies beyond appearances. As He took on a servant's task, Jesus demonstrated His true nature—that He loved His disciples absolutely and would do the lowliest of labors for them.

We live in a world that is built on deception. Tremendous sums of money are spent on advertising to create illusions. "If you buy this beautiful sports car, you will be surrounded by beautiful women," the advertisement suggests. "If you drink a particular brand of soda, you will be part of the 'in' crowd." Politicians spend fortunes trying to establish an image for themselves, veiling their true character with what they want the public to believe. However, falsely created images are almost always eventually exposed. Greed, ambition, and selfishness will raise their ugly heads in the form of pride.

Jesus showed by his humble actions that the only way to lead others is to be a real servant. "This is as true in public life and the business world as it is in the church. No number of corporate memos or rah-rah speeches exhorting workers to commit themselves to an organization or its clients will have as powerful an impact as a person of authority modeling consistently and clearly the attitude of a servant: placing others' needs before one's own, committing oneself to doing concrete things to meet those needs, and looking for neither favors nor reciprocity from the people one serves" *(The Word in Life Study Bible, New Testament Edition).*

True servanthood never fails. It will endear others to you and prove your leadership of them. In washing His disciples' feet, Jesus left a lasting impression they would never forget. He spoke of Himself to them as truth personified, but His humble acts of servanthood shouted volumes louder than even His words.

I. MOTIVATED BY LOVE (John 13:1-5)

A. Knowledge of the Father's Will (v. 1)

1. Now before the feast of the passover, when Jesus knew that his hour was come that he should depart out of this world unto the Father, having loved his own which were in the world, he loved them unto the end.

Jesus had entered Jerusalem five days before the Passover Feast to the wild cheers of misguided people who thought He was going to deliver them from Roman oppression (John 12:12, 13). He knew there was a price on His head and that His personal safety was at risk, but He came anyway. He was fully aware of His mission and what its cost would be. The authorities and power figures in the city might think that they could destroy Him, but Jesus had the upper hand. He had stated this earlier: "The Father loves the Son and has placed everything in his hands" (John 3:35, *NIV*). His total purpose for living was to carry out the plan the Father had given Him.

Paul commented on Jesus' mission: "For he 'has put everything under his feet.' Now when it says that 'everything' has been put under him, it is clear that this does not include God himself, who put everything under Christ" (1 Corinthians 15:27, *NIV*). Events in Jerusalem may seem to have been out of control, and justice a scarce commodity, but the Creator was still in charge.

B. The Betrayer's Heart (v. 2)

2. And supper being ended, the devil having now put into the heart of Judas Iscariot, Simon's son, to betray him.

Judas had already betrayed his own false motives. Earlier in His ministry, when many disciples were deserting Jesus, Judas had remained. Jesus, however, recognized his motive in the midst of apparent faithfulness: "Have I not chosen you, the Twelve? Yet one of you is a devil!' (He meant Judas, the son of Simon Iscariot, who, though one of the Twelve, was later to betray him.)" (John 6:70, 71, *NIV*). Judas had stayed with Jesus—but only for personal gain. Evil had already entered his heart. There was no servanthood in him.

He betrayed himself even further as he complained about Mary's apparent waste of the expensive ointment when she anointed Jesus (John 12:1-8). He tried to hide behind a pious phrase when he asked, "Why was not this ointment sold for three hundred pence, and given to the poor?'" (v. 5). Obviously, his real interest was greed. To see a year's worth of wages "wasted" on Jesus was more than he could stand. Like the other disciples, he had been hoping for an important place in the Lord's kingdom; but apparently he had come to realize that Jesus would never be the king he expected Him to be. His greed and hope for status could not be realized if he remained loyal to Jesus.

Could there have been another motive in Judas' heart? "Every age has pondered the motive. John believed that Satan entered Judas Iscariot's soul. The most popular conjectures other than greed or jealousy are disappointment that Jesus refused to launch a rebellion; or a belief that if Jesus were arrested he would summon heavenly hosts to his rescue and precipitate his kingdom on earth" (John Pollock, *The Master, A Life of Jesus*).

C. Knowledge of His Own Identity (v. 3)

3. Jesus knowing that the Father had given all things into his hands, and that he was come from God, and went to God.

There is a tremendous freedom that comes from a knowledge of who you are. When you are confident in your identity, you need not worry about what anyone else thinks. You don't have to prove anything. Jesus was the Son of God. The Father had given Him authority over all things. This liberated Him to love His disciples—even those who would betray and deny Him.

We each should realize that we have purpose in Christ's kingdom and are all equally loved. There is truth in the statement "All men are created equal." We may not have equal talents, abilities, or opportunities—but God loves us all the same. Therefore, there is no reason to compare ourselves to one another.

Jesus was confident in who He was, and could take a servant's role without thinking about how this might appear to others.

D. A Slave's Task (vv. 4, 5)

4. He riseth from supper, and laid aside his garments; and took a towel, and girded himself.

5. After that he poureth water into a bason, and began to wash the disciples' feet, and to wipe them with the towel wherewith he was girded.

Everyone present at the Passover Feast knew that Jesus was in charge of the occasion. It was His prerogative to orchestrate the evening. "Before eating, the head of the household or company must ceremonially wash his hands. Jesus again rose from his place, but he did not place his hands in the basin. Instead, he removed his robe. John watched perplexed as Jesus pulled off his sleeveless tunic, woven from top to bottom without seam, and stood before them stripped to his loincloth like a slave. John never forgot the love and tenderness, the serenity on Jesus' face as he wound a towel round his waist, took the basin, and knelt down to wash Judas' feet. He wiped them with the towel, then moved to the next. Disciples watched in total silence as their Master worked as if he were the lowest slave" (John Pollock, *The Master: A Life of Jesus*).

Was there any intention on Jesus' part to embarrass or shame His disciples into humility by washing their feet? What do you think was the purpose of His actions?

II. MISUNDERSTOOD SERVICE (John 13:6-11)

A. Peter's Confusion (vv. 6-9)

6. Then cometh he to Simon Peter: and Peter saith unto him, Lord, dost thou wash my feet?

7. Jesus answered and said unto him, What I do thou knowest not now; but thou shalt know hereafter.

8. Peter saith unto him, Thou shalt never wash my feet. Jesus answered him, If I wash thee not, thou hast no part with me.

9. Simon Peter saith unto him, Lord, not my feet only, but also my hands and my head.

It was a common courtesy in Middle Eastern homes for a servant to wash the feet of guests to remove the dust. However, Jesus had requested privacy for Himself and the disciples, and thus the absence of a servant. One might argue that there was no money for such added extravagance. However, given the details of how Jesus told Peter and John to set up the meal (Matthew 26:17-19; Mark 14:12-16; Luke 22:7-13), it is obvious that Jesus could have had anyone there He wished.

Luke's account of the Last Supper includes bickering for position and rank in the Lord's kingdom by the disciples (22:24). They were wrapped up in their own concerns and failed to perceive the gravity of the situation. We can only imagine the sudden shame they felt upon seeing their Master perform the most menial service to them.

The incongruity of such an act—Jesus, their Master, acting like a slave—was unsettling to Peter. True to his usual outspoken nature, he was quick to respond. Perhaps he remembered the attitude John the Baptist had expressed: ". . . whose sandals I am not fit to carry" (Matthew 3:11, *NIV*) and "I need to be baptized by you, and do you come to me?" (v. 14, *NIV*). Being the burly, rough fisherman he was, Peter was not used to having anyone treat him with such lowliness and respect. Peter's response to Jesus' proposed action to wash his feet was similar to his response when at Jesus' word their catch of fish had been so large the boats were sinking: "When Simon Peter saw this, he fell at Jesus' knees and said, 'Go away from me, Lord; I am a sinful man!'" (Luke 5:8, *NIV*).

Peter was both ashamed and confused. Impulsively, he refused to let Jesus wash his feet. Jesus' response to him implied there was a greater meaning to this than just the physical act being carried out. He told Peter that if he refused the footwashing, he could have no part with Him. Peter, still thinking the Lord was speaking of a physical washing, impetuously requested that in that case Jesus wash his head and hands also. A tremendous fear of rejection had struck Peter's heart, but Jesus was speaking in spiritual terms. "Just as in the natural life a man who has bathed needs only to wash the dust off his sandaled feet when he returns home, so in the spiritual life a man who has been cleansed from sin need not think that all is lost when he sins in his walk through life. He needs only confess these sins to be entirely clean again." (*Ryrie Study Bible*, note on John 13:10).

Though Peter may have been dumbfounded by the symbolism of Jesus' act at the time, eventually he himself would mature to such a point that he used similar metaphorical language: "And this water symbolizes baptism that now saves you also—not the removal of dirt from the body but the pledge of a good conscience toward God. It saves you by the resurrection of Jesus Christ" (1 Peter 3:21, *NIV*).

B. Knowledge of the Betrayer (vv. 10, 11)

10. Jesus saith to him, He that is washed needeth not save to wash his feet, but is clean every whit: and ye are clean, but not all.

11. For he knew who should betray him; therefore said he, Ye are not all clean.

Imagine the pain Jesus experienced as He washed the feet of the one He knew would betray Him. The even greater agony was His foreknowledge that there was no hope for this man. Though the other disciples would forsake the Master, they would be restored and ultimately become great instruments in the Kingdom. No such future awaited Judas. His decision forever separated him from the Lord. Jesus knew this would be the last act of kindness He could ever do for Judas. In broken despair and hopelessness, this man would turn away from the redeeming love that was available to him.

Why didn't one of the disciples intervene to stop Jesus from washing the other disciples' feet and take over the lowly task himself?

III. CHALLENGE TO SERVE (John 13:12-17)

12. So after he had washed their feet, and had taken his garments, and was set down again, he said unto them, Know ye what I have done to you?

13. Ye call me Master and Lord: and ye say well; for so I am.

14. If I then, your Lord and Master, have washed your feet; ye also ought to wash one another's feet.

15. For I have given you an example, that ye should do as I have done to you.

16. Verily, verily, I say unto you, The servant is not greater than his lord; neither he that is sent greater than he that sent him.

17. If ye know these things, happy are ye if ye do them.

Having performed the humble chore for His disciples, Jesus now questioned them about what His actions meant. If they really recognized Him as their Master and Lord, they must become willing to do the same lowly tasks.

Obviously, He was talking about more than just the outward act of washing one another's feet. His higher purpose was to show them the importance of humbling themselves, serving others, and guarding against pride. They must come to see that no act of service was beneath them. The King of kings and Lord of lords had not come to earth just to sit on a throne. Neither would His disciples be given such a privilege. If He was to be a servant, they must become servants too.

When Jesus came to earth, He totally immersed Himself in obedience to His Father's will. The disciples now must strip themselves of pride, selfishness, and ambition—and immerse their lives in walking in obedience to Christ. They would ultimately have a great place in His kingdom, but this would come only when they had learned not to seek glory for themselves but to give glory to God.

A new mind-set must be learned by all believers. Paul said, "Let this mind be in you, which was also in Christ Jesus" (Philippians 2:5). Servanthood is not a spontaneous fruit of the Spirit. Servanthood is a conscious, willful action in response to the Holy Spirit. It requires constant doing—it does not just happen.

Jesus humbled Himself in order to carry out the Father's plan. Every believer must also humble himself in order to walk in obedience to Christ. As servants following the example of Jesus, we must not look at any job as too lowly in our efforts for the Lord. We must also be constantly absorbed in doing His will, forgetting our own lives, interests, and desires.

Do you think the disciples understood at this point what Jesus was teaching them?

REVIEW QUESTIONS

1. If servanthood is one of the qualities of a true follower of Christ, how much of this attribute was demonstrated by the 12 disciples during the three years they spent with Him?
2. Is servanthood a natural desire on the part of the believer, or does it have to be cultivated and learned?
3. "He that is washed needeth not save to wash his feet, but is clean every whit." What did Jesus mean by this statement?
4. When Jesus told His disciples to follow His example, did He mean literally to wash each other's feet?
5. What are some practical ways people in leadership positions can exhibit servanthood?

GOLDEN TEXT HOMILY

"I HAVE GIVEN YOU AN EXAMPLE, THAT YE SHOULD DO AS I HAVE DONE TO YOU" (John 13:15).

Martin Luther once said, "A Christian man is the most dutiful servant of all, and subject to everyone." His statement was based on the principle and example set forth by Christ in the Golden Text.

Christ set an example for the disciples to follow when He washed their feet (v. 5). The term *example* indicates that not merely the principle of humility expressed by the act but also the act itself was commanded by the Lord.

The grammar of the phrase "that ye should do" in the Greek text indicates it was a command with continuing application. It was not to be simply a onetime event for the disciples. It was something the Lord expected them and other disciples to continually follow.

The essence of the principle represented by the act of washing the saints' feet is given in verse 16: "The servant is not greater than his lord; neither he that is sent greater than he that sent him." Obedience to the command to wash the feet of another believer represents servanthood. The Christian concept of servanthood means there are distinctions of functions and leadership within the body of Christ, but no one is "greater" than anyone else. The grace of God is applied to all, and we must all serve each other. **—Excerpts from the *Evangelical Sunday School Lesson Commentary*, Vol. 40**

SENTENCE SERMONS

CHRISTIANS are to follow Christ's example in serving others.

—Selected

LOVE LOOKS NOT for limits, but opportunities.

—H. Bert Ames

LOVE IS the medicine for all moral evil. By it the world is to be cured of sin.

—Henry Ward Beecher

GOD NEVER GAVE a man a thing to do concerning which it were irreverant to ponder how the Son of God would have done it.

—George Macdonald

EVANGELISM APPLICATION

LOVING SERVICE TO OTHERS, HOWEVER MENIAL, CAN BE AN EFFECTIVE WITNESS.

What men seek most is power. Think of the powerful people around you: politicians, national leaders, business tycoons, law enforcement officials, teachers, pastors, parents—and often children. There is an inborn trait in man that causes him to strive to exert influence over others.

Jesus was also a power figure. In fact, He was the most powerful man who ever lived. He had formed the universe, and He could alter it with the snap of a finger. This was part of His deity.

However, he was also totally human. He submitted all His divine attributes to the Father when He became a baby and lived out the life of a man. Therefore, everything He did on earth had to be by the Father's direction. He acted only as the Father told Him to. He made this clear many times. On one occasion He said, "I tell you the truth, the Son can do nothing by himself; he can do only what he sees his Father doing, because whatever the Father does the Son also does. For the Father loves the Son and shows him all he does" (John 5:19, 20, *NIV*).

Jesus had no power in Himself, yet He was powerful. How do we explain this? It was power that came from the most pure servanthood this world has ever known. It accomplished what was intended because God directed it completely. As long as the Father instructed Him to do so and the Holy Spirit empowered Him, Jesus could turn water into wine, heal the sick, and raise men from the dead. Undaunted, He could also face men's disapproval and hatred.

Matthew 19:30 says, "But many who are first will be last, and many who are last will be first" (*NIV*). In the same sense, to be strong you must become weak. One of the enigmas of Christianity is that those who would be the strongest—

must first become the weakest. Only as we recognize that we are here to serve others can Christ fully use us and give us the unction we need to accomplish the work of His kingdom. The Lord told Paul, "My grace is sufficient for thee: for my strength is made perfect in weakness" (2 Corinthians 12:9).

ILLUMINATING THE LESSON

The freshman congressman knew that his position in Washington was tentative at best. He had been elected by a district totally distrustful of the political establishment. He realized that he must stick firmly to the positions that had won his constituents' votes in the recent election.

One thing he did was to sleep in his office. Instead of renting an expensive apartment, he worked extra hours and then used a mattress from his closet to sleep on. He showered and shaved at the congressional health club facilities in his office building. He rarely ventured away from his work, knowing he could not let himself get caught up in the whirlwind life of celebrity politicians.

Thinking that his actions were simply good stewardship and a visible symbol of his servanthood to his district, he was caught off guard when another member of the House publicly chastised him for his alleged misuse of government properties. In essence, he was being accused of freeloading on Uncle Sam by not renting an apartment.

One point of interest: Although this new congressman owned a nice home back in his home state (and was in fact financially well-off), his accuser owned only a simple condominium in his home state—but maintained an upscale home in Washington.

Which politician demonstrated the better quality of servanthood?

DAILY BIBLE READINGS

M. Pride's Downfall.
2 Chronicles 33:21-25
T. Pride's Embarrassment.
Esther 6:1-11
W. Humility's Reward.
1 Kings 3:3-15
T. Humility's Blessings.
2 Chronicles 7:12-18
F. Humility Demonstrated.
John 3:25-31
S. Humility Commanded.
Colossians 3:12-17

Where Can I Serve

Study Text: Daniel 1:17-20; 2:48, 49; Luke 10:38-42; Romans 12:3-8; 16:23; Philippians 4:22; 1 Timothy 5:4; 1 Peter 4:9

Objective: To explore opportunities for Christian service and serve wherever God directs.

Golden Text: "Whatsoever ye do in word or deed, do all in the name of the Lord Jesus, giving thanks to God and the Father by him" (Colossians 3:17).

Central Truth: Opportunities for Christian service are found everywhere.

Evangelism Emphasis: To reach others with the gospel often means building bridges of selfless service.

PRINTED TEXT

Luke 10:38. Now it came to pass, as they went, that he entered into a certain village: and a certain woman named Martha received him into her house.

39. And she had a sister called Mary, which also sat at Jesus' feet, and heard his word.

40. But Martha was cumbered about much serving, and came to him, and said, Lord, dost thou not care that my sister hath left me to serve alone? bid her therefore that she help me.

41. And Jesus answered and said unto her, Martha, Martha, thou art careful and troubled about many things:

42. But one thing is needful: and Mary hath chosen that good part, which shall not be taken away from her.

1 Timothy 5:4. But if any widow have children or nephews, let them learn first to shew piety at home, and to requite their parents: for that is good and acceptable before God.

1 Peter 4:9. Use hospitality one to another without grudging.

Romans 12:5. So we, being many, are one body in Christ, and every one members one of another.

6. Having then gifts differing according to the grace that is given to us, whether prophecy, let us prophesy according to the proportion of faith;

7. Or ministry, let us wait on our ministering: or he that teacheth, on teaching;

8. Or he that exhorteth, on exhortation: he that giveth, let him do it with simplicity; he that ruleth, with diligence; he that sheweth mercy, with cheerfulness.

Daniel 2:48. Then the king made Daniel a great man, and gave him many great gifts, and made him ruler over the whole province of Babylon, and chief of the governors over all the wise men of Babylon.

49. Then Daniel requested of the king, and he set Shadrach, Meshach, and Abednego, over the affairs of the province of Babylon: but Daniel sat in the gate of the king.

Romans 16:23. Gaius mine host, and of the whole church, saluteth you. Erastus the chamberlain of the city saluteth you, and Quartus a brother.

Philippians 4:22. All the saints salute you, chiefly they that are of Caesar's household.

DICTIONARY

Shadrach (SHAYD-rak) Meshach (MEE-shack) and Abednego (ah-BED-nee-go)—Daniel 2:49—Friends of Daniel whom God protected from the fiery furnace.

Gaius (GAY-us) Erastus (ee-RAS-tus) Quartus (KWOR-tus)—Romans 16:23—Three persons who served with Paul in ministry and from whom Paul sent greetings to the Romans.

LESSON OUTLINE

I. IN THE HOME
  A. The Martha Syndrome
  B. The Family's Responsibility
  C. Showing Hospitality

II. IN THE CHURCH
  A. Healthy Respect for Self and Others
  B. Members of One Body
  C. The Variety of Gifts

III. IN PUBLIC SERVICE
  A. Integrity Wins Respect
  B. Faithful Service Rewarded
  C. Servanthood Through Friendship
  D. Servanthood Gains Access

LESSON EXPOSITION

INTRODUCTION

The opportunities for service in Christ's kingdom are countless. One can work for the Lord wherever he is, whatever the circumstances. For too long many have undervalued themselves by thinking that what they are capable of has little worth, while those whose activities are highly visible they consider to be the only ones "doing the Lord's work." It is obvious that the great apostle Paul recognized the need for people to serve in all areas of life. He compared the body of Christ to the human body and insisted that each part was of great value to the whole: "The body is a unit, though it is made up of many parts; and though all its parts are many, they form one body. So it is with Christ" (1 Corinthians 12:12, *NIV*).

Therefore, we should encourage all believers to recognize the ways they can serve, both in their occupations and as needs arise within the church. The idea is not so much *where* one serves but, rather, to motivate the individual to do his best "as unto the Lord."

In this lesson we will examine the three major arenas of service—the home, the church, and in the public—to see not only the opportunities but also the attitudes we should express as we give ourselves to the Lord's work.

No one is exempt from working in the Kingdom. There is a job for each one to do. We must recognize our place and fill that need.

I. IN THE HOME (Luke 10:38-42; 1 Timothy 5:4; 1 Peter 4:9)

A. The Martha Syndrome (Luke 10:38-42)

38. Now it came to pass, as they went, that he entered into a certain village: and a certain woman named Martha received him into her house.

39. And she had a sister called Mary, which also sat at Jesus' feet, and heard his word.

40. But Martha was cumbered about much serving, and came to him, and said, Lord, dost thou not care that my sister hath left me to serve alone? bid her therefore that she help me.

41. And Jesus answered and said unto her, Martha, Martha, thou art careful and troubled about many things:

42. But one thing is needful: and Mary hath chosen that good part, which shall not be taken away from her.

When it comes to Christian service, we are often tempted to classify people into two categories: the Marys and the Marthas. The Marys are very worshipful but are generally of little help when it comes to getting work done. The Marthas handle every detail, making sure nothing is left out. However, they are frequently so busy working in the Kingdom that they seem to have little time for worship.

The story of Mary and Martha as told in Luke's Gospel has often been interpreted to show Martha in a negative light. She has been caricatured as obsessively busy as opposed to her more spiritual sister. Some use this to say that religious pursuits are more important than carrying out routine tasks.

However, we cannot take this one gentle rebuke by Jesus as a condemnation of Martha's serving heart. Someone had to prepare the meal for the Master and His disciples. In the church today, someone has to maintain the buildings, clean the bathrooms, cut the grass, prepare and mail the newsletter, prepare food for the sick, and so forth. The list of necessary mundane activities stretches infinitely long.

The simple point Jesus was making is that in addition to taking care of details, Martha needed to maintain a sensitivity to spiritual concerns. The Master, however, was not drawing a line to separate the two. Martha had lost sight of why Jesus had come to her home. He was not there just for her hospitality, but because they were friends. And this special time needed to be enjoyed.

Martha seems to have learned her lesson well, for when Jesus came after Lazarus' death, she recognized Him as the only one who could raise her brother from the dead (John 11:20-27).

Also, there is an interesting statement that John made in recounting the story of this family: "Jesus loved Martha, and her sister, and Lazarus" (John 11:5). Notice that Martha's name is listed first. Ultimately, there was no difference in Jesus' love for Martha and Mary, and likely there was no difference in the degree of the two sisters' love for Him. There was merely a difference in personality, which indicated a different means of expressing that love. Like Martha, however, we are all called to maintain a balance between diligent service and a consistent attitude of dependence on the Lord.

B. The Family's Responsibility (1 Timothy 5:4)

4. But if any widow have children or nephews, let them learn first to shew piety at home, and to requite their parents: for that is good and acceptable before God.

In New Testament times widows were abundant. Women tended to marry very young (in their early teens), while men usually did not marry until well into their 20s or 30s. Thus, wives most often outlived their husbands. Added to the age difference were the ravages of war, diseases, and other difficult aspects of earning a living. The mortality rate left many women without support while they were still quite young. It is generally assumed that is why we hear nothing about Joseph in Jesus' adult years, while Mary is very much in the picture. We can also note that as He was dying on the cross, Jesus left the responsibility of His mother in the hands of John. The Lord was setting an example for us even in this extreme moment.

In Jewish society, widows were considered the responsibility of the community (see Deuteronomy 24:19-21). The system also called for a brother of the deceased husband to marry the widow if there had been no male child born in that marriage. Other widows were left to manage the best they could, with help from the synagogues and other civic programs. In many cases, however, these women had to resort to begging to survive.

Paul made it absolutely clear that widows were to be cared for. They must not be abandoned to fall into destitution. However, he was making it equally clear that the responsibility belongs first to family members.

The same holds true today. In this century of governmental social programs, many families have defected from their responsibility. As Christians, we must take an active role in the welfare of our less fortunate relatives. This is a priority of Christian service.

The church has also quietly forsaken its duty to the widowed and needy. We cannot continue in this direction. As the century comes to a close, we find governmental programs shrinking. The church and its constituents must reclaim its role in caring for those within the body of Christ who cannot care for themselves.

C. Showing Hospitality (1 Peter 4:9)

9. Use hospitality one to another without grudging.

Hospitality should be the rule rather than the exception in Christian homes. This is a legitimate form of service for the Lord. Just as Peter encouraged hospitality, Paul also encouraged believers to open their homes to fellowship. He said, "Share with God's people who are in need. Practice hospitality" (Romans 12:13, *NIV*). When writing to both Timothy and Titus, he placed this among the qualifications for pastors and elders (1 Timothy 3:2; Titus 1:8). The writer of Hebrews elevated the practice to a spiritual plane, indicating that often we are doing more than we think: "Do not forget to entertain strangers, for by so doing some people have entertained angels without knowing it" (Hebrews 13:2, *NIV*).

It does not take wealth or social standing to be hospitable. Often the greatest moments of true Christian fellowship take place over a simple cup of coffee. The idea is to focus on your guests, not on yourself—providing food, a listening ear to their needs, a place to spend the night, or just simple acceptance.

How do you classify yourself—as a Mary or a Martha? Why? Was either of these women more spiritual than the other? Explain.

II. IN THE CHURCH (Romans 12:3-8)

A. Healthy Respect for Self and for Others (v. 3)

(Romans 12:3 is not included in the printed text.)

Christians should never let themselves get caught in the trap of comparing themselves with others. This is a poor measure of self-worth. However, it is easy to succumb to the temptation to belittle oneself or, vise versa, to look down on someone else by making such comparisons. Either extreme reduces our effectiveness as worthwhile servants in the Lord's kingdom.

God does not look at our gender, social class, race, ethnic background, family heritage, or physical appearance to determine our usefulness in the Kingdom. Therefore, neither should we. We need to view all people as God's children and, as such, be willing to reach out to them without prejudice, envy, conceit, or self-consciousness. None of us are any more than what God's grace has molded us into: "But by the grace of God I am what I am" (1 Corinthians 15:10, *NIV*).

B. Members of One Body (vv. 4, 5)

(Romans 12:4 is not included in the printed text.)

5. So we, being many, are one body in Christ, and every one members one of another.

Paul used the human body to show a metaphorical picture of how the family of God operates. All believers should live and work together cooperatively, each recognizing his own particular function as essential to the health of the total body. We are all "labourers together with God" (1 Corinthians 3:9). Each of us has been given gifts to use in service to help build the church. We must recognize that we are not all given the same gifts; therefore, we need not compare ourselves to anyone else in the Body. Our great task is to do what we *can* do wholeheartedly.

C. The Variety of Gifts (vv. 6-8)

6. Having then gifts differing according to the grace that is given to us, whether prophecy, let us prophesy according to the proportion of faith;

7. Or ministry, let us wait on our ministering: or he that teacheth, on teaching;

8. Or he that exhorteth, on exhortation: he that giveth, let him do it with simplicity; he that ruleth, with diligence; he that sheweth mercy, with cheerfulness.

Think for a moment of all the various gifts that have been given to different individuals in the church. Pastors are given responsibility for the tender care and efficient oversight of the flock. Prophets are articulate mouthpieces for what God has to say. Teachers are logical thinkers who can communicate the Word effectively. Marthas are detail people, helping to create an atmosphere so that others can worship. Marys are compassionate people and good listeners. Encouragers lift the spirits of those who are disheartened. Givers bring monetary and substantive gifts to help others. Leaders provide organization and good management.

The list goes on and on. However, none of us are all of these wrapped up into one, although many have more than one gift. We must use the gifts we have been given but at the same time recognize those gifts that have been given to others. Their strengths balance our weaknesses. Together, we all serve in the Lord's church.

What happens when we try to exercise a gift that we have not been given? Should we ever be envious of the gifts God has granted to others in the body?

III. IN PUBLIC SERVICE (Daniel 1:17-20; 2:48, 49; Romans 16:23; Philippians 4:22)

A. Integrity Wins Respect (Daniel 1:17-20)

(Daniel 1:17-20 is not included in the printed text.)

From the moment they were taken into captivity, Daniel and the other three Hebrew young men determined that they would serve God. The Babylonians intended to remold them, even changing their names and putting them through a long education process. However, "Daniel resolved not to defile himself" (Daniel 1:8, *NIV*), choosing to remain committed to God's will and ways.

Daniel did not show himself rebellious; but, rather, he found ways to live by God's standards without unnecessary confrontations. Choosing to negotiate rather than to be obstinate, Daniel suggested that he and the others be given healthy foods rather than the rich royal-table fare. This creative idea saved their lives. Sometimes God's people are required to make certain adjustments to the culture of their times. And this is possible without compromising God's law.

Daniel and the others worked hard to learn the culture they had been thrown into, but they still maintained their allegiance to God. In the process, they gained great wisdom. This proved invaluable to God's plan for bringing an end to the Captivity and returning His chosen people to Jerusalem.

There is a great need for believers to serve in the public arena. However, this is an area in which the temptation to sacrifice one's values is great. Daniel proved that he could be true to God's commands and still serve with honor.

B. Faithful Service Rewarded (Daniel 2:48, 49)

48. Then the king made Daniel a great man, and gave him many great gifts, and made him ruler over the whole province of Babylon, and chief of the governors over all the wise men of Babylon.

49. Then Daniel requested of the king, and he set Shadrach, Meshach, and Abednego, over the affairs of the province of Babylon: but Daniel sat in the gate of the king.

The integrity Daniel established through years of faithfulness paid off. King Nebuchadnezzar recognized not only Daniel's wisdom but also that the God Daniel served is the "God of gods and the Lord of kings and a revealer of mysteries" (v. 47, *NIV*). Daniel's consistent character ultimately gave the king a picture of what God is like. "Our acts of love and compassion may impress people, and if we give God credit for our actions, they will want to know more about him" (*Life Application Bible*, Tyndale House

Publishers, notes on Daniel 2:47).

Daniel was unselfish in the glory being given him. He asked that his companions be given posts in the province he was to govern. Daniel knew that he had to have capable assistants who were godly. We too must be careful in choosing whom we work with. It has been said that the people we get our advice from are the most important people in our lives. Daniel chose men he knew he could trust—other godly servants.

C. Servanthood Through Friendship (Romans 16:23)

23. Gaius mine host, and of the whole church, saluteth you. Erastus the chamberlain of the city saluteth you, and Quartus a brother.

The entire 16th chapter of Romans is a series of greetings to friends and fellow workers of Paul's—from Paul and other of his friends and fellow workers. The great apostle recognized that it took many people to carry on the work of the Kingdom—Jews and Gentiles, men and women, Greeks and Romans, free men and slaves. The church had a broad base, crossing cultural, social, and economic lines. Paul had friends in all these places and positions. He recognized the value of people in general and showed no prejudice in his choice of friends. He did not just use people for the sake of spreading the gospel; he genuinely loved the people he worked with. We should follow his example.

D. Servanthood Gains Access (Philippians 4:22)

22. All the saints salute you, chiefly they that are of Caesar's household.

There were many Christians in Rome when Paul wrote this epistle while imprisoned there. Even though he was awaiting trial in the Roman courts, there were actually believers working in Caesar's household! The message of the gospel was taking hold in all levels of society. Christianity is not just for one class of people but for all men. We should recognize this and find a place of service wherever we can, from the lowest ranks of society to the highest plateaus.

Many people feel it is impossible to work in the political arena and still be a Christian. Do you believe this? Explain your answer.

REVIEW QUESTIONS

1. Mary sat devotedly at the Lord's feet, listening attentively to His teachings but leaving her sister to do the serving alone. Can people be "so heavenly minded they are no earthly good"? How should we view the attitudes of the two sisters?
2. What is the difference between hospitality and social entertaining?
3. Are you guilty of comparing yourself to others in the body of Christ?
4. Should Christians regard public service (politics, public office) as something to be desired or, rather, to be avoided?

GOLDEN TEXT HOMILY

"WHATSOEVER YE DO IN WORD OR DEED, DO ALL IN THE NAME OF THE LORD JESUS, GIVING THANKS TO GOD AND THE FATHER BY HIM" (Colossians 3:17).

In this life we may never know the extent of our influence on other people. I am convinced everything we say or do is an influence for either good or evil. No matter how trivial the word or deed, the conclusion is the same. Therefore, our Christian faith must be consistent in our everyday life. Then we can be the influence our society needs.

The Christian has a mission to influence the lives of those around him. Often the mission is lost in the frustration of the moment. In modern society so much is required that we hardly have time to minister to our fellowman. However, Christ exhorts us to pick up our cross daily and follow Him (Luke 9:23). Christian virtues, love for others, and personal character are a most convincing argument for the cause of Christ. All Christians should walk circumspectly before God and the world, doing all things in the name of the Lord Jesus.

A Christian life must be a life of self-discipline and commitment. Jesus said, "Ye are the salt of the earth. . . . Ye are the light of the world" (Matthew 5:13, 14). A godly life and a Christian witness have a healthy influence on society. As we see the world sinking in immorality, corruption, and intemperance, it is urgent that Christians witness daily by word and deed.

Therefore, let us never grow weary in well doing. May what people see and hear from you and me be a Christian attitude in word, deed, and spirit! Then we can fulfill the command of Jesus in Matthew 5:16: "Let your light so shine before men, that they may see your good works, and glorify your Father which is in heaven."—**Jerry Puckett, Customer Service Representative, Pathway Press, Cleveland, Tennessee**

SENTENCE SERMONS

OPPORTUNITIES for Christian service are found everywhere.

—Selected

THE CHURCH is a workshop, not a dormitory.

—Selected

THE DUTIES of home are discipline for the ministries of heaven.

—Anonymous

GOD DOES NOT do anything with us, only through us.

—Oswald Chambers

EVANGELISM APPLICATION

TO REACH OTHERS WITH THE GOSPEL OFTEN MEANS BUILDING BRIDGES OF SELFLESS SERVICE.

Which jobs are the most important in the Kingdom? In 1 Corinthians Paul listed a hierarchy of gifts, saying that God "has appointed first of all apostles, second prophets, third teachers, then workers of miracles, also those having gifts of healing, those able to help others, those with gifts of administration, and those speaking in different kinds of tongues" (12:28, *NIV*). Does this mean the Lord values some people's service more highly because of the gifts He has given them? Most believers down through the centuries have generally felt so. We put pastors, missionaries, teachers, and evangelists on pedestals, while thinking that those who work in "secular" jobs are at the bottom of the spiritual ladder.

However, all work is of importance to God. He uniquely designed each of us to carry out different kinds of tasks. Some of these may seem spiritual, while others appear to have no benefit to the furtherance of the gospel.

What is most important is the attitude with which we conduct our occupations. A spirit of humility, cooperation, and thanksgiving should permeate our daily routine, thereby giving a quiet witness to those we associate with. There may have been a ranking to the "gifts" God assigns, but not to the vocations we work in.

After Paul listed the order of spiritual gifts in 1 Corinthians 12, he quickly moved to write the great *love* chapter (1 Corinthians 13). If we want to excel in God's kingdom, we must do our service with love. This is the one commodity that is of greatest value to God.

ILLUMINATING THE LESSON

Most people feel that they could serve the Lord so much better if they had a different job, had more education, lived in a different city, went to a different church, had greater talents, and so forth. Yet God wants us to serve Him wherever we are. Certainly there are many people called to work in full-time ministries, but the majority in the church need to "bloom where they are planted."

The important idea is that we take Christ with us to wherever our workplace is. This is sometimes a difficult concept for people to accept. Once an individual becomes a Christian, he has a new set of ideals. These make him want to escape the harsh language, crude jokes, competitive atmosphere, immoral conduct, and so forth, that pervades the general secular workplace. It would seem so much easier to work in a Christian atmosphere. However, Jesus never intended that believers escape from the world and set up an exclusive society. Our faith should be an *insulation*, not an *isolation*, from the world. It really is a form of servanthood for us to work alongside unbelievers and allow our lives and actions to communicate the gospel by how we do our work.

DAILY BIBLE READINGS

M. Obedient Servant. Genesis 24:1-10
T. Listening Servant. 1 Samuel 3:1-10
W. Advised to Serve. 1 Kings 12:1-8
T. Christ, the Wise Servant. Isaiah 11:1-10
F. Faithful Servant. Matthew 24:42-51
S. Servant of the Lord. 2 Timothy 2:15-26